to Maria Luisa

Roberto L. Quercetani

A World History of the JUMPING EVENTS

1860-2010
Men and Women

editVallardi

Lamine Diack
President of the International Athletics Foundation
President of the International Association of Athletics Federations

Foreword

The International Athletics Foundation is once more proud to support the publication of the latest work of the renowned and respected historian and journalist, Roberto L. Quercetani.

A World History of Jumping Events is the latest volume from this prolific author who with his great dedication to and love for our sport has been progressively focussing on the various categories of event disciplines, describing in even greater detail the stories and stars first captured in his authoritative, all-event- encompassing publication 'ATHLETICS - A history of Modern Track and Field Athletics'.

To say I am delighted to read this publication would be a gross understatement as of course as a former long jumper I must declare an avid interest in the subject matter which remains so close to my heart.

All the jumping events which are included in the programme of the Olympic Games and the World Championships - High Jump, Pole Vault, Long Jump, Triple Jump - for men and women are covered in this edition.

As with all of his previous historical surveys of the Olympics' number one sport, Quercetani has again deftly managed to place the progression and development of these field events within their rightful cultural and historical context, allowing the personalities of the protagonists to figuratively jump out from the page.

On behalf of the International Athletics Foundation, the International Association of Athletics Federations and the entire Athletics Family I congratulate my friend and colleague, Roberto, for his latest contribution to the definitive documentation of our sport's history.

Lamine Diack

ACKNOWLEDGEMENTS

We wish to thank the following authorities for their contribution:

International Association of Athletics Federations (IAAF)
International Athletics Foundation (IAF)
Lamine Diack, Sergey Bubka, Pierre Weiss, Nick Davies.

We also wish to express our appreciation to All Sports Photographic for their important contribution.

As well as to the following friends:
John Hendershott ("Track & Field News"),
Jacques Carmelli, Gérard Dumas, Gérard Leconte, Peter Matthews,
Mel Watman and graphics expert Diego Galbiati.

Text: Roberto L. Quercetani
Graphics: Diego Galbiati
Produced by: EditVallardi - Cassina de Pecchi (Milan) ITALY
Printing and binding: A.G.S. - Città di Castello (PG) ITALY
Picture acknowledgements: All Sports Photographic (UK), Roberto L. Quercetani

PRINTED IN ITALY - July 2011

Member of the
World Sportpublisher's
Association

Via Roma 74 - 20060 Cassina de Pecchi - Milan (ITALY)
segreteria@editvallardi.com - www.editvallardi.com

ISBN 978-88-95684-47-5

CONTENTS

WOMEN:

INTRODUCTION

by Roberto L. Quercetani

My series of history books dedicated to the various sections of athletics, which started in 1973, now tackles the jumping events – i.e. high jump, pole vault, long jump and triple jump. As far as the modern history of the sport is concerned, in the men's section this range was set in motion in the second half of the 19th century, whereas in the women's section things really began to move only in the 20th century as far as high jump and long jump were concerned, while pole vault and triple jump joined the parade only in relatively recent days.

Jumping conditions have changed noticeably throughout the years, particularly in the vertical jumps. In particular, the introduction of poles made with synthetic materials such as fibreglass caused a major revolution in that event. Within twenty years, from 1960 to 1980, the transition from bamboo to metal poles and then to fibreglass ones caused an advance of just about one metre in record heights. For example, one cannot honestly compare Cornelius Warmerdam with Sergey Bubka. Both deserve to be considered as the undisputed kings of their respective epochs. In the high jump, the transition from the original "scissors" to the Western Roll, down to the Straddle of our days, had a great effect on the evolution of marks. The so-called horizontal events – long and triple jump – have shown a more consistent pattern throughout the years, yet they too have obviously benefited from ever changing factors in training methods and medicine. As regards the latter, it should be said that the cost of major victories and records has risen rather visibly in recent years. Few champions, if any, seem now able and lucky enough to escape the Moloch of injuries for a considerable amount of time.

At the time of writing the current men's world records in the jumping events all date from the 20th century, more exactly from the years between 1991 and 1995. In the women's ranks the oldest world record dates from 1987 – Stefka Kostadinova's 2.09 in the high jump, the youngest is Yelena Isinbayeva's 5.06 in the pole vault (2009). With the 2011 "Worlds" in Daegu and the 2012 Olympics in London we can look forward to some furious assaults even in this department though.

MEN 1860-1900

1

HIGH JUMP

The irrepressible Sweeney

There is no explicit reference to competitive jumping for height in Greek mythology. The Irish, however, had such an event on the programme of their Tailteann Games, which were first held long before the beginning of the Christian Era. In the Middle Ages evolutions in vertical jumping were linked as often as not with acrobatic feats (somersault, "wall" jump, and the like). In the British Isles the high jump in various forms remained popular through the centuries. First to clear the magic height of 6 feet (1.829 m.) was an Englishman, **Marshall Jones Brooks** (born on 30 May 1855; 1.83 m. / 75 kg.), who on 17 March 1876 at Marston near Oxford went over a bar set at 1.831. Three weeks later, on 7 April in London, he easily mastered 1.892. Spectators were in ecstasy as Brooks went back under the bar! He wound up his eventful season by annexing the English AAA title with 1.829, reportedly without troubling to remove his top hat ! Montague Shearman, the master of British athletics historians, described his form as follows:

"He took very little run, and in fact walked up to the bar, springing straight over it, with his legs tucked up high and well in front of him, and invariably looked, when his legs were once over, as if his body would fall crashing into the bar, but he nearly always managed to jerk his body forward again, and to alight upon his toes".

In those days most high jumpers apparently had little or no concern for the position of their centre of gravity vis-à-vis the cross-bar. They simply drove all parts of the body as high as possible, generally using a slow approach.

Brooks' record was shattered by another Briton, Patrick Davin, who mastered 1.90 (6/2- 3/4) at Carrick/on Suir on 5 July 1880. Quite amazing, even if seen through modern glasses, are the feats of the man who succeeded him as record holder, **William Byrd Page,** an American, born on 23 February 1886 (1.70 m & 64 kg.), who in 1887 first mastered 1.91, then 1.93 at Philadelphia on 7 October, in what was actually an exhibition - a mark the AAU later ratified as a record. This man provided history's first notable height vs. record differential, 23 centimetres. In the words of an American observer he used "a slight backward layout". A good but somewhat questionable performance of 1.965 was credited to George Rowdon of England in 1890, but the record was disallowed by the AAA on account of a sloping ground, although a commentator of the time said "It is possible that the run-up to the bar was sloping, but not at the take-off place".

In the last decade of the 19th century jumping form improved noticeably, chiefly thanks to the efforts of **Michael Francis Sweeney,** an Irishman transplanted in USA (born on 27 October 1872 1.74 m. 70 kg.). He was the first man to achieve a certain degree of proficiency with the Eastern cut-off style, particularly in an essential detail, that of converting horizontal speed generated in the approach run into a fair amount of vertical drive.His remarkable career spanned over 14 years, from 1888 till 1902. He broke Page's record just before turning twenty in New York on 8 October 1892 with 1.935 (6-4 ¼). Then followed a short interlude by James Ryan of Britain, with a 1.945 (6-4 ½) record jump at Tipperary on 19 August 1895, after which the irrepressible Sweeney took over and bettered the record three times in a row later in the same season, with the following marks: 6-5 (1.955) in New York on 28 August, 1.965 (6-5 ⅜) at Bayonne on 2 September and finally 1.971 (6-5 ⅝) again in New York on 21 September. The last mark occurred in the frame of what is generally considered history's first meet of international significance, the New York AC vs London AC affair. About which Sweeney later confided his feelings in these terms: "I had a strong spiritual experience when I broke the record. The bar was at 6-5 5/8 and I thought it was impossible to clear. I tried twice. The second time I could hear the groans of the crowds as I struck the bar on the way down. I walked back praying silently. I seemed to feel I needed supernatural help. The bar had looked at least 7 feet. After my prayer I turned round and to my astonishment it did not seem higher than 5-8 (1.727 m.). I came to the mark on my take-off exclaiming: I've got, I've got it. And as I jumped I went blind, but I had cleared the bar. The next thing I remember was Teddy Roosevelt picking me out of the pit. He was New York Police Commissioner in those days, and was an official of the Games". (Roosevelt later became the 26th President of the United States).

In 1896 Sweeney took the position of athletic director at Hill School, thus giving up amateur competition. However he continued to excel as a "pro", showing great versatility: 14.60 in the triple jump and 3.09 in the pole vault.

In the first two editions of the modern Olympics high jump results were rather mediocre, partly due to far from good conditions.

1896 Olympics, Athens - High Jump (10 April): 1.Ellery Clark (USA) 1.81; 2.James Connolly (USA) 1.72; 3.Robert Garrett (USA) 1.71; 4.Fritz Hofmann (Germany) 1.70; 5.Henrik Sjöberg (Sweden) 1.70.

1900 Olympics, Paris - High Jump (15 July): 1.Irving Baxter (USA) 1.90; 2.Patrick Leahy (GB) 1.78; 3.Lajos Gönczy (Hungary) 1.75; 4.Carl Albert Andersen (Norway) 1.70; 5.Eric Lemming (Sweden) 1.70; 6.Waldemar Steffen (Germany) 1.70; 7.Louis Monnier (France) 1.60; 8.Tore Blom (Sweden) 1.60.

1900 Olympics, Paris – Standing High Jump (16 July): 1.Raymond Ewry (USA) 1.65; 2.Irving Baxter (USA) 1.525; 3.Lewis Sheldon (USA) 1.50.

POLE VAULT

"Til the frail bamboo"

The pole vault is one of the most spectacular events in athletics and some experts consider it the most difficult to learn. Its origin is connected with man's earliest wartime activities, since jumping with a pole over streams and fences and other obstacles was a useful medium to escape enemies or wild beasts. In an excellent book on the Olympics of ancient Greece by Iris Douskou it is claimed that a vaulting exercise was invariably a jump over horses. On a red-figured cylix, a youth is depicted getting ready to leap over some horses with the aid of a pole.

An event called "pole jumping" figured in the programme of the ancient Tailteann Games of Ireland. An expression such as "spear-high jump" is occasionally encountered in classic Greek literature, yet there is no trace of an athletic event of that type in writings dealing with the ancient Olympics. It is, however, interesting to note that the Germans use a strikingly similar word ("Stabhochsprung", i.e. staff-high jump) for this event in its modern version.

Under the influence of Guts Muths (author of "Gymnastik für die Jugend", 1793), pole vaulting as a gymnasium sport was practised in Germany early in the 19th century. In the British Isles the exercise probably originated in the Fen country, where poles had long been a must for negotiating ditches and canals. In the early days, pole jumping was for distance rather than for height. It fell to some members of the Ulverston (Lancashire) Cricket Club to launch pole vaulting for height as an athletic contest in England, about the middle of the 19th century. These pioneers used long, heavy poles, usually of ash or hickory, with a tripod of iron at the lower end. This was planted in the ground about three feet (91.4 cm.) in front of the crossbar. The vaulting act, made in a sitting position, came as the combined result of climbing and swinging. One of the most famous English "climbers" was **Thomas Ray** (born on 5 February 1862; 1.82 m. / 76 kg.), who enjoyed a long career before meeting a premature death at 42. He achieved a top performance of 3.555 on 22 September 1888 at Barrow. According to our friend Richard Hymans, however, Ray's mark was not ratified by the AAA "as headed nails were used to support the bar".

The last record holder of the "climbing set" was another Briton, **Richard Dickinson** (born in 1867), who scaled 3.58 at Kidderminster on 4 July 1891.

By such a time the event already figured in American and Japanese college meets. And the Americans soon abandoned the hand shift, thus laying the foundations of modern vaulting. **Hugh Baxter**, a great athlete, thus vaulted 3.48 in 1887. It may be of interest to recall that back in 1878 he had experimented with a bamboo pole, only to return to a hickory one the following year.

A long period of American domination began in

1898, when **Raymond Gustavus Clapp** (born on 31 May 1875) of Yale University scaled a height of 3.62 at Chicago on 18 June 1898, which was to remain the best mark of the 19th century.

The first Olympic winners were William Hoyt of USA in 1896 and William Baxter, another American, in 1900, both with 3.30. Strange things happened on the latter occasion, at Athens: to begin with, some of the best Americans decided to stay away from the competition on religious grounds, since the event was to be held on a Sunday. In subsequent days French organizers allowed them to appear in special events. In one of these Dan Horton (USA) cleared 3.45 to win from another American, Charles Dvorak, 3.35 – performances which obviously had no bearing on Olympic results. Baxter, the official champion, had won the high jump an hour earlier. Not surprisingly, such a double has never been matched in Olympic history !

From the days of "free enterprise" in vaulting

The so-called "climbing technique", prevalent in Britain in the early days of modern pole vaulting, especially in the Ulverston clan, had several varieties of sort, according to Montague Shearman. The famed English historian relates that a friend of his "once saw a small acrobat at a circus clear far greater heights by the simple process of clambering up the pole like a monkey as soon as it was poised, and then dropping over the bar". Shearman goes on to say: "Something of the trick suggested is employed by (Thomas) Ray, who shifts his hands up the bar when his pole is poised in the air".

1896 Olympics, Athens: pole vault (10 April): 1.William Hoyt (USA) 3.30; 2.Albert Tyler (USA) 3.25; 3.Joannis Theodoropoulos (Greece) 2.85; 4.Evangelos Damaskos (Greece) 2.80; 5.Basilios Xydas (Greece) 2.80.

1900 Olympics, Paris: pole vault (15 July): 1.Irving Baxter (USA) 3.30; 2.M.B. Colkett (USA) 3.25; 3.Carl Albert Andersen (Norway) 3.20; 4.(tie): Eric Lemming (Sweden), Jakob Kauser (Hungary) and Emile Gontier (France) 3.10; 7.K.G.Staaf (Sweden) 2.80; 8.August Nilsson (Sweden) 2.60.

LONG JUMP

A strange duel

This is one of the most natural events in track and field athletics. The long jumper has no implements to deal with and invariably follows a specified direction of run. That is probably the chief reason why jumping for distance has always been a popular practice among men of all races. In fact, this was the only jumping event included in the programme of the ancient Olympic Games. The Greeks, however, used jumping weights ("halteres"), swinging them forwards and backwards while in the air to supplement the action of arms and legs. In his book "Greek athletes and athletics", Prof. H.A.Harris ventures the opinion that the Greeks called long jump what was in fact a double, if not triple jump.

Even in the early days of modern athletics long jumping with dumb-bells was a popular exercise among British "pros". John Howard was credited with a mark of 9.01, apparently with a 5 lb. (2.27 kg.) dumb-bell at Chester in 1854. The first 7-metre jump of modern times is commonly attributed to **John Godwin Lane,** a sturdy little Irishman (born in 1853, 1.73 m. / 71 kg.): 7.05 at College Park, Dublin, on 11 June 1874, alas with suspected wind assistance (a factor which was seldom taken into consideration in the early days) and apparently on a gently sloping runway. More acceptable perhaps was a 7.06 (23-2) mark which Patrick Davin, another Irishman (born on 4 June 1857; 1.82 m./ 76 kg.) achieved on two occasions in 1883, at Monasterevan on 30 August and at Portarlington on 13 September, both from grass runways. In the same year John Parsons of England joined the "7-Metre Club" with 7.01. Like Davin, he also excelled as a high jumper.

America soon entered the picture and in 1886 a fast man like **Malcolm Worthington Ford** (born on 7 February 1862) brought the world record to the other side of the Atlantic with a leap of 7.08 (23-3). He was a most versatile athlete, a three-time winner of the AAU 100 y. title as well as holder of the best on record mark for the triple jump with 13.45 (1884).

1986 saw the introduction of the take-off board. Until then, the boundary simply consisted of a white line marked on the ground. The take-off board, 1.21 m. in length, 20 cm. in width and 10 cm. in depth, has since been the crux of long jumpers. It is commonly felt that if the jumper could be relieved of that psychological burden while going down the runway, his distances would automatically improve by several centimeters.

Among those who took turns in breaking the world record during the Nineties was **Charles Burgess Fry** (born on 25 April 1872; 1.79 m. / 79 Kg.), a famous English all-round sportsman who jumped 7.17 (23-6 ½) at Oxford on 4 March 1893.

1896 Olympics, Athens: long jump (7 April) – 1.Ellery Clark (USA) 6.35; 2.Robert Garrett (USA) 6.18; 3.James Connolly (USA) 6.11; 4.Alexandre Tuffère (France) 5.98; 5.Alphonse Grisel (France) 5.83; 6.Alexandros Chalkokondylis (Greece) 5.74; 7.Karl Schumann (Germany) 5.70; 8.D.Wein (Hungary) 5.64; 9.A.Skaltsoyiannis (Greece) 5.64.

The struggle for world supremacy between Irish and American long jumpers reached a climax near the turn of the century. **Meyer Prinstein** (born in Poland in December 1890; died on 10 March 1928; 1.80 / 74 Kg.), a student from Syracuse University, long jumped 7.23 (23-8 7/8) at New York on 11 June 1898, only to be excelled later in the season by **Walter Joseph May Newburn** (born in 1874; 1.90 m. / 91 Kg.), a big Irishman from Syracuse University, who did 7.25, then 7.33 (24-0 1/2) both times from a board take-off, the latter at Dublin on 16 July 1898. The following year it was the turn of versatile **Alvin Christian Kraenzlein** (born at Augsburg, Germany on 12 December 1876; died at Willes Barre, Pa., on 6 January 1928; 1.83 m. / 75 kg.). His parents migrated to USA when he was three. As a student at Pennsylvania University (where he was to get a degree in odontology in 1901) he rose to the highest standards of his time in the long jump and in the hurdles and could vie with the best in the sprints as well. He set world records in the 120 y. (and 110 m.) hurdles, in the 220 yard hurdles and in the long jump with 7.29 (twice) and 7.40 on 29 April 1899 at Franklin Field, Philadelphia, then 7.42 and 7.43 (24-4 ½) on 26 May at Manhattan Field, New York. His best times over the flat route were 10.0 (100 y.) and 21.8 (220 y.). This outstanding athlete had his most glorious days at the 1900 Olympics in Paris where he was able to run 8 races in the space of just 3 days (14/16 July) and won four titles for USA: 110 m. hurdles in 15 2/5, 70 m. flat in 7.0, long jump (7.185) and 200 m. hurdles (25 2/5).

Kraenzlein's most serious rival in the long jump was the above-mentioned Meyer Prinstein. The 1900 Olympic final in Paris was held on 15 July, a Sunday, and Prinstein was among those American athletes who chose to stay away on religious grounds. In his absence, Kraenzlein did 7.185, one centimeter beyond the distance reached by his rival in the qualifying round, and thus won the gold medal. Rumour has it that after the qualifying rounds both agreed not to compete on Sunday. As the story goes, Prinstein was ostensibly outraged when his team-mate failed to keep his word.

Thoughts of an athlete

In the first edition of the modern Olympics (Athens 1896) results were generally poor and the long jump was no exception. The winner, Ellery Clark of USA, then a 22-year old Harvard student, did no better than 6.43 (although, interestingly enough, he came back three days later to annex the high jump crown as well). He later recalled that day in his book "Reminiscences of an Athlete". In that event, competitors were allowed only three jumps. He fouled on his first two, then …… "I shall never forget my feelings as I stood at the end of the path for my third – and last – try. Five thousand miles, I reflected, I had come; and was it to end in this ? Three fouls and then five thousand miles back again, with that for my memory of the Games". Luckily enough, on that crucial last jump Clark was able to do himself justice.

Our friend Hubert Hamacher, a German who has probably studied the 19th century history of our sport more profoundly than anyone else, supplies an amusing consideration re: Clark – his best long jump mark in 1896, 6.426 m., barely sufficed to earn him a place among the top fifty in the World List of that year ! Yet he managed to earn a gold medal in the inaugural Olympics at Athens ! But then those Games were far from being fully representative of the best athletic power of those days.

1900 Olympics, Paris: long jump (15 July) – 1.Alvin Kraenzlein (USA) 7.185; 2.Meyer Prinstein (USA) 7.175 (made in qualifying round, 14 July); 3.Patrick Leahy (GB) 6.95; 4.William Remington (USA) 6.825; 5.Albert Delannoy (France) 6.755; 6. John McLean (USA) 6.435.

1900 Olympics, Paris: standing long jump (16 July) – 1.Raymod Ewry (USA) 3.30; 2.Irving Baxter (USA) 3.135; 3.Emile Torcheboeuf (France) 3.03; 4.Lewis Sheldon (USA).

TRIPLE JUMP

The jump-as-you-please era

The triple jump (or hop, step and jump) has been for many years one of the most neglected events in athletics. To this ostracism have largely contributed some of the major powers of the sport. In USA, for example, the event appeared on the AAU Championships programme in 1893, was dropped the following year and resumed only in 1906. What is more, it was not incorporated in college competition till 1959. In Germany, a country usually interested in all athletic events, the triple jump was at one stage ousted from the Championship programme for several years. In Britain the event made its first appearance in the AAA Championships only in 1914.

This event is a deceptively easy but in actual fact a most exacting test of athletic skill, requiring as it does a high combination of strength and technique. In few other events are the muscles subjected to such a strain as in the triple jump. During the 20th century. countries such as Japan and Australia in the Thirties and USSR and Poland in the Fifties have done much to popularize the triple jump, devoting full attention to its complicated technical aspects.

The first Olympic champion

The first title to be awarded at the Athens Olympics, on 6 April 1896, was won by James Connolly, a 30-year-old Harvard freshman. By winning the triple jump with 13.71 he became the first "olympionikos" of modern times. There are good reasons to believe that such a distinction could hardly have gone to a more deserving athlete. Historian Bill Mallon relates that "when he (Connolly) heard that several Bostonians were going to Athens (for the Games), he requested permission from his dean to leave school .... But his grades were not so good and permission was refused. Connolly then decided to drop out of school and made the trip anyway". But to achieve his end and make history he needed financial help. This was provided with money raised through a "cake sale" arranged in his parish! Connolly (born at South Boston, MA. on 28 November 1865) later became a writer of sea-faring novels.

The rules now governing the triple jump are reflected in the name which was given to it until not so long ago in English-speaking countries: hop, step and jump. In fact the three leaps are essentially different from one another. The first leap ("hop") is made with take-off and landing on the same foot; the second leap ("step") implies landing on the other foot, the third leap ("jump") has much in common with a normal long jump. It was only recently that the definition "triple jump" supplanted the older one.

The Irish and the Scots are the acknowledged fathers of this event, at least in modern times. The 19th century fashion in the Emerald Isle consisted in taking two hops and a jump, in which the best leg was used twice before the final jump. The leading Irish exponents of this form were John Daly (13.81 in 1873), John Purcell (15.11 in 1887, Daniel Shanahan (15.25 in 1888) and Matthew Roseingrave (15.26 in 1895). Two Scottish "pros" were also credited with fine marks: David Johnstone (15.39 in 1881) and Robert Hogg (15.16 in 1893). With the form now in use, Shanahan did 14.50 in 1886 and Purcell reached 14.70 in 1887. However, it should be noted that the book "1906 Irish Athletic Record" generally makes no distinction between different forms. This explains why Irish statisticians, e.g. Tony O'Donoghue, have been working hard to identify marks made with the now prevailing form.

Purcell's mark was excelled at the 1893 AAU Championships in Chicago, when Edward Bloss won with 14.78. This man was also credited with an interesting mark in an ultra-short indoor event: 2 4/5 over 20 yards (18.28 m.) in 1892.

At the 1896 Olympics in Athens an American of Irish extraction, **James B. Connolly** (born on 28 November 1865; 1.75 m. / 72 Kg.) won with 13.71, taking two hops and a jump. It was a "jump-as-you-please" contest, every competitor being free to use the form he liked best. Four years later, at the Paris Olympics, Connolly improved to 13.97 but had to be content with second place behind the redoubtable Meyer Prinstein (14.47).

Olympics, Athens – Triple jump (6 April): 1.James Connolly (USA) 13.71; 2.Alexandre Tuffère (France) 12.70; 3.Joannis Persakis (Greece) 12.52; 4.Alajos Szokolyi (Hungary) 12.30; 5.Christos Zumis (Greece); 6.Alexandros Chalkokondylis (Greece).

1900 Olympics, Paris – Triple Jump (16 July): 1.Meyer Prinstein (USA) 14.47; 2.James Connolly (USA) 13.97; 3.Lewis Sheldon (USA) 13.64; 4.Patrick Leahy (GB) 13.36; 5.Albert Delannoy (France); 6.Alexandre Tuffère (France).

1900 Olympics, Paris – Standing triple jump (16 July): 1.Ray Ewry (USA) 10.58; 2.Irving Baxter (USA) 9.95; 3.Robert Garrett (USA) 9.50; 4.Lewis Sheldon (USA) 9.45.

MEN 1901-1920

2

HIGH JUMP

Horine, a smart inventor

In the first decade of the new century Olympic laurels in the high jump were won with relatively unimpressive performances. In 1904 Samuel Jones of USA won at St. Louis with 1.80 and two years later Con Leahy of Northern Ireland needed no better than 1.775 to win at the "interim" Games in Athens – an edition now regarded as unofficial by historians. Among place winners on both occasions was Lajos Gönczy of Hungary, one of the first "continentals" to emerge in this event, who could claim a personal best of 1.82 (1904).

In the 1906 Games in Athens there was also a contest in the standing high jump, won by a most versatile American, Ray Ewry.

1904 Olympics, St.Louis - High Jump (29 August): 1.Samuel Jones (USA) 1.80; 2.Garrett P. Serviss (USA) 1.778; 3.Paul Weinstein (Germany) 1.778; 4.Lajos Gönczy (Hungary) 1.75; 5.Emil Freymark (USA), 6.Ervin Barker (USA) 1.70.

1904 Olympics, St.Louis - Standing High Jump (31 August): 1.Ray Ewry (USA) 1.60; 2.Joseph Stadler (USA) 1.45; 3.Lawson Robertson (USA) 1.45; 4.John Biller (USA) 1.42; 5.Lajos Gönczy (Hungary) 1.35.

1906 Interim Olympics, Athens - High Jump (26 April): 1.Con Leahy (GB/Ireland) 1.775; 2.Lajos Gönczy (Hungary) 1.75; 3.(tie) Themistoklis Diakidis (Greece) and Herbert Kerrigan (USA) 1.725. 5.Gunnar Rönström (Sweden) 1.675.

1906 Interim Olympics, Athens - Standing High Jump (30 April): 1.Ray Ewry (USA) 1.56; 2.(tie) Léon Dupont (Belgium), Lawson Robertson (USA) and Martin Sheridan (USA) 1.40; 5.Lajos Gönczy (Hungary) 1.35; Disqualified for breaking rules: K Tsiklitiras (Greece) (1.30).

A good overall standard was first attained in the 1908 Olympics in London, with seven men mastering the 6 ft. (1.829 m.) barrier.

1908 Olympics, London - High Jump (21 July): 1.Harry Potter (USA) 1.905; 2.(tie) Géo André (France), Con Leahy (GB/Ire), István Somody (Hungary) 1.88; 5.(tie) Herbert Gidney (USA), Thomas Moffitt (USA) 1.85; 7.Neil Patterson (USA) 1.83.

1908 Olympics, London - Standing High Jump (18 July): 1.Ray Ewry (USA) 1.57; 2.(tie) Konstantin Tsiklitiras (Greece) and John Biller (USA) 1.55; 4.Leroy Holmes (USA) 1.52; 5.(tie) Platt Adams (USA), Géo André (France) and Alfred Motte (France) 1.47.

But the first man who really made history in the event was **George Horine** of USA (born at Escondido, California, on 3 February 1890; 1.80 m. / 73 kg.). Like most jumpers of his generation he began with the scissors style, i.e. approaching the bar from the right side and jumping off his left foot. His best with this form, while a school boy, was 1.549. Here is how, in his own words (from an article he wrote for Dink Templeton's book "The High Jump") he "invented" the new form:

"I was forced into the "Western" form through an accident. I was trying a few jumps with some of the other fellows (before entering college) and as the available grounds were about 12 feet (3.66 m.) wide and 40 feet (12.19 m.) long we had to place the standards in a certain way and leave them there" ... "So I tried taking off from my left foot. This was the beginning of my new form. ... Within a week after my discovery of the new jump action in 1909, I cleared 5 ft. 9 in. (1.75 m.) and a few days later made 6 ft. 1 in. (1.85 m.)". In rolling over the bar his body was virtually parallel with the ground and his centre of gravity lay much lower than in previous styles of jumping – hence the economy of the operation. The smart inventor hailed from the West Coast, and so the new form was aptly named "Western Roll".

After enrolling at Stanford University, however, Horine was induced to abandon his unorthodox form in favour of a straight-on jump. Even so, he continued to improve: 1.87 in 1910, 1.93 in 1911. It looked as if his "reactionary" coach was right after all. But Horine had different views and eventually returned to his self-developed form. From then on he really scaled the heights. Early in 1912 he set a new American Collegiate record of 1.949 and on 29 March, at Palo Alto, he did 1.984 for a new world record. A few weeks later, on 18 May, still on the Stanford campus at Palo Alto, he went over a crossbar set at 6 ft. 7 in. (2.007 m.), after a hard fight with his team-mate Edward Beeson, who was second with 1.943. As Horine later admitted in one of his writings, "My jump at 6 ft. 7 in. was not clean", inasmuch as he touched the bar in going over (which is, of course, all but rare in record efforts). On the other hand, he claimed that he had "one-to-two inches (2.5 to 5 cm.) to spare" in his previous jump at 1.948 m. Be it as it may, he became history's first 2-metre jumper. (Whether he "knew" or not, that is of course another story – even nowadays, almost a century later, Americans ignore the metric system).

The new record holder was awaited at the Olympic Games in Stockholm with mixed feelings of anxiety and incredulity. Unluckily enough, he was apparently past his peak for the season by the time he faced the élite of the world, two months after his greatest achievement. He had to be content with a bronze medal at 1.89. Another American, tall Alma Richards, won at 1.93 after a great battle with the lithe and nervous Hans Liesche of Germany (1.91). Among other place winners was Jim Thorpe, the famous all-rounder, who wound up fifth at 1.87 but was disqualified. It should be noted that only a few weeks earlier, in New York, Thorpe had mastered 1.956, beating Richards (1.93) and Horine (1.905).

1912 Olympics, Stockholm – High Jump (8 July): 1.Alma Richards (USA) 1.93; 2.Hans Liesche (Germany) 1.91; 3.Gedorge Horine (USA) 1.89; 4.Egon Erickson (USA) 1.87; 5.Harry Grumpelt (USA) 1.85; 6.John Johnstone (USA) 1.85; 7.K Kullerstrand (Sweden) 1.83; 8.(tie) I.Wardener (Hungary) and T.Carroll (GB) 1.75.

1912 Olympics, Stockholm – Standing High Jump (13 July): 1.Platt Adams (USA) 1.63; 2.Benjamin Adams (USA) 1.60; 3.Constantin Tsiklitiras (Greece) 1.55; 4.(tie) E. Möller (Sweden), Richard Byrd (USA) and Leo Goehring (USA) 1.50.

Horine's contribution to the progress of this event was certainly great, no matter if critics of the time generally regarded his style of jumping as a bit difficult to learn. The advantages in clearance form were so obvious, however, that the new form gradually caught on, first in the States, and much later in the rest of the world. A curious detail: Horine won the AAU title just once, in 1915, with no better than 1.848. In the six-year span of his career, however, he won 59 of his 64 competitions.

Memories of a star performer

As often as not, the great pioneers of modern athletics used to write extensively about their past experiences. George Horine, for example, contributed a long and interesting article to Dink Templeton's book "The High Jump" (published in 1927). As an American, Horine thought in feet and inches rather than metres and centimetres – no matter if, in the eyes of the major part of the outer world, he owed his fame mostly to having been the first member of the Two-Metre Club - or better as the pioneer of the Western Roll. In said article he revealed, among other things, that he cleared 6 feet (1.829 m.) or higher no less than 57 times during his career. And he did 6 feet 4 inches (1.93) or better ten times. He also said that his best practise mark was 6-8 ¼ (2.038).

In terms of "technical tricks", Horine wrote that in training he always used **two** handkerchiefs on the bar. "I watched these and tried to clear between them. I never took my eyes off these markers".

Another Californian, **Edward Beeson** (born on 2 June 1890; 1.84 m. / 66 Kg.) was the next record-breaker. Using a variant of the Western Roll and reportedly taking advice from … shotputter Ralph Rose, on 2 May 1914 at Berkeley he bettered the world record with 2.014. On that occasion he and Horine began by mastering 1.84, then they chose to try the new record height. Beeson made it on his second attempt, while Horine failed three times.

Next to appear on the American scene was a truly amazing jumper hailing from the Rocky Mountains – Clinton Larson. In a way he can be credited with using a "Fosbury Flop" ante-litteram, with a face-upward, back-to-the-bar position resulting in a complete lay-out. Indifferent in height (1.76 m.) but capable of running the 100 y. in 10 1/5, he laid the stress on the approach run. In 1917 he won the AAU title (1.892 m.) and cleared 2.029 in an unsanctioned meet at Provo, Utah. In 1919 he came to Europe and won his event at the Inter-Allied Games in Paris with 1.864. In 1924, when he was nearly 32, he went over a bar set at 2.07 in the course of an exhibition at Magna, Utah. In 1920 the Olympic title was won by Richmond Landon of USA with a jump of 1.94. Third in the event was Bo Ekelund of Sweden, who in later years was to become one of his country's leading athletic personalities.

1920 Olympics, Antwerp – High Jump (17 August): 1.Richmond Landon (USA) 1.94; 2.Harold Muller (USA) 1.90; 2.Bo Ekelund (Sweden) 1.90; 4.Walther Whalen (USA) 1.85; 5.John Murphy (USA) 1.85; 6.Howard Baker (GB) 1.85; 7.(tie) Einar Thulin (Sweden) and Pierre Lewden (France) 1.80; 9.(tie) René Labat (France), Tim Carroll (GB), Hans Jagenburg (Sweden), Thorvig Swahn (Sweden) 1.75.

POLE VAULT

Lex Americana (with a French interference)

American domination in pole vaulting was to continue for nearly …. three- quarters of the new century, with rare interferences by specialists from other countries. The first record-breaker of the 20th century was Norman Dole, an American who vaulted 3.69 in 1904. He was not present at the St.Louis Olympics of that year though and the title was won by another American, Charles Dvorak (3.50). Another famous absentee on that occasion was **Fernand Gonder,** a fore-runner of the French vaulting school of our days. This man of medium build (1.70 m./ 56 Kg.) was born at Rochefort on 12 June 1883. He first became acquainted with pole vaulting while in military service at Bordeaux in the spring of 1904. A few weeks later he set his French record with 3.38. Then he went on to win the national title in Paris with 3.69, thereby equalling Norman Dole's world record, set only a few weeks earlier. On 4 June 1905, at Gradignan, Gonder improved to 3.74 to become the only owner of the record. In the same year he reportedly cleared 4.00 during an exhibition. Contrary to what was said and written in other countries, Gonder was not a "pole climber". His form conformed with the rules. He became internationally known in 1906, when he won his event at the "Interim" Olympics in Athens with 3.50, beating among others Bruno Söderström of Sweden and Edward Glover of USA, runner-up at the 1905 AAU Championships.

1904 Olympics, St.Louis - Pole Vault (3 September): 1.Charles Dvorak (USA) 3.50; 2.Leroy Samse (USA) 3.43; 3.Louis Wilkins (USA) 3.43; 4.Ward McLanahan (USA) 3.35; 5.Claude Allen (USA) 3.35; 6.Walter Dray (USA) 7.Paul Weinstein (Germany).

1906 Interim Olympics, Athens – Pole Vault (25 April): 1.Fernand Gonder (France) 3.50; 2.Bruno Söderström (Sweden) 3.40; 3.Edward Glover (USA) 3.35.

Fernand Gonder turned to rugby shortly afterwards and thus missed the 1908 Olympics in London, where Edward Cook and Alfred Gilbert, both of USA, were bracketed in an unusual tie for first at 3.71, **each earning a gold medal** !

1908 Olympics, London - Pole Vault (24 July): 1.(tie) Edward Cook (USA) & Alfred Gilbert (USA) 3.71; 3.(tie) Ernest Archibald (Canada), Charles Jacobs (USA) and Bruno Söderström (Sweden) 3.58; 6.(tie) Sam Bellah (USA) and Georgios Banikas (Greece) 3.50; 8.C. Szathmary (Hungary) 3.35.

By that time, Americans had regained the pole position even in the record department: by the end of 1908 the new "ceiling" was 3.90 by Walter Dray. The above-mentioned Alfred Gilbert cleared a bar set at 4 metres during an exhibition at Westville in 1909. When his career was over he turned to business and eventually made a fortune as president of a toy factory.

History's first official 13-footer was a Yale man, **Robert Gardner** of USA (born on 9 April 1890 (1.83 m. / 60 Kg.), who did 13 ft. 1 in. (3.98 m.) at

Philadelphia on 1 June 1912. Exactly a week later the metric minded world received a more intelligible message when **Marcus Snowell Wright** (born at Chicago on 21 April 1890; 1.70 m. / 69 Kg.), a left-hander of medium build, cleared 4.02 in the U.S. Olympic Trials at Cambridge, MA. on 8 June 1912. Wright's form included some of the vital elements of modern vaulting technique, like a run of about 30 m., a prolonged "swing", a single-hand release, first with the lower (left) hand, then with the upper one (right) and an arch position in going over the bar. Same as a contemporary "inventor", high jumper George Horine, however, he failed to do himself justice at the 1912 Olympics in Stockholm. In a hotly contested event, six men went over 3.80 and victory went to Harry Babcock of USA at 3.95 while his compatriots Marcus Wright and Frank Nelson tied for second at 3.85.

1912 Olympics, Stockholm - Pole Vault (11 July): 1.Harry Babcock (USA) 3.95; 2.(tie) Frank Nelson (USA) and Marcus Wright (USA) 3.85; 4.(tie) William Happenny (Canada), Frank Murphy (USA) and Bertil Uggla (Sweden) 3.80; 7.Sam Bellah (USA) 3.75; 8.Gordon Dukes (USA), Frank Coyle (USA), Bill Fritz (USA) 3.65; 11.Robert Pasemann (Germany) 3.40.

Frank Foss (USA), the Olympic pole vault champion of 1920, surrounded by a good number of bewildered eye-witnesses. In those days landing (on unsound surfaces) was not the easiest part of the game.

First of the great post-war vaulters was **Frank Kent Foss** of USA (born on 9 May 1895; 1.72 m. / 66 Kg.), who perfected the "jackknife" clearance form, so called after the figure described by the body in going over the bar. In 1919 at Chicago he bettered Wright's record with a 4.05 vault. The following year he improved to 4.09 in winning the Olympic title at Antwerp. He was to remain for many years (till 1980) the only vaulter to have won both honours with a single stroke. Foss achieved the record height in what we may call a "modern" way: after failing in his first attempt at 4.00, he asked to take the remaining trials at 4.09 – and succeeded. Of course he had previously secured his victory at a lower height.

1920 Olympics, Antwerp - Pole Vault (20 August): 1.Frank Foss (USA) 4.09 (world record); 2.Henry Petersen (Denmark) 3.70; 3.Edwin Meyers (USA) 3.60; 4.Edward Knourek USA) 3.60; 5.Ernfrid Rydberg (Sweden) 3.60; 6.Lauritz Jörgensen (Denmark) 3.60; 7.Eldon Jenne (USA) 3.60; 8.Georg Högström (Sweden) 3.50; Johan Mattsson (Sweden) 3.50, Paul Lagarde (France) 3.50, Jussi Ruoho (Finland) 3.50; André Franquenelle (France) 3.50; René Joannes-Powell (Belgium) 3.50. Etienne Gajan (France) also did 3.50, in the qualifying round.

LONG JUMP

O'Connor, a peculiar record breaker

At the dawn of the new century Ireland had a man who was seemingly in a class with the American duo Kraenzlein-Prinstein. He was **Peter O'Connor** (born in County Wicklow on 18 October 1874; 1.86 m. / 66 Kg.). Like other leading athletes of his time, he missed the Paris Olympics (1900), but a few weeks later, at New Ross on 29 August, he beat Prinstein's world record with a 7.51 effort. It should be noted, however, that shortly before the Paris Games the man from the Emerald Isle had lost to Kraenzlein in the AAA Championships in London – 6.81 to 6.96.

The slender O'Connor had his vintage year in 1901, when he improved through 7.54 (Dublin, 27 May), 7.60 (Dublin, 15 July), 7.605 (Dublin, 28 July) and finally to 7.61 (Ballsbridge, Dublin on 5 August). These marks were made from a hard board take-off. In the same year O'Connor also did 7.63 at Portlaoise , but on a downhill runway. His marks in his relatively few appearances outside of Ireland were not so impressive, yet he won the English AAA title for six years in a row (1901-06), his best mark of the series being 7.25. In 1904 he missed the Olympics again, but two years later he showed up at the "Interim" Games in Athens, where he lost to Prinstein, 7.025 to 7.20, but evened the count with the American in the triple jump, after Prinstein called it a day due to an ankle injury. O'Connor, who was also a leading high jumper (1.88), had a technique all of his own – "he drew the knees up towards the chin and relied on his initial velocity to carry him sailing through the air". He jumped, mainly if not exclusively, on nervous energy. So poor were the competitive conditions in those days that during his long career he sprained his take–off (left) foot on seven occasions.

"A veritable steam-engine"

Peter O'Connor was undoubtedly one of Ireland's greatest pioneers in athletics. In his book "Champions of the Athletic Arena" (1946), William Dooley supplies interesting details about him: "Our stand-out long jumper – he writes – although not recommending smoking for aspiring athletes, has himself always smoked, in the words of a contemporary like a veritable steam-engine. Yet he is as well preserved at 73 years (at the time of Dooley's writing) as the average man a quarter of a century his junior, retaining the erect bearing, and much of the elasticity of movement of the athlete." Mr. Dooley went on to say: "the rough grass surfaces on which he competed were not conducive to record breaking performances such as those made by his successors several decades later".

The last sentence should obviously be fit whenever one indulges in the risky business of comparing top athletes of a past era with those of the present time.

Prinstein made amends for his bad luck at the 1900 Paris Games by scoring a fine double four years later in St.Louis. He won the long jump with 7.34 and the triple jump with 14.35 – a feat **no one** has been able to duplicate as of today ! In both events he achieved his best distance on the last trial.

1904 Olympics, St.Louis - Long jump (1 September): 1.Meyer Prinstein (USA) 7.34; 2. Daniel Frank (USA) 6.89; 3.Robert Stangland (USA)

6.88; 4.Fred Englehardt (USA) 6.63; 5.George Van Cleaf (USA); 6.John Hagerman (USA).

1904 Olympics, St.Louis – Standing Long Jump (29 August): 1.Ray Ewry (USA) 3.47; 2.Charles King (USA) 3.27; 3.John Biller (USA) 3.25; 4.Henry Field (USA) 3.18; 5.Paul Weinstein (Germany).

1906 Interim Olympics, Athens - Long Jump (27 April): 1.Meyer Prinstein (USA) 7.20; 2.Peter O'Connor (Ireland) 7.025; 3.Hugo Friend (USA) 6.96; 4.Hjalmar Mellander (Sweden) 6.585; 5.Sidney Abrahams (GB) 6.21; 6.Thomas Cronan (USA) 6.185; 7.Gunnar Rönström (Sweden) 6.15; 8.István Somodi (Hungary) 6.045; 9.Vasilios Stournaras (Greece) 6.03.

Ray Ewry (USA), "the Human Frog", a dominant figure in the standing jumps in the early days of the century.

1906 Interim Olympics, Athens – Standing Long Jump (27 April): 1.Ray Ewry (USA) 3.30; 2.Martin Sheridan (USA) 3.095; 3.Lawson Robertson (USA) 3.05; 4.Léon Dupont (Belgium) 2.975; O'Connor's world record was threatened for the first time in 1908, when his countryman Tim Ahearne did 7.57 at Kanturk, barely two weeks after finishing no better than eighth (with 6.72) in the Olympic final in London, which was won by Frank Irons of USA with 7.48.

1908 Olympics, London – Long Jump (22 July): 1.Frank Irons (USA) 7.48; 2.Daniel Kelley (USA) 7.09; 3.Calvin Bricker (Canada) 7.08; 4.Edward Cooke (USA) 6.97; 5.John Brennan (USA) 6.86; 6.Frank Mount-Pleasant (USA) 6.82; 7.Albert Weinstein (Germany) 6.77; 8.Timothy Ahearne (GB) 6.72; 9.D. Murray (GB) 6.71; 10.Gunnar Rönström (Sweden) 6.66.

1908 Olympics, London – Standing Long Jump (16 July): 1.Ray Ewry (USA) 3.33; 2.Constantin Tsiklitiras (Greece) 3.22; 3.Martin Sheridan (USA) 3.22; 4.John Biller (USA) 3.21; 5.Olle Ekberg (Sweden) 3.19.

America's lucky streak remained unbroken four years later in Stockholm, when Albert Gutterson improved on his previous best by almost a foot with a 7.60 effort.

1912 Olympics, Stockholm – Long Jump (12 July): 1.Albert Gutterson (USA) 7.60; 2.Calvin Bricker (Canada) 7.21; 3.Georg Åberg (Sweden) 7.18; 4.Harry Worthington (USA) 7.03; 5.Eugene Mercer (USA) 6.97; 6.Fred Allen (USA) 6.94; 7.Robert Pasemann (Germany) 6.82; 8.Frank Irons (USA) 6.80; 9.H.S.O. Ashington (GB) 6.78; 10. R.F.Bie (Norway) 6.75. Disqualified: Jim Thorpe (USA) 6.89.

1912 Olympics, Stockholm – Standing Long Jump (8 July): 1.Constantin Tsiklitiras (Greece) 3.37; 2.Platt Adams (USA) 3.36; 3.Benjamin Adams (USA) 3.28; 4.C. Malmsten (Sweden) 3.20; 5.(tie) E. Möller (Sweden) and Leo Goehring (USA) 3.14; 7.A. Baronyi (Hungary) 3.13; 8.Richard Byrd (USA) 3.12.

The great tradition of black long jumpers was inaugurated in the early post-war days by Sol Butler, an American who distinguished himself on both sides of the Atlantic. In 1919, at the Inter-Allied Games in Paris he won with 7.557, a mark curiously accompanied in press reports by what was then a seldom heard verdict

- wind assisted. In 1920 Butler earned a berth on the US Olympic team with a 7.51 effort, leaving his nearest rival 38 cm. behind. But at the 1920 Antwerp Olympics (the first of the post-World War I era) the strongly built Butler was unlucky enough to injure himself in the qualifying round. He wound up seventh with 6.60. This opened the door to Europe's first victory in the event: William Petersson of Sweden (who later changed his name to Björneman) clinched the gold medal with 7.15.

1920 Olympics, Antwerp - Long Jump (18 August): 1.William Petersson (Sweden) 7.15; 2.Carl Johnson (USA) 7.095; 3.Eric Abrahamsson (Sweden) 7.08; 4.Dink Templeton (USA) 6.95; 5.Erling Aastad (Norway) 6.885; 6.Rolf Franksson (Sweden) 6.73; 7.Sol Butler (USA) 6.60; 8.Einar Raeder (Norway) 6.585; 9.Gösta Bladin (Sweden) 6.57; 10.Johan Johannesen (Norway) 6.565.

TRIPLE JUMP

Ahearne & Ahearn Ltd.

The first man to achieve notable distances in international competition was Meyer Prinstein of USA, no matter if his winning efforts in the Olympics – 14.47 in 1900 and 14.35 in 1904 – appear rather irrelevant if compared with his known potential as a long jumper. The programme of the 1900 and 1904 Olympics also included a standing hop, step and jump, which was won on both occasions by **Raymond Charles Ewry** of USA (born at Lafayette, Indiana, on 14 October 1873; 1.85 m. / 79 Kg.), legendary athlete who is remembered as the greatest specialist of all time in the standing jumps. During his career, which lasted nearly twenty years, he massed a huge number of championship titles, including eight Olympic gold medals (plus two at the "Interim" Games of 1906).

1904 Olympics, St.Louis - Triple Jump (1 September): 1.Meyer Prinstein (USA) 14.35; 2.Fred Englehardt (USA) 13.90; 3.Robert Stangland (USA) 13.36, 4.John Fuhler (USA) 12.91; 5.George Van Cleaf (USA); 6.John Hagerman (USA); 7.Samuel Jones (USA).

1904 Olympics, St. Louis - Standing Triple Jump (3 September): 1.Ray Ewry (USA) 10.54; 2.Charles King (USA) 10.16; 3.Joseph Stadler (USA) 9.60; 4.Garrett Serviss (USA) 9.53.

The last internationally visible sparks of the Irish tradition – apart from Eamonn Fitzgerald's unheralded fourth place at the 1932 Olympics in Los Angeles – were offered by the Ahearne brothers of County Limerick. Timothy and Daniel. The former won the triple jump in the colours of Great Britain at the 1908 Olympics in London, at the age of twenty-two, with 14.92. His younger brother **Daniel Ahearn** (born in County Limerick on 2 April 1888; 1.78 m. / 72 Kg.) soon emigrated to America, where he dropped the final "e" of his family name. He was probably the first of the great triple jumpers. Between 1910 and 1918 he won the AAU title 8 times, that is every year except once, in 1912, when victory went to Platt Adams, a famous all-round jumper. As a record-breaker, Daniel did 15.12 in 1910 and 15.52 in 1911, both times at Celtic Park, Long Island, New York. The latter mark consisted of a 6.10 hop, a 3.50 step and a 5.92 jump. But he was to join that legion of athletes who just could no do themselves justice in the Olympic Games. He did not compete at Stockholm in 1912, and eight years later, at Antwerp, he was past his peak and had to be content with a sixth place (14.08). Winner at Stockholm was Gustaf ("Topsy") Lindblom of Sweden with 14.76. Incidentally, Lindblom shared with the famous Torsten Tegnér (for many years editor and publisher of "Idrottsbladet", Stockholm) the honour of pioneering Swedish sports journalism. The Olympic final of 1920, held under poor conditions, was won by a Finn, Vilho Tuulos, with 14.505. By then the heydays of Irish and American triple jumpers were virtually over.

1908 Olympics, London - Triple jump (25 July): 1.Timothy Ahearne (GB/Ireland) 14.92; 2.J.Garfield MacDonald (Canada) 14.76; 3.Edvard Larsen (Norway) 14.39; 4.Calvin Bricker (Canada) 14.09; 5.Platt Adams (USA) 14.07; 6.Frank Mount-Pleasant (USA) 13.97; 7.Karl Fryksdahl (Sweden) 13.65; 8.J.J.Brennan (USA) 13.59; 9.Martin Sheridan (USA) 13.42; 10. D.A.Stupart (South Africa) 13.40.

1912 Olympics, Stockholm - Triple Jump (15 July): 1.Gustaf Lindblom (Sweden) 14.76; 2.Georg Åberg (Sweden) 14.51; 3.Erik Almlöf (Sweden) 14.17; 4.Erling Vinne (Norway) 14.14; 5.Platt Adams (USA) 14.09; 6.Edvard Larsen (Norway) 14.06; 7.Hjalmar Ohlsson (Sweden) 14.01; 8.Nils

Fixdal (Norway) 13.96; 9.Charles Brickley (USA) 13.88; 10.Gustaf Nordén (Sweden) 13.81.

1920 Olympics (Antwerp) – Triple Jump (21 August): 1.Vilho Tuulos (Finland) 14.505; 2.Folke Jansson (Sweden) 14.48; 3.Erik Almlöf (Sweden) 14.27; 4.Ivar Sahlin (Sweden) 14.175; 5.Sherman Landers (USA) 14.17; 6.Daniel Ahearn (USA) 14.08; 7.Ossian Nylund (Finland) 13.74; 8.Howard Baker (GB) 13.675; 9.Kaare Bache (Norway) 13.64; 10.Sven Runström (Sweden) 13.63.

MEN 1921-1940

3

HIGH JUMP

The advent of the "Straddle"

The outstanding figure of the Twenties in the high jump was **Harold Marion Osborn** of USA (b. at Butler, Illinois, on 13 April 1899; d. on 5 April 1975; 1.81 m. / 73 Kg.). A keen student of form, he developed a very efficient side-to-the-bar clearance and outshone all his predecessors in brilliance and consistency of performance. As a great all-round man, he holds a unique record, being the only athlete to this day to have coupled an Olympic victory in an individual event with a victory in the decathlon. This happened in Paris in 1924: first he annexed the high jump crown at 1.98, then he won the ten-event grind with a record score. His best official mark in the high jump was 2.038 at Urbana, Illinois, on 27 May 1924.

Harold Osborn (USA), double Olympic champion in 1924 (high jump & decathlon). In 1925 he showed Europeans how 2 metres heights, or just about, could be mastered, even in a queer setting.

1924 Olympics, Colombes, Paris - High Jump (7 July): 1.Harold Osborn (USA) 1.98; 2.Leroy Brown (USA) 1.95; 3.Pierre Lewden (France) 1.92; 4.Thomas Poor (USA) 1.88; 5.Jenö Gáspár (Hungary) 1.88; 6.Helge Jansson (Sweden) 1.85; 7.Pierre Guilloux (France) 1.85; 8.(tie) Sverre Helgesen (Norway) and Lawrence Roberts (South Africa) 1.83.

The following year, at the Texas Relays in Austin, Osborn did 2.056 in an exhibition. He was the first American to master the classic 2-metre barrier on several occasions under the eyes of European crowds. It was as a result of his trick of pressing the bar back in towards the uprights with his hand that the IAAF introduced a new rule to the effect that the bar should be able to fall on either side. This bespectacled American, who was to become a doctor of osteopathy, had a long career: he managed to clear 1.981 at the age of 37 and in the same year, 1936, he set a world record of 1.676 in the standing high jump. Third in the 1924 Olympic final in Colombes near Paris was Pierre Lewden of France, whose name was to symbolize a modified scissors style which practically cornered the market in continental Europe for many years.

Lewden's best in the high jump, 1.95 in 1925, was fractionally inferior to the best-on-record for Europe, jointly held by Tim Carroll of Ireland (1913) and Benjamin Howard Baker of Britain (1921) with 1.956.

By the end of 1932, i.e. twenty years after Horine's historic record, only ten men had jumped 2 metres or higher. The only non-American in that group was Simeon Toribio of the Philipppines, who cleared exactly that height in the Ninth Far Eastern Games at Tokyo in 1930. In the Olympics, however, long drawn competitions made it difficult for anyone to reach record heights. So at Amsterdam, in 1928, Robert King of USA won the Olympic title with 1.94, while Osborn finished fifth.

1928 Olympics, Amsterdam – High Jump (29 July): 1.Robert King (USA) 1.94; 2.Ben Hedges (USA) 1.91; 3.Claude Ménard (France) 1.91; 4.Samujel Toribio (Philippines) 1.91; 5.Harold Osborn (USA) 1.91; 6.Kazuo Kimura (Japan) 1.88; 7.(tie) Pierre Lewden (France), Charles McGinnis (USA), Mikio Oda (Japan) and André Cherrier (France) 1.88.

Four years later, at Los Angeles, Duncan McNaughton of Canada broke the long chain of American victories by defeating Robert Van Osdel, Toribio and Cornelius Johnson in a jump-off, after all four had cleared 1.97 in the competition proper. The Canadian, who chose that occasion to make the best jump of his career, had matured as a star athlete while a student at the University of Southern California in Los Angeles. One of his team-mates was Van Osdel, the American who placed second in the Olympic event. Dean Cromwell, famous coach of the "Trojans" (battle name of the USC students), had been teaching his two pupils how to beach each other while beating all others. Seldom, if ever, did two men learn the same lesson so well ! A PS seems to be in order: if the fewer trials-and-misses rule had been in force then, Van Osdel would have won, having cleared 1.97 on his first attempt. Johnson, McNaughton and Toribio would have followed in that order. In those days, of course, placings for the medals were decided in a jump-off.

1932 Olympics, Los Angeles – High Jump (31 July): 1.Duncan McNaughton (Canada) 1,97; 2.Robert Van Osdel (USA) 1.97; 3.Simeon Toribio (Philippines) 1,97; 4.Cornelius Johnson (USA) 1.97; 5.Ilmari Reinikka (Finland) 1.94; 6.Kazuo Kimura (Japan) 1.94; 7.(tie) Jerz Plawczyk (Poland) and Misao Ono (Japan) 1.90; 9.(tie) Jack Portland (Canada), Claude Ménard (France), George Spitz (USA), Birger Haug (Norway), Angiolino Tommasi (Italy) 1.85; 14.Paul Riesen (Switzerland) 1.80.

Europe had to wait till 1934 to welcome her first 2-metre jumper. This was **Kalevi Kotkas** (born at Reval, now Tallinn, on 10 August 1913; 1.94 m. / 96 Kg.). This Estonian-born athlete opted for the Finnish nationality in 1932. His first clearance of the magic height occurred in South America during a night meet at Rio de Janeiro on 7 March 1934, when he mastered a bar set at 2.01. Later in the year he won the European Championship title at Turin with 2.00. This was the inaugural edition of this continental meet.

Even a modern observer is astonished to learn that Kotkas could lift his massive frame rather consistently over 1.98 while using a modified version of the scissors. More understandably, perhaps, he was also a first-class discus thrower (51.27 in 1937) and a good shot putter (15.55 in 1938). Later in 1934, two other Europeans quickly followed in Kotkas' footsteps: Mihály Bodosi of Hungary and Veikko Peräsalo of Finland did 2.005. In 1935 two Japanese jumpers, Hiroshi Tanaka and Yoshiro Asakuma, raised the Asian record to 2.01.

All these men used the Eastern cut-off, or slight variations of it. In USA the last major exponent of this jumping form was George Spitz, appropriately enough an Easterner, who flirted with the record heights in the early Thirties, with top marks of 2.045 indoors (1932) and 2.032 outdoors (1934).

The man who succeeded Osborn as world record holder was a Western Roll jumper from California, Walter Marty, who did 2.048 in 1933 and 2.061 in 1934. Still in '34, he cleared 2.07 in an unsanctioned meet. The tradition of great black high jumpers was inaugurated by **Cornelius Cooper Johnson** (born in Los Angeles on 21 August 1913; died in 1946; 1.91 m. / 79 Kg.), who is remembered as one of the most invincible performers in the annals of the event. As previously related, this precocious Western Roller finished fourth at the Los Angeles Olympics, aged nineteen. He had improved from 1.828 in 1930 through 1.93 in 1931 till 1.997 in the Olympic year. "Corny", whose legs accounted for 49% of his height, first mastered a record height in the AAU Indoor Championships at New York's Madison Square Garden on 22 February 1936, when he cleared 2.055 from a board take-off. Rather unexpectedly, he got company at that height from another American jumper, Edward Burke, who eventually won the title in a jump-off. Exactly on the same day, possibly a few hours later, at Fort Collins, Colorado, Gilbert Cruter cleared 2.054 from a dirt take-off in another indoor meet. Both Burke and Cruter were only 21 at the time.

Johnson conquered the official world record, i.e. the outdoor one, at the US Olympic Tryouts on 12 July, still in New York. On that occasion several good jumpers folded up under the pressure of the occasion. Marty, Spitz, Burke and Mel Walker (who had done 2.032 at the AAU Championships a week earlier) were unable to clear 1.981. Delos Thurber, a Californian, secured the vital third place and a berth on the Olympic team by going over that height, leaving Johnson and Dave Albritton alone to fight it out between themselves after that. Having by then got the tickets they wanted so much, the two men mastered 2.032, then had the bar raised to 2.076. Both made the record height on their second try, first Johnson, then Albritton. By then, Johnson had enough of co-ownerships. At the Berlin Olympics he was all alone over 2.03, thus winning the most coveted of titles. Albritton, Thurber and Kalevi Kotkas of Finland followed in that order, all with 2.00. All the first four thus broke Osborn's twelve-year old Olympic record (1.98). And Kotkas became the first man in history to jump 2 metres and go unrewarded by a medal.

In the four-year period between Los Angeles and Berlin, Johnson was outjumped only once, by Al Threadgill in an indoor meet in 1936. He continued through the 1938 indoor season. He died under tragic conditions in 1946.

Kotkas had his greatest day at Göteborg on 1 September 1936, when he raised the European record to 2.04, beating Olympic runner-up Albritton (2.02). In subsequent seasons, the Finn put on further weight, and his standard as a high jumper went down slowly but steadily.

A forgotten record

One relatively little known European high jumper of the late Thirties was Nikolay Kovtun of USSR, who in a meet held in Moscow on 17 June 1937, cleared a bar set at 2.01 – second best ever by a European up to that time. An estimated 50,000 spectators saw this meet, yet Kovtun's name was to remain virtually unknown outside of Russia – and, for that matter, also in the eyes of future Russian generations. This sad story was brought to light by Yevgeniy Malkov in the daily paper "Sovyetskiy Sport" on 24 June 1988. The article, titled "A Jump in the Unknown" and subtitled "Truth from Distant Years", revealed that "after his record performance Kovtun had little time to rejoice. Before the year was out some people in uniform came to his training camp and took him aside. After that, he was never seen again. Those were the days when thousands of guiltless individuals were branded as enemies of the people. And nobody was given further explanations".

Kovtun was in fact sentenced to ten years in jail, a time he spent in the North under hard circumstances. He was freed in 1947, but only three years later he was arrested once more and sentenced to another five years, a time he spent in the Urals. Meanwhile, Soviet statisticians had been given lessons in putting back the clock of history: Kovtun's name and records (he also held the USSR triple jump mark: 14.66 in 1936) were expunged from all books. In early post-war years Yuriy Ilyasov was credited with a new national record of .... 1.99. As destiny would have it, Kovtun was set free in 1955, the year in which Yuriy Styepanov moved a step forward and raised the USSR record to 2.02.

Another jumper of Kovtun's generation, Edmund Rokhlin, recalls meeting Kovtun after the liberation: "He in no way resembled the strong man I knew from pre-war days. Silent, reserved, he hardly spoke with anybody. And he no longer had any interest in sport". Kovtun died of a heart attack in 1981. In 1988 the monthly magazine "Lyogkaya Atletika" published revised summaries of the USSR Championships for the period 1920-40. The names of once expunged athletes appeared in bold type. In addition to Kovtun's, I counted **38 such entries !**

PS. In a previous book of mine ("Athletics", 2000) I wrote that Kovtun was one of the earliest European adepts of the "straddle". I have since learnt that he used in fact a conventional "Western Roll".

1936 Olympics, Berlin – High Jump (2 August): 1.Cornelius Johnson (USA) 2.03; 2.David Albritton (USA) 2.00; 3.Delos Thurber (USA) 2.00; 4.Kalevi Kotkas (Finland) 2.00; 5.Kimio Yada (Japan) 1.97; 6.(tie) Hiroshi Tanaka (Japan), Lauri Kalima (Finland), Yoshiro Asakuma (Japan), Gustav Weinkötz (Germany) 1.94; 10.(tie) Aksel Kuuse (Estonia), Günther Gehmert (Germany) 1.90.

David Donald Albritton (born at Danville, Alabama on 13 April 1913; 1.905 m. / 71 Kg.) was then only at the beginning of a fabulous career. Between 1936 and 1950 he won the AAU title five times and matched the height of the eventual winner on two other occasions. He was also the first jumper of international renown to adopt a prone position over the crossbar, thus introducing what came to be known as the "belly roll" or straddle style of jumping. This form was used for the first time in championship competition as early as in 1930 by a Dean Cromwell pro-

Dave Albritton (USA) tying an ultra-fresh world record in the high jump (2.076) at the 1936 Olympic Tryouts in New York. First to master that height, a few minutes earlier, was Cornelius Johnson, here lying on the grass.

tégé, Jim Stewart of the University of Southern California, who in that year cleared 1.988. This most economical of all clearance forms calls for great co-ordination and perfect timing. Another early exponent of the belly roll was Gilbert Cruter, a tall man from Colorado, mentioned earlier in this chapter.

Last in the chain of prominent American jumpers of those days was Melvin Walker, who cleared 2.076 from a dirt take-off indoors in 1937, then came to Europe later in the same year and twice bettered the official world record, first with 2.08 (Stockholm, 6 August), then with 2.09 at Malmö on 12 August. Walker used the "Western Roll".

POLE VAULT

American symphony

Early in the Twenties, Europeans in general and Scandinavians in particular were becoming familiar with the art of pole vaulting. Henry Petersen, a Danish gymnast, was an Olympic finalist on two occasions - second in 1920, fourth in 1924. He emerged at 18 with a national record of 3.69 (1918), a great achievement for a junior in those days. Seven years later he wound up with 4.038. In the meantime, however, another Scandinavian had risen to more spectacular heights.

Charles Hoff of Norway (born at Fredrikstad on 9 May 1902; 1.88 m. / 76 Kg.) came to athletics through cross country running. He took up vaulting in 1920. The following year he captured the Norwegian record at 3.545 and brought it to 3.87 before the season was out. The latter mark was good enough to earn him a third place in the 1921 World List ! Such a detail certainly points to the relative paucity of competition in those days. In 1922 Hoff became Europe's first 4-metre man with a 4.02 clearance and later in the season he set a new world record of 4.12 (Copenhagen, 3 September). In subsequent years he built up a substantial lead over his American and European opponents by achieving record marks of 4.21 in 1923, 4.23 and 4.252 in 1925. The last performance, made at Turku, Finland on 2 September, remained unsurpassed as a European record till 1937. Hoff was, however, denied the supreme satisfaction of winning Olympic laurels. In 1924 an injured ankle forced him to give up vaulting in the weeks preceding the Paris Olympics, but apparently allowed him to do a fair amount of running. So the world's no.1 vaulter appeared at Stade de Colombes only as a runner: he reached the semi-finals of the 400 m. and earned eighth place in the 800 m. final ! His absence from the pole vault competition was historically important, in that it allowed America's winning streak to continue. (It was finally broken in ....1972). The title went to Lee Barnes, a high school boy who won with 3.95, after a jump-off with his teammate Glenn Graham. The winner was one week short of his eighteenth birthday. He has remained to this day the youngest Olympic champion in vaulting history.

1924 Olympics, Colombes, Paris - Pole Vault (10 July): 1.Lee Barnes (USA) 3.95; 2.Glenn Graham (USA) 3.95; 3.James Brooker (USA) 3.90; 4.Henry Petersen (Denmark) 3.90; 5.Victor Pickard (Canada) 3.80; 6.Ralph Spearow (USA) 3.70; 7.Maurice Henrijean (Belgium) 3.66.

Maybe Hoff could have vied for a gold medal also in 1928, if in the meantime he had not been ousted from international competition for infringing the amateur code. Before then, in 1926, he had given lessons to his American rivals during a memorable US tour, which curiously coincided with his honeymoon trip. While there, he improved on the US (all-comers) record many times, with bests of 4.17 indoors and 4.19 outdoors. Hoff, the first major exponent of the "flyaway" style, continued to perform as a "pro". In 1931 he vaulted 4.32 (a mark superior to the official world record) and in 1930 he amassed 7,629.215 points in the decathlon. As an amateur he had shown his versatility with such marks as 10.8, 21.8, 49.2 and 1:55.9 in the flat races, 16.2 in the 110 m. hurdles, 7.41 in the long jump and 14.38 in the triple jump. In Norway he was re-qualified as a "national amateur" and in 1933 he won his last championship title with 3.80. He must be considered one of the greatest talents ever to come out of Europe. When he disappeared from the amateur scene, no continental vaulter was able to match or even remotely approach his feats. The Americans therefore lost no time in regaining full control of the situation.

Only one year after Hoff's American visit, the 14 ft. (4.26 m.) barrier was broken for the first time by a twenty-three-year-old Yale man, Sabin Carr. This well built athlete had improved from 3.96 in 1925 to 4.04 in 1926. He captured the world record at Philadelphia on 27 May 1927 with a 14-foot clearance and the following year he vaulted 4.29 from a board runway indoors.

Charles Hoff (Norway) in one of his world record efforts in the pole vault: 4.235 at Oslo in 1925.

The Paris Olympic champion, Lee Barnes, fought back in 1928, when he raised the world mark to 4.31 in a spring meet at Fresno, California, with Ward Edmonds second at 4.26. Both represented California schools. At the Amsterdam Olympics, however, Carr had the upper hand and won with 4.20, while Barnes, the tiny type of vaulter, finished no better than fifth, ironically enough with the same mark (3.95) that had earned him a gold medal four years earlier in Paris.

1928 Olympics, Amsterdam – Pole Vault (1 August): 1.Sabin Carr (USA) 4.20; 2.William Droegemuller (USA) 4.10; 3.Charles McGinnis (USA) 3.95; 4.Victor Pickard (Canada) 3.95; 5.Lee Barnes (USA) 3.95; 6.Yenataro Nakazawa (Japan) 3.90; 7.Henry Lindblad (Sweden) 3.90; 8.János Karlovits (Hungary) 3.80; 9.Julius Müller (Germany) 3.65.

Sixth in the Amsterdam final, ahead of the best Europeans, thus went to a man from the country of the Rising Sun, Yenataro Nakazawa. The following year another Japanese, Shuhei Nishida, raised the national record over the 4-metre barrier, to 4.10. In 1932 Nishida went to the Los Angeles Olympics with a personal best of 4.15, seemingly not good enough to stamp him as a potential danger to the all-conquering Americans. In fact, US vaulters had gone wild at their Olympic Trials in Palo Alto, with Bill Graber raising the world record to 4.37 and Bill Miller clearing 4.30 to take second place. In the Olympic battle, however, Graber failed to live up to expectations. After clearing 4.15, he passed the next height (4.20), then failed at 4.25. He even lost the bronze medal, which went to his countryman George Jefferson at 4.20. Miller was left alone to battle it out with Nishida. The Japanese, a light vaulter of medium build endowed with great stamina, amazingly improved on his personal best **three times**, finally clearing 4.30. But Miller stood the challenge bravely and won the day by going over 4.315 at his third attempt. The bar jiggled but stayed on, and Uncle Sam was again the master of the vaulting fraternity.

1932 Olympics, Los Angeles – Pole Vault (3 August): 1.William Miller (USA) 4.315; 2.Shuhei Nishida (Japan) 4.30; 3.George Jefferson (USA) 4.20; 4.William Graber (USA) 4.15; 5.Shizuo Mochizuki (Japan) 4.00; 6.Lucio de Castro (Brazil) 3.90; 7.Petros Chlentzos (Greece) 3.75.

Even in later years Nishida continued to achieve his best marks in "hot" competition. During a European tournée in 1935 he twice equalled his personal best (4.30), first at the World University Games in Budapest, then in a Five.Nations (Sweden, Germany, Hungary, Japan, Italy) match in Berlin. His travel companion was Sueo Oe, who had previously beaten Nishida at Tokyo with a 4.25 vault. But during their European tour they were defeated by the leading Americans of that year, Keith Brown and Bill Sefton. Brown, the last major exponent of the Yale tradition, had raised the world record to 4.39 in a spring meet at Cambridge, Massachusetts, on June 1. Besides being a very consistent vaulter, he was also a 1.984 high jumper. Much to the regret of his Eastern fans he was sidelined with an injury in 1936 and had to give up his Olympic hope.

The USA vs Japan feud reached its acme in 1936, the year of the Berlin Olympics. Shortly before leaving for Europe, Oe upped the Japanese and Asian record to 4.34. At the same time American vaulters were fighting hard to secure tickets for the Olympics. In the AAU Championships at Princeton on 4 July, 22-year-old George Varoff topped a fine field with a new world record of 4.43. Only a few months earlier he was a virtual unknown, lost in the cohort of America's 13-foot-plus men.Now he seemed to have the inside lane in the race to Berlin. Had he been superstitious, he might have been worried in remembering what had happened to other world record holders – Dray, Wright, Hoff, Barnes, Graber – before or during previous Olympics. In the Final Tryouts, held on 12 July in New York, Varoff ran into unsuspected trouble. When the bar was raised to 4.34 he was still in the game, but so were three California vaulters, Bill Sefton, Earle Meadows and Bill Graber. A few minutes later Graber and Meadows (both on first try) and Sefton (on third try) had mastered the height, while Varoff was at the end of the runway, facing his last chance. At the decisive moment, pressure got the best of him – and he failed.

Les Barnes (USA), a student at the University of Southern California, who won the Olympic pole vault title in 1924, just a few days before turning 18.

A newly crowned world record holder thus had to bypass the Games. Such a thing could only happen in America: that was the favourite comment of foreign observers. A few moments after the drama had come to an end, Varoff was at the "mike" wishing good luck to his conquerors, all of whom incidentally were (or had been) pupils at Dean Cromwell at the University of Southern California.

In the Olympic final at Berlin, Graber duplicated his mark of 1932 in Los Angeles (4.15) and had to be content with fifth place. The America vs. Japan battle finally involved four men: Sefton and Meadows on one side, Oe and Nishida on the other. All four cleared 4.25, after which the bar was raised to 4.35. The competition had been going on for nearly five hours. Performing under floodlights, amid the cheers of their respective fans, the four men offered the full measure of their resources. Sefton, Oe and Nishida all came close at least once, but failed. Only Meadows, who had a personal best of 4.37, made it on his second attempt. The two Japanese beat Sefton in a jump-off and were bracketed in a tie for second place. The leader of the Japanese team, in an ante-litteram application of the fewer misses rule, thought Nishida should have the silver medal (he had gone over 4.25 on his first try, while Oe needed two), but the two athletes finally decided to cut the medals in two parts, so that each had his share of both silver and bronze ! P.S. A few days later, George Varoff vaulted 4.38 in a "consolation" meet held in New York !

1936 Olympics, Berlin – Pole Vault (5 August): 1.Earle Meadows (USA) 4.35; 2.Shuhei Nishida (Japan) 4.25; 3.Sueo Oe (Japan) 4.25; 4.William Sefton (USA) 4.25; 5.William Graber (USA) 4.15; 6.(tie) Kiyoshi Adachi (Japan), Richard Webster (GB), Josef Haunzwickel (Austria), Alfred Proksch (Austria), Peter Bácsalmási (Hungary), Viktor Zsuffka (Hungary), Jan Koreis (Czechoslovakia), Wilhelm Schneider (Poland), Sylvanus Apps (Canada), Danilo Innocenti (Italy) and Bo Ljungberg (Sweden), all with 4.00.

Early in 1937 Oe competed successfully in American indoor meets. In his first appointment on boards, at New York's Madison Square Garden, he had to use a borrowed pole (his own implements were badly damaged during a long trip by land and sea), yet he managed to beat Olympic champion Earle Meadows, 4.34 to 4.26. At the end of his US tour, the medium built (1.75 m. / 60 Kg.) Keio University student was 2-to-2 vs. his American rival, plus a tie.

The 1937 outdoor season was marked by the duel between **Bill Sefton** and **Earle Meadows.** The former (born at Los Angeles on 21 January 1915; 1.90 m. / 82 Kg.) got the ball rolling with a new world record of 4.45 at Los Angeles on 10 April. But Meadows (born at Corinth, Mississippi, on 29 June 1913; 1.85 m. / 72 Kg.) lost little time in joining the parade. Early in May at Palo Alto both cleared 4.48. In the Pacific Coast Conference meet, held at Los Angeles on 29 May, the "Heavenly Twins" (as they were by then called) faced a crossbar set at 14 ft. 11 in. (4.54 m.). Sefton made it on his first try and was declared Conference champion. Meadows needed three tries to master the record height and thus became the most illustrious non-winner in vaulting annals. In June the consistent Sefton won the NCAA title with 4.49. The AAU Championships at Milwaukee on 3 July offered a gigantic four-way battle, in which the two record-holders were matched at 4.46 by George Varoff and Cornelius Warmerdam. For once, the fewer misses count was used to decide positions: 1.Sefton, 2.Warmerdam, 3.Meadows, 4.Varoff. About two months later Sefton and Meadows visited Japan. By then they were past their peak for the season and the reliable Sueo Oe won the first round at Tokyo at 4.30, with Sefton second (4.20). Then Meadows injured a shoulder and could do no better than 4.10. He was out for the rest of the tour. Sefton lost one more before finally winning at 4.35 in the last meet of the tour. Before the year was out, Oe achieved his lifetime best: 4.35. He was to die in the Philippines during World War II. Sefton called it a day after his brilliant 1937 campaign. He thus retired at 22, his potentialities still untapped. Not the last of his admirers was Meadows, who for his part remained in action for many more years.

In 1948, at thirty-five years of age, he mastered 4.42 in two different indoor meets !

Hoff's European record was finally shattered on 17 June 1937 at Moscow, when Nikolay Ozolin, the first world class athlete produced by the USSR, vaulted 4.26. Ozolin reached the major heights after many years of hard work, thereby setting a pattern which was to be followed in later years by many of Russia's best athletes. He captured the USSR record for the first time in 1927 with a 3.435 vault, at the age of twenty-one. To establish himself as Russia's best, however, he had to battle it out, first with Vladimir Dyachkov, then with Gavriil Rayevskiy. Ozolin improved on his European record twice, with 4.29 in 1938 and 4.30 at Moscow on 31 July 1939. Much to his dismay, USSR was not a member of the IAAF at the time, and his record efforts could not be ratified at the international level. When this was remedied at the end of World War II, Ozolin finally got a chance to vie for a European title. But at the ripe age of 40, in 1946, he had to be content with second place with 4.10 at the European Championships in Oslo, behind Sweden's Allan Lindberg (4.17). The pole vault was in any case Russia's first parade event: Dyachkov cleared 4.20 in 1939 and Rayevskiy did 4.23 in 1940. At the end of their careers, both Ozolin and Dyachkov earned an international reputation as coaches of the jumping events.

The first European vaulter to receive international recognition for a mark over Charles Hoff's old record was Erling Kaas of Norway, who did 4.27 in 1939. It should be noted that in the first two editions of the European Championships (Turin 1934 and Paris 1938), with USSR not taking part, marks of 4 metres or slightly superior were good enough to earn first place. In the third edition (Oslo 1946), Kaas was in the game but just like Ozolin he could do no better than 4.10 and finished fourth. The continental title went to Allan Lindberg of Sweden with 4.17.

Few athletes have ever made so much history in any event as **Cornelius Anthony Warmerdam** (born at Long Beach, California, on 22 June 1915; 1.83 m. / 72 Kg.) did in the pole vault during the early Forties. "Dutch", as he was known because of his Dutch origin, took up vaulting at fourteen, while at Hanford High School. From 1929 to 1932 his annual progress was steady: 2.74, 3.04, 3.32, 3.73. Then, as related by Cordner Nelson in his book "Track's Greatest Champions", "he chose to work on his father's ranch, 40 acres of peaches and apricots", instead of going to college. Now and then, however, he would continue to practice vaulting, "on their fruit drying field". Until one day in 1933, when he caught the eye of a curious observer, who felt bound to approach Fresno State coach Flint Hanner and told him: "I just saw a kid jumping over 13 feet (3.96) ..... in a spinach patch". Hanner casually observed: "That's not much of a broad jump". By the time the coach realized his mistake, Warmerdam was bound to enlist at Fresno State. From then on his progress was more remarkable: 4.11 in 1934, 4.28 in 1935, 4.31 in 1936 and 4.46 in 1937, his last year in college. By then he was one of America's premier vaulters, but if he had called it a day at that stage (as did most of his compatriots after leaving college) he would now be remembered only by a select group of statisticians. But he chose to go on, combining sport with his job, and joined the San Francisco Olympic Club. In 1938 he raised his best to 4.42, won the AAU title at 4.40 and was first in the Germany vs. USA dual meet at Berlin. The following year he set a US and world record of 4.42 but was content with 4.40 outdoors and lost to George Varoff in the AAU meet. In the meantime he had raised his grip on the pole to 13 feet (3.96). His rise to heights then rigidly regarded as stratospheric began in 1940, by which time he was teaching history and geometry in a mountain high school. On 13 April of that year, at Berkeley, he delighted a small crowd with history's first 15-foot (4.57) vault, a height he cleared on his second attempt. After breaking that psychological barrier he went from strength to strength. He closed his 1940 account with a new record, 4.60, at the AAU Championships in Fresno on 29 June. And that was by no means the end.

LONG JUMP

Owens, the greatest

Peter O'Connor's long awaited successor as world record holder finally appeared in the person of Edwin Gourdin, an American from Harvard University, who in 1921 climaxed a season of consistent long jumping with a 7.69 effort during an Anglo-American Inter-Varsity meet at Cambridge, Massachusetts. He was a better-than-average sprinter and on the same occasion he beat Harold Abrahams of Britain in the 100 yards, as well as in the long jump. Unfortunately Gourdin was to join that group of athletes who had reached their peak in non-Olympic years.

William DeHart Hubbard (USA), the world's leading long jumper in the Twenties. He was also an excellent sprinter.

By 1924 a new man had appeared on the scene: **William DeHart Hubbard** (born at Cincinnati on 25 November 1903, died on 23 June 1976). A man of medium build endowed with great speed and stamina, Hubbard was to prove the outstanding long jumper of the pre-Owens era. He won the AAU title for six consecutive years (1922-27), an astounding achievement in such a nerve-wrecking event as the long jump. His style included a run of less than 30 m., a remarkable acceleration and a single, fast kick of the lead leg. He was at one time co-holder of the world's 100 y. record (9 3/5 n 1926) and won that event at the 1925 NCAA Championships. On the same occasion (Chicago, 13 June) he achieved his best official mark, a new world record of 7.89, winning from F.Morgan Taylor (7.37), the great 400 m. hurdles specialist. Two years later, at Cincinnati on 17 September, Hubbard reached 7.98, a mark which was not accepted because the landing pit was one inch (2.54 cm.) lower than the take-off board. He was the first long jumper to show consistency in the 25 ft. (7.62 m.) range. He won the 1924 Olympic title with 7.445 – and on that jump he fell back, thus losing vital centimetres. The day before, spectators had been treated to an even greater display of long-jumping ability when another American, Robert LeGendre, was credited with an amazing 7.765 during the pentathlon. This effort came as a surprise. In fact, it transcended the known ability of the 26-year-old LeGendre, who in the States had always played second fiddle to Hubbard.

1924 Olympics, Colomes, Paris – Long Jump (8 July): 1.William DeHart Hubbard (USA) 7.445; 2.Edwin Gourdin (USA) 7.275; 3.Sverre Hansen (Norway) 7.26; 4.Vilho Tuulos (Finland) 7.07, 5.Louis Wilhelme (France) 6.99; 6.Christopher Mackintosh (GB) 6.92; 7.Virgilio Tommasi (Italy) 6.89; 8.Jac Boot (Holland) 6.86; 9.Albert Rose (USA) 6.855; 10.(tie) Mikio Oda (Japan) and Pauli Sandström (Finland) 6.83; 12.Sylvio Cator (Haiti) 6.81.

An ever lasting record

The ATFS (Association of Track & Field Statisticians), founded in 1950, can point to a rich number of books which have paid a wholesome tribute to the history of the world's oldest sport. One of the most precious ones is "National Athletics Records for all countries in the world", which enshrines record marks for the 200-plus countries represented in the IAAF. Collecting this material year after year is no mean task, as there are still quite a few countries from which it is pretty hard to obtain reliable information. This project was first conceived and realized by Luigi Mengoni of Italy in 1973. The latest version (2010) was edited by two Germans, Winfred Kramer and Heinrich Hubbeling, a Syrian, Fouad Habash, and a Frenchman, Yves Pinaud.

From such a work we learn that the oldest national record is now 7.93 by Sylvio Cator of Haiti in the long jump, made in 1928, which at that time happened to be a world record as well. According to Bernard Linley of Trinidad, the best known statistician from Central America, the second best LJ mark made in the intervening time by a Haitian was 7.75 by Marc Narcisse in 2005.

In his heydays, Cator (born on 9 Oct 1900, died on 22 July 1952) was also captain of the Haiti national soccer team. The main stadium of Haiti's capital, Port-au-Prince, bears his name. In January 2010, thousands of homeless people affected by a major earthquake that hit that country took refuge in the stadium.

In 1928, with Hubbard injured and probably past his peak, two men engaged in a fierce battle for the conquest of that elusive 26-foot (7.92 m.) barrier. They were **Edward Barton Hamm,** an American, and **Sylvio Cator,** who was from Haiti but mostly operated in France. The former (born on 13 April 1906; died on 25 June 1982; 1.79 m. / 70 Kg.) succeeded Hubbard as record holder with a jump of 7.90 in the US Olympic Tryouts at Cambridge, Massachusetts, on 7 July. He went on to win the Olympic title from Cator, 7.73 to 7.58. But the Haitian got partial revenge when he became history's first official 26-footer at Colombes, Paris, on 9 September, reaching 7.93 on his sixth and last try.

1928 Olympics, Amsterdam - Long Jump (31 July): 1.Edward Hamm (USA) 7.73; 2.Sylvio Cator (Haiti) 7.58; 3.Alfred Bates (USA) 7.40; 4.Willi Meier (Germany) 7.39; 5.Erich Köchermann (Germany) 7.35; 6.Hannes de Boer (Holland) 7.32; 7.Edward Gordon (USA) 7.32; 8.Erik Svensson (Sweden) 7.29; 9.Chuhei Nambu (Japan) 7.25; 10.Olle Hallberg (Sweden) 7.18.
** de Boer won 6th place from Gordon in a jump-off.*

A prominent figure in the world long-jumping picture in the fall of 1931 was **Chuhei Nambu** (born on 27 May 1904; 1.67 m. / 62 Kg.), a stocky little man from Japan who on 27 October at Tokyo achieved a surprising leap of 7.98. A good sprinter (10.5 for 100 m. in 1933), Nambu was equally proficient in both long jump and triple jump, two events which in reality are not so closely related as one might think. This double capacity enabled him to win two medals in the 1932 Los Angeles Olympics: bronze in the long jump (7.45) and gold in the triple jump with a new world

Edward Gordon (USA), the Olympic long jump champion of 1932.

Eulace Peacock (USA), the sprinter/long jumper Jesse Owens feared most.

record of 15.72. The former event was won by Edward Gordon of USA with 7.64. This athlete was to have a long career, no matter if he performed at generally inferior levels in subsequent years.

1932 Olympics, Los Angeles – Long jump (2 August): 1.Edward Gordon (USA) 7.64; 2.Lambert Redd (USA) 7.60; 3.Chuhei Nambu (Japan) 7.45; 4.Erik Svensson (Sweden) 7.41; 5.Richard Barber (USA) 7.39; 6.Naoto Tajima (Japan) 7.15; 7.Hector Berra (Argentina) 6.66; 8.Clovis de Figueiredo Reposo (Brazil) 6.43; 9.Sylvio Cator (Haiti) 5.93; 10.Esteban Crespo (Mexico) 5.83; 11.Erich Köchermann (Germany) 5.72.

In the Thirties the long jump fraternity was gratified by the appearance of a man who was to outshine all his predecessors by no mean margin. This super athlete was **James Cleveland Owens** (born at Oakville, Alabama on 12 September 1913; died at Tucson, Alabama on 31 March 1980; 1.78 m. / 71 Kg.), possibly less impressive than his main rivals Ralph Metcalfe and Eulace Peacock in sheer muscular power but built on well-proportioned statuesque lines. Owens combined the agility and strength of a panther. Known as Jesse (pronunciation of J.C.) since his schoolboy days, he was such a born talent that he lost no time in joining the top ranks: from 7.35 in 1932 he improved to 7.60 in the following year and to 7.81 in 1934, by which time he was firmly established as the no.1 master of the art. In 1935, his sophomore year at Ohio State University, Owens began to set his eyes on Nambu's world record. At the Drake Relays in April he missed the target by a fractional margin with a 7.97 jump, on which he fell back in landing, thereby losing something like 15 cm. ! But on his Day of Days, 25 May 1935 at Ann Arbor, Michigan, he found the time to capture the long jump mark as well – with a history making 8.13, a world record that would remain unbeaten for 25 years ! The detailed story of that giant effort in told in the adjoining aside.

A delightful effrontery

Jesse Owens had his Days of Days at Ferry Field, Ann Arbor, on 25 May 1935, in the "Big Ten Conference", a championship for the 10 best colleges of the Middle West. In the space of **three quarters of an hour** or so he set **four world records** – in chronological order, 9.4 (100 y. rec. equalled), 8.13 (long jump), 20.3 (220 y.) and 22.6 (220 y. hurdles). In between his record breaking chores on the track, at 3.25 pm he paid a visit to the long jump pit, a newly laid grass runway, placed directly in front of the stands. The announcer had the delightful effrontery to suggest that Owens would try for a new world record ! After a run of about 30 m. he took off and after a simple kick, more of a swing perhaps, he landed at 26 feet 8 ¼ inches (8.13 m.). That was to remain his only jump for the day and the best in the world for the next 25 years ! Even though there was no international wind rule at the time, careful officials recorded the wind in Jesse's favour as 1.49 m/s, which would be legal even in relation to the present rule.

In the eyes of the metric minded world Owens was the first 8-metre long jumper. (Claims that Sylvio Cator had reached 8 metres-even in his native country in 1929 had never been substantiated). Second to Owens in that memorable event at 7.66 was Willis Ward, a 2.01 high jumper.

To everybody's surprise, Owens learned the taste of defeat only a few weeks after his Ann Arbor triumph. It happened at the AAU meet in Lincoln, Nebraska, on 4 July, and his conqueror was muscular Eulace Peacock, who chose the occasion to reach a personal best of exactly 8 metres. Owens came close to that distance twice but could go no farther than 7.98. Peacock, who as previously related was a great sprinter, did not possess Owens' floating style, but was endowed with tremendous power. Unfortunately, a muscular ailment forced him down early in 1936. At the US Olympic Tryouts (to which he was exceptionally admitted by the AAU even though he did not have a qualifying mark) he made a desperate attempt but his condition did not carry him beyond a pitiful (for him) 7.08.

In the meantime, Europeans were showing improved form. O'Connor's time honoured continental record (7.61) was finally surpassed in 1928, when Rudolf Dobermann of Germany reached 7.645, an achievement which was virtually matched later in the year by another German, Erich Köchermann, with 7.64. Not surprisingly, the country with the richest reservoir of good sprinters was taking the leadership in the European long jump department. One should however mention a great might-have-been, Harold Abrahams of Britain, a first class sprinter who reached 7.38 in 1924 but was for ever barred from further progress the following year when he sustained a serious injury.

In the Thirties Germany had two excellent specialists, Luz Long and Wilhelm Leichum. The former eventually wound up with superior marks, best of which was a 7.90 effort in 1937. The latter, a 10.4 metric sprinter, was European champion (1934 and 1938) and won the event in the dual meet with USA in 1938. In the 1936 Berlin Olympics Long rose to the challenge of the great Owens, drawing level with the American at 7.87 mid-way in the competition. But Owens quickly reacted with jumps of 7.94 and 8.06 in the conclusive rounds. That was the hottest long jump event of pre-war days, no matter if the marks benefited from a favourable wind. Naoto Tajima of Japan was third at 7.74, followed by Arturo Maffei of Italy and Leichum, both with 7.73, while decathlon man Robert Clark of USA had to be content with sixth place (7.67). Long made up for his unimpressive speed with a well synchronized, polished "hang" style of jumping. On the other hand, it is generally admitted that Owens did not contribute anything new to the technique of the event. Yet no one until then had been able to perform the exercise with the supreme confidence and the unparalleled smoothness of action that were characteristic of the American. Posterity is obviously inclined to regret that such a unique talent quit the arena at the age of 23, after his triumphs at Berlin, where he won 4 events: 100, 200 m., long jump, 4x100 m. relay.

Luz Long (Germany), Owens' great rival in the long jump at the Berlin Olympics (1936). He was an exponent of the "hang style".

1936 Olympics, Berlin – Long Jump (4 August): 1.Jesse Owens (USA) 8.06; 2.Luz Long (Germany) 7.87; 3.Naoto Tajima (Japan) 7.74; 4.Arturo Maffei (Italy) and Wilhelm Leichum (Germany) 7.73; 6.Robert Clark (USA) 7.67; 7.John Brooks (USA) 7.41; 8.Robert Paul (France) 7.34; 9.Arthur Bäumle (Germany) 7.32; 10. Åke Stenqvist (Sweden) and Otto Berg (Norway) 7.30; 12.Gianni Caldana (Italy) 7.26.

With Owens out of the picture right after his 1936 heroics, Luz Long of Germany raised the European record to 7.90 at Berlin on 1 August 1937, which allowed him to top the World List for that year. He was to lose his life in World War II, namely in Sicily in 1943. The same destiny befell his countryman Wilhelm Leichum, who died on the Eastern front in 1941.

In the late Thirties America regained the leadership of the event, but Owens' record was to remain unchallenged for many years to come.

TRIPLE JUMP

Oda opens Japan's vintage season

Europe's most proficient triple jumper during the Twenties was **Vilho Tuulos** of Finland (born at Tampere on 26 March 1895, died in 1967; 1.83 m. / 77 Kg.). His active career spread over twenty years but he reached the zenith of his condition in 1923, when he scored a fine double at the International Games in Göteborg with 7.31 in the long jump and 15.39 in the triple jump. A few days later, namely on 6 July at Borås, Sweden, he reached 15.48, which was to stand as a European triple jump record for 16 years. He was one of the first specialists to lay an adequate stress on the "step", in which he maintained a good elevation, thereby achieving a remarkable degree of uniformity throughout his three leaps.

The 1924 Olympic final produced startling results. Luis Brunetto of Argentina, the South American champion, took an early lead with 15.425, far better than anything he had done at home. Anthony ("Nick") Winter, a 30-year-old Australian, led the other series of qualifiers with 15.18, three centimetres beyond his personal best. On his last try of the final Winter went wild with a feat of sheer strength and reached 15.525, dislodging Dan Ahearn's world record by a fractional margin. His leaps were as follows: 6.11, 5.09, 4.32. Curiously enough, the record mark was initially registered with the IAAF as 15.53, and corrected after World War II to 15.52. Tuulos was third with 15.37. Finnish historians still rave about a hairline foul in which their countryman was said to have landed at 15.72. The pit was by then in such a poor state that it was virtually impossible to clearly identify the "foul line".

1924 Olympics, Colombes, Paris – Triple Jump (12 July): 1.Anthony Winter (Australia) 15.525 (world record); 2.Luis Brunetto (Argentina) 15.425; 3.Vilho Tuulos (Finland) 15.37; 4.Väinö Rainio ((Finland) 15.01; 5.Folke Jansson (Sweden) 14.97; 6.Mikio Oda (Japan) 14.35; 7.Earle Wilson (USA) 14.235; 8.Ivar Sahlin (Sweden) 14.16; 9.Merwin Graham (USA) 14.00; 10.Con O'Connor (Ireland) 13.99; 11 Willem Peters (Holland) 13.86; 12. Hans J. Odde (GB) 13.40.

A young Japanese thus finished a hardly noticed sixth in that memorable event. He was **Mikio Oda** (born at Hiroshima on 30 March 1905; died at Kamakura on 2 December 1998; 1.67 m. / 65 Kg.) and in the course of that battle he gathered many useful hints. After returning home, he worked more and more assiduously to develop his potential. In doing so he acted as an eye-opener in making his countrymen realize fully their vocation for the jumping events. While waiting to see "the rest of the world" again at the Amsterdam Olympics (1928), he showed steady improvement: 14.805 in 1925, 15.343 and 15.355 in 1927, 15.41 in 1928. Encouraged by such achievements and the titles won at the Far Eastern Games, he came back with a lot of self-confidence. At Amsterdam, in 1928, he won Asia's first Olympic gold medal with 15.21, after a fierce battle with Levi Casey of USA (15.17). Veteran Tuulos of Finland, who shortly before the Games had reached 15.58 with the aid of a breeze, won his third Olympic medal, finishing third.

1928 Olympics, Amsterdam – Triple Jump (2 August): 1. Mikio Oda (Japan) 15.21; 2.Levi Casey (USA) 15.17; 3.Vilho Tuulos (Finland) 15.11; 4.Chuhei Nambu (Japan) 15.01; 5.Toimi Tulikoura (Finland) 14.70; 6.Erkki Järvinen (Finland) 14.65; 7.Willem Peters (Holland) 14.55; 8.Väinö Rainio (Finland) 14.41; 9.Sidney Bowman (USA) and Jan Blankers (Holland) 14.35; 11.Lloyd Bourgeois (USA) 14.28; 12.Anthony Winter (Australia) 14.15.

Japan's guiding light

Mikio Oda performed a rare pioneering job in Japan. In his book "Great Asian athletes" (1989) Cdr.P.K.Mahanand pays adequate tribute to him, the first Asian male athlete to win a gold medal in the Olympic Games (1928) and set a world record (1931). "He inspired a whole generation of Japanese and put them on the golden streak. When he retired, he had already trained his successor, Chuhei Nambu, to continue his tradition. And the test of a great teacher is to produce a pupil who will outshine him. Chuhei Nambu was such an obedient and determined pupil". Performance-wise, during his career he bettered 15 metres in the triple jump on 9 occasions, at a time when such a distance was very rare merchandise indeed.

In the years that followed Oda continued to be Japan's guiding light in athletics, both as a coach and as a journalist. He was also one of the earliest members of the ATFS (Association of Track & Field Statisticians), founded in 1950.

That was the dawn of a brilliant era for Japan's triple jumpers. Oda, an excellent all-round jumper (personal bests of 7.52 in the long jump, 1.92 in the high jump and 3.80 in the pole vault) set a new world record of 15.58 at Tokyoon 27 October 1931, when he was extended by a new challenger, Kenkichi Oshima (15.44). That was a historic day for Japanese athletics: in the same meet Nambu captured the world's long jump record with 7.98. Early in 1932 Oda was sidelined with an injury after a most promising start (15.55) and was thus prevented from performing at his best in the Los Angeles Olympics. Few athletes, if any, have made such a great contribution to the advancement of athletics in their own country.

Chuhei Nambu, who had been Oda's chief rival for several years, filled the gap more than adequately in Los Angeles. He used a long hop of 6.40, a step of 4.39 ad a jump of 4.93 to achieve a new world record of 15.72. Consistent Eric ("Spänst") Svensson of Sweden took second place ahead of Kenkichi Oshima.

1932 Olympics, Los Angeles – Triple Jump (4 August): 1.Chuhei Nambu (Japan) 15.72, world record; 2.Eric Svensson (Sweden) 15.32; 3.Kenkichi Oshima (Japan) 15.12; 4.Eamonn Fitzgerald (Ireland) 15.01; 5.Willem Peters (Holland) 14.93; 6.Sol Furth (USA) 14.88; 7.Sidney Bowman (USA) 14.87; 8.Rolland Romero (USA) 14.85; 9.Péter Bácsalmsási (Hungary) 14.33; 10.Francesco Tabai (Italy) 14.29; 11.Onni Rajasaari (Finland) 14.20; 12.Mikio Oda (Japan) 13.97.

The Japanese continued to dominate the event throughout the Thirties. Next in the line of world class jumpers were Oshima and Masao Harada, who had their field day at Koshien Grounds, Osaka, on 16 September 1934, during the Japan vs. USA match. Each had five valid efforts over 15 m. On his second try Harada reached 15.75, but in the last round Oshima rose to the occasion with 15.82, a feat in which he was aided by a wind of 2.2 m/s. The mark was ratified as a Japanese record but never made the IAAF book (nor did, for that matter, Harada's 15.75) even though the "wind rule" in force nowadays was not introduced until 1936.

Of all countries in the world, Australia was then the only one capable of challenging Japan. Jack Metcalfe, a fine all-rounder, had won the 1934 British Empire Games event in London with 15.63. He really let himself go in December of the following year in Sydney, when he broke Nambu's world record with 15.78. On that occasion he was spurred on by Basil Dickinson (15.64). Metcalfe's distribution of efforts in his winning mark was unusual, to say the least: a hop of 5.64, a step of 4.02 and a jump of 6.12. At the end of his career Metcalfe could point to marks of 1.988 in the high jump and 7.42 in the long jump. At the 1936 Olympics in Berlin he managed a triple jump of 15.50 but had to be content with third place behind two Japanese jumpers. The event, held on 6 August, was featured by the "explosion" of Naoto Tajima, who began with 15.76 in the first round of the final and then sailed for an unprecedented 16.00 on his fourth attempt. The new world record was achieved with a hop of 6.20, a step of 4.80 and a jump of 5.00. Masao Harada was second with 15.66. **Naoto Tajima** (born at Iwakuni on 15 August 1912; died in Tokyo on

Mikio Oda (Japan), winner of the triple jump at the 1928 Olympics - Asia's first gold medal in the annals of the Games.

4 December 1990; 1.78 m. / 67 Kg.) was previously known as a long jumper, with a personal best of 7.74 in 1935, a mark he duplicated in finishing third in the Olympic event. His best triple jump mark prior to the Games was only 15.40, but his best comethrough performance did not surprise those who had watched him in his training spins.

1936 Olympics, Berlin – Triple Jump (6 August): 1.Naoto Tajima (Japan) 16.00, world record; 2.Masao Harada (Japan) 15.66; 3.Jack Metcalfe (Australia) 15.50; 4.Heinz Wöllner (Germany) 15.27; 5.Rolland Romero (USA) 15.08; 6.Kenkichi Oshima (Japan) 15.07; 7.Erich Joch (Germany) 14.88; 8.Dudley Wilkins (USA) 14.83; 9.Olavi Suomela (Finland) 15.72; 10.Luz Long (Germany) 14.62; 11.Edward Luckhaus (Poland) 14.61; 12.Lajos Somló (Hungary) 14.60; 13.Onni Rajasaari (Finland) 14.59.

Most of the Japanese triple jumpers of pre-war days were primarily good long jumpers, with marks ranging from Oshima's 7.47 to Nambu's 7.98. They generally used a long hop, and consequently had to apply the principle of progressive elevation in the remaining leaps. In post-war years, however, interest for what was once considered a national event began to fade considerably.

In Europe interest in the triple jump was kept alive by the Scandinavians. Nordic specialists generally had a good technique and relied on elasticity (Swedish: spänst) to make up for their insufficient speed. After Tuulos and Svensson, the leading exponent was Onni Rajasaari of Finland, who in the summer of 1939 succeeded his countryman Tuulos as European record holder with 15.52. In the same year Kaare Ström of Norway had a mark of 15.82 nullified (at least for record purposes) by an aiding wind.

Naoto Tajima (Japan) in his winning effort in the triple jump at the Berlin Olympics (1936): a new world record of 16.00.

MEN 1941-1960

4

HIGH JUMP

Russians upset Thomas

American jumpers broke into the world record department again in 1941. It all started with a most unusual coincidence: on 26 April 1941, Melvin Walker's world record (2.09) was bettered twice within a few hours – at different sites. First Bill Stewart jumped 2.092 at Provo, Utah; then Les Steers went over a crossbar set at 2.102 at Seattle, Washington. The latter showed great consistency throughout the entire season and crowned an unprecedented campaign wit a jump of 2.108 at Los Angeles on 17 June. (Strangely enough, the IAAF ratified the mark as 2.11). **Lester LeRoy Steers** (born at Eureka, California, on 16 June 1917; died at Richland, Washington, on 23 January 2003; 1.87 m. / 88 Kg.) perfected the straddle to a most remarkable degree. His body sometimes appeared to be draped around the crossbar. The heavy type of jumper, he was a precision instrument the like of which the world had never seen before. One day, during a training session, he jumped at 6 ft. 6 in. (1.981) thirteen times, just one after another, and made twelve of them. Early in 1941, during an indoor exhibition at Eugene, he went over a bar set at 2.146 – the first known effort over 7 feet (2.134), no matter if unofficial. Steers had emerged as a high school boy in 1936 with 1.965. He continued to progress regularly: 1.981 in 1937 and 1938, 2.038 in 1939, and 2.067 in 1940, when he also mastered 2.086 in an exhibition. He was AAU champion twice (1939-40), but strangely lost to Bill Stewart on the fewer misses count in the 1941 meet, after both had cleared 2.076. World War II obviously put a premature end to his career, but for many years to come he was recalled by coaches and athletes as a steady reference point in terms of technique. At a Coaches Clinic in 1941, Steers revealed that his weight had increased from 80 Kg. in 1940 to 88 kg. in 1941. His best with the Western Roll was 2.038.

The crisis brought about by years of limited activity was well reflected in the results of the 1948 Olympics in London. John Winter of Australia, who could point to a personal best of 2.013, won the gold medal at 1.98. He had a wrenched back and made the winning height in a gallant effort, after which he had to call it a day. Fortunately for him, not one of his rivals was able to fight back successfully. For once the Americans had to be content with third and fourth place.

1948 Olympics, London - High Jump (30 July): 1.John Winter (Australia) 1.98; 2.Björn Paulsen (Norway) 1.95; 3.George Stanich (USA) 1.95; 4.Dwight Eddleman (USA) 1.95; 5.Georges Damitio (France) 1.95; 6.Art Jackes (Canada) 1.90; 7.(tie) Alan Paterson (GB) and Hans Wahli (Switzerland) 1.90; 9.(tie) Göran Widenfelt (Sweden), A.Jadresic Vargas (Chile) and Pierre Lacaze (France) 1.90; 12.Agdeboyega Folaranmi Adedoyin (GB) 1.90; 13.Birger Leirud (Norway) 1.90.

Steers' successor appeared in the early Fifties in the person of **Walter "Buddy" Davis** (born at Beaumont, Texas, on 5 January 1931; 2.03 m. / 95 Kg.), an American who was a victim of polio in the early years of his life. He gamely recovered and, like other great athletes, used sport as a vehicle towards complete physical rehabilitation. In 1952 he won the Olympic title with a mark, 2.04, that just exceeded his own height.

1952 Olympics, Helsinki - High Jump (20 July): 1.Walter Davis (USA) 2.04; 2.Kenneth Wiesner (USA) 2.01; 3.José Telles da Conçeicao (Brazil) 1.98; 4.Gösta Svensson (Sweden) 1.98; 5.Ronald Pavitt (GB) 1.95; 6.Ion Söter (Rumania) 1.95; 7.Arnold Betton (USA) 1.95; 8.Björn Gundersen (Norway) 1.90; 9.(tie) Jacques Delelienne (Belgium) and J. Olatunji Majekodunmi (Nigeria) 1.90.

On 27 June 1953, at the AAU Championships in Dayton, Ohio, Davis rose the world record to 2.124. He even went over 7 feet (2.13) in unofficial tries. Davis had a relatively short career and left the athletic arena without having explored his full potential. Telles da Conçeicao of Brazil, the Olympic bronze medallist of the Helsinki Olympics, was one of the most versatile talents ever to come out of South America. In 1954 he became the first 2 metre jumper from that continent and in 1956 he finished sixth in the 200 m. at the Melbourne Olympics. At the end of his career he could point to such marks as 10.2 (100 m.), 20.8 (200 m.), 7.40 (long jump) and 6173 pts (decathlon, 1950 scoring table). In athletics, conventional limits likely to give food for thought often amount to a psychological barrier. The 7-foot (2.134 m.) high jump had been a most elusive target for leading English speaking jumpers for decades. The trouble lies in the fact that the athlete knows exactly what he is up against, and that often makes him "sick". A typical example was **Ernest "Ernie" Shelton** (born on 28 October 1932 at Chanute, Kansas, 1.83 m. / 72 Kg.), a very consistent Californian, who in 1953-55 collected no less than 21 competitive marks in the range 2.08/2.115. He was probably the first among world class jumpers to effectively combine the straddle with a dive. The rule under which at least one of the competitor's feet should clearly precede the head over the bar had been repealed late in the Thirties, and as time went by the advantages offered by the new situation were being grasped by an ever growing number of jumpers. Shelton flirted with the 7-foot barrier for years, reportedly failing to make it by infinitesimal margins. In few events, if any, can the difference between a failure by a hair's breadth and a lucky clearance (with the bar quivering) be as little as in the high jump. But athletics history, like all history, does not consider near failures. A worthy "pendant" to Shelton in form and consistency was **Bengt Nilsson** of Sweden (born at Härnösand on 17 February 1934; 1.81 m. / 67 Kg.), who put Europe back on the world high jump map. For years, results at the European Championships had been indicative of a low ebb. Anton Bolinder of Sweden won at Oslo in 1946 with 1.99, a personal best. Four years later, at Brussels, Alan Paterson, a Scotsman who held the British record with 2.019 (1947), topped the field with 1.96. Incidentally, Paterson was only 19 when he achieved his record mark. As for Nilsson, he used a polished version of the dive straddle and eventually became Sweden's most popular athlete since the days of milers Hägg and Andersson. He first mastered 2 meters in 1953 with a 2.01 effort. He had his best year in 1954. After breaking Kotkas' European record at Halmstad with a 2.05 clearance, he really went wild at Göteborg on 15 July: jumping from the same take-off that had yielded Kotkas' record (2.04) in 1936, he improved on his fresh best three times in the space of 14 minutes, clearing 2.06, 208 and 2.10 – a true masterpiece in the art of concentration. Following an easy win in the European Championships at Bern (2.02), Nilsson closed his 1954 account with a 2.114 jump on 19 September, still at Göteborg. That was an improvement of 10 cm. over his 1953 best.

Between 1953 and 1955, Nilsson and Shelton met several times in Scandinavian meets and each had his share of victories. After collecting ten marks at 2.08 or higher in 1954-56, Nilsson was unlucky enough to be hit by injury on the eve of the 1956 Olympics, in which he competed as a severely handicapped man. After that bitter experience, he lost interest and consequently disappeared from the picture. Curiously enough, 1956 also proved to be the swan song of Ernie Shelton. Either or both of them may have run out of nervous energy as a result of their most exacting schedule in the preceding years.

The decline of Shelton and Nilsson curiously coincided with the arrival of history's first (official) 7-foot jumper. This was **Charles Dumas** of USA (born at Tulsa, Oklahoma, on 12 February 1937; died at Inglewood, Los Angeles on 5 January 2004; 1.87 m. / 81 Kg.). He used a rather slow run but had a tremendous lift. He matured to athletic greatness in the favourable California climate and progressed from 1.969 in 1954 to 2.089 in 1955. He was crowned world record holder on a most significant occasion – the US Olympic Trials (formerly Tryouts) at Los Angeles on 29 June 1956. This agile athlete straddled over a bar set at 2.15 on his second attempt and thus broke by a clear margin one of the toughest mental barriers – 7 English feet. Shelton, fifth with 2.045, failed to qualify for Melbourne. The ever turning wheel of life: an old champion was "dead", a new champion was "born". In Australia Dumas, who had not turned 20 yet, found a hard nut to crack in Charles "Chilla" Porter of Brisbane, his senior by only one year. Inspired by a familiar atmosphere, the Australian made the day of the Olympic final the greatest of his athletic career. During that competition he managed to improve on his personal best (2.038) **three times**, a fantastic achievement in such a long drawn event as an Olympic final. Finally he sailed over 2.10. Dumas, who appeared to have no nerves, gathered himself together and clinched the gold medal by going over 2.12 on his third attempt. Igor Kashkarov was third (2.08), while Stig Pettersson, then regarded as Nilsson's hair apparent, took fourth place with 2.06.

1956 Olympics, Melbourne - High Jump (23 November): 1.Charles Dumas (USA) 2.12; 2.Charles Porter (USA) 2.10; 3.Igor Kashkarov (SU) 2.08; 4.Stig Pettersson (Sweden) 2.06; 5.Kenneth Money (Australia) 2.03; 6.Vladimir Sitkin (SU) 2.00; 7.(tie) Colin Ridgeway (Australia) and Phil Reavis (USA) 2.00; 9.Julius Chigbolu (Nigeria) 2.00; 10.Vernon Wilson (USA) 2.00.

Experts were greatly impressed by the excellent co-ordination of Kashkarov, a heavy jumper weighing 88 Kg. That was the earliest sign of Russia's coming of age as a new high jump power. In 1954 **Yuriy Stepanov** (born at Leningrad on 30 August 1932; 1.85 m. / 75 Kg.) had placed fifth in the European Championships with an unprepossessing 1.93, but the following year he raised the SU record to 2.02, thus bettering by one centimetre the pre-war mark of Nikolay Kovtun, a man whose incredible vicissitudes have been related in a previous chapter.

By 1956 Stepanov had changed from the Eastern cut-off to the dive straddle, improving to 2.04. In June 1957 he upped his best to 2.09 and on 13 July of the same year at Leningrad, his native town, he sailed over 2.11, and then raised the world record to 2.16 (actual height, 2.162). Quite obviously, the spectacular feat of the 25-year-old Russian aroused a great deal of curiosity, which increased further when later in 1957 two other Russians, Vladimir Sitkin and Igor Kashkarov, came up with marks of 2.15 and 2.14 respectively. No matter how good the technique of these men, their progress seemed somewhat unreal to certain observers. Very soon it transpired that these and other Russian jumpers were using a thick (2 to 4 cm.) sole in the shoe of their take-off foot. Such a device, which offered obvious advantages, was not a Russian invention though. Experiments along that line had been made in other countries long before then, e.g. by Bengt Nilsson of Sweden, even though he was once quoted as saying that he had never used a built-up shoe in any of the major meets. Be that as it may, the new fashion quickly caught on, and very soon every top class jumper in Europe had a built-up shoe of his own. Marks well over 2 metres became commonplace. The IAAF, reacting to urges from several quarters, finally banned the "orthopaedic shoe" and set the maximum permissible thickness of soles at 13 millimetres.

But the stable door was closed only in 1958, with no retro-active measures, and in the meantime Stepanov's 2.16 had been ratified as a world record. At the 1958 European Championships in Stockhollm, Stepanov did 2.06 and had to be content with sixth place. The event was a real thriller and victory finally went to a Swedish outsider, Rickard Dahl, who came through with 2.12, his best ever. Jirí Lánsky of Czechoslovakia and Stig Pettersson of Sweden were second and third respectively (both 2.10). Russia's spectacular rise as a major high jump power continued well beyond the interlude of the built-up shoe. In the two earliest USA vs SU dual meets (1958-59), former world record holder Charles Dumas was beaten, first by Stepanov, then by Robert Shavlakadze. Early in 1960, however, the appearance of a new and truly gigantic American prospect seemed likely to shift the balance in favour of USA again. **John Curtis Thomas** (born at Boston on 3 March 1941; 1.96 m. / 88 Kg.) was the pro-type of what technicians call a natural talent. This powerfully built man improved from 1.73 in 1956 to 1.95 in 1957, then 2.10 during a "tournée" in Japan in 1958. He mastered 7 feet (2.134) for the first time indoors in 1959, and a few weeks later he improved to 2.165, still from boards. On the eve of the outdoor season he caught his left (take-off) foot in an elevator shaft. The injury was so serious that he only returned to action towards the end of the year. But in 1960 he resumed his ascension. First he raised the indoor record to 2.197, then he moved outdoors and in the

John Thomas (USA), a great high jumper in the early Sixties.

space of two months he bettered the official world record time and again, with 2.171, 2.178, 2.184 and finally 2.229. The last effort (actually measured at 2.232 but later rounded down to the nearest quarter of an inch) occurred in the US Olympic Tryouts at Palo Alto, California, on 1 July. The other two qualifiers for the trip to Rome, 18-year old Joe Faust and Charles Dumas, were left far behind, with 2.134 and 2.108 respectively. The amazing consistency of the new world record holder stamped him as an odds-on favourite for the Olympic crown. In the meantime, however, the Russians were working really hard to make up for lost ground. The trio they selected for Rome was a redoubtable one. It consisted of Robert Shavlakadze, a moustached Georgian with a personal best of 2.13; Viktor Bolshov, a 21-year-old talent who had improved in two years from 1.95 to 2.15; and Valeriy Brumel, then eighteen, who was picked at the last moment: after placing no better than sixth at the SU Championships, he suddenly rose to a spectacular European record of 2.17 in mid-August. Yet few international experts, if any, interpreted the latest Russian pre-Olympic news as an alarm signal for John Thomas.

But on September 1st, at Rome's Stadio Olimpico, things took an unexpected turn. Thomas, who until then had been fighting against records rather than opponents, found himself confronted with a different challenge. As the contest unfolded, his mood changed from over-confidence to fear. At first he neglected to warm up between jumps, and by the time he rose to the challenge mentally, nervous tension did the rest. Best he could do for the day was a second-time clearance at 2.14, but so did Brumel and Bolshov, while Shavlakadze needed only one jump to clear that height. At 2.16 the 27-year-old Georgian was over on his first attempt, Brumel on his second, while Thomas and Bolshov failed three times. On the fewer trials and misses rule, Thomas barely salvaged third place, ahead of Bolshov, while veteran Shavlakadze edged Brumel for the gold medal.

1960 Olympics, Rome – High Jump (1 September): 1.Robert Shavlakadze (SU) 2.16; 2.Valeriy Brumel (SU) 2.16; 3.John Thomas (USA) 2.14; 4.Viktor Bolshov (SU 2.14; 5.Stig Pettersson (Sweden) 2.09; 6.Charles Dumas (USA) 2.03; 7.(tie) Kjell-Åke Nilsson (Sweden) 2.03, Jiri Lansky (Czechoslovakia) 2.03 and Theo Püll (Germany) 2.03; 10.Robert Kotei (Ghana) 2.03; 11.Cornel Porumb (Rumania) 2.03; 12.Mahamat Idriss (France) 2.03; 13.Sándor Noszály (Hungary) 2.03.

The three Soviets were athletes of strong but not exceptional build: Shavlakadze 1.86 m. / 82 Kg; Brumel 1.85 m. / 77 Kg.; Bolshov 1.83 m. / 80 Kg. Their splendid co-ordination in every phase of the exercise allowed them to make up for their physical inferiority vis-à-via Thomas. They came to Rome "oiled" to perfection and fully determined to make things difficult for the fresh world record holder. Shavlakadze, a smooth belly-roller, was by Rome time the most experienced of the trio, but Brumel was the rising star and on 25 October, at Uzhgorod, he raised the European record to 2.20 (actual height, 2.203). **Valeriy Brumel** (born at Tolbuzhino, Siberia, on 14 April 1942; died at Moscow on 26 January 2003; 1.85 m. / 77 Kg.) had hardly shown a particular vocation for high jumping as a youth: his best at 14 was 1.40. The next two years were of decisive importance for his future career: between 1957 and 1958 he improved from 1.75 to 1.95. His first coach was Pyotr Stein, who introduced him to weight training, by then regarded as one of the most effective media for the conditioning of an athlete. In 1959 Brumel upped his best to 2.01. Early in 1960 he came under the wing of Vladimir Dyachkov, a former pole vaulter (4.20 in 1939), by then regarded as the most knowledgeable coach in Russia and possibly in the world. More on Brumel and his major deeds in the chapter devoted to the period 1961-1980.

POLE VAULT

From the incomparable "Dutch" to the Metal Era

After breaking the 15-foot (4.57) barrier in 1940, Cornelius Warmerdam went from strength to strength. From then on his ability practically knew no bounds. With unmatched perseverance he went higher and higher: 4.64 and 4.71 in 1941, 4.74 and 4.77 in 1942. The last mark occurred at Modesto, California, on 23 May, and his clearance of the record height was so ample that an official estimated his effort as worth 4.82. Spectators broke the crossbar into bits for souvenirs ! From board runways, indoors, Warmerdam did 4.58 and 4.75 in 1942, and finally 4.78 at Chicago on 20 March 1943. He achieved the last of his forty-three vaults over 15 feet (4.57) in winning the 1944 AAU outdoor title at New York. He was then a naval lieutenant, and that was to remain his last appearance in big-time competition. Eight years later, at the age of thirty-seven, he cleared 4.37 in an exhibition. With World War II draining the ranks of America's active vaulters, Warmerdam had no competition to spur him on during his best years. All the greater, therefore, was his merit for conquering previously unexplored heights the way he did. At the end of 1944 his lead vis-à-vis history's second best performer was as great as 23 cm. ! Yet in the opinion of American technicians he contributed little new, if anything, to the art of pole vaulting. As Ken Doherty once put it, "he simply did everything right that others had been trying to do for years". Above all, "Dutch" maintained that all phases of the exercise should unfold as one continuous movement, with no pauses or hitches of any kind. In his vaults at the major heights he would use a grip of 4.03 m., measured from the lower part of the upper hand to the ground. Remarkably enough, in training he would never try anything above 14 feet (4.26).

After the retirement of this phenomenon, the debate among the world's leading vaulters was resumed at pre-Warmerdam heights. It was as if someone had put the clock of history back several years. At the 1948 Olympics in London, Guinn Smith of USA won the title of world champion with a 4.30 vault. After doing 4.43 as early as in 1941, aged twenty-one, he had lost his best athletic years because of war. He qualified for the Games with a 4.47 effort, and in London he braved the risk of a water-logged runway and the pain of a tightly strapped knee to win the title from Erkki Kataja of Finland and Bob Richards of USA, who finished in that order, both with 4.20.

1948 Olympics, London - Pole Vault (2 August): 1.Guinn Smith (USA) 4.30; 2.Erkki Kataja (Finland) 4.20; 3.Robert Richards (USA) 4.20; 4.Erling Kaas (Norway) 4.10; 5.Ragnar Lundberg (Sweden) 4.10; 6.Richmond Morcom (USA) 3.95; 7.(tie) Hugo Göllors (Sweden) and Valto Olenius (Finland) 3.95; 9.(tie) José Barbosa (Puerto Rico), José Vicente (Puerto Rico), Victor Sillon (France) and Allan Lindberg (Sweden) 3.80.

By that time, however, the bamboo pole was being replaced with a metal pole of carefully blended alloys. Whether the new material represented a definite improvement over the best bamboo types is still a matter of debate. The metal pole was generally considered to be slightly less flexible, but safer than the bamboo pole. Be as it may, the "fashion" of 15-foot vaults introduced by Warmerdam did not catch on until 1951. The ice was broken in an indoor meet early in the year, when Bob Richards, the London bronze medallist, slipped over a bar set at 4.59. Less than two months later he was up to 4.69, still indoors. Meanwhile another vaulter, Don Laz, had mastered 4.59 under similar conditions. It is generally conceded that boards provide some additional spring. On 21 April there were two 15-foot efforts outdoors too, at different sites and within a few hours of each other: first by Don Cooper with 4.57 at Lawrence, Kansas, then by Laz with 4.61 at Los Angeles. Laz in particular was acknowledged to have a great potential, but for some reason he fell somewhat below expectations. By the end of his career his best outdoors was 4.62, and he went 2 cms. higher indoors. Cooper, who was a 9.7 100 y. man, had a somewhat sporadic career and failed to improve further.

The deceptive side of progress

Bob Richards and Don Laz, two great vaulters who won gold and silver respectively at the 1952 Olympics, both had sons who aimed at surpassing their parents in the same art. Markwise, Bob Richards Jr. and Doug Laz can be said to have been successful: in fact, they scaled heights of 5.33 (1973) and 5.30 (1976) respectively, i.e. well beyond their fathers' marks (4.72 for the Reverend Richards, 4.64 for Laz). Apart from the fact that "juniors" had the advantage of using fiber-glass poles, it is however a fact that neither managed to make an impact on the vaulting élite of the Seventies. Doug Laz had to be content with fifth place at the 1976 US Olympic Trials, and Richards Jr. never made the grade in top-class competition. In the meantime there had been a revolution in vaulting standards and the "price of glory" had risen to spectacular heights. Hence the deceptive side of progress.

Something similar had previously happened to the offspring of another famous champion, Morgan ("Buzz") Taylor Jr., a son of the 1924 Olympic 400 m. hurdles champion. "Buzz" elected to specialize in what had been his father's second love, the long jump. He excelled daddy's best with a 7.77 effort but did not go beyond a fourth place at the 1952 US Olympic Tryouts.

Robert Richards (born at Champaign, Illinois, on 20 February 1926; 1.78 m. / 74 Kg.) was the first vaulter who managed to lift himself to heights in the

The reverend Bob Richards (USA), Olympic pole vault champion twice (1952 and '56).

"Warmerdam region". Like "Dutch", he was a good but not exceptional performer in his early years. By 1947, his last year in college, his best was 4.30. But he had plenty of strength and determination, and by dint of hard work he eventually managed to reach the top. At the end of his long career he could point to personal records of 4.70 outdoors (1956) and 4.72 indoors (1957). This dedicated athlete, who as a youth had known some of the difficult sides of life, failed in his repeated attempts to surpass Warmerdam, whom he once described as "part sprinter, part shock-absorber, part acrobat and part strong man - simply not human". Even so, Richards had great success as a competitor. He became the first vaulter in history to win the Olympic title twice. At Helsinki in 1952 he won from Don Laz, 4.55 to 4.50, and four years later in Melbourne he won from Bob Gutowski, 4.56 to 4.53, each time at the end of a long-drawn contest.

1952 Olympics, Helsinki - Pole Vault (22 July): 1.Robert Richards (USA) 4.55; 2.Donald Laz (USA) 4.50; 3.Ragnar Lundberg (Sweden) 4.40; 4.Pyotr Denisenko (SU) 4.40; 5.Valto Olenius (Finland) 4.30;6.Bunkichi Sawada (Japan) 4.20; 7.Vladimir Brazhnik (SU) 4.20; 8.Viktor Khnyezhev (SU 4.20; 9.George Mattos (USA) 4.20; 10.Erkki Kataja (Finland) 4.10; 11.(tie) Tamás Homonnay (Hungary) and Lennart Lind (Sweden) 4.10; 13.Milan Milakov (Yugoslavia) 4.10.

In AAU competition Richards won 9 outdoor and 8 indoor pole vault titles. He exceeded Warmerdam in quantity, if not in quality, amassing a tally of 126 vaults over 15 feet (4.57). As a minister of religion he once apologized for having done no better than 4.67 in a big night meet, to which he had gone after making five sermons in as many different cities over the preceding five days ! As a decathlon man, far from polished in some events, he was good enough to win the AAU title three times. His best under the 1950 scoring table was 7313 pts (1954).

In the early Fifties, European vaulting standards showed an encouraging upward trend. For many years in the past, several of the best vaulters from Europe had been good gymnasts with little basic speed. This situation was now being remedied, and the two men who dominated the continental picture in those years were both capable of 14.7 in the "high" hurdles. They were Ragnar ("Ragge") Lundberg of Sweden and Pyotr Denisenko of SU. The former was European champion in 1950 with 4.30 and figured prominently in three editions of the Olympics: fifth in 1948 and 1956, third in 1952. He held the European record for several years and wound up with a lifetime best of 4.46 in 1956. Denisenko was fourth at the 1952 Olympics, and achieved his best, 4.46 in 1954, when he was thirty-four. In terms of longevity he nearly matched his predecessor Nikolay Ozolin, in that he still managed 4.30 at thirty-nine. Denisenko also amassed 6680 pts in the decathlon (under the1950 scoring table). Further progress towards American heights was achieved by Eeles Landström of Finland and Georgios Roubanis of Greece, both of whom, however, learned some of the finer points as students in American universities. Landström was European champion twice, with 4.40 in 1954 and 4.50 in 1958. Roubanis mastered 4.60 in 1958 and was probably the first man to use a fiberglass pole in a major meet: it happened at the 1956 Olympics in Melbourne, where he won a bronze medal with 4.50. By that time the advancement in overall standards in the States was such as to suggest that Warmerdam's world record (4.77) would be beaten pretty soon. The long-awaited successor was **Robert**

Allen Gutowski (born at San Pedro, California, on 25 April 1935; died on 2 August 1960; 1.83 m. / 68 Kg.). After a rather unimpressive start, this light-footed American made the big jump between nineteen and twenty-one: 4.00 in 1954, 4.43 in 1955, 4.70 in 1956. The last mark came several weeks after the USA Olympic Tryouts, in which Gutowski had finished fourth, thus failing to make the team under the rigid selective system followed by the AAU. Later in the summer, the man who had shunted Gutowski to the unpleasant fourth place, Jim Graham, dislocated an ankle. On the eve of the Melbourne Games, Graham was still struggling to regain top form, just when Gutowski was beginning to reveal his great potential. In this peculiar situation, Graham generously gave up his right to compete in the Olympics so that a better man could represent the States. As an outstanding commentator put it:

"Gutowski's 4.70 convinced Graham that America needed Gutowski more than Graham needed the very great honour of competing in the Olympics."

Incidentally, Jim was a son of Glenn Graham, the man who lost the 1924 Olympic pole vault title in a jump-off. As related above, Gutowski proved worthy of the sensitive choice of his companion by finishing second at Melbourne.

1956 Olympics, Melbourne: Pole vault (26 November): 1.Robert Richards (USA) 4.56; 2.Robert Gutowski (USA) 4.53; 3.Georgios Roubanis (Greece) 4.50; 4.George Mattos (USA) 4.35; 5.Ragnar Lundberg (Sweden) 4.25; 6.Zenon Wazny (Poland) 4.25; 7.Eeles Landström (Finland) 4.25; 8.Manfred Preussger (Germany) 4.25; 9.(tie) Vladimir Bulatov (SU) and Giulio Chiesa (Italy) 4.15; 11.Anatoliy Petrov (SU) 4.15; 12.Zbigniew Janiszewski (Poland) 4.15.

Gutowski's greatest hour came on 27 April 1957 at Palo Alto, California, when he succeeded Warmerdam as world record holder with a 4.78 clearance. Gutowski, a 9.9 100 y. sprinter, made his record with an aluminium pole. On 15 June of the same year, at Austin, Texas, he improved to 4.82, but owing to a difference of opinion over a technicality the mark was accepted by the AAU but not by the IAAF. It may be of interest to record that Gutowski long jumped 7.39 some forty minutes before beating Warmerdam's vault record for the first time. In 1960 he raised his best for the horizontal jump to 7.54. At the same time, however, he slipped to seventh in the pole vault at the US Olympic Tryouts. Later in the summer he died in a car accident. Last of the great metal pole vaulters was **Donald George Bragg** (born at Penns Grove, New Jersey on 15 May 1935; 1.90 m. / 89 Kg.). This powerful acrobat, aptly nicknamed "Tarzan", was a precocious talent. He managed 4.19 at eighteen and mastered 15 feet (4.57) for the first time at twenty. In 1959 he raised the indoor record to 4.81 and on 2 July 1960 at Palo Alto, California, he won the event at the US Olympic Tryouts with a new world outdoor record of 4.80, which mark was curiously inferior to Gutowski's American record. Bragg, one of the biggest men in the annals of the event up to that time, went on to capture the Olympic title in Rome with a 4.70 clearance, a remarkable achievement after nearly six hours of a tantalizing contest. His compatriot Ron Morris was second at 4.60, while two "American educated" vaulters, Eeles Landström of Finland and Rolando Cruz of Puerto Rico, took third and fourth respectively, both with 4.55. Among those who fell below expectations were Janis Krasovskis of the SU and Manfred Preussger of Germany, who held the European record at 4.65. Vladimir Bulatov of the SU, a Siberian who in 1959 had matched Bragg at Philadelphia with a 4.64 vault, sustained a severe ankle injury in a practice vault and could not compete. Bragg was to retire after a low-key season in 1961.

1960 Olympics, Rome - Pole Vault (7 September): 1.Donald Bragg (USA) 4.70 (OR); 2.Ronald Morris (USA) 4.60; 3.Eeles Landström (Finland) 4.55; 4.Rolando Cruz (Puerto Rico) 4.55; 5.Günter Malcher (Germany) 4.50; 6.(tie) Matti Sutinen (Finland) and Igor Petrenko (SU) 4.50; 8.Rudolf Tomásek (Czechoslovakia) 4.50; 9.Leon Lukman (Yugoslavia) 4.40; 10.Christo Christov (Bulgaria) 4.40; 11.Dimiter Chlebarov (Bulgaria) 4.30; 12.Andrzej Krzesinski (Poland) 4.30; 13.Janis Krasovskis (SU) 4.30.

LONG JUMP

Owens' successor finally arrives

Not surprisingly, the post-Owens era was marked by a definite regress in top performances. It was only in the Forties that a real menace to Owens' record (8.13) appeared in the person of Willie Steele, an American who had the muscular power of Eulace

Peacock. In the spring of 1942, just before turning nineteen, Steele reached 7.80. Then World War II put a halt to his development. After serving with the US Army in the Mediterranean area, Steele returned to civilian life and athletics and in 1947 he came dangerously close to Owens' mark with a leap of 8.07. This occurred in Salt Lake City (altitude, 1338 m.). He qualified for the 1948 Olympics with 7.97 and on that occasion he had a hairline foul of 8.18. In London, not even a bad leg could prevent him from clinching the gold medal with 7.825. And he won with almost a foot to spare !

1948 Olympics, London - Long Jump (31 July): 1.Willie Steele (USA) 7.825; 2.Thomas Bruce (Australia) 7.555; 3.Herbert Douglas (USA) 7.545; 4.Lorenzo Wright (USA) 7.45; 5.Adegboyea Adedoyin (GB) 7.27; 6.Georges Damitio (France) 7.07; 7.Harry Whittle (GB) 7.03; 8.Felix Würth (Austria) 7.00; 9.Harry Askew (GB) 6.935; 10.Erich Kistenmacher (Argentina) 6.80; 11.Eward Adamczyk (Poland) 6.735.

A man whose potentialities were never fully tapped was Andy Stanfield, the Olympic 200 m. champion of 1952. In one of his relatively few attempts, in 1951, he reached 7.85. At the 1952 Olympics in Helsinki the event was dominated by two Americans, Jerome Biffle and Meredith Gourdine, who finished one-two in that order.

1952 Olympics, Helsinki - Long Jump (22 July): 1.Jerome Biffle (USA) 7.57; 2.Meredith Gourdine (USA) 7.53; 3.Ödön Földessy (Hungary) 7.30; 4.Ary Façanha De Sa (Brazil) 7.23; 5.Jorma Valtonen (Finland) 7.16; 6.Leonid Grigoryev (SU) 7.14; 7.Karl-Erik Israelsson (Sweden) 7.10; 8.Paul Faucher (France) 7.02; 9.Pentti Snellman (Finland) 7.02; 10.Masaji Tajima (Japan) 7.00; 11.Neville Price (Soth Africa) 6.40. George Brown (USA) and Henk Visser (Holland) had no valid jumps.

The three medallists of 1960 in the Olympic long jump. From left, Irvin Roberson (USA), second; Ralph Boston (USA), first; Igor Ter-Ovanesyan (Soviet Union), third.

The first white jumper beyond the 8. metre line did not appear until 1955. This man was John Bennett of USA, whose 8.01 at the Pan-American Games in Mexico City was not good enough for victory, since his compatriot Ross Range sailed 8.03 on the same occasion.

A man who chased Owens' record for years was **Gregory Bell** of USA (born at Terre Haute, Indiana, on 7 November 1930; 1.75 m. / 68 Kg.), who over a period of four years (1956-1959) had three competitive efforts between 8.09 and 8.10. He won the Olympic title at Melbourne in 1956. That competition provided a typical example of how athletic performances can be influenced by atmospheric conditions. During the long jump final the wind ranged from 14 m/s adverse to 9 m/s favourable ! Bell and Bennett finished one-two and achieved their best marks in the face of the wind: 7.83 and 7.68 respectively. The bronze medal went to consistent Jorma Valkama of Finland (7.48).

1956 Olympics, Melbourne - Long Jump (24 November): 1.Gregory Bell (USA) 7.83; 2.John Bennett (USA) 7,68; 3.Jorma Valkama (Finland) 7.48; 4.Dmitriy Bondarenko (SU) 7.44; 5.Karim Olowu (Nigeria) 7.36; 6.Kazimierz Kropidlowski (Poland) 7.30; 7.Neville Price (South Africa) 7.28; 8.Olyeg Fyedoseyev (SU) 7.27; 9.Arthur Cruttenden (GB) 7.15; 10.Henryk Grabowski (Poland) 7.15; 11.Kenneth Wilmshurst (GB) 7.14; 12.Fermin Donazar (Uruguay) 6.57; 13.Igor Ter-Ovanesyan (SU) no valid jump.

As time went on, Owens' record tended to become a myth. But even in the so-called natural events, progress cannot be delayed indefinitely. In Europe, Long's continental record from pre-war days (7.90) was finally beaten at Bucharest in 1956 by a Dutchman hailing from Curacao, Henk Visser, who reached 7.98. A great stylist but rather nervous and prone to injuries, Visser probably missed the chance of his lifetime later in the same year, when the Dutch team withdrew from the Melbourne Olympics in protest of the SU invasion of Hungary, as did a few other European countries.

Europe's first 8-metre man was **Igor Ter-**

A pioneer from Senegal

At the present time Africa rules the roost in the middle and long distance races, but about half a century ago it moved its first internationally visible steps in other events, notably including the jumps. Diack Lamine of Senegal was one such pioneer in the long jump. Shortly before his native country became independent (1960), he lived and studied in France. After playing soccer for some time, he turned to athletics at 25 and quickly became a class long jumper. In 1958 he was "champion de France" with 7.63, leaving the runner-up (7.21) the whale of a distance behind. Such a mark placed him 21st in the 1958 World List. The following year he improved to 7.72, which actually exceeded the French record, but was aided by a 2.80 m/s wind. A serious knee injury in 1960 put a definite halt to what could have been a great career. Diack Lamine found other ways to serve Senegal and Africa though. He crowned a brilliant career as a sport authority by becoming Senegal's minister for youth and sport in 1969 and the first non-European President of the IAAF in 1999.

Ovanesyan (born at Kiev on 19 May 1938; 1.86 m. / 78 Kg.), a man of Armenian extraction whose father Aram had been SU record holder in the discus (42.595 in 1933). Acknowledged to possess great natural gifts, Igor showed remarkable versatility: 10.4 (100 m.), 2.00 (high jump) and 7184 pts. (decathlon, 1950 scoring table). With his high aggregate of speed and elevation, he was obviously attracted by the long jump. At eighteen, in 1956, he made the headlines with a jump of 7.74, but the Melbourne Olympics found him too "green" and he did not go beyond the qualifying round. Two years later he was crowned European champion in Stockholm with 7.81. On 16 May 1959 in Moscow he bettered the continental record with 8.01, even though he fell back in landing. Europe finally had a man capable of threatening America's best. By 1960 Germany had an excellent prospect in Manfred Steinbach, who had emerged as a good sprinter (10.4 and 21.2) while living in East Germany. After taking up residence in the Federal Republic, he concentrated on the long jump. He "exploded" on 24 July 1960 in Berlin: after breaking Long's German record with 7.93, he took advantage of a gust of wind (officially given as 3.2 m/s) to reach 8.14. This mark was fractionally superior to Owens' world record, but conditions obviously made it unacceptable. Thereby hangs a tale though, first related by Ekkehard zur Megede, an ATFS member from Germany – the chief officer on the pit, Walter Blume, later admitted there was no reading on the 8.14 jump. "We would have been blamed by the public, if we had confessed our mistake. So I decided to give a fictitious reading of +3.2 m/s, of course more than the permitted 2.0 m/s, so that it was not necessary to fill in a record protocol. Blume added: "You may publish this after my death".

That was the lightning. The thunder came on 12 August 1960 at Walnut, California, when a lean American by the name of Ralph Boston made a tremendous leap of 8.21 in windless conditions. This phenomenal effort capped a brilliant series: 7.26 (he sat back in the pit!) – 7.94 – 8.07 – 7.96 – 8.21 – pass. He took a 37 m. run for his record jump. **Ralph Boston** (born at Laurel, Mississippi, on 9 May 1939; 1,87 m. / 74 Kg.) had come to the fore at twenty with an excellent 7.69. In his junior days he was, like Owens, a 24-foot (7.31) jumper. At the peak of his career he could point to the following marks: 13.7 (120 y. hurdles), 22.4 (220. hurdles, straightaway), 2.057 (high Jump) and 15.45 (triple jump). He had fair speed and could do a 9.7 100 y.

With three 8-metre men in the field, the Rome Olympic final not surprisingly outshone even the great Olympic event of 1936. Boston won, as expected, with a new Olympic record of 8.12, achieved on his third attempt. But the next three place winners were close on his heels. The most serious challenger was his compatriot Irvin "Bo" Roberson, a tall, muscular man who produced the finest leap of his career, 8.11, on the very last jump of the competition. While waiting for Roberson's jump to be measured, Boston certainly experienced the most dramatic moments of his athletic career. ("My heart was really thumping", he said). If Roberson had tied his rival at 8.12 he would have been the winner on the basis of having the longer second best leap. Ter-Ovanesyan was third with a new European record of 8.04 and Manfred Steinbach fourth with 8.00, a new German record. Jorma Valkama, a consistent Finn, took fifth: he was to die only two years later. In this hotly contested event, measurement was made with an efficient new sighting device which eliminated the use of a tape. The electric scoreboard then flashed the distance.

1960 Olympics, Rome - Long Jump (2 September): 1.Ralph Boston (USA) 8.12, 2.Irvin Roberson (USA) 8.11; 3.Igor Ter-Ovanesyan (SU) 8.04; 4.Manfred Steinbach (Germany) 8.00; 5.Jorma Valkama (Finland) 7.69; 6.Christian Collardot (France) 7.68; 7.Henk Visser (Holland) 7.66; 8.Dmitriy Bondarenko (SU) 7.58; 9.Manfred Molzberger (Germany) 7.49; 10.Attilio Bravi (Italy) 7.47; 11.Dimitrios Manglaras (Greece) 7.45; 12.Paul Foreman (West Indies) 7.26; 13.Frederick Alsop (GB) 7.25. Takayuki Okazaki (Japan), injured, did not jump in the final.

TRIPLE JUMP

A soloist from Brazil: A.F.da Silva

Last of the great Japanese triple jumpers was **Genken Kin**, actually a Korean by the name of **Won Kwon-kim,** who in the geopolitical situation of the early Forties represented the land of the Rising Sun. He was born in Korea on 13 December 1918. As a junior, in 1937, he reached 15.23, and two years later he had a successful European "tournée". He was the world leader for several years, with top marks of 15.82 in 1941 and 15.86 in 1943, and also did 7.66 in the long jump. In the early years of his career he was apparently criticized by some experts for using a "hop" definitely shorter than that prevalent in the Oda school. But later on he was acknowledged to possess a fine balance in the various phases of the exercise, He is said to have bettered Tajima's world record (16.00) in training. After World War II he was able to represent his native country at the 1948 Olympics in London: by then past his peak, he finished an undistinguished twelfth with 14.25, six centimetres behind one A.F.Da Silva (more about him later in this chapter).

The winner in London was Arne Åhman of Sweden, who beat George Avery of Australia in a tight duel, 15.40 to 15.365. Ruhi Sarialp of Turkey was third with 15.025. Åhman was to excel also as a high jumper (1.99).

1948 Olympics, London - Triple Jump (3 August): 1.Arne Åhman (Sweden) 15.40 (15.40 – 14.68 – 14.89 – 14.58 – foul – foul); 2.George Avery (Australia) 15.365; 3.Ruhi Sarialp (Turkey) 15.025; 4.Preben Larsen (Denmark) 14.83; 5.Geraldo de Oliveira (Brazil) 14.825; 6.Valdemar Rautio (Finland) 14.70; 7.Leslie McKeand (Australia) 14.53; 8.Helio Coutinho da Silva (Brazil) 14.49; 9.Åke Hallgren (Sweden) 14.485; 10. William Albans (USA) 14.33; 11.Adhemar Ferreira da Silva (Brazil) 14.31; 12. Won Kwon-kim (Korea) 14.25; 13.Lennart Moberg (Sweden) 14.215. Henry Rebello (India), no valid jump.

The first phenomenon of the post-Japan era came from a country hitherto undistinguished in athletics – Brazil. This was **Adhemar Ferreira da Silva** (born at São Paulo on 29 September 1927; died at São Paulo on 12 January 2001; 1.77 m. / 69 Kg.). Prior to his appearance on the scene, Brazil had a couple of 15 m. triple jumpers, but it is generally conceded that Adhemar's rise to fame was that of a solitary genius. The natural talent of this magnificent athlete was adequately exploited through the methodical approach of his European coach, Dietrich Gerner of Germany (a 55.1 "intermediate" hurdler in 1927). From 13.05 in his first competition in 1947, Adhemar improved to 16.56 in his 100th competition in 1955. As a record breaker he first entered the picture on 3 December 1950 at São Paulo, when he equalled Tajima's fourteen-year-old mark (16.00). The following year, namely on 30 September at Rio de Janeiro, he became the sole owner of the record with a 16.01 effort. A menace to the throne of this "Paulista" was by then looming in the person of his compatriot Helio Coutinho da Silva, a "Careca" (i.e. a native of Rio de Janeiro) who late in 1951 did 15.99. Unfortunately, a serious injury put paid to the chances of the talented Helio, who was a 10.4 metric sprinter. Adhemar continued to improve and his ability as a big-time jumper came in full evidence at the 1952 Olympics in Helsinki, when he beat his own world record in four of his six trials and won the gold medal with 16.22. Trailing him in that memorable event were Leonid Shcherbakov of the SU (15.98) and Arnoldo Devonish of Venezuela (15.52).

1952 Olympics, Helsinki - Triple Jump (23 July): 1.Adhemar Ferreira da Silva (Brazil) 16.22 (WR) (15.95 - 16.12 - 15.54 - 16.09 - 16.22 - 16.05); 2.Leonid Shcherbakov (SU) 15.98; 3.Arnoldo Devonish (Venezuela) 15.52; 4.Walter Ashbaugh (USA) 15.39; 5.Rune Nilsen (Norway) 15.13; 6. Yoshio Iimuro (Japan) 14.99; 7.Geraldo de Oliveira (Brazil) 14.95; 8.Roger Norman (Sweden) 14.89; 9.Reino Hiltunen (Finland) 14.85; 10.Zygfryd Weinberg (Poland) 14.76; 11.James Gerhardt (USA) 14.69; 12.Rui Ramos (Portugal) 14.69; 13.Preben Larsen (Denmark) 14.62; 14.Tadashi Yamamoto (Japan) 14.57; 15.Arne Åhman (Sweden) 14.05.

Shcherbakov was the "chef de file" of a new dynasty of triple jumpers. Soviet technicians had spotted he triple jump as one of the weakest points in the armour of rival countries in Europe and North America. So they began to work hard to take full advantage of the situation. **Leonid Shcherbakov** (born at Olyebino on 7 April 1927; 1.78 m. / 73 Kg.) broke the ice at the 1950 European Championships in Brussels, annexing the continental title at 15.39. After his brilliant second place in the 1952 Olympics, he continued to improve. He worked assiduously to strengthen his leg muscles, using weights around his waist in training sessions. After reaching maximum height in the "hop", he would take advantage of his hyper-strong ankles for a low and long "step", and would finally regain height in the "jump". Being a man of relatively mediocre speed, however, he needed eight seasons to improve from 15.43 in 1949 to 16.46 in 1956. He won his second European title at Bern in 1954 with 15.90 and wrested the world record from Adhemar Ferreira da Silva on 19 July 1953 in Moscow with 16.235. The Brazilian took up the gauntlet, and again chose a major competition as the occasion for his reply. At the Pan-American Games in Mexico City on 16 March 1955 he topped all his previous efforts with a magnificent 16.56. This record performance was achieved with an aiding wind of merely 0.2 m/s. and with a ratio of 6.28 (hop), 4.95 (step) and 5.33

Adhemar Ferreira da Silva (Brazil), a twotime triple jump winner in the Olympics (1952 and 1956), the first great field event man produced by Latin America.

(jump). Arnoldo Devonish was second at 16.13. At the 1956 Olympics in Melbourne (27 November) Adhemar Ferreira da Silva became the first triple jumper since Prinstein's pioneer days to successfully defend his title of world champion. His chief opponent was Vilhjálmur Einarsson, a strong man from Iceland who took the lead in the second round with 16.26. The Brazilian rose to the challenge with 16.35 in the fourth round – and that was the winning jump. Vitold Kreer of the SU was third, while former world record holder Shcherbakov had to be content with sixth. Adhemar was a man of moderate speed and his ability as a long jumper was just fair (7.33). Brit even so he became the greatest athlete in South American history. He had first appeared in the Olympics in 1948: eleventh. And he was to make his fourth appearance in 1960 in Rome: fourteenth.

1956 Olympics, Melbourne - Triple jump (27 November): 1.Adhemar Ferreira da Silva (Brazil) 16.35 (OR); (15.69 – 16.04 – 15.90 – 16.35 – 16.26 – 16.21) 2.Vilhjálmur Einarsson (Iceland) 16.26; 3.Vitold Kreer (SU) 16.02; 4.William Sharpe (USA) 15.88; 5.Martin Rehák (Czechoslovakia) 15.85; 6.Leonid Shcherbakov (SU) 15.80; 7.Koji Sakurai (Japan) 15.73; 8.Teruji Kogake (Japan) 15.64; 9.Kenneth Wilmshurst (GB) 15.54; 10.Ryszard Malcherczyk (Poland) 15.54; 11.Ira Davis (USA) 15.40; 12.George Shaw (USA) 15.33; 13.Hiroshi Shibata (Japan) 15.25; 14.Karl Rahkamo (Finland) 15.21; 15.Mohinder Singh (India) 15.20.

Józef Schmidt (Poland), twotime triple jump champion in the Olympics (1960 and 1964).

The Russians recaptured the world record during the inaugural SU vs. USA dual meet in Moscow in July 1958, when Olyeg Ryakhovskiy jumped 16.59, mainly by virtue of a 6.46 "hop". The following month, at the European Championships in Stockholm, Ryakhovskiy was decisively beaten by Józef Schmidt of Poland, who braved the adverse elements and a poor runway to reach a personal best of 16.43. Ryakhovskiy, who was actually an Asian, barely held off Einarsson of Iceland in a close fight for second place, 16.02 to 16.00. SU fought back in 1959, when Olyeg Fyedoseyev used his potential as a long jumper (7.77) to reach 16.70 for a new world mark at Nalchik (Caucasus) on 3 May. But **Józef Schmidt** (born at Michalkowice on 28 March 1935; 1.84 m. / 77 Kg.) was to top them all in the Olympic year 1960. This Pole was regarded as a real comer even before his breakthrough in 1958. His annual progression was as follows: 14.40 in 1955, 15.10 in 1956, 15.61 in 1957. A pulled tendon slowed him down in 1959, but he was back in stride the following year. He made history in the Polish Championships at Olsztyn on 5 August 1960, when in the first round of the final he compiled a ratio of 6.00, 5.02 and 6.01 for a new world record of 17.03, aided by a legal wind of 1.0 m/s. And he was said to have lost several centimetres due to an imperfect landing ! Schmidt went on to win the Olympic title in Rome with 16.81, then the second best performance of his career. Vladimir Goryayev (16.63) and Vitold Kreer (16.43), both of the SU, relegated to fourth place Ira Davis, who could nevertheless rejoice for having set a new US record (16.41).

1960 Olympics, Rome - Triple Jump (6 September): 1.Józef Schmidt (Poland) 16.81 (16.78 – foul – 16.81 – foul – 16.63 – 13.48); 2.Vladimir Goryayev (SU) 16.63; 3.Vitold Kreer (SU) 16.43; 4.Ira Davis (USA) 16.41; 5.Vilhjalmur Einarsson (Iceland) 16.37; 6.Ryszard Malcherczyk (Poland) 16.01; 7.Manfred Hinze (Germany) 15.93; 8.Kari Rahkamo (Finland) 15.84; 9.Ian Tomlinson (Australia) 15.71; 10.Yevgeniy Mikhailov (SU) 15.67; 11.Sten Erickson (Sweden) 15.49; 12.Frederick Alsop (GB) 15.49; 13.John Baguley (Australia) 15.22; 14.Adhemar Ferreira da Silva (Brazil) 15.07; 15. Pierluigi Gatti (Italy) no valid jump.

MEN
1961-1980

5

HIGH JUMP

From Brumel to the "Wizard of Fox"

After the Rome Olympics, Brumel soon proved the most talented of the Soviets who had upset John Thomas in the Eternal City. He was a high jump "addict" since the age of fourteen, when he cleared 1.40. His progress since then had been remarkably quick: 1.76 in 1957, 1.95 in '58, 2,01 in '59, 2.20 in '60. He rose to world record heights for the first time in an indoor meet at Leningrad on 28 January 1961, when he cleared 2.25. This was well above Thomas' official world record, but the mark, made from a dirt take-off, could not be ratified, since the IAAF continued to ignore anything that happened "under a roof". But Brumel lost little time in meeting the demand even under outdoor conditions. He succeeded Thomas as world record holder on 18 June 1961 in Moscow with 2.236 (ratified as 2.23). In the same year he had two more record performances: 2.243 (ratified as 2.24) on 16 July in Moscow and 2.25 during the Universiade at Sofia on 31 August.

Brumel dominated the high jump scene for five years, 1961 through 1965. His matchless straddle allowed him to better the world record on three more occasions: 2.26 at Palo Alto, California, on 22 July 1962, 2.27 in Moscow on 29 September 1962 and 2.28 (his lifetime best, on third try) in Moscow on 21 July 1963. A clear indication of his competitive ability is provided by the fact that three of his six world records occurred in connection with SU vs. USA dual meets, a confrontation which was given tremendous publicity at the time. He won the 1962 European title with 2.21 and two years later, in Tokyo, he won the Olympic gold medal. On the latter occasion he again faced his old rival John Thomas. It was a close duel, and Brumel felt the pressure as never before. After both had cleared 2.18 and failed at 2.20, the Russian got the nod on the fewer misses rule. John Rambo, a young American who stood 2 metres in his socks, took third place with 2.16.

1964 Olympics, Tokyo – High Jump (21 October): 1.Valeriy Brumel (SU) 2.18 (OR); 2.John Thomas (USA) 2.18 (OR); 3.John Rambo (USA) 2.16; 4.Stig Pettersson (Sweden) 2.14; 5.Robert

Valeriy Brumel (USSR), a great exponent of the "dive straddle". He brought the world's high jump record to 2.28.

Shavlakadze (SU) 2.14; 6.(tie) Kjell-Åke Nilsson (Sweden) and Ralf Drecoll (Germany) 2.09; 8.Edward Caruthers (USA) 2.09; 9.Mahamad Idriss (Chad) 2.09; 10.Lawrence Peckham (Australia) 2.09.

In the fall of 1965 a motor accident put a premature end to the career of the phenomenal Brumel, then only twenty-three. (The story is told in the adjoining aside). What he had done during his five-year reign was of course largely sufficient to earn him a special niche in the Hall of Fame of athletics. Few adepts of the straddle, if any, had brought that style to such a degree of near perfection. Brumel's assets notably included a fast approach run (he once did 10.5 for the 100 m.) and great strength in the left (take-off) leg. The latter virtually acted as a pole in converting propulsive force from horizontal to vertical. Brumel offered glimpses of great talent even as a long jumper (7.65 in 1961).

"Second attempt"

Brumel's athletic adventure came to an abrupt stop in October 1965 as a result of a motor accident . He was riding on the back of a motorcycle driven by a personal friend (actually a champion in this sport). The vehicle went out of control and hit a tree. Brumel's right leg was pinned under the machine and both men were still unconscious when help arrived. Brumel underwent surgery for two simple fractures below the knee and one multiple fracture of the ankle. Undamaged was his left (take-off) leg, ironically the one that had given him some problems recently. (He went no higher than 2.21 in 1965). That was the beginning of a long Odyssey. Several other operations followed and Brumel was in a cast for nearly three years. Then he spent many tantalizing hours in rehabilitation exercises. In the autumn of 1969 he was able to resume competition. He managed 2.00, then 2.06, but his tortured leg did not respond adequately and his comeback, already miraculous, ended there and then. A few years later, a theatrical work bearing the significant title "Second attempt" reached the stage. It was inspired by Brumel's untiring efforts to regain his former physical prowess and was chiefly a tribute paid to his main "saviour", Prof. G.A.Ilizarov, who for a number of years had given him medical and psychological assistance.

Next to the incomparable Brumel, one of the most interesting figures during the Sixties was **Ni Chi-chin** of China (under Pinyin, the new phonetic alphabet adopted in 1979, his name is spelled **Ni Zhiqin**). Curiously enough, he and Brumel were "astrological twins", sharing the same birthday. Ni was born in South Western Fukien on 14 April 1942, and was strikingly similar to the Russian even in build, being 1.84 m. tall and weighing 82 Kg. The Chinese was credited with 2.05 at eighteen. In 1961 he made a tour of Eastern Europe, taking lessons from Russian jumpers. After undergoing ankle surgery, he rose to world class in 1966, clearing 2.27 at the Games of the New Emerging Forces, held at Phnom–Penh. After another accident, he made the world headlines on 8 November 1970 at Changsha with a 2.29 jump, one centimetre over Brumel's official record. But in those days the People's Republic of China was not a member of the IAAF and so Ni's mark could not be ratified.

In the meantime there had been new technical developments which in a relatively short time were to have a great impact on the evolution of the event. The man behind this "revolution" was an American, **Richard ("Dick") Fosbury** (born at Portland, Oregon, on 6 March 1947; 1.93 m. / 83 Kg.). He began with the old scissors style, clearing 1.625 at fifteen. He then reasoned that he might do better by simply .... "lying down". In fact he lowered the centre of gravity by laying out on his back. His new technique included a curved run-up, which placed him side-on to the bar. Then he rotated his body and crossed the bar head first, legs last before landing on his shoulders. By the time Fosbury entered Oregon State University in 1965, he could point to a personal best of 2.007. But then his new coach Bernie Wagner, one of America's best known technicians, asked him to try the roll, straddle version. Fosbury regarded the conventional style as rather complicated, yet agreed to try – but eventually returned to his own style six months later, with the intelligent Wagner entirely on his side. Progress followed quickly and in 1967 Fosbury cleared 2.102. By then his story was reminiscent of another one which had occurred, still on West Coast high jump pits, some fifty-odd years earlier.... The new style came to be known as the "Fosbury Flop". In a lighter vein, the inventor was nicknamed "The Wizard of Fox", a free rendering of the title of a famous book for children by L.F.Baum. As it usually happens whenever a revolution breaks out, the new "invention" was looked upon with marked scepticism by several observers – especially in Europe. Chances are that the "breakthrough" of the new jumping form would have been delayed rather considerably if the inventor had not carried his style to victory in the noblest of competitions, the Olympic Games, a spectacle relayed to millions of TV-viewers around the world. 1968 was easily Fosbury's best year, yet his pre-Olympic season was not exceptional. He went to Mexico with a personal best of 2.21, curiously achieved in placing third at the US Olympic Trials behind Ed Caruthers and Reynaldo Brown, who cleared the same height but had fewer misses. But in the Olympic final he made no mistakes and finally topped a crack field with 2.24, a new Olympic record. Two "conventional" jumpers finished second and third - Caruthers and Valentin Gavrilov of the SU, with 2.22 and 2.20 respectively.

1968 Olympics, Mexico City - High Jump (20 October): 1.Richard Fosbury (USA) 2.24 (OR); 2. Ed Caruthers (USA) 2.22; 3.Valentin Gavrilov (SU) 2.20;4.Valeriy Skvorzov (SU) 2.16; 5.Reynald Brown (USA) 2.14; 6.Giacomo Crosa (Italy) 2.14; 7.Gunther Spielvogel (Germany) 2.14; 8.Lawrence Peckham (Australia) 2.12; 9.Robert Sainte-Rose (France) 2.09; 10.Ingomar Sieghart (Germany) 2.09; 11.Luis Garriga (Spain) 2.09; 12.Ahmed Sénoussi (Chad) 2.09; 13.Miograd Todosijevic (Yugoslavia) 2.06.

Fosbury's "winning product" was sweeping the board in America. At the same time it began to catch the imagination of young jumpers in other parts of the world as well – and most of them were quick to adopt it. In Europe, however, established performers and coaches generally remained faithful to the "conventional" (straddle) style. Valentin Gavrilov of the SU won the European title at Athens in 1969 with 2.17. The first continental jumper to achieve fine results with the "Flop" was István Major of Hungary, who was at his best indoors and had a top mark of 2.24. Fosbury had a fairly good season in 1969, then disappeared from the scene. He joined the Mike O'Hara "pro" group in 1973, with limited success. Curiously enough, he never won the AAU title (he was second in 1969).

Brumel's official successor as world record holder was an American exponent of the straddle, Pat Matzdorf. On 3 July 1971 at Berkeley, during a triangular meet USA-SU-"World All Stars", he cleared 2.29 on his third attempt. Just like Fosbury, he had just one great season. But four years later he managed 2.24 .... with the "Flop". For many years he was to remain the only jumper credited with top-class marks with both styles.

The first European to win a continental outdoor title using the "Flop" was Kestutis Sapka of the SU, a Lithuanian who won at Helsinki in 1971 with 2.20. But in the 1972 Olympics in Munich the adepts of the straddle regained the top with Jüri Tarmak of the SU, who won the gold medal with 2.23 from Stefan Junge of East Germany. Third went to an American Flopper, Dwight Stones.

Ni Chih-chin was China's first great high jumper. In 1970 he did 2.29, which mark was a world best at the time but could not be ratified as such since China was not yet a member of the IAAF. This picture was taken in 1966.

1972 Olympics, Munich - High Jump (10 September): 1.Jüri Tarmak (SU) 2.23; 2.Stefan Junge (East Germany) 2.21; 3.Dwight Stones (USA) 2.21; 4.Hermann Magerl (West Germany) 2.18; 5.Adam Szepesi (Hungary) 2.18; 6.(tie) John Beers (Canada) and István Major (Hungary) 2.15; 8.Rustam Akhmyetov (SU) 2.15; 9.John Hawkins (Canada) 2.15; 10.Enzo Dal Forno (Italy) 2.15; 11.Jan Dahlgren (Sweden) 2.15; 12.(tie) Vassilios Papadimitriou (Greece) and Kestutis Sapka (SU) 2.15; 14.Bernard Gauthier (France) 2.15.

Jacek Wszola (Poland) won the Olympic high jump title (1976) shortly before turning 20.

Dwight Stones (born at Los Angeles on 6 December 1953; 1.95 m. / 81 Kg.) was an American of Swedish extraction, barely eighteen and a half at the time of the Munich Olympics. He had adopted the Flop early, overcoming a fear which was quite common in those days: the "danger factor" in landing head and shoulders first on sawdust pits. (This was to disappear only with the advent of synthetic materials). He made rapid progress: 1.918 in 1969, 2.007 in 1970, 2.171 in 1971 and 2.21 in winning the event at the US Olympic Trials in 1972. On 11 July 1973 at Munich he captured the world record at the unripe age of 19 years and seven months, clearing 2.30 on his third attempt. That was his eighteenth jump of the afternoon, and it is curious to note that in some of his jumps at the lower heights he used the straddle ! In 1976 Stones bettered the world record on two more occasions: 2.31 on 5 June and 2.32 on 4 August, both at Philadelphia's time honoured Franklin Field. In between these happy days, however, he had a gloomy one in Montreal's Olympic arena. That was in fact a rainy day and Stones, who relied on speed so much, found himself unable to do better than 2.21, the same height he had cleared in his bright Olympic debut four years earlier – and again worth a bronze medal. Gold went to his rival and friend Jacek Wszola olf Poland, who cleared 2.25, a great achievement under such conditions. Greg Joy of Canada was second at 2.23.

1976 Olympics, Montreal – High Jump (31 July): 1.Jacek Wszola (Poland) 2.25 (OR); 2.Greg Joy (Canada) 2.23; 3.Dwight Stones (USA) 2.21; 4.Sergey Budalov (SU) 2.21; 5.Sergey Senyukov (SU) 2.18; 6.Rodolfo Bergamo (Italy) 2.18; 7.Rolf Beilschmidt (East Germany) 2.18; 8.Jesper Törring (Denmark) 2.18; 9.Terje Totland (Norway) 2.18; 10.Rune Almén (Sweden) 2.18; 11.James Barrineau (USA) 2.14; 12.Claude Ferragne (Canada) 2.14; 13. Bill Jankunis (USA) 2.10; 14.Leif-Roar Falkum (Norway) 2.10.

Fruits of a rivalry

It does not happen everyday that three athletes from as many different countries, after meeting on the steps of an Olympic dais, may decide to join efforts and produce a book on their "art". This unusual circumstance materialized with Jacek Wszola of Poland, Greg Joy of Canada and Dwight Stones of USA, who finished in that order in the Olympic high jump final at Montreal in 1976. The book came out in 1983, under the inevitable title: "High Jump". The driving force behind the project was Dr. David Martin of Georgia State University, Atlanta, noted physiologist and track historian as well as a close friend of the three champions. The book they produced is a fine compendium of high jump technique, told through the experiences and reflections of three dedicated Floppers.

Dwight Stones, a very consistent jumper, was no.1 in "Track & Field News" World Ranking for four consecutive years (1973-76). Early in the "Seventies" the "Flop" gradually conquered Europe as well. After his victory in the 1971 European Championships, Kestutis Sapka came close to successfully defending his title in Rome in 1974. On that occasion he was second with 2.25, the same height cleared by Jesper Törring of Denmark, who won on the fewer misses rule. SU and East Germany were at any rate the last strongholds of the straddle. The former produced another good exponent of that jumping form with **Vladimir Yashchenko** (born at Zaporozhe, Ukraine, on 12 January 1959; 1.93 m. / 84 Kg.). A truly gifted athlete, "Volodya" jumped 2.03 at fifteen. Three years later, on 3 July 1977, he cleared a bar set at 2.33, thus breaking Stones' world record. This happened at Richmond, Virginia, during a USA vs SU Junior match, and the feat of the 18-year-old Ukrainian, who had a previous best of 2.26 indoors, greatly impressed US experts. Yashchenko went on to clear 2.35 in the European Indoor Championships at Milan on 12 March 1978. And later in the same year, namely on 16 June at Tbilisi, he raised the official outdoor mark to 2.34. These results came as the sum total of great talent and plenty of hard work, possibly too hard for a boy of his age. The wear and tear of hyper-intensive training soon began to tell. Yashchenko managed to annex the 1978 European title in Prague with 2.30, but that was to remain his last cry. Stress fractures put a premature end to his meteoric career. Another "great" among latter-day straddle jumpers was Rolf Beilschmidt of East Germany, a consistent performer who achieved his best, 2.31, in the 1977 European Cup. Another interesting jumper was Franklin Jacobs of USA, a Flopper who on 27 January 1978 in New York set an indoor record of 2.32 – 59 cm. above his head ! As at the end of 2010 this "differential" was still the equal greatest on record for jumpers who have done 2.30 or better. Jacobs' most notable victory was in the 1979 World Cup at Montreal, when he beat **Jacek Wszola** (both 2.27). The latter (born at Warsaw on 30 December 1956; 1.94 m. / 71 Kg.) has been one of the most gifted and consistent jumpers of the modern era. He was for years Stones' most serious rival in international competition. Wszola, he too a Flopper, won his gold medal at Montreal before turning 20. Four years later, namely on 25 May 1980 at Eberstadt, he succeeded Yashchenko as world record holder with 2.35. By the way, this German city was to become the Mecca of élite high jumpers, who would gather there every year for a High Jump Festival. Eberstadt had no stadium worthy of the name, only a high jump installation – and spectators gather around it to create a warm atmosphere. Among the men beaten by Wszola there in 1980 was a 19-year-old German, Dietmar Mögenburg, who gave the Pole an indirect "reply" within 24 hours. In a meet at Rehlingen on 26 May, Mögenburg cleared 2.35, thus equalling the ultra-fresh world record. As a West German, however, young Mögenburg had to stay away from the 1980 Moscow Olympics, just like the Americans. Defending champion Jacek Wszola thus loomed as an odds-on favourite. In the Olympic final the Pole cleared 2.31, yet found his effort good only for a silver medal, with Jörg Freimuth of East Germany third at the same height on the misses rule. The upset winner was a 21-year-old East German, Gerd Wessig, who on that day achieved the seemingly impossible, improving on his pre-Games record (2.30) **three times**, with 2.31, 2.33 and finally 2.36 on his second attempt for the first men's high jump world record ever in the long history of the Games ! Wessig, a Flopper who stood 2.01 in height, celebrated with a complete backward somersault ! Yet he was to remain the phenomenon of a single day. In the years that followed recurrent injuries, and possibly other factors as well, kept him well below his Moscow "plafond".

1980 Olympics, Moscow - High Jump (1 August): 1.Gerd Wessig (East Germany) 2.36 (WR & OR); 2.Jacek Wszola (Poland) 2.31; 3.Jörg Freimuth (East Germany) 2.31; 4.Henry Lauterbach (East Germany) 2.29; 5.Roland Dalhäuser (Switzerland) 2.24; 6.Vasa Komenic (Yugoslavia) 2.24; 7.Adrian Proteasa (Rumania) 2.21; 8.Aleksandr Grigoryev (SU) 2.21; 9.Mark Naylor (GB) 2.21; 10.Gennadiy Byelkov (SU) 2.21; 11.Aleksey Demyanyuk (SU) 2.21; 12.Janusz Trzepizur (Poland) 2.18; 13.Sorin Matei (Romania) 2.18; 14.Guy Moreau (Belgium) 2.18; 15.Marco Tamberi (Italy) 2.15; 16.Roberto Cabrejas (Spain) 2.10.

POLE VAULT

The fibreglass revolution

The year 1961 marked the advent of a new pole which was to revolutionize the standards of the event. It came to be known as the fibreglass pole. Implements made of such material had been experimented in USA since the early Fifties and one was actually used by Georgios Roubanis of Greece when he placed third in the 1956 Olympic final at Melbourne. According to Dr. Richard Ganslen, a former vaulter (NCAA champion in 1939 with 4.39, using a bamboo pole) and a keen student of vaulting materials and technique, experiments with flexible poles of a substantially similar nature had been made by Nikolay Ozolin of the SU as early as in 1928.

Such were the qualities of the new pole that 15-foot (4.57) or better vaults soon became commonplace occurrences. The relatively rigid metal poles used in early post-war years had yielded only minor advantages vis-à-vis the best bamboo models of previous years. Fibreglass brought about the most exciting change in the history of the event. Its main value lay in its flexion at take-off. It also permitted a higher (by 30/40 cms.) hand grip on the pole, and aided upward momentum during the push-up. Above all, the new pole had a great tensile strength. Given all these advantages, it would be unfair to compare marks made from 1961 onwards with those of the bamboo and/or metal era. Even so, I do not agree with those observers who claim that if bamboo poles were still in use today, the world record would still belong to the great Corny Warmerdam. Such a view obviously ignores or underestimates other important factors which have contributed to the evolution of this event, such as superior conditioning methods and the ever stiffer competition prevailing at the international level.

At any rate, fibreglass poles caused a real earthquake: between 1961 and 1980 the world record, which on the eve of the new era belonged to "Tarzan" Bragg with 4.80, was bettered forty-odd times (counting official marks plus a few others which were never ratified). By the end of 1980 the "ceiling" was up to 5.78, an improvement of nearly one metre in twenty years ! Progress was great even in "depth", as can be seen from the following table, showing the marks of the first and fiftieth performers in the World Year Lists for 1960, virtually the last year of the Metal Era, 1961-64, i.e. the years of transition, 1970 and 1980.

	1st	50th
1960	4.80	4.45
1961	4.83	4.47
1962	4.94	4.56
1963	5.20	4.65
1964	5.28	4.75
1970	5.49	5.03
1980	5.78	5.40

No other athletic event had ever offered such an upward trend in a similarly short period of time.

The first vaulter to set a world record with fibreglass was George Davies of USA: 4.83 on 20 May 1961 at Boulder, Colorado. Shortly afterwards there was a European interlude thanks to **Pentti Nikula** of Finland (born at Somero on 3 February 1939; 1.79 m. / 67 Kg.). On 22 June 1962 at Kauhava he broke a 35-year-old US monopoly by capturing the world record with a 4.94 effort. And he was also the first man to break the 5-metre barrier, alas under unofficial conditions. This was during an indoor meet at Pajulahti on 2 February 1963, when he cleared 5.00, 5.05 and 5.10 in close succession. Later in the same year, on 5 May at Pori, he cleared 5.00 outdoors, but this earned him only a European record because in the intervening time the Americans had fought back successfully. For official purposes, history's first 5-metre vaulter was **Brian Sternberg** of USA (born at Seattle, Washington, on 21 June 1943; 1.85 m. / 76 Kg.), who cleared 5 metres even a few weeks before turning twenty, on 27 April 1963 at Philadelphia. In the following weeks, Sternberg and his compatriot John Pennel took turns in bettering the record. A few weeks after improving to 5.08, however, Sternberg was put off the track by a hideous accident. It happened during a training session on the trampoline, while attempting to perform a double back somersault. He lost control and instead of landing on his feet he came down on the back of his neck and shoulders. He suffered dislocation of cervical vertebrae, with damage to the spinal cord. Despite surgical treatment, he was to remain paralyzed from his neck down. Quite revealing of Sternberg's modesty was his comment after clearing 5.08: "I don't attach much importance to records made with the fibreglasspole. Cornelius Warmerdam still is the greatest".

Progress with the "catapult pole" – as Don Bragg chose to call it – continued at relentless speed. By the end of 1963 John Pennel had upped the world record to 5.20.

At the Tokyo Olympics (1964) the US first string, Fred Hansen, by then the new world record holder at 5.28, was put to a hard test by three Germans. After a 9-hour struggle he finally emerged the winner with 5.10. Wolfgang Reinhardt (5.05) and Klaus Lehnertz (5.00), both of West Germany, followed in that order, while Manfred Preussger of East Germany, who also cleared 5.00, had to be content with fourth place. (N.B. Prior to the Games, West & East Germany had agreed to hold a national trial meet, in which the first three in each event were to qualify for a united Olympic team).

1964 Olympics, Tokyo – Pole Vault (17 October): 1.Fred Hansen (USA) 5.10; 2.Wolfgang Reinhardt (Germany) 5.05; 3.Klaus Lehnertz (Germany) 5.00; 4.Manfred Preussger (Germany) 5.00; 5.Gennadiy Bliznyetsov (SU) 4.95; 6.Rudolf Tomasek (Czechoslovakia) 4.90; 7.Pentti Nikula (Finland) 4.90; 8.Billy Pemelton (USA) 4.80; 9.Igor Feld (SU) 4.80; 10.Guerrino Moro (Canada) 4.70; 11.John Pennel (USA) 4.70; 12.Risto Ankio (Finland) 4.70; 13.Roman Lesek (Yugoslavia) 4.70; 14.Taisto Laitinen (Finland) 4.60.

Even though fibreglass poles were particularly favoured by young vaulters, there were some established performers from the Metal Era who managed to convert to the new implement with remarkable success. Foremost in this group were Ron Morris of USA, the 1960 Olympic silver medallist, who improved from 4.70 (metal) to 5.03 (fibreglass), and Manfred Preussger of East Germany (from 4.65 to 5.15). The most prominent role in the record breaking spree was played by **Robert Seagren** of USA (born at Pomona, California, on 17 October 1946; 1.83 m. / 79 Kg.). A "son of fibreglass", he bettered the world record time and again, beginning with 5.32 in 1966 and winding up with 5.63 in 1972 ! He won the 1968 Olympic title at Mexico City, exactly one day before turning twenty, with 5.40. It was a hard fought event and Seagren won on fewer misses from Claus Schiprowski of West Germany ad Wolfgang Nordwig of East Germany, who also cleared 5.40 and were classified in that order. It was clear that Europeans were finally able to talk on even terms with America's best.

1968 Olympics, Mexico City - Pole Vault (16 October): 1.Robert Seagren (USA) 5.40 (OR); 2.Claus Schiprowski (West Germany) 5.40 (OR); 3.Wolfgang Nordwig (East Germany) 5.40 (OR); 4.Christos Papanikolaou (Greece) 5.35; 5.John Pennel (USA) 5.35; 6.Gennadiy Bliznyetsov (SU) 5.30; 7.Hervé D'Encausse (France) 5.25; 8.Heinfried Engel (West Germany) 5.20; 9.Ignacio Sola (Spain) 5.20; 10.Kjell Isaksson (Sweden) 5.15; 11.Kiyoshi Niwa (Japan) 5.15; 12.Aleksandr Malyutin (SU) 5.00; 13.Michael Bull (GB) 5.00; 14.Altti Alarotu (Finland) 5.00. Erkki Mustakari (Finland) no valid jump.

Pentti Nikula had won the 1962 European title with 4.80. Then came Nordwig, who scored three consecutive victories in the continental meet, with 5.10 in 1966, 5.30 in '69 and 5.35 in '71. Always a great competitor, **Wolfgang Nordwig** (born at Siegmar, Chemnitz, on 27 August 1943; 1.84 m. / 72 Kg.) bettered the world record twice in 1970, with 5.45 and 5.46, but was excelled towards the end of the season by Christos Papanikolaou of Greece, who at Athens on 24 October treated his countrymen to a rare sight with a 5.49 clearance.

A memorable event occurred at the 1972 Olympics in Munich. After sixteen consecutive victories (1896 through 1968), American vaulters had to leave the highest step of the Olympic dais to a foreigner, the reliable Wolfgang Nordwig. Unfortunately, this event was

Wolfgang Nordwig (East Germany) won the pole vault title at the 1972 Olympics, breaking a US monopoly dating from 1896.

preceded and partly clouded by a bitter controversy. Manufacturers had never ceased to devise new types of fibreglass poles and the latest models were definitely better than those used at the dawn of the new era. The newest ones had been used for months on both sides of the Atlantic and it was with one of them that Seagren raised the world record to 5.63 at the US Olympic Trials at Eugene on 2 July. The IAAF displayed a certain degree of inconsistency by first banning the new poles from the Olympics on 25 July, readmitting them on 27 August and finally banning them for good on 30 August, i.e. two days before the qualifying round. This meant that Seagren and several others were compelled to abandon the poles they had been using throughout the major part of the season. It was rumoured that Nordwig too had tried the latest models, only to discard them in pre-Olympic weeks. At any rate, Nordwig had his greatest day on 2 September in Munich and won the gold medal at 5.50, his lifetime best. Seagren was second (5.40), ahead of another American, Jan Johnson (5.35). Among those who fell by the wayside chiefly as a result of the pole controversy were two of the best Europeans, Kjell Isaksson of Sweden and Renato Dionisi of Italy. Both failed to make the final, a bitter pill especially for Isaksson, who early in the season had bettered the world record several times, up to 5.55 (plus an unratified 5.59), before finally losing it to Seagren.

1972 Olympics, Munich – Pole vault (2 September): 1.Wolfgang Nordwig (East Germany) 5.50 (OR); 2.Robert Seagren (USA) 5.40; 3.Jan Johnson (USA) 5.35; 4.Reinhard Kuretzky (West Germany) 5.30; 5.Bruce Simpson (Canada) 5.20; 6.Volker Ohl (West Germany) 5.20; 7.Hans Lagerqvist (Sweden) 5.20; 8.François Tracanelli (France) 5.10; 9.Ingemar Jernberg (Sweden) 5.10; 10.Wojciech Buciarski (Poland) 5.10; 11.Christos Papanicolaou (Greece) 5.00. No valid jump: Hervé D'Encausse (France), Tadeusz Slusarski (Poland) and Antti Kalliomäki (Finland).

Despite his class and longevity, Kjell Isaksson had to be content with two silver medals in the European Championships (1969 and '71). As for Dionisi, he won the event in the Europe vs. America dual meet in 1969 and a European indoor title in 1973. His lifetime best was 5.45.

The great Nordwig decided to step out after his Munich victory. From that time onwards three vaulting schools began to fight it out for supremacy in Europe: France, Poland and SU. The combined effect of their efforts was that USA finally had to relinquish its leadership of the event. At the 1974 European Championships in Rome victory went to Vladimir Kishkun of the SU with 5.35. In the Olympic year 1976 the Americans were predictably thirsty for revenge. In the meantime they had recaptured the world record with Dave Roberts, who did 5.65 in 1975, aged 24. What followed in the early stages of 1976 seemed to confirm that US vaulters were back in lane 1. The world record was bettered time and again, first by Earl Bell, 5.67, then by Roberts himself, who won at the US Olympic Trials at Eugene on 22 June with 5.70. But the Montreal Olympic event gave partly unexpected results. The battle was featured by a lot of "poker strategy", with leading contenders passing this or that height in order to keep down the number of their trials in the light of the final countback of trials and failures, which would be decisive in breaking ties. Three men cleared 5.50 and Tadeusz Slusarski of Poland won "on points" from Antti Kalliomäki of Finland and world record holder Roberts.

Wladyslaw Kozakiewicz (Poland), winner of a hotly contested pole vault competition at the 1980 Olympics in Moscow with a record shattering 5.78.

1976 Olympics, Montreal – Pole vault (26 July): 1.Tadeusz Slusarski (Poland) 5.50; 2.Antti Kalliomäki (Finland) 5.50; 3.Dave Roberts (USA) 5.50; 4.Patrick Abada (France) 5.45; 5.Wojciech Buciarski (Poland) 5.45; 6.Earl Bell (USA) 5.45; 7.Jean-Michel Bellot (France) 5.40; 8.Itsuo Takanezawa (Japan) 5.40; 9.Günther Lohre (West Germany) 5.35; 10.Yuriy Prokhoryenko (SU) 5.25; 11.Wladyslaw Kozakiewicz (Poland) 5.25; 12.Don Baird (Australia) 5.25; 13.(tie) Vladimir Kishkun (SU) and Terry Porter (USA) 5.20; 15.Tapani Haapakoski (Finland) 5.20.

The French school made spectacular advances under the stimulus of two dedicated coaches, Jean-Claude Perrin and Maurice Houvion (the latter was a former national record holder with 4.87 in 1963). The first Frenchman to be crowned world record holder, seventy-five years after the legendary Fernand Gonder, was Thierry Vigneron, who mastered 5.75 at Colombes on 1 June 1980. Then came Philippe Houvion, a son of the above-mentioned Maurice, who raised the mark to 5.77 two weeks before the Moscow Olympics.

With the Americans not in the game as a result of the boycott, the Olympic final loomed as a three-side affair involving SU, France and Poland. Victory went to **Wladyslaw Kozakiewicz** of Poland (born at Solyechniki, SU, on 8 December 1953; 1.87 m. / 84 Kg.), a sturdy vaulter who could point to a long, gradual progress, from 2.00 at the age of twelve till 5.02 at nineteen. Earlier in 1980 he had raised the world record to 5.72, before the French took over. In Moscow he won in the face of a seemingly hostile Russian crowd, mastering a height of 5.78. This was the first time since 1920 that an Olympic gold medal was won with a world record.

1980 Olympics, Moscow – Pole vault (30 July): 1.Wladyslaw Kozakiewicz (Poland) 5.78 (OR & WR); 2.(tie) Konstantin Volkov (SU and Tadeusz Slusarski (Poland) 5.65; 4.Philippe Houvion (France) 5.65; 5.Jean-Michel Bellot (France) 5.60; 6.Mariusz Klimczyk (Poland) 5.55; 7.Thierry Vigneron (France) 5.45; 8.Sergey Kulibaba (SU) 5.45; 9.Tapani Haapakoski (Finland) 5.45; 10.Miro Zalar (Sweden) 5.35; 11.Brian Hooper (GB) 5.35; 12.Rauli Pudas (Finland) 5.25.

LONG JUMP

Beamon: "Tell me I'm not dreaming"

After the 1960 Olympics in Rome, Ralph Boston and Igor Ter-Ovanesyan dominated the long jump scene for a long time. They took turns in beating the world record – a feud the like of which was not to be found in the history of the event. In the last sixty years, that is prior to Boston's breakthrough, only eight men had made the IAAF record book in the long jump. The ding-dong battle between Ralph and Igor was marked by the following record performances:

° *Modesto, 27 May 1961: Boston 8.24*
Moscow, 16 July 1961: Boston 8.28
(Ter-Ovanesyan 2nd with 8.01)
Yerevan, 10 June 1962: Ter-Ovanesyan 8.31
Kingston, 15 August 1964: Boston 8.31
Los Angeles, 12 September 1964: Boston 8.34
Modesto, 29 May 1965: Boston 8.35
Mexico City, 19 October 1967: Ter-Ovanesyan 8.35

Boston, extraordinary in his consistency in the 8-metre-plus range, was first in "Track & Field News" World Ranking for **eight straight years** (1960-67), a superlative feet. Ter-Ovanesyan also showed great consistency and set a record in longevity, figuring in said Ranking **for fifteen straight years,** 1957 through 1971, although he was ranked first only once, in 1969. A marvel of durability in an event which taxes physical and mental resources like few others in athletics.

Boston had one of his greatest days at the 1964 Olympic Trials in Los Angeles, when he compiled the following series: 8.49 (wind + 2.6 m/s, hence illegal) – 8.21 – 8.34 (world record, wind +1.0 m/s) – 8.11 – 8.14 – pass. Later in the year, at the 1964 Olympics in Tokyo, the two great rivals, Ralph and Igor, got tough competition from a sturdy Welshman, **Lynn Davies** (born at Nantymoel near Bridgend, Glamorgan, on 20 May 1942; 1.85 m. / 76 Kg.). He was a talented sprinter with such marks as 9.5 and 21.2 over the English distances. On that basic speed he built a remarkable condition, especially through weight training. He thus improved from 7.14 in 1961 to 7.72 in '62. The latter mark earned him a fourth place at the British Commonwealth Games in Perth, the winner being Mike Ahey of Ghana with a wind-assisted 8.05. Davies was a great fighter and as such he offered his masterpiece in the 1964 Olympics in Tokyo, on a cold, rainy day, when he took the lead with his penultimate jump with 8.07 (wind – 0.70 m/s). Boston replied with 8.03 on his last try (against a wind of – 2.02 m/s) but had to be content with silver, while Ter-Ovanesyan took bronze with 7.99.

1964 Olympics, Tokyo – Long Jump (18 October): 1.Lynn Davies (GB) 8.07 (7.45, foul, 7.59, 7.78, 8.07, 7.74); 2.Ralph Boston USA) 8.03; 3.Igor Ter-Ovanesyan (SU) 7.99; 4.Wariboko West (Nigeria) 7.60; 5.Jean Cochard (France) 7.44; 6.Luis Felipe Areta (Spain) 7.34; 7.Michael Ahey (Ghana) 7.30; 8.Andrzej Stalmach (Poland) 7.26; 9.Hiroomi Yamada (Japan) 7.16; 10. Wolfgang Klein (W.Germany) 7.15; 11.John Michael Morbey (GB) 7.09; no valid jump: Gayle Hopkins (USA).

In 1965 at Modesto, on what was called "the fastest runway in the world", Ralph Boston had a great series: foul – 8.15 - 8.26 – 8.24 – 8.06 – 8.35 (world record, wind 0.0 m/s). It was a windy day and before taking his last jump Boston stationed his rival and friend Gayle Hopkins (he too an 8-metre plus man) at the wind gauge. Boston stood at the end of the runway and waited for Hopkins to give his "hi-sign". This enabled the champion to take off in a windless moment. The result was a new world record.

Ter-Ovanesyan was somewhat prone to injuries, hence more cautious in spreading himself. He was a technical marvel and had a great competitive heart. He had his best day, mark-wise at least, in a pre-Olympic meet at Mexico City in 1967, when he put together the following series: 8.33 – 7.97 – foul – 8.35 (equalling Boston's world record, wind 0.0 m/s) – 8.17 – 8.16. Among those who offered congratulations was Jesse Owens, visibly impressed by Ter's technical prowess. His comment: "I was lucky to do 8.13 with an almost primitive form".

In subsequent years Davies continued to be a threat to both Boston and Ter-Ovanesyan, even though he

Bob Beamon (USA) in his famous "jump into the XXI century": 8.90 at the 1968 Olympics in Mexico City.

was a bit behind them in general standard of performance. "Ter" had won his second European title at Belgrade in 1962 with a wind-assisted 8.19, but four years later in Budapest he lost to the irrepressible Davies, 7.88 to 7.98.

In 1968 the world of sport in general and the long jump fraternity in particular were shocked by what appeared to be a "super-natural" event – a leap of eight meters ninety centimetres ! It happened in the Olympic final at Mexico City on 18 October 1968. The man who turned that incredible trick was an American, **Robert Beamon** (born at Jamaica, New York, on 29 August 1946; 1.90 m. / 75 Kg.) great natural talent if ever there was one, Beamon scaled the heights rapidly, improving from 7.80 in 1966 to 8.11 in 1967. A 9.5 100 y. sprinter, he was acknowledged to possess tremendous potential. Boston was once quoted as saying: "Beamon has terrific abdominal strength, and just as amazing strength in his hamstrings. He can hold his legs up forever". Before going to Mexico, Beamon had a great season in USA: undefeated, he beat Boston six times. His best pre-Olympic marks were 8.33 in the AAU meet at Sacramento and a wind-assisted 8.39 in the US Olympic Trials at Echo Summit, hence in rarefied atmosphere. As destiny would have it, in Mexico he had his most difficult hour during the qualifying rounds in the morning of 17 October. After fouling on his first two tries, he decided to have a "safety jump" in his third and last - he took off with about 30 cm. to spare and hit the sand at 8.19 ! That was certainly an alarm bell for his rivals, no matter if Boston had qualified majestically on his first jump with a new Olympic record of 8.27. Even so, the track world was hardly prepared for what happened in the early afternoon of 18 October. Yet there was an "insider" like Ralph Boston who said: "I'm always nervous when Beamon goes down the runway, because I know that some day he might put all his great talent together in one big jump". The final started at 3.40 p.m. in cool temperature, following a rain shower. In the opening round the first three jumpers fouled. Then came Beamon's turn. As Tom McNab, noted British coach and commentator, put it: "Beamon attacked the runway with incredible ferocity and seemed to leap as if from a trampoline". In fact, he hit the board with great precision and took off from his right foot (his shoe had six spikes). A 1.956 high jumper, in his flight he reached a peak which was estimated as 1.78 m. He landed well beyond the operational range of a special Cantabrian device which was used for measuring jumps. Judges thus had to resort to a conventional steel tape. Finally, the official announcement came: 8.90. There was an aiding wind, which was officially given as 2.0 m/s, the maximum allowable under IAAF rules. The listed world record, jointly held by Boston and Ter-Ovanesyan, was thus eclipsed by a giant margin – 55 cms ! When he realized the immensity of his feat, Beamon exclaimed: "Tell me I'm not dreaming". Still in that momentous first round, Charlie Mays, the third US string and an 8.01 man, had a narrow foul, said to be worth 8.61. Then it started raining – as Ter-Ovanesyan was taking his first jump. He managed 8.12, and shortly after that Boston did 8.16. But that was all the "Big Two" could do for the day. Beamon's phenomenal jump was bound to have a paralyzing effect on all his rivals. Yet it is curious to note that a "lesser light" such as Klaus Beer of East Germany surpassed himself in round 2 to clinch the silver medal with 8.19, his best ever. In his fifth try Boston himself had a foul which was said to be worth 8.48. He finally had to be content with a bronze medal – still a remarkable achievement, after his gold in 1960 and his silver in '64. Ter-

Ovanesyan was fourth. Under better weather conditions somebody could have bridged at least part of the gulf separating Beamon from his nearest rival – 71 cms. ! But this is of course idle speculation. When it was all over, experts began to search for details which might explain Beamon's explosion or at least make it more "digestible" for common mortals. High altitude and wind assistance were obviously taken into account immediately. Dr. Donald H. Potts, a noted US mathematician and statistician, estimated that "the two elements gave him (Beamon) about 4% advantage over dead-calm sea-level conditions", which would make his record worth about 8.56 under normal conditions, still a fantastic improvement vis-à-vis all previous efforts. (And it would be worth more than that if the wind "bonus", legal under IAAF rules, was not obliterated).

1968 Olympics, Mexico City – Long Jump (18 October): 1.Bob Beamon (USA) 8.90 (WR & OR) (8.90, 8.04, passed up the last 4 trials); 2.Klaus Beer (East Germany) 8.19; 3.Ralph Boston (USA) 8.16, 4.Igor Ter-Ovanesyan (SU) 8.12; 5.Tönu Lepik (SU) 8.09; 6.Alan Crawley (Australia) 8.02; 7.Jack Pani (France) 7.97; 8.Andrzej Stalmach (Poland) 7.94; 9.Lynn Davies (GB) 7.94; 10.Hiroomi Yamada (Japan) 7.93w; 11.Leonid Barkovskiy (SU) 7.90; 12.Reinhold Boschert (West Germany) 7.89; 13.Michael Ahey (Ghana) 7.71; 14.Lars-Olof Höök (Sweden) 7.66; 15.Victor Brooks (Jamaica) 7.51; 16.Gérard Ugolini (France) 7.44. Charles May (USA) no valid jump.

After Beamon's fantastic achievement, long jump standards obviously returned to "normal". And experts learnt to appreciate what was happening without necessarily referring to that "impossible" world record. In 1970 Sepp Schwartz of West Germany earned wide acclaim when he equalled Ter-Ovanesyan's European record (8.35) during a dual meet with USA at Stuttgart. And hardly anybody showed dismay when Max Klauss of East Germany won the 1971 European title in Helsinki with 7.92, almost one metre shy of "The Jump". The evergreen Ter-Ovanesyan was a close second with 7.91, thus collecting his fifth medal in just as many appearances in the European title meet. Lynn Davies was fourth. The 1972 Olympics in Munich crowned the youngest champion in the history of the event: **Randy Williams** of USA (born at Fresno on 23 August 1953; 1.75 m. / 72 Kg.), who jumped 8.34 in the qualifying rounds, then won the final with 8.24, a few weeks after turning nineteen. Hans Baumgartner of West Germany edged Arnie Robinson of USA for the silver medal.

History reread

Like all history in general, even athletics history is sometimes subject to rereading exercises. A book wearing the title "Anthology of the Olympic Games" appeared in 2003. It was authored by Dick Ganslen of USA. An excellent vaulter in his younger days (4.39 in 1939), he was a keen student of sport under a scientific viewpoint. As such he studied Bob Beamon's phenomenal long jump (8.90), made in the 1968 Olympics at Mexico City. During a visit to the Mexican capital toward the end of the Seventies, he got a chance to carefully examine the anemometer which was used to measure wind speed in the horizontal jumps at those Games, when world records were broken - by Beamon in the long jump, by Viktor Saneyev (SU) and Nelson Prudencio in the triple jump. Ganslen came to the conclusion that the instrument "had not been calibrated for altitude. In other words, no compensation was made to balance the fact that such events were held at an altitude of 2248 metres, hence in a rarefied atmosphere for which it would have been necessary to apply a differential of "at least 3%" in reading the wind factor, which in the case of Beamon's 8.90 was given as + 2.0 m/s – the maximum allowed under IAAF rules. The same of course could be said for Saneyev's and Prudencio's record marks in the triple jump (17.39 and 17.27 respectively), for both of which the same (miraculous ?) wind reading of +2.0 m/s was officially given. Said Ganslen: "That's the kind of calculation a voyager is used to make when trying to determine air speed in high altitude locations".

Whenever one happens to be at altitudes of 1000 feet (304.80 m.) or more above sea level, air speed cannot be read correctly without making appropriate adjustments. One can of course conclude that the differential suggested by Ganslen, if properly applied, would have made Beamon's record jump "windy" beyond the maximum allowed under IAAF rules (+2.0 m/s), hence illegal. It is obvious, however, that this kind of reasoning is apt to remain "unofficial" as long as the IAAF will continue to ignore the altitude factor. The Association of Track & Field Statisticians (ATFS) denotes with an "A" all sprint marks made at altitudes of 1000 metres or more.

Post-miracle atmosphere

No athletic performance in modern history has ever evoked such strong feelings as Bob Beamon's famous leap of 8.90 at the 1968 Olympics in Mexico City. When it happened, somebody called it "a jump into the XXI century". *(This definition was valid till 1991 ...)*

In the inner circle of Beamon's closest rivals, the best comment probably came from witty Ralph Boston: "Fourteen years of jumping in the sand is a long time, and now I gotta find something else to do". Beamon himself retired soon afterwards. I recall his appearance in the Europe vs. America dual meet at Stuttgart in 1969 – more for the tail-coat and derby hat he was sporting upon entering the stadium than for his show in the competition itself (he was fourth and last with 7.75). As far as athletics was concerned, by then he had no incentives. And in his heart of hearts he probably felt he would never come close to his "miracle jump". As for his colleagues in the long jump fraternity, they soon learnt that it would by extremely difficult to come reasonably close to Beamon's mark, let alone excel it. In 1980, at the dawn of the Lewis Era, the second best jumper of all time was in statistical books with 8.54, still light years away from Beamon's world record flag.

1972 Olympics, Munich – Long Jump (9 September): 1.Randy Williams (USA) 8.24 (8.24 – 7.32 – 7.72 – 7.80 – 7.77 – foul); 2.Hans Baumgartner (West Germany) 8.18; 3.Arnie Robinson (USA) 8.03; 4.Joshua Owusu (Ghana) 8.01; 5.Preston Carrington (USA) 7.99; 6.Max Klauss (East Germany) 7.96; 7.Alan Lerwill (GB) 7.91; 8.Leonid Barkovskiy (SU) 7.75; 9.Valeriy Podluzhniy (SU) 7.72; 10.Jacques Rousseau (France) 7.65; 11.Ari Väänänen (Finland) 7.62; 12.Grzegorz Cybulski (Poland) 7.58.

The best jumpers of the Seventies generally resisted the temptation of trying their luck in high altitude sites, even though most experts agreed that Beamon's record seemed virtually unassailable under sea-level conditions. One of the best jumpers in the early Seventies was Valeriy Podluzhniy of the SU, who won the 1974 European title in Rome with 8.12, beating Nenad Stekic of Yugoslavia (8.05). Podluzhniy, who had an excellent technique, compiled an amazing series at Munich in the fall of 1971: six valid jumps between 8.17 and 8.00, with an average of 8.09. Stekic, a rather unpredictable jumper, had his great day on 25 July 1975 at Montreal, when he used a wind of 1.95 m/s to reach 8.45, a new European record. The big jump came on his first try, after which he was content with 7.97 and a wind-aided 7.99. At the 1978 European Championships in Prague the winner was Jacques Rousseau of France, who beat Stekic in a close battle, 8.18 to 8.12. The Yugoslav never won a major title, yet continued to jump well for many years, and at 39 he was still capable of marks close to the 8-metre line. The 1976 Olympic title in Montreal was won by **Clarence "Arnie" Robinson** (born at San Diego on 7 April 1948; 1.88 m. / 75 Kg.), who did 8.35 in perfectly windless conditions, a feat for which he was lauded by spectator Bob Beamon. Defending champion Randy Williams was second.

1976 Olympics, Montreal – Long Jump (29 July): 1.Arnie Robinson (USA) 8.35; 2.Randy Williams (USA) 8.11; 3.Frank Wartenberg (East Germany) 8.02; 4.Jacques Rousseau (France) 8.00; 5.João C. de Oliveira (Brazil) 8.00; 6.Nenad Stekic (Yugoslavia) 7.89; 7.Valeriy Podluzhniy (SU) 7.88; 8. Hans Baumgartner (West Germany) 7.84; 9.Rolf Bernhard (Switzerland) 7.74; 10.Aleksey Pereverzyev (SU) 7.66; 11.Fletcher Lewis (Bahamas) 7.61. Larry Myricks (USA) no tries (qualified for final but sustained an injury in warming up and could not compete).

Robinson, a very consistent jumper, also won the 1977 World Cup event at Düsseldorf with 8.19. By then USA also found a man who could outshine everybody in terms of durability – **Larry Myricks** (born at Clinton, Mississippi, on 10 March 1956; 1.88 m. / 77 Kg.). Although a most reliable performer, Myricks missed his rendezvous with "Lady Luck" on important occasions. After improving from 7.83 in 1975 to 8.09 early in 1976, Myricks began to loom as a possible medallist for the Montreal Olympics, but as reported above he was stopped by an injury just before the final.

After a one-year lay-off, Myricks came back more determined than ever and in 1979 he moved to the no.1 position. His brightest victory occurred, of all places in the world, in Montreal. It happened in the final of the World Cup and Myricks won on his last jump with 8.52, wresting the lead from Lutz Dombrowski of East Germany (8.27). Then came 1980 and Myricks again faced an "adverse wind": the US boycott kept him away from the Moscow Olympics. The gold medal went to **Lutz Dombrowski** (born at Karl-Marx-Stadt, now Chemnitz, on 25 June 1959; 1.87 m. / 87 Kg.), who won with his best – ever mark, 8.54, with a legal wind of 0.9 m/s. That was also the second longest jump in history. The no-man's land separating Beamon from the rest of the world was gradually getting narrower. With Americans and West Germans not in the meet, the other medals went to Frank Paschek of East Germany, second, and Valeriy Podluzhniy of the SU, third. Dombrowski, a fast, powerful jumper, was later handicapped by recurrent injuries.

The 1980 Olympics, Moscow – Long Jump (28 July): 1.Lutz Dombrowski (East Germany) 8.54 (8.15 – 8.32 – pass – 8.21 – 8.54 – 8.34); 2. Frank Paschek (East Germany) 8.21; 3.Valeriy Podluzhniy (SU) 8.18; 4.László Szalma (Hungary) 8.13; 5.Stanislaw Jaskulka (Poland) 8.13; 6.Viktor Byelskiy (SU) 8.10; 7.Antonio Corgos (Spain) 8.09; 8.Yordan Yanev (Bulgaria) 8.02; 9.Rolf Bernhard (Switzerland) 7.88; 10.Philippe Deroche (France) 7.77; 11.Kayode Elegbede (Nigeria) 7.49. João C. de Oliveira (Brazil) qualified for final but did not compete.

Ralph Boston (USA), a dominant figure in the long jump during the Sixties.

TRIPLE JUMP

Nearly four of a kind for Saneyev

Józef Schmidt of Poland, history's first 17-metre man, although occasionally hampered by muscular ailments, had a long and noble career. He was a good sprinter (10.4 for the 100 m.) and an excellent long jumper (7.84, plus a wind-aided 7.96). Form-wise, he showed a low trajectory in hop and step, then regained height in the third leap, which thus resembled a full-fledged long jump. Always a great competitor, he won his second European title at Belgrade in 1962 with 16.55, beating Vladimir Goryayev (16.39) and former world record holder Olyeg Fyedoseyev (16.24), both of the SU.

In 1964 Schmidt, then 29, had to undergo knee surgery a few months before the Tokyo Olympics. His one and only mark prior to the Games, 15.81 in Rome, gave scarce indications about the extent of his recovery. But a couple of weeks later, in Tokyo, the Pole was his real self and successfully defended his title with 16.85, a new Olympic record. The Russians again had to be content with silver and bronze, which went to Fyedoseyev and Viktor Kravchenko respectively. Schmidt thus joined Meyer Prinstein and A.F.da Silva as a two-time winner of the triple jump in the Games.

1964 Olympics, Tokyo – Triple Jump (16 October): 1.Józef Schmidt (Poland) 16.85 (16.37 – 16.65 – 16.58 – foul – 14.55 – 16.85) (OR); 2.Olyeg Fyedoseyev (SU) 16.58; 3.Viktor Kravchenko (SU) 16.57; 4.Fred Alsop (GB) 16.46; 5.Serban Ciochina (Rumania) 16.23; 6.Manfred Hinze (E.Germany) 16.15; 7.Georgi Stoikovski (Bulgaria) 16.10; 8.Hans-Jürgen Rückborn (E.Germany) 16.09; 9.Ira Davis (USA) 16.00; 10.Takayuki Okazawa (Japan) 15.90; 11.William Sharpe (USA) 15.84; 12.Jan Jaskolski (Poland) 15.82; 13.Mansour Dia (Senegal) 15.44.

In 1965, however, Schmidt had another accident, and the following year, at Budapest, he did no better than fifth in the European title meet. Victory went to Georgi Stoikovski of Bulgaria at 16.67, with Hans-Jürgen Rückborn of East Germany second, one centimetre back. Schmidt fought back bravely and in 1967 he jumped 16.84. But the wave of progress had brought other jumpers closer and closer to the 17-metre line. One of these was Giuseppe Gentile, Italy's first triple jumper of international calibre. Tall and powerful although somewhat prone to injuries, he was a

16.32 man on the eve of the Olympic year 1968. A good combination of long jumper / triple jumper, he began to loom as an Olympic prospect in August 1968 with new national records of 7.91 and 16.74 on consecutive days. Yet there was a Finn, Pertti Pousi, who did even better, with 8.04 and 17.00, he too on consecutive days. Another serious candidate for Olympic honours was Viktor Saneyev, a Georgian representing the SU, who had done 16.67 in 1967 and 16.87 in July 1968. Hardly anybody talked about Nelson Prudencio of Brazil, whose pre-Olympic best was a "mere" 16.30. In the cauldron of Estadio Olimpico at Mexico City, Pousi was eliminated in the qualifying round (16 October), but Gentile rose to the occasion with a stunning world record, 17.10, achieved in windless conditions at 11.10 in the morning. The double effect of a Tartan runway and a rarefied atmosphere was by then evident, yet the final on the following day went above expectations. Within less than two hours, Gentile's fresh world mark was bettered four times ! The dramatic sequence was as follows:

° 3.15 p.m. - Gentile 17.22 (wind nil)
4.05 p.m. - Saneyev 17.23 (+2.0 m/s)
5.00 p.m. - Prudencio 17.27 (+2.0 m/s)
5.05 p.m. - Saneyev 17.39 (+2.0 m/s)

Saneyev thus won the titanic battle from Prudencio and Gentile. Other place winners, "inspired" by the thin air, also surpassed themselves, as can be seen from the table that follows. Mark-wise, defending champion Józef Schmidt had done better than in his winning ventures of 1960 and '64, yet placed only seventh. But it was obvious that conditions prevailing in Mexico City could hardly be compared with those of previous Games.

1968 Olympics, Mexico City – Triple Jump (17 October): 1.Viktor Saneyev (SU) 17.39 (WR & OR) (16.49 – 16.84 – 17.23 – 17.02 – 16.81 – 17.39); 2.Nelson Prudencio (Brazil) 17.27; 3.Giuseppe Gentile (Italy) 17.22; 4.Arthur Walker (USA) 17.12; 5.Nikolay Dudkin (SU) 17.09; 6.Philip May (Australia) 17.02; 7.Józef Schmidt (Poland) 16.89; 8.Mansour Dia (Senegal) 16.73; 9.Georgi Stoikovski (Bulgaria) 16.46; 10.Henrik Kalocsai (Hungary) 16.45; 11.Joachim Kugler (West Germany) 15.90; 12.Luis Felipe Areta (Spain) 15.75; 13.Serban Ciochina (Rumania) 15.62.

After his bitter-sweet experience in Mexico, Giuseppe Gentile continued to be hampered by injuries now and then and could do no better than 16.72. The world at large was to see him again in 1970, when he played Jason to the Medea of singer Maria Callas in the movie "Medea".

Far more impressive was the career record of **Viktor Saneyev** (born at Sukhumi, Georgia, on 3 October 1945; 1.88 m. / 80 Kg.). He eventually became the most durable top-class performer in the history of the event. This Georgian was an athlete of multiform capabilities, credited with such marks as 10.5 (100 m.), 7.90 (long jump) and 1.90 (high jump). He chose to concentrate on the triple jump in 1963, when he did 14.88. Four years later he was good enough to beat some of the best continental triple jumpers in the final of the European Cup at Kiev with 16.67. From then on he reigned supreme for several years, collecting three golds and a silver in the Olympic Games, two golds and two silvers in the European Championships.

On 5 August 1971, during the Pan-American Games at Cali, Colombia (altitude, 1046 m.), a 19-year-old Cuban, Pedro Pérez Duenas, created a sensation with a new world record of 17.40 (wind + 0.5 m/s), leaving Nelson Prudencio of Brazil far behind (16.82). Pérez had a great series: ° *16.92 – 17.40 – 14.92 – 17.04 – 17.12 – 17.19.*

A great improvement vis-à-vis his pre-Games best: 16.86. That was to remain, easily and by far, Pérez's greatest day. In later years injuries prevented him from rising to similar heights again. Saneyev annexed his first European title at Athens in 1969 with a "windy" 17.34, leaving his nearest opponent almost half a metre behind. Early in the Seventies the Georgian jumper had a fine rival in Jörg Drehmel of East Germany. At the 1971 European Championships in Helsinki, Drehmel edged his great opponent, 17.16 to 17.10 (both wind-assisted), but Saneyev fought back successfully in the Munich Olympics the following year, finally keeping Drehmel at bay by a narrow margin, 17.35 to 17.31. It should be noted, however, that in his winning effort Saneyev was aided by a wind slightly over the limit (2.2 m/s.), whereas Drehmel reached his best distance with a legal wind (1.5 m/s). These are the inevitable vagaries of field event competitions, but on occasion they can play a significant, if not decisive, role.

1972 Olympics, Munich – Triple Jump (4 September): 1.Viktor Saneyev (SU) 17.35w; (17.35w – 16.71 – 17.19 – foul – 16.98 – foul); 2.Jörg Drehmel (East Germany) 17.31;3.Nelson Prudencio (Brazil) 17.05; 4.Carol Corbu (Rumania) 16.85; 5.John Craft (USA) 16.83; 6.Mansour Dia

(Senegal) 16.83; 7.Michael Joachimowski (Poland) 16.69; 8.Kristen Flögstad (Norway) 16.44; 9.Mikhail Bariban (SU) 16.30; 10.Bernard Lamitié (France) 16.27; 11.Samuel Igun (Nigeria) 16.03: 12.Toshiaki Inoue (Japan) 15.88.

Saneyev closed his 1972 account on a high note, recapturing the world record with 17.44 in a meet held in his native town, Sukhumi, on 17 October. He did this without the benefit of thin air and against a wind of 0.5 m/s.

The indefatigable Saneyev went on to win his second European title at Rome in 1974 with 17.23. But as the Montreal Olympics drew near he found a new challenger in **João Carlos de Oliveira** of Brazil (born at Pindamanhangaba near São Paulo on 28 May 1954; 1.86 m. / 76 Kg.). This exceptional athlete had first bettered 16 m. in 1974 with 16.34. The following year he went to Mexico City for the Pan-American Games, and astounded the athletics world. He began by beating Arnie Robinson of USA in the long jump, 8.13 to 7.94, and two days later (15 October) he uncorked a triple jump of 17.89, thus excelling Saneyev's world record by 45 cms. And unlike Beamon in his miracle long jump in the same stadium seven years earlier, the Brazilian received no help from the wind. The record came in the second round. For the rest João had two fouls and three passes. Tommy Haynes of USA was second with 17.20. But the fresh record holder was hampered by sciatica in the spring of 1976 and the Olympic rendezvous in Montreal found him short on condition and he had to be content with the bronze medal (16.90). The irrepressible Saneyev was again the winner, this time at 17.29, while James Butts of USA was second with 17.18, a lifetime best, curiously achieved in perfect coincidence with the crack of the starter's pistol in getting a race off. Former world record holder Pérez Duenas was fourth.

1976 Olympics, Montreal - Triple Jump (30 July): 1.Viktor Saneyev (SU) 17.29 (foul – 16.71 – 17.06 – foul – 17.29 – foul); 2.James Butts (USA) 17.18; 3.João Carlos de Oliveira (Brazil) 16.90; 4. Pedro Pérez Duenas (Cuba) 16.81; 5.Tommy Haynes (USA) 16.78; 6.Wolfgang Kolmsee (West Germany) 16.68; 7.Eugenius Biskupski (Poland) 16.49; 8.Carol Corbu (Rumania) 16.43; 9.Jiri Vycichlo (Czechoslovakia) 16.28; 10.Pentti Kuukasjärvi (Finland) 16.23; 11.Bernard Lamitié (France) 16.23; 12.Rayfield Dupree (USA) 16,23.

João Carlos de Oliveira took partial consolation with a nice string of victories in the World Cup, his marks being 16.68 at Düsseldorf in 1977, 17.02 at Montreal in '79 and 17.37 in Rome in '81. Meanwhile, the great Saneyev was battling with ankle injuries. Despite several operations he could not regain his condition of old, yet stayed in line and at the 1978 European Championships in Prague he missed his third gold by a trifle in losing to Milos Srejovic of Yugoslavia, 16.93 to 16.94.

Viktor Saneyev (USSR) won three golds and a silver in the triple jump at the Olympic Games (1968 through 1980).

João Carlos de Oliveira, the latest "pearl" in the Brazilian collection of triple jumpers.

Despite his physical ailments, Saneyev still entertained a dream for 1980: match Al Oerter's stupendous record of four consecutive victories in the same event in the Olympics. In the Games final Saneyev, wearing a bandage below his right knee, managed an excellent 17.24, but had to bow to his compatriot Jaak Uudmäe, an Esthonian who won with the mark of his lifetime, 17.35. João Carlos de Oliveira, the pre-meet favourite of many, was only third at 17.22. It should be said, however, that strange things happened that day. Some very good efforts by João and Australia's Ian Campbell (fifth), which in the opinion of foreign observers seemed to excel Uudmäe's winning mark, were inexplicably ruled fouls by Soviet judges. Officials apparently contended that in Campbell's best jump the athlete's left foot had dragged along the runway during his step phase, but films failed to prove their point in a convincing manner. In 1990 the following sentence was added to IAAF rules concerning the triple jump: "It shall not be considered a failure if the competitor, while jumping, touches the ground with the "sleeping leg".

1980 Olympics, Moscow – Triple Jump (25 July): 1.Jaak Uudmäe (SU) 17.35 (foul – 16.83 – 17.35 – foul – 17.08 - 17.28); 2.Viktor Saneyev (SU) 17.24; 3.João Carlos de Oliveira (Brazil) 17.22; 4.Keith Connor (GB) 16.87; 5.Ian Campbell (Australia) 16.72; 6.Atanas Chochev (Bulgaria) 16.56; 7.Béla Bakosi (Hungary) 16.47; 8.Kenneth Lorraway (Australia) 16.44; 9.Yevgeniy Anikin (SU) 16.12; 10.Milan Spasojevic (Yugoslavia) 16.09; 11.Armando Herrera (Cuba) 16.03w; (Christain Valétudie (France) 1 foul, injured).

MEN 1981-2000

6

HIGH JUMP

Sotomayor, the one and only 2.45 m. man.

By the early Eighties the "Flop" had taken over as the ruling style. At the top the most notable leap forward was assured by a Chinese, **Zhu Jianhua** (born at Shanghai on 29 May 1963; 1.96 m. / 74 Kg.). As related in the previous chapter, the most populated country on earth had already had a top-notch high jumper, Ni Zhiqin (whose 2.29 from 1970 was not ratified as a world record because at the time the Chinese People's Republic was not a member of the IAAF), yet there was no relation between him and his successor of the early Eighties. Ni was one of the last "straddlers", while Zhu soon developed into a fine "Flopper", mastering 2.13 at sixteen. Still as a junior, in 1982, he jumped 2.33. He first bettered the world record with 2.37 (Beijing, 11 June 1983). However, Zhu was a temperamental athlete and as such he failed to reproduce his best form in the major tests of his career. This first happened at Helsinki in 1983, when the Finnish capital hosted the inaugural edition of the World Championship, a new global test launched by the IAAF and first conceived to take place every four years – in pre-Olympic seasons. Winner of the event at Helsinki was a Russian who came out of nowhere to top a crack field with 2.32. He was **Gennadiy Avdeyenko** (born at Odessa on 4 November 1963; 2.02 m. / 82 Kg.)and his name was to be heard time and again in the years that followed, were it only .... on occasions that really mattered.

1983 World Championships, Helsinki – High Jump (13 August): 1.Gennadiy Avdeyenko (SU) 2.32; 2.Tyke Peacock (USA) 2.32; 3.Zhu Jianhua (China) 2.29; 4.(tie) Igor Paklin (SU) and Dietmar Mögenburg (West Germany) 2.29; 6.Dwight Stones (USA) 2.29; 7.Carlo Thränhardt (West Germany) 2.26; 8.Valeriy Sereda (SU) 2.26; 9.Milt Ottey (Canada) 2.26; 10.Luca Toso (Italy) 2.26; 11.Patrik Sjöberg (Sweden) 2.23; 12.Leo Williams (USA) 2.23; 13.Jacek Wszola (Poland) 2.23.

The 1984 Olympics in Los Angeles were expected to show a partly different situation, were it only for the fact that the SU and most of her alleys (with the notable exception of Rumania) decided to stay away from this rendez-vous, ostensibly as a "reply" to the boycott of the 1980 Olympics in Moscow by USA. High jump winner at Los Angeles was **Dietmar Mögenburg** of West Germany (born at Leverkusen on 15 August 1961; 2.01 m. / 78 Kg.). His early break-

Zhu Jianhua (China) held the world record for the high jump: 2.39 in 1984.

through as a junior was related in a previous chapter. As time went on he developed into a most reliable competitor. In Los Angeles he won the Olympic gold medal with 2.35 from Sjöberg and Zhu. Veteran Dwight Stones of USA, in his third Olympic adventure, jumped higher than ever before in the Games yet finished no better than fourth.

1984 Olympics, Los Angeles – High Jump (11 August): 1.Dietmar Mögenburg (West Germany) 2.35; 2.Patrik Sjöberg (Sweden) 2.33; 3.Zhu Jianhua (China) 2.31; 4.Dwight Stones (USA) 2.31; 5.Doug Nordquist (USA) 2.29; 6.Milt Ottey (Canada) 2.29; 7.Liu Yupeng (China) 2.29; 8.Cai Shu (China) 2.27; 9. Erkki Niemi (Finland) 2.24; 10.Carlo Thränhardt (West Germany) 2.15. No height: Roland Dalhäuser (Switzerland) and Milton Goode (USA).

On 11 August 1985 a news item from the SU stunned the athletics world: in a regional meet at Donyetsk, a virtual unknown named Rudolf Povarnitsin had mastered a height of 2.40, a new world record. The surprise was due to the fact that prior to his magic day Povarnitsin had done no better than 2.26 ! He was a tall (2.01 m.), born 23 years ago at Votkinsk in the Udmurtsk Republic – the birthplace of composer Pyotr Ilich Tchaikovskiy. At Donyetsk he improved on his personal best four times in quick succession, with 2.29, 2.32, 2.35 and 2.40 ! That was to remain easily and by far his happiest day. He was a factor in major meets only once, when he earned a tie for third at the 1988 Olympics in Seoul. A more consistent competitor was his countryman Igor Paklin, who raised the world record to 2.41 at the Universiade in Kobe on 4 September 1985 and was crowned European champion the following year at Stuttgart. In times of relative poverty for Scandinavian athletics, Sweden had an outstanding man in **Patrik Sjöberg** (born at Göteborg on 5 January 1965; 2.00 m. / 82 Kg.), who proved a tough competitor on many occasions and won his good share of honours, notably including a world title at Rome in 1987. Earlier in the same year, on 30 June at Stockholm, he succeeded Paklin as world record holder with 2.42.

In 1987 Rome was the seat of the second edition of the "Worlds". The standard of top performers in the high jump reached new levels as all medal winners mastered a height of 2.38. This was all the more surprising as the contest was frequently interrupted by medal ceremonies, during which the athletes could not jump. The reliable Sjöberg mastered 2.38 on his first try and thus won on fewer misses from Igor Paklin and Gennadiy Avdeyenko, who managed 2.38 on their third trial and thus tied for second.

1987 World Championships – High Jump (6 September): 1.Patrik Sjöberg (Sweden) 2.38; 2.(tie) Igor Paklin and Gennadiy Avdeyenko (both SU) 2.38; 4.Dietmar Mögenburg (West Germany) 2.35; 5.Nick Saunders (Bermuda) 2.32; 6.Sorin Matei (Rumania) 2.32; 7.Jan Zvara (Czechoslovakia) 2.32; 8.Carlo Thränhardt (West Germany) 2.29; 9.Javier Sotomayor (Cuba) 2.29; 10.(tie) Krzysztof Krawczyk (Poland) and Geoff Parsons (GB) 2.25; 12. (tie) Tom McCants (USA) and Arturo Ortiz (Spain) 2.25; 14.Gerd Nagel (West Germany) 2.20; 15.Robert Marinov (Bulgaria) 2.20. No height: Sergey Malchenko (SU).

The last record breaker of the XX century was **Javier Sotomayor** of Cuba (born at Limonar, Matanzas province, on 13 October 1967; 1.95 m. / 82 Kg.). A pupil of José Godoy, he reached spectacular heights very early: 2.00 at fifteen, 2.33 at seventeen and a world record 2.43 at Salamanca, Spain, on 8 September 1988 – incidentally the first world record ever set on Spanish soil. With Cuba boycotting the Seoul Olympics, he was unable to meet the world's best in that meet, in which victory went to Gennadiy Avdeyenko, who raised the Olympic record to 2.38, equalling his personal best.

1988 Olympics, Seoul - High Jump (25 September): 1.Gennadiy Avdeyenko (SU) 2.38; 2.Hollis Conway (USA) 2.36; 3.(tie) Rudolf Povarnitsin (SU) and Patrik Sjöberg (Sweden) 2.36. 5.Clarence

Patrik Sjöberg (Sweden), world high jump champion in 1987, seen here in the 1995 edition at Göteborg - by then past his peak, he finished 6th.

Saunders (Bermuda) 2.34; 6.Dietmar Mögenburg (West Germany) 2.34; 7.(tie) Dalton Grant (GB), Igor Paklin (SU) and Carlo Thränhardt (West Germany) 2.31; 10. Jim Howard (USA) 2.31; 11.Brian Stanton (USA) 2.31; 12.Krzysztof Krawczyk (Poland) 2.31; 13.Luca Toso (Italy) 2.25; 14.Arturo Ortiz (Spain) 2.25.

Sotomayor returned to action immediately and won at the 1989 World Indoor Championships at Budapest, where he mastered 2.43. Later in the same year, namely on 29 July at San Juan, Puerto Rico, he reached a milestone of great international appeal, going over a bar set at 8 feet (2.44 m.). On the eve of the event, Puerto Rican TV launched an urgent appeal:

"Vengan a ver el primer ser umano saltar ocho pies" (Come and see the first human being jump over 8 feet).

The appeal was obviously meant for the English speaking world. (By then 33 years had gone by since Charles Dumas of USA first conquered 7 feet (2.13 m.). "Soto" did not let them down. After his first two jumps (2.20 and 2.30) he was the only man left in the contest and thus able to fully concentrate on major heights. He cleared 2.35 and 2.40 in swift succession. At 22.20 hrs the bar was set at 2.44, one centimetre above his own world record. He brushed the bar off in his first attempt before clearing it on his second. By doing so he captured the imagination of the world of sport in a twofold manner. First, that metric height was a shade (actually, 1.5 mm.) over 8 English feet. Secondly, it happened to be just the height of the crossbar in the world's most popular sport – soccer. But history often reminds us that the difference between one man's success and another's failure can be infinitesimal. The previous week in New York "Soto" was defeated by his arch rival Patrik Sjöberg, 2.34 to 2.37. After which he sat and watched the long-haired Swede narrowly miss at 8 feet not once but three times ! Both Sotomayor and Sjöberg, no matter how gifted in terms of talent, fought with the Moloch of Injuries for the greater part of their careers. In 1990 the Swede was quoted as saying: "It is too much for me. I have lost the touch: it is too hard training and then getting injured all the time". Even so, he struggled on for several more years before calling it quits. As for Sotomayor, he averaged two injuries per year, some of them requiring surgery, between 1987 and '91. In a book dedicated to him, he was quoted as saying: "The physical and mental stress characterizing modern competition at the highest level entails great dangers. He added:

"Los atletas constantemente estan jugando con fuego" (athletes are constantly playing with fire).

Javier Sotomayor (Cuba), the first man to conquer 8 feet (2.44) and 2.45 m. in the hight jump.

Despite his frequent injuries, always affecting his take-off (left) foot, the Cuban ace managed to resurrect time and again.

At the 3rd edition of the World Championships, held in Tokyo in 1991, USA briefly recaptured the limelight thanks to a 24-year-old Texan jumper, Charles Austin, who defeated "Soto" in a close duel, 2.38 to 2.36, while Sjöberg had to be content with no higher than seventh.

1991 World Championships, Tokyo – High Jump (1 September): 1.Charles Austin (USA) 2.38; 2.Javier Sotomayor (Cuba) 2.36; 3.Holls Conway (USA) 2.36; 4.Dalton Grant (GB) 2.36; 5. (tie) Marino Drake (Cuba) and Troy Kemp (Bahamas) 2.34; 7. Patrik Sjöberg (Sweden) 2.31; 8.Rick Noji (USA) 2.28; 9.Dragutin Topic (Yugoslavia) 2.28; 10.(tie) Arturo Ortiz (Spain) and Igor Paklin (SU) 2.24; 12.Artur Partyka (Poland) 2.24; 13.Rudolf Povarnitsin (SU) 2.24; 14.Steinar Hoen (Norway) 2.20.

Sotomayor fought back bravely and later in the Nineties he collected more laurels. At the 1992 Olympics in Barcelona he confirmed his good feelings for the Spanish atmosphere and emerged the winner at the end of a gigantic battle. Spectators were treated to the greatest "blanket finish" in the history of the event. Five men cleared 2.34, but none could go higher. Sotomayor, as the only one to master that height on his first try, won and thus fulfilled his Olympic dream.

1992 Olympics, Barcelona - High Jump (2 August): 1.Javier Sotomayor (Cuba) 2.34; 2.Patrik Sjöberg (Sweden) 2.34; 3.(tie) Artur Partyka (Poland), Hollis Conway (USA) and Tim Forsyth (Australia) 2.34;

6.Ralf Sonn (West Germany) 2.31; 7.Troy Kemp (Bahamas) 2.31; 8.(tie) Charles Austin (USA), Dragutin Topic (Yugoslavia) and Marino Drake (Cuba) 2.28; 11.Gustavo Becker (Spain) 2.28; 12.Steve Smith (GB) 2.24; 13.Sorin Matei (Rumania) 2.24; 14.Georgi Dakov (Bulgaria) 2.24.

Sotomayor also managed to improve on his world record. On 27 July 1993 he returned to Salamanca, an ancient city in West-Central Spain where he had set his first global record in 1988 and upped his mark to 2.45. His work on that occasion was confined to five jumps: he cleared 2.23, 2.32 and 2.38, always on his first try. Then he mastered the record height on his second attempt, when the bar quivered but remained on the pegs. Three men followed with 2.26 and second place went to Troy Kemp of Bahamas. When it was all over, "Soto" indulged in a brief discussion about future possibilities in his event. He felt that up-and-coming jumpers could aim at heights in the range 2.46/2.48 but added that the next big barrier – 2.50 – was way off. "At any rate – he added – it's nothing I'm planning on". At the time of writing these lines – 17 years later - "Soto" 's mark is still unsurpassed.

Throughout the rest of the Nineties, the Cuban constantly remained at or near the top, notwithstanding his injury problems. He caught his second victory in a global meet at the 1993 World Championships, held in Stuttgart. He won at 2.40, then had two tries at 2.46 - the second was described as "quite reasonable". The IAAF had decided to make this meet a biennial affair. As a result, from then on only one year out of four would be without a "global" (Worlds / Olympic) rendezvous.

1993 World Championships, Stuttgart – High Jump (22 August): 1.Javier Sotomayor (Cuba) 2.40; 2.Artur Partyka (Poland) 2.37; 3.Steve Smith (USA) 2.37; 4.Ralf Sonn (Germany) 2.34; 5.Troy Kemp (Bahamas) 2.34; 6.Hollis Conway (USA) 2.34; 7.Arturo Ortiz (Spain) 2.31; 8.Tony Barton (USA) 2.31; 9.Tim Forsyth (Australia) 2.28; 10.Olyeg Zhukovskiy (Byelarus) 2.28; 11.(tie) Jean-Charles Gicquel (France) and Róbert Ruffini (Slovakia) 2.25.

In 1995 Sotomayor was again hampered by a foot injury and had to be content with second at the World Championships, held at Göteborg. Troy Kemp of Bahamas, a former student at Boise State University in USA, by then 29, went over a bar set at 2.37 on his second try, while the Cuban needed three attempts. The sun was shining into the faces of the jumpers as the world record holder, wearing sunglasses, came reasonably close to clearing 2.39. Kemp was not so close at that height, yet won on the fewer misses count.

1995 World Championships, Göteborg – High Jump (8 August): 1.Troy Kemp (Bahamas) 2.37; 2.Javier Sotomayor (Cuba) 2.37; 3.Artur Partyka (Poland) 2.35; 4.(tie) Steve Smith (GB) and Steinar Hoen (Norway) 2.35; 6.Patrik Sjöberg (Sweden) 2.32; 7.Tony Barton (USA) 2.29; 8. (tie) Tim Forsyth (Australia), Dragutin Topic (Yugoslavia) and Jaroslaw Kotewicz (Poland) 2.25; 11.Ian Thompson (Bahamas) 2.25; 12.Bi Hongyong (China) 2.15.

The no.1 American throughout the greater part of the Nineties was **Charles Austin** (born at Bay City, Texas on 19 December 1967; 1.84 m. / 77 Kg.), a consistent performer who, as previously related, had won a world title in 1991, beating Sotomayor. Austin triumphed again at the Atlanta Olympics in 1996, after overcoming the effects of a serious injury. On the day that counted "Soto" himself was even worse off as he continued to be plagued by ankle woes. The Cuban had to be content with a dismal (for him) 2.25. Inspired by the home atmosphere, Austin finally raised the Olympic record to 2.39 and won from a strong European duo - Artur Partyka (Poland) and Steve Smith (GB).

1996 Olympics, Atlanta – High Jump (28 July): 1.Charles Austin (USA) 2.39 (OR); 2.Artur Partyka (Poland) 2.37; 3.Steve Smith (GB) 2.35; 4.Dragutin Topic (Yugoslavia) 2.32; 5.Steinar Hoen (Norway) 2.32; 6.Lambros Papakostas (Greece) 2.32; 7.Tim Forsyth (Australia) 2.32; 8.Lee Jin-Taek (So.Korea) 2.29; 9.Wolfgang Kreissig (Germany) 2.29; 10.Przemyslaw Radkiewicz (Poland) 2.29; 11.(tie) Jaroslaw Kotewicz (Poland) and Javier Sotomayor (Cuba) 2.25; 13.Troy Kemp (Bahamas) 2.25; 14.Tomás Janku (Czechoslovakia) 2.25.

The indefatigable Sotomayor fought back again in 1997, winning his third global title at the World Championships in Athens with 2.37. Second went to Europe's no.1, **Artur Partyka** of Poland (born at Stalowa Wola on 25 July 1969; 1.92 m. / 71 Kg.). In global title meets this Pole thus won silver in the 1996 Olympics as well as in the 1993 and '97 World Championships, and bronze in the 1992 Olympics and the '95 World Championships. Son of an Algerian father and a Polish mother, he had a superb competitive record, even though he never went higher than 2.38.

1997 World Championships, Athens - High Jump (6 August): 1.Javier Sotomayor (Cuba) 2.37; 2.Artur Partyka (Poland) 2.35; 3.Tim Forsyth (Australia) 2.35; 4.(tie) Steinar Hoen (Norway) and Dalton Grant (GB) 2.32; 6.Lambros Papakostas (Greece) 2.32; 7.Konstantin Matusevich (Israel) 2.29; 8.Lee Jin-Taek (South Korea) 2.29; 9.Martin Buss (Germany) 2.29; 10.Gilmar Mayo (Colombia) 2.29; 11.Sergey Klyugin (Russia) 2.29; 12.Jan Janku (Czechoslovakia) 2.25.

Sotomayor had so to say a "traffic accident" at the 1999 Pan-American Championships in Winnipeg. The Cuban, by then 32, fell foul of a doping control as traces of cocaine were detected in his urine sample. He was thus deprived of the title he had won at 2.30. Strongly supported by the Cuban State and press, he denied using cocaine and said he was simply "the victim of sabotage". The IAAF allowed him to compete again from August 2000. An affair which was to remain controversial. The 1999 World Championships in Sevilla thus went on stage in the absence of the world record holder. Victory went to Vyacheslav Voronin of Russia at 2.37. (The SU as such had finished to exist in 1991, after which its various republics appeared in sporting events as separate entities).

1999 World Championships, Sevilla - High Jump (23 August): 1.Vyacheslav Voronin ((Russia) 2.37; 2.Mark Boswell (Can) 2.35; 3.Martin Buss (Germany) 2.32; 4.Dragutin Topic (Yugoslavia) 2.32; 5.Staffan Strand (Sweden) 2.29; 6.(tie) Kwaku Boateng (Canada) and Lee Jin-Taek (South Korea) 2.29; 8.(tie) Charles Austin (USA) and Brendan Reilly (Ireland) 2.29; 10.(tie) Wilbert Pennings (Holland), Abderrahmane Hammad (Algeria) and (GB), Stefan Holm (Sweden) 2.25. No height: Steve Smith (GB).

Sotomayor returned just in time to compete in the 2000 Olympics, held in Sydney. This edition of the Games was a marvel from several standpoints, first of all in terms of attendances – over 100,000 in most of the evening sessions. The pre-meet favourite in the high jump was Vyacheslav Voronin, a 26-year-old Russian, who had mastered 2.40 several weeks earlier in London. But on the occasion that counted most he did no better than 2.29 and finished only tenth. His training companion Sergey Klyugin was clever and lucky enough to jump 2.35 just before a heavy rain entered the picture and ruined the rest of the competition. Sotomayor had to be content with 2.32 and second.

2000 Olympics, Sydney - High Jump (24 September): 1.Sergey Klyugin (Russia) 2.35; 2.Javier Sotomayor (Cuba) 2.32; 3.Abderrahmane Hammad (Algeria) 2.32; 4.Stefan Holm (Sweden) 2.32; 5.Konstantin Matusevich (Israel) 2.32; 6.(tie) Staffan Strand (Sweden) and Mark Boswell (Canada) 2.32; 8.Wolfgang Kreissig (Germany) 2.29; 9.Sergey Dymchenko (Ukraine) 2.29; 10.Vyackeslav Voronin (Russia) 2.29; 11.Nathan Leeper (USA) 2.25; 12.Kwaku Boateng (Canada) 2.25; 13.Kenny Evans (USA) 2.20.

As at the end of 2000 there had been 33 marks at 2.40 or higher. World record holder Sotomayor had 21, i.e. 63.9 % of the total. The phenomenal "hausse" of the Eighties, when the world record was raised from 2.35 to 2.44, had been followed by a standstill in later years. The "Flop" had admittedly accounted for earlier progress to a large extent, hyper-intensive training being another factor.

POLE VAULT

Sergey, the Czar

Vaulting standards continued to go up incessantly throughout the Eighties. Between 1981 and '89 the world record was bettered 14 times, in a debate involving two countries – France and the SU. The best exponent of the French school was **Thierry Vigneron** (born in Paris on 9 March 1960; 1.81 m. / 73 Kg.), who achieved five world record performances between 1980 and 1984, all of them outdoors, plus one indoors. Last of the series was a 5.91 at Rome in 1984, strangely enough in an event he did not win, because ten minutes later Sergey Bubka of the SU cleared 5.94. Another Frenchman, **Pierre Quinon** (born at Lyon on 20 February 1962; 1.80 m. / 74 Kg.) had earlier held the world record with 5.82 (1983). Both these men were eventually outshone by **Sergey Bubka of the SU** (born at Voroshilovgrad, Ukraine, on 4 December 1963; 1.83 m. / 80 Kg.), who in the course of time became the undisputed master of the art. He made his début on the international scene at the 1981 European Junior Championship tying for seventh with 5 metres even. Only two years later he was selected at the last moment to represent the SU at the inaugural World Championships in Helsinki, mainly on the strength of a 5.72 vault. He surprised a lot of people by outlasting his older and more experienced rivals in a long, nerve-wrecking competition. The qualifying round was abandoned due to heavy rains and the final thus lasted almost seven hours. Bubka, not yet 20, finally won at 5.70. That was the beginning of a long reign.

1983 World Championships, Helsinki – Pole Vault (14 August): 1.Sergey Bubka (SU) 5.70; 2.Konstantin Volkov (SU) 5.60; 3.Atanas Tarev (Bulgaria) 5.60; 4.Tadedusz Slusarski (Poland) 5.55; 5.Tom Hintnaus (USA) 5.50; 6.Patrick Abada (France) 5.50; 7.Miro Zalar (Sweden) 5.50; 8.(tie) Wladyslaw Kozakiewicz (Poland) and Thierry Vigneron (France) 5.40; 10.(tie) Felix Böhni (Switzerland), Frantisek Jansa (Czechoslovakia) and Vladimir Polyakov (SU) 5.40; 13.Jeff Buckingham (USA) 5.40; 14.Veijo Vannesluoma (Finland) 5.40.

What "czar" Sergey has done from 1983 onwards entitles him to be considered as the greatest vaulter of our time and probably of all time, without wishing in any way to detract from the great achievements of "Dutch" Warmerdam, the king of the Bamboo Era. Here is a summary of Bubka's feats:

Seventeen world outdoor records: 5.85, 5.88, 5.90 and 5.94 in 1985, 6.00 in '85, 6.01 in '86, 6.03 in '87, 6.05 and 6.06 in '88, 6.07, 6.08, 6.09 and 6.10 in '91, 6.11, 6.12 and 6.13 in '92 and 6.14 in '94.

Eleven world indoor records: 5.83 in 1984, 5.97 in '87, 6.03 in '89, 6.05 in '90, 6.08, 6.10, 6.11 and 6.12 in '91, 6.13 in '92, 6.14 and 6.15 in '93.

He was the most "cosmopolitan" of record breakers in choosing the sites of his record performances: 24 in Europe, 3 in Asia and 1 in North America.

Apart from the 1984 Olympics in Los Angeles, from which he had to stay away as the citizen of a boycotting country, he won every major honour at stake. Outdoors he was world champion 6 times in a row, from 1983 up to and including 1997 ! He was European champion in 1986. Indoors he was world champion 4 times.

"Helsinki 1983:
in my mind and in my heart forever"
by Sergey Bubka

Helsinki, 1983, the historic 1st IAAF World Championships in Athletics. My debut, my entry step into the mainstream of the world pole vaulting – and the victory I will never forget. Even now, years later, I still remember the amazing twists and turns of this event to the smallest details.

A 19-year-old young hopeful, as I was then considered, I was sent to Finland to gain my first experience in an international tournament of such caliber. No grand expectations, no big responsibility. "If you clear 5.60, be sure you completed your mission" – this was the minimum program the team coaches set for me.

That was the first time I found myself competing against the élite pole vaulters – the famous, the titled, and what was more important, the experienced. But regardless of our skill and practices, the 27 of us faced one more rival to beat – the weather. A cold drizzle that later grew into a heavy shower, pouring non-stop for two consecutive days forced the organizers to cancel the qualifying round and allow everyone straight into the final – a decision totally without precedent.

The unusually large number of competitors caused huge intervals between attempts, which made muscles cool down while stirring up the nerves. The gusty wind made competing even a bigger challenge. I remember myself sitting on a bench edge after two misses at 5.60, trying to gear up for my third attempt, visualizing the future jump from the first steps on the runway and to the moment of landing ..... The tension was immense, but it all dispelled when I realized I was on the mats with the height cleared, this followed by a first-attempt success at 5.70.

Then – a moment of unexpected triumph, when I realized I was a World Champion. The podium, the national anthem, and the weight of a golden medal on my chest – everything like in a dream .... There were not many people at that time who believed I would stay on the pole vaulting throne for long. It was not before the following spring that I strengthened my position by clearing 5.85 in Bratislava.

It was many years ago, but anyway the moments of Helsinki '83 are in my mind and heart forever.

Note - Sergey Bubka, the author of the above story, is now Senior Vice President of the IAAF.

In the absence of this great Ukrainian warrior, the 1984 Olympic crown went to the above-mentioned Pierre Quinon of France, who baffled the Americans on their own ground.

1984 Olympics, Los Angeles – Pole Vault (8 August): 1.Pierre Quinon (France) 5.75; 2.Mike Tully (USA) 5.65; 3.(tie) Earl Bell (USA) and Thierry Vigneron (France) 5.60; 5.Kimmo Pallonen (Finland) 5.45; 6.Doug Lytle (USA) 5.40; 7.Felix Böhni (Switzerland) 5.30; 8.Mauro Barella (Italy) 5.30; 9. Alberto Ruiz (Spain) 5.20; 10.Yang Weimin (China) 5.10; 11.Jeff Gutteridge (GB) 5.10. No height: Tom Hintnaus (Brazil), Serge Ferreira (France) and Tomomi Takahashi (Japan).

Bubka became history's first 6-metre man on 13 July 1985 at Stade Jean-Bouin in Paris, when he cleared exactly that height on his third attempt. At record heights he used a grip of 5.10 (or slightly higher). His coach Vitaliy Petrov once timed him in 0.9 secs. (with a digital watch) for the last 10 m. of his run – a speed of 36 km. per hour !

All Bubka needed to successfully defend his title at the 2nd World Championsips, held in Rome in 1987, was just two jumps – one at 5.70 and one at 5.85. By then his rivals had nothing left. He himself failed three times at 6.05. On his first try at that height he was visibly disturbed by a fanfare which entered in action exactly at that time for the medal ceremony of another event.

1987 World Championships, Rome – Pole Vault (5 September): 1.Sergey Bubka (SU) 5.85 (CR); 2.Thierry Vigneron (France) 5.80; 3.Rodion Gataullin (SU) 5.80; 4.Marian Kolasa (Poland) 5.80; 5. (tie) Earl Bell (USA) and Nikolay Nikolov (Bulgaria) 5.70; 7.Delko Lesov (Bulgaria) 5.60; 8.Atanas Tarev (Bulgaria) 5.60; 9.Aleksandr Obizhayev (SU) 5.50; 10.Ferenc Salbert (France) 5.50; 11.Gianni Stecchi (Italy) 5.40; 12.Miro Zalar (Sweden) 5.30; No height: Hermann Fehringer (Austria) and Zdenek Lubensky (Czechoslovakia).

A serious challenger for Bubka emerged in his own country in the person of **Rodion Gataullin** (born at Tashkent on 23 November 1965; 1.89 m. / 78 Kg.), who first beat the "czar" in the final of the Grand Prix IAAF/Mobil in 1988. But Bubka quickly turned the tables on his challenger in the Seoul Olympics. That was when he managed to win what was to remain his one and only Olympic "gold". He went over 5.90 on his third and last try, yet he did so in a very impressive manner – slow-motion replays indicated it may well have been a 20-ft. (6.09 m) clearance.

Sergey Bubka (SU), the king of pole vaulting throughout most of the Eighties and Nineties.

1988 Olympics, Seoul – Pole Vault (28 September): 1.Sergey Bubka (SU) 5.90 (OR); 2.Rodion Gataullin (SU) 5.85; 3.Grigoriy Yegorov (SU) 5.80; 4.Earl Bell (USA) 5.70; 5.(tie) Philippe Collet (France) and Thierry Vigneron (France) 5.70; 7.István Bagyula (Hungary) 5.60; 8.Philippe D'Encausse (France) 5.60; 9.Asko Peltoniemi (Finland) 5.60; 10.Kory Tarpenning (USA) 5.50; 11.Zdenek Lubensky (Czechoslovakia) 5.50; 12.Billy Olson (USA) 5.50; 13.Hermann Fehringer (Austrria) 5.40. No height: Miroslaw Chmara (Poland) and Marian Kolasa (Poland).

By 1990, however, Gataullin appeared ready to take over and did in fact defeat Bubka at the European Championships in Split. The challenger won with 5.85, while Bubka, for once not his real self, finished only sixth with 5.70. Taller and slimmer than his great rival, Gataullin was once credited with 14.4 in the 110 m. hurdles. He became history's second 6-metre man during the 1989 indoor season (6.00 at Leningrad, then 6.02) and later in the season, at Tokyo, he turned the trick outdoors as well, with exactly 6 metres. At the dawn of the Nineties, the SU dominated the pole vault scene just as USA had done thirty and more years ago. Suffice it to say that in 1990 five Russians credited with marks in the 5.85/5.90 range were not rated good enough to make the SU team for the afore-mentioned European Championships in Split ! France had by then a good vaulter in Philippe Collet, a stocky little man who did 5.94 indoors in 1990, reportedly after "steadying the bar with his hands", thus saving an otherwise doomed jump. This "technique" was known as "Volzing" in USA, after the name of the vaulter (Dave Volz) who had been using it most frequently in recent years. There was no provision in the rule book for any attempt aimed at "corriger la fortune", as the French say. The prevailing idea probably was that one could hardly do such refined "handwork" while up in the air. Yet simlar practices had been occasionally used in the past. My friend Prof. Luciano Fracchia of Asti, Italy, owner of a fantastic collection of films on athletic competitions, told me that such a phenomenon was clearly discernible during the 1980 Olympic final in Moscow. But it was only in 1998 that the IAAF added a new clause to rule 172/6, reading as follows: "A competitor fails if ..... during the vault he replaces deliberately with his hands or fingers a bar which is about to fall off the supports". The man most instrumental for causing such a change was Jeff Hartwig, the first American to conquer 6 metres (6.00, then 6.01 in 1998 and 6.02 in '99), who had apparently perfected his "Volzing technique" to an admirable degree. At the 1999 World Indoor Championships in Maebashi, Japan, the new rule was in force and Hartwig conformed to it and finished second with 5.95. Ironically enough, victory went to Jean Galfione of France, who went over 6.00, a personal best, steadying the bar with his left hand. A protest from the U.S. delegation was denied by the Jury of Appeal.

Maksim Tarasov (Russia) succeeded "Czar" Sergey Bubka as world's pole vault champion in 1999.

Sergey Bubka was forced to assume a low profile in 1989-90, mostly on account of injuries. But he was back in harness by 1991. He not only regained the top but managed to maintain it for .... seven more seasons (1991 through 1997). After which he could claim the longest reign as no.1 in "Track & Field News" World Ranking – 13 "victories" (1983-88 and 1991-97).

1991 World Championships - Pole Vault (29 August): 1.Sergey Bubka (SU) 5.95 (CR); 2.István Bagyula (Hungary) 5.90; 3.Maksim Tarasov (SU) 5.85; 4.Rodion Gataullin (SU) 5.85; 5.Peter Widén (Sweden) 5.75; 6.Tim Bright (USA) 5.75; 7.Hermann Fehringer (Austria) 5.60; 8.Thierry Vigneron (France) 5.60; 9. Bernhard Zinti (Germany) 5.50; 10.Jean Galfione (France) 5.40; 11.Doug Wood (Canada) 5.40; 12. Galin Nikov (Bulgaria) 5.30. No height: Philippe Collet (France).

Bubka experienced the main failure of an otherwise splendid career at the 1992 Olympics in Barcelona. The detailed story is told in the adjoining aside. The man who took the czar's seat, so to say, was **Maksim Tarasov** (born at Yaroslavl on 2 December 1970; 1.94 m. / 80 Kg.). Outstanding since his schoolboy days (5.60 at 18, 5.80 at 19) he inevitably played second fiddle to Bubka for a long while, then took advantage of Sergey's unlucky day at Barcelona to win the Olympic gold medal in 1992, edging his countryman Igor Trandenkov on the fewer misses rule, after both had cleared 5.80. Following the disruption of the SU, athletes from that vast country momentarily competed under the banner of a united team (EUN). Javier Garcia, a medium size 26-year-old from Spain, was a surprise third. He received a really huge ovation for clearing 5.75 (a national record) on his second try.

1992 Olympics, Barcelona - Pole Vault (7 August): 1.Maksim Tarasov (EUN) 5.80; 2.Igor Trandenkov (EUN) 5.80; 3.Javier Garcia (Spain) 5.75; 4.Kory Tarpenning (USA) 5.75; 5.Dave Volz (USA)

5.65; 6.Asko Peltoniemi (Finland) 5.60; 7.Philippe Collet (France) 5.55; 8.Yevgeniy Krasnov (Israel) 5.40; 9.István Bagyula (Hungary) 5.30; 10.Alberto Ruiz (Spain) 5.30; No height: Tim Bright (USA) and Sergey Bubka (EUN).

"It looked as if the clock was running faster than usual"

Even a superstar like Sergey Bubka often experienced the difference between "cold" meets in a friendly atmosphere, ideal for record attempts, and "hot" competition in major championship meets governed by stricter rules. In the latter type of meet his best ever was 6.01 (1997 World Ch.).

His failure at the Barcelona Olympics in 1992 was thus recounted in "Track & Field News": "Having been spoiled on the international circuit by accommodating judges, (at Barcelona) Bubka was constantly rushed for time as the strictly enforced 2-minute limit (for every try) was not long enough for him to catch a usable run-up without a headwind. On his first attempt at 5.70 he was forced to go with only 2 seconds remaining on the clock. His second attempt, also a failure, was similar. He took his third attempt at 5.75 so as to have more time to prepare, but he balked on his run and when he went again he was not in a position to make a complete vault as the pole he had selected was too soft for the speed he generated, now with a slight tailwind. After that final failure he admitted that nerves were a problem. To me it looked like the clock was running faster than usual", he said.

Bubka was his real self again in 1993. He improved on the world's indoor record twice: with 6.14 at Liévin on 13 February and 6.15 in his backyard at Donyetsk on 21 February. The latter mark is still the highest ever in the history of the event. On that occasion he took seven jumps in all, clearing 5.70 first time, 5.90 and 6.15 third time. Later in the season, he retained his title at the World outdoor Championships in Stuttgart with 6 metres even. On this occasion he represented his native Ukraine, which was by then an independent country.

1993 World Championships, Stuttgart – Pole Vault (19 August): 1.Sergey Bubka (Ukraine) 6.00 (CR); 2.Grigoriy Yegorov (Kazakhstan) 5.90; 3.(tie) Maksim Tarasov (Russia) and Igor Trandenkov (Russia) 5.80; 5.Scott Huffman (USA) 5.80; 6.Denis Petushinskiy (Russia) 5.80; 7.Valeriy Bukreyev (Est) 5.75; 8.Jean Galfione (Fra) 5.70; 9.Vasiliy Bubka (Ukraine) 5.70; 10.István Bagyula (Hungary) 5.70; 11.Peter Widén (Sweden) 5.60.

Sergey Bubka posted his best outdoor mark at Sestriere, a mountain resort in Northwestern Italy (altitude, 2.050 m.) on 31 July 1994. Once again his work was clear-cut: he needed two attempts at 5.70, then went over 5.90 and 6.14 always on his first attempt, using a perfect tailwind. By doing so he also became the first athlete to win a shiny red Ferrari, the prize awarded to athletes who would break a global mark in that meet.

In 1995 Bubka won his fifth consecutive title of world outdoor champion. True to his style, he needed only three jumps to achieve his goal: two at 5.70 and just one at 5.92, a height he made with plenty to spare. Then he tried 6.15, and just failed by a trifle on his last attempt. Tarasov edged Jean Galfione of France for second. On the fewer misses rule, after both had cleared 5.86.

1995 World Championships, Göteborg – Pole Vault (11 August): 1.Sergey Bubka (Ukraine) 5.92; 2.Maksim Tarasov (Russia) 5.86; 3.Jean Galfione (France) 5.86; 4.Okkert Brits (South Africa) 5.80; 5.Rodion Gataullin (Russia) 5.70; 6.Scott Huffman (USA) 5.70; 7.Igor Trandenkov (Russia) 5.70; 8.Dean Starkey (USA) 5.60; 9.(tie) Andrei Tiwontchik (Germany) and Igor Potapovich (Kazakhstan) 5.60; 11.Tim Lobinger (Germany) 5.40; No height: Valeri Bukreyev (Estonia).

Bad luck continued to follow Bubka closely in Olympic years. Achilles tendon trouble forced him to leave the infield during the qualifying round in the Atlanta Games. In the final three men went over 5.92, a new Olympic record, and Jean Galfione, a brilliant exponent of the French school, won on fewer misses. Almost incredible but true, Americans for once played a minor role on their home ground: their best man for the day, Lawrence Johnson, placed no higher than eighth.

1996 Olympcs, Atlanta – Pole Vault (2 August): 1.Jean Galfione (France) 5.92 (OR); 2.Igor Trandenkov (Russia) 5.92 (=OR); 3.Andrei Tiwontchik (Germany) 5.92 (=OR); 4.Igor Potapovich (Kazakhstan) 5.86; 5.Pyotr Bochkaryov (Russia) 5.86;

6.Dmitriy Markov (Byelarus) 5.86; 7.Tim Lobinger (Germany) 5.80; 8.Lawrence Johnson (USA) 5.70; 9.(tie) Alain Andji (France) and Michael Stolle (Germany) 5.70; 11.(tie) Jeff Hartwig (USA) and Danny Krasnov (Israel) 5.60; 13.Scott Huffman (USA) 5.60; 14.Riaan Botha (South Africa) 5.60.

The irrepressible Bubka crowned a splendid career with his sixth and last global title at the 1997 Worlds in Athens. And he did so with a new championship record, 6.01, a height he cleared on his first try. Tarasov, probably the toughest of his rivals, was second at 5.96. The happy winner, by then almost 34, described that as his most difficult title.

1997 World Championships, Athens – Pole Vault (10 August): 1.Sergey Bubka (Ukraine) 6.01 (CR); 2.Maksim Tarasov (Russia) 5.96; 3.Dean Starkey (USA) 5.91; 4.Tim Lobinger (Germany) 5.80; 5.Nick Buckfield (GB) 5.70; 6.Pat Manson (USA) 5.70; 7.Vadim Strogalyov (Russia) 5.70; 8.Yevgeniy Smiryagin (Russia) 5.70; 9.(tie) Danny Kasnov (Israel) and Martin Eriksson (Sweden) 5.50; 11.Trond Barthel (Norway) 5.50. No valid jump: Riaan Botha (South Africa) and Jean Galfione (France).

During the Nineteens, the dismantling of the SU led Bubka, by then a full-time professionial, to expatriate. He settled down in Berlin for a while, then took residence in Monaco with his wife Lilyana and sons Vitaliy and Sergey Jr. Now and then he would visit his native Ukraine, mostly in connection with the Donyetsk indoor meet, of which he had been the central figure for a long time. In more recent years he began to work for the IAAF Headquarters in Monaco. At the time of writing he is Senior Vice President of that body.

The 1999 World Championships event, held at Sevilla, was strictly an affair for former SU aces. Russia's Maksim Tarasov, who had been living in Budapest since 1992, won with 6.02 – an imposing mark for "global" meets, always characterized by long-drawn competitions. Second went to Dmitriy Markov, a Russian-born athlete who had settled down in Australia, becoming a citizen of that country early in 1999; and third went to Aleksandr Averbukh, a Siberian-born vaulter who appeared in the colours of his country of election, Israel, and gave it its first ever medal. Tying for fourth at 5.70 was Germany's Danny Ecker, a son of Heide Rosendahl, the heroine of the 1972 Olympic Games.

1999 World Championships, Sevilla – Pole Vault (26 August): 1.Maksim Tarasov (Russia) 6.02 (CR); 2.Dmitriy Markov (Australia) 5.90; 3.Aleksandr Averbukh (Israel) 5.80; 4.(tie) Danny Ecker (Germany) and Nick Hysong (USA) 5.70; 6.Tim Lobinger (Germany) 5.70; 7.(tie) Michael Stolle (Germany) and Igor Potapovich (Kazakhstan) 5.70; 9.Danny Krasnov (Israel) 5.50; 10.Okkert Brits (South Africa) 5.50; No valid jump: Jean Galfione and Romain Mesnil (both France).

Bubka finally had to bid farewell in 2000. Although still hampered by an injury, he was bold enough to enter the qualifying competition of the Olympic Games in Sydney when the bar was raised to no less than 5.70. He failed - and an era thus came to an end. Rather surprisingly, USA scored its first victory for 32 years thanks to Nick Hysong , who scaled 5.90 at his first attempt. His countryman Lawrence Johnson mastered the same height on his second try, Tarasov and Germany's Michael Stolle with their third. No one went higher and Hysong thus won the closest battle in the history of the event.

2000 Olympics, Sydney – Pole Vault (29 September): 1.Nick Hysong (USA) 5.90; 2.Lawrence Johnson (USA) 5.90; 3.Maksim Tarasov (Russia) 5.90; 4.Michael Stolle (Germany) 5.90; 5.(tie) Dmitriy Markov (Australia) and Viktor Chistyakov (Australia) 5.80; 7.Okkert Brits (South Africa) 5.80; 8.Danny Ecker (Germany) 5.80; 9.Montxu Miranda (Spain) 5.70; 10.(tie) Yevgeniy Smiryagin (Russia), Aleksandr Averbukh (Israel) and Giuseppe Gibilisco (Italy) 5.50; 13. Tim Lobinger (Germany) 5.50.

As at the end of 2000 no more than nine men had conquered the once magic 6-metre barrier, for a total of 71 marks. Sergey Bubka was easily and by far the best of them, with 44 marks at 6.00 or higher, followed by Tarasov and Gataullin (7 each), Hartwig (5), Brits (3), Lobinger (2), Galfione, Trandenkov and Markov (1 each). It should further be noted that 22 of the 71 six-metre marks (i.e. 30,9 %) were made **indoors.**

LONG JUMP

Lewis is the greatest, but Powell conquers Fort Beamon

From 1981 onwards an American dominated the long jump scene as no one else had ever done since the days of Jesse Owens. Like his great predecessor, this man dominated the sprints as well. And like Owens, he too came from Alabama. He was **Frederick Carlton ("Carl") Lewis** (born at Birmingham, Alabama, on 1 July 1961; 1.88 m. 79 Kgs). His deeds as a junior were truly impressive. At sixteen he jumped 7.26 while at Willingboro High School in New Jersey. Only two years later, in 1979, he was good enough to place third at the Pan-American Games in San Juan, Puerto Rico, with a leap of 8.13, curiously the same distance reached by Jesse Owens in his "Day of Days" at Ann Arbor in 1935. Lewis suffered his last defeat as a junior on 27 February 1981 at the US indoor Championships in New York, when Larry Myricks beat him, 8.13 to 8.08. After that he went unscathed through **64 long jump competitions spaced over 10 seasons**. Lewis often said that the long jump was his first love. Most of his wins in this event were by wide margins. He had a close call now and then, for instance in his appearance in Rome for the 1981 World Cup, when he won by 4 centimetres (8.15 to 8.11) from Gary Honey of Australia.

Lewis won his first "global" title at the inaugural World Championships, held in Helsinki in 1983. And he did so under difficult circumstances: A few minutes after anchoring the US sprint relay to victory in their 4x100 m. heat, he made a delayed appearance in the long jump final. And he soared out to 8.55, a distance which allowed him to win the event with 26 cms. to spare !

1983 World Championships, Helsinki – Long Jump (10 August): 1.Carl Lewis (USA) 8.55 (CR, +1.2 m/s wind); 2.Jason Grimes (USA) 8.29 (+0.6 m/s); 3.Mike Conley (USA) 8.12 (+1.1 m/s); 4.László Szalmá (Hungary) 8.12 (+1.5 m/s); 5.Nenad Stekic (Yugoslavia) 8.09 (1.1 m/s); 6.Gary Honey (Australia) 8.06 (+1.4 m/s); 7.Antonio Corgos (Spain) 8.06 (+0.3); 8.Yusuf Alli (Nigeria) 7.89 (+0.6 m/s); 9.Georgios Cojocaru (Rumania) 7.88w (+2.6 m/s); 10.Jan Leitner (Czechoslovakia) 7.84w (+2.3 m/s); 11.Oganes Stepanyan (SU) 7.74 (-0.4 m/s); 12.Atanas Atanasov (Bulgaria) 7.69w (+2.1 m/s); 13.Lee Mu-Tsai (Taipeh) 7.57 (+0.2 m/s).

Yet Beamon's famous world record (8.90) continued to be an elusive target even for Lewis. Carl did 8.79 on two occasions: on 19 June 1983 at Indianapolis and on 27 January 1984 at New York – the latter was still the world indoor record at the end of 2010. In an outdoor meet at Indianapolis on 24 July 1982 Lewis had a hairline foul which in the opinion of expert observers was definitely worth **9-metres plus.**

At the 1984 Olympics in Los Angeles, Lewis literally re-edited the triumphs of Jesse Owens at Berlin in 1936 by winning four gold medals in exactly the same events (100 m., 200 m., long jump, 4x100 m.). He won the long jump with astounding ease. In fact, he took only two tries: in his first, after hitting the board with about 10 cms. to spare, he reached 8.54 – good enough to leave his nearest rivals – **thirty centimetres** behind ! Lewis fouled on his second jump, after which he decided to call it a day ("I didn't want to take any chances" he said, obviously thinking of other events that still had to unfold). Gary Honey of Australia and Giovanni Evangelisti of Italy finished in that order, both with a new personal best of 8.24.

1984 Olympics, Los Angeles – Long Jump (6 August): 1.Carl Lewis (USA) 8.54 (-1.6 m/s); 2.Gary Honey (Australia) 8.24 (-0.8 m/s); 3.Giovanni Evangelisti (Italy) 8.24 (-0.7 m/s); 4.Larry Myricks (USA) 8.16; 5.Liu Yuhuang (China) 7.99; 6.Joey Wells (Bahamas) 7.97; 7.Junichi Usui (Japan) 7.87; 8.Kim Jong-Il (South Korea) 7.81; 9.Yussuf Alli (Nigeria)

Larry Myricks (USA), winner of the long jump at the 1979 World Cup in Montreal.

7.78; 10.Antonio Corgos (Spain) 7.69; 11.Mike McRae (USA) 7.63; 12.Jubobaraye Kio (Nigeria) 7,57.

Larry Myricks was Lewis' chief rival for more than ten years. Between 1976 and 1994 he put together a mammoth series of classy marks: 269 over 8 metres ! He topped Lewis in quantity, but not in quality. By comparison, Myricks' competitive record at the international level was relatively "thin". He won a bronze at the 1987 World Championships in Rome and another at the 1988 Olympics in Seoul. On both occasions Lewis was a superlative winner. The Roma event was tarnished by a nasty episode which is related in an adjoining aside.

A sad story

Giovanni Evangelisti of Italy was in the limelight at the 1987 Worlds, helas as the victim of a nasty episode. This was when his sixth and last jump was "lengthened" by nearly half a metre by Italian judges, affected by an ill-conceived patriotism. The false mark, 8.38, moved the Italian to third. It was signalled on the flashboard and momentarily gave Italy a bronze medal, besides adding lustre to Evangelisti's curriculum, which in itself happened to be a good one already. That error was crystal clear to spectators who happened to sit in the Tribuna Tevere section, alongside the long jump runway. Inevitably, however, it became a matter for the gossip column as soon as the mark and its doubtful nature reached audio-visual media. It thus became the bitterest pill in the annals of Italian athletics. The Italian Olympic Committee (CONI) started an investigation, which eventually clarified the misbehaviour of the judges, who were consequently ousted from federation ranks. The report also hinted to "negligence" on the part of higher officials in dealing with the case. A few months later the Council of the IAAF annulled the mark and adjusted results accordingly. Larry Myricks (8.33) thus moved to third and Evangelisti to fourth with his best legitimate mark (8.19). The history of athletics offers several examples of marks which were "inflated" one way or another to benefit certain athletes, mostly members of the home team. At any rate the "Evangelisti affair" of Rome '87 is worth a choice place in the "Museum of (not-so-casual) Errors".

1987 World Championships, Rome – Long Jump (5 September): 1.Carl Lewis (USA) 8.67 (CR, +0.4 m/s); 2.Robert Emmiyan (SU) 8.53 (-0.2 m/s); 3.Larry Myricks (USA) 8.33 (-0.9 m/s); 4.Giovanni Evangelisti (Italy) 8.19 (+0.3); 5.Jens-Uwe Hirschberg (East Germany) 8.16 (-0,68 m/s); 6.Jaime Jefferson (Cuba) 8.14 (-0.8 m/s); 7.Vladimir Amidzhinov (Bulgaria) 8.11 (-0.3 m/s); 8.Mike Conley (USA) 8.10 (+0.5 m/s); 9.George Layevskiy (SU) 8.08 (-0.5 m/s); 10.Heiko Reski (West Germany) 8.03 (+0.4 m/s); 11.Yusuf Alli (Nigeria) 8.00 (-1.9 m/s); 12.Junichi Usui (Japan) 8.00 (+2.0 m/s); 13.Vladimir Bobylyov (SU) 7.90w (+2.6 m/s); 14.Jarmo Kärnä (Finland) 7.83 (+0.5 m/s); 15. Norbert Brige (France) 7.82 (-0.4 m/s); 16.Pol Emordi (Nigeria) 7.80 (-0.1 m/s); 17.Ivo Krsek (Czechoslovakia) 7.72 (-1.1 m/s).

Lewis scored yet another smashing victory at the 1988 Olympics in Seoul. With a winning jump of 8.72, he left his nearest rivals and team-mates, Mike Powell and Larry Myricks, 23 and 45 cms. behind respectively. Giovanni Evangelisti curiously reiterated his fourth place of the year before in Rome.

1988 Olympics, Seoul – Long Jump (26 September): 1.Carl Lewis (USA) 8.72 (-0.2 m/s); 2.Mike Powell (USA) 8.49(+1.8 m/s); 3.Larry Myricks (USA) 8.27(+1.2 m/s); 4.Giovanni Evangelisti (Italy) 8.08w (+2.2 m/s); 5.Antonio Corgos (Spain) 8.03 (+0.5 m/s); 6.László Szalma (Hungary) 8.00 (+1.8 m/s); 7.Norbert Brige (France) 7.97 (+0.4 m/s); 8. Leonid Voloshin (SU) 7.89 (-0.2 m/s); 9. Yan Pang (China) 7.86 (+0.9); 10.Jarmo Kärnä (Finland) 7.82 (+0.2); 11.Emiel Mellaard (Holland) 7.71 (+0.1 m/s); 12.Mark Forsythe (GB) 7.54 (+1.1).

Myricks' imposing career record was tarnished when the IAAF announced that he was found "positive" to a forbidden stimulant on three different occasions during the 1990 indoor season. He was originally disqualified for life but the ban was later shortened to 1 year.

The outstanding figures of the decade on the European scene were Lutz Dombrowski of East Germany and Robert Emmiyan of the SU. After his victory at the 1980 Olympics in Moscow, the German continued to be a factor for several years, although hampered by injuries from time to time. He won the 1982 European title but had to stay away from the 1984 Olympics in Los Angeles, his contry being in the boycotters' camp.

Robert Emmiyan (born at Leninakan, Armenia, on 16 February 1965; 1.78 m. / 69 Kg.) was a fine adept of the "hang" style. A precocious talent, he mastered 8 metres at the tender age of 18 . Three years later, during the Goodwill Games in Moscow, he captured the European record with a leap of 8.61, beating Larry Myricks (8.41). Born and brought up in a mountainous area, he had his longest jump on 22 May 1987 at Tsakhkadzor (altitude, 1980 m.), when he offered a replica of the Beamon classic with a stupendous 8.86 on his first try, aided by a legal wind of 1.85 m/s. He continued with 8.65 and 8.53, then decided to call it a day. As irony would have it, a few days later he went down to Turin for the Italy vs. SU match and narrowly lost to Giovanni Evangelisti, 8.09 to 8.10. As previously reported, Emmiyan did himself justice by finishing second to Carl Lewis at the World Championships in Rome. In later years injuries made things more difficult for him. But he was lucky at least in one way: he happened to be in Moscow the day a terrific earthquake hit Armenia in December 1988. The loss of his father and extensive damage to his hometown, Leninakan, obviously affected him in more than one way. Several months later he was back in stride, but seemed to lack his former consistency. Mark-wise, his high altitude / sea level differential was merely 25 cms. (8.86 – 8.61), as opposed to 57 cms. for Beamon (8.90 – 8.33).

Meanwhile, another excellent prospect had emerged from the ever-rich reservoir of the US long jump fraternity - **Mike Powell** (born on 10 November 1963 at Philadelphia; 1.88 m. / 77 Kg.). Basket was for some time his first love but later on he turned his attention to athletics, and the long jump in particular. As destiny would have it, the joyous and talented Mike found himself chasing Carl Lewis instead of Michael Jordan, his hero .... He first conquered 8 metres in 1983 (8.06). The following year he was sixth at the US Olympic Trials. During the Los Angeles Olympics he used to drive a bus taking the Swedish team to the Memorial Coliseum. But he continued to make progress, first under the tutelage of John Smith, then under coach Randy Huntington. By 1988 he was ready to challenge everybody but Lewis. In the Seoul Olympics – as previously reported - he managed to shunt Larry Myricks to third but finished well behind. Powell reached the top, statistically at least, in 1990, when his 8.66 was the best mark of the season on a world-wide scale. But Lewis continued to be untouchable in head-to-head confrontations. By then "King Carl" was confining his long jumping to a couple of meets per season. In 1991 he and Powell met twice and both tussles were real thrillers. At the national championships, serving as Trials for the World title meet in Tokyo, Lewis won by the narrowest of margins, 8.64 to 8.63. Their wind readings in such jumps (+1.7 and +0.6 respectively) gave Lewis a certain advantage. After that close call, Lewis could claim 15 straight wins over Powell in an 8-year span (1983-91), but the latter felt more confident than ever ..... Then came the World Championships in Tokyo. In the qualifying round (29 August) Powell advanced with 8.19 on first try. Lewis needed two: after a "monster" foul of about 8.80, he qualified with 8.56.

At the end of the greatest long jump battle in history, Mike Powell (USA) consoles teammate Carl Lewis after beating him and the world record in Tokyo (1991), 8.95 to 8.91w.

The final the following day offered the most exciting and dramatic competition in the long history of the event. Powell jumped ahead of Lewis and opened with a cautious 7.85. Lewis, looking sharper than ever, answered with 8.68. In round 2 Powell improved to 8.54 and Lewis fouled. In round 3 Powell did 8.29 and Lewis replied with a superb 8.83, his longest jump ever but windy (+2.3). Powell began to look dangerous in the next round with a foul of about 8.76. Then Lewis landed just beyond Bob Beamon's world record flag, but his 8.91 was spoiled by an aiding wind (+2.9). In round 5 Powell had a dream jump: he made a near-perfect take-off and had a fantastic landing, getting maximum extension. A wondrous figure - 8.95 – was flashed on the board. The wind was a mere +0.3 and Fort Beamon thus fell after resisting all attacks for 23 years. Lewis reacted as only a great champion could be expected to do under such circumstances. He closed with his best legal jumps ever, 8.87 (-0.2) and 8.84 (+1.7), but that was not enough for the day. With his fantastic series (four jumps in the range 8.83/8.91) he probably qualified as the **greatest loser** in athletic history. Powell closed with a foul. When it was all over he really let himself go, running crazily across the infield and startling a seemingly cold Japanese judge with a bearhug. He had killed two birds with a stone, breaking the most famous of athletic records and beating arch rival Lewis for the first time !

On that famous day Larry Myricks was a distant and hardly noticed third, with 8.42.

A PS about Powell's record jump. Scientific analysis revealed that he had actually jumped 8.98 as the toe-to-plasticine distance was measured at 3 cms.

Ivan Pedroso (Cuba), a threetime winner of the long jump at the world championships (1995, '97 and '99).

1991 World Championships, Tokyo – Long Jump (30 August): 1.Mike Powell (USA) 8.95 (WR, + 0.3 m/s); 2.Carl Lewis (USA) 8.91w (2.9 m/s); 3. Larry Myricks (USA) 8.42 (+0.8 m/s); 4.Dietmar Haaf (Germany) 8.22w (+3.3m/s); 5.Bogdan Tudor (Rumania) 8.06 (+1.7 m/s); 6.David Culbert (Australia) 8.02 (+1.9 m/s); 7.Giovanni Evangelisti (Italy) 8.01 (+0.7 m/s); 8.Volodymyr Ochkan (SU) 7.99w (+2.1 m/s); 9.Jaime Jefferson (Cuba) 7.94 (-0.5 m/s); 10.Andre Müller (Germany) 7.94w (+3.1); 11.Chen Zunrong (China) 7.92 (+0.5 m/s); 12.Konstantinos Koukodimos (Greece) 7.92 (-1.5 m/s); 13. George Ogbeide (Nigeria) 7.78 (+0.8 m/s).

From then on, all clashes between Powell and Lewis were touch-and-go affairs. Between 1992 and '96 they met six more times and Powell edged Lewis 4 to 2. But the old lion had the upper hand on the occasions that counted most, the Olympics of 1992 and '96. In the former, at Barcelona, Lewis beat Powell by 3 cms - 8.67 to 8.64. And another American, Joe Greene, made it a clean sweep for USA by finishing third.

1992 Olympics, Barcelona – Long Jump (6 August): 1.Carl Lewis (USA) 8.67 (-0.7 m/s); 2.Mike Powell (USA) 8.64 (-0.5 m/s); 3.Joe Greene (USA) 8.34 (+0.2 m/s); 4.Ivan Pedroso (Cuba) 8.11 (0.0 m/s); 5.Jaime Jefferson (Cuba) 8.08 (+0.5 m/s); 6.Konstantinos Koukodimos (Greece) 8.04 (-0.1 m/s); 7.Dmitriy Bagryanov (EUN) 7.98 (+0.1 m/s); 8.Huang Geng (China) 7.87 (+0.1 m/s); 9.Borut Bilac (Slovenia) 7.76 (+0.6 m/s); 10. Chen Zunrong (China) 7.75 (0.0 m/s); 11.David Culbert (Australia) 7.73 (-0.4 m/s); 12: Bogdan Tudor (Rumania) 7.61 (+0.2 m/s).

In 1993 Lewis took the year off from jumping and Powell went unscathed through 25 competitions ! He retained his title at the World Championships in Stuttgart with 43 cms. to spare vis-à-vis his nearest rival, Stanislav Tarasenko of Russia.

1993 World Championships, Stuttgart – Long Jump (20 August): 1.Mike Powell (USA) 8.59 (+0.4 m/s); 2.Stanislav Tarasenko (Russia) 8.16 (-0.1 m/s); 3.Vitaliy Kirilenko (Ukraine) 8.15 (+1.0); 4.Erick Walder (USA) 8.05 (+0.9 m/s); 5.Ivaylo Mladenov (Bulgaria) 8.00 (+0.3); 6.Nikolay Antonov (Bulgaria) 7.97 (-0.1); 7.Aleksandr Glovatskiy (Byelarus) 7.95 (+0.6 m/s); 8.François Fouche (South Africa) 7.93 (+0.5 m/s); 9. Andre Müller (Germany) 7.83 (-0.1 m/s); 10.Spyros Vasdekis (Greece) 7.80 (+1.1); 11.

Milan Gombala (Czechoslovakia) 7.69 (+0.2 m/s). No valid jump: Ivan Pedroso (Cuba).

Another great jumper of the Nineties was **Ivan Pedroso** (born on 17 December 1972 at Ciudad Habana; 1.72 m. / 66 Kg.), a Cuban who in the latter part of the decade wrested the lead from US aces. He emerged at the 1990 World Junior Championships in Plovdiv, Bulgaria, finishing fourth with 7.81 at the unripe age of 17 years 8 months. Two years later he joined the elite of the event with 8.53 (and a wind-aided 8.79) and placed fourth in the Barcelona Olympics, well behind a US trio.

The Cuban was a man of medium build, endowed with a very fine technique. In the eyes of the outer world he "exploded", so to say, in a meet held at Sestriere, Italy (altitude 2050 m.) on 29 July 1995, when he was credited with a great 8.96, one centimetre over Mike Powell's world record. At first the wind reading was given as legal (+1.2 m/s), but there were allegations of interference by an Italian coach standing right in front of the anemometre – especially, if not exclusively, during Pedroso's jumps. When the competition was over it emerged that only 4 out of a total of 60 jumps had been wind-legal, and three of those four were by Pedroso, who had the following series: foul, 8.89w (+2.4), foul, 7.80 (+1.0), 8.30 (+1.0), 8.96 (+1.2). FIDAL, the Italian Athletics Federation, badly burnt by the Evangelisti scandal of 1987 (as related in an aside earlier in this book), decided that it would not submit Pedroso's 8.96 to the IAAF for ratification, being convinced that without the interference of the man blocking the anemometer, the wind reading would have been well over the allowable limit (+2.0 m/s), as it was in the overwhelming majority of the other jumps. Notwithstanding such odd circumstances, it was generally felt that Pedroso was capable of 9-metre jumps. He actually went that far early in 1995 at the Pan-American Games at Mar del Plata, Argentina, when he won with 8.50 but also had a narrow foul of 9.03 which eyewitnesses considered to be worth no less than 9.00 in actual fact.

A few days after the Sestriere interlude, Pedroso won his first major title - in the World Championships at Göteborg. He did so by an imposing margin – 40 cms. vis-à-vis James Beckford of Jamaica, while Powell was only third.

1995 World Championships, Göteborg – Long Jump (12 August): 1. Ivan Pedroso (Cuba) 8.70 (+1.6 m/s); 2.James Beckford (Jamaica) 8.30 (0.0 m/s); 3.Mike Powell (USA) 8.29 (-0.3 m/s); 4.Georg Ackermann (Germany) 8.14 (-1.2 m/s); 5. Bogdan Tudor (Rumania) 8.01 (-0.1 m/s); 6.Kostas Koukodimos (Greece) 8.00 (0.0 m/s); 7.Huang Geng (China) 7.94 (-0.9 m/s); 8.Ivaylo Mladenov (Bulgaria) 7.93 (+0.5 m/s); 9.Andrey Ignatov (Russia) 7.93 (+1.5 m/s); 10.Franck Zio (Burkina Faso) 7.87 (-0.9 m/s); 11.Robert Emmiyan (Armenia) 7.77 (0.0 m/s); 12. Nobuharu Asahara (Japan) 7.77 (+1.2 m/s); 13.Galin Georgiev (Bulgaria) 7.72 (-1.1 m/s); 14.Kareem Streete-Thompson (USA) 7.43 (-2.1).

Carl Lewis was back in stride in 1996, year of the Atlanta Olympics. He needed only one good jump (8.50) to clinch his fourth gold in the history of the event at the quadrennial Games. He thus equalled discus thrower Al Oerter's record for victories in the same event. Oerter had turned the trick between 1956 and '68. Powell entered the Atlanta competition with a frail groin muscle and could do only 8.17 for fifth place. On his last try, a heart-rending foul, he aggravated his condition dramatically. Ivan Pedroso, clearly not yet fully recovered from a leg operation, finished 12th.

1996 Olympics, Atlanta – Long Jump (29 July): 1.Carl Lewis (USA) 8.50 (-1.3 m/s); 2.James Beckford (Jamaica) 8.29 (-1.4 m/s); 3.Joe Greene (USA) 8.24 (+0.1 m/s); 4.Emmanuel Bangué (France) 8.19 (+0.6 m/s); 5.Mike Powell (USA) 8.17 (-0.2 m/s); 6.Gregor Cankar (Slovenia) 8.11 (-0.4 m/s); 7.Aleksandr Glovatskiy (Byelarus) 8.07 (-1.4 m/s); 8. Mattias Sunneborn (Sweden) 8.06 (-0.5 m/s); 9.Huang Geng (China) 7.99; 10.Yuriy Naumkin (Russia) 7.96; 11.Andrey Ignatov (Russia) 7.83; 12.Ivan Pedroso (Cuba) 7.75; 13.Erik Nijs (Belgium) 7.72.

At the end of the Lewis Era, Pedroso took over and won the last three "global" titles of the XX century. In the 1997 Worlds at Athens he had an 8.42 opener, after which he tried, in a relaxed mood, to go for a record jump. He exceeded 8.70 in two fouls, but that was all he could do. He finally won by no more than 4 centimetres from Erick Walder of USA.

1997 World Championships, Athens – Long Jump (5 August): 1.Ivan Pedroso (Cuba) 8.42 (+0.1 m/s); 2.Erick Walder (USA) 8.38 (-0.2 m/s); 3.Kiril Sosunov (Russia) 8.18 (+0.9 m/s); 4.James Beckford (Jamaica) 8.14 (+0.6 m/s); 5.Nelson Ferreira (Brazil) 8.04 (+0.4 m/s); 6.Aleksandr Glovatskiy (Byelarus) 8.03 (+0.3 m/s); 7.Cheikh Touré (Senegal) 7.98 (0.0 m/s); 8.Kevin Dilworth (USA) 7.88 (-0.4 ms); 9.Masaki Morinaga (Japan) 7.86 (+0.1 m/s); 10.Lao

Jianfeng (China) 7.76 (+1.2 m/s); 11.Bogdan Tudor (Rumania) 7.66 (0.0 m/s); no valid jump: Maurice Wignall (Jamaica).

Meanwhile, Europe had no worthy successor for Armenian Robert Emmiyan, yet Yago Lamela of Spain appeared to be a good prospect. He did 8.56 in 1999, both indoors and out, and was second to Pedroso in the World Championships at Sevilla.

1999 World Championships, Sevilla - Long Jump (28 August): 1.Ivan Pedroso (Cuba) 8.56 (+1.1 m/s); 2.Yago Lamela (Spain) 8.40 (+0.6 m/s); 3.Gregor Cankar (Slovenia) 8.36 (+1.6 m/s); 4.Jai Taurima (Australia) 8.35 (+0.7 m/s); 5.Shane Hair (Australia) 8.24 (+1.9 m/s); 6.Huang Le (China) 8.01 (+0.5 m/s); 7.Kevin Dilworth (USA) 8.00 (+1.4 m/s); 8.Younés Moudrik (Morocco) 7.99 (+1-6 m/s); 9.Emmanuel Bangué (France) 7.94 (+1.5 m/s); 10.Ciaran McDonagh (Ireland) 7.90 (+0.8 m/s); 11.Erik Nijs (Belgium) 7.83 (+0.3 m/s); 12.Hussein Al-Sabee (Saudi Arabia) 7.62 (+0.8 m/s).

Pedroso was again the winner at the Sydney Olympics in 2000. He had a troubled day though: after qualifying for the final only on his third and last attempt (8.32), he had to fight hard to emerge victorious against the local favourite Jai Taurima. The latter took the lead with his second jump, 8.18, but was overtaken in the second round by Pedroso's 8.34. The Aussie star, a well-built 28-year-old who could point to a personal best of 13.95 in the "high" hurdles, brought the crowd (110,000 souls) to its feet when he did 8.40, then 8.49. a new Oceania record, but the reliable Pedroso, amid unbearable tension, reached 8.55 on his last trial, and that settled the issue in his favour.

2000 Olympics, Sydney - Long Jump (28 September): 1.Ivan Pedroso (Cuba) 8.55 (+0-4 m/s); 2.Jai Taurima (Australia) 8.49 (+0.6 m/s); 3.Roman Shchurenko (Ukraine) 8.31 (+0.3 m/s); 4.Aleksey Lukashevich (Ukraine) 8.26 (-0.2 m/s); 5.Kofi Amoah Prah (Germany) 8.19 (-0.6 m/s); 6.Peter Burge (Australia) 8.15 (+0-7 m/s); 7.Luis Felipe Meliz (Cuba) 8.08 (+0.1 m/s); 8.Dwight Phillips (USA) 8.06 (-0.1 m/s); 9.Bogdan Tarus (Rumania) 8.00 (-0.8 m/s); 10. Carlos Calado (Portugal) 7.94 (+0.3); 11.Petar Dachev (Bulgaria) 7.80 (+0.2 m/s); 12.Vladimir Malyavin (Russia) 7.67 (-0.6 m/s).

At the end of the century Carl Lewis could claim 39 "legal" marks over 8.50. In this special ranking he led from Pedroso (30), Myricks (17) and Powell (16).

TRIPLE JUMP

Edwards breaks barriers for all tastes: 18 metres and 60 feet.

A few weeks after his third victory in the World Cup (1981) João Carlos de Oliveira was involved in a traffic accident and suffered heavy fractures, finally necessitating the amputation of his right leg. A sad end to a great career. Few triple jumpers, if any, have ever had João's natural gifts. He was a 10.1 sprinter and an 8.36 long jumper. His successor as a world record holder was **Willie Banks** of USA (born at Travis Air Force Base, California, on 11 March 1956; 1.90 m. / 77 Kg.). He grew up as an athlete alternating long jump and triple jump, first in High School and then at UCLA, once bringing his college to a widely acclaimed victory in a dual meet with crosstown rival USC. In 1981 he topped the World List in the triple jump with 17.56 and also long jumped 8.11. Then he alternated ups and downs, like placing second in the inaugural 1983 World Championships in Helsinki, where lost to Zdzislaw Hoffmann of Poland. Spectators were delighted when the American asked them to clasp rhythmically as he was going down the runway. He tried to "respond" as well as he could but Hoffmann first equalled Banks' best (17.18) then improved further on his last effort (17.42). True, Banks had a borderline foul around 17.50. As "Track & Field News" put it, Banks' "efforts to get spectators pumped up may have sown the seeds of his own doom".

1983 World Championships, Helsinki - Triple Jump (8 August): 1.Zdzislaw Hoffmann (Poland) 17.42 (CR, +0.6 m/S); 2.Willie Banks (USA) 17.18 (+0.4 m/s); 3.Ajayi Agbebaku (Nigeria) 17.18 (+1.4 m/s); 4.Mike Conley (USA) 17.13 (+1.6 m/s); 5.Vlastimil Marinec (Czechoslovakia) 17.13 (0.0 m/s); 6.Jan Cado (Czechoslovakia) 17.06 (+1.4 m/s); 7.Béla Bakosi (Hungary) 16.83 (0.0 m/s); 8.Al Joyner (USA) 16.76 (+0.2); 9.Peter Bouschen (West Germany) 16.70 (+1.8 m/s); 10.Gennadiy Valyukevich (SU) 16.41w (+2.6 m/s), 11.Bedros Bedrosian (Rumania) 16.18 (+0.3 m/s); 12.Steve Hanna (Bahamas) 14.96 (-1.0 m/s).

Next on the line of major winners was an American, Alphonzo ("Al") Joyner, who pulled off a golden upset at the 1984 Olympics in Los Angeles. In the first round of the final he reached 17.26, aided somewhat by a following wind of 2.1 m/s. No one of his rivals managed to do better. He left behind, among others, his team-mates Mike Conley and Willie Banks, the favourites of most prognosticators. It should be mentioned, however, that Conley had reached a longer distance, 17.36, in the qualifying rounds (wind + 0.8 m/s), before spraining an ankle early in the final. The winner was a brother of Jackie Joyner-Kersee, who in those Games won a silver medal in the heptathlon. Al later married Florence Griffith, to this day the greatest of sprinters on the distaff side.

1984 Olympic Games, Los Angeles – Triple Jump (4 August): 1.Al Joyner (USA) 17.26w (+2.1 m/s); 2.Mike Conley (USA) 17.18 (-0.4 m/s); 3.Keith Connor (GB) 16.87 +0.4 m/s); 4.Zehnxian Zou (China) 16.83 (-1.0 m/s); 5.Peter Bouschen (Germany) 16.77 (-0.9 m/s); 6.Willie Banks (USA) 16.75 (-0.6 m/s); 7.Ajayi Agbebaku (Nigeria) 16.67 (-1.6 m/s); 8.Eric McCalla (GB) 16.66 (-0.2 m/s); 9.Joseph Taiwo (Nigeria) 16.64 (-1.1 m/s); 10.John Herbert (GB) 16.40 (-0.9 m /s); 11.Hassan Badra (Egypt) 16.07 (-0.5 m/s); 12.Mamadou Diallo (Senegal) 15.99 (-1.5 m/s).

Willie Banks finally came into his own on 16 June 1985 at Indianapolis, when he won a hot triple jump battle at the US Championships with a record-shattering 17.97, aided by a legal wind of 1.47 m/s. He won from Mike Conley (17.71), Charles Simpkins (17.52) and 1984 Olympic champion Al Joyner (17.46).

The eccentric and popular Willie Banks (USA), holder of the world record in the triple jump (17.97 in 1985).

On a strictly competitive basis, however, the most successful triple jumper of the post-Saneyev era was long-haired **Khristo Markov** of Bulgaria (born at Dimitrovgrad on 27 January 1965; 1.84 m. / 78 Kg.). Between 1986 and '88 he scored a perfect triple, annexing European, World and Olympic titles. His lifetime best and European record, 17.92, was made on the second of such occasions, on 31 August 1987 in Rome. The Bulgarian was also an excellent long jumper: 8.23 indoors in 1985.

1987 World Championships, Rome – Triple Jump (31 August): 1.Khristo Markov (Bulgaria) 17.92, ER (+1.6 m/s); 2.Mike Conley (USA) 17.67 (-1.0 m/s); 3.Oleg Sakirkin (SU) 17.43 (+1.4 m/s); 4.Aleksandr Kovalenko (SU) 17.38 (-1.0 m/s); 5. Jacek Pastusinski (Poland) 17.35 (+1.7 m/s); 6.Joseph Taiwo (Nigeria) 17.29w (+3.9 m/s); 7.Peter Bouschen (West Germany) 17.26w (+3.6 m/s); 8. Oleg Protsenko (SU) 17.23w (+3.9 m/s); 9.Norbert Elliott (Bahamas) 16.79 (+1.9 m/s); 10.Ivan Slanar (Czechoslovakia) 16.69 (+0.9 ms); 11.Dario Badinelli (Italy) 16.63 (+0.5 m/s); 12.Zdzislaw Hoffmann (Poland) 16.58 (+1.9 m/s); No valid jump: Norifumi Yamashita (Japan).

A year later, at he Seoul Olympics, Markov reached 17.61. a new Olympic record right on his first attempt. That settled the issue. Athletes from Eastern Europe found the hot weather rather unbearable, yet managed to make a medal sweep. On the US side, Mike Conley had lost the game in advance by finishing no better than fourth at the Olympic Trials.

1988 Olympics, Seoul – Triple Jump (24 September): 1.Khristo Markov (Bulgaria) 17.61 OR (+0.7 m/s); 2.Igor Lapshin (SU) 17.52 (+0.1 m/s); 3.Aleksandr Kovalenko (SU) 17.42 (-0-8 m/s); 4.Oleg Protsenko (SU) 17.38 (0.0 m/s); 5.Charlie Simpkins (USA) 17.29 (+0.2 m/s); 6.Willie Banks (USA) 17.03 (+0.9 m/s); 7.Ivan Slanar (Czechoslovakia) 16.75 (0.0 m/s); 8.Jacek Pastusinski (Poland) 16.72 (-0.6 m/s); 9.Joseph Taiwo (Nigeria) 16.46 (+0.8 m/s); 10.Norbert Elliott (Bahamas) 16.19 (-0.2 m/s); 11.Didier Falise (Belgium) 16.17 (+0.2 m/s); 12. Norifumi Yamashita (Japan) 15.62 (-0.4 m/s).

The first American to be crowned world champion was **Kerry "Kenny" Harrison** (born at Milwaukee on 13 February 1965; 1.78 m. / 75 Kg.). He turned the trick at Tokyo in 1991 after years of gradual progress. A 17-metre man since 1986, he had reached the top

Zdzislaw Hoffmann (Poland), winner of the triple jump at the 1983 World Championships.

in the "Dagens Nyheter" Games on 2 July 1990 with 17.93 (wind + 1.6 m/s), the second best mark of all time, four centimetres shy of the world record set by his countryman Willie Banks in 1985. The World Championships event offered a terrific battle involving three men – Harrison and Mike Conley of USA, Leonid Voloshin of the SU. The last one had turned to the triple jump after finishing 8th in the long jump of the Seoul Olympics, an event in which he had a personal best of 8.46. In the Tokyo triple jump Harrison and Conley took the leading positions in round 2 with 17.78 and 17.62 respectively. In the next round Voloshin managed to move to second with 17.75, but that was all he could do. Curiously enough, both Americans were inferior to their Russian rival in terms of long jump potential (Conley 8,43, Harrison 8.17).

Harrison had a flawless season in 1991, yet it is worth noticing that his winning margin vis-à-vis Voloshin the only two times they met was the same tiny 3 cm.

1991 World Championships, Tokyo – Triple Jump (26 August): 1.Kenny Harrison (USA) 17.78 (-0.8 m/s); 2.Leonid Voloshin (SU) 17.75 (+1.0 m/s); 3.Mike Conley (USA) 17.62 (+0.4 m/s): 4.Vasiliy Sokov (SU) 17.28 (-0.4 m/s); 5.Tord Henriksson (Sweden) 17.12 (+0.5 m/s); 6.Brian Wellman (Bermudas) 16.98 (-0.5 m/s); 7.Yoelvis Quesada (Cuba) 16.94 (-0.4 m/s); 8.Georges Sainte-Rose (France) 16.92 (-0.3 m/s); 9.Ralf Jaros (Germany) 16.76 (-2.1 m/s); 10.Oleg Denishchik (SU) 16.61 (-0.2 m/s); 11.Norifumi Yamashita (Japan) 16.26 (-0.4 m/s); 12.Andrzej Grabarczyk (Poland) 16.23 (0.2 m/s).

Conley had his brightest day at the 1992 Olympics in Barcelona, when he reached 17.63 in round 2 and improved to a great 18.17 in what was his favoured try, the last. He thus won the title he had been dreaming of for years, but a baffling wind of +2.1 m/s nullified his effort for record purposes. Having once met him on the way to the stadium during those days, I know that his joy for the gold medal he had won by far excelled his sorrow for missing the record.

1992 Olympics, Barcelona – Triple Jump (3 August): 1.Mike Conley (USA) 18.17w (+2.1 m/s), best legal mark 17.63 (+0.5 m/s); 2.Charlie Simpkins (USA) 17.60 (+0.7 m/s); 3.Frank Rutherford (Bahamas) 17.36 (+1.1 m/s); 4.Leonid Voloshin (EUN) 17.32 (+1.1 m/s); 5.Brian Wellman (Bermudas) 17.24 (-0.6 m/s); 6.Yoelvis Quesada (Cuba) 17.18 (+1.9 m/s); 7.Aleksandr Kovalenko (EUN) 17.06 (-0.1 m/s); 8.Zou Sixin (China) 17.00 (+1.2 m/s); 9.Vasiliy Sokov (EUN) 16.86 (0.0 m/s); 10.Maris Bruziks (Latvia) 16.80 (+1.3 m/s); 11.Pierre Camara (France) 16.52 (0.0 m/s); 12.Eugeniusz Bedeniczuk (Poland) 16.23 (+0.7 m/s).

Even after his great Olympic victory, Mike Conley was still thirsty. Now his main target was the World Championship title. From 1983 onwards he had competed in the first three editions of that meet, placing fourth (1983), second ('87) and third ('91). The coveted gold medal finally came his way at Stuttgart in 1993, where he won with 17.86, beating the very tough Voloshin by 21 cms. It is to be noted that the American usually achieved his best in the latest phase of his efforts. His mastery in this aspect is discussed in an adjoining aside.

1993 World Championships, Stuttgart – Triple Jump (16 August): 1.Mike Conley (USA) 17.86 (+0.3 m/s); 2.Leonid Voloshin (Russia) 17.65 (0.0 m/s); 3.Jonathan Edwards (GB) 17.44 (+0.1); 4.Ralf Jaros (Germany) 17.34 (+0.1 m/s); 5.Pierre Camara (France) 17.28 (+0.5 m/s); 6.Denis Kapustin (SU) 17.19 (+0.6 m/s); 7.Anisio Silva (Brazil) 17.19 (+0.2 m/s); 8.Brian Wellman (Bermudas) 17.12 (0.0 m/s); 9.Serge Hélan (France) 17.09 (+1.1 m/s); 10.Kenny Harrison (USA) 17.06 (+0.5 m/s); 11.Jerome Romain (Dominica) 16.98 (+0.1 m/s); 12. Yoelvis Quesada (Cuba) 16.77 (-0.1 m/s); 13.Oleg Denishchik (Byelarus) 16.61 (+0.2 m/s).

The 18-metre barrier continued to be an elusive target for triple jumpers. The man who finally turned the trick was **Jonathan Edwards** of Great Britain (born in London on 10 May 1966; 1.81 m. / 70 Kg.). For all its glory in the annals of the sport, Albion had a rather meagre tradition here. Her first Olympic medal was a bronze by Keith Connor in the 1984 Olympics. A vicar's son and himself a committed Christian, prior to 1993 Edwards would not compete on Sunday, which caused him to bypass the 1991 World Championships, where the qualifying round was scheduled for that very day. He later changed his mind as he thought he should at any time "honour God for the gift of athletic ability" he had given him. Edwards, who had first bettered 17 metres in 1989, reaped the first major reward for his hard and meticulous training by placing third at the 1993 World Chammpionships with 17.44, a personal best. He had his greatest season in 1995. In June/July he bettered 18 metres four times, always with the aid of a wind over the limit: 18.43 (+2.4 m/s) and 18.39 (+3.7 m/s) in the European Cup at Villeneuve-d'Ascq on 25 June; 18.03 (+2.9 m/s) at Gateshead on 2 July; and 18.08 (+2.5 ms) at Sheffield on 23 July. Shortly before the last meet, however, he managed to succeed Willie Banks as world record holder with a legal 17.98 (+1.8 m/s) at Salamanca on 18 July. He had his Day of Days on 7 August at the World Championships in Göteborg, breaking barriers for everybody's taste: 18 metres, for the major part of the world, and 60 feet (18.28) for nostalgic lovers of the English measuring system. His series was as follows; 18.16 (+1.3 m/s) – 18.29 (+1.3 m/s) – pass – pass, 17.49 – pass.

Last-attempt phenomenon in every sense

Mike Conley's ability in often reaching his best results on his sixth and last trial was simply amazing. Throughout his brilliant career the American had ten legal marks in the range 17.87 / 17.67 and **seven** of these were achieved in the sixth round ! The longest distance he ever reached was 18.17 in the Barcelona Olympics, when a dire wind of 2.1 m/s nullified his claim for a new world record. Well, even that great mark came in the very last round.

Conley's devilish ability as a last-attempt phenomenon was shining in another sense – even in the effort proper he had a tendency to concentrate on the all-important jump phase of each triple jump attempt. In connection with his victory in the 1993 Worlds at Stuttgart, "Track & Field News" offered some interesting figures in this respect. Conley achieved his victory with 17,86 – helas, in round 5 – with a hop of 5.75, a step of 5.47 and a jump of 6.64 In percentages the ratio was as follows: 32 %, 31 %, 37 %.

He thus bettered Banks' 10-year-old world record twice and won the world title by an awesome margin: 67 cms. In a post-meet interview he said: "My edge at the moment is that I have very good foot speed on the ground. My last phase (jump) is very long because of the speed I maintain". He surely maximized his potential to a great extent. His other personal bests (10.48 in the 100 m. and 7.41 in the long jump) look rather deceptive in that respect.

1995 World Championships, Göteborg – Triple Jump 7 August): 1.Jonathan Edwards (GB) 18.29 WR (+1.3 m/s); 2.Brian Wellman (Bermudas) 17.62w (+2.7 m/s); 3.Jerome Romain (Dominica) 17.59w (+2.1 m/s); 4.Yoelvis Quesada (Cuba) 17.59w (+2.6 m/s); 5.Yoel Garcia (Cuba) 17.16 (+1.2 m/s); 6.James Beckford (Jamaica) 17.13w (2.5 m/s); 7.Mike Conley (USA) 16.96w (+3.6 m/s); 8.Galin Georgiev (Bulgaria) 16.93 (-0.2 m/s); 9. Tord Henriksson (Sweden) 16.92 (+0.1 m/s); 10.Maris Bruziks (Latvia) 16.80 (+1.4 m/s); 11. Roger Nachum (Israel) 16.69 (+1.7 m/s); 12.Sergey Arzamasov (Kazakhstan) 16.68 (+0.8 m/s).

The **breakdown** of Edwards' best performances in 1995 – at the time of writing still ranking as the best ever in the history of the triple jump - was as follows:

Hop	Step	Jump		
Villeneuve d'Ascq, 25 June 1995				
6.50w	5.60w	6.33w	=	18.43w
Göteborg, 7 August 1995				
6.05	5.22	7.02	=	18.29

Edwards and his "choirboy smile" graced European crowds for several more years although he never duplicated his magic moments of 1995, save perhaps for a mark of 18.01 at Oslo in 1998. At the 1996 Olympics in Atlanta he had to bow to Kenny Harrison. This rather unpredictable American re-emerged in the summer of 1996 after a layoff of 15 months due to "numerous injuries". His comeback at the U.S. Olympic Trials was sensational. In his one and only try he flew to 18.01, aided by a generous wind (+3.7 m/s) – good enough for an easy victory over veteran Mike Conley (17.57). In the Olympics he was again scarce in quantity but superb in quality. He had only two valid jumps: 17.99 and 18.09, both legal and superior to Banks' U.S. record. Edwards had to be content with 17.88 and second place. It should be noted that

Harrison also excelled as a long jumper: 8.17 indoors, way back in 1986.

1996 Olympics, Atlanta – Triple Jump (27 July): 1.Kenny Harrison (USA) 18.09 (-0.4 m/s) ; 2. Jonathan Edwards (GB) 17.88 (+0.9 m/s); 3.Yoelvis Quesada (Cuba) 17.44 (+0.2 m/s); 4.Mike Conley (USA) 17.40 (+0.2 m/s); 5.Armen Martirosyan (Armenia) 16.97 (+1.1 m/s); 6.Brian Wellman (Bermuda) 16.95; 7.Galin Georgiev (Bulgaria) 16.92; 8.Robedrt Howard (USA) 16.90; 9.Viktor Sotnikov (Russia) 16.84; 10.Volodomyr Kravchenko (Ukraine) 16.62; 11.Frank Rutherford (Bahamas) 16.38; No valid try: Jerome Romain (Dominica).

The last two world champions of the Nineties were Yoelvis Quesada of Cuba in 1997 and Charles-Michael Friedek of Germany in 1999. The former was a boy prodigy in his younger days, with 17.13 at 18 and 17.23 at 19. At the World Championships he was 7th in 1991, 12th in '93 and 4th in '95, before finally winning in '97 with 17.85, a personal best.

1997 World Championships, Athens – Triple Jump (8 August): 1.Yoelvis Quesada (Cuba) 17.85 (+0.9 m/s); 2.Jonathan Edwards (GB) 17.69 (+0.3 m/s); 3.Aliecer Urrutia (Cuba) 17.64 (0.0 m/s); 4.Denis Kapustin (Russia) 17.59 (-0.2 m/s); 5.Brian Wellman (Bermuda) 17.22 (0.0 m/s); 6.Jerome Romain (Dominica) 17.17 (-0.4 m/s); 7.Hristos Melétoglou (Greece) 17.12 (-0.2 m/s); 8.Andrew Owusu (Canada) 17.11 (+0.4 m/s); 9.Kenny Harrison (USA) 17.05 (-1.6 m/s); 10.Serge Hélan (France) 16.97 (-0.6 m/s); 11.Charles-Michael Friedek (Germany) 16.86 (0.0 m/s); 12.Armen Martirosyan (Armenia) 16.70 (-0.2 m/s).

Jonathan Edwards (Great Britain) on his greatest day, after setting a new world triple jump record (18.29) at Göteborg in 1995.

Charles-Michael Friedek, a law student from Germany, won a close battle at the 1999 Worlds in Sevilla. Due to a heel injury, it was only at the last moment that he decided to compete. He came out the winner with 17.59, equalling his personal best from 1997. He did so in round 4 and world record holder Jonathan Edwards had to be content with third.

1999 World Championships, Sevilla – Triple Jump (25 August): 1.Charles-Michael Friedek (Germany) 17.59 (+1.9 m/s); 2.Rostislav Dimitrov (Bulgaria) 17.49 (+1.4 m/s); 3.Jonathan Edwards (GB) 17.48 (+0.4 m/s); 4.Andrew Murphy (Australia) 17.32 (+1.7 m/s); 5.Paolo Camossi (Italy) 17.29 (+1.5 m/s); 6.LaMark Carter (USA) 17.10 (+0.2 m/s); 7.Jérome Romain (France) 17.10 (-0.2 m/s); 8.Jiri Kuntos (Czechoslovakia) 17.00 (1.8 m/s); 9.Denis Kapustin (Russia) 16.89 (+1.7 m/s); 10.Yoelvis Quesada (Cuba) 16.88 (+0.4 m/s); 11.Larry Achike (GB) 16.59 (+1.4 m/s); 12.Vasiliy Sokov (Russia) 16.53 (+0.8 m/s).

Old gentle warrior Jonathan Edwards was not ready to give up yet. In 2000, aged 34, he finally won the title that was still missing in his "palmarès" – the Olympic one. On his third try he reached 17.71 and nobody was able to threaten him. Like many Commonwealth-heritage athletes, he rode a strong wave of support from the Sydney crowd. When it was all over, he was visibly overwhelmed and said: "I was on the point of crying and had to choke back the tears .... To come here at 34 and win the gold medal has been fabulous". In fact, he was the oldest Olympic gold medallist in the history of the event.

Friedek of Germany sprained a knee in pre-meet training and could not do himself justice in the final.

2000 Olympics, Sydney – Triple Jump (25 September): 1.Jonathan Edwards (GB) 17.71 (+0.2 m/s); 2.Yoel Garcia (Cuba) 17.47 (+0.1 m/s); 3.Denis Kapustin (Russia) 17.46 (+0.3 m/s); 4.Yoelvis Quesada (Cuba) 17.37 (+0.3 m/s); 5.Larry Achike (GB) 17.29 (+0.5 m/s); 6.Phillips Idowu (GB) 17.08 (0.0 m/s); 7.Robert Howard (USA) 17.05 (+ 0.5 m/s); 8.Paolo Camossi (Italy) 16.96 (+0.3 m/s); 9.Rostislav Dimitrov (Bulgaria) 16.95 (+0.4 m/s); 10.Andrew Murphy (Australia) 16.80 (+0.4 m/s); 11.Walter Davis (USA) 16.61 (-0.1 m/s). No valid mark: Charles-Michael Friedek (Germany).

At the end of the century Edwards had 5 of the top 10 best (valid) marks in history – namely marks no. 1, 3, 4, 5 and 6.

MEN 2001-2010

7

HIGH JUMP

An ever changing hierarchy

Javier Sotomayor re-emerged rather comfortably from the intermezzo that befell him at the Pan-American Games of 1999, when he turned positive to cocaine. The "Federaciòn Cubana de Atletismo" appealed to the Arbitration Commission of the IAAF, which finally decided to readmit him to international competition as of August 2000. He was thus able to compete in the World Championships held at Edmonton, Canada, in 2001. By then 34, the Cuban lion fought bravely, was one of four jumpers who went over 2.33 and finally missed the medal circle only on the misses count, finishing fourth. Victory went to Martin Buss of Germany, a tall jumper (1.95 m.) who chose the occasion to set a new personal record, 2.36. Buss had entered the close circle two years before, placing third at the Sevilla Worlds.

However, there was a PS. to Sotomayor's fourth place. After the championships it was revealed that he had failed yet another doping control test in July 2001. He later admitted to the offence, which resulted in a life ban as this came on top of his previous (1999) suspension. Consequently, his Edmonton performance was annulled.

2001 World Championships - Edmonton (8 August): 1.Martin Buss (Germany) 2.36; 2.(tie) Yaroslav Rybakov (Russia) and Vyacheslav Voronin (Russia) 2.33; 4.(tie) Sergey Klyugin (Russia) and Stefan Holm (Sweden) 2.30; 6.(tie) Mark Boswell (Canada) and Staffan Strand (Sweden) 2.25; 8.Kwaku Boateng (Canada) 2.25; 9.(tie) Abderrahmane Hammad (Algeria) and Charles Austin (USA) 2.20; 11.Gilmar Mayo (Columbia) 2.20. Disqualified: Javier Sotomayor (Cuba) 2.33.

Mr. Shorty can jump high and is a clever statistician too

As a rabid statistician of old, I can bear witness that time is the "Lord of Changers" in this field too. Fifty or more years ago, when athletics statistics was a rarity even in specialized sporting publications, I sometimes happened to be questioned by certain athletes on something like "What is my position in the current World List ?" In this respect I also remember a gag played the other way round. During the 1950 European Championhips in Brussels, I asked a British 400-metre runner about his personal best in that event. He said: "As far as I can remember, it's 47 seconds plus".

Nowadays, the world of athletics abounds in statistical compilations of all sorts. Web sites and Internet can furnish you with virtually everything you may be interested in. There are athletes who excel in such a game. In this respect Stefan Holm of Sweden, the Olympic high jump champion of 2004, is a most valid example. In his web site one can find all his marks through the years, the history of his clashes with leading contenders, etc. Mind you, he can also tell you exactly who are the best high jumpers in terms of personal best / own height differential. Only 1.81 m. tall, (not impressive for a top high jumper), Holm can point to a personal record of 2.40 (indoors, in 2005). His differential is therefore an imposing 59 cm. In the history of the event only one jumper can match that differential: Franklin Jacobs of USA, 1.73 m. tall, jumped 2.32 (he too indoors) in 1978.

In the years that followed the most consistent jumpers at the highest level were **Yaroslav Rybakov** of Russia and **Stefan Holm** of Sweden. The former (born at Mogilyev on 22 November 1980; 1.98 m. /

84 Kg.) won the European Championship title in 2002 with 2.31. Right behind him, with 2.29, was Holm (born at Forshaga on 25 May 1976; 1.81 m. / 70 Kg.). These two jumpers thus differed greatly in terms of tally. Holm was a Mr. Shorty in the family of leading performers. More in this respect is told in the adjoining aside. From the standpoint of style, the Swede exhibited a perfect "Flop".

The 2001 season projected into the limelight a jumper from South Africa, Jacques Freitag, who was just the opposite of Stefan Holm in terms of physical build: 2.04 m. tall, he weighed 83 Kg. On occasion, however, his long legs seemed to pose him problems in terms of co-ordination. He emerged early and in 2000 he was world junior champion. Three years later, at the senior world meet in Paris-St.Denis, he won from Holm himself with 2.35. The Swede, **23 centimetres shorter** than his rival, did 2.32. Freitag's mother, Hendrina Pieters, had been South African champion in the same event in 1973. She had a personal best of 1.74 (1973).

2003 World Championships, Paris-St.Denis – High Jump (25 August): 1.Jacques Freitag (South Africa) 2.35; 2.Stefan Holm (Sweden) 2.32; 3.Mark Boswell (Canada) 2.32; 4.Mikhail Tsvetkov (Russia) 2.29; 5.Germaine Mason (Jamaica) 2.29; 6.Grzegorz Sposob (Poland) 2.29; 7.Jamie Nieto (USA) 2,29; 8.Andrey Sokolovskiy (Ukraine) 2.29; 9.Yaroslav Rybakov (Russia) 2.29; 10.Aleksander Walerianczyk (Poland) 2.25; 11.Jaroslav Bába (Czechoslovakia) 2.25; 12.Matt Hemingway (USA) 2.25; 13.Roman Fricke (Germany) 2.20.

More than a century after the inaugural Olympics of 1896, Athens hosted the Games again in 2004. It was there that Stefan Holm had his Day of Days as a competitor. It was a hard fought battle though. At one point, he found himself in fourth place on the countback after taking two jumps to clear 2.32 and three at 2.34. But he turned the tables on his rivals with a first-time clearance of 2.36. Second went to Matt Hemingway of USA, whose grandfather was the cousin of a famous author, Ernest Hemingway. World champion Jacques Freitag, nursing an ankle injury, fell in the qualifying round.

2004 Olympics, Athens – High Jump (22 August): 1.Stefan Holm (Sweden) 2.36; 2.Matt Hemingway (USA) 2.34; 3.Jaroslav Bába (Czechoslovakia) 2.34; 4.James Nieto (USA) 2.34; 5.Andrey Sokolovskiy (Ukraine) 2.32; 6.Yaroslav Rybakov (Russia) 2.32; 7.Mark Boswell (Canada) 2.29; 8.Svatoslav Ton (Czechoslovakia) 2.29; 9.Vyacheslav Voronin (Russia) 2.29; 10.Dragutin Topic (Serbia & Montenegro) 2.29; 11.Lisvany Pérez (Cuba) 2.25; 12.Alessandro Talotti (Italy) 2.25.

In the following years no jumper towered consistently above all others. And major titles went to an ever changing hierarchy of men. Yuriy Krymarenko of Ukraine won at the 2005 World Championships in Helsinki with no more than 2.32, a height he cleared on his last attempt. In his wake there were no fewer than sedven men at 2.29, one of them being favourite Stefan Holm, who said: "I don't know why I didn't have any power in my legs today".

2005 World Championships, Helsinki – High Jump (14 August): 1.Yuriy Krymarenko (Ukraine) 2.32; 2.(tie) Victor Moya (Cuba) and Yaroslav Rybakov (Russia) 2.29; 5.Mark Boswell (Canada) 2.29; 5.(tie) Jaroslav Bába (Czech Rep.) and Nicola Ciotti (Italy) 2.29; 7.Stefan Holm (Sweden) 2.29; 8.Vyacheslav Voronin (Russia) 2.29; 9.Dragutin Topic (Serbia & Montenegro) 2.25; 10.Kyriakos Ioannou (Cyprus) 2.25; 11.(tie) Matt Hemingway (USA) and Oskari Frösen (Finland) 2.20; 13.Andrey Sokolovskiy (Ukraine) 2.20.

A major surprise occurred at the 2007 World Championships in Osaka with the victory of Donald Thomas, a newcomer from Bahamas, who won with a first-time clearance at 2.35, equalling his personal best. He won on the fewer misses count from two Europeans, the well-known Rybakov and Kyriakos Ioannou, who thus became the first Cypriot to win a medal at any event in these Championships. The 23-year old Thomas, a former basketball player, had made a sensational debut in the event in January 2006, going over 2.22. As a student at Auburn University in USA, he rose to 2.24 later in the same year. His progress in 2007 was eye-catching: a few weeks before the Osaka rendez-vous he rose to 2.35 at Salamanca, a Spanish rendezvous once so dear to the great Sotomayor.

2007 World Championships, Osaka – High Jump (29 August): 1.Donald Thomas (Bahamas) 2.35; 2.Yaroslav Rybakov (Russia) 2.35; 3.Kyriakos Ioannou (Cyprus) 2.35; 4.Stefan Holm (Sweden) 2.33; 5.(tie) Victor Moya (Cuba) and Tomás Janku (Czech Republic) 2.30; 7.Eike Onnen (Germany) 2.26; 8.Jaroslav Bába (Czech Rep.) 2.26; 9.Kabelo Kgosiemang (Botswana) 2.26; 10.Tom Parsons (GB)

2.26; 11.(tie) Andrey Silnov (Russia) and Michal Bieniek (Poland) 2.21; 13.Jesse de Lima (Brazil) 2.21; 14.Martyn Bernard (GB) 2.21; 15.Linus Thörnblad (Sweden) 2.16.

After his surprising victory at Osaka, Thomas admitted that he still had technical problems, yet he was quite optimistic about his future: "When I get things together I think I can even start raving about the world record". As it was, in the three years that followed he could not go higher than 2.32.

Russia, still the no.1 power in terms of quality jumpers, fought back bravely in 2008 and won two of the three medals at stake in the 2008 Olympics at Beijing. Andrey Silnov, who had been no.1 in "Track & Field News" World Ranking in 2006, was selected for the Games even though he placed no higher than fourth at the Russian Championships, the trial meet. Earlier in the season he had cleared 2.38 in London and the Russian Athletics Federation decided to select him for the team. They had no reason to repent for their impromptu choice because Silnov had a great day in Beijing – he cleared all heights, up to and including 2.36, on his first try. And he had two very close tries at 2.42. When it was all over, the happy winner was quoted as saying: "I am grateful to the people who decided that I should come to Beijing .... I felt I had no alternative but to win gold in order to justify their faith in me". One of his interviewers was crisp enough to ask him whether he considered calling Andrey Tereshin, "the poor guy he had replaced" (who was third in the Russian Championships). Silnov's reply was as simple as this: "It was the decision of the authorities. I don't think I have to call anyone".

The 2008 Olympics, Beijing – The high jump (19 August): 1.Andrey Silnov (Russia) 2.36; 2.Germaine Mason (GB) 2.34; 3.Yaroslav Rybakov (Russia) 2.34; 4.Stefan Holm (Sweden) 2.32; 5.Raul Spank (Germany) 2.32; 6.Jaroslav Bába (Czech Rep.) 2.29; 7.Tomás Janku (Czech Rep.) 2.29; 8.Tom Parsons (GB) 2.25; 9.Martyn Bernard (GB) 2.25; 10.(tie) Jessé de Lima (Brazil) and Filippo Campioli (Italy) 2.20; 12.Rozle Prezelj (Slovenia) 2.20.

Rybakov, probably the most consistent competitor in recent years, won his first World Championhip title in 2009, after placing second in three previous editions. In a tough, rain-delayed final, he won on the fewer misses count at 2.32, a height which was cleared by three other contenders, all from Europe. The decadence of U.S. high jumpers, once the rulers of the event, was crystal clear: their best man, Andra Manson, had to be content with ninth place at 2.23.

The 2009 World Championships - Berlin (21 August: 1.Yaroslav Rybakov (Russia) 2.32; 2.Kyriakos Ioannou (Cyprus) 2.32; 3.(tie) Sylvester Bedmarek (Poland) and Raul Spank (Germany) 2.32; 5.(tie) Mickaël Hanany (France), Linus Thörnblad (Sweden), Jaroslav Bába (Czech Rep.) and Martin Nuyens (Holland) 2.23; 9.Andra Manson (USA) 2.23; 10.Ivan Ukhov (Russia) 2.23; 11.(tie) Giulio Ciotti (Italy) and Keith Moffatt (USA) 2.23; 13.Kabelo Kgosiemang (Botswana) 2.18.

The most recent 2.40 performer is another Russian, **Ivan Ukhov** (born at Chelyabinsk on 29 March 1986; 1.92 m. / 83 Kg.), who cleared exactly that height in an indoor meet at Pireás on 25 February 2009. Performance-wise he was no. 1 even in 2010, when he could point to four marks in the range 2.39 / 2.35. But he has yet to win a major title. At the 2010 European Championships he had to be content with second (at 2.31) to his countryman Aleksandr Shustov, who cleared 2.33.

As at the end of 2010, eleven men had jumped 2.40 or higher. Only two – Holm and Ukhov – have done so in the first ten years of the 21st century.

POLE VAULT

Bubka is still a mirage

The dissolution of the SU and the consequent emergence of its various republics as independent states obviously had repercussions on the athletics scene. In the family of pole vaulters there was a tendency toward migration. **Dmitri Markov** (born at Vitebsk, Belarus, on 14 March 1975; 1.82 m. / 85 Kg.) emigrated to Australia ad became a citizen of that country in 1999. **Alex Averbukh** (born at Irkutsk, Siberia, on 1 October 1974; 1.78 m. / 76 Kg.) emigrated to Israel and took the citizenship of that country in 1999. Both thus opened new frontiers to said countries, which had practically no traditions in pole vaulting. As we noted in the previous chapter, both the above-mentioned athletes managed to win medals at the 1999 World Championships in Sevilla: silver for Markov and bronze for Averbukh. They did even better two years later in the Worlds at Edmonton, Canada.

The Australian, although hampered by a bad foot, was so clever as to master on second try a height of 6.05, which won gold for him; Averbukh was second with 5.85. Markov's mark in particular is worthy of notice. In such "global" meets this is as often as not a long-drawn event and up to that moment no one had ever been as brilliant as Markov. The great Sergey Bubka, for example, had never done better than 6.01 (1997 Worlds). After his victory, Markov gave three bottles of champagne to the doctors who had treated his injured toe prior to the final.

2001 World Championships, Edmonton – Pole Vault (9 August): 1.Dmitri Markov (Australia) 6.05 (CR); 2.Alex Averbukh (Israel) 5.85; 3.Nick Hysong (USA) 5.85; 4.Michael Stolle (Germany) 5.85; 5.Romain Mesnil (France) 5.85; 6.(tie) Richard Spiegelburg (Germany) and Christian Tamminga (Holland) 5.75; 8.Adam Kolasa (Poland) 5.75; 9.Tim Mack (USA) 5.75; 10.Viktor Chistyakov (Australia) 5.75; 11.Danny Ecker (Germany) 5.65; 12.Martin Eriksson (Sweden) 5.50; No height: Rems Blom (Holland).

Averbukh went on to win the European Ch. title in 2002 with 5.85 and thus gave Israel its first ever "gold" in the annals of that meet. And he was clever enough to win that title once more in 2006.

In the early years of the new century Italy entered the game with a vaulter who proved to be one of the best in the world, which had never happened since the distant days of Renato Dionisi. The man in question was **Giuseppe Gibilisco** (born at Siracusa on 5 January 1979; 1.83 m. / 78 Kg.). He began "to play with a pole" at the tender age of 13, when he did 2.40. His big progress was between 1994 and '95, when he went from 3.80 to 4.80. By 2000 he was pretty close to the best European class with 5.70 and finished tenth at the Sydney Olympics with 5.50, after going over 5.70 in the qualifying round. By then he was advised by Vitaliy Petrov, the man who had coached the great Sergey Bubka. The Ukrainian expert soon discovered that Gibilisco had plenty of talent, even though he was at times hampered by a complex character. 2003 was Gibilisco's best year. At the Golden Gala in Rome he beat the Italian record, first with 5.77 and then with 5.82, finishing second to Roland Mesnil of France (5.92). The Italian had his Day of Days at the World Championships, held in a huge stadium at St.Denis, just outside Paris. He went through a critical moment at 5.75, a height at which he failed twice. True to his complex mentality, he chose to move to 5.80 for his third and last try. For that purpose, however, he used a heavier pole as per Petrov's suggestion. He went over that, then mastered 5.85 and 5.90 always first time to finally nail victory, ahead of Okkert Brits (South Africa), Patrik Kristiansson (Sweden) and Markov (Australia). Just as he had done in Rome, Gibilisco thus bettered the Italian record twice – a truly **rare** happening in such "global" meets.

2003 World Championships, Paris-St.Denis – Pole vault (28 August): 1.Giuseppe Gibilisco (Italy) 5.90; 2.Okkert Brits (South Africa) 5.85; 3.Patrik Kristiansson (Sweden) 5.85; 4.Dmitri Markov (Australia) 5.85; 5.Tim Lobinger (Germany) 5.80; 6.(tie) Denis Yurchenko (Ukraine), Tim Mack (USA) and Derek Miles (USA) 5.70; 9.(tie) Adam Kolasa (Poland) and Vadim Strogalyov (Russia) 5.70; 11.Viktor Chistyakov (Australia) 5.60.

USA, the country which had ruled the roost in this event for many years, was back on top at the 2004 Olympics in Athens. The man who turned the trick for Uncle Sam was a 32-year-old veteran, **Tim Mack** (born at Cleveland on 15 September 1972; 1.88 m. / 78 Kg.). His road to progress was a long one – 5.31 in 1993, 5.60 in '95, 5.70 in '98, 5.81 in 2000. His best year, easily and by far, was 2004. He won the US title with 5.90, then rose to 5.95 in the Olympic event and wound up with 6.01 in a late season meet at Monaco, thus becoming the 11th 6-metre vaulter in history. His team-mate Toby Stevenson, credited with 6 metres even earlier in the season, was a good second with 5.90. World champion Gibilisco of Italy again indulged in his strange game of taking his remaining jump(s) at a higher height after failing at a lower one, but his strategy did not pay this time and he had to be content with 5.85 and third. The man who took fifth with 5.75 was Germany's Danny Ecker, a son of the famous Heide Rosendahl, heroine of the 1972 Olympics.

2004 Olympics, Athens – Pole Vault (27 August): 1.Tim Mack (USA) 5.95 (OR); 2.Toby Stevenson (USA) 5.90; 3.Giuseppe Gibilisco (Italy) 5.85; 4.Igor Pavlov (Russia) 5.80; 5.Danny Ecker (Germany) 5.75; 6.Lars Börgeling (Germany) 5.75; 7.Derek Miles (USA) 5.75; 8.Alex Averbukh (Israel) 5.65; 9.(tie) Rens Blom (Holland) and Denis Yurchenko (Ukraine) 5.65; 11.(tie) Paul Burgess (Australia) and Tim Lobinger (Germany) 5.55; 13.(tie) Pavel Gerasimov (Russia), Daichi Sawano (Japan) and Ruslan Yeremenko (Ukraine) 5.55; 16.Oleksandr Korchmid (Ukraine) 5.55.

In subsequent years the picture in the commanding positions changed time and again and especially in major meets the formbook was often cast to the winds. At the 2005 World Championships in Helsinki, Rens Blom of Holland, the son of a 10.5 sprinter, emerged victorious over better known quantities with 5.80, barely 1 cm. shy of his personal best. He thus became the first Dutch athlete to win a gold medal at the World Championships.

2005 World Championships, Helsinki - Pole Vault (11 August): 1.Rens Blom (Holland) 5.80; 2.Brad Walker (USA) 5.75; 3.Pavel Gerasimov (Russia) 5.65; 4.Igor Pavlov (Russia) 5.65; 5.(tie) Nick Hysong (USA), Tim Lobinger (Germany) and Giuseppe Gibilisco (Italy) 5.50; 8.Daichi Sawano (Japan) 5.50; 9.Partrik Kristiansson (Sweden) 5.50; 10.Kevin Rens (Belgium) 5.35. No height: Dmitri Markov (Australia) and Danny Ecker (Germany).

One of the most consistent performers was Alex Averbukh of Israel, who won his second European title in 2006. Former world champion Giuseppe Gibilisco of Italy never regained his best form. Being no longer in connection with Vitaliy Petrov, he went through troubled years. In 2007 he was inflicted a suspension by FIDAL, the Italian Athletics Federation for "the use or attempted use of a banned substance or of a prohibited practice". However, he had never tested positive and said suspension was finally lifted.

Brad Walker led USA to yet another victory at the 2007 World Championships in Osaka, at the end of a close battle with Romain Mesnil of France. Both cleared 5.86 and the overall standard was higher than ever, with no fewer than 8 men at 5.81 or better.

2007 World Championships, Osaka - Pole Vault (1 September): 1.Brad Walker (USA) 5.86; 2.Romain Mesnil (France) 5.86; 3.Danny Ecker (Germany) 5.81; 4.Igor Pavlov (Russia) 5.81; 5.Björn Otto (Germany) 5.81; 6.Yevgeniy Lukyanenko (Russia) 5.81; 7.Alex Averbukh (Israel) 5.81; 8.Tim Lobinger (Germany) 5.81; 9.Steve Hooker (Australia) 5.76; 10. Fábio da Silva (Brazil) 5.76; 11.Maksym Mazuryk (Ucraine) 5.76; 12.Denys Yurchenko (Ukraine) 5.66.

The Olympic year 2008 produced three new 6-metre men. The most eye-catching subject was an Australian, **Steve Hooker** (born on 16 July 1982 in Melbourne, 1.87 m. / 85 Kg.), the offspring of two excellent athletes. His father Bill was good in the 800 m. (1:45.36) and in the 400 m. hurdles (50.6); his mother

Steve Hooker of Australia (left) and Renaud Lavillenie of France are currently the world's best pole vaulters. Here they congratulate each other after a Golden League meet at Split in 2010, in which they finished first and second in that order. Both aim to succeed the great Sergey Bubka as holders of the world record.

Erica (née Nixon) was prominent in the long jump and the pentathlon. Steve played Australian football before turning to the pole vault. From 5.00 in 1999 he improved steadily and by 2006 he was up to 5.96. He joined the "6-Metre Club" on 27 January 2008 at Perth, clearing a bar set at 6.00 on his third attempt. That select fraternity got two more members later in the season when Brad Walker raised the US record to 6.04 and Yevgeniy Lukyanenko of Russia cleared 6.01.

With such prosperity the Olympic event in Beijing promised to be a thrilling affair. In fact it was more like a comedy of errors, with Walker failing to clear a height in the qualifying round and Hooker making 5.65 only at his third attempt in the final. Lukyanenko was first over 5.80, but the Aussie star proved a great competitor: he had four successive last gap clearances, including one at 5.96 (new Olympic record), which proved decisive for the outcome of the battle. That is a very unusual happening for "global" meets at such stages.

2008 Olympics (Athens) - Pole Vault (22 August): 1.Steve Hooker (Australia) 5.96 (OR); 2. Yevgeniy Lukyanenko (Russia) 5.85; 3.Denis Yurchenko (Ukraine) 5.70; 4.Derek Miles (USA) 5.70; 5.Dmitriy Starodubtsev (Russia) 5.70; 6.Danny Ecker (Germany) 5.70; 7.Jérôme Clavier (France) 5.60; 8. Raphael Holzdeppe (Germany) 5.60; 9.Igor Pavlov (Russia) 5.60; 10.Jan Kudlicka (Czech Rep.) 5.45; 11.Przemyslaw Czerwinski (Poland) 5.45; no height: Giuseppe Gibilisco (Italy) and Leonid Andreyev (Uzbekistan).

"The hardest thing I've done in my life"

Steve Hooker's victory in the 2008 Olympic event must rank as one of the most dramatic ever seen in the history of pole vaulting. In Beijing's huge Bird Nest, truly a peculiar stadium if ever there was one, the Aussie star claimed the title after clearing the last four heights (5.80, 5.85, 5.90 and 5.96) **all on his third and last try!** When it was all over, the Aussie star rightly described his work as "without question the hardest thing I've done in my life, physically and mentally". His work at the victory height (5.96) was in itself dramatic: after one miss he stood around on his second try, incurring a time foul – but he lost little or no time in trying once more, quite successfully.

At the time of writing (2011) Hooker is still considered – along with France's stylish Renaud Lavillenie – as a possible successor of the immortal Sergey Bubka, whose world records (6.14 outdoors and 6.15 indoors) date from the early Nineties of the last century.

Hooker was great during the 2009 indoor season, raising his best to 6.06 in Boston. That was a height exceeded only by Sergey Bubka. On that occasion the Aussie star had three unsuccessful tries at 6.16, i.e. one centimetre over Bubka's best ever (an indoor mark). In his last attempt he cleared the bar with his hips but came down with his chest and arms. Hooker went on by winning the world's outdoor title in Berlin with 5.90 – and did so in difficult circumstances: suffering from an adductor injury, he gambled, just taking one jump in qualifying and not entering the final until 5.85. His physical state was such that he thought it advisable to take only one more jump: he did so at 5.90 and succeeded, finally winning from two Frenchmen, Romain Mesnil and Renaud Lavillenie. The latter, not yet 23, was a fine all-rounder who had mastered 6.01 only a few weeks earlier.

2009 World Championships, Berlin – Pole vault (22 August): 1.Steve Hooker (Australia) 5.90; 2.Romain Mesnil (France) 5.85; 3.Renaud Lavillenie (France) 5.80; 4.Maksim Mazuryk (Ukraine) 5.75; 5.Aleksandr Gripich (Russia) 5.75; 6.Damiel Dossévi (France) 5.75; 7.(tie) Giuseppe Gibilisco (Italy), Steven Lewis (GB) and Alexander Straub (Germany) 5.65; 10.(tie) Viktor Chistyakov (Russia) and Daichi Sawano (Japan) 5.50; 12.(tie) Alhaji Jeng (Sweden) and Kevin Rans (Belgium) 5.50; 14.Malte Mohr (Germany) 5.50; No height: Derek Miles (USA).

In 2010 Hooker got started in a most promising way: in the World Indoor Championships, held at Doha, he won with 6.01 and had at least one decent try at 6.16. Later in the season, being at times in far-from-perfect physical conditions, he had ups and down and on the whole he was less consistent than Lavillenie, who won the French national title with 5.94 and the European one with 5.85.

As at the end of 2010 seventeen men had joined the "6-metre-Club". Sergey Bubka, by now Senior Vice President of the IAAF, still towers above them all with his world records from the Nineties. Hooker is second with 6.06 (indoors).

LONG JUMP

Phillips, the most consistent

Ivan Pedroso of Cuba added to his impressive list of honours by winning his event at the 2001 World Championships in Edmonton. He defeated Savante Stringfellow of USA, 8.40 to 8.24. The ace from La Habana, by then 29, could thus point to an impressive list of "global" titles: 4 World and 1 Olympic. It should be added that unlike several other long jumpers he loved indoor competition too. He won the world indoor title five times in a row (1993-2001).

2001 World Championships (Edmonton) – Long Jump (11 August): 1.Ivan Pedroso (Cuba) 8.40 (+1.2 m/s); 2.Savante Stringfellow (USA) 8.24 (+1.6 m/s); 3.Carlos Calado (Portugal) 8.21 (+1.1 m/s); 4.Miguel Pate (USA) 8.21w (+2.7 m/s); 5.Kareem Streete-Thompson (Cayman Islands) 8.10 (+0.7 m/s); 6.Oleksey Lukashevich (Ukraine) 8.10 (+0.8 m/s); 7.James Beckford (Jamaica) 8.08 (-0.4 m/s); 8.Dwight Phillips (USA) 7.92 (+0.8 m/s); 9.Grzegorz Marciniszyn (Poland) 7.92 (+1.4 m/s); 10.Hussein Al-Sabee (Saudi Arabia) 7.90 (0.0 m/s); 11.Abdurahman Al-Nubi (Qatar) 7.63 (+0.7 m/s); 12.Vitaliy Shkurlatov (Russia) 7.61 (+0.9 m/s).

In the wake of Pedroso there followed another superb competitor – **Dwight Phillips** of USA (born at Decatur, Georgia, on 1 October 1977; 1.81 m. / 82 kg.), who in the course of three years (2003, '04 and '05) managed to win 34 of his 42 competitions. He reached world class in 2000 (8.21 plus a wind-aided 8.30) and won his first "global" title three years later in Paris-St.Denis after a close battle with James Beckford of Jamaica, 8.32 to 8.28. The American had a wide range as he could point to personal bests like 10.14 (100 m.), 46.80 (400 m.) and 16.41 (triple jump).

2003 World Championships, Paris-St.Denis – Long Jump (29 August): 1.Dwight Phillips (USA) 8.32 (+0.5 m/s); 2.James Beckford (Jamaica) 8.28 (+0.1 m/s); 3.Yago Lamela (Spain) 8.22 (+0.5 m/s); 4.Ignisious Gaisah (Ghana) 8.13 (0.0 m/s); 5.Hussein Al-Sabee (Saudi Arabia) 8.10 (0.0 m/s); 6.Vladimir Zyuskov (Ukraine) 8.08 (-0.2 m/s); 7.Walter Davis (USA) 8.02 (+0.4 m/s); 8.Osbourne Moxey (Bahamas) 7.93 (+0.5 m/s); 9.Chris Tomlinson (GB) 7.93 (+0.6 m/s); 10. Bogdan Tarus (Rumania) 7.84 (+0.4 m/s); 11.Luis Felipe Méliz (Cuba) 7.73 (+0.8 m/s); 12. Loúis Tsátoumas (Greece) 7.72 (+0.1 m/s).

Phillips went to Athens for the 2004 Olympics with a new personal best of 8.60 and hit gold with his very first try (8.59). His countryman John Moffitt won silver with a new personal best of 8.47. Third went to Joan Lino Martinez, a Cuba-born Spaniard, whose best jump (8.32) should have been ruled a foul according to some observers as TV replays showed clearly that his toe was over the board. There was no mark in the plasticine though and that would justify the ruling. Even so, he got no.4 in "Track & Field News" World Ranking at the end of the year.

Dwight Phillips (USA), the most consistent long jumper of the last decade.

2004 Olympics, Athens – Long Jump (26 August): 1.Dwight Phillips (USA) 8.59 (+1.0 m/s); 2. John Moffitt (USA) 8.47 (+0.9 m/s); 3.Joan Lino Martinez (Spain) 8.32 (+1.3 m/s); 4.James Beckford (Jamaica) 8.31 (+0.8 m/s); 5.Chris Tomlinson (GB) 8.25 (+1.6 m/s); 6.Ignisious Gaisah (Ghana) 8.24 (+0.8 m/s); 7.Ivan Pedroso (Cuba) 8.23 (+0.7 m/s); 8. Bogdan Tarus (Rumania) 8.21 (+0.7 m/s); 9.Vitaliy Shkurlatov (Russia) 8.04 (+1.3 m/s); 10.Jonathan Chimier (Mauritius) 8.03 (+1.4 m/s); 11.Yago Lamela (Spain) 7.98 (+1.0 m/s); 12.Salim Sdiri (France) 7.94 (+0.9 m/s).

In 2005 Phillips won his third "global" title in just as many years. As per his trademark, the American won the Helsinki event with a "killer" of 8.60 in the first trial of the final. No one managed to come close to that, yet Ignisious Gaisah of Ghana produced a personal best of 8.34 to nail second place.

2005 World Championships, Helsinki – Long Jump (13 August): 1.Dwight Phillips (USA) 8.60 (+1.6 m/s); 2.Ignisious Gaisah (Ghana) 8.34 (+0.2 m/s): 3.Tommi Evilä (Finland) 8.25w (+2.9 m/s); 4.Joan Lino Martinez (Spain) 8.24w (+2.9 m/s); 5.Salim Sdiri (France) 8.21w (+2.4 m/s); 6.Irving Saladino (Panama) 8.20w (+2.8 m/s); 7.Khotso Mokoena (South Africa) 8.11w (+2.6 m/s); 8.Volodomyr Zyuskov (Ukraine) 8.06w (+2.3 m/s); 9.James Beckford (Jamaica) 8.02 (+0.1 m/s); 10.Vitaliy Shkurlatov (Russia) 7.88 (+1.4 m/s); 11.Issam Nima (Algeria) 7.73 (+0.6 m/s); 12.Nils Winter (Germany) 7.72 w (+3.2 m/s).

Italy had by then a promising prospect in **Andrew Howe** (born on 12 May 1985 in Los Angeles; 1.84 m. / 73 Kg.). The son of American parents, he migrated to Italy at the tender age of 5 when his mother, physiotherapist Renée Felton, a good hurdler, married again, this time with an Italian, Ugo Besozzi. The boy grew in the Rieti area, a favourable one for Italian athletics lovers. Andrew revealed great talent early. As a long jumper he did 5.88 at age 13, 7.52 at 15. As a

Irving Saladino, winner of the long jump at the 2007 "Worlds" – on his last attempt. He put Panama on the map of athletics half a century after the heydays of sprinter Lloyd LaBeach.

sprinter he ran the 200 m. in 20.99 at 16. He made a sensational debut in the international competition: at the 2004 World Junior Championships at Grosseto, Italy, he won the long jump with 8.11 and the 200 m. in 20.28. Two years later, at 21, he won the European title with 8.20. In 2007 he long jumped 8.41, then went to Osaka for the World Championships, where he improved to 8.47, a new Italian record, on his very last trial. He thus took the lead, but only for a few minutes as experienced **Irving Saladino** of Panama closed with 8.57, a new South American record. The latter (born at Ciudad de Colón on 23 January 1983; 1.83 m. / 70 Kg.) was less precocious than his Italian rival but later went farther. From 7.51 at 20 he improved steadily and dominated the picture in 2006/07.

2007 World Championships, Osaka – Long Jump (30 August): 1.Irving Saladino (Panama) 8.57 (0.0 m/s); 2.Andrew Howe (Italy) 8.47 (-0.2 m/s); 3.Dwight Phillips (USA) 8.30 (+0.4 m/s); 4.Oleksiy Lukashevych (Ukraine) 8.25 (+0.2 m/s); 5.Khotso Mokoena (South Africa) 8.19 (-0.1 m/s); 6.James Beckford (Jamaica) 8.17 (+0.1 m/s); 7.Ndiss Kaba Badji (Senegal) 8.01 (+0.1 m/s); 8.Ahmad Fayez Marzouk (Saudi Arabia) 7.98 (0.0 m/s); 9.Christian Reif (Germany) 7.95 (-0.4 m/s); 10.Miguel Pate (USA) 7.94 (-0.6 m/s); 11.Hussein Al-Sabee (Saudi Arabia) 7.84 (+0.4 m/s). No valid jump: Trevell Quinley (USA).

In 2008 Irving Saladino went to the Beijing Olympics – the first ever held in China – as an odds-on favourite. He became the first Panamanian Olympic champion by winning rather comfortably with 8.34. His most serious rivals, Phillips and Howe, had off seasons on account of physical disorders. For the first time in the long history of the Games no American made the long jump final.

2008 Olympic Games, Beijing – Long Jump (18 August): 1.Irving Saladino (Panama) 8.34 (-0.3 m/s); 2.Khotso Mokoena (South Africa) 8.24 (0.0 m/s); 3.Ibrahin Camejo (Cuba) 8.20 (+0.2 m/s); 4. Ngonidzashe Makusha (Zimbabwe) 8.19 (+0.6 m/s); 5.Wilfredo Martinez (Cuba) 8.19 (-0.4 m/s); 6.Ndiss Kaba Badji (Senegal) 8.16 (+0.2 m/s); 7.Luis Felipe Méliz (Spain) 8.07 (-0.1 m/s); 8.Roman Novotny (Czech Rep.) 8.00 (-0.3 m/s); 9.Gabie Garenamotse (Botswana) 7.85 (+0.1 m/s); 10.Greg Rutherford (GB) 7.84 (-0.4 m/s); 11.Hussein Al-Sabee (Saudi Arabia) 7.80 (0.0 m/s). No valid jump: Louis Tsátoumas (Greece).

A major surprise occurred at the 2009 European Indoor Championships, held in Turin, Italy. Sebastian Bayer of Germany went into the meet with a personal best of 8.17. He began by improving to 8.29, then had four fouls and finally exploded with a surprising .... 8.71, a new European indoor record. He himself could hardly believe it, yet our friend Alain Bouillé, who can point to a good career as a judge, told me that Bayer took off with 6.2 cm. to spare on that wondrous leap. When the year was over Bayer could point to a second best of 8.49.

In 2009 Phillips had a near perfect season, with a top mark of 8.74 in the Prefontaine Classic at Eugene on 7 June – a new personal best and at the time of writing the best mark made so far in the new century. Phillips regained the world title he had won in 2003 and 2005. In the final he began with 8.40 and increased to 8.54 in the second round. That sufficed to stay ahead of the rest till the end. Khotso Mokoena of South Africa took second, exactly as in the 2008 Olympics. Defending champion Saladino had three fouls early in the final and was therefore eliminated. Andrew Howe, physically not at his best, failed to qualify and had to undergo Achilles surgery in September.

"Per aspera ad astra"

Dwight Phillips, the most consistent long jumper of recent years, really came from nowhere, so to say. Relatively few observers apparently know that at age 14 both his legs were broken in a motorcycle accident. As he himself related: "My brother's friend hit me while I was in the street playing football with other boys. I did not know where he was coming from and I moved in the wrong direction to try to get out of the way". Dwight's legs were left twisted, requiring eight months of rehabilitation and using a walker after the casts were removed.

Even so, he managed to resurge .... as a long jumper. Just before turning 19 he managed to jump 7.14.In 1999 he joined the 8-metre class. At the time of writing he can claim four "global" titles: one in the Olympics, three at the Worlds. At 8.74 (2009) he ranks seventh in the All Time World List. His most glorious moments coincided with his victory at the 2009 World Championships in Berlin – the town where his famous countryman Jesse Owens made history at the 1936 Olympics. He joined his predecessor in a special Hall of Fame as winner of the event at the two major long jump competitions ever held at the Berlin Olympic Stadium. Phillips received his gold medal from Jesse Owens' granddaughter Marlene Dortch. The granddaughter of Luz Long, the German who finished second to Owens in 1936, awarded the silver medal to Khotso Mokoena of South Africa, second to Phillips in the 2009 competition.

2009 World Championships, Berlin – Long Jump (22 August): 1.Dwight Phillips (USA) 8.54 (+0.1 m/s); 2.Khotso Mokoena (South Africa) 8.47 (+0.1 m/s); 3.Mitchell Watt (Australia) 8.37 (-0.4 m/s); 4.Fabrice Lapierre (Australia) 8.21 (-0.2 m/s); 5.Greg Rutherford (GB) 8.17 (+0.7 m/s); 6.Salim Sdiri (France) 8.07 (+0.2 m/s); 7.Gable Garenamotse (Botswana) 8.06 (-0.2 m/s); 8.Chris Tomlinson (GB) 8.06 (-0.2 m/s); 9.Brian Johnson (USA) 7.86 (+0.1 m/s); 10.Yahya Berrabah (Morocco) 7.83 (+0.4 m/s); Louis Tsátoumas (Greece) 7.59 (+0.4 m/s). No valid jump: Irving Saladino (Panama).

Phillips was no.1 again in 2010, winning most if not all his main competitions. At 33 he can point to one of the longest high-class careers in the annals of the event.

Andrew Howe has been constantly hampered by injuries in recent years. He now feels more at ease in sprinting than in jumping. In 2010 he chose to return to the 200 metres and clocked 20.30, third best by a European for that season.

TRIPLE JUMP

The "unbreakable" Olsson

World record holder Jonathan Edwards added one more jewel to his splendid career when he won the triple jump at the 2001 World Championships in Edmonton, Canada. He did so with an excellent 17.92, which as at the end of 2010 is still the second best mark made in the new century. Second to him on that occasion was **Christian Olsson** of Sweden (born at Göteborg on 25 January 1980; 1.92 m. / 74 Kg.), with 17.47. For several years to come the Swede proved an excellent competitor, although hampered by injuries from 2005 onwards. In 2001, his first year in the high ranks, he beat Edwards twice in a sequence of 7 clashes.

2001 World Championships, Edmonton, Canada – Triple Jump (6 August): 1.Jonathan Edwards (GB) 17.92 (+0.7 m/s); 2.Christian Olsson (Sweden) 17.47 (+1.2 m/s); 3.Igor Spasovkhodskiy (Russia) 17.44 (+0.9 m/s); 4.Yoel Garcia (Cuba) 17.40 (+1.2 m/s); 5.Walter Davis (USA) 17.20 (+0.3 m/s); 6.Brian Wellman (Bermuda) 16.81 (-1.3 m/s); 7.Larry Achike (GB) 16.79 (+0.8 m/s); 8.Rozstislav Dimitrov (Bulgaria) 16.72w (+2.4 m/s); 9.Phillips Idowu (GB) 16.60 (+0.3 m/s); 10.Johan Meriluoto (Finland) 16.54 (+1.1 m/s); 11.Paolo Camossi (Italy) 16.18 (-1.7 m/s); 12.Konstantinos Zalagitis (Greece) 16.13 (+1.6 m/s).

In 2002 Edwards and Olsson had nine head-to-head confrontations. The world record holder again emerged the victor, but only by a narrow margin (5 to

4). And Olsson won the European Championship title with 17.53, while the Briton – 14 years his elder ! – had to be content with third. 2003 marked the real turning point in this great rivalry. Edwards was by then spending more time as a BBC television commentator than on athletics training. Even so the British lion continued to perform most honourably. Early in the season, at Gateshead, he and Olsson had a close battle, from which the Swede emerged victorious – 17.92w to 17.61. Then Edwards was bogged down by an injury and in the World Championships at Paris-St.Denis he had to be content with 12th place. The Swede won with 17.72, leaving runner-up Yoandri Betanzos of Cuba almost half a metre behind ! That was for Edwards the end of a fabulous career.

2003 World Championships, Paris-St.Denis – Triple Jump (25 August): 1.Christian Olsson (Sweden) 17.72 (-0.3 m/s); 2.Yoandri Betanzos (Cuba) 17.28 (+0.2 m/s); 3.Leevan Sands (Bahamas) 17.26 (-0.4 m/s); 4.David Giralt (Cuba) 17.23 (+0.1 m/s); 5.Jadel Gregório (Brazil) 17.11 (+0.2 m/s); 6.Kenta Bell (USA) 17.08 (0.0 m/s); 7.Hristos Melétoglou (Greece) 16.92 (+1.2 m/s); 8.Andrew Owusu (Ghana) 16.86 (0.0 m/s); 9.Yoelbi Quesada (Cuba) 16.84 (-0.1 m/s); 10.Ivaylo Rusenov (Bulgaria) 16.66 (+0-1 m/s); 11.Aleksandr Glavatskiy (Bulgaria) 16.40 (-0.3 m/s); 12. Jonathan Edwards (GB) 16.31 (+0.3 m/s).

Christian Olsson (Sweden), a good collector of gold medals in the triple jump in the early years of the 21st century.

In 2004 Olsson had a near perfect season: He began by taking the World Indoor title with 17.83, his lifetime best. Outdoors he won 12 of his 13 competitions, including the Olympic final at Athens (17.79). Then serious injuries put him out of the game in 2005: he had four operations in nine months! Triple jumpers seem to be particularly exposed to the Moloch of injuries.

2004 Olympics, Athens – Triple Jump (22 August): 1.Christian Olsson (Sweden) 17.79 (+1.4 m/s); 2.Marian Oprea (Rumania) 17.55 (+0.7 m/s); 3.Danila Burkenya (Russia) 17.48 (+0.4 m/s); 4.Yoandri Betanzos (Cuba) 17.47 (+0.4 m/s); 5.Jadel Gregório (Brazil) 17.31 (0.0 m/s); 6.Hristos Melétoglou (Greece) 17.13 (+0.6 m/s); 7.Viktor Gushchinskiy (Russia) 17.11 (+0.7 m/s); 8.Yoelbi Quesada (Cuba) 16.96 (+0.9 m/s); 9.Kenta Bell (USA) 16.90 (+0.7 m/s); 10.Julian Kapek (France) 16.81 (+0.1 m/s); 11.Walter Davis (USA) 16.78 (+0.9 m/s). No valid mark: Phillips Idowu (GB).

With Olsson not in the game, the gold medal at the 2005 World Championships went to an American, Walter Davis, a former basketball player. Marian Oprea of Rumania, who had done 17.81 earlier in the season, had to be content with third.

2005 World Championships, Helsinki – Triple Jump (11 August): 1.Walter Davis (USA) 17.57 (+0.3 m/s); 2.Yoandri Betanzos (Cuba 17.42 (+0.4 m/s); 3.Marian Oprea (Rumania) 17.40 (+2.0 m/s); 4.Leevan Sands (Bahamas) 17.39w (+2.3 m/s); 5.Karl Taillepierre (France) 17.27 (+2.0 m/s); 6. Jadel Gregório (Brazil) 17.20 (0.0 m/s); 7.Kenta Bell USA) 17.11 (+2.0 m/s); 8.David Giralt (Cuba) 17.09 (+0.7 m/s); 9.Viktor Yastrebov (Ukraine) 16.90w (+2.3 m/s); 10.Dmitrij Valukevic (Slovakia) 16.79w (+2.8 m/s); 11.Momchil Karailev (Bulgaria) 16.70w (+2.2 m/s); 12.Anders Moller (Denmark) 16.16w (+2.7 m/s).

The irrepressible Olsson was back in harness in 2006. He won his second European title at Göteborg, leaving runner-up Nathan Douglas (GB) almost half a metre behind (17.67 to 17.21). Olsson was as good as usual even in the first part of the 2007 season, when he defeated his strongest rival, Nelson Evora of Portugal, three times in a row. But a hamstring injury put him down again at the most crucial stage of the year, just before the World Championships at Osaka. In his absence, Evora produced a new personal best of 17.74 and became Portugal's first male world champion. Actually born in Côte d'Ivoire, Evora had come to Portugal at 18. He was actually a great all-arounder, with 2.07 in the high jump and 8.10 in the long jump. Second at Osaka was Jadel Gregório, a giant (2.02 m. / 102 kg.) from Brazil, who earlier in the season had jumped 17.90, succeeding the great João Carlos de Oliveira as South American record holder.

2007 World Champioships, Osaka - Triple Jump (27 August): 1.Nelson Evora (Portugal) 17.74 (+1.4 m/s); 2.Jadel Gregório (Brazil) 17.59 (+0.3 m/s); 3.Walter Davis (USA) 17.33 (+1.0 m/s); 4.Osniel Tosca (Cuba) 17.32 (+1.1 m/s); 5.Aarik Wilson (USA) 17.31 (+0.6 m/s); 6.Phillips Idowu (GB) 17.09 (-0.9 m/s); 7.David Giralt (Cuba) 16.91 (+0.7 m/s); 8.Alexander Martinez (Switzerland) 16.85 (+1.3 m/s); 9.Kim Deok-hyeon (South Korea) 16.71 (+1.1 m/s);10.Aleksandr Petrenko (Russia) 16.66 (+0.8 m/s); 11.Zhong Minwei (China) 16.66 (+1.5 m /s); 12.Dimitrios Tsiámis (Greece) 16.59 (-1.1 m /s).

Christian Olsson competed only once in 2008 (17.00) and had to stay away from the circus of major competitions in general and the Beijing Olympics in particular. Reigning world champion Nelson Evora had another excellent season and had Phillips Idowu, a 30-year-old Briton, as his main rival. The latter opened his 2008 account on an excellent note, winning the world's indoor title with a new personal best of 17.75. Evora managed to reverse positions at Beijing though, beating his British rival in a pretty close contest, 17.67 to 17.62. Both these marks were actually worth more: measured from take-off, 17.80 and 17.71 respectively.

2008 Olympics, Beijing - Triple Jump (21 August): 1.Nelson Evora (Porrtugal) 17.67 (+1.1 m/s); 2.Phillips Idowu (GB) 17.62 (+0.9 m/s); 3.Leevan Sands (Bahamas) 17.59 (+0.9 m/s); 4.David Giralt (Cuba) 17.52 (+0.2 m/s); 5.Marian Oprea (Rumania) 17.22 (-0.2 m/s); 6.Jadel Gregório (Brazil) 17.20 (+0.2 m/s); 7.Larry Adkins (GB) 17.17 (-0.2 m/s); 8.Viktor Kuznyetsov (Ukraine) 16.87 (-0.3 m/s); 9.Igor Spasovkhodskiy (Russia) 16.79 (-0.6 m/s); 10.Li Yanxi (China) 16.77 (+1.2 m/s); 11.Momchil Karailiev (Bulgaria) 16.48 (-0.2 m/s); 12.Héctor Fuentes (Cuba) 16.28 (-0.6 m/s).

Teddy Tamgho (France), best of the rising stars in triple jump circles.

The Evora vs Idowu feud continued in 2009, in inverted roles that is true. At the World Championships in Berlin the Briton reached 17.73, his outdoor best, in round 3 – after barely touching the take-off board (which is 20 cms. long). Evora had to be content with 17.55 and second.

2009 World Championships, Berlin - Triple Jump (18 August): 1.Phillips Idowu (GB) 17.73 (0.0 m/s); 2. Nelson Evora (Portugal) 17.55 (+0.1 m/s); 3.Alexis Copello (Cuba) 17.36 (-0.1 m/s); 4.Leevan Sands (Bahamas) 17.32 (-0.5 m/s); 5.David Giralt (Cuba) 17.26 (0.0 m/s); 6.Li Yanxi (China) 17.23 (+1.1 m/s); 7.Igor Spasovkhodskiy (Russia) 16.91 (-0.3 m/s); 8.Jadel Gregório (Brazil) 16.89 (-0.1 m/s); 9.Momchil Karailiev (Bulgaria) 16.82 (+0.3 m/s); 10.Nathan Douglas (GB) 16.79 (-0.1 m /s); 11.Teddy

Tamgho (France) 16.79 (-0.6 m/s); 12.Dmitrij Valukevich (Slovakia) 16.54 (+0.3 m/s).

Back in 11th place in the Berlin meet was a young man who could emerge as the star of the near future. He is **Teddy Tamgho** of France (born in Paris on 15 June 1989; 1.86 m. / 76 Kg.). As a junior he improved from 16.35 in 2007 to 17.19 in 2008. At 20 he was up to 17.58 (indoors). His real breakthrough was in 2010. He first made the headlines at the World Indoor Championships at Doha, Qatar, when he beat a good Cuban duo (Betanzos and Giralt) and a resurging Olsson with a fine 17.90, a new world indoor record. He did even better outdoors: at New York on 12 June he reached 17.98, moving to no.3 in the World All Time List, behind Jonathan Edwards and Kenny Harrison. He did not have a flawless season's record though: in particular he did no better than 17.45 and third at the European Championships, finishing behind Idowu (17.81) and Marian Oprea of Rumania (17.51). Even so, several experts – notably including Jonathan Edwards himself – see him as a possible threat to the world record.

At the end of 2010 the World All Time List notably showed no fewer than 7 Cubans among the top 50. Only Russia and USA (both 8) have more.

A guessing game

Many things have changed in the world of track and field throughout the first decade of the new century. On the morning of an Adidas Grand Prix meeting to be held in New York in June of 2010, a poll appeared on the IAAF website asking if Jonathan Edwards' triple jump world record (18.29 in 1995) would stand to celebrate its 15th anniversary on August 7 of that year – a guessing game the IAAF of yesteryear would have never thought of. That looked like a bold question, yet in the meet concerned Teddy Tamgho of France reached 17.98, a new French record and the world's longest leap in nearly 12 years. Tamgho has since been regarded as a possible successor of the great Briton, who as a TV commentator has been praising the Frenchman's qualities in no restrictive terms. Curiously enough, neither Edwards nor his successor "in fieri" have ever done superlative things as broad jumpers – Tamgho has a p.b. of 7.72, while Edwards had a legitimate best of 7.41.

MEN: 2011

This is being written on 26 June, when the outdoor season in Europe is still in its initial phase. Earlier in the year, some classy marks were registered in the European Indoor Championships held at Paris-Bercy in mid-March. In the triple jump, Terry Tamgho of France set a new world indoor record of 17.92 and won from an Italian veteran, Fabrizio Donato, who raised his all-time best to 17.73. In the same meet Ivan Ukhov (Russia) won the high jump with 2.38 and Renaud Lavillenie (France) took the pole vault with 6.03, moving to equal sixth in the World All-Time List.

Outdoors, an interesting 8.44 in the long jump was credited to Mitchell Watt of Australia, 23. In USA, Christian Taylor reached 17.80 in the triple jump, aided by an excessive wind.

WOMEN 1895-1940

8

Jumping ways: the Vassar pioneers

Women's athletics was relegated to a back seat in the games of ancient Greece. Contrary to what is thought by a majority of non-believers, however, there was a quadrennial festival for women too, celebrated at Olympia and named after Hera, the "goddess of matrimony". The long jump formed part of the pentathlon but is also mentioned by some historians as an independent event, held at Eleusis, which was, however, a long way from the main centres of athletic activity.

In modern times the honour to have introduced women in the world of athletics is commonly attributed to Vassar College, a private school (then for women only) which was located at Poughkeepsie in the state of New York and was founded by Matthew Vassar. The first "Field Day" for women was held there on 9 November 1895, when a group of "nimble, supple and vivacious girls" engaged in 11 different battles. There were three jumping events on the programme. The high jump went to Laura Brownell, who beat Emma Baker – 1.22 to 1.17. The latter won the running long jump with 3.48. There was also a standing long jump on the programme and the winner was Camille Sabie with 2.485. Most of the athletes appeared in more than one event. There was also a "fence vault", which historian Dave Carey describes as follows: "It appears to be like the high jump, except that the bar is rigidly in place. In fact it looked like several boards, one above the other, held firmly in place on their sides. The women could rest their hands on it for support as they vaulted over". Obviously, this was not the pole vault as we know it today. As for the triple jump, historians trace its origin to 1899, when such an event, held indoors, appeared in another US school, at Bryn Mawr, and was won by Mary Ayer with 6.72.

The revivers of the modern Olympics did not have progressive views on the subject of women participating in sporting events, Pierre de Coubertin himself being no exception. Yet, in addition to USA, other English speaking countries such as Great Britain, Australia, New Zealand and South Africa held women's meets in the first decade of the XX century. However, the real boost came from France, more exactly from a fervent "suffragette" named Alice Milliat, who in 1917 founded the "Fédération Féminine Sportive de France". Two years later, her request to have women's events included in the Olympic programme was refused by the IOC. The tenacious French pioneer and her associates went ahead by themselves and decided to organize the first multi-national women's meet. This was held in the Principauté de Monaco from 24 to 31 March 1921 and was essentially an Anglo-French festival. There were two jumping events on the programme. The high jump went to Hilda Hatt with 1.40 and the long jump to Mary Lines with 4.70 – both from Great Britain. **Mary Lines** (born on 3 December 1893; 1.65 m. / 60 Kg.) was reportedly in her first year of competition, yet she really had the lion's share as she also won the 60 m. (8 1/5), the 150 m. (36 3/5) and anchored two victorious British relay teams. Just for good measure, she also placed second in the 800 m. !

Later in 1921 Madame Milliat and her associates founded the "Fédération Sportive Féminine Internationale" (FSFI). Six countries were represented : France, Great Britain, Czechoslovakia, Italy, Spain and USA. Madame Milliat was elected President of the newly born organisation, which held its inaugural Women's World Games at Stade Pershing, Paris, on 20 August 1922. The whole programme, 11 events partly with preliminary rounds, was completed in one day and the meet was witnessed by 20.000 spectators !

The FSFI held on and organized three more editions of the World Games: Göteborg (1926), Prague (1930) and London (1934), by which time the number of countries involved was up to nineteen and the programme included 12 events. In the meantime, however, the ostracism of the powers that be of men's sport had come to a predictable and just end: in 1926 the

CIO finally took notice of the serious purposes that animated M.me Milliat and her associates and voted (12 to 5) to include women's events in the Olympics. The occasion for this historic event were the Games of 1928 in Amsterdam. The women's programme was very thin though, including only five events, one of these being the high jump. It must be said that this début was saluted with mixed feelings by the press in general, then a virtual monopoly of the male sex. There were witty remarks too, e.g. by a Swedish paper which carried a picture showing a woman athlete in training, with the caption:

"Eva tränar för A'dam" (i.e. Eve training for A'dam, an obvious contraction for Amsterdam).

Delving into sport papers of the Twenties, one is confronted with the scarcity of reports on women's meets. Even the German weekly "Der Leichtathlet", believed to be the best magazine of those days in our sport, had only a relatively short coverage of the FSFI World Games.

At this stage, however, we deem it advisable to proceed with an event-by-event survey.

HIGH JUMP

"The Saskatoon Lily"

In the high jump the first mark officially recognized by the FSFI as a world record was a 1.46 (actually 1.463) effort by Nancy Vorhees of USA, made at Simsbury, Connecticut on 20 May 1922. A few months later, the American did 1.45 in the inaugural World Games in Paris, yet she had to be content with a tie for first with Hilda Hatt of Great Britain.

High jumping at Vassar College late in the 19th century.

1922 World Games, Paris - High Jump (20 August): 1. (tie) Hilda Hatt (GB) and Nancy Vorhees (UA) 1.45; 3.Ivy Lowman (GB) 1.42; 4.Cécile Gerner (France) 1.40; 5.Mado Bracquemond (France) 1.40; 6.Lida Havlickova (Czechoslovakia) 1.38.

We must add, however, that Waltraude Schmidt of Germany had an unratified 1.50, made at Dresden on 17 July 1921.

The first official mark over 1.50 was credited to Phyllis Green of Great Britain: 1.524 (5 feet) in the English AAA Championships, held in London on 11 July 1925. Hilda Hatt was second with 1.485.

1926 was a momentous season in the women's high jump and the record was bettered time and again. In the second edition of the World Games, held at Göteborg, Sweden, victory went to Hélène Bons of France with 1.50, made in a jump-off, after she and Hilda Hatt had done 1.45 in the regular competition. But the find of the year was **Ethel Catherwood** of Canada (born in Ontario on 2 May 1910; 1.78 m. / 58 Kg.). At the tender age of 16 she made the FSFI record, jumping 1.585 at Regina on 6 September. This was in a "mixed competition" and young Ethel did in fact win from Beren Lawson, Saskatchevan Men's champion !

1926 World Games, Göteborg – High Jump (27 August): 1.Hélène Bons (France) 1.45 (won with 1.50 in jump-off); 2.Hilda Hatt (GB) 1.45; 3.Inga Broman (Sweden) 1.45; 4.(tie) Ana Margret Ahlmstrand (Sweden) and Evelyne Cloupet (France) 1.40; 6.(tie) Barbara Holliday (GB) and Jolan Jaborovizowna (Poland) 1.40.

Catherwood had joined the athletic world thanks to Teddy Oke, an unusual mining millionaire. Along with a job in his brokerage offices, she had access to a club of girl athletes and got a coach, Walter Knox. In 1928 she went to Amsterdam to participate in the Olympic Games as a clear favourite. Her most serious rival was supposed to be Marjorie Clark, a 19-year-old South African who went over a bar set at 1.60 in an exhibition held at Stamford Bridge, London on 23 June. Mind you, Catherwood was credited with exactly the same height in a regular competition, in the Canadian Championships at Halifax on 2 July. Also to be considered was Carolina Gisolf of Holland, who did 1.58

at Bruxelles on 23 July. In the Olympic Games at Amsterdam she would have the advantage of competing on home ground. Yet Catherwood lived up to the expectations of her many fans. In the final she took 7 jumps, and cleared 1.51, 1.54, 1.56, 1.58 always first time. By then she was the only competitor still "alive", since Gisolf could do no better than 1.56. The Canadian then tried 1.60 – and made it on her last attempt. Later re-measured as 1.595, her mark was ratified as such by the FSFI.

Canadian sport writers were by then going into rhapsodies in extolling the virtues of their 18-year-old marvel. One went like this:

"From the instant this tall, slim, graceful girl from the prairies tossed aside her long, flowing cloak of purple and made her first leap, the fans fell for her. A flower-like face of rare beauty above a long, slim body simply clad in pure white, she looked like a tall, strange lily – and was immediately christened by the crowd "The Saskatoon Lily". Such beautiful words notwithstanding, not all Canadians felt this way. At a meeting of Olympic officials in Amsterdam an appeal led by several Canadian men had been forwarded to eliminate women's sport from future Games, mainly on the grounds that "strenuous sport was physiologically and psychologically unsuitable for women". Fortunately, Ethel Catherwood and quite a few others were valid refutations of such arguments.

The high jump happened to be one of the (only) five events included in the women's programme of the 1928 Olympics in Amsterdam.

1928 Olympics, Amsterdam – High Jump (5 August): 1.Ethel Catherwood (Canada) 1.59 (OR); 2.Carolina Gisolf (Holland) 1.56; 3.Mildred Wiley (USA) 1.56; 4.Jean Shiley (USA) 1.48; 5.Helma Notte (Germany) 1.48; 6.Marjorie Clark (South Africa) 1.48; 7.Inge Braumüller (Germany) 1.48; 8.Catherine Maguire (USA) 1.48; 9.Marion Holley (USA) 1.48; 10.Louise Stevens (Belgium) 1.48.

In 1929 Catherwood moved to USA, after which her career strangely came to a premature end. Her successor as a world record holder was Carolina Gisolf, who cleared 1.605 at Maastricht in 1929. But the Dutch woman had to be content with silver again in the third edition of the FSFI World Games, held at Prague in 1930. She lost to Inge Braumüller of Germany on the fewer misses account, after both had cleared 1.57.

1930 World Games, Prague – High Jump (7 September): 1.Inge Braumüller (Germany) 1.57; 2.Carolina Gisolf (Holland) 1.57; 3.Helma Notte (Germany) 1.53; 4.Marjorie Okell (GB) 1.50; 5.Mary Milne (GB) 1.50; 6.Jelka Tratnic (Yugoslavia) 1.45; 7.Lucienne Laudre (France) 1.40; 8.(tie) Hélène Verdie (France), Elise van Truyen (Belgium) and Anna Kael (Hungary) 1.40; 11.(tie) Chiyo Hamasaki (Japan), Katalin Vertessy (Hungary), Wilma Lebet (Austria), Votavova (Czechoslovakia) and Marie Ulrichova (Czechoslovakia) 1.35.

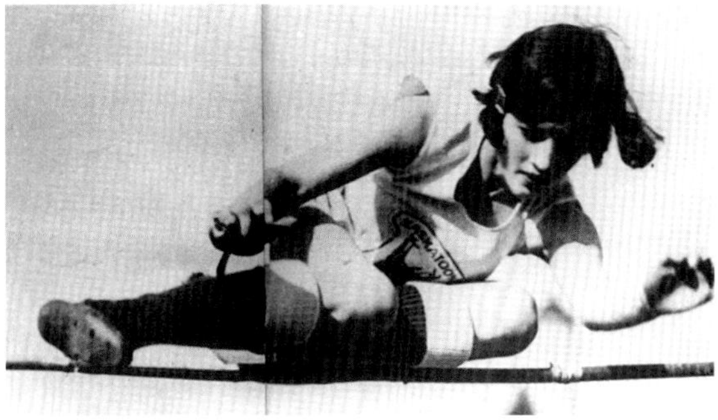

Ethel Catherwood (Canada), know as "the Saskatoon Lily", became an Olympic high jump champion at 18 years of age.

Resistance to the expansion of women's events was still extant though. In the Olympic Games of 1932, held in Los Angeles, there were no more than six. However, within the IAAF the advocates of progress were growing in number. Proof of this was to be found in the decision to ratify as IAAF world records marks made from 1932 onwards. As far as the high jump was concerned, the last mark approved by the FSFI was Carolina Gisolf's 1.62, made at Amsterdam on 12 June 1932. But in the Games event at Los Angeles she was opposed to a very strong American duo, composed of Jean Shiley and Mildred Didrikson. In the early days of women's athletics the paucity of competition made it relatively easy for the best talents to shine in more than one event. Typical in this respect was **Mildred Didrikson** (born at Port Arthur, Texas, on 26 June 1911; died in 1956; 1.69 m. / 46 Kg.). "Babe", as she was called, had a rather short career in athletics, yet conquered virtually all there was to conquer. At the 1932 AAU Championships, which also served as Olympic Tryouts, held at Evanston, Illinois on 16 July, she competed in **eight events, in the space of two and a half hours !** She won 80 m. hurdles, shot, javelin and baseball throw, tied for first in the high jump with Jean Shiley at 1.60, was fourth in the discus and failed to make the final in the 100 m. and the 220 y. She thus won the team title for Employers' Casualty AA of Dallas all by herself ! At the Los Angeles Olympics the following month she won the javelin with 43.86, the 80 m. hurdles in 11.7, a new world record, and was second to Jean Shiley in the high jump. Carolina Gisolf, the fresh world record holder, had to be content with 1.58 and fourth. "Babe" and Shiley cleared 1.65 for a new world record, then failed at 1.68. In a jump-off at 1.67, both girls cleared first time. At that stage, however, the judges declared Didrikson's jump illegal because she dived over the bar head first, which was against the rule in those days. She told the judges she had been using the same style all afternoon, but they retorted: "If you were diving before, we didn't see it. We just saw it this time". At any rate it should be noted that under present rules Shiley would have won anyhow, since she had achieved the winning height (1.65) at her first attempt, while Didrikson cleared second time.

1932 Olympics, Los Angeles – High Jump (7 August): 1.Jean Shiley (USA) 1.65 (WR); 2.Mildred Didrikson (USA) 1.65 (WR); 3.Eva Dawes (Canada) 1.60; 4.Carolina Gisolf (Holland) 1.575; 5.Marjorie Clark (South Africa) 1.575; 6.Annette Rogers (USA) 1.575; 7.Helma Notte (Germany) 1.55; 8.Yuriko Hirohashi (Japan) 1.485; 9.Yayeki Sagara (Japan) 1.46; 10.Ellen Braumüller (Germany) 1.41.

Age riddles

Even in this time and age statisticians are sometimes confronted with controversial information about the age of certain athletes, particularly those born in Africa. Age riddles were met even more frequently in days long gone by. Mildred "Babe" Didrikson, regarded by many as the greatest sportswoman America has ever had (25 lines of text in the "Encyclopaedia Britannica", 1963 edition), appears to be a case in point. On entry lists of the 1932 Olympics in Los Angeles she apparently gave her birthyear as 1913. Later on, other sources gave the year as 1914, a version accepted by "Britannica" itself and to be found also on a Texas state historical marker near her gravesite. In his excellent book "Track's Greatest Women", Jon Hendershott reveals that Didrikson was actually born on 26 June 1911, as per three sources: 1) The headstone above her grave; 2) a baptismal certificate; 3) a family Bible. He also found that her family name was Didriksen (she was the daughter of Norwegian immigrants), but "Babe", as a fervent patriot, chose to write it as Didrikson. Minor details, of course, which do not change history. They just reveal certain tendencies sometimes prevailing in human nature.

Didrikson, who married "pro" wrestler George Zaharias in 1938, was until then the only woman to have won Olympic medals on the track as well as on the field. She excelled in several other sports, notably including golf, in which she won the US Open title three times, the last one in the comeback of her life, after undergoing surgery for cancer. She died in 1956, at the age of forty-five.

The IAAF finally decided to inherit, so to say, the meritorious work of the FSFI and take women's athletics in its own hands. M.me Milliat and her associates agreed, yet decided to stage one more edition of their "World Games" before giving up though – the meeting took place in London in 1934. In the high jump there had been no further progress of late and a jump of 1.57 sufficed to earn the title.

1934 World Games, London – High Jump (9 August): 1.Selma Grieme (Germany) 1.574; 2.Mary Milne (GB) 1.525; 3.Margaret Bell (Canada) 1.525; 4.Eva Dawes (Canada) 1.525; 5.Marjorie R. Clark (South Africa) 1.525; 6.Elfriede Kaun (Germany) 1.495.

New prospects emerged on the way to the 1936 Olympics. One of these was **Dorothy Odam** of Great Britain (born at Stockwell, London, on 14 March 1920; 1.68 m. / 52 Kg.). She blossomed to world class as a teen-ager and in 1935, aged 15, ranked equal fourth in the world with 1.60 ! Early in 1936 at Brentwood she did 1.65, which however was never ratified by the IAAF. Later in the season she won a silver medal at the Berlin Olympics, matching the height of Ibolya Csák of Hungary at 1.60. Under the rule now in force, the English girl would have won gold because she cleared 1.60 at the first attempt, while Csák needed two. At that time, however, places were decided with a jump-off, in which the Hungarian did 1.62 and won the gold medal. At 21, she was an "oldie" if compared with the 16-year-old winner !

1936 Olympics, Berlin - High Jump (9 August): 1.Ibolya Csák (Hungary) 1.60; 2.Dorothy Odam (GB) 1.60; 3.Elfriede Kaun (Germany) 1.60; 4.Marguerite Nicolas (France) 1.58; 5.(tie) Doris Carter (Australia). Annette Rogers (USA) and Francina Koen (Holland) 1.55; 8.(tie) Nelly Carrington (GB), Margaret Bell (Canada), Alice Arden (USA), Kathlyn Kelly (USA) and Wanda Nowak (Austria) 1.50.

Women entered the arena of the European Championships in 1938, when a meet exclusively for them was organized in Vienna. The high jump event caused mixed feelings though. Dora Ratjen of Germany won with a record height, 1.70, but following protests from delegations representing other countries, she was subjected to a sex control and found to be ineligible for women's sport. A few days later the German weekly "Der Leichtathlet" published a communiqué from the main body of German sport which said: "Severe instructions have been imparted to make sure that no similar cases will henceforth occur in National-Socialist Germany". Ratjen took a new surname, Hermann, and her record was deleted. The official winner at Vienna was Olympic champion Ibolya Csák with 1.64.

Dorothy Odam was in the news again in 1939, when she raised the world record to 1.66 at Brentwood on 29 May. That was to remain the last official record before World War II. In 1940 she married Richard Tyler and it was only until after the birth of two sons that she returned to athletic competition in 1945.

POLE VAULT

As related in the introduction to this chapter, an event called "fence vault" was practised by the Vassar College pioneers, but this was hardly reconcilable with the pole vault as we know it today. In his book on the progression of World Records, Richard Hymans gives the following mark as the earliest record set in a proper pole vault event: 1.725 by Ruth Spencer (USA) at Painesville on 15 May 1911. The United States thus acted as pioneers in this event. After World War II, Germany and USSR joined the parade and by the end of 1940 the best known performance was 2.535 by one Zoya Grigoryevna Romanova of the SU, made at Moscow on 26 August 1935. She was 28 years old at the time.

LONG JUMP

The long jump, as a most natural exercise, was on the programme of the very first Vassar Field Day, on 9 November 1895. It was won by the versatile Emma Baker, a 19-year-old girl who reached 3.48. In what was obviously a "rarefied atmosphere", the record remained the property of American college women for several years – one of them, Ellen Hayes, was the first to reach the 5-metre barrier, with a jump of 5.00 exactly, at Sweetbriar on 7 April 1913. The first mark to be ratified by an international body, FSFI, was a 5.16 by Maria Mejzliková of Czechoslovakia, made at Prague on 6 August 1922. In those days when versatility was the rule, the Czech woman apparently did not compete in this event at the inaugural FSFI World Games, held at Stade Pershing, Paris, on 20 August 1922. She won the 60 metres instead (7.6), beating Mary Lines of Great Britain. The latter, aged 29, took the long jump with 5.06.

There was also a standing long jump on the programme. It was won by yet another versatile performer, Camille Sabie of USA.

1922 World Games, Paris - Long Jump (20 August): 1.Mary Lines (GB) 5.06; 2.Elizabeth Stine (USA) 5.025; 3.Camille Sabie (USA) 4.96; 4.Hilda Hatt (GB) 4.68; 5.Marie Jirasková (Czechoslovakia); 6.Cécile Maugars (France).

Standing long jump (20 August): 1.Camille Sabie (USA) 2.485; 2.Mary Hughes (GB) 2.405; 3.Henriette Comte-Anavoisard (France) 2.34; 4.Florence Birchenough (GB) 2.33; 5.Bozena Sramková (Czecoslovakia); 6.Lucie Frost (France).

The world's best for the long jump was bettered time and again during the Twenties. The outstanding figure was **Kinue Hitomi** of Japan (born on 1 January 1907; died in 1931; 1.57 m. / 45 Kg.), the first Asian woman to make the headlines in athletics. She was only 19 when she appeared at the second World Games, held in Göteborg, Sweden, in 1926. Only a handful of Western experts apparently knew of an unratifed record jump of 5.75, achieved by her on 5 June of that year in Tokyo.

Shortly before the Göteborg rendez-vous, in the British Games held in London on 2 August, Muriel Gunn of Great Britain was credited with 5.485, a mark which was ratified as a world record by the FSFI. In their Göteborg clash, however, Hitomi had the upper hand and won with 5.50, officially a new world's best, while Gunn was second with 5.44. This was only one of the six events (!) in which Hitomi appeared during the Games. She won both running and standing long jumps, was second in the discus, third in the 100 yards, fifth in the 60 m. and sixth in the 250 m. !

1926 World Games, Göteborg – Long Jump (28 August): 1.Kinue Hitomi (Japan) 5.50, WR; 2.Muriel Gunn (GB) 5.44; 3.Zdenka Smolova (Czechoslovakia) 5.28; 4.Asta Plathino (Sweden) 5.16; 5.Zinaida Liepina (Latvia) 5.00; 6.Josephine Matthews (GB) 4.82; 7.Waclawa Sadkowska (Poland) 4.77; 8.Marta Johansson (Sweden) 4.65; 9.Lucienne Laudré (France) 4.63; 10.Louise Stevens (Belgium) 4.51.

Standing Long Jump (29 August): 1.Kinue Hitomi (Japan) 2.49; 2.Zdena Smolova (Czechoslovakia) 2.47; 3.Barbara Holliday (GB) 2.37; 4.Florence Birchenough (GB) 2.32; 5.Marta Johansson (Sweden) 2.29; 6.Vera Jacobsson (Sweden) 2.28; 7.Evelyne Cloupet (France) 2.22.

Muriel Gunn fought back in 1927, raising the world record for the long jump to 5.575 in London on 1 August. But Hitomi was to have the last word – at Osaka on 20 May 1928 she jumped 5.78, then 5.98. The latter was the first world record ratified by the IAAF in this event.

The long jump was not included in the restricted women's programme adopted by the IAAF for the 1928 Olympics.

"A master at translating theory into praxis"

If there was ever a woman who acted as the pioneer of athletics in her mother country, that was unquestionably Kinue Hitomi, a light-weight wonder from Japan. In fact, authoritative students of Asian athletics have long recognized her as the standard-bearer of sport as a whole for the vast Asian continent.

In terms of versatility she certainly shone like no other woman of her generation. In her relatively short career she set world records in a wide range of events, her best marks being as follows: 100 m. 12.2 (1928), 200 m. 24.7 (1929), 220 y. 25.8 (1928), 400 m. 59.0 (1928), long jump 5.98 (1928), triple jump 11.62 (1926), triathlon 217 pts. (1929).

Hitomi was also the first Asian athlete to win a medal in the Olympic Games. In the inaugural edition of 1928 at Amsterdam the women's programme consisted of barely 5 events, yet the Japanese girl managed to finish second ... in the 800 metres. Without forgetting, of course, her exploits in the FSFI World Games, detailed in the main text. And she was only 19 at the time of her first appearance in such a meet.

In the eyes of her contemporaries Hitomi's most amazing performance was a long jump of 6.07, achieved during a Japan vs. Germany match at Seoul on 17 October 1929. Even though the wind was measured as +5.8 m/s, the FSFI ratified the mark as a world record simply because that body – just like the IAAF – had no specific "wind rule" at that time.

As a graduate from a Tokyo college of physical education Hitomi was, in the words of a keen student of Asian sport, Cdr. P.K.Mahanand, "the greatest exponent in translating theory into praxis".

Unfortunately her Prague heroics were the last flashes of brilliance from this unique athlete, because in 1931 she fell the victim of tuberculosis when only 24 years of age.

In the meantime a new outstanding talent had emerged in Poland, **Stanislawa Walasiewicz** (born at Wierzchownia on 11 April 1911; died in Cleveland, Ohio, on 4 December 1960; 1.62 m. / 54 Kg.). She was actually baptized as Stefania, but the world of athletics always knew her as Stanislawa. She emigrated to USA while still a teen-ager and over there she became, for all and sundry, Stella Walsh, even though she always represented Poland, her native country, in international competition. She was primarily a sprinter, yet she shone also as a long jumper. In 1930, aged 19, she took advantage of a following wind to beat Hitomi's official world record with 6.02. Later in the same year she went to Prague for the third edition of the World Games, where she concentrated in the sprint distances with great success. In the long jump there was yet another Hitomi vs. Gunn duel. And the Japanese star won by a fair margin – 5.90 to 5.76. Here again the marks were aided by a favourable breeze.

1930 World Games, Prague – Long Jump (8 September): 1.Kinue Hitomi (Japan) 5.90; 2.Muriel Gunn-Cornell (GB) 5.76; 3.Selma Grieme (Germany) 5.71; 4.Mai Jacobsson (Sweden) 5.65; 5.Felicitas

Schlarp (Germany) 5.52; 6.Saara Teitelbaum (Esthonia) 5.38; 7.Germaine Jacobs (France) 5.21; 8.Mary Seary (GB) 5.17; 9.Sumiko Watanabe (Japan) 5.07; 10.Ondina Valla (Italy) 4.92.

N.B. Most if not all the above marks were favoured by the wind (unspecified velocity).

The fourth and last edition of the SFFI World Games was held in London in 1934. Walasiewicz chose to concentrate on the sprints and the long jump title went to 23-year-old Traude Göppner of Germany, who beat her team-mate Bauschulte by the narrowest of margins.

1934 World Games, London - Long Jump (11 August): 1.Traude Göppner (Germany) 5.80; 2.Hedwig Bauschulte (Germany) 5.79; 3.Sumiko Watanabe (Japan) 5.46; 4.Evelyn Gohawk (Canada) 5.38; 5.Phyllis Bartholomew (GB) 5.36. Zdeňka Koubková (Czechoslavkia), 3rd with 5.69, was later identified as a man.

Walasiewicz continued to treat the long jump as a "side activity", yet she managed to revise her own world best, reaching 6.095 at Worcester, Massachusetts on 28 June 1937. She tried the event in the first European Championships for women, held in Vienna in 1938, but had to bow to Irmgard Praetz of Germany – 5.81 to 5.88.

Out of the ever-growing phalanx of German stars there emerged yet another prospect, Christel Schulz. In a meet held at Berlin's Olympic Stadium on 30 July 1939 this girl, aged 18, brought the world record to 6.12. Her nearest rival was a young Dutch woman, Fanny Koen (5.97), who was to rise to greater heights in the following decade. In IAAF books Schulz was the first woman to be officially credited with a 6-metre-plus mark.

TRIPLE JUMP

Early Tries

The triple jump is, so to say, the youngest of the four jumping events for women. It was not included in the programme of "global" championships until 1992, yet it was practised in USA as far back as by the end of the XIX century, namely at Bryn Mawr College, Pennsylvania. One Mary Ayer is in fact credited with a 6.72 mark, made right there on 21 April 1899 – apparently indoors. Some time later the event appeared on the programme of another US school, Vassar College, with vastly superior marks, up to 9.00, a distance achieved right there by Charlotte Hand on 7 May 1910. In the course of time other countries adopted it, and in the Twenties a famous Japanese all-arounder, Kinue Hitomi, bettered the "record" time and again, up to 11.62 in 1926. Another Japanese girl, Rie Yamaguchi, improved to 11.68 in 1939.

9 WOMEN 1941-1970

The incomparable Fanny Blankers-Koen (Holland) was primarily a sprinter-hurdler, yet she managed to set world records in the high jump and the long jump as well.

HIGH JUMP

Fanny et al

In 1941 Dorothy Odam's world record for the high jump (1.66) was equalled by two different athletes, first by Esther van Heerden of South Africa at Stellenbosch on 29 March, then by Ilsebill Pfenning of Switzerland at Lugano on 27 July. The latter record had quite a strange story. As a result of unfortunate circumstances it remained lying in the archives of SLV (the Swiss Athletics Association), most probably because somebody there assumed that the world record stood at 1.70. As reported earlier in this chapter, such a mark had been achieved at the European Championships of 1938 by Dora Ratjen of Germany, who was later found to be ineligible for women's competition, and consequently deprived of her record. To put things right there came at last our friend Fulvio Regli, one of the founders of the ATFS, who informed SLV officials about this. It was only in 1976 that the documents reached the IAAF and Pfenning's mark was finally accorded official recognition !

To outshine all these brave women there came in 1943 a bright new star from Holland, **Francina ("Fanny") Blankers née Koen** (born in Amsterdam on 26 April 1918; died in Amsterdam on 25 January 2004; 1.75 m. / 63 Kg.), the first "queen" of modern athletics in a truly international perspective. Through

her smashing victories, her many records and, last but not least, her unassuming behaviour, she put women's athletics in a new and fully delightful dimension. As a most versatile talent, she emerged in 1935, aged 17, with a 2:29.0 in the 800 metres, her first national record. From 1938 till 1952 she set world records in .... **ten** different events. She won her international crowns in the sprint and hurdle events, but early in her career she was able to set world records also in the high jump, the long jump and the pentathlon. In 1940 she married her coach Jan Blankers, a former triple jumper of international calibre (in 1933 he won the AAA title in London with 14.69).

"Fanny" was first to conquer the 1.70 m. barrier: at Amsterdam on 30 May 1943 she bettered the listed world record no less than three times – 1.66, 1.69, both on second try, and 1.71, on third try. By then the mother of a two-year-old boy, "Fanny" concentrated mostly on the running events for the rest of her career. She seldom found the time to use her "scissors" style

Iolanda Balas (Romania) ruled over the high jump sorority for many years.

in major high jump competitions. A fourth place (at 1.57) in the 1946 European Championships at Oslo is just one of the rare exceptions. Therefore she virtually left the high jump to the tender care of the so-called specialists.

At the 1948 Olympics in London there was a torrid duel between an American, Alice Coachman, and a Britisher, Dorothy Odam-Tyler. Both jumped 1.68 and the former won on the fewer misses' count, which had by then been adopted as a new rule. The English woman, by then 28, thus earned her second silver medal, twelve years after she got her first in Berlin. The adjoining aside tells readers how changing rules can sometimes change results.

1948 Olympics, London - High Jump (7 August): 1.Alice Coachman (USA) 1.68 (OR); 2.Dorothy Odam-Tyler (GB) 1.68 (OR); 3.Micheline Ostermeyer (France) 1.61; 4.(tie) Vinton Beckett (Canada) and Doreen Dredge (Canada) 1.58; 6.Bertha Crowther (GB) 1.58; 7.Ilse Steinegger (Austria) 1.55; 8.Dorothy Gardner (GB) 1.55; 9.(tie) Simone Ruas (France) and Anne Iversen (Denmark) 1.50; 11.(tie) Carmen Phipps (Jamaica), Shirley Gordon (Canada) and Cynthia Robinson (USA) 1.50.

When rules change "the wrong way"

Dorothy Odam-Tyler of Great Britain was one of those rare athletes who managed to perform at the very top before and after World War II. She won Olympic silver medals in the high jump in two editions of the Olympic Games - **twelve years apart.** What makes her case truly unique is the fact that she missed gold on both occasions because ..... changing rules played against her. At Berlin in 1936, aged only 16, she jumped 1.60 at her first attempt, while Ibolya Csák of Hungary cleared the same height at the second try. Under the rule now in effect, Dorothy would have been the winner. But in 1936 the outcome was decided in a jump-off and here the Hungarian did better than her rival and thus won gold.

Twelve years later in London Dorothy was obviously eager to "redeem" herself under the eyes of so many English spectators. Here the battle was between her and America's Alice Coachman. When the bar was raised to 1.68, a new Olympic record, both women succeeded and Coachman won on the fewer misses rule, which had lately been adopted as a new rule. In sport - as in quite a few other things in life - there is unquestionably an element called luck.

Dorothy's career was simply marvellous in terms of longevity: in the space of **twenty years** she competed in four editions of the Olympic Games: second in 1936 and 1948, tied for 7th in 1952 and for 12th in 1956 ! In 1961, aged 41, she ranked fifth in Great Britain !

"Fanny" Koen's world record was broken by Sheila Lerwill of Great Britain, who raised it to 1.72 in the AAA Championships held in London on 7 July 1951. She met defeat in a major test though: in the 1952 Olympics in Helsinki she lost to Esther Brand of South Africa – 1.65 to 1.67. Veteran Odam-Tyler, by then 32, tied for seventh.

1952 Olympics, Helsinki – High Jump (27 July): 1.Esther Brand (South Africa) 1.67; 2.Sheila Lerwill (GB) 1.65; 3.Aleksandra Chudina (SU) 1.63; 4.Thelma Hopkins (GB) 1.58; 5.Olga Modrachová (Czechoslovakia) 1.58; 6.Theodora Solms-Schenk (Austria) 1.58; 7.(tie) Nina Kosova (SU) and Dorothy Odam-Tyler (GB) 1.58; 9.Gunhild Larking (Sweden) 1.55; 10.Alice Whitty (Canada) 1.55; 11.Galina Ganeker (SU) 1.55.

Great Britain and the SU were the leading powers for a few more years. Their representatives took turns in bettering the world record – up to the advent of a new jumper who was to re-write the history of the event time and again. If there has ever been an athlete who towered head and shoulders above her contemporaries for a seemingly endless time this was **Iolanda Balas** of Rumania (born at Timisoara on 12 December 1936; 1.85 m. / 72 Kg.). She set **fourteen** world record marks, starting with 1.75 at Budapest on 14 July 1956 and ending with 1.91 at Sofia on 16 July 1961. At the 1956 Olympics she had a rare gloomy day, winding up no better than fifth. The winner was Mildred McDaniel of USA, who set a new world record with a 1.76 clearance.

1956 Olympics, Melbourne - High Jump (1 December): 1.Mildred McDaniel (USA) 1.76 (WR); 2.(tie) Thelma Hopkins (GB) and Maria Pisareva (SU) 1.67; 4.Gunhild Larking (Sweden) 1.67; 5.Iolanda Balas (Rumania) 1.67; 6.Micheline Mason (Australia) 1.67; 7.Mary Donaghy (New Zealand) 1.67; 8.(tie) Jirina Voborilová (Czechoslovakia) and Hermina Geyser (South Africa) 1.64; 10. Olga Modrachová (Czechoslovakia) 1.64; 11.Valentina Ballod (SU) 1.60; 12.(tie) Reinalde Knapp (Austria) and Dorothy Odam-Tyler (GB) 1.60.

Balas' defeat was her last for ... **eleven years** to come ! In the intervening time **she compiled a wondrous streak of 140 consecutive victories,** an all-time record in modern athletics. She was well above average in height (1,85 m.) on the yardstick of her time. She could not adapt to either the Western Roll or the Straddle, so she used a modified version of the Scissors. She was coached by Ion Söter, a former high jumper of international class (2.055 in 1956), who later became her husband. Balas won her event twice in both the Olympics (1960 and '64) and the European Championships (1958 and '62). By the time she raised the world record to her career best of 1.91 she had a 13 cm. lead vis-à-vis the second best performer of all time ! Her reign was long, happy and even tedious at times. She once put it this way: "Sometime it was hard to compete; there was no opposition for me". Balas' last world record (1.91 in 1961) resisted all assaults for a full decade. In the intervening time the Rumanian won all there was to win. At the 1960 Olympics in Rome she outclassed her nearest rivals, and so did she at Tokyo four years later.

Alice Coachman: first ebony gold

In the men's ranks, the first black to win an Olympic gold medal in an individual event was William DeHart Hubbard of USA (long jump, 1924). In the ranks of the fair sex such a "first" belongs to another American, **Alice Coachman** (born at Albany, Georgia on 9 November 1923; 1.70 m. / 57 Kg.), who won the high jump at the 1948 Olympics in London with a personal best of 1.68.

During her career she won 25 AAU titles, indoors and out, 10 of which in the outdoor high jump (1939-48). She won the first of these titles before turning sixteen. At the 1943 AAU Championships in Cleveland she finished a close second to "Stella" Walsh in the 100 metres, with an estimated 11.7.

1960 Olympics, Rome – High Jump (8 September): 1.Iolanda Balas (Rumania) 1.85 (OR); 2.(tie) Jaroslawa Józwiakowska (Poland) and Dorothy Shirley (GB) 1.71; 4.Galina Dolya (SU) 1.71; 5.Taisiya Chenchik (SU) 1.68; 6.(tie) Helen Frith (Australia), Inga-Britt Lorentzon (Sweden) and Frances Slaap (GB) 1.65; 9.(tie) Ingrid Becker (Germany), Pertronella Zwier (Holland), Florence Petry (France), Marlene Schmitz-Porz (Germany) and Olga Gere (Yugoslavia) 1.65; 14.(tie) Noemia Rogers (USA) and Valentina Ballod (SU) 1.65.

1964 Olympics, Tokyo – High Jump (15 October): 1.Iolanda Balas (Rumania) 1.90 (OR); 2.Michele Brown (Australia) 1.80; 3.Taisya Chenchik (SU) 1.78; 4.Aida Dos Santos (Brazil) 1.74; 5.Dianne Gerace (Canada) 1.71; 6.Frances Slaap (GB) 1.71; 7.Olga Pulic (Yugoslavia) 1.71; 8.Eleanor Montgomery (USA) 1.71; 9.Karin Rüger (Germany) 1.71; 10. Jaroslawa Bieda (Poland) 1.71; 11.Robyn Woodhouse (Australia) 1.71; 12.Liina Kaarna (Finland) 1.68.

After the retirement of Iolanda Balas, several Eastern European figures alternated at the top of the event, alas with lower marks. At the 1968 Olympics in Mexico City an 18-year-old Czech girl, Miloslava Rezkova, upset better known candidates with 1.82, equalling her personal best.

1968 Olympic Games, Mexico City – High Jump (17 October): 1.Miloslava Rezkova (Czechoslovakia) 1.82; 2.Antonina Okorokova (SU) 1.80; 3.Valentina Kossyr (SU) 1.80; 4.Jaroslava Valentova (Czechoslovakia) 1.78; 5.Rita Schmidt (East Germany) 1.78; 6.Maria Faithova (Czechoslovakia) 1.78; 7.Karin Schulze (East Germany) 1.76; 8.Ilona Gusenbauer (Austria) 1.76; 9.(tie) Magdolna Csabi (Hungary) and Ghislane Barnay (France) 1.71; 11.Mariac Cypriano (Brazil) 1.71; 12.Vera Gruschkina (SU) 1.71; 13.Barbara Inkpen (GB) 1.68; 14.Snezana Hrepevnik (Yugoslavia) 1.68.

POLE VAULT

For the world of athletics, women pole vaulters remained a virtually unknown factor even for the period under examination, at the end of which the best known mark belonged to two Americans, Diane Bragg and Brenda Walker, with 2.59 (in 1952 and 1969 respectively).

LONG JUMP

Versatile "Fanny" Blankers-Koen had the long jump as one of her "secondary" events. She managed to break the world record though: she did so in the midst of World War II, with a jump of 6.25 at Leiden on 19 September 1943. The event was first included in the Olympic programme in the Games of 1948 in London. The Dutch woman would have started as the favourite, but in those days the rules allowed women to compete in only three individual events and she decided to give up the long jump to concentrate on sprint and hurdle races. The first Olympic title thus went to Olga Gyarmati of Hungary with 5.695.

1948 Olympics, London - Long Jump (4 August): 1.Olga Gyarmati (Hungary) 5.695 (OR);

2.Noemi Simonetto de Portela (Argentina) 5.60; 3.Ann-Britt Leyman (Sweden) 5.575; 4.Gerda van der Kade-Koudijs (Holland) 5.57; 5.Neltje Karelse (Holland) 5.545; 6.Kathleen Russell (Jamaica) 5.495; 7.Judy Canty (Australia) 5.38; 8.Yvonne Curtet-Chabot (France) 5.35; 9.Maria Oberbreyer (Austria) 5.24; 10.Ilse Steinegger (Austria) 5.195; 11.Vinton Beckett (Jamaica) 5.14; 12.Emma Reed (USA) 4.83.

Blankers-Koen's successor as world record holder was Yvette Williams of New Zealand, who reached 6.28 at Gisborne on 20 February 1954. She had missed the target by an infinitesimal margin at the Helsinki Olympics in 1952, where she won the most coveted of titles with 6.24.

1952 Olympics, Helsinki – Long Jump (23 July): 1.Yvette Williams (New Zealand) 6.24 (OR); 2.Aleksandra Chudina (SU) 6.14; 3.Shirley Cawley (GB) 5.92; 4.Irmgard Schmelzer (Germany) 5.90; 5.Wilhelmina Lust (Holland) 5.81; 6.Nina Tyurkina (SU) 5.81; 7.Mabel Landry (USA) 5.75; 8.Verna Johnson (Australia) 5.74; 9.Marie Österdahl (Finland) 5.73; 10.Olga Gyarmati (Hungary) 5.67; 11.Valentina Lituyeva (SU) 5.65; 12.Elzbieta Dunska (Poland) 5.65.

In 1955 the SU, by then a major power in women's athletics, had her first world record holder in this event – Galina Vinogradova-Popova, 23, who first equalled Williams' mark (6.28), then bettered it with 6.31 at Tbilisi on 18 November.

In 1956 the leadership passed to Elzbieta Krzesinska née Dunska, a 22-year-old Polish girl who set a new world record of 6.35 at Budapest on 20 August, then equalled it in the Olympic final at Melbourne. On both occasions she was helped by a legal wind, i.e. under 2 m/s.

1956 Olympics, Melbourne – Long Jump (27 November): 1.Elzbieta Dunska-Krzesinska (Poland) 6.35 (eq.WR); 2.Willye White (USA) 6.09; 3.Nadezhda Khnykina-Dvalishvili (SU) 6.07; 4.Erika Fisch (West Germany) 5.89; 5.Marthe Lambert (France) 5.88; 6.Valentina Shaprunova (SU) 5.85; 7.Beverley Weigel (New Zealand) 5.85; 8.Nancy Borwick (Australia) 5.82; 9.Maria Kusion (Poland) 5.79; 10.Helga Hoffmann (West Germany) 5.73; 11.Olga Gyarmati (Hungary) 5.66 12.Genowefa Minicka (Poland) 5.64.

In those days Olympic years were easily and by far the dominant peak in the world of athletics and leading women tried hard to be at their best at the right time. 1960, year of the Rome Games, was no exception. At that time, however, German athletes had to go through a double task – West vs. East Trials and Games. In other words, they experienced what their American colleagues knew since long ago. A so-called "Olympia-Qualifikation" was held at Erfurt early in August three weeks before the Games. Hildrun Claus, a 21-year-old East German, twice bettered Krzesinska's world record, with 6.36 on her fourth try and 6.40 (zero wind) on her sixth and last. Such a feat stamped her as the favourite for the Rome event. But she was unable to peak twice within three weeks. In Rome she took the lead with her first jump, 6.21 – but thast's all she could do. In the fourth trial Vera Krepkina of SU jumped 6.37 and former record holder Krzesinska reached 6.27. The Russian, an 11.3 100 m. performer, thus won the gold medal.

1960 Olympics, Rome – Long Jump (31 August): 1.Vera Krepkina (SU) 6.37 (OR); 2.Elzbieta Krzesinska (Poland) 6.27; 3.Hildrun Claus (Germany)

Mary Rand (GB), first in the long jump and second in the pentathlon at the 1964 Olympics in Tokyo.

6.21; 4.Renate Junker (Germany) 6.19; 5.Ludmila Radchenko (SU) 6.16; 6.Helga Hoffmann (Germany) 6.11; 7.Johanna Bijleveld (Holland) 6.11; 8.Valentina Shaprunova (SU) 6.01; 9.Mary Bignal (GB) 6.01; 10.Beverley Weigel (New Zealand) 5.98; 11.Maria Chojnacka (Poland) 5.98; 12.Fumiko Ito (Japan) 5.98; 13.Maria Bibro (Poland) 5.86.

Places only third but is sole owner of the world record !

Claus took a revenge of sorts in an international match held at Berlin on 23 June 1961. Mind you, there again she was only third, but the anemometer spoke in her favour. She did 6.42, aided by a legal wind of +1.4 m/s. The two who beat her did so with aiding winds over the limit: Tatyana Shchelkanova (SU), first with 6.50 (+3.2m/s) and Valentina Shaprunova (SU), second with 6.46 (+5.4 m/s). Claus thus became the new world record holder – a privilege she lost less than a month later when the above-mentioned Shchelkanova did 6.48 n Moscow on 16 July. The last mentioned was to better her own record three times: 6.53 and 6.62 in 1962, 6.70 in Moscow on 4 July 1964.

By that time there were two rare examples of jumpers who managed to win an Olympic crown and set a new world record in one gulp, that is on one and the same occasion. Mary Rand of Great Britain did so in the Tokyo Olympics of 1964 with 6.76 and Viorica Viscopoleanu of Rumania turned such a trick at the Mexico City Olympics in 1968 with 6.82. In the former case Rand did it against a wind of 1.69 m/s and from a clay runway that was rain-soaked. Having crowned her boldest dream, she continued to compete for a few more years but without ever approaching her 1964 form.

As for Viscopoleanu, it must be said that her Mexico City record jump (6.82) was made in windless conditions. However, the high altitude of the Mexican capital (2300 m.) was a strong aiding factor due to the rarefied atmosphere. In those Games this was amply confirmed by Bob Beamon's historic world record in the men's long jump (8.90).

1964 Olympics, Tokyo - Long Jump (14 October): 1.Mary Rand (GB) 6.76 (WR); 2.Irena Kirszenstein (Poland) 6.60; 3.Tatyana Shchelkanova (SU) 6.42; 4.Ingrid Becker (Germany) 6.40; 5.Viorica Viscopoleanu (Rumania) 6.35; 6.Diana Yorgova (Bulgaria) 6.24; 7.Hildrun Claus-Laufer (Germany)

Heide Rosendahl (West Germany) first in the long jump and second in the pentathlon at the 1972 Olympics in Munich. She also anchored the victorious 4x100 m. relay team.

6.24; 8.Helga Hoffmann (Germany) 6.23; 9.Berit Berthelsen (Norway) 6.19; 10.Tatyana Talysheva (SU) 6.18; 11.Aida Chuiko (SU) 6.13; 12.Willye White (USA) 6.07; 13.Sheila Parkin (GB) 6.04.

1968 Olympics, Mexico City - Long Jump (14 October): 1.Viorica Viscopoleanu (Rumania) 6.82 (WR); 2.Sheila Sherwood (GB) 6.68; 3.Tatyana Talysheva (SU) 6.66; 4.Burghild Wieczorek (Germany) 6.48; 5.Miroslawa Sarna (Poland) 6.47; 6.Ingrid Becker (Germany) 6.43; 7.Berit Berthelsen (Norway) 6.40; 8.Heidemarie Rosendahl (Germany) 6.40; 9.Violet Odogwu (Nigeria) 6.23; 10.Martha Watson (USA) 6.20; 11.Willye White (USA) 6.08; 12.Maureen Barton (GB) 5.95.

West Germany had one of her brightest stars in **Heidemarie Rosendahl** (born at Hückeswagen on 14 February 1947; 1.74 m. / 66 Kg.), who broke Viscopoleanu's world record at the 1970 Universiade in Turin on 3 September with 6.84. This performance, achieved on the last try (zero wind), partly softened the disappointment she had experienced a few minutes earlier when an intrinsically better jump worth about 6.90 was declared a foul. But Heide's chief glory was yet to come.

TRIPLE JUMP

This event was long regarded as the "parent pauvre" of the women's programme. Virtually ignored at the international level, it continued to appear sporadically in some countries such as USA and Japan. At the end of the period under review the unofficial world record set by Rie Yamaguchi of Japan (11.66 in 1939) was still standing though. British sources credit Mary Bignal-Rand with a 12.21 mark, apparently made in 1959 during a training session.

WOMEN 1971-2000

10

HIGH JUMP

Rosemarie opens 2-Metre Club

Iolanda Balas' last world record (1.91 in 1961) remained unbeaten for ten years, in spite of the fact that in the meantime the majority of élite high jumpers had adopted the more efficient Straddle style. Iolanda's successor finally arrived in the person of Ilona Gusenbauer of Austria, who mastered 1.92 at Vienna on 4 September 1971. The 1972 Olympic final in Munich was featured by a major upset: a 16-year-old West German, **Ulrike Meyfarth** (born at Frankfort/Main on 4 May 1956; 1.86 m. / 71 Kg.) outjumped a bunch of seasoned performers, including Gusenbauer, and struck gold with 1.92, equalling the world record and becoming the youngest individual event winner in Olympic history. A fantastic achievement for a girl whose pre-1972 best was 1.80, although it should be noted that at that stage of her development Ulrike stood 1.84, well above the average height of élite jumpers in those days.

1972 Olympics, Munich - High Jump (4 September): 1.Ulrike Meyfarth (West Germany) 1.92 (eq. WR); 2.Yordanka Blagoeva (Bulgaria) 1.88; 3.Ilona Gusenbauer (Austria) 1.88; 4.Barbara Inkpen (GB) 1.85; 5.Rita Schmidt (East Germany) 1.85; 6.Sara Simeoni (Italy) 1.85; 7.Rosemarie Witschas (East Germany) 1.85; 8.Debbie Brill (Canada) 1.82; 9.Andrea Bruce (Jamaica) 1.82; 10.Ellen Mundinger (West Germany) 1.82; 11.Audrey Redid (Jamaica) 1.82; 12.(tie) Rita Gildemeister (East Germany) and Grit Ejstrup (Denmark) 1.82; 14.Renate Gärtner (West Germany) 1.82; 15.Miroslava Hübnerova (Czechoslovakia) 1.82.

Meyfarth's exploit had a curious aftermath: years of utter mediocrity for the precocious Ulrike, including a tie for second (at 1.80) in the 1973 European Junior Championships and a dismal 1.78 at the 1976 Olympics in Montreal, where she failed to qualify for the final.

The first woman to conquer the 2-metre barrier was a Straddle jumper from East Germany, **Rosemarie Ackermann née Witschas** (born at Lohsa on 4 April 1952; 1.75 m. / 59 Kg.). At twenty she made the Olympic final in Munich, placing seventh at 1.85. Two years later she produced her first world record (1.94), then kept improving steadily, in the process winning European (1974) and Olympic (1976) titles.

1976 Olympics, Montreal - High Jump (28 July): 1.Rosemarie Witschas-Ackermann (East Germany) 1.93 (OR); 2.Sara Simeoni (Italy) 1.91; 3.Yordanka Blagoeva (Bulgaria) 1.91; 4.Mária Mrachnová (Czechoslovakia) 1.89; 5.Joni Huntley (USA) 1.89; 6.Tatyana Shlyakhto (SU) 1.87; 7.Annette Tånnander (Sweden) 1.87; 8.Cornelia Popa (Rumania) 1.87; 9.Andrea Matay (Hungary) 1.87; 10. Julie White (Canada) 1.87; 11.Brigitte Holzapfel (West Germany) 1.87.

Ulrike Meyfarth (Germany), a twotime winner of the Olympic high jump title - twelve years apart (1972 and '84).

Sara Simeoni (italy) won high jump medals in three editions of the Olympics, striking gold in 1980.

On 26 August 1977, at Berlin's Olympic Stadium, Rosemarie Ackermann made history by clearing 2 metres even. In this meet she cleared 1.75, 1.80, 1.86, 1.89, 1.92, 1.97 and 2.00, always first time, before failing 3 times at 2.02. Woman's breakthrough at 2 metres thus came sixty-five years after George Horine's pristine 2-metre effort in the male ranks. By 1978, however, Ackermann had a worthy rival in **Sara Simeoni** of Italy (born at Rivoli Veronese on 19 April 1953; 1.77 m. / 60 Kg.), one of the greatest competitors in the annals of women's athletics. Sara had her first major clash with life at twelve, when she applied for the "corps de ballet" at the Arena, Verona's famous open-air theatre. The recruiter turned her down on the grounds that she had big feet and was a bit too tall for her age. But the girl was able to use those "big feet" to good advantage in another walk of life and eventually became the "prima ballerina" of high jumping. To achieve that goal, however, she had to work and toil for twelve years, starting from the day of her début in 1966, when she cleared 1.25 using a most rudimentary style. She improved steadily year after year, passing from the Scissors to the Flop. As regards the latter style, it should be said that it was put on the map of women's athletics by Debbie Brill, a Canadian who first used it as a teen-ager, more or less at the time Dick Fosbury introduced it in the male ranks. To preserve her identity, Debbie chose to call it "Brill Bend". She had a long but somewhat troubled career, with a personal best of 1.99 (indoors) in 1982.

Simeoni made the great leap forward between 1977 and 1978, when she improved by 8 cm. – from 1.93 to a record smashing 2.01. She achieved the latter height during an international meet at Brescia on 4 August 1978. That set the stage for a great showdown with Ackermann at the European Championships in Prague four weeks later. Until then, the German had always had the upper hand in her clashes with the Italian. The Prague event was a see-saw battle, which Sara finally won by equalling her fresh world record, while Ackermann had to be content with 1.99 and second place. The Italian cleared the winning height on her second try. As an eye-witness, I still remember that Ackermann made it too ..... except that the bar fell seconds later, while she was standing in the pit with arms raised. In few events, if any, can the difference between success and failure be so infinitesimal as in a high jump contest.

Simeoni had a unique ability in excelling herself under pressure. Between 1971 and 1978 she did just that in every major international meet, as one can see from the following chart (PB = personal best):

		Result	Pre-meet PB	Diff. cm.
1971	Euro. Ch.	1.78 (9.)	1.76	+2
1972	Olympics	1.85 (6.)	1.80	+5
1974	Euro. Ch.	1.89 (3.)	1.86	+3
1976	Olympics	1.91 (2.)	1.90	+1
1978	Euro. Ch.	2.01 (1.)	2.01	=

In 1979 Sara and Rosi split, 1-1. By then, however, the German was plagued by recurrent tendon problems. Not even repeated surgery was able to put an end to her torment. At the 1980 Olympics in Moscow, jumping with a wrap just under the knee of her take-off leg, she had to be content with a fourth place at 1.91. Simeoni won with 1.97. Soon after that glorious day, she too began to suffer the effects of countless hours of intensive training. While Ackermann said farewell to the sport, the Italian struggled on for several more years, with ups and downs.

1980 Olympics, Moscow – High Jump (26 July): 1.Sara Simeoni (Italy) 1.97 (OR); 2.Ursula Kielan (Poland) 1.94, 3.Jutta Kirst (East Germany) 1.94; 4.Rosemarie Witschas-Ackermann (East Germany) 1.91; 5.Marina Sisoyeva (SU) 1.91; 6.(tie) Christine Stanton (Australia) 1.91 and Andrea Reichstein (East Germany) 1.91; 8.Cornelia Popa (Rumania) 1.88; 9.Tamara Bykova (SU) 1.88; 10.Andrea Matay (Hungary) 1.85; 11.Louise Miller (GB) 1.85; 12.Chris Soetewey (Belgium) 1.80.

A step backward may be in order. Young Ulrike

Meyfarth's victory at the 1972 Olympics had a curious aftermath: years of utter mediocrity for the precocious Ulrike, including a tie for second (at 1.80 !) in the 1973 European Junior Championships and a dismal 1.78 at the 1976 Olympics in Montreal, where she failed to qualify for the final. It was only in 1978 that she finally improved further. She reached the top again in 1982, winning the European Championship title at Athens with a new world record – 2.02. She cleared such a height on her third attempt. The following year the German found a new rival in **Tamara Bykova** of the SU (born at Azov, Rostov region, on 21 December 1958; 1.79 m. / 62 Kg.). In a European Cup event, held in London, both raised the world record to 2.03. The Russian had the record all for herself later in the season as she did 2.04 at Pisa, Italy. This was a few days after she had won the World Championship title in the inaugural edition of this meet at Helsinki, beating Meyfarth – 2.01 to 1.99.

1983 World Championships, Helsinki – High Jump (9 August): 1.Tamara Bykova (SU) 2.01 (CR); 2.Ulrike Meyfarth (West Germany) 1.99; 3.Louise Ritter (USA) 1.95; 4.Colleen Sommer (USA) 1.95; 5.Kerstin Brandt (East Germany) 1.92; 6.Debbie Brill (Canada) 1.88; 7.Susanne Helm (East Germany) 1.88; 8.Olga Juha (Hungary) 1.88; 9.Vanessa Brown (Australia) 1.88; 10.(Tie) Andrea Bienias (East Germany) and Silvia Costa (Cuba) 1.84; 12.(Tie) Maryse Ewanje-Epée (Francia), Katalin Sterk (Hungary) and Minna Vehmästo (Finland) 1.84; 15.Chris Soetewey (Belgium) 1.84; 16.Yang Wenqin (China) 1.84.

1984, year of the Los Angeles Olympics, began on a high note for Bykova, who raised her record mark to 2.05 at Kiev on 22 June. The following month Lyudmila Andonova of Bulgaria raised the record to 2.07 at Berlin on 20 July, beating Bykova (1.98). But the hideous boycott that kept the SU and Bulgaria out of the Olympics opened the way to Meyfarth's victory – **twelve years after her first.** The German, by then 28, won with a new Olympic record, 2.02. Her strongest rival that day was Sara Simeoni, who despite her ailments managed to grab the silver medal with 2.00, a height she had last mastered six years earlier. The "Track & Field News" World Ranking, issued as per tradition at the end of the year, had Meyfarth no higher than third and Simeoni only seventh. The top spot went to Lyudmila Andonova of Bulgaria, who scored 2-0 in her clashes with Bykova and had a superior seasonal record.

1984 Olympics, Los Angeles – High Jump (10 August): 1.Ulrike Meyfarth (West Germany) 2.02 (OR); 2.Sara Simeoni (Italy) 2.00; 3.Joni Huntley (USA) 1.97; 4.Maryse Ewanje-Epée (France) 1.94; 5.Debbie Brill (Canada) 1.94; 6.Vanessa Brown (Australia) 1.94; 7.Zheng Dazhen (China) 1.91; 8.Louise Ritter (USA) 1.91; 9. (Tie) Diane Elliott (GB) and Yang Wenquin (China) 1.88; 11.(tie) Brigitte Holzapfel (West Germany), Heike Redetzky (West Gernany), Pam Spencer (USA), Chris Stanton (Australia) and Niculina Vasile (Rumania) 1.85.

After missing the Los Angeles Games because of the boycott, Tamara Bykova was tenacious enough to go on for several more years. She had made her first appearance in the Olympics in 1980, placing ninth with 1.88. She went on to win a silver medal at the 1987 World Championships and bronze at the 1988 Olympics. The most recent holders of the world record have come from Bulgaria: Lyudmila Andonova and Stefka Kostadinova. The former, daughter of a Bulgarian father and a Russian mother, reached her peak in 1984, a year after giving birth to a daughter. On 20 July at Berlin, she shattered Bykova's fresh mark with a 2.07 clearance. As a Bulgarian she was of course among the unlucky athletes who missed the Los Angeles Olympics. In 1985 tragedy struck her in a more serious way when she was found "positive" to a stimulant (amphetamine) during a doping test. She was consequently suspended by the IAAF. When she returned to action in 1987, she was merely a shadow of her former self.

Stefka Kostadinova (born at Plovdiv on 25 March 1965; 1.80 m. / 60 Kg.) had a more solid career. A precocious talent, she cleared 2 metres for the first time at nineteen. Two years later, in 1986, she equalled Andonova's world record, 2.07, at Sofia n 25 May. And exactly six days later, at the same venue – Vasil Levski Stadium – she jumped 2.08. In 1987 she crowned a perfect season with a victory at the World Championships in Rome, where she raised the record to 2.09, winning a tough duel with Bykova (2.04). Kostadinova's seasonal record in 1987 stands as the greatest ever in the annals of the event. Between 21 January and 26 September she had 32 competitions, indoors and out, and lost only three. Her average for the year was a hair over 2.00 !

1987 World Championships, Rome – High Jump (30 August): 1.Stefka Kostadinova (Bulgaria) 2.09 (WR); 2.Tamara Bykova (SU) 2.04; 3.Susanne Beyer (East Germany) 1.99; 4.Silvia Costa (Cuba)

1.96; 5.Larisa Kositsyna (SU) 1.96; 6. Heike Redetzky (West Germany) 1.96; 7.Svetlana Isayeva (Bulgaria) 1.93; 8.(tie) Lyudmila Avdeyenko (SU) and Louise Ritter (USA) 1.93; 10.Madely Beaugendre (France) 1.93; 11.Coleen Sommer (USA) 1.93; 12.Lyudmila Andonova (Bulgaria) 1.85.

In athletics, however, the balance of powers can change anytime anywhere, and at the 1988 Olympics in Seoul the Bulgarian unexpectedly lost to Louise Ritter, a 30-year-old American. Both cleared 2.01 in the competition proper, then failed at 2.03. But Ritter mastered 2.03 in a jump-off, equalling her personal best, while Kostadinova failed again. That settled the issue and added to the long list of Olympic upsets. The American, who prior to 1988 had been a good but not exceptional jumper (her highest honour being a bronze at the 1983 World Championships), certainly timed her peak condition perfectly. At the end of the year, however, "Track & Field News" ranked Kostadinova first (for the fourth time in a row) and Ritter second as the Bulgarian won 2-1 in direct cash-es and had a better season's record.

1988 Olympics, Seoul - High Jump (30 September): 1.Louise Ritter (USA) 2.03 (OR); 2.Stefka Kostadinova (Bulgaria) 2.01; 3.Tamara Bykova (SU) 1.99; 4.Olga Turchak (SU) 1.96; 5.(tie) Lyudmila Andonova (Bulgaria) and Alina Astafei (Rumania) 1.93; 7.Christine Stanton (Australia) 1.93: 8.(tie) Diana Davies (GB) and Kim Hee-Sun (S.Korea) 1.90; 10.Maryse Ewanje-Epée (France) 1.90; 11.Megumi Satoh (Japan) 1.90; 12.Janet Boyle (GB) 1.90.

Stefka Kostadinova (Bulgaria), holder of the world's high jump record with 2.09 (1987).

The Seoul event was at any rate a turning point in Kostadinova's career. Subsequently plagued by a knee injury, she was unable to reproduce her 1987 form. Winner of the World Cup event at Barcelona in 1989 was Silvia Costa of Cuba, who chose the occasion to raise her lifetime best to 2.04.

The only jumper who came fairly close to Stefka Kostadinova's world record (2.09 in 1987) during the Nineties was **Heike Henkel** of Germany (born Redetzky on 5 May 1964 at Kiel; 1.82 m. / 63 Kg.). A gifted athlete no doubt, yet she had been active for more than ten years when she mastered 2 metres for the first time, in 1989. But only two years later she reached the top, wining at the World Championships in Tokyo with 2.05, leaving runner-up Yelena Yelesina of the SU 7 centimetres behind.

1991 World Championships, Tokyo - High Jump (31 August): 1.Heike Henkel (Germany) 2.05; 2.Yelena Yelesina (SU) 1.98; 3.Inga Babakova (SU) 1.96; 4.Beata Holub (Poland) 1.96; 5.Birgit Kähler (Germany) 1.93; 6.Stefka Kostadinova (Bulgaria) 1.93; 7.Tamara Bykova (SU) 1.93; 8.Judit Kovács (Hungary) 1.90; 9.Sárka Nováková (Czechoslovakia) 1.90; 10.Vanessa Ward (Australia) 1.90; 11.Alison Inverarity (Australia) 1.87; 12.Heike Balck (Germany) 1.84.

Heike Henkel had her best-ever mark in an indoor meet at Karlsruhe in 1992 – 2.07. Later in the same year she was crowned Olympic champion at Barcelona with 2.02. She thus matched her countrywoman Ulrike Meyfarth both mark-wise and in honours. She had a son in 1994, after which she repeatedly attempted a comeback, but persistent injuries hampered her and she never regained top form.

1992 Olympics, Barcelona - High Jump (8 August): 1.Heike Henkel (Germany) 2.02; 2.Alina Astafei (Rumania) 2.00; 3.Ioamnet Quintero (Cuba) 1.97; 4.Stefka Kostadinova (Bulgaria) 1.94; 5.Sigrid Kirchmann (Austria) 1.94; 6.Silvia Costa (Cuba) 1.94; 7.Megumi Satoh (Japan) 1.91; 8.Alison Inverarity (Australia) 1.91; 9.Debbie Marti (GB) 1.91; 10.Donata Jancewicz (Poland) 1.88; 11.(tie) Tanya Hughes (USA) and Birgit Kähler (Germany) 1.88.

Three highly touted jumpers failed rather badly at the 1993 World Championships. World record holder Kostadinova narrowly failed to qualify for the final, Henkel did but withdrew injured and Astafei merely tied for fourth. Two Cuban jumpers, Ioamnet Quintero and Silvia Costa, finished one-two in that order. The winner, aged 21, was 1.89 m. tall.

1993 World Championships, Stuttgart - High Jump (21 August): 1.Ioamnet Quintero (Cuba) 1.99; 2.Silvia Costa (Cuba) 1.97; 3.Sigrid Kirchmann (Austria) 1.97; 4.(tie) Alina Astafei (Rumania) and Yelena Rodina (Russia) 1.94; 6.Antonella Bevilacqua (Italy) 1.94; 7.Tanya Hughes (USA) 1.91; 8.Valentina Gotovska (Latvia) 1.91; 9.(tie) Hanne Haugland (Norway) and Katarzyna Majchrzak (Poland) 1.88; 11.Britta Bilac (Slovenia), Yelena Topchina (Russia) and Svetlana Zalevskaya (Kazakhstan) 1.88.

Kostadinova had a long spell at the top. She too gave birth to a son, in January 1995, yet a few months later she won her second world title at Göteborg with a 2.01 clearance. Such a quick comeback amazed even her husband and coach Nikolay Petrov. Quite an achievement, eight years after her first gold. Astafei had been given a three-year suspension by the Rumanian federation for refusing to compete at the 1994 European Indoor Championships. However, she migrated to Germany and gained German citizenship. Her silver medal was thus credited to her new country.

1995 World Championships, Göteborg - High Jump (13 August): 1.Stefka Kostadinova (Bulgaria) 2.01; 2.Alina Astafei (Germany) 1.99; 3.Inga Babakova (Ukraine) 1.99; 4.Tatyana Motkova (Russia) 1.96; 5.Tatyana Shevchik (Byelarus) 1.96; 6.Hanne Haugland (Norway) 1.96; 7.Svetlana Leseva (Bulgaria) 1.93; 8.(tie) Amy Acuff (USA) and Nele Zilinskiené (Lithuania) 1.93; 10.Yelena Topchina (Russia) 1.93; 11.Viktoriya Fyodorova (Russia) 1.90; 12.Tatyana Khramova (Byelarus) 1.85.

In 1996 Kostadinova went on to annexe her first Olympic title at Atlanta with 2.05 - a great achievement, 10 years after her first world record performance. This was in fact one of the highest summits ever, with Bakoyanni of Greece a surprise second at 2.03 and Babakova of Ukraine third at 2.01.

1996 Olympics, Atlanta - High Jump (3 August): 1.Stefka Kostadinova (Bulgaria) 2.05 (OR); 2.Niki Bakoyanni (Greece) 2.03; 3.Inga Babakova (Ukraine) 2.01; 4.Yelena Gulyayeva (Russia) 1.99; 5.(tie) Galina Astafei (Germany), Tatyana Motkova (Russia) and Nelé Zilinskiené (Lithuania) 1.96; 8.Hanne Haugland (Norway) 1.96; 9.(tie) Britta Bilac (Slovenia) and Tisha Waller (USA) 1.93; 11.(tie) Olga Bolshova (Moldavia) and Zuzana Kovácikovà (Czechoslovakia) 1.93; 13.Svetlana Zalevskaya (Kazakhstan) 1.93.

PS. Antonella Bevilacqua (Italy) finished fourth with 1.99 but was later disqualified for doping offence.

The imperishable Kostadinova won her last major title a the 1997 World Indoor Championships. Incidentally, this was her fifth victory in the annals of the undercover championships as opposed to two outdoor titles. As it happened to many great high jumpers, the wear and tear of training and competition with the resulting injuries finally put an end to Kostadinova's incredible career.

There was a relative standstill in high jump standards in the last years of the XX century. The last two world championship titles were won at 1.99, by Hanne Haugland olf Norway in 1997 and by Inga Babakova of Ukraine in 1999. The latter had collected medals in most if not all the major championships of the decade.

1997 World Championships, Athens - High Jump (10 August): 1.Hanne Haugland (Norway) 1.99; 2.(tie) Inga Babakova (Ukraine) and Olga Kaliturina (Russia) 1.96; 4.Yulya Lyakhova (Russia) 1.96; 5.(tie) Kajsa Bergqvist (Sweden) and Tatyana Motkova (Russia) 1.93; 7.(tie) Antonella Bevilacqua (Italy), Britta Bilac (Slovenia) and Alina Astafei (Germany) 1.93; 10.(tie) Heike Balck (Germany) and Hestrie Storbeck (South Africa) 1.90; 12.Pia Zinck (Denmark) 1.90.

1999 World Championships, Sevilla - High Jump (29 August): 1.Inga Babakova (Ukraine) 1.99; 2.Yelena Yelesina (Russia) 1.99; 3.Svetlana Lapina (Russia) 1.99; 4.(tie) Tisha Waller (USA), Kajsa Bergqvist (Sweden) and Zuzana Hlavonová (Czechoslovakia) 1.96; 7.Viktoriya Styopina (Ukraine) 1.96; 8.Svetlana Zalevskaya (Kazakhstan) 1.93; 9.Ami Acuff (USA) 1.93; 10.(tie) Hanne Haugland (Norway) and Monica Dinescu (Rumania) 1.93; 12.Yelena Gulyayeva (Russia) 1.93.

2000 was a year of mixed fortunes for most of the leading performers. Yelena Yelesina, a Russian by then living in Australia, won the Olympic title in a close battle with Hestrie Cloete of South Africa as both cleared 2.01. Sweden's Kajsa Bergqvist tied for third with the surprising Oana Pantelimon of Rumania, who improved on her personal best twice during the final. At the end of the season, however, Bergqvist was no.1 in "Track & Field News" World Ranking thanks to her solid seasonal record.

2000 Olympics, Sydney - High Jump (30 September): 1.Yelena Yelesina (Russia) 2.01; 2.Hestrie Cloete (South Africa) 2.01; 3.(tie) Kajsa Bergqvist (Sweden) and Oana Pantelimon (Rumania) 1.99; 5.Inga Babakova (Ukraine) 1.96; 6.Svetlana Zalevskaya (Kazakhstan) 1.96; 7.Viktoriya Palamar (Ukraine) 1.96; 8.Amewu Mensah (Germany) 1.93; 9.(tie) Venelina Veneva (Bulgaria) and Monica Dinescu (Rumania) 1.93; 11.(tie) Yoko Ota (Japan) and Zuzana Hlavonová (Czechoslovakia) 1.90; 13.Eleonora Milusheva (Bulgaria) 1.90.

At the end of the XX century there were 41 women in the 2-Metre Club, with two Bulgarians – Kostadinova and Andonova – on top.

POLE VAULT

Emma, the trail blazer; Stacy, the first world champion

Sometime during the Eighties the most active explorer of women's talent in this event was China. It was only in 1991, however, that an athlete from that country managed to clear a bar set at exactly 4 metres. This was Zhang Chunzhen, aged 21, and she did just that at Guangzhou on 24 March of that year. Another Chinese woman, Sun Caiyun, went up to 4.23 outdoors (1995) and 4.28 indoors (1996), alas after suffering a 3-month ban through a positive test for stimulants in 1994.

Pioneer of the event in Europe was Daniela Bartová of Czechoslovakia, who bettered the world best time and again, up to 4.22 at Salgótarján on 11 September 1995. This mark was achieved in an international town square event – an obviously unofficial variety which was quite popular with both male and female vaulters.

The first woman to really make history in the event was an Australian, **Emma George** (born at Beechworth, Victoria, on 1 November 1974; 1.72 m. 64 Kg.). As a teen-ager she was a trapeze artist in the Flying Fruit Flies Circus for several years. Her early interest in athletics was for the sprints and the long jump. Late in 1994 she entered her first pole vault competitions, clearing 2.55. That was the start of a meteoric rise. Exactly a year later, on 30 November 1995 in Melbourne, she set the first of a long series of world

Emma George (Australia), a trail blazer in the evolution of the women's pole vault.

records with 4.25. That was incidentally the year when the IAAF began to ratify record performances. George acted as a trail blazer to an ever growing number of women who in various parts of the world had taken up the event. As she went higher and higher she adopted the approved Sergey Bubka strategy, improving by one centimetre at a time. A barrier which over half a century ago had captured the imagination of men, namely 15 feet (4.57), was mastered by George on 20 February 1998 at Auckland. On that occasion she exhibited a change in her technique, jumping off 12 steps instead of her regular 16. "I didn't think it would be possible", she said. "To do this off my shorter run is just fantastic for me". Later in the same year she did 4.58, then 4.59. With her 11th official world, at Sydney on 20 February 1999, she conquered another barrier, more significant in the eyes of the metric-minded world – 4.60. In terms of competitive ability, however, she was clearly outshone by an American, **Stacy Dragila** (born Mikaelsen at Auburn on 25 March 1971; 1.72 m. / 63 Kg.). In fact, Dragila had been at work a bit longer than her Aussie rival, but her progress was slower. Yet, when the IAAF decided to award the first major PV title at the

1997 World Indoor Championships in Paris, Dragila beat George, 4.40 to 4.35. Wrote "Track & Field News": "Emma George forgot one of the elemental rules of vaulting: it doesn't matter how high you jump, it's how high you jump when the bar gets high. In fact, the Aussie star produced some spectacular clearances at lower heights, but when push came to shove, she couldn't clear the bar.

And surprising Stacy Dragila could". This was confirmed time and again in subsequent seasons. George just could not do herself justice in hot competitions.

The women's pole vault first appeared in a "global" outdoor meet at the 1999 World Championships in Sevilla. George was the shadow of herself: just back from injury after a disastrous European campaign, she merely managed 4.15 and finished unplaced. Anzhela Balakhonova of Ukraine held the lead for a long time, but when the bar was raised to 4.60, Dragila turned the tables on her, going over on her second try. The American thus equaled George's world record. Balakhonova was second at 4.55 and Tatyana Grigoryeva, a born Russian now competing for Australia, was third at 4.45.

1999 World Championships, Sevilla - Pole Vault (21 August): 1.Stacy Dragila (USA) 4.60 (eq.WR); 2.Anzhela Balakhonova (Ukraine) 4.55; 3.Tatyana Grigoryeva (Australia) 4.45; 4.Zsuzsanna Szabó (Hungary) 4.40; 5.Nicole Humbert (Germany) 4.40; 6.(tie) Pavla Hamácková (Czechoslovakia) and Daniela Bártová (Czechoslovakia) 4.40; 8.Yelena Belyakova (Russia) 4.35; 9.Kellie Suttle (USA) 4.35; 10.Elmarie Gerryts (South Africa) 4.25; 11.Alejandra Garcia (Argentina) 4.25; 12.Vala Flosadóttir (Iceland) 4.25.

Stacy Dragila (USA), the first outdoor world champion (1999) in the women's pole vault.

Stacy Dragila became the sole owner of the world record on 23 July 2000 at Sacramento, in a meet that served as both National Championships and US Olympic Trials. She cleared 4.63 on her first attempt, leaving her nearest rival, Kellie Suttle, twenty centimetres behind. Later in the year, at Sydney, the American won the Olympic title with 4.60. This was the official première of the event in the Olympics. She also went over 4.70 in a so-called Beach Pole Vault Challenge, held at Santa Barbara on 11 June. The competition was held on an elevated board runway on Leadbetter Beach. Obviously unacceptable for official purposes, although statistically valid.

Emma George was below her best for most of the season and failed to qualify for the Olympic final. At the end of the year she had surgery on her feet for three stress fractures.

2000 Olympics, Sydney – Pole Vault (25 September): 1.Stacy Dragila (USA) 4.60 (OR); 2.Tatyana Grigoryeva (Australia) 4.55; 3.Vala Flosadóttir (Iceland) 4.50; 4.Daniela Bártová (Czechoslovakia) 4.50; 5.Nicole Humbert (Germany) 4.45; 6.Yvonne Buschbaum (Germany) 4.40; 7.Monika Pyrek (Poland) 4.40; 8.Marie Rasmussen (Denmark) 4.35; 9.Doris Auer (Austria) 4.25; 10.Gao Shuying (China) 4.15; 11.Kellie Suttle (USA) 4.00. No valid jump: Elmarie Gerryts (South Africa) and Anzhela Balakhonova (Ukraine).

At the end of 2000 thirteen women had gone 4.50 or higher.

LONG JUMP

Lithuanian breaks 7-metre barrier

I have already hinted to the all-round ability of Heide Rosendahl. The daughter of a good discus thrower, she showed great promise as a junior, winning a silver medal in the pentathlon at the 1966 European Championships in Budapest. By then the long jump was her parade event. After capturing the world record in 1970 (6.84), she annexed the Olympic crown in the 1972 Games in Munich, edging Diana Yorgova of Bulgaria in a close contest, 6.78 to 6.77. Those Games were in fact the high-water mark in Heide's career. She also won a silver medal in the pentathlon and capped an unforgettable week with a fantastic anchor leg in the sprint relay, winning gold for West Germany. She had given the competitor's oath at the opening ceremony and was the "coqueluche" of the crowd throughout the Games.

1972 Olympics, Munich – Long Jump (31 August): 1.Heidemarie Rosendahl (West Germany) 6.78; 2.Dana Yorgova (Bulgaria) 6.77; 3.Eva Suranová (Czechoslovakia) 6.67; 4.Marcia Garbey (Cuba) 6.52w; 5.Heldi Schüller (West Germany) 6.51; 6.Meta Antenen (Switzerland) 6.49; 7.Viorica Viscopoleanu (Rumania) 6.48; 8.Margit Olfert (East Germany) 6.46; 9.Sheila Sherwood (GB) 6.41; 10.Ilona Bruzsenyak (Hungary) 6.39; 11.Willie White (USA) 6.27; 12.Jarmila Nygrynová (Czechoslovakia) 6.24.

Rosendahl's "Kämpfer-Herz"

Heide Rosendahl had her brightest hours as a versatile star in the 1972 Olympics.

Playing in Munich, hence "at home", was certainly a major advantage to the bespectacled West German star. As related in the text, she won her parade event, the long jump, beating Dana Yorgova of Bulgaria by one centimetre (6.78 to 6.77) and was second in the pentathlon. But where she really showed her great "Kämpfer-Herz" (as the Germans say – fighting heart) was in the last leg of the 4x100 m. relay. She took the baton for the final leg with a lead of about 3/4 m. vis-à-vis the massive Renate Stecher of East Germany, who had previously triumphed in both sprints (100 and 200 m.) and was therefore rated as the world's fastest woman. Most observers obviously thought that Stecher would reverse positions. But in the most hectic seconds of her career Heide really out-passed herself. The prevalently West German crowd obviously rooted for her. The advantage of "playing at home" is generally regarded as important, especially in team games, but less so in individual sports. Yet Rosendahl was not to be denied – she held on bravely and actually increased her lead vis-à-vis Stecher, winning comfortably, 42.81 (a new world record) to 42.95. That was in my view one of the greatest competitive efforts I have ever witnessed.

PS. Five years later, Rosendahl gave birth to a son, Danny (known as Ecker, as per his father's surname). He too fell in love with athletics: in an honourable career he managed to join the select group of 6-metre pole vaulters (6.00 indoors in 2001), but in terms of honours he never came close to matching his mother's record.

Rosendahl's successor as a world record holder was Angela Voigt of East Germany, who did 6.92 at Dresden on 9 May 1976. Only ten days later, still at Dresden, she was beaten by her compatriot Siegrun Siegl, who wrested the record from her with a 6.99 effort, while Voigt had to be content with 6.78. The latter eventually won the rubber race at the Montreal Olympics with 6.72, while Siegl was only fourth. (The latter won the pentathlon in a photo finish decision a few days later).

1976 Olympics, Montreal – Long Jump (23 July): 1.Angela Voigt (East Germany) 6.72; 2.Kathy McMillan (USA) 6.66; 3.Lidiya Alfeyeva (SU) 6.60; 4.Sigrun Siegl (East Germany) 6.59; 5.Ildikó Szabó (Hungary) 6.57; 6.Jarmila Nygrynová (Czechoslovakia) 6.54; 7.Heidemarie Wycisk (East Germany) 6.39; 8.Elena Vintila (Rumania) 6.38; 9.Susan Reeve (GB) 6.27; 10.Aniko Milassin (Hungary) 6.19; 11.Diane Jones (Canada) 6.13; No valid jump: Liliana Panayotova (Bulgaria).

The elusive 7-metre barrier was broken in 1978 by a Lithuanian representing the SU, **Wilma Bardauskiene née Augustinaviciute** (born at Pakruojis, Lithuania, on 15 June 1953; 1.72 m. / 61 Kg.). She emerged as a topnotch performer at twenty-four with 6.82. On 18 August 1978 at Kishinyov she mastered 7 metres not once but three times: 7.07 (wind +1.83 m/s), 7.07 (wind over the limit) and 7.06. At the European Championships in Prague, eleven days later, she improved on her record mark in the qualifying round with 7.09 (wind zero), then won the title with 6.88. With such marks as 11.2 in the 100 m. and 1.68 in the high jump, she certainly had a great potential. An expert like Igor Ter-Ovanesyan once described her as "7.50 stuff". But like so many other great athletes of our time she had to pay a heavy tribute to the Moloch of injuries. A stress fracture severely hampered her in 1980 and she was unable to qualify for the Moscow Olympics. That was the end of her career.

As it often happens when a conventional barrier finally crumbles, other jumpers soon entered 7-metre territory. The 1980 Olympic event in Moscow offered a hot battle, at the end of which a jump of 6.95 only sufficed for fourth place. Winner of a tight contest was Tatyana Kolpakova of the SU at 7.06, with the other two medal winners also mastering the 7-metre barrier.

1980 Olympics, Moscow – Long Jump (31 July): 1.Tatyana Kolpakova (SU) 7.06 (OR); 2.Brigitte Wujak (East Germany) 7.04; 3.Tatyana Skachko (SU) 7.01; 4.Anna Wlodarczyk (Poland) 6.95; 5.Siegrun Siegl (East Germany) 6.87; 6.Jarmila Nygrynová (Czechoslovakia) 6.83; 7.Siegrid Heimann (East Germany) 6.71; 8.Lidiya Alfeyeva (SU) 6.71; 9.Susan Hearnshaw (GB) 6.50; 10.Susan Reeve (GB) 6.46; 11.Barbara Wojnar-Baran (Poland) 6.33; 12.Lidia Gousheva (Bulgaria) 6.24. 13.Jennifer Inniss (Guyana) 6.10.

In the early Eighties, two Rumanians took turns in bettering the world record. On 1 August 1982 Anisoara Stanciu née Cusmir succeeded Bardauskiene during the Rumanian Championships at Bucharest with a 7.15 effort, but five minutes later she was outshone by Valeria Ionescu, who went 7.20 and thereby clinched title and record. But Stanciu had the last word in this "internal struggle" when she reached 7.27, then 7.43, still at Bucharest on 4 June 1983.

At the "première" of the World Championships, held at Helsinki later in 1983, both Rumanians had to bow to a talented East German, Heike Daute, who won with a wind-aided 7.27. Cusmir was second and third went to Carol Lewis of USA, younger sister of the great Carl, then the no.1 sprinter and long jumper in the men's ranks.

1983 World Championships, Helsinki – Long Jump (14 August): 1.Heike Daute (East Germany) 7.27w (+2.2 m/s); 2.Anisoara Cusmir-Stanciu (Rumania) 7.15w (+3.4 m/s); 3.Carol Lewis (USA) 7.04w (+4.3 m/s); 4.Tatyana Proskuryakova (SU) 7.02; 5.Beverly Kinch (GB) 6.93w; 6.Zsuzsa Vanyek (Hungary) 6.81; 7.Eva Murková (Czechoslovakia) 6.80w; 8.Robyn Lorraway (Australia) 6.85; 9.Valy Ionescu (Rumania) 6.62; 10.Jarmila Strejcková (Czechoslovakia) 6.56; 11.Jennifer Inniss (Guyana) 6.54; 12.Helga Radtke (East Germany) 6.44.

At the 1984 Olympics in Los Angeles, Rumania was the only Eastern European country to take part. Stanciu and Ionescu seized the opportunity and finished one-two in that order.

1984 Olympics, Los Angeles – Long Jump (9 August): 1.Anisoara Cusmir-Stanciu (Rumania) 6.96; 2.Valy Ionescu (Rumania) 6.81; 3.Sue Hearnshaw (GB) 6.80w; 4.Angela Thacker (USA) 6.78w; 5.Jackie Joyner-Kersee (USA) 6.77; 6.Robyn Lorraway (Australia) 6.67; 7.Glynis Nunn (Australia) 6.53w; 8.Shonel Ferguson (Bahamas) 6.44; 9.Carol Lewis (USA) 6.43; 10.Dorothy Scott (Jamaica) 6.40; 11.Linda Garden (Australia) 6.30; 12.Snezana Dancetovic (Yugoslavia) 5.88.

Heike Drechsler née Daute of East Germany (born on 16 December 1964 at Gera, 1.81 m. / 68 Kg.) eventually put an end to the Rumanian intermezzo when she reached 7.44 in Berlin on 22 August 1985. This new world record was reached on her sixth and last trial, with a wind of exactly 2.0 m/s. The following year

Heike Drechsler (Germany), for many years a topclass long jumper. In her early years she was also a leading sprinter, equalling the world's 200 m. record in 1986 with 21.71.

she did 7.45 twice, first at Tallinn on 21 June, then at Dresden on 3 July, with legal aiding winds of 0.9 m/s and 1.1 m/s respectively. By then also a co-holder of the world's 200 m. record (21.71), Drechsler excelled all her predecessors in basic speed. She scored a great double in the European Championships, held in Stuttgart, later in 1986, with 21.71 and 7.27. However, even this talented athlete was to find a tough nut to crack – tough enough to beat her in both the 1987 World Championships and the 1988 Olympics. The woman in question was **Jackie Joyner-Kersee** of USA (born at East St.Louis, Illinois, on 3 March 1962; 1.78 m. / 70 Kg.), who gradually developed into the greatest all-rounder in the annals of women's athletics. This agile but solidly built American, sister of triple jumper Al Joyner (the 1984 Olympic champion) married her coach Bob Kersee in 1986. The long jump was her best event. She first landed in 7-metre territory at twenty-three and by 1987 she was able to challenge all comers. She equalled Drechsler's world record, 7.45, during the Pan-American Games at Indianapolis on 13 August 1987, with a mild aiding breeze (+0-6 m/s). The following month she had her first major clash with Drechsler at the World Championships in Rome, where she defeated the German, 7.36 to 7.13. In fairness to Drechsler, it should be added that she injured her left knee in her fourth trial and was unable to take her remaining jumps. She actually finished third, close behind Yelena Byelevskaya of the SU (7.14).

Jackie Joyner-Kersee (USA), the greatest of all in the multiple events, was also a topclass long jumper.

1987 World Championships, Rome – Long Jump (4 September): 1.Jackie Joyner-Kersee (USA) 7.36 (CR) (+0.4 m/s); 2.Yelena Byelevskaya (SU) 7.14 (-0.6 m/s); 3.Heike Drechsler (East Germany) 7.13 (-0.7 m/s); 4.Helga Radtke (East Germany) 7.01; 5.Galina Chistyakova (SU) 6.99; 6.Irina Valyukyevich (SU) 6.89, 7.Jennifer Inniss (USA) 6.80; 8.Nicole Boegman (Australia) 6.63; 9.Lyudmila Ninova (Bulgaria) 6.50; 10.Silviya Moneva (Bulgaria) 6.45; Sheila Echols (USA) 6.39; 12.Lene Demsitz (Denmark) 6.11.

The woman who set the last world record of the century was **Galina Chistyakova** of the SU (born at Izmail, Ukraine, on 26 July 1962; 1.69 m. / 54 Kg.). At 22 she managed 7.29, while no faster than 11.6 as a sprinter. She broke the world mark held by Drechsler (7.45) during the Znamenskiy Memorial meet at Leningrad on 11 June 1988, landing at 7.52 (wind + 1.31 m/s). This was on her sixth and last trial, after she had equalled the record on her fourth (wind +0.92 m/s). Before and after such an exploit, however, she had to be content with a fifth place at the 1987 "Worlds" and a third at the 1988 Olympics. She was married to a world class triple jumper, Aleksandr Beskrovniy (17.53 in 1983). Joyner eventually won the re-match with Drechsler at the 1988 Seoul Olympics – 7.40 to 7.22. Drechsler had injured her back two days before this competition. Yet she also managed to compete in the 200 metres, finishing third.

1988 Olympics, Seoul – Long Jump (29 September): 1.Jackie Joyner-Kersee (USA) 7.40 (+0.9 m/s, OR); 2.Heike Drechsler (East Germany) 7.22 (+0.5 m/s); 3.Galina Chistyakova (SU) 7.11 (+1.3 m/s); 4.Yelena Byelevskaya (SU) 7.04; 5.Nicole Boegman (Australia) 6.73w; 6.Fiona May (GB) 6.62; 7.Agata Karczmarek (Poland) 6.60; 8.Sabine John (E.Germany) 6.55; 9.Xiong Qiying (China) 6.50; 10.Inessa Kravets (SU) 6.46; 11.Liu Shuzhen (China) 6.40; 12.Lene Demsitz (Denmark) 6.38.

Joyner-Kersee, a great competitor if ever there was one, won yet another major duel wit Heike Drechsler at the 1991 World Championships in Tokyo. That was a close duel though. She opened with 7.32 on her first jump, to which Drechsler responded with 7.29 on her third. The American then tried to improve further but stepped on the plasticine and twisted her right foot. She landed heavily in the sand and looked to be severely injured. But it wasn't so bad after all and she closed with 7.11 in the sixth round.

Throughout the Nineties Galina Chistyakova's world record (7.52 in 1988) withstood all assaults – like many other records established in the preceding decade which we may recall as the "Smoky Eighties". Begrimed with smoke, yes, were it only in the sense that drug tests left much to be desired at the time in terms of both frequency and effectiveness. However, at least one jumper managed to menace Chistyakova's record, namely Heike Drechsler, who did 7.63 at Sestriere on 31 July 1994, an effort which was nullified by an aiding wind of 2.1 m/s – i.e. over the allowable limit by an infinitesimal margin. However, if we consider that Sestrière, an Italian ski resort, is located 2.050 metres above sea level, then we may conclude that in intrinsic value Drechsler's 7.63 was surely no better than several other marks in the range 7.52 / 7.48 made with legal winds at or near sea level. That notably includes a mark of 7.48 made by Drechsler herself at Lausanne on 8 July 1992 with an aiding wind of merely 0.4 m/s.

As a top-class athlete Drechsler managed to survive the downfall of the GDR Communist regime better than most other champions of that country, whose names – just like hers – appear on several occasions with circumstantial evidence in Brigitte Berendonk's book "Doping". In the Nineties she definitely preferred the long jump to her other love, the sprints, and although failing in her repeated efforts to break Chistyakova's record she performed at 7.20-plus levels more consistently than any other jumper. After giving birth to a son in 1989, she returned to action and barely lost to her arch-rival Jackie Joyner-Kersee, 7.29 to 7.32, at the 1991 World Championships in Tokyo.

1991 World Championships, Tokyo – Long Jump (25 August): 1.Jackie Joyner-Kersee (USA) 7.32 (wind 0.0 m/s); 2.Heike Drechsler (Germany) 7.29 (-0-2 m/s); 3.Larisa Berezhnaya (SU) 7.11 (0.0 m/s); 4.Yelena Sinchukova (SU) 7.04 (1.8 m/s); 5.Susen Tiedtke (Germany) 6.77; 6.Marieta Ilcu (Rumania) 6.72; 7.Ljudmila Ninova (Austria) 6.72; 8.Yelena Byelevskaya (SU) 6.69; 9.Ringa Ropo-Junnila (Finland) 6.63; 10.Jackie Edwards (Bahamas) 6.37; 11.Christy Opara-Thompson (Nigeria) 6.28; 12.Yinka Idowu (GB) 6.16.

Drechsler regained the top a year later at the Barcelona Olympics with 7.14, winning from Inessa Kravets and Joyner-Kersee.

1992 Olympics, Barcelona – Long Jump (7 August): 1.Heike Drechsler (Germany) 7.14; 2.Inessa Kravets (Ukraine) 7.12; 3.Jackie Joyner-Kersee (USA) 7.07; 4.Mirela Dulgheru (Rumania) 6.71; 5.Irina Mushayilova (Russia) 6.68; 6.Sharon Couch (USA) 6.66; 7.Sheila Echols (USA) 6.62; 8.Susen Tiedtke (Germany) 6.60; 9.Flora Hyacinth (Virgin Islands) 6.52; 10.Agatha Karczmarek (Poland) 6.41; 11.Renata Nielsen (Denmark) 6.06; Disqualified for doping offence: Niole Medvedyeva (Lithuania).

Galina Chistyakova (USSR) holds the current women's world record for the long jump - 7.52 in 1988.

Drechsler won yet another world title at Stuttgart in 1993 (7.11) – ten years after her first victory in Helsinki. In later years injuries, necessitating surgery on both Achilles tendons, hampered her more than somewhat. Yet she was able to resist rust till the end of the century, as will be related later on.

1993 World Championships, Stuttgart – Long Jump (15 August): 1.Heike Drechsler (Germany) 7.11 (-0.3 m/s); 2.Larisa Berezhnaya (Ukraine) 6.98 (+0.4 m/s); 3.Renata Nielsen (Denmark) 6.76 (+0.6 m/s); 4.Yelena Khlopotnova (Ukraine) 6.75; 5.Lyudmila Galkina (Russia) 6.74; 6.Lyudmila Ninova (Austria) 6.73; 7.Nicole Boegman (Australia) 6.70; 8.Agata Karczmarek (Poland) 6.57; 9.Susen Tiedtke (Germany) 6.54; 10.Yelena Sinchukova (Russia) 6.52; 11.Mrela Dulgheru (Rumania) 6.48; 12.Valentina Uccheddu (Italy) 6.38.

The most consistent medal winner in the latter part of the Nineties was **Fiona May** (born on 12 December 1969 at Slough, England; 1.82 m. / 61 Kg.). In the early part of her career she competed in the colours of her native country, Great Britain. Following her marriage with an Italian athlete, Gianni Iapichino (national record holder in the pole vault with 5.70), she became eligible to represent Italy from 1994 onwards. A tall, stream-lined girl, she had shown great promise as a youngster, winning a world junior title in 1988. Then, after years of a relative standstill, she blossomed again under Italian colours. She won her first major title at the 1995 World Championships, not without the assistance of the wind, which blew in her favour (4.3 m/s) during her best trial. She had a second best of 6.93 with a legal wind (0.8 m/s) which would have sufficed for victory anyhow. Former greats Joyner-Kersee and Drechsel had to be content with minor placings. The versatile Jackie had nonetheless remained at or near the top for a long time, reaching her best-ever in 1994 - 7.49 twice, first in New York, then at Sestrière.

1995 World Championships, Göteborg – Long Jump (6 August): 1.Fiona May (Italy) 6.98w (+4.3 m/s); 2.Niurka Montalvo (Cuba) 6.86 (+0.5 m/s); 3.Irina Mushayilova (Russia) 6,83w (+3.0 m/s); 4.Olga Rublyova (Russia) 6.78; 5.Valentina Uccheddu (Itly) 6.76; 6.Jackie Joyner-Kersee (USA) 6.74w; 7.Agata Karczmarek (Poland) 6.71; 8.Viktoriya Vershinina (Ukraine) 6.66; 9.Heike Drechsel (Germany) 6.64w; 10.Inessa Kravets (Ukrane) 6.57; 11.Yelena Khlopotnova (Ukraine) 6.53; 12.Chantal Brunner (New Zealand) 6.43. No valid mark: Jackie Edwards (Bahamas).

In the 1996 Olympics at Atlanta victory went to Chioma Ajunwa of Nigeria, who thus became her country's no.1 "gold" in the history of the Games. She was just returning to competition after a four-year drugs ban and won from Fiona May, 7.12 to 7.02.

Fiona May (Italy), a British-born long jumper, was a steady collector of medals, including a world title (1995), toward the end of the century.

1996 Olympics, Atlanta - Long Jump (2 August): 1.Chioma Ajunwa (Nigeria) 7.12 (+0.9 m/s); 2.Fiona May (Italy) 7.02 (+1.4 m/s); 3.Jackie Joyner-Kersee (USA) 7.00 (+0.5 m/s); 4.Niki Xanthou (Greece) 6.97, 5.Yelena Shekhovtsova (Ukraine) 6.97; 6.Agata Karczmarerk (Poland) 6.90; 7.Nicole Boegman (Australia) 6.73; 8.Tünde Vaszi (Hungary) 6.60; 9.Chantal Brunner (New Zealand) 6.49w; 10.Voula Patoulidou (Greece) 6.37; No valid jump: Sharon Jaklofsky (Holland). Disqualified for drug offence: Iva Prandzheva (Bulgaria) 6.82.

Fiona May continued to rank among the world's best for the rest of the century, winning medals in two more editions of the World Championships – bronze in 1997 and silver in 1999. For all her competitive achievements, however, she wound up with a personal best of "merely" 7.11 in 1998, plus a wind-aided 7.23 in the altitude of Sestrière (2050 m.) in 1995. World champion at Athens in 1997 was Lyudmila Galkina of Russia with a personal best of 7.05. Chioma Ajunwa looked most promising in the qualifying rounds, leading with 7.01, but she hurt herself on her first jump in the final and was carried off on a stretcher.

1997 World Championships, Athens – Long Jump (9 August): 1.Lyudmila Galkina (Russia) 7.05 (+0.6 m/s); 2.Niki Xanthou (Greece) 6.94 (+0.1 m/s); 3.Fiona May (Italy) 6.91 (+0.8 m/s); 4.Heike Drechsler (Germany) 6.89; 5.Jackie Joyner-Kersee (USA) 6.79; 6.Susen Tiedtke-Greene (Germany) 6.78; 7.Viktoriya Vershinina (Ukraine) 6.71; 8.Erica Johansson (Sweden) 6.64; 9.Magdalena Khristova (Bulgaria) 6.64; 10.Marion Jones (USA) 6.63; 11.Sharon Jaklofsky (Holland) 6.61; 12.Chioma Ajunwa (Nigeria) 5.21.

The last world championship title of the century went to Niurka Montalvo of Spain, whose best jump, 7.06, came in her final attempt. Some observers, notably including runner-up Fiona May, doubted its validity, yet TV replays showed that there may have been no impression on the plasticine. The Spaniard jumped upwards without rotating her foot.

1999 World Championships, Sevilla – Long Jump (23 August): 1.Niurka Montalvo (Spain) 7.06 (-0.1 m/s); 2.Fiona May (Italy) 6.94 (-0.2 m/s); 3.Lyudmila Galkina (Russia) 6.82 (0.0 m/s); 4.Joanne Wise (GB) 6.75; 5.Dawn Burrell (USA) 6.74; 6.Susen

Tiedtke (Germany) 6.68; 7.Maurren Maggi (Brazil) 6.68; 8.Nicole Boegman (Australia) 6.63; 9.Erica Johansson (Sweden) 6.63; 10.Olga Rublyova (Russia) 6.56; 11.Shana Williams (USA) 6.52. Disqualified for doping offence: Marion Jones (USA) 6.83 (-0.2 m/s).

By the end of the century an American, Marion Jones, began to look as possibly the greatest prospect of them all. She was in the first place a sprinter, no. 1 in the world to be sure. As a long jumper she showed technical flaws, yet she did 7.31 in 1998. After finishing no better than tenth at the 1997 "Worlds", she rose to third in the 1999 edition at Sevilla. Close observers of her training deeds rated her as "7.60 stuff". At the 2000 Olympics in Sydney she won 100 and 200 metres (10.75 and 21.84 respectively) and helped the US sprint relay to place third. However, her athletic figure was severely damaged years later. At the end of a long controversy, she confessed that she had been using drugs in 1999/2000, under the guidance of her coach Trevor Graham. She also pled guilty to having previously lied to investigators about such a felony. The IAAF deprived her of the medals she had won at the 1999 Worlds and the 2000 Olympics. Such mendacity finally cost her several months in jail. All this probably amounted to the most serious case ever seen in the domain of "private vices" characteristic of democratic countries, an expression we chose to use alongside that of "state vices", those perpetrated in dictatorships (e.g. DDR or East Germany).

2000 Olympics (Sydney) - Long Jump (29 September): 1.Heike Drechsler (Germany) 6.99 (+1.9 m/s); 2.Fiona May (Italy) 6.92 (+1.1 m/s); 3.Tatyana Kotova (Russia) 6.83 (+1.4 m/s); 4.Olga Rublyova (Russia) 6.79; 5.Susen Tiedtke (Germany) 6.74; 6.Jackie Edwards (Bahams) 6.59; 7.Tünde Vaszi (Hungary) 6.59; 8.Lyudmila Galkina (Russia) 6.56w; 9.Elva Goulbourne (Jamaica) 6.43; 10.Dawn Burrell (USA) 6.38; 11.Yelena Shekhovtsova (Ukraine) 6.37. Disqualified for doping offence: Marion Jones (USA) 6.92 (+1.0 m/s).

TRIPLE JUMP

Kravets put it on the map

The triple jump is among the latest additions to the standard programme of women's athletics. The IAAF first included it in the programme of the World Championships in 1993. As an international event it had begun to blossom in the Eighties, especially in USA. Japan, the SU and China. The last unofficial world record was credited to Galina Chistyakova of the SU, 14.52 in 1989. The IAAF book was opened the following year and Li Huirong of China, 24, became the first official holder of the world record – 14.54 at Sapporo on 25 August 1990.

The first winner at the "Worlds" was a Russian, **Anna Biryukova** (born on 27 September 1967 at Sverdlovsk; 1.74 m. / 58 Kg.). who chose the occasion to break the 15-metre barrier with 15.09. She was a good but not exceptional long jumper (6.89 in 1990). In fact, she had failed to qualify for the final of that event a few days earlier.

1993 World Championships, Suttgart - Triple Jump (21 August): 1.Anna Biryukova (Russia) 15.09 (WR) (+0.5 m/s); 2.Iolanda Chen (Russia) 14.70 (+0.1 m/s); 3.Iva Prandzheva (Bulgaria) 14.23 (-0.2 m/s); 4.Niurka Montalvo (Cuba) 14.22; 5.Helgha Radtke (Germany) 14.19; 6.Antonella Capriotti (Italy) 14.18; 7.Sárka Kaspárková (Czech Rep.) 14.16; 8.Urszula Wlodarczyk (Poland) 13.80; 9.Michelle Griffith (GB) 13.69; 10.Jelena Blazevica (Latvia) 13.57; 11.Ljudmila Ninova (Austria) 13.30; 12.Monica Toth (Rumania) 12.87. No valid jump: Inna Lasovskaya (Russia).

Then came the woman who really put the event on the map: **Inessa Kravets** of Ukraine (née Shulyak on 5 October 1966 at Dnyepropetrovsk; 1.78 m. / 58 Kg.). She was a first-class long jumper with a personal best of 7.37 plus a second place in the Olympics, both in 1992. In fact, she had been one of Biryukova's predecessors as holder of the world's triple jump record too (14.95 in 1991). At the 1995 World Championships in Göteborg she had a poor day in the long jump, finishing no better than tenth. She was thirsty for revenge and on 10 August she made history in the triple jump. Three days earlier she had watched Jonathan Edwards sail to a world record of 18.29 in the men's event. The Ukrainian girl very much wanted to emulate him, but she had a poor start, fouling her first two tries, apparently because "she found the runway so fast that she had increased the length of her usual run-up". After that she badly needed a "safe" jump, still good enough to make the top 8 who were allowed to go on. Here again she misjudged things, but in a different way for she "exploded" with a mighty 15.50 – 41 centimetres beyond Biryukova's world record ! The wind was a legal +0.9 m/s. Later in round 3 Biryukova reacted with a gallant 15.08 and in round 5 Prandzheva of Bulgaria took second place with 15.18. Kravets' last three tries were anti-climactic: foul, pass, 14.55. She amazingly described her world record as "an imperfect jump".

1995 World Championships, Göteborg – Triple Jump (10 August): 1.Inessa Kravets (Ukraine) 15.50 (WR) (+0.9 m/s); 2.Iva Prandzheva (Bulgaria) 15.18 (+0.3 m/s); 3.Anna Biryukova (Russia) 15.08 (+1.4 m/s); 4.Inna Lasovskaya (Russia) 14.90; 5.Rodica Petrescu (Rumania) 14.82w; 6.Ren Ruiping (China) 14.25; 7.Zhanna Gureyeva (Byelarus) 14.22; 8.Barbara Lah (Italy) 14.18w; 9.Jelena Blazevica (Latvia) 14.09; 10.Olena Govorova (Ukraine) 14.07; 11.Iolanda Chen (Russia) 14.05; 12.Michelle Griffith (GB) 13.59.

In 1996 Kravets annexed the Olympic title as well, with 15.33. It should be mentioned that back in 1993 she had been inflicted a 3-months drugs ban for stimulants. In 1997 she had an operation on a serious right thigh injury.

1996 Olympics, Atlanta – Triple Jump (31 July): 1.Inessa Kravets (Ukraine) 15.33 (OR) (-0.1 m/s); 2.Inna Lasovskaya (Russia) 14.98 (+1.1m/s); 3.Sárka Kaspárková (Czech Rep.) 14.98 (-0.6 m/s); 4.Ashia Hansen (GB) 14.49; 5.Olga Vasdeki (Greece) 14.44; 6.Ren Ruiping (China) 14.30; 7.Rodica Mateescu (Rumania) 14.21; 8.Jelena Blazevica (Latvia) 14.12; 9.Olena Govorova (Ukraine) 14.09; 10.Sheila Hudson (USA) 14.02; 11.Olena Khlusovych (Ukraine) 13.81; Disqualified for doping offence: Iva Prandzheva (Bulgaria) 14.92.

Inessa Kravets (Ukraine), an excellent long jumper who reached the top when she turned to a new event, the triple jump.

In the last three "global" meets of the century Kravets' world record was never really threatened. Yet Sárka Kaspárková of the Czech Republic in 1997 and Tereza Marinova of Bulgaria in 2000 both won major titles with 15.20. It fell to a Russian, Tatyana Lebedeva, to move to second best of all time with a mark of 15.33, made at Yokohama in 2000.

1997 World Championships, Athens – Triple Jump (4 August): 1.Sárka Kaspárková 15.20 (0.0 m/s); 2.Rodica Mateescu (Rumania) 15.16 (+0.1 m/s); 3.Yelena Govorova (Ukraine) 14.67 (+0.7 m/s); 4.Olga Vasdéki (Greece) 14.62; 5.Ashia Hansen (GB) 14.49; 6.Tereza Marinova (Bulgaria) 14.34; 7.Jelena Blazevica (Latvia) 14.06; 8.Betty Lise (France) 14.03; 9.Gundega Sproge (Latvia) 13.98; 10.Petra Lobinger (Germany) 13.86; 11.Cynthea Rhodes (USA) 13.79; 12. Zhanna Gureyeva (Byelarus) 13.59.

1999 World Championships, Sevilla – Triple Jump (24 August): 1.Paraskevi Tsiamita (Greece) 14.88 (+0.2 m/s). (She did 15.07 (-0.6 m/s) in the qualifying round on 22 Aug.); 2.Yamilé Aldama (Cuba) 14.61 (-0.4 m/s); 3.Olga Vasdéki (Greece) 14.61 (+0.2 m/s); 4.Tatyana Lebedeva (Russia) 14.55; 5.Iva Prandzheva (Bulgaria) 14.54; 6.Sárka Kaspárková (Czech Rep.) 14.54; 7.Yelena Govorova (Ukraine) 14.47; 8.Cristina Nicolau (Rumania) 14.38; 9.Oksana Rogova (Russia) 14.16; 10.Baya Rahouli (Algeria) 14.00; 11.Adelina Gavrila (Rumania) 13.87; 12.Ashia Hansen (GB) 13.39.

2000 Olympics, Sydney – Triple Jump (24 September): 1.Tereza Marinova (Bulgaria) 15.20 (-0.3 m/s); 2.Tatyana Lebedeva (Russia) 15.00 (+1.3 m/s); 3.Yelena Govorova (Ukraine) 14.96 (+0.7 m/s); 4.Yamilé Aldama (Cuba) 14.30; 5.Baya Rahouli (Algeria) 14.17; 6.Cristina Nicolau (Rumania) 14.17; 7.Olga Vasdéki (Greece) 14.15; 8.Oksana Rogova (Russia) 13.97; 9.Anja Valant (Slovenia) 13.59; 10.Françoise Mbango (Cameroon) 13.53; 11.Ashia Hansen (GB) 13.44. No valid jump: Sárka Kaspárková (Czech Rep.).

Eleven women had bettered the 15-metre mark as at the end of 2000. Four of them represented Russia.

WOMEN 2001-2010

11

HIGH JUMP

The stars: Cloete, Bergqvist and Vlasic

Stefka Kostadinova's world record (2.09 in 1987) withstood all assaults throughout the first decade of the new century. The first outstanding figure of this period was **Hestrie Cloete** of South Africa (née Storbeck at Germiston on 26 August 1978; 1.85 m. / 68 Kg.), who won medals in three "global" championships: gold in the 2001 and 2003 "Worlds", with 2.00 and 2.06 respectively, silver at the 2004 Olympics with 2.02, behind Yelena Slesarenko of Russia (2.06). She thus became the first South African woman to win any World Championship medal. The Springbok ace had shown great talent since the beginning of her career. At 19 years of age she was the top junior in the world, with 1.94. Two years later she jumped 2.04 and in 2000 she won a silver medal at the Sydney Olympics.

2001 World Championships, Edmonton – High Jump (12 August): 1.Hestrie Cloete (South Africa) 2.00; 2.Inga Babakova (Ukraine) 2.00; 3. Kajsa Bergqvist (Sweden) 1.97; 4.Venelina Veneva (Bulgaria) 1.97; 5.Vita Palamar (Ukraine) 1.94; 6.Blanka Vlasic (Croatia) 1.94; 7.(tie) Dóra Györffy (Hungary) and Monica Lagar (Rumania) 1.90; 9.Oana Pantelimon (Rumania) 1.90; 10.(tie) Amy Acuff (USA) and Yelena Gulyayeva (Russia) 1.90; 12. Antonietta Di Martino (Italy) 1.85.

At the 2003 "Worlds" Cloete retained her title with impressive superiority. She had no failures up to and including 2.06, a height which was to remain her all-time best. She then tried to break Kostadinova's world record. Her tries at 2.10 were unsuccessful – but "still close enough to bring a smile of satisfaction" on her face, as one reporter put it. Even so, that magic height, 2.10, was to prove unattainable for many years to come … …

A great career, even in terms of longevity, was that of Sweden's **Kajsa Bergqvist** (born at Sollentuna on 12 October 1976; 1.75 m. / 59 Kg.). Following her third place ex-aequo) in the 2000 Olympics at Sydney, she collected an imposing series of medals – gold at the 2002 European Championships (1.98) and the 2005 "Worlds" (2.02), bronze at the 2001 and 2003 "Worlds" and in the 2006 Europeans. Her outdoor best was 2.06 at Eberstadt in 2003. This German town is dear to high jumpers because it has a yearly festival devoted to them. Bergqvist also has a 2.08 which still stands as a world indoor record. It was made at Arnstadt on 4 February 2006. After a not so brilliant season in 2007, the Swedish star decided to call it a day. More about this outstanding jumper can be found in an adjoining aside.

Kajsa Bergqvist (Sweden) can look back to a long and glorious career as a high jumper. She holds the world indoor record with 2.08.

Blanka Vlasic (Croatia) is currently the world's no. 1 high jumper. She has a personal best of 2.08 and still aims at succeeding Stefka Kostadinova (2.09 in 1987) as world record holder.

2003 World Championships, Paris-St.Denis - High Jump (31 August): 1.Hestrie Cloete (South Africa) 2.06; 2.Marina Kuptsova (Russia) 2.00; 3.Kajsa Bergqvist (Sweden) 2.00; 4.Venelina Veneva (Bulgaria) 1.98; 5.Vita Palamar (Ukraine) 1.95; 6.Anna Chicherova (Russia) 1.95; 7.BlankaVlasic (Croatia) 1.95; 8.Juana Rosario Arrendel (Rep. Dominicana) 1.95; 9.(tie) Amy Acuff (USA) and Viktoriya Styopina (Ucraine) 1.90; 11.(tie) Ruth Beitia (Spain) and Olga Kaliturina (Russia) 1.90.

2004 Olympics, Athens – High Jump (28 August): 1.Yelena Slesarenko (Russia) 2.06 (OR); 2.Hestrie Cloete (South Africa) 2.02; 3.Viktoriya Styopina (Ukraine) 2.02; 4.Amy Acuff (USA) 1.99; 5.Iryna Mikhalchenko (Ukraine) 1.96; 6.Anna Chicherova (Russia) 1.96; 7.Oana Pantelimon (Rumania) 1.93: 8.Monica Lagar (Rumania) 1.93; 9.Inha Babakova (Ukraine) 1.93; 10.Marta Mendia (Spain) 1.93: 11.Blanka Vlasic (Croatia) 1.89; 12.Tia Hellebaut (Belgium) 1.85.

2005 World Championships, Helsinki – High Jump (8 August): 1.Kajsa Bergqvist (Sweden) 2.02; 2.Chaunte Howard (USA) 2.00; 3.Emma Green (Sweden) 1.96; 4.Anna Chicherova (Russia) 1.96; 5.Viktoriya Palamar (Ukraine) 1.93; 6.Tia Hellebaut (Belgium) 1.93; 7.Viktoriya Styopina (Ukraine) 1.93; 8.Amy Acuff (USA) 1.89; 9.Dóra Györffy (Hungary) 1.89; 10.Venelina Veneva (Bulgaria) 1.85; 11.Iva Straková (Czech Rep.) 1.85; 12.Iryna Mikhalchenko (Ukraine) 1.85.

The outstanding performer of recent years was unquestionably **Blanka Vlasic** of Croatia (born at Split on 8 November 1983; 1.92 m. / 75 Kg.). Being well above the average of women jumpers in height, at 18 years of age she was able to place sixth at the 2001 World Championships in Edmonton. Two years later, at 20, she jumped 2.01. As a competitor she reached a high level of consistency in 2007, when she won a gold medal at the World Championships in Osaka. A title she successfully defended two yeas later in Berlin. Her best as at the end of 2010 is 2.08 (Zagreb, 2009). She can claim a record of sorts though: as of now she has had 60 record attempts at 2.10, a height which would exceed the long standing world record of Stefka Kostadinova (2.09 in 1987). On several occasions she came very close ....

One such was in an international meet at Split late in 2010. Her third attempt, a close failure, so thrilled the home crowd that they gave her a standing ovation. That's sport at its best, I believe.

"Mission accomplished"

Kajsa Bergqvist, the second best high jumper of all time with her indoor world record (2.08 in 2006), reached a very high degree of popularity in her home country, Sweden. Thanks to her competitive ability, no doubt, but also on account of her sprightly temperament which invariably ignited spectators. Toward the end of 2007, the 20th year of her athletic activity, she said "it was time to call it a day". "I reached the point where I can consider my mission as accomplished. It's time for me to enter a new life".

High jumping is an event that taxes nervous and physical energies to a high degree. Especially when it comes to doing "the right thing at the right moment". That a woman like Kajsa, 1.75m. tall, may have been able to successfully compete against generally taller rivals and collect 52 marks over 2 metres, is in itself a marvellous thing.

Italy's Antonietta Di Martino, who tied for second at the 2007 World Championships, is an interesting case. She is only 1.69 m. tall and has a personal best of 2.03. That implies a p.b.-vs.- height differential of 34 centimetres, the highest on record. The previous record, 33 cms., was held by Niki Bakoyiánni of Greece (2.03 – 1.70) and Kajsa Bergqvist of Sweden (2.08 – 1.75).

2007 World Championships, Osaka - High Jump (2 September): 1.Blanka Vlasic (Croatia) 2.05; 2.(tie) Anna Chicherova (Russia) 2.03 and Antonietta Di Martino (Italy) 2.03; 4.Yelena Slesarenko (Russia) 2.00; 5.Yekaterina Savchenko (Russia) 2.00; 6.Ruth Beitia (Spain) 1.97; 7.(tie) Marina Aitova (Kazakhstan), Kajsa Bergqvist (Sweden), Emma Green (Sweden), Vita Palamar (Ukraine) and Melanine Skotnik (France) 1.94; 12.Amy Acuff (USA) 1.94.

Blanka Vlasic had another great season in 2008, yet she lost the Olympic title on countback to Tia Hellebaut of Belgium, after both had cleared 2.05. The latter reached this goal at the age of 30, two years after joining the 2-metre club.

2008 Olympics, Beijing - High Jump (23 August): 1.Tia Hellebaut (Belgium) 2.05; 2.Blanka Vlasic (Croatia) 2.05; 3.Anna Chicherova (Russia) 2.03; 4.Yelena Slesarenko (Russia) 2.01; 5.Vita Palamar (Ukraine) 1.99; 6.Chaunté Howard (USA) 1.99; 7.(tie) Ruth Beitia (Spain) and Ariane Friedrich (Germany) 1.96; 9.Emma Green (Sweden) 1.96; 10. (tie) Marina Aitova (Kazakhstan), Antonietta Di Martino (Italy), Iva Straková (Czech Rep.) and Viktoriya Styopina (Ucraine) 1.93; 14. Svetlana Shkolina (Russia) 1.93.

Vlasic, easily and by far the most consistent of all in the 2-metre-plus range, annexed her second world title outdoors at Berlin, where she beat among others Ariane Friedrich of Germany, the local favourite. The latter had beaten Vlasic earlier in the season, still in Berlin – 2.06 (a German outdoor record) to 2.03.

Antonietta Di Martino (Italy) can claim a record of sorts as a high jumper. With her recent 2.04 indoors she has the record for the greatest ever differential (height – personal best) – 35 cms.

2009 World Championships, Berlin - High Jump (20 August): 1.Blanka Vlasic (Croatia) 2.04; 2.Anna Chicherova (Russia) 2.02; 3.Ariane Friedrich (Germany) 2.02; 4.Antonietta Di Martino (Italy) 1.99; 5.Ruth Beitia (Spain) 1.99; 6.Svetlana Shkolina (Russia) 1.96; 7.(tie) Chaunté Howard (USA) and Emma Green (Sweden) 1.96; 9.Mélanie Melfort (France) 1.92; 10.Yelena Slesarenko (Russia) 1.92; 11.Meike Kröger (Germany) 1.87; 12.Amy Acuff (USA) 1.87.

There were no major developments in 2010. Blanca Vlasic was once again no.1, adding to her list of honours with victories in the World Indoor Championships and in the European Championships. She again proved unlucky in her attempts to break Kostadinova's 23-year-old world record but was awarded the "Woman Athlete of the Year" title by the IAAF.

POLE VAULT

Isinbayeva, first member of the 5-Metre Club

The second edition of the World Championships for women vaulters took place at Edmonton, Canada, in 2001. At the end of a four-hours battle in hot sunshine, Stacy Dragila won again, beating Svetlana Feofanova of Russia on the countback, after both had cleared 4.75. Even apart from that, 2001 was a magic season for the American, who bettered her world record time and again – four times indoors, up to 4.70 (Pocatello, 17 February) and three outdoors, up to 4.81 (Palo Alto, 9 June). By then pole vaulting in its female version had captured the imagination of track fans. Cordner Nelson, co-founder with his brother Bert of the American magazine "Track & Field News", put it this way: "They are the darlings of the track world, these women vaulters, with their entrancing mix of spectacular acrobatics, hugging friendliness and fierce competitive fire".

2001 World Championships, Edmonton - Pole Vault (6 August): 1.Stacy Dragila (USA) 4.75 (CR); 2.Svetlana Feofanova (Russia) 4.75 (CR); 3.Monika Pyrek (Poland) 4.55; 4.Tatyana Grigorieva (Australia) 4.55; 5.Gao Shuying (China) 4.50; 6.Thórey Elisdóttir (Iceland) 4.45; 7.Yvonne Buschbaum (Germany) 4.45; 8.Pavla Hamacková

(Czech Rep.) 4.45; 9.Janine Whitlock (GB) 4.35; 10.Caroline Hingst (Germany) 4.25; 11.Doris Auer (Austria) 4.25; 12.Mary Sauer (USA) 4.25.

Svetlana Feofanova of Russia (born in Moscow on 16 July 1980; 1.64 m. / 53 Kg.) was originally a very good gymnast. In spite of her unimpressive build, she proved a tough competitor down pole vault runways. She improved from 4.10 as a junior in 1999 to 4.75 in 2001 and gradually moved to the role of Dragila's no.1 opponent. In 2003 the Russian shot ahead of her American rival, only to find that in the meantime a potentially superior prospect was ready to wrest the lead from both of them. The new star also came from Russia. She was **Yelena Isinbayeva** (born at Volgograd on 3 June 1982; 1.74 m. / 66 Kg.). She too a former gymnast, Isinbayeva had shown tremendous talent as a vaulter since her school days, winning world titles as Youth and Junior. At 16 years of age she mastered 4 metres even. From then on, her march was fantastic and by 2003 she was able to set a new world record: 4.82 at Gateshead on 13 July. Later in the same year, in the World Championships at Paris-St.Denis, she had to bow to Feofanova's competitive fire and be content with third place. She was beaten also by Annika Becker of Germany, who in 2002 had been for a short time the European record holder at 4.77. As for Dragila, that meet virtually marked the end of her long reign: she only tied for fourth.

Yelena Isinbayeva of Russia, currently the one and only member of the "5-Metre Club" in the women's pole vault.

2003 World Championships, Paris. St.Denis - Pole Vault (25 August): 1.Svetlana Feofanova (Russia) 4.75 (eq. CR); 2.Annika Becker (Germany) 4.70; 3.Yelena Isinbayeva (Russia) 4.65; 4.(tie) Stacy Dragila (USA) and Monika Pyrek (Poland) 4.55; 6.Yvonne Buschbaum (Germany) 4.50; 7.Anna Rogowska (Poland) 4.45; 8.Yelena Belyakova (Russia) 4.45; 9.Gao Shuying (China) 4.35; 10.Mary Sauer (USA) 4.35; No height: Thórey Elisdóttir (Iceland) and Marie Poissonier (France).

2004 marked the actual opening of the Isinbayeva Era. She broke the world record time and again, winding up with 4.92 at Brussels on 3 September. Her main rivals fought bravely but had to surrender to her superior stature. In the meet of the year, the Athens Olympics, Feofanova fought bravely but was finally beaten by a wide margin – 4.75 to 4.91, the latter being by then a new world record. Stacy Dragila, who back in 2000 had won the first Olympic title, found herself unable to make the final.

2004 Olympics, Athens - Pole Vault (24 August): 1.Yelena Isinbayeva (Russia) 4.91 (WR); 2.Svetlana Feofanova (Russia) 4.75; 3.Anna Rogowska (Poland) 4.70; 4.Monika Pyrek (Poland) 4.55; 5.Thórey Elisdóttir (Iceland) 4.55; 6.(tie) Naroa Agirre (Spain), Anzhela Balakhonova (Ukraine), Vanessa Boslak (France) and Dana Ellis (Canada) 4.40; 10.Stephanie McCann (Canada) 4.40; 11.Pavla Hamácková (Czech Rep.) 4.40; 12.Katerina Badurová (Czech Rep.) 4.20; 13.(tie) Alejandra Garcia (Argentina) and Silke Spiegelburg (Germany) 4.20. No height: Dana Cervantes (Spain).

By the end of 2004 it was clear that marks over the 5-metre barrier were quite possible for Isinbayeva. At the Athens Olympics of that year she admitted having cleared that height in practice. For all official purposes, however, the historic milestone was first reached at London's Crystal Palace on 22 Jul 2005 when she broke the 5-metre barrier with an "even 5". English spectators cheered enthusiastically - even older ones not yet familiar with metric landmarks.

Dragila, by then 33, was obviously declining. In addition to her history making deeds in the pole vault, she had been an excellent all-around athlete who could point to personal bests such as 13.88 in the 100 m. hurdles, 1.70 in the high jump, 5.89 in the long jump, 10.80 in the shot put an d 44.28 in the javelin throw.

2005 World Championships, Helsinki – Pole Vault (12 August): 1.Yelena Isinbayeva (Russia) 5.01 (WR); 2.Monika Pyrek (Poland) 4.60; 3.Pavla Hamácková (Czech Rep.) 4.50; 4.Tatyana Polnova (Russia) 4.50; 5.Gao Shuying (China) 4.50; 6.(tie) Dana Ellis (Canada) and Anna Rogowska (Poland) 4.35; 8.Vanessa Boslak (France) 4.35; 9.Naroa Agirre (Spain) 4.35; 10.Caroline Hingst (Germany) 4.35; 11. Jillian Schwartz (USA) 4.20; 12.Tatiana Grigorieva (Australia) 4.00. No height: Tracy O'Hara (USA).

Between 2006 and 2009 Isinbayeva added to her laurels, raising the world record time ad again up to 5.06, a height she cleared on 28 August 2009 at Zurich. She won "global" titles at the Bejing Olympics in 2008 and at the World Championships in 2007. Defeat knocked at her door in the 2009 "Worlds" in Berlin, when she failed to qualify for the final - with one failure at 4.75 and two at 4.80, thus ending a superb sequence of major titles. After that she decided to allow herself a sabbatical in 2010, just to rest her aching muscles and revive her competitive fire. The 2009 world title went to Anna Rogowska of Poland at 4.75. A record 21 women cleared 4.40 in the qualifying round, a clear indication that the near future will see further advances.

2007 World Championships, Osaka – Pole Vault (28 August): 1.Yelena Isinbayeva (Russia) 4.80; 2.Katerina Badurová (Czech Rep.) 4.75; 3.Svetlana Feofanova (Russia) 4.75; 4.Monyka Pyrek (Poland) 4.75; 5.Vanessa Boslak (France) 4.70; 6.(tie) Yuliya Golubchikova (Russia) and Fabiana Murer (Brazil) 4.65; 8.Anna Rogowska (Poland) 4.60; 9.Tatyana Polnova (Russia) 4.60; 10.Jennifer Stuczynski (USA) 4.50; 11.Kym Howe (Australia) 4.50. No height: Silke Spiegelburg (Germany).

2008 Olympics, Beijing – Pole Vault (18 August): 1.Yelena Isinbayeva (Russia) 5.05 (WR); 2.Jennifer Stuczynski (USA) 4.80; 3.Svetlana Feofanova (Russia) 4.75; 4.Yuliya Golubchikova (Russia) 4.75; 5.Monika Pyrek (Poland) 4.70; 6.Caroline Hingst (Germany) 4.65; 7.Silke Spiegelburg (Germany) 4.65; 8.April Steiner (USA) 4.55; 9.Vanessa Boslak (France) 4.55; 10. (tie) Fabiana Murer (Brazil) and Anna Rogowska (Poland) 4.45; 12. Gao Shuying (China) 4.45.

Chief collectors of records and titles

Sergey Bubka and Yelena Isinbayeva can easily be classified as the greatest exponents of pole vaulting, each for his/her own sex of course. Both have towered above their contemporaries to such an extent as to defy comparison with most if not all the greatest champions from other events. Sergey, an Ukrainian, was the first member of the men's 6-metres club. Yelena, a Russian, achieved a similar distinction in the female ranks by breaking the 5-metre barrier. (Whoever is tempted to make comparisons should of course be reminded that the event was included in the women's international programme only at the beginning of the present century).

Let's anyhow indulge in a comparison of records and titles collected by the two phenoms.

World Records:

Bubka 28	(17 outdoors, 11 indoors)
Isinbayeva 27	(15 outdoors, 12 indoors)

"Global" titles:

Bubka 4	(3 "Worlds", 1 Olympic)
Isinbayeva 4	(2 "Worlds", 2 Olympic)

One should of course remember that Bubka had to stay away from the 1984 Los Angeles Olympics when the SU decided to boycott those Games. If we consider that Isinbayeva is still active (she was 28 at the time of writing) it is easy to conclude that she still has a chance to excel the great Ukrainian.

2009 World Championships, Berlin – Pole Vault (17 August): 1.Anna Rogowska (Poland) 4.75; 2.(tie) Chelsea Johnson (USA) and Monyka Pirek (Poland) 4.65; 4.Silke Spiegelburg (Germany) 4.65; 5.Fabiana Murer (Brazil) 4.55; 6.Kate Dennison (GB) 4.55; 7.(tie) Anna Battke (Germany) and Tatyana Polnova (Russia) 4.40; 9.Aleksandra Kiryashova (Russia) 4.40; 10.Kristina Gadschiew (Germany) 4.40. No valid jump: Yelena Isinbayeva (Russia) and Yuliya Golubchikova (Russia).

At the end of 2010 Isinbayeva had to her credit the 14 best marks of all time, seven of which in the 5-metre-plus category. Second place on such a list belonged to Jennifer Stuczynski of USA – 4.92 in 2008, the year that saw her win a silver medal at the Beijing Olympics. In her younger days Stuczynski was a leading baseball player at Roberts Wesleyan University .

LONG JUMP

Shorter Jumps

Even in the long jump there is a world record – 7.52 by Galina Chistyakova – which dates from the Eighties of the XX century. The best mark of the most recent years is 7.42 by another Russian, **Tatyana Kotova** (born at Kokand, Uzbekistan, on 11 December 1976; 1.82 m. / 59 Kg.). This athlete, who now lives in Central Siberia, can point to a good competitive record: three times second at the World Championships (2001, '03 and '05), third at the Athens Olympics (2004) and European champion in Munich (2002).

Fiona May of Italy won her second World Championship title at Edmonton, Canada, in 2001, just ahead of Kotova – 7.02 to 7.01, both with favouring winds. It may be interesting to note that both these jumps turned out to be considerably longer if measured from the actual take-off points: 7.16w for May, 7.12w for Kotova. That was Fiona's last major cry, because in the 2003 edition of the same meet she had to be content with a ninth place. Taken for all in all, she had an excellent competitive record in her career, in excess of her best marks. On the eve of her victory at Edmonton, for example, she had a seasonal best of just 6.79.

2001 World Championships, Edmonton – Long Jump (7 August): 1.Fiona May (Italy) 7.02w (+ 2.6 m/s); 2.Tatyana Kotova (Russia) 7.01w (+3.6 m/s); 3.Niurka Montalvo (Spain) 6.88w (+2.1 m/s); 4.Tünde Vaszi (Hungary) 6.86 ; 5.Valentina Gotovska (Latvia) 6.84w; 6.Niki Xánthou (Greece) 6.76w; 7.Maureen Maggi (Brazil) 6,73; 8.Lyudmila Galkina (Russia) 6.70; 9.Guan Yingnan (China) 6,69w; 10.Elva Goulbourne (Jamaica) 6.62; 11.Kumiko Ikeda (Japan) 6.44. No valid mark: Jenny Adams (USA).

In 2002, with May taking a sabbatical (she had a daughter midway in the year), Kotova had a dominant position and achieved a personal best of 7.42. But in 2003 the Russian again had to be content with silver at the World Championships in Paris-St.Denis, where she was upset in the very last round by Eunice Barber, a Sierra Leone jumper who had migrated to France. The latter closed with 6.99, which sufficed to give France her first gold in those championships. Her actual jump, if measured from the take-off board, would have been 7.10. May, in a half-hearted effort to come back, was only ninth.

2003 World Championships, Paris-St.Denis – Long Jump (30 August): 1.Eunice Barber (France) 6.99 (+0.4 m/s); 2.Tatyana Kotova (Russia) 6.74 (+0.1 m/s); 3.Anju Bobby George (India) 6.70 (+1.2m/s); 4.Jade Johnson (GB) 6.63; 5.Olga Rublyova (Russia) 6.58; 6.Tünde Vaszi (Hungary) 6.53; 7.Bronwyn Thompson (Australia) 6.48; 8.Grace Upshaw (USA) 6.47; 9.Fiona May (Italy) 6.46; 10.Lyudmila Galkina (Russia) 6.45; 11.Valentina Gotovska (Latvia) 6.43; 12.Concepción Montaner (Spain) 6.37.

Russia by then showed a great long jump-triple jump sample: **Tatyana Lebedeva** (born at Sterlitamsk, Bashkortostan, on 21 July 1976; 1.71 m. / 61 Kg.), who between 2001 and 2004 was able to collect three "global" titles – two in the long jump and one in the triple jump. In the 2004 Olympics, held in Athens, she won the long jump with 7.07, four days after placing third in the triple jump, which was regarded as her no.1 event. In this meet the standard of competition was excellent in depth, but relatively unimpressive at the top. Russia scored a big 1-2-3 sweep.

2004 Olympics, Athens – Long Jump (27 August): 1.Tatyana Lebedeva (Russia) 7.07 (+1.3 m/s); 2. Irina Simagina (Russia) 7.05 (+0.8 m/s); 3. Tatyana Kotova (Russia) 7.05 (+1.8 m/s); 4.Bronwyn Thompson (Australia) 6.96; 5.Marion Jones (USA) 6.85w (+3.1 m/s); 6.Anju Bobby George (India) 6.83; 7.Jade Johnson (GB) 6.80; 8. Tünde Vaszi (Hungary) 6.73w; 9.Bianca Kappler (Germany) 6.66; 10.Grace Upshaw (USA) 6.64; 11.Caroline Klüft (Sweden) 6.63; 12. Yelena Kashcheyeva (Kazakhstan) 6.53.

Tatyana Kotova suffered an unexpected defeat at the 2005 "Worlds". The winner was Tianna Madison of USA, who became a world champion 20 days before turning twenty, with a personal best of 6.89 (she had a wind-aided 6.92 earlier in the season).

Tatyana Lebedeva (Russia), the no.1 performer in the long jump / triple jump combination.

Kotova, second, and Barber, third, added to their medal collection.

2005 World Championships, Helsinki - Long Jump (10 August): 1.Tianna Madison (USA) 6.89 (+1.1 m/s); 2.Tatyana Kotova (Russia) 6.79 (+1.5 m/s); 3.Eunice Barber (France) 6.76w (+2.3 m/s); 4.Yargelis Savigne (Cuba) 6.69; 5.Anju Bobby George (India) 6.66; 6.Oksana Udmurtova (Russia) 6.53; 7.Grace Upshaw (USA) 6.51; 8.Kelly Sotherton (GB) 6.42w; 9.Jackie Edwards (Bahamas) 6.42w; 10. Tünde Vaszi (Hungary) 6.32; 11.Concepción Montaner (Spain) 6.21; 12. Elva Goulbourne (Jamaica) 6.21.

Iron woman Lebedeva returned to her winning ways, winning the long jump world title at Osaka and placing second in the triple jump three days later. In the former event Russia had a clean sweep.

2007 World Championships, Osaka - Long Jump (28 August): 1.Tatyana Lebedeva (Russia) 7.03 (+0.3 m/s); 2.Lyudmila Kolchanova (Russia) 6.92 (-0.3 m/s); 3.Tatyana Kotova (Russia) 6.90 (+0.5 m/s); 4.Naide Gomes (Portugal) 6.87; 5.Bianca Kappler (Germany) 6.81; 6.Maurren Maggi (Brazil) 6.80; 7.Keila Costa (Brazil) 6.69; 8.Brittney Reese (USA) 6.60; 9.Anju Bobby George (India) 6.53; 10.Tianna Madison (USA) 6.47; 11.Viktoriya Rybalko (Ukraine) 6.45; 12.Jana Veldáková (Slovakia) 6.21.

In 2008 Maurren Maggi, a former gymnast, became the first Brazilian woman to win an Olympic title. And she did this at 32 years of age, beating the irrepressible Lebedeva by the narrowest of margins, 7.04 to 7.03. In 1999 she had made her first breakthrough with 7.26, a mark favoured by the high altitude of Bogota (2644 m.)

2008 Olympics, Beijing - Long Jump (22 August): 1.Maurren Maggi (Brazil) 7.04 (+0.2 m/s); 2.Tatyana Lebedeva (Russia) 7.03 (+0.4 m/s); 3. Blessing Okagbare (Nigeria) 6.91 (+0.1 m/s); 4.Chelsea Hammond (Jamaica) 6.79; 5.Brittney Reese (USA) 6.76; 6.Oksana Udmurtova (Russia) 6.70; 7.Jade Johnson (GB) 6.64; 8.Grace Upshaw (USA) 6.58; 9.Caroline Klüft (Sweden) 6.49; 10.Tabia Charles (Canada) 6.47; 11.Keila Costa (Brazil) 6.43; 12.Funmi Jimoh (USA) 6.29.

In 2009 Tatyana Lebedeva was again beaten by an outsider, Brittney Reese of USA, 23, in the most important meet of the year, the "Worlds". In order to turn such a trick the 23-year-old American produced a new personal best of 7.10 – and did so after "giving away" 7.7 cm. in hitting the board !

2009 World Championships, Berlin - Long Jump (23 August): 1.Brittney Reese (USA) 7.10 (+1.0 m/s); 2.Tatyana Lebedeva (Russia) 6.97 (+1.0 m/s); 3.Karin Melis Mey (Turkey) 6.80 (+0.4 m/s); 4.Naide Gomes (Portugal) 6.77; 5.Olga Kucherenko (Russia) 6.77; 6.Shara Proctor (Anguilla) 6.71; 7.Maurren Maggi (Brazil) 6.68; 8.Ksenja Balta (Esthonia) 6.62; 9.Brianna Glenn (USA) 6.59; 10.Teresa Dobija (Poland) 6.58; 11.Natasha Mironchik (Byelarus) 6.29. No valid jump: Keila Costa (Brazil).

Brittney Reese had another good season in 2010 and even in the absence of "global" meets she again ranked no.1 in the world.

The first decade of the new century produced generally inferior marks - especially if compared with the standard of the roaring Eighties of the preceding century.

TRIPLE JUMP

The indefatigable Lebedeva

Tatyana Lebedeva of Russia continued to rule the roost even in the first decade of the new century. And did so while riding two horses, as per her custom. Here is a summary of her outstanding record in "global" (Olympics / World Ch.) meets during her career:

	Long Jump	Triple Jump
1999 (WC)	4th	-
2000 (OG)	-	2nd
2001 (WC)	-	1st
2003 (WC)	-	1st
2004 (OG)	1st	3rd
2005 (WC)	-	-
2007 (WC)	1st	2nd
2008 (OG)	2nd	2nd
2009 (WC)	2nd	6th

She never scored a double in such meets but came pretty close to it. She did turn such a trick at the 2004 World Indoor Championships in Budapest, with 15.36 (her personal best) and 6.98 on consecutive days. Taken for all in all, she did relatively better in the triple jump, in which at the time of writing (end of 2010) she ranks third in the World All Time List with the above-mentioned 15.36, whereas in the long jump she ranks eighth with 7.33 (2004).

At the 2001 "Worlds", held at Edmonton, Canada, she outclassed all her rivals, winning with an incredible 65 cm. to spare. In her best trial, 15.25, she had a hop of 5.52, a step of 4.21 and a jump of 5.52.

2001 World Championships, Edmonton – Triple Jump (10 August): 1.Tatyana Lebedeva (Russia) 15.25 (-0.8 m/s); 2.Françoise Mbango (Cameroon) 14.60 (-0.6 m/s); 3.Tereza Marinova (Bulgaria) 14.58 (-1.3 m/s); 4.Magdelin Martinez (Italy) 14.52; 5.Heli Koivula (Finland) 14.28; 6.Cristina Nicolau (Rumania) 14.17; 7.Ashia Hansen (GB) 14.10; 8.Trecia Smith (Jamaica) 13.92; 9.Olga Bolshova (Moldova) 13.86; 10.Yelena Govorova (Ucraine) 13.85; 11.Camilla Johansson (Sweden) 13.84; 12.Natalya Safronova (Byelarus) 13.82.

Lebedeva missed the entire 2002 season when pregnant with her daughter Anastasiya. but joined the circus again in 2003.

Françoise Mbango-Etone of Cameroon (born at Yaoundé on 14 April 1976; 1.72 m. / 63 Kg.), a well beaten second at the 2001 "Worlds", continued to improve and in 2003 she gave Lebedeva a good run for her money at the next edition of said meet, in the giant stadium of Paris-St.Denis. In the second round of the final Mbango moved ahead with 15.05, a new African record, only to be surpassed by Lebedeva with 15.16 and 15.18.

2003 World Championships, Paris-St.Denis – Triple Jump (26 August): 1.Tatyana Lebedeva (Russia) 15.18 (-0.2m/s); 2.Françoise Mbango (Cameroon) 15.05 (-0.7 m/s); 3.Magdelin Martinez (Italy) 14.90 (-0.2 m/s); 4.Anna Pyatykh (Russia) 14.72; 5.Mabel Gay (Cuba) 14.52; 6.Barbara Lah (Italy) 14.38; 7.Yelena Govorova Ukraine) 14.38; 8.Hrisopiyi Devetzi (Greece) 14.34; 9.Adelina Gavrila (Rumania) 14.29; 10.Kéne Ndoye (Senegal) 14.29; 11.Baya Rahouli (Algeria) 14.26; 12.Ólga Vasdéki (Greece) 14.08.

Lebedeva, the never-say-die type, came back early in 2004, winning at the World Indoor Championships in Budapest with 15.36, good enough to place her second in the World All-Time List. But things took a different turn later in the season, at the Athens Olympics, when Mbango, the sturdy African jumper, finally hit gold with yet another African record, 15.30. She thus became the first athlete from Cameroon to win an Olympic title. Lebedeva placed only third, behind Hrisopiyi Devetzi of Greece – 15.14 to 15.25. It should be noted that the latter had done even better in the qualifying round two days earlier, with 15.32 (+0.9 m/s). The right mark in the wrong place, that is – if made in the final it would have earned her pure gold.

2004 Olympics, Athens – Triple Jump (23 August): 1.Françoise Mbango (Cameroon) 15.30 (+0.6 m/s); 2.Hrisopiyi Devetzi (Greece) 15.25 (-0.1 m/s); 3.Tatyana Lebedeva (Russia) 15.14 (+0.7 m/s); 4.Trecia Smith (Jamaica) 15.02; 5.Yamilé Aldama

(Sudan) 14.99; 6.Baya Rahouli (Algeria) 14.86; 7.Magdelin Martinez (Italy) 14.85; 8.Anna Pyatykh (Russia) 14.79; 9.Yusmay Bicet (Cuba) 14.57; 10.Elena Hovorova (Ukraine) 14.35; 11.Ólga Vasdéki (Greece) 14.34; 12.Huang Qiuyan (China) 14.33.

Lebedeva was out of the game in the 2005 "Worlds" due to an injury and the title, in the meet held at Helsinki, went to a Jamaican, Trecia-Kaye Smith, a student in physiotherapy at the University of Pittsburgh, USA, who won with 15.11, barely 5 cms. shy of her personal best from 2004. She excelled the more experienced jumpers in height, being 1.85 m. tall.

2005 World Championships, Helsinki - Triple Jump (7 August): 1.Trecia Smith (Jamaica) 15.11 (+0.8 m/s); 2.Yargelis Savigne (Cuba) 14.82 (+0.7 m/s); 3.Anna Pyatykh (Russia) 14.78 (-0.5 m/s); 4.Yamilé Aldama (Sudan) 14.72; 5.Hrisopiyi Devetzi (Greece) 14.64; 6.Kéne Ndoye (Senegal) 14.47; 7.Baya Rahouli (Algeria) 14.40; 8.Magdelin Martinez (Italy) 14.31; 9.Huang Qiuyan (China) 14.21; 10.Viktoriya Gurova (Russia) 13.96; 11.Carlotta Castrejana (Spain) 13.86.

Lebedeva, hampered by an Achilles tendon injury, did 14.15 in the qualifying round but withdrew from the final.

Lebedeva's toughest rival in the latter part of the decade was a Cuban, **Yargelis Savigne** (born at Niceto Pérez, Guantánamo on 13 November 1984; 1.65 m. / 63 Kg.), who was clever enough to beat the experienced Russian in two editions of the World Championships, 2007 and 2009. On the first occasion she produced a personal best of 15.28, while Lebedeva had to be content with 15.07. In terms of long jump potential, the Cuban lagged well behind Lebedeva – their personal bests being 6.79 (indoors) and 7.33 respectively.

2007 World Championships, Osaka - Triple Jump (31 August): 1.Yargelis Savigne (Cuba) 15.28 (+0.9 ms); 2.Tatyana Lebedeva (Russia) 15.07 (+0.8 m/s); 3.Hrisopiyi Devetzi (Greece) 15.04 (-0.2 m/s); 4.Anna Pyatykh (Russia) 14.88; 5.Marija Sestak (Slovenia) 14.72; 6.Magdelin Martinez (Italy) 14.71; 7.Olga Saladuha (Ukraine) 14.60; 8.Xie Limei (China) 14.50; 9.Keila Costa (Brazil) 14.40; 10.Olesya Bufalova (Russia) 14.39; 11.Olga Rypakova (Kazakhstan) 14.32; 12.Dana Veldáková (Slovakia) 14.09.

Françoise Mbango, the girl from Cameroon, had a serious mishap in 2007, when she was suspended indefinitely by the athletics federation of her country following her absence from the All Africa Games in Algiers and her subsequent withdrawal from the World Championships in Osaka after she had confirmed her participation. She managed to redeem herself in 2008 though. In the Beijing Olympics she retained her title and again had Tatyana Lebedeva as her main victim.

2008 Olympics, Beijing - Triple Jump (17 August): 1.Françoise Mbango (Cameroon) 15.39 (OR) (+0.5 m/s); 2.Tatyana Lebedeva (Russia) 15.32 (+0.5 m/s); 3.Hrisopiyi Devetzi (Greece) 15.23 (+1.6 m/s); 4.Olga Rypakova (Kazakhstan) 15.11; 5.Yargelis Savigne (Cuba) 15.05; 6.Marija Sestak (Slovenia) 15.03; 7.Viktoriya Gurova (Russia) 14.77; 8.Anna Pyatykh (Russia) 14.73; 9.Olga Saladuha (Ukraine) 14.70; 10.Kaire Leibak (Estonia) 14.13; 11.Trecia Smith (Jamaica) 14.12; 12.Xie Limei (China) 14.09.

Yargelis Savigne of Cuba, winner of the women's triple jump at the 2009 World Championships.

The last "global" meet of the decade saw Yargelis Savigne a class apart. The Cuban easily retained her title and won with 34 cm. to spare. Lebedeva had a serious back problem and had to be content with sixth, right behind a Serbian. Biljana Topic, wife of Dragutin Topic, one of the most durable high jumpers in the men's ranks.

2009 World Championships, Berlin – Triple Jump (17 August): 1.Yargelis Savigne (Cuba) 14.95 (+1.3 m/s); 2.Mabel Gay (Cuba) 14.61 (-0.2 m/s); 3.Anna Pyatykh (Russia) 14.58 (-0.4 m/s); 4.Biljana Topic (Serbia) 14.52; 5.Trecia Smith (Jamaica) 14.48; 6.Tatyana Lebedeva (Russia) 14.37; 7.Cristina Bujin (Rumania) 14.26; 8.Dana Veldáková (Slovakia) 14.25; 9.Xie Limei (China) 14.16; 10.Olga Rypakova (Kazakhstan) 13.91; 11.Teresa Nzola Meso Ba (France) 13.79; 12.Gisele de Oliveira (Brazil) 13.19.

At the end of the decade Kravets' world record (15.50) was still unchallenged, while Mbango and Lebedeva came next in that order in the All-Time List. In 2010 the best performance was 15.25 by Olga Rypakova of Kazakhstan, a new Asian record.

WOMEN: 2011

High jumper Antonietta Di Martino, a 33-year-old Italian veteran, raised her personal record to 2.04 in an indoor meet at Banska Bystrica. She thereby increased her height (1.69) / mark differential to 35 cms, the largest ever for a woman. Still indoors, Jennifer Stuczynski-Suhr of USA did 4.86 in the pole vault.

In the same event, Anna Rogowska of Poland did 4.85 indoors, a new personal best. World record holder Yelena Isinbayeva returned to her native surroundings in Volgograd and is expected to resume competition in July.

STATISTICS
MEN

WORLD YEAR LISTS 1860 - 1900

HIGH JUMP

Year	Name	Nat	Born	Mark	Pos	Venue	Date
1860	Robert Burton	GB	41	1.70	1)	Harrow	27 Mar
	Henry Powell	GB	38	1.675	1)	Oxford	15 Mar
	Victor Brooke	Ire	43	1.675	2)	Harrow	27 Mar
	Professional:						
	Andre Milne	GB		1.775	1)	Forfar	10 Aug
1861	Henry Powell	GB	38	1.65	1)	Oxford	26 Nov
	Professional:						
	Donald Dinnie	GB	37	1.775	1)	Montrose	08 Aug
1862	Francis Gooch	GB		1.65	1)	Oxford	04 Nov
1863	William Maitland	GB		1.675	)	Harrow	Mar
	Henry Sampson	GB		1.675	)	Liverpool	13 Jun
	G. Bayley	GB		1.675	)	Liverpool	13 Jun
	Francis Gooch	GB		1.675	)	Durham	02 Sep
1864	Thomas Mitchell	GB	39	1.705	1)	Liverpool	09 Jul
	Professional:						
	Thomas Russell	GB		1.775	1)	Alva	10 Aug
1865	Francis Gooch	GB		1.65	)	Cambridge	25 Mar
	Professional:						
	Andrew Milne	GB		1.775	1T)	Alloa	09 Aug
	Samuel Muir	GB		1.775	1T)	Alloa	09 Aug
1866	Thomas Little	GB	45	1.75	1T)	Beaufort House	23 Mar
	John Roupell	GB	45	1.75	1T)	London	23 Mar
	Herbert W. Brooks	GB		1.75	1T)	London	26 Nov
	John A. Harwood	GB	45	1.751	1T)	London	26 Nov
	Professional:						
	John Bell	GB		1.775	1T)	Galashiels	28 Jul
	Gavin Tait	GB	34	1.775	1T)	Galashiels	28 Jul
1867	Thomas Little	GB	45	1.75	1)	London (BH)	12 Apr
	Fellows	GB		1.75	1)	Aldershot	10 Oct
	Charles Green	GB	46	1.73	2T)	London (BH)	12 Apr
	Frederick O'Grady	GB	47	1.73	2T)	London (BH)	12 Apr

1868	Charles Green	GB	46	1.735	1T)	Cambridge	19 Mar
	Gurney Hoare	GB	47	1.735	1T)	Cambridge	19 Mar
	Guy Pym	GB	41	1.73	1)	Beaufort House London (BH)	30 May
	Robert Mitchell	GB	47	1.73	1)	Beaufort House London (BH)	20 Jun
	Professional:						
	Andrew Milne	GB		1.775	1)	Alloa	12 Aug
1869	Robert Mitchell	GB	47	1.73	1)	Sheffield	03 May
	Hugh Miller	GB		1.73	1)	Liverpool	26 Jun
	C. Grundy	GB		1.70	2T)	Liverpool	26 Jun
	F. Corbett	GB		1.70	2T)	Liverpool	26 Jun
	John Duckworth	GB	45	1.70	4)	Liverpool	26 Jun
	Professional:						
	Andrew Milne	GB		1.79	1)	Dundee	21 Aug
1870	Robert Mitchell	GB	47	1.755	1)	London (LB) Lillie Bridge	09 Apr
	Frededrick Hargreaves	GB	50	1.755	1)	Liverpool	25 Jun
	John Harwood	GB	45	1.715	1)	Croydon	11 Jun
	J. C. Greaves	GB		1.715	1)	Rochdale	11 Jun
1871	Robert Mitchell	GB	47	1.765	1)	London (LB) Lillie Bridge	03 Apr
	Frederick Hargreaves	GB	50	1.75	1)	Pendlebury	05 Aug
	J. B. Hurst	GB	47	1.73	1)	Louth	07 Aug
	Professional:						
	Milne	GB		1.765	1)	Perth	27 Jul
1872	John Gurney	GB	49	1.74	1)	Cambridge	13 Mar
	Edward Prior	GB	52	1.71	2)	Cambridge	13 Mar
	Robert Mitchell	GB	47	1.71	1)	Sheffield	13 May
	William Curteis	GB	49	1.71	1)	Camberley	04 Oct
1873	Thomas Davin	Ire	52	1.785	1)	Dublin	07 Jul
	John Gurney	GB	49	1.76	1)	Cambridge	26 Mar
	Michael Brannigan	Ire		1.75	)	Ballinakil	
1874	Marshall Brooks	GB	55	1.80	1)	London (L.B.) Lillie Bridge	30 Mar
	Thomas Davin	Ire	52	1.78	2)	London (L.B.)	30 Mar
	P. Cadogan	Ire		1.78	1)	Dublin	27 Jun
1875	Michael Glazebrook	GB	53	1.80	1)	London (L.B.) Lillie Bridge	22 Mar
	George Martin Kenny	Ire	55	1.79	1)	Dublin	26 Jun
	Samuel Walker	GB	55	1.75	1)	Torquay	30 Aug
1876	Marshall Brooks	GB	55	1.89	1)	London (L.B.) Lillie Bridge	07 Apr
	Thomas Davin	Ire	52	1.815	1)	Dublin	01 Jun
	William Kelly	Ire		1.79	1)	Cork	17 May
1877	"Lieutenant" L. T. Carden	Ire		1.80	)	Maryborough	30 Jun
	Patrick Davin	Ire	57	1.775	)	Dublin	
	Thomas Tomlinson	GB		1.75	1)	Ilkley	11 Aug
1878	C. W. Power	Ire		1.80	)	Garlow	02 Jul
	Patrick Davin	Ire	57	1.80	1)	Kilkenny	19 Aug
	William Kelly	Ire		1.79	)	Cork	29 May
	Exhibition:						
	Thomas Tomlinson	GB		1.80	-)	Windsor	07 Sep
1879	Patrick Davin	Ire	57	1.865	1)	Kilkenny	16 Jul
	William Kelly	Ire		1.75	1)	Mardyke	22 Apr
	J. P. Conover	USA		1.73	1)	Mott Haven, NY	09 May
1880	Patrick Davin	Ire	57	1.90	1)	Carrick-on-Suir	05 Jul
	John Parsons	GB	59	1.77	1)	London (L.B.)	03 Jul

HIGH JUMP 1881 1890

Year	Athlete	Nation	Born	Mark	Pos	Venue	Date
1881	Patrick Davin	Ire	57	1.865	1)	Carrick-on-Suir	05 Jul
	Michael Connery	Ire		1.84	)		
	Tom Malone	Ire	57	1.84	)	Kilkenny	
	Professional:						
	H. Andrews	GB		1.85	1)	Stirling	12 Aug
1882	Patrick Davin	Ire	57	1.88	1)	Dublin	19 Aug
	Professional:						
	E. W. Johnston	Can		1.84	)		
1883	Patrick Davin	Ire	57	1.84	1)	Portington	27 Sep
	John Parsons	GB	59	1.835	1)	London	30 Jun
	D. A. Foreman	USA		1.825	1)	San Francisco	26 Jun
	Professional:						
	Tom Malone	Ire	57	1.84	1)		
1884	John Parsons	GB	59	1.825	1)	Partrtick	Apr
	W. Cummings	USA		1.80	1)	Philadelphia	25 Aug
	G. W. Hamilton	USA		1.775	1)	Omaha	30 Aug
	Professional:						
	J. N. Byrnes	Ire		1.775	1)	Botany Bay	Jul
1885	William Byrd Page	USA	66	1.835	1)	Philadelphia	14 May
	Patrick . J. Kelly	Ire	64	1.80	1)	Southp Port	27 Jun
	E.J. Walsh	Ire		1.80	1)	Haddiington	04 Jul
1886	William Byrd Page	USA	66	1.865	1)	Tralee	01 Aug
	Michael R. Conneryway	Ire		1.84	1)	Kilmallock	15 Aug
	A. Scott	Can		1.825	1)	London, Ont.	24 May
	Professional:						
	T.F. Kearny	USA		1.845	)	Brooklyn	05 Sep
1887	William Byrd Page	USA	66	1.91	1)	Stourbridge	15 Aug
	George Rowdon	GB	64	1.88	1)	Paignton	24 Aug
	Patrick Kelly	Ire	64	1.865	1)	Mallow	24 Jul
	Patrick McGrath	Ire		1.865	1)	Tralee	01 Aug
	Exhibition:						
	William Byrd Page	USA	66	1.93	-)	Philadelphia	07 Oct
1888	William Byrd Page	USA	66	1.89	1)	Philadelphia	30 Jun
	William Montgomery	GB		1.825	1)	Manchester	09 Jun
	Isaac Webster	USA	65	1.815	1)	New York (MF)	26 May
	Exhibition:						
	Geoge Rowdon	GB	64	1.85	-)	Haytor Camp	10 Aug
1889	George Rowdon	GB		1.90	1)	Dartmouth	01 Jun
	P.M. McGrath	Ire		1.825	1)	Dublin	09 Jun
	George Rowdon	GB	64	1.825	1)	Dawlish	04 Jul
	Tom Jennings	GB	69	1.815	1)	London (SB)	01 Jun
	R. K. Pritchard	USA		1.815	1)	Rosedale	28 Sep
	Exhibition:						
	George Rowdon	GB	64	1.90	-)	Dartmouth	01 Jun
	Professional / Exhibition:						
	John Fitzpatrick	Ire/USA		1.94	1)	Boston	15 Jul
1890	Patrick Davin	Ire	57	1.895	1)	Boston	25 Aug
	James M. M. Ryan	Ire	71	1.865	1)	Dublin	17 Aug
	W. Schlerf	USA		1.86	1)	Philadelphia	28 Jun

	Exhibition:						
	George Rowdon	GB	64	1.96	-)	Haytor Camp	06 Aug
1891	G.R.eorge R. Fearing	USA		1.885i	1)	Boston	14 Feb
	Alvah Nickerson	USA	70	1.88	1)	Travers Island, N.Y.	13 Jun
	W. M. Fletcher	Ire		1.87	1)	Durrow	22 Jul
	Professional / Downhill:						
	Michael Conroy	Aus		1.955	-)	St. Kilda	22 Jun
1892	Michael Sweeney	USA	72	1.935	1)	Travers Island, N.Y.	08 Oct
	Herbert L. Herrick	USA		1.88	2)	Travers Island, N.Y.	08 Oct
	Murty O'Brien	Ire		1.855	1)	Dublin	10 Sep
1893	James M. Ryan	Ire	71	1.91	1)	Nenagh	03 Aug
	Michael Sweeney	USA	72	1.905i	1)	Philadelphia	17 Feb
	Murty O'Brien	Ire		1.90	1)	Coachford	30 Jul
1894	Michael Sweeney	USA	72	1.92			
	Murty O'Brien	Ire		1.905	1)	Kildorrey	08 Sep
	Eugene Goff	USA	72	1.825	-)	Bergen Point	04 Jul
1895	Michael Sweeney	USA	72	1.97	1)	New York	21 Sep
	James M. Ryan	Ire	71	1.94	1)	Tipperary	19 Aug
	Richard Sjöberg	Swe	90	1.90	1)	Uppsala	28 May
	Exhibition:						
	James M. Ryan	Ire	71	1.98	-)	Tipperary	Sep
1896	Michael Sweeney	USA	72	1.89i	1)	New York	22 Feb
	W.C.Pattersonn	USA		1.88	1T)	Madison	09 May
	B.Herbert Kerrigan	USA	75	1.88	1T)	Madison	09 May
	M.J.James M. Ryan	Ire	71	1.88	1)	Dublin	18 Jul
1897	J.ames D. Winsor	USA		1.915	1)	New Haven	08 May
	E.C. Waller	USA		1.905i	1)	Chicago	27 Dec
	R.C. Mervin	USA		1.885	1)	New Haven	15 May
	Irving Baxter	USA	76	1.885	1)	New York	28 Aug
1898	Patrick Leahy ??	Ire	77	1.965 ?	1)	Cork Millstreet	14 Aug

(according to the book, "Irish Athletic Record 1906" he held the Irish record with 6-4 ¾ (1.95), made at Millstreet on 6 Sep 1898).

	Irving Baxter	USA	76	1.905	1)		
	G. Gernandt	Ger/USA		1.89	1)	New York	15 Aug
	Exhibition:						
	Patrick Leaky	Ire	77	1.965	-)	Limerick	24 Jul
1899	Patrick Leahy	Ire	77	1.96	1)	Mallow	15 Aug
	Irving Baxter	USA	76	1.915i	1)	Georgetown	11 Mar
	Garrett Serviss	USA	78	1.895	1)	Travers Island, N.Y.	10 Jun
1900	Irving Baxter	USA	76	1.915	1)	Baltimore	30 May
	Patrick Leahy	Ire	77	1.89	1)	Nenagh	24 May
	J.S. Spraker	USA		1.89	1)	New Haven	31 Oct

ALL TIME WORLD LIST AS AT THE END OF 1900

Michael Sweeney	USA	72	1.97	1)	New York	21 Sep 95
Pat Leahy	Ire	77	1.965	1)	Cork	14 Aug 98
James M. Ryan	Ire	71	1.94	1)	Tipperary	19 Aug 95
James D.Windsor	USA		1.915	1)	New Haven	08 May 97
Irving Baxter	USA	76	1.915	1)	Georgetown	11 Mar 99
William Page	USA	66	1.91	1)	Philadelphia, Stourbridge	15 Aug 87
E.C. Waller	USA		1.905il	1)	Chicago	27 Dec 97
Murty O'Brien	Ire		1.905	1)	Kildorrey	08 Sep 94

HIGH JUMP 1901 1912

Year	Athlete	Nat	Born	Mark	Pos	Venue	Date
1901	Garrett Serviss	USA	78	1.905	1)	Buffalo	07 Sep
	Samuel Jones	USA	79	1.895	1)	Philadelphia	27 Apr
	Irving Baxter	USA	76	1.88	)		
	G. Howard-Smith	GB	80	1.88	1)	Montreal	14 Sep
	Exhibition:						
	Patrick Leahy	Ire	77	1.95	1)	Charleville	25 Aug
1902	Patrick Leahy	Ire	77	1.915	1)	Kilkenny	11 Aug
	Samuel Jones	USA	79	1.905	1)	London	05 Jul
	Cornelius Leahy	Ire	77	1.89	)		
1903	Garrett Serviss	USA	78	1.93	1)		
	Cornelius Leahy	Ire	77	1.89	1)	Dublin	30 Aug
	William Lowe	USA		1.875	1)	Syracuse	16 May
1904	Cornelius Leahy	Ire	76	1.94	1)	Limerick	18 Sep
	Samuel Jones	USA	79	1.88	)		
	William Hennessey	USA		1.88	)		
1905	Cornelius Leahy	Ire	77	1.93	1)	Westport	23 Aug
	Channing Hall	USA	85	1.885	)	Berkeley	08 Apr
	William Hennessey	USA		1.88	)	SDt.Louis	12 Oct
1906	Channing Hall	USA	85	1.90	1)	New York	01 Sep
	Cornelius Leahy	Ire	77	1.89	1)	Macroom (?)	19 Aug
	Ewan Munger	USA		1.855	)		
1907	Thomas Moffitt	USA	84	1.91	1)	Cambridge, MA	01 Jun
	John Marshall	USA		1.89	2)	Cambridge, MA	01 Jun
	Channing Hall	USA	85	1.885i	1)	San Francisco	Jan
1908	Harry Porter	USA	82	1.99	)		
	Ewan Munger	USA		1.905	)		
	James Burke	Ire	84	1.905	)	Rome, N.Y.	Sep
	Exhibition:						
	Cornelius Leahy	Ire	77	1.95	-)	Adare	15 Aug
1909	Harry Porter	USA	82	1.93	1)	New York	08 May
	Egon Erickson	USA	88	1.93	1)	New York	06 Jun
	Michael Creed	Ire		1.905	1)	Dundalk	18 Jul
1910	Timothy Leahy	Ire	90	1.915	1)	Mitchellstown	08 Aug
	Jarvis Burdick	USA	89	1.91	1)	Philadelphia	14 May
	George Horine	USA	90	1.905	)		
1911	George Horine	USA	90	1.930	1)	Palo Alto	01 Apr
	Robert Pasemann	Ger	86	1.92	1)	Braunschweig	13 Aug
	Samuel Lawrence	USA	88	1.915i	1)	Cambridge, MA	21 Mar
	Edward Beeson	USA	90	1.905	1T)	Berkeley	15 Apr
	Harry Grumpelt	USA	85	1.905	1)	Pittsburgh	01 Jul
	Harry Porter	USA	82	1.905	2)	Pittsburgh	01 Jul
	Jervis Burdick	USA	89	1.905	3)	Pittsburgh	01 Jul
	István Wardener	Hun	89	1.90	1)	Budapest	24 Sep
1912	George Horine	USA	90	2.005	1)	Palo Alto	18 May
	James Thorpe	USA	88	1.955	1)	New York	12 Jun
	Samuel Lawrence	USA	88	1.94i	1)	Boston	10 Feb
	Edward Beeson	USA	90	1.94	2)	Palo Alto	18 May
	Alma Richards	USA	90	1.93	2)	New York	12 Jun
	Arthur Moffat	USA		1.925	)		
	Wesley Oler	USA	92	1.92	1)	Cambridge, MaA	25 May
	Hans Liesche	Ger	91	1.91	2)	Stockholm	08 Jul
	Timothy Leahy	Ire	90	1.905	1)	Kanturk	25 Aug
	Harry Grumpelt	USA	85	1.905	1)	New York	07 Sep
	John Johnstone	USA	92	1.905	1)	Pittsburgh	21 Sep
	M.J. Cullinan	USA		1.905			

Year	Athlete	Nat	Born	Mark	Place	Venue	Date
1913	Edward Beeson	USA	90	1.965	1)	Berkeley	10 May
	Timothy Carroll	Ire	88	1.955	1)	Kinsale	04 Aug
	Timothy Leahy	Ire	90	1.955	1)	Limerick	31 Aug
	Ben Howard Baker	GB	92	1.955	1)	Rochdale	20 Aug
	Egon Erickson	USA	88	1.91i	1)	Boston	08 Feb
	Jenö Gáspár	Hun	96	1.91	1)	Budapest	20 Aug
	Hanns Steigauf	Ger	90	1.91	1)	Ingolstadt	29 Aug
	Warren Sargent	USA	90	1.905i	1)	Ann Arbor	22 Mar
	Ivar Reimers	Swe	86	1.905	1)	Reijmyre	10 Aug
	George Horine	USA	90	1.905	1)	San Francisco	21 Sep
1914	Edward Beeson	USA	90	2.015	1)	Berkeley	02 May
	Jenö Gáspár	Hun	96	1.915	1)	Budapest	11 Jun
	Hanns Steigauf	Ger	90	1.90	-)	Budapest	21 Jun
	Wesley Oler	USA	92	1.89	1)	London	04 Jul
	Robert Wahl	USA		1.88i	1)	Evanston	24 Mar
	Luther Nichols	USA		1.88	1T)	Cambridge, MA	30 May
	Eugene Jenning	USA		1.88	2)hc	New York	30 May
	Harry Grumpelt	USA	85	1.88	1)	New York	06 Jun
	Paulus Af Uhr	Swe	92	1.88	1)	Stockholm	14 Jun
	Ivàn Wardener	Hun	92	1.88	1)	Budapest	21 Jun
	Alma Richards	USA	90	1.88	1)	Dayton	04 Jul
	Ben Howard Baker	GB	92	1.88	2)	London	04 Jul
	George Horine	USA	90	1.88	1)	Berkeley	19 Sep
1915	Wesley Oler	USA	92	1.965	1)	New York	05 Jun
	Alma Richards	USA	90	1.955	1)	Philadelphia	24 Apr
	Richard Sjöberg	Swe	90	1.92	1)	Kristiania	12 Sep
	George Horine	USA	90	1.915	1)	Berkeley	03 Apr
	Joseph Loomis	USA		1.915	1)	Chicago	03 Jul
	Fritz Warendorph	Nor	94	1.90	1)	Fredrikstad	29 Aug
	Egon Erickson	USA	88	1.89i	2)	New York	04 Mar
	Maurice James	USA		1.88	3T)	Philadelphia	24 Apr
	John Johnstone	USA	92	1.88	3T)	Philadelphia	24 Apr
	Bidwell	USA		1.87	1T)	Los Angeles	27 Mar
	Earl Thomson	Can	95	1.87	1T)	Los Angeles	27 Mar
1916	Luther Nichols	USA		1.94	1)	Palo Alto	15 Apr
	Wesley Oler	USA	92	1.905	1T)	Philadelphia	24 Apr
	Alma Richards	USA	90	1.905	1T)	Philadelphia	24 Apr
	Frank Maker	USA		1.88	1)	Palo Alto	15 Apr
	Harry Barwise	USA		1.88	2)	Newark	09 Sep
	Egon Erickson	USA	88	1.88	1)	New York	26 Aug
	Muirhead	USA		1.875	1)	Pullman	03 Jun
	Webster	USA		1.865	1T)	Madison	20 May
	Nelson	USA		1.865	1T)	Madison	20 May
	Al Fisher	USA		1.865	)		
	Bo Ekelund	Swe	94	1.86	1)	Kristiania	04 Jun
	Karl-Axel Kullerstrand	Swe	92	1.86	)	Göteborg	23 Jul
1917	Clinton Larsen	USA	92	1.965	1)	Philadelphia	28 Apr
	Luther Nichols	USA		1.93	1)	Palo Alto	14 Apr
	Richard Templeton	USA	97	1.93	2)	Palo Alto	14 Apr
	J. P. Jackson	USA		1.89	1)	Berkeley	07 Apr
	Karl-Axel Kullerstrand	Swe	92	1.89	1)	Eskilstuna	10 Jun
	Joseph Loomis	USA		1.88i	1)	New York	17 Mar
	Axel Peterson	Swe	93	1.86	2)	Eskilstuna	10 Jun
	Exhibition:						
	Clinton Larsen	USA	92	2.025	-)	Provo	01 Jun
1918	John Murphy	USA		1.905	)		
	Georg Högström	Swe	93	1.90	1)	Karlstad	04 Aug
	Hans Jagenburg	Swe	94	1.86	)		
	Ivar Reimers	Swe	86	1.85	)	Falun	09 Jun
	Fritz Warendorph	Nor	94	1.85	1)	Kristiania	18 Aug
	Louis Watson	USA		1.85	1)	New York	08 Sep
	A. Abromet	USA		1.85	2)	New York	08 Sep

	Carl Rice	USA		1.85	1)	Great Lakes	21 Sep
	J. Frank Osborn	USA		1.84	1T)	Columbia	25 May
	Lauritz Schibbye	Nor	92	1.83	1)	Kristiania	11 Aug
	Gustaf Holmér	Swe	91	1.83	)	Jönköping	25 Aug
1919	Bo Ekelund	Swe	94	1.93	1)	Köbenhavn	21 Sep
	John Murphy	USA		1.91	1)	Philadelphia	13 Sep
	John Jackson	USA		1.905	1)	Berkely	03 May
	Ben Howard Baker	GB	92	1.905	1)	Crewe	02 Aug
	Carl Johnson	USA	98	1.885	1)	Chicago	07 Jun
	Richmond Landon	USA	98	1.88	1T)	Cambridge, MA	31 May
	William Shanahan	Ire	97	1.88	)	Belfast	17 Aug
	Harry Barwise	USA		1.88	1)	Cambridge, MA	23 Aug
	Walter Whalen	USA		1.88	3)	Philadelphia	13 Sep
	Gaston Ribot	Fra		1.865	1T)	Bordeaux	29 Jun
	Armand Estang	Fra	86	1.865	1T)	Bordeaux	29 Jun
1920	Richmond Landon	USA	98	1.94	1)	Antwerpen	17 Aug
	Dink Templeton	USA	97	1.935	1)	Palo Alto	15 May
	John Murphy	USA		1.935	1)	Cambridge, MA	17 Jul
	Harold Muller	USA	01	1.92	1)	Pasadena	26 Jun
	Walter Whalen	USA	98	1.915i	1)	New York	13 Mar
	Ben Howard Baker	GB	92	1.915	1)	London	04 Sep
	Egon Erickson	USA	88	1.905i	1)	New York	10 Feb
	Louis Watson	USA	95	1.905	2)	Philadelphia	26 Jun
	Jonathan Murphy	Ire		1.905	1)		
	Bo Ekelund	Swe	94	1.90	3)	Antwerpen	17 Aug

ALL TIME WORLD LIST AS AT THE END OF 1920

Clinton Larsen	USA	92	2.025	1)	Provo	01 Jun 17
Edward Beeson	USA	90	2.015	1)	Berkeley	02 May 14
George Horine	USA	90	2.005	1)	Palo Alto	18 May 12
Michael Sweeney	USA	72	1.97	1)	New York	21 Sep 95
Wesley Oler	USA	92	1.965	1)	New York	05 Jun 19
George Rowdon	GB	64	1.96	1)	Haytor Camp	06 Aug 90
Timothy Carroll	Ire	88	1.955	1)	Kinsale	04 Aug 13
Alma Richards	USA	90	1.955	1)	Philadelphia	24 Apr 15
Pat Leahy	Ire	77	1.945	)	Millstreet	06 Sep 98
Frank Maker	USA		1.945	1)	Palo Alto	15 Apr 16

1921	R. P. Chamberlain	USA		1.972	1)	Charlottesville,VA	30 Mar
	Dewey Alberts	USA		1.959	1)	Urbana, IL	20 May
	Howard Baker	GB	92	1.956	1)	Huddersfield	25 Jun
	Mint Howell	USA		1.940	1)	Palo Alto, CA	07 May
	Richmond Landon	USA	98	1.934	1)	Travers Island, NY	04 Jun
	Harold Muller	USA	01	1.930	1)	Berkeley, CA	14 May
	John Murphy	USA		1.930	2)	Pasadena, CA	04 Jul
	Oliver Corey	USA		1.905	3)	Pasadena, CA	04 Jul
	Leroy Brown	USA	02	1.892i	2)	Boston	05 Feb
	Edwin Weatherdon	USA		1.892	2)	Travers Islnd, NY	04 Jun
	Pierre Lewden	Fra	01	1.89	1)	Auxerre	21 Aug
	Extra trial:						
	Einar Thulin	Swe	96	1.90	-)	Malmö	06 Jun
1922	Harold Osborn	USA	99	1.981	1)	Des Moines, IA	29 Apr
	Dewey Alberts	USA		1.959	1)	Newark, NJ	09 Sep
	John Murphy	USA		1.957	1T)	Iowa City, IA	03 Jun
	Leroy Brown	USA	02	1.953i	1)	New York	11 Mar
	Peter Platten	USA	00	1.949	1)	Minneapolis	20 May
	Oliver Corey	USA		1.927	1)	Redlands, CA	18 Feb
	R. P. Chamberlain	USA		1.905	1)	Charlottesville, VA	15 Apr
	Pierre Lewden	USA	01	1.905	1)	London	29 Jul
	Robert Clark	USA		1.895	2T)	Cambridge, MA	27 May

	Harold Muller	USA	01	1.895	2T)	Cambride, MA	27 May
1923	Harold Osborn	USA	99	1.994	1)	Peoria, IL	05 May
	Leroy Brown	USA	02	1.972	1)	Chicago	01 Sep
	Richmond Landon	USA	98	1.962i	2)	New York	31 Jan
	John Murphy	USA		1.937i	1)	Boston	03 Feb
	Tom Poor	USA	03	1.930	1)	Des Moines, IA	28 Apr
	Pierre Lewden	Fra	01	1.930	1)	London	07 Jul
	Emerson Norton	USA	00	1.915	1T)	Philadelphia	28 Apr
	David MacEllven	USA		1.905i	1)	Evanston, IL	17 Mar
	Clarence Flahive	USA		1.886i	2)hcp	Boston	03 Feb
	Robert Juday	USA	00	1.883	1)	Chicago	31 Aug
1924	Harold Osborn	USA	99	2.038	1)	Urbana, IL	27 May
	Leroy Brown	USA	02	1.994	1)	New York	07 Jun
	Richmond Landon	USA	98	1.962i	1)	New York	07 Mar
	Tom Poor	USA	03	1.930	1)	Lawrence, KS	19 Apr
	Oather Hampton	USA	05	1.930	1)	Palo Alto, CA	17 May
	Pierre Lewden	Fra	01	1.930	1)hcp	Glasgow	02 Aug
	Robert Juday	USA	00	1.930	1)	West Orange, NJ	06 Sep
	Wright	USA		1.924	1)	South Bend, IN	03 May
	Justin Russell	USA		1.921i	1)	Evanston, IL	15 Mar
	Emerson Norton	USA	00	1.92	D)	Colombes	11 Jul
	Jump-off:						
	Raymond Smith	USA		1.937	-)	Ann Arbor, MI	31 May
1925	Harold Osborn	USA	99	2.01	1)	Malmö	30 Aug
	Justin Russell	USA		1.981	1)	Columbus, OH	06 Jun
	Tom Poor	USA	03	1.969	1)	Austin, TX	27 Mar
	Tom Work	USA	05	1.964	1)	Seattle	30 May
	Robert Juday	USA	00	1.956	3)	San Francisco	04 Jul
	Karl Österberg	Swe	94	1.95	1)	Stockholm	19 Jun
	Pierre Lewden	Fra	01	1.95	1)	Stockholm	30 Aug
	Henry Coggeshall	USA		1.937	1)	Los Angeles	16 May
	Oather Hampton	USA	05	1.937	4T)	San Francisco	04 Jul
	Alden Ross	USA		1.937	6)	San Francisco	04 Jul
	Exhibition:						
	Harold Osborn	USA	99	2.055	(-)	Austin, TX	27 Mar
1926	Rufus Haggard	USA		2.013	1)	Chicago	12 Jun
	Anton Burg	USA	04	1.988	2)	Chicago	12 Jun
	Lloyd Stern	USA		1.981i	1)	Chicago	29 Jan
	Robert King	USA	06	1.975	1)	Cambridge, MA	29 May
	Charles Anson	USA		1.956	2)	Columbus, OH	15 May
	Harold Osborn	USA	99	1.949i	1)	New York	04 Feb
	Henry Coggeshall	USA		1.937	3T)	Chicago	12 Jun
	Garland Shepherd	USA		1.930	1)	Lawrence, KS	17 Apr
	Justin Russell	USA		1.930	1)	Chicago	26 Jun
	Ivan Nilsson	Swe	04	1.93	1)	Oslo	29 Jul
	Torbern Cassel	Swe	00	1.93	1)	Linköping	12 Sep
	Exhibition:						
	Garland Shepherd	USA		1.964	-)	Austin, TX	03 Apr
	Doubtful conditions:						
	Con O'Connor	EIR		1.969	1)	Abbeyleix	22 Aug
1927	Robert King	USA	06	1.988	1)	Palo Alto, CA	19 Mar
	Harold Osborn	USA	99	1.981i	1)	Chicago	01 Mar
	Anton Burg	USA	04	1.978	1)	Columbus, OH	23 Apr
	Charles Major	USA		1.972i	1)	New York	02 Feb
	Garland Shepherd	USA		1.969	1T)	Chicago	11 Jun
	Henry Coggeshall	USA		1.967	1)	Los Angeles	19 Feb
	Charles McGinnis	USA	06	1.956i	1)	Evanston, IL	12 Mar
	William Robusch	USA	01	1.956	1)	Pittsburgh	27 Aug

	Tom Maynard	USA		1.943	1)	Philadelphia	28 May
	Kornél Késmárki	Hun	03	1.94	1)	Budapest	18 Sep
	Intrasquad meet:						
	Nils Bergström	Swe	09	1.95i	1)	Falkenberg	27 Feb
1928	Robert King	USA	06	1.997	1)	Chicago	09 Jun
	Anton Burg	USA	04	1.981	1)	Chicago	03 Sep
	Rufus Haggard	USA		1.978	1)	St.Louis	02 Jun
	Joe Abernathy	USA		1.956	1)		
	Charles McGinnis	USA	06	1.956	1)	Detroit	01 Jul
	Jack McIntosh	USA		1.946i	1T)	South Bend, IN	03 Mar
	John Cline	USA		1.946i	1T)	South Bend, IN	03 Mar
	Simeon Toribio	Phi	05	1.946	1)	Manila	22/27 Apr
	Bert Nelson	USA		1.943	2)	Chicago	03 Sep
	Ben Hedges	USA	07	1.943	1)	Travers Island, NY	13 Oct
	Exhibition:						
	Henry Lasallette	USA		1.943	-)	Selma, CA	05 May
1929	Henry Lasallette	USA		1.994	1)	Vancouver	13 Jul
	Henry Coggeshall	USA		1.985	1)	Berkeley	06 Apr
	Robert Van Osdel	USA	10	1.956	1T)	Los Angeles	08 Jun
	Bert Nelson	USA		1.953	1)	Denver	03 Jul
	Kazuo Kimura	Jap	09	1.94	1)	Seoul	17 Oct
	Walter Marty	USA	10	1.937	1)	Fresno	26 Apr
	Leo Sexton	USA	09	1.930i	1)	New York	09 Feb
	William Filmer	USA		1.930	2)	Berkeley	06 Apr
	Howard Arthur	USA		1.930	3)	Los Angeles	08 Jun
	Geoffrey Turner	GB		1.930	1)	Burnley	03 Aug
	Jump-off:						
	Kornél Késmárki	Hun	03	1.93	-)	Budapest	10 Aug
	Extra Trial:						
	Robert King	USA	06	1.943	-)	Fresno	27 Apr
	No qualified officials:						
	Geoffrey Turner	GB		1.956	1)	Widnes	20 Jul
1930	Robert Van Osdel	USA	10	2.013	1)	Los Angeles	22 Mar
	Bert Nelson	USA		2.000i	1)	South Bend	01 Feb
	Simeon Toribio	Phi	05	2.00	1)	Tokyo	24 May
	James Stewart	USA	05	1.988	1)	Palo Alto	17 May
	Ted Shaw	USA		1.986	1)	Lawrence	19 Apr
	Parker Shelby	USA		1.967	1)		
	Walter Marty	USA	10	1.962	1)	Chicago	27 Aug
	Kazuo Kimura	Jap	09	1.96	2)	Tokyo	24 May
	Anton Burg	USA	04	1.953	1)	Pittsburgh	23 Aug
	Willis Ward	USA	12	1.943i	1)	Detroit	08 Mar
	Exhibition/Extra Trial:						
	Herny Lasallette	USA		1.981	-)	El Monte, CA	29 Mar
1931	George Spitz	USA	12	2.014	1)	Travers Island, N.Y.	19 Sep
	Walter Marty	USA	10	2.000	1)	Taft, CA	12 Jun
	Harold Osborn	USA	899	1.981i	2)	New York	02 Feb
	Anton Burg	USA	04	1.981i	1)	New York	25 Feb
	Willis Ward	USA	12	1.981	1)	Detroit	25 Apr
	Howard Spencer	USA	12	1.975i	2)	New York	14 Mar
	James Stewart	USA	05	1.969	1)	Los Angeles	20 Mar
	Darrell Jones	USA		1.964	1)	Lafayette, IN	16 May
	Robert Schroeder	USA		1.956	1)	Pittsburg, KA	23 May
	William O'Connor	USA		1.956	1)	Philadelphia	30 May
1932	George Spitz	USA	12	2.045i	1)	Boston	13 Feb
	Bert Nelson	USA		2.029	1)	Milwaukee	03 Jun

Year	Athlete	Nat	Born	Mark	Place	Venue	Date
	Willis Ward	USA	12	2.010	1)	Chicago	11 Jun
	Robert Van Osdel	USA	10	1.997	1T)	Palo Alto	16 Jul
	Cornelius Johnson	USA	13	1.997	1T)	Palo Alto	16 Jul
	Walter Marty	USA	10	1.994	1)	Sacramento	07 May
	Henry Lasallette	USA		1.988	1)	Long Beach	05 Mar
	Ben Hedges	USA	07	1.981i	2)	New York	06 Feb
	Worth Watkins	USA		1.978	1)		
	Howard Spencer	USA	12	1.972	1)	Beaver Falls	23 Apr
1933	Walter Marty	USA	10	2.048	1)	Fresno	13 May
	George Spitz	USA	12	2.038i	1)	New York	25 Feb
	Howard Spencer	USA	12	2.013i	2)	New York	25 Feb
	Cornelius Johnson	USA	13	2.007	1)	Chicago	30 Jun
	Lloyd Richey	USA	12	1.984	1)		
	Keith Brown	USA	13	1.984	1)	New Haven	20 May
	John Metcalfe	Aus	12	1.984	1)	Sydney	07 Dec
	Bert Nelson	USA		1.981i	2)	New York	18 Feb
	Veikko Peräsalo	Fin	12	1.98	1)	Oslo	01 Jul
	Kimio Yada	Jap	13	1.98	1)	Tokyo	12 Sep
1934	Walter Marty	USA	10	2.070	1)	Fresno	07 Apr
	Cornelius Johnson	USA	13	2.048	1T)	Milwaukee	30 Jun
	George Spitz	USA	12	2.032	1)	Travers Island, NY	02 Jun
	Kalevi Kotkas	Fin	13	2.01	1)	Rio de Janeiro	07 Mar
	Mihály Bodosi	Hun	09	2.005	1)	Pécs	15 Apr
	Veikko Peräsalo	Fin	12	2.005	1)	Seinäjoki	27 May
	Yoshiro Asakuma	Jap	14	2.00	1)	Nishinomiya	16 Sep
	Douglas Barham	USA		1.988	1)	Norman	12 May
	Lloyd Richey	USA	12	1.984	)		
	Delos Thurber	USA	16	1.981	2)	Long Beach	03 Mar
	Exhibition / Extra Trial:						
	Harold Osborn	USA	899	2.045	-)	Atlantic City	26 May
	George Spitz	USA	12	2.038	-)	Philadelphia	28 Apr
	Unknown irregularity:						
	John Metcalfe	Aus	12	1.988	1)	Marton	17 Mar
1935	George Spitz	USA	12	2.032i	1)	New York	16 Mar
	Cornelius Johnson	USA	13	2.032	1)	Santa Barbara	27 Apr
	Vincent Murphy	USA		2.013i	1)	Notre Dame	09 Mar
	Hiroshi Tanaka	Jap	15	2.01	1)	Tokyo	15 Jun
	Yoshiro Asakuma	Jap	14	2.01	1)	Tokyo	20 Jun
	Al Threadgill	USA		2.007i	1)	Toronto	Mar
	Kalevi Kotkas	Fin	13	2.00	1)	Paris	29 Sep
	Worth Watkins	USA		1.984	1)	Fort Worth	23 Mar
	Harold Osborn	USA	899	1.981i	2T)	New York	16 Mar
	Dave Albritton	USA	13	1.981	1)	Cleveland	09 Jun
	Exhibition:						
	Harold Osborn	USA	899	1.981	-)	St.Louis	30 Jun
1936	Cornelius Johnson	USA	13	2.076	1T)	New York	12 Jul
	Dave Albritton	USA	13	2.076	1T)	New York	12 Jul
	Edward Burke	USA	15	2.055i	1)	New York	22 Feb
	Gilbert Cruter	USA	15	2.054i	1)	Fort Collins	22 Feb
	Walter Marty	USA	10	2.051	1)	Palo Alto	09 May
	Valevi Kotkas	Fin	13	2.04	1)	Göteborg	01 Sep
	Melvin Walker	USA	14	2.032	1T)	Princeton	04 Jul
	Al Threadgill	USA		2.026i	1)	New York	11 Jan
	Delos Thurber	USA	16	2.019	1T)	Columbus	13 Jun
	Lauri Kalima	Fin	16	2.01	1)	Jyvaskyla	05 Sep
	Exhibition / Extra Trial:						
	Humbert Smith	USA	16	2.013	-)	Palo Alto	11 Apr
1937	Melvin Walker	USA	14	2.09	1)	Malmö	12 Aug
	Edward Burke	USA	15	2.064i	1)	New York	27 Feb

Year	Athlete	Nat	Born	Mark	Pl	Venue	Date
	Dave Albritton	USA	13	2.048	1)	Milwaukee	03 Jul
	Nikolay Kovtun	USSR	14	2.01	1)	Moskva	17 Jun
	Cornelius Johnson	USA	13	2.01	1)	Paris	07 Sep
	Al Threadgill	USA		2.007i	1)	Boston	13 Feb
	Jack Vickery	USA		2.007	1)	Austin	03 Apr
	Humbert Smith	USA	16	2.007	1)	Los Angeles	17 Apr
	Delos Thurber	USA	16	2.007	1)	Palo Alto	08 May
	Juan Luyanda	PR		2.007	1)	Rio Piedras	14 Nov
	Extra Trial:						
	Delos Thurber	USA	16	2.032	-)	Fresno	15 May
1938	Dave Albritton	USA	13	2.051	1T)	Minneapolis	18 Jun
	Gil Cruter	USA	15	2.051	1T)	Minneapolis	18 Jun
	Mel Walker	USA	14	2.05	1)	Milano	11 Sep
	Cornelius Johnson	USA	13	2.032i	1)	Brooklyn, NY	08 Jan
	Lloyd Thompson	USA		2.019i	1)	Providence, R.I.	15 Feb
	Humbert Smith	USA	16	2.019	1)	Berkeley	30 Apr
	Delos Thurber	USA	16	2.013	3T)	Minneapolis	18 Jun
	Wesley Allen	USA		2.013	3T)	Minneapolis	18 Jun
	Edward Burke	USA	15	2.013	3T)	Minneapolis	18 Jun
	Gil LaCava (Greene)	USA	20	2.010	1)	Hollister, CA	28 May
	Exhibition:						
	Lester Steers	USA	17	2.007	-)	Palo Alto	16 Apr
1939	Lester Steers	USA	17	2.038i	1)	San Francisco	04 Mar
	Mel Walker	USA	14	2.032i	1)	New York	25 Feb
	William Eipel	USA	13	2.007i	2)hcp/scr	New York	21 Jan
	Arthur Byrnes	USA	17	2.007i	3)hcp/scr	New York	21 Jan
	Dave Albritton	USA	13	2.007i	2)	New York	04 Feb
	John Wilson	USA	20	2.007	1)	Los Angeles	18 Feb
	J. C. Devall	USA		2.007	1)	Baton Rouge	May
	William Stewart	USA	21	2.007	2)	Lincoln	04 Jul
	Joe Batiste	USA	19	2.003	1)	Phoenix, AZ	15 Apr
	William Hunt	USA		2.00	1)		May
	Sanshi Okamoto	Jap		2.00	1)	Stuttgart	29 Jul
	Hiroshi Tanaka	Jap	15	2.00	1)	Helsinki	11 Aug
	Nils Nicklén	Fin	17	2.00	1)	Stockholm	17 Aug
1940	Lester Steers	USA	17	2.067	1T)	Los Angeles	27 Apr
	John Wilson	USA	20	2.067	1T)	Los Angeles	27 Apr
	Don Boydston	USA		2.038	1)	Fort Worth	16 Mar
	Joshua Williamson	USA		2.038	1)	Kingston, NY	21 Jul
	Tetsuo Akima	Jap		2.02	1)	Kashihara	02 Jun
	Don Canham	USA	18	2.013i	1T)	Minneapolis	22 Jun
	Kelly Horn	USA		2.010	1)		27 Apr
	Mel Walker	USA	14	2.007i	2)	Boston	10 Feb
	Bill Wakefield	USA		2.007	2)	Los Angeles	06 Apr
	J. C. Devall	USA		2.003	1)	Baton Rouge	13 Apr
	Adam Berry	USA	20	2.003	)		
	Exhibition (no accredited officials):						
	Lester Steers	USA	17	2.086	-)	Tuolumne City	09 Jun
1941	Lester Steers	USA	17	2.108	1)	Los Angeles	17 Jun
	William Stewart	USA	21	2.092	1)	Provo	26 Apr
	John Wilson	USA	20	2.054	2)	Palo Alto	21 Jun
	Adam Berry	USA	20	2.051	3)	Philadelphia	29 Jun
	Jerry Walters	USA		2.029	1T)	Austin	05 Apr
	Don Boydston	USA		2.029	1T)	Austin	05 Apr
	Keith O'Rourke	USA	21	2.029	3)	Palo Alto	21 Jun
	Henry Coffman	USA	19	2.026	1)	Austin	10 May
	Mel Walker	USA	14	2.019i	1)	Boston	08 Feb
	Pete Watkins	USA	21	2.007	1)	Waco, TX	19 Apr
	Extra Trial:						
	Don Boydston	USA		2.057	-)	Austin	05 Apr

Year	Name	Nat	Age	Mark	Pos	Venue	Date
	Exhibition:						
	Lester Steers	USA	17	2.146i	-)	Eugene	27 Feb
1942	Pete Watkins	USA	21	2.032	)		
	Gil (LaCava) Greene	USA	20	2.026	1)	Los Angeles	04 Apr
	Adam Berry	USA	20	2.026	1)	Lincoln	13 Jun
	Henry Coffman	USA	19	2.019	)		
	Kelly Horn	USA		2.019	1)	Atlanta	25 Apr
	Searles Tally	USA	20	2.000	1)	Los Angeles	25 Apr
	Dwight Eddleman	USA	22	2.000	1)	Bridgeport, IL	09 May
	Joshua Williamson	USA		1.994i	1T)	New York	28 Feb
	Fred Bolduck	USA		1.981	1)	Los Angeles	16 Apr
	A. Richmond Morcom	USA	21	1.981	2)	New York	20 Jun
	Exhibition:						
	Pete Watkins	USA	21	2.051	-)		
	Unconfirmed performance:						
	Searles Tally	USA	20	2.032	1)	Los Angeles	28 Mar
1943	Bill Vessie	USA	22	2.032i	1)	New York	13 Mar
	Pete Watkins	USA	21	2.032	1)	Des Moines	24 Apr
	Fred Sheffield	USA	23	2.032	1)	Evanston	12 Jun
	Willard Smith	USA		2.026	1)	Fresno	22 May
	Jerry Donovan	USA	22	2.013	1T)	Austin	03 Apr
	Les Barnes	SA		2.013	1)	Johannesburg	04 Oct
	Joshua Williamson	USA		2.000	2)	New York	20 Jun
	John Vislocky	USA	21	1.981i	2)	New York	06 Feb
	Dwight Eddleman	USA	22	1.981i	1)	Chicago	20 Mar
	Adam Berry	USA	20	1.981	)		
	Robert Hodgell	USA	22	1.981	2T)	Evanston	12 Jun
	Billy Christopher	USA		1.981	2T)	Evanston	12 Jun
1944	John Wilson	USA	20	2.032	1)	Los Angeles	22 Apr
	Kenneth Wiesner	USA	25	2.011	1)	Milwaukee	10 Jun
	Hermann Nacke	Ger	20	2.01	P)	Kiel	20 Aug
	Bill Vessie	USA	22	2.007i	1)	Boston	12 Feb
	Dave Albritton	USA	13	2.007i	1)	Chicago	18 Mar
	Willard Smith	USA		2.007	1T)	New York	18 Jun
	Fred Sheffield	USA	23	2.007	1T)	New York	18 Jun
	Dwight Eddleman	USA	22	1.984	1)	Chicago	24 Jun
	Robert Thackeray	USA		1.981i	1T)	Cleveland	15 Jan
	Estel Harper	USA		1.981i	1T)	Cleveland	15 Jan
	Monte Kinder	USA		1.981	1)	Austin	01 Apr
	George Heddy	USA		1.981	1)	New York	17 Jun
	Kenneth Whitney	USA		1.981	3T)	New York	18 Jun
	Unknown irregularity:						
	Les Barnes	SA		2.029	-)	Johannesburg	07 Oct
	Unconfirmed performance:						
	Les Barnes	SA		2.007	-)		
1945	Pete Watkins	USA	21	2.007	1)	Frankfurt/M.	26 Aug
	Ken Wiesner	USA	25	2.000	1)	Milwaukee	21 Apr
	Fred Sheffield	USA	23	1.997	1T)	Milwaukee	09 Jun
	Dwight Eddleman	USA	22	1.988i	1)	Cleveland	23 Mar
	John Vislocky	USA	21	1.981i	1)	New York	03 Feb
	Joshua Williamson	USA		1.981i	1T)	New York	24 Feb
	Don Barksdale	USA	23	1.981	1T)	Los Angeles	26 May
	Gil (LaCava) Greene	USA	20	1.981	1T)	Los Angeles	26 May
	Richard Schnacke	USA		1.981	D)	Bloomfield, NJ	07 Jul
	Kalervo af Ursin	Fin	20	1.98	1)	Pilhava	04 Sep
1946	Ken Wiesner	USA	25	2.041	1)	Minneapolis	22 Jun
	Tom Scofield	USA		2.016	2T)	Minneapolis	22 Jun
	Fred Sheffield	USA	23	2.016	2T)	Minneapolis	22 Jun

Year	Athlete	Nat	Born	Mark	Pos	Venue	Date
	Gunnar Lindecrantz	Swe	21	2.01	1)	Praha	11 Jul
	Dwight Eddleman	USA	22	2.003i	1)	Champaign, IL	11 May
	John Vislocky	USA	21	2.003	1)	New York	15 Iun
	Dava Albritton	USA	13	2.003	1)	San Antonio	29 Jun
	Alan Paterson	GB	28	2.00	1)	Antwerpen	07 Jul
	Henry Coffman	USA	19	1.994	1)		
	Bill Vessie	USA	22	1.994	1)	Traver Island, NY	01 Jun
1947	Bill Vessie	USA	22	2.032	1)	New York	10 May
	Irving Mondschein	USA	24	2.029i	1)	New York	12 Feb
	Tom Scofield	USA		2.022	1)	Lincoln, NE	24 May
	John Vislocky	USA	21	2.019i	1)	Boston	08 Feb
	Alan Paterson	GB	28	2.019	2)	Glasgow	02 Aug
	Dwight Eddleman	USA	22	2.010i	1)	Champaign, IL	08 Mar
	Charles Hanger	USA		2.010	1)	Berkeley, CA	28 Jun
	John Winter	Aus	24	2.007	1)	Perth	22 Feb
	Lester Steees	USA	17	2.007	1)	Portland	31 May
	Henry Coffman	USA	19	1.998	2)	Lincoln, NE	04 Jul
1948	George Stanich	USA	28	2.04	1)	Praha	18 Aug
	Dave Albritton	USA	13	2.038	1)	Berea, OH	26 Jun
	Verne McGrew	USA	29	2.038	1)	Evanston, IL	09 Jul
	Bill Vessie	USA	22	2.032i	1)	New York	31 Jan
	John Vislocky	USA	21	2.032i	1T)	New York	14 Feb
	Tom Scofield	USA		2.022	1T)	Milwaukee	03 Jul
	John Winter	Aus	24	2.013	1)	Perth	28 Feb
	Roland Knecht	USA	28	2.013	1)	Baton Rouge, LA	10 Apr
	Charles Hanger	USA		2.013	1)	Berkeley, CA	05 Jun
	Dwight Eddleman	USA	22	2.013	3)	Evanston, IL	09 Jul
	Exhibition / Extra Trial:						
	Henry Coffman	USA	19	2.032	-)	Austin	03 Apr
	John Winter	Aus	24	2.032	-)	Adelaide	28/29 May
1949	Bob Walters	USA		2.036	1)	Lawrence, KS	23 Apr
	Dick Phillips	USA		2.032i	1)	Boston	05 Mar
	John Vislocky	USA	21	2.032	1)	New York	17 Sep
	Irving Mondschein	USA	24	2.029	1T)	New York	28 May
	Georges Damitio	Fra	24	2.02	1)	Casablanca	29 Oct
	Bill Vessie	USA	22	2.016i	1)	Baltimore	12 Mar
	Jack Heintzman	USA	26	2.013i	1)		
	Alan Paterson	GB	28	2.007	1)	Glasgow	11 Jun
	Dwight Eddleman	USA	22	2.003	19	Milwaukee	04 Jun
	Rune Reiz	Swe	24	2.00	1)	Stockholm	09 Sep
	Yuriy Ilyasov	SU	26	2.00i	1)	Leningrad	08 Nov
1950	Bob Walters	USA		2.048	1)	Austin	13 May
	Virgil Severns	USA	29	2.038	1T)	Austin	01 Apr
	Jack Razzetto	USA		2.038	1T)	Austin	01 Apr
	Papa Gallo Thiam	Sen/Fra	30	2.03	1)	Dakar	27 Apr
	Vern McGrew	USA	29	2.026	1T)	Dallas	03 Jun
	Bob Gordon	USA	28	2.026	1T)	Dallas	03 Jun
	Christiaan de Jongh	SA	30	2.026	1)	Pretoria	23 Sep
	John Vislocky	USA	21	2.019i	1)	Boston	04 Feb
	Alan Paterson	GB	28	2.007	1)	Helensburgh	22 Jul
	Wilfred Dancer	USA		1.994	1)	Pasadena, CA	18 Mar
	Extra trial:						
	Georges Damitio	Fra	24	2.00	-)	Casablanca	24 Jun
	Unknown irregularity:						
	Andries du Preez	SA	26	2.007	-)	Pretoria	04 Apr
1951	Charles Holding	USA	30	2.076	1)	Fort Worth	17 Mar
	Walter Davis	USA	31	2.057	1)	Austin	07 Apr
	J. Lewis Hall	USA	31	2.057	1)	Seattle	16 Jun
	Arnold Betton	USA	32	2.057	1)	St.Louis	19 Jun

Year	Athlete	Nat	Born	Mark	Place	Venue	Date
	William Miller	USA		2.030	D)	Santa Barbara, CA	03 Jul
	Virgil Severns	USA		2.026	2)	Austin	07 Apr
	Chris de Jongh	SA		2.007	1)	Pretoria	07 Mar
	Richard Jones	USA		2.007	1)	Stillwater, OK	31 Mar
	Herb Neff	USA		2.007	1)	Atalnta	21 Apr
	Richard Meissner	USA		2.007	1)	Des Moines	28 Apr
	Fred Pratley	USA		2.007	1)	Provo, UT	05 May
	Barney Dyer	USA	31	2.007	1) ??	Provo, UT	05 May
	Herman Wyatt	USA	31	2.007	2)	Berkeley	23 Jun
	Extra Trial:						
	Herman Wyatt	USA	31	2.029	-)	Compton	01 Jun
1952	Walter Davis	USA	31	2.095	1)	Dallas	10 May
	Charles Holding	USA	30	2.067	1)	Beaumont, TX	10 May
	Emmy Barnes	USA		2.041	2)	Long Beach, CA	21 Jun
	Arnold Betton	USA	32	2.041	2)	Long Beach, CA	21 Jun
	Herman Wyatt	USA	31	2.032	1)	Palo Alto, CA	29 Mar
	J. Lewis Hall	USA	31	2.032	1)	Miami, FL	03 May
	Ion Söter	Rum	27	2.03	1)	Cluj	06 Oct
	Peron DuBard	USA		2.029	1)	Columbus, OH	03 May
	Kenneth Wiesner	USA	25	2.029	2)	Los Angeles	28 Jun
	Gösta Svensson	Swe		2.02	1)	Göteborg	22 May
1953	Walter Davis	USA	31	2.124	1)	Dayton, OH	27 Jun
	Herman Wyatt	USA	31	2.080	1)	San Jose, CA	10 Apr
	Ernest Shelton	USA	32	2.08	1)	Turku	17 Jul
	Charles Holding	USA	30	2.076	1)	Commerce, TX	17 Apr
	Calvin Clark	USA	29	2.061	1)	Logan, UT	21 Apr
	J. Lewis Hall	USA	31	2.041	1)	Birmingham, AL	04 Apr
	Barney Dyer	USA	31	2.041	1)	Salt Lake City	30 May
	Milton Mead	USA		2.038	1)	Ann Arbor, MI	16 May
	Mark Smith	USA		2.035	1)	Lincoln, NE	20 Jun
	Floyd Jeter	USA	34	2.029	1)	Long Beach, C A	14 Mar
	Arnold Betton	USA	32	2.029	1)	Peoria, IL	02 May
	Extra Trial:						
	Bengt Nilsson	Swe	34	2.03	-)	Svängasta	19 Jul
	Exhibition:						
	Kennet Wiesner	USA	25	2.083	-)	Houston	Mar
1954	Bengt Nilsson	Swe	34	2.114	1)	Göteborg	19 Sep
	Ernest Shelton	USA	32	2.110	1)	Pasadena	31 Jul
	Charles Holding	USA	30	2.083	1)	Commerce, TX	15 May
	Floyd Jeter	USA	34	2.051	2)	St. Louis	18 Jun
	Ron Mitchell	USA	31	2.035i	1)	Champaign, Il	27 Feb
	Les Vanover	USA		2.032	2)	Odessa, TX	27 Mar
	Doug Spainhower	USA		2.032	1)	Salt Lake City	14 May
	Art Carder	USA		2.032	1T)	Abilene, TX	05 Jun
	Emmanuel Ifeajuna	Nig		2.032	1)	Vancouver	31 Jul
	Ion Söter	Rum	27	2.03	1)	Bucuresti	30 Jun
	Jiri Lánsky	CZE	33	2.03	1)	Praha	24 Oct
1955	Ernest Shelton	USA	32	2.115	1)	Los Angeles	10 Jun
	Bengt Nilsson	Swe	34	2.10	1)	Stockholm	07 Jul
	Charles Dumas	USA	37	2.089	2)	Los Angeles	10 Jun
	Charles Holding	USA	30	2.051	)	Tulsa, OK	30 Apr
	Jaroslav Kovár	CZE	34	2.05	)	Bratislava	25 Sep
	Vladimir Sitkin	SU	34	2.05	1)	Odessa	23 Oct
	Floyd Smith	USA	35	2.048	)	DeKalb, Il	16 Apr
	Stig Pettersson	Swe	35	2.04	)	Göteborg	31 Jul
	Julius O. Chigbolu	Nig	29	2.038	)	Lagos	16 Apr
	Robert Barksdale	USA	34	2.038	)	Baltimore	16 Apr
	Exhibition:						
	Barney Dyer	USA	31	2.051	-)	Los Angeles	19 Mar

Year	Athlete	Nation	Born	Mark	Place	Venue	Date
1956	Charles Dumas	USA	37	2.149	1)	Los Angeles	29 Jun
	Igor Kashkarov	SU	33	2.10	1)	Tashkent	21 Oct
	Charles Porter	Aus	36	2.10	2)	Melbourne	23 Nov
	Bengt Nilsson	Swe	34	2.09	1)	Stockholm	02 Sep
	Donald Stewart	USA	37	2.089	1)	Dallas	03 May
	Ernest Shelton	USA	32	2.083	1)	Los Angeles	05 May
	Walter Mangham	USA	38	2.076	1)	Mt.Lebanon, PA	28 Apr
	Vernon Wilson	USA	31	2.07	2T)	Los Angeles	29 Jun
	Philip Reavis	USA	36	2.07	2T)	Los Angeles	29 Jun
	Vladimir Polyakov	SU	36	2.07	2)	Tashkent	21 Oct
	Extra Trial:						
	Charles Dumas	USA	37	2.153	-)	Los Angeles	01 Nov
1957	Yuriy Stepanov	SU	32	2.162	1)	Leningrad	13 Jul
	Vladimir Sitkin	SU	34	2.15	1)	Odessa	29 Sep
	Igor Kashkarov	SU	33	2.14	1)	Moskva	08 Aug
	Floyd Smith	USA	35	2.115	1)	Chicago	23 Jun
	Don Stewart	USA	37	2.105	1)	Austin	11 May
	Charles Dumas	USA	37	2.096	1)	Compton	31 May
	Charles Porter	Aus	36	2.089	1)	Brisbane	09 Feb
	Jirí Lánsky	CZE	33	2.08	1)	Praha	06 Oct
	Stig Pettersson	Swe	35	2.07	1)	Stockholm	14 Sep
	Jaroslav Kovár	CZE	34	2.06	1)	Praha	18 Sep
	Vladimir Omyelchuk	SU	37	2.06	1)	Odessa	20 Oct
	Extra Trial:						
	Björn Thorkildsen	Nor	26	2.06	-)	Bergen	08 Sep
1958	Charles Dumas	USA	37	2.121	1)	Los Angeles	26 Apr
	Yuriy Stepanov	SU	32	2.12	1)	Moskva	28 Jul
	Rickard Dahl	Swe	33	2.12	1)	Stockholm	24 Aug
	Stig Pettersson	Swe	35	2.10	1)	Borås	08 Aug
	Jirí Lánsky	CZE	33	2.19	2)	Stockholm	24 Aug
	Igor Kashkarov	SU	33	2.10	1)	Moskva	27 Aug
	John Thomas	USA	41	2.10	1)	Odawara	14 Sep
	Bertil Holmgren	Swe	33	2.095	1)	Dallas	10 May
	Don Stewart	USA	37	2.095	1)	Houston	07 Jun
	Boris Ribak	SU	34	2.09	1)	Yalta	12 Oct
	Robert Shavlakadze	SU	32	2.09	1)	Tbilisi	28 Oct
	Made with a thick soled shoe:						
	Robert Shavlakadze	SU	32	2.10	1)	Erivan	18 May
1959	Charles Dumas	USA	37	2.134	1)	Fresno	09 May
	Robert Shavlakadze	SU	32	2.13	1)	Moskva	28 Jun
	Igor Kashkarov	URSS	33	2.12	1)	Warszawa	27 Jun
	John Thomas	USA	41	2.111i	1)	Hanover, N.H.	10 Jan
	Stig Pettersson	Swe	35	2.11	1)	Malmö	26 Jul
	Boris Ribak	SU	34	2.10	1)	Odessa	18 Jul
	Eero Salminen	Fin	33	2.10	1)	Helsinki	16 Aug
	Vasiliy Khoroshilov	SU	39	2.10	1)	Yalta	11 Oct
	Viktor Bolshov	SU	39	2.09	1)	Leningrad	13 Jul
	Jirí Lansky	CZE	33	2.09	1)	Plzen	17 Jul
	Extra Trial:						
	Robert Gardner	USA	35	2.083	-)	N'changa	29 Apr
	Exhibition:						
	Robert Gardner	USA	35	2.108	-)	Pittsburgh	Aug
1960	John Thomas	USA	41	2.229	1)	Palo Alto	01 Jul
	Valeriy Brumel	SU	42	2.203	1)	Uzhgorod	25 Oct
	Robert Shavlakadze	SU	33	2.16	1)	Roma	01 Sep
	Viktor Bolshov	SU	39	2.153	1)	Moskva	12 Jun
	Charles Dumas	USA	37	2.14	1)	Tempe	08 Apr
	Joseph Faust	USA	42	2.134	2)	Palo Alto	01 Jul

	Stig Pettersson	Swe	35	2.13	1)	Charlottenberg	07 Aug
	Ed Costa	USA	40	2.111	1)	Provo	23 Apr
	Henry Wyborney	USA	40	2.108	1)	Eugene	02 Apr
	Teodoro Flores Palacios	Gua	39	2.105	1)	Quezaltenango	26 Feb
1961	Valery Brumel	SU	42	2.25i	1)	Leningrad	28 Jan
	John Thomas	USA	41	2.19	2)	Moskva	16 Jul
	Viktor Bolshov	SU	39	2.16	1)	Grozniy	28 Oct
	Stig Pettersson	Swe	35	2.15	1)	Skövde	07 Aug
	Bob Avant	USA	39	2.134	1)	Walnut, CA	29 Apr
	Robert Shavlakadze	SU	33	2.11	2)	Leselidze	10 May
	Igor Kashkarov	SU	33	2.11	2)	Moskva	18 Jun
	Ni Chih-chin	Chi	42	2.11	1)	Beijing	30 Sep
	Joe Faust	USA	42	2.102	2)	Walnut,CA	29 Apr
	Robert Gardner	USA	35	2.102	1)	Philadelphia	30 May
	Exhibition:						
	Mahamat Idriss	Fra	42	2.11	-)	Vichy	21 Jun
1962	Valeriy Brumel	SU	42	2.27	1)	Moskva	29 Sep
	Ni Chih-chin	Chi	42	2.17	1)	Beijing	16 Jun
	Joe Faust	USA	42	2.165	1)	Norwalk, KA	19 Apr
	Stig Pettersson	Swe	35	2.16	1)	Stockholm	23 Aug
	Robert Shavlakadze	SU	33	2.15	1)	Erivan	26 May
	John Thomas	USA	41	2.15	1)	Göteborg	20 Aug
	Colin Ridgway	Aus	39	2.146	1)	Laredo	10 Mar
	Gene Johnson	USA	41	2.146	1)	Chicago	30 Jun
	Viktor Bolshov	SU	39	2.14	1)	Warszawa	18 Aug
	Robert Gardner	USA	35	2.134	1)	Nashville	15 May
	Bob Avant	USA	39	2.134	1)	Albuquerque	16 Jun
1963	Valeriy Brumel	SU	42	2.28	1)	Moskva	21 Jul
	Ni Chih-chin	Chi	42	2.20	1)	Beijing	17 Aug
	Tony Sneazwell	Aus	42	2.20	1)	Tokyo	14 Oct
	John Thomas	USA	41	2.184	1)	Nashville	30 Mar
	Viktor Bolshov	SU	39	2.15i	1)	Leningrad	23 Mar
	Gene Johnson	USA	41	2.15	2)	Moskva	21 Jul
	Lew Hoyt	USA	43	2.146	1)	Los Angeles	23 Feb
	Joe Faust	USA	42	2.140	1)	Los Angeles	16 Mar
	John Rambo	USA	43	2.134	1)	Walnut	18 May
	Otis Burrell	USA	44	2.134	2)	Walnut	18 May
	Paul Stuber	USA	41	2.134	2)	St.Louis	22 Jun
1964	Valeriy Brumel	SU	42	2.24	1)	Zurich	23 Jun
	Ni Chih-chin	Chi	42	2.21	1)	Shanghai	11 Oct
	Edward Czernik	Pol	40	2.20	1)	Hässleholm	30 Jul
	John Thomas	USA	41	2.18	2)	Tokyo	21 Oct
	Robert Shavlakadze	SU	33	2.17	1)	Kiev	28 Aug
	John Rambo	USA	43	2.165	1)	Long Beach	02 May
	Mahamat Idriss	Fra	42	2.16	1)	Fort Lamy	28 Mar
	Richard Ross	USA	41	2.16	1)	Houston	08 May
	Ed Caruthers	USA	45	2.16	1)	New Brunswick	28 Jun
	Andrey Khmarskiy	SU	43	2.15	2)	Leselidze	16 May
	Extra Trial:						
	John Rambo	USA	43	2.175	-)	Fresno	13 Jun
1965	Ni Chih-chin	Chi	42	2.25	1)	Wuhan	20 Nov
	Valeriy Brumel	SU	42	2.19	1)	Oslo	21 Aug
	Lawrie Peckham	Aus	44	2.19	1)	Melbourne	23 Oct
	Tony Sneazwell	Aus	42	2.19	2)	Melbourne	23 Oct
	Viktor Bolshov	SU	39	2.18	1)	Minsk	03 Jul
	Otis Burrell	USA	44	2.18	1)	Warszawa	08 Aug
	Ed Caruthers	USA	45	2.17	1)	Norwalk, CA	15 Apr
	Edward Czernik	Pol	40	2.17	1)	Zielona Gora	10 Oct
	Gene Johnson	USA	41	2.16	1)	Nairobi	05 May
	Valeriy Skvortsov	SU	45	2.15	1)	Kiev	24 Jul

Year	Name	Nat	Born	Mark	Pl	Venue	Date
1966	Ni Chih-chin	Chi	42	2.27	1)	Phnom-Penh	30 Nov
	Valeriy Skvortsov	SU	45	2.21	1)	Moskva	29 May
	Otis Burrell	USA	44	2.185	1)	New York	26 Jun
	Steve Herndon	USA	46	2.175	1)	Notre Dame	04 Jun
	Ron Tull	USA	46	2.17	1)	Norman, OK	09 Apr
	Mahamat Idriss	Fra	42	2.17	1)	Fort-Lamy	10 Apr
	Frank Costello	USA	44	2.16	1)	Chapel Hill, NC	16 Apr
	John Hartfield	USA	44	2.16	1)	Houston	08 May
	Stan Albright	USA	47	2.16	3)	New York	26 Jun
	Lawrie Peckham	Aus	44	2.16	2)	Los Angeles	24 Jul
	Edward Czernik	Pol	40	2.16	2)	Minsk	26 Jul
	Extra Trial:						
	Jacques Madubost	Fra	44	2.18	-)	Saint Brieuc	08 May
1967	Clarence Johnson	USA	47	2.215	1)	Palo Alto	06 May
	Ed Caruthers	USA	45	2.195	1)	Santa Barbara	25 Mar
	Ken Brown	USA		2.17	1)		May
	Valentin Gavrilov	SU	46	2.17	1)	Chorzów	02 Jul
	Lawrie Peckham	Aus	44	2.17	1)	Stockholm	05 Jul
	John Hartfield	USA	44	2.16	1)	Laredo	11 Mar
	Stephen Brown	USA	48	2.16	1)	Provo	17 Jun
	Robert Sainte-Rose	Fra	43	2.16	1)	Paris	29 Jul
	Otis Burrell	USA	44	2.16	2)	Winnipeg	30 Jul
	Ralf Drecoll	WG	44	2.15	1)	Göttingen	13 Jul
	Jan Dahlgren	Swe	47	2.15	1)	Stockholm	22 Jul
	Werner Pfeil	EG	37	2.15	1)	Cottbus	28 Sep
1968	Dick Fosbury	USA	47	2.24	1)	Mexico City	20 Oct
	De Caruthers	USA	45	2.22	2)	Mexico City	20 Oct
	Peter Boyce	Aus	46	2.21	1)	Fresno	30 Mar
	Reynaldo Brown	USA	50	2.21	2)	South Lake Tahoe	16 Sep
	Valentin Gavrilov	SU	46	2.20	1)	Dnyepropetrovsk	31 May
	Mike Bowers	USA	45	2.19	1)	Ypsilanti	04 May
	Robert Sainte-Rose	Fra	43	2.19	1)	Font Romeu	01 Sep
	John Hartfield	USA	44	2.185	4)	South Lake Tahoe	16 Sep
	Valeriy Skvortsov	SU	45	2.18	1)	Leninakan	16 Aug
	Gunter Spielvogel	WG	44	2.175	1)	Cali	03 Nov
1969	Valentin Gavrilov	SU	46	2.21	1)	Los Angeles	19 Jul
	Dick Fosbury	USA	47	2.195	1)	Knoxville	21 Jun
	Otis Burrell	USA	44	2.19	1)	Orange, CA	14 Jun
	Ross Jourdan	USA	47	2.185	1)	Gainesville	18 Jan
	Lawrie Peckham	Aus	44	2.185	1)	Melbourne	06 Dec
	Bo Jonsson	Swe	47	2.18	1)	Stockholm	11 May
	Kenneth Lundmark	Swe	46	2.18	2)	Stockholm	11 May
	Rudi Köppen	EG	43	2.18	1)	Berlin	19 Jun
	Valeriy Skvortsov	SU	45	2.18	1)	Odessa	01 Jul
	Sergey Martinov	SU	45	2.18	1)	Moskva	12 Jul
1970	Ni Chih-chin	Chi	42	2.29	1)	Changsha	08 Nov
	Kestutis Sapka	SU	49	2.23	1)	Sochi	03 Oct
	Bill Elliott	USA	46	2.215	1)	Modesto	23 May
	Reynaldo Brown	USA	50	2.215	2)	Modesto	23 May
	István Major	Hun	49	2.20	1)	Budapest	24 May
	Valentin Gavrilov	SU	46	2.20	1)	Kiev	03 Jul
	Thomas Zacharias	WG	47	2.20	1)	Mayen	27 Sep
	Endre Kelemen	Hun	47	2.19	1)	Warszawa	28 Jun
	Viktor Bolshov	SU	39	2.19	1)	Kishinyov	04 Sep
	Ron Jourdan	USA		2.185	1)	Gainesville	31 Mar
	Barry Shepard	USA		2.185	1)	Tempe	31 Mar
	Extra Trial:						
	Endre Kelemen	Hun	47	2.21	-)	Sotkamo	05 Jul
1971	Pat Matzdorf	USA	42	2.29	1)	Berkeley	03 Jul
	Ni Chih.chin	Chi	42	2.25	1)	Tirana	16 Jul

Year	Athlete	Nat	Born	Mark	Pl	Venue	Date
	Rustam Akhmyetov	SU	50	2.23	1)	Moskva	18 Jul
	István Major	Hun	49	2.23	1)	Siena	19 Sep
	Kestutis Sapka	SU	49	2.22	1)	München	05 Sep
	Reynaldo Brown	USA	50	2.21	1)	Seattle	19 Jun
	John Dobroth	USA	41	2.20	1)	Westwood, LA	03 Apr
	Hidehiko Tomizawa	Jap	46	2.20	1)	Tokyo	28 May
	Jan Dahlgren	Swe	47	2.20	1)	Stockholm	15 Jun
	Hermann Magerl	WG	49	2.20	1)	Bonn	24 Jul
	Csaba Dozsa	Rum	51	2.20	2)	Helsinki	14 Aug
	Sergey Budalov	SU	49	2.20	1)	Moskva	29 Aug
	Roman Moravec	Cze	50	2.20	1)	Praha	05 Sep
1972	Jüri Tarmak	SU	46	2.25	Q)	Moskva	18 Jul
	István Major	Hun	49	2.24i	1)	Grenoble	11 Mar
	Kestutis Sapka	SU	49	2.24	1)	Augsburg	24 Jun
	Hermann Magerl	WG	49	2.24	1)	Cham	16 Sep
	Reynaldo Brown	USA	50	2.235i	1)	College Park	14 Jan
	Stefan Junge	EG	50	2.23	1)	Potsdam	10 Jun
	Vladimir Abramov	SU	49	2.23	1)	Moskva	11 Aug
	Jan Dahlgren	Swe	47	2.22i	1)	Göteborg	12 Feb
	Tom Woods	USA	53	2.215	1)	Eugene	03 Jun
	Ron Jourdan	USA	47	2.21	1)	Hato Rey	06 Feb
	Barry Shur	USA	51	2.21	1)	Boulder	20 May
	József Tihányi	Hun	46	2.21	1)	Budapest	10 Jun
	Adám Szepesi	Hun	45	2.21	2)	Budapest	10 Jun
	Valyentin Gavrilov	SU	46	2.21	Q)	Moskva	28 Jun
	Dwight Stones	USA	53	2.21	1)	Eugene	09 Jul
	Chris Dunn	USA	51	2.21	3)	Eugene	09 Jul
	Rustam Akhmyetov	SU	50	2.21	2)	Moskva	19 Jul
	Viktor Bolshov	SU	39	2.21	4)	Moskva	19 Jul
	Jaroslav Alexa	Cze	49	2.21	1	Praha	19 Aug
1973	Dwight Stones	USA	53	2.30	1)	München	11 Jul
	Ni Chih-chin	Chi	42	2.25	1)	Pyongyang	28 Jun
	Tom Woods	USA	53	2.245	1)	Corvallis	07 Apr
	John Beers	Can	52	2.24	1)	Burnaby, B.C.	09 Sep
	István Major	Hun	49	2.24	1)	Budapest	28 Sep
	Rey Brown	USA	50	2.235	1)	Baton Rouge	09 Jun
	Paul Poaniewa	Fra	53	2.22	1)	Colombes	22 Jul
	Vladimir Abramov	SU	67	2.22	1)	Leningrad	05 Aug
	Robert Joseph	USA	21	2.21	1)	Tucson	17 Mar
	Claude Ferragne	Can	52	2.21i	1)	Montreal	23 Mar
	Kestutis Sapka	SU	49	2.21	1)	Nalchik	01 Apr
	Vassilios Papadimitriou	Gre	48	2.21	1)	Athinai	24 Aug
	Professional:						
	John Radetich	USA	48	2.255i	1)	Pocatello	03 Mar
1974	Dwight Stones	USA	53	2.28	1)	Oslo	30 Jul
	Jesper Törring	Den	47	2.25	1)	Roma	04 Sep
	Kestutis Sapka	SU	49	2.25	2)	Roma	04 Sep
	Vladimir Abramov	SU	49	2.24	1)	Moskva	21 Jun
	Sergey Budalov	SU	49	2.23i	1)	Moskva	02 Mar
	Imants Karlsons	SU	55	2.23	1)	Praha	19 Jun
	Rune Almén	Swe	52	2.23	1)	Helsinki	17 Aug
	Tom Woods	USA	53	2.22i	1)	Pocatello	18 Jan
	Vladimir Maly	Cze	52	2.22	1)	Praha	28 Jun
	John Radetich	USA	48	2.21i	1)	Pocatello	23 Feb
	Bill Jankunis	USA	55	2.21i	1)	Boulder	10 Mar
	Valentin Gavrilov	SU	46	2.21i	1)	Praha	26 Feb
	Vello Lumi	SU	49	2.21i	1)	Bryansk	28 Feb
	Endre Kelemen	Hun	47	2.21i	1)	Trinec	28 Feb
	Enzo Del Forno	Ita	50	2.21i	1)	Udine	23 Mar
	Paul Underwood	USA	53	2.21	1)	Tempe	06 Apr
	Sergey Senyukov	SU	55	2.21	1)	Alushta	08 Apr
	Mike Fleer	USA	52	2.21	1)	Des Moines	26 Apr
	Stanislav Molotilov	SU	55	2.21	2)	Siena	21 Jul

Year	Athlete	Nat	Born	Mark	Place	Venue	Date
	Rory Kotinek	USA	53	2.21	1)	Aarhus	22 Jul
	Teymour Ghiassi	Irn	46	2.21	2)	Teheran	13 Sep
	Exhibition:						
	Leif-Roar Falkum	Nor	49	2.23	-)	Oslo	10 Aug
1975	Dwight Stones	USA	53	2.28i	1)	New York	21 Feb
	Tom Woods	USA	53	2.27	1)	Eugene	20 Jun
	Paul Poaniewa	Fra	53	2.26	1)	Saint-Etienne	29 Jun
	Vladimir Maly	Cze	52	2.24i	1)	Praha	26 Feb
	Pat Matzdorf	USA	49	2.24	1)	Chicago	24 May
	Rolf Beilschmidt	EG	53	2.24	1)	Dresden	21 Jun
	Ron Livers	USA	55	2.24	1)	Berea	23 Jul
	Aleksandr Grigoryev	SU	55	2.24	1)	Nice	16 Aug
	Greg Joy	Can	56	2.235i	1)	Albuquerque	08 Feb
	Bill Jankunis	USA	55	2.235	1)	Norman	17 May
	Rory Kotinek	USA	53	2.235	2)	Eugene	20 Jun
	Keith Guinn	USA	55	2.235	1)	Eugene	16 Aug
1976	Dwight Stones	USA	53	2.32	1)	Philadelphia	04 Aug
	Jacek Wszola	Pol	56	2.29	1)	Koblenz	08 Sep
	John Radetich	USA	48	2.285i	1)	Salt Lake City	20 Feb
	Bill Jankunis	USA	55	2.28	1)	Eugene	27 Jun
	Rory Kotinek	USA	53	2.26i	2)	New York	20 Feb
	Sergey Senyukov	SU	55	2.26	1)	Ostrava	05 Jun
	Mike Winsor	USA	56	2.26	2)	Philasdelphia	05 Jun
	Tom Woods	USA	53	2.26	1)	Athinai	30 Jun
	Greg Joy	Can	56	2.26	1)	Regina	29 Aug
	Sergey Budalov	SU	49	2.25	1)	Kiev	23 Jun
	James Barrineau	USA	55	2.25	3)	Eugene	27 Jun
1977	Vladimir Yashchenko	SU	59	2.33	1)	Richmond	03 Jul
	Rolf Beilschmidt	EG	53	2.31	1)	Helsinki	13 Aug
	Aleksandr Grigoryev	SU	55	2.30	1)	Riga	05 Jun
	Dwight Stones	USA	53	2.30	1)	Nice	21 Aug
	Jacek Wszola	Pol	56	2.30	1)	Fürth	11 Sep
	Rory Kotinek	USA	53	2.29	1)	Rieti	28 Aug
	Kyle Arney	USA	56	2.285	1)	Champaign	04 Jun
	Sergey Senyukov	SU	55	2.28	1)	Podolsk	17 Jul
	Staislav Molotilov	SU	55	2.27i	2)	Minsk	25 Jan
	Franklin Jacobs	USA	57	2.27	2)	Westwood	11 Jun
	Mike Winsor	USA	56	2.27	1)	Karlstad	10 Aug
1978	Vladimir Yashchenko	SU	59	2.35i	1)	Milano	12 Mar
	Franklin Jacobs	USA	57	2.32i	1)	New York	27 Jan
	Greg Joy	Can	56	2.31i	1)	College Park	13 Jan
	Rolf Beilschmidt	EG	53	2.31	1)	Leipzig	01 Jul
	Dwight Stones	USA	53	2.30	1)	Westwood	09 Jun
	Henry Lauterbach	EG	57	2.30	1)	Potsdam	19 Aug
	Benn Fields	USA	54	2.30	1)	Valparaiso	01 Nov
	Wolfgang Killing	WG	53	2.28i	1)	Cosford	01 Mar
	Aleksandr Grigoryev	SU	55	2.28	2)	Praha	02 Sep
	Ruud Wielart	Hol	54	2.27	1)	Torino	04 Jun
	Gennadiy Byelkov	SU	56	2.27	2)	Vilnius	25 Jun
1979	Dietmar Mögenburg	WG	61	2.32	1)	Torino	04 Aug
	Rolf Beilschmidt	EG	53	2.30	1)	Leipzig	02 Jun
	Carlo Thränhardt	WG	57	2.30	2)	Eberstadt	09 Jun
	Gerd Nagel	WG	57	2.30	3)	Eberstadt	09 Jun
	Aleksandr Grigoryev	SU	55	2.30	1)	Malmö	30 Jun
	André Schneider	WG	58	2.30	1)	Berlin	17 Aug
	Vladimir Yashchenko	SU	59	2.29i	1)	Fort Worth	03 Mar
	Jacek Wszola	Pol	56	2.29	1)	Stockholm	03 Jul
	Franklin Jacobs	USA	57	2.285i	1)	Inglewood	02 Feb
	Gennadiy Byelkov	SU	56	2.28i	1)	Vilnius	04 Feb
	Ruud Wielart	Hol	54	2.28	1)	Leiden	01 Sep
	Aleksey Demyanyuk	SU	58	2.28	1)	Tbilisi	09 Sep

1980	Gerd Wessig	EG	59	2.36	1)	Moskva	01 Aug
	Jacek Wszola	Pol	56	2.35	1)	Eberstadt	25 May
	Dietmar Mögenburg	WG	61	2.35	1)	Rehlingen	26 May
	Carlo Thränhardt	WG	57	2.31	1)	Stuttgart	05 Jun
	Jörg Freimuth	EG	61	2.31	3)	Moskva	01 Aug
	Aleksandr Grigoryev	SU	55	2.30	1)	Moskva	05 Jul
	Gerd Nagel	WG	57	2.30	2)	Hannover	16 Aug
	Adrian Proteasa	Rum	59	2.29i	3)	Sindelfingen	02 Mar
	James Frazier	USA	59	2.29i	1)	Tucson	10 May
	Massimo Di Giorgio	Ita	58	2.29	1)	Pisa	05 Jul
	Henry Lauterbach	EG	57	2.29	4)	Moskva	01 Aug

ALL TIME WORLD LIST AS AT THE END OF 1980

Gerd Wessig	EG	59	2.36	1)	Moskva	01 Aug 80
Vladimir Yashchenko	SU	59	2.35i	1)	Milano	12 Mar 78
Jacek Wszola	Pol	56	2.35	1)	Eberstadt	25 May 80
Dietmar Mögenburg	WG	61	2.35	1)	Rehlingen	26 May 80
Dwight Stones	USA	53	2.32	1)	Philadelphia	04 Aug 76
Franklin Jacobs	US	57	2.32i	1)	New York	27 Jan 78
Rolf Beilschmidt	EG	53	2.31	1)	Helsinki	13 Aug 77
Greg Joy	Can	56	2.31i	1)	College Park	13 Jan 78
Carlo Thränhardt	WG	57	2.31	1)	Stuttgart	05 Jun 80
Jörg Freimuth	EG	61	2.31	3)	Moskva	01 Aug 80

1981	Jeff Woodard	USA	58	2.33i	1)	New York	27 Feb
	Aleksey Demyanyuk	SU	58	2.33	1)	Leningrad	11 Jul
	Roland Dalhäuser	Swz	58	2.31	1)	Eberstadt	07 Jun
	Gerd Nagel	WG	57	2.31	2)	Eberstadt	07 Jun
	Dwight Stones	USA	53	2.31	1)	Nice	23 Aug
	Jianhua Zhu	Chi	63	2.30	1)	Tokyo	06 Jun
	Massimo Di Giorgio	Ita	58	2.30	1)	Udine	13 Jun
	Valeriy Serena	SU	59	2.30	1)	Tbilisi	27 Jun
	Vladimir Granyenkov	SU	59	2.30	2)	Leningrad	11 Jul
	Franck Verzy	Fra	61	2.30	1)	Montgeron	12 Jul
	Dietmar Mögenburg	WG	61	2.30	1)	Lausanne	14 Jul
1982	Dietmar Mögenburg	WG	61	2.34i	1)	Milano	06 Mar
	Jianhua Zhu	Chi	63	2.33	1)	New Delhi	01 Dec
	Janusz Trzepizur	Pol	59	2.32i	2)	Milano	06 Mar
	Roland Dalhäuser	Swz	58	2.32i	3)	Milano	06 Mar
	Gennadiy Belkov	SU	56	2.32	1)	Tashkent	29 May
	Milton Ottey	Can	59	2.32	1)	Provo	04 Jun
	Del Davis	USA	60	2.32	2)	Provo	04 Jun
	Milton Goode	USA	60	2.31i	1)	New York	12 Feb
	Dwight Stones	USA	53	2.31i	2)	New York	12 Feb
	Stephen Wray	Bah	62	2.31	2)	Brisbane	07 Oct
	Gerd Nagel	WG	57	2.30	2T)	Eberstadt	30 May
	Carlo Thränhardt	WG	57	2.30	4)	Eberstadt	30 May
	Tyke Peacock	USA	61	2.30	1)	Civitanova Marche	10 Jul
	Aleksey Demyanyuk	SU	58	2.30	1)	Kiev	22 Aug
1983	Jianhua Zhu	Chi	63	2.38	1)	Shanghai	22 Sep
	Valeriy Serena	SU	59	2.35	1)	Moskva	19 Jun
	Paul Frommeyer	WG	57	2.34	1)	Recke	17 Jun
	Carlo Thränhardt	WG	57	2.34	1)	Aachen	06 Jul
	Eddy Annijs	Bel	58	2.34	1)	Bruxelles	23 Jul
	Igor Paklin	SU	63	2.33	1)	Tashkent	13 May
	Patrik Sjöberg	Swe	65	2.33	1)	Oslo	09 Jul
	Tike Peacock	USA	61	2.33	1)	Berlin	17 Aug
	Juan F. Centelles	Cub	61	2.32	1)	Bratislava	04 Jun
	Dietmar Mögenburg	WG	61	2.32	1)	München	26 Jul
	Gennadiy Avdeyenko	SU	63	2.32	1)	Helsinki	13 Aug
	Frank Verzy	Fra	61	2.32	1)	London	10 Aug

	Extra Trial:						
	Dennis Lewis	USA	59	2.32i	-)	Ypsilanti	28 Dec
1984	Jianhua Zhu	Chi	63	2.39	1)	Eberstadt	10 Jun
	Carlo Thränhardt	WG	57	2.37i	1)	Berlin	24 Feb
	Valeriy Serena	SU	59	2.37	1)	Rieti	02 Sep
	Igor Paklin	SU	63	2.36i	1)	Milano	01 Feb
	Sergey Zasimovic	SU	62	2.36	1)	Tashkent	05 May
	Dietmar Mögenburg	WG	61	2.36	3)	Eberstadt	10 Jun
	Sorin Matei	Rum	63	2.34	1)	Bucuresti	09 Jun
	Dwight Stones	USA	53	2.34	1)	Los Angeles	24 Jun
	Javier Sotomayor	Cub	67	2.33	1)	Habana	19 May
	Aleksandr Kotovic	SU	61	2.33	1)	Sofia	20 May
	Patrik Sjöberg	Swe	65	2.33	4	Eberstadt	10 Jun
	Vladimir Granyenkov	SU	59	2.33	1)	Moskva	05 Aug
	Aleksey Demyanyuk	SU	58	2.33	2)	Moskva	05 Aug
	Jim Howard	USA	59	2.33	1)	London	18 Aug
1985	Igor Paklin	SU	63	2.41	1)	Kobe	04 Sep
	Rudolf Povarnitsin	SU	62	2.40	1)	Donyetsk	11 Aug
	Dietmar Mögenburg	WG	61	2.39i	1)	Köln	24 Feb
	Patrik Sjöberg	Swe	65	2.38i	1)	Berlin	22 Feb
	Eddy Annys	Bel	58	2.36	1)	Ghent	26 May
	Aleksandr Kotovich	SU	61	2.35i	1)	Vilnius	13 Jan
	Jim Howard	USA	59	2.35i	1)	Richfield	17 Feb
	Jianhua Zhu	Chi	63	2.35	1)	Guangzhou	04 Mar
	Sorin Matei	Rum	63	2.35	1)	Bucuresti	01 Jun
	Gennadiy Avdeyenko	SU	63	2.35	1)	Leningrad	26 Jul
	Ján Zvara	Cze	63	2.35	1)	Praha	14 Sep
1986	Igor Paklin	SU	63	2.38	1)	Rieti	07 Sep
	Jim Howard	USA	59	2.36i	1)	Albuquerque	25 Jan
	Carlo Thränhardt	WG	57	2.36i	1)	Berlin	14 Feb
	Javier Sotomayor	Cub	67	2.36	1)	Santiago de Cuba	23 Feb
	Gennadiy Avdeyenko	SU	63	2.35	1)	Sofia	01 Jun
	Aleksandr Kotovich	SU	61	2.34i	1)	Minsk	18 Jan
	Dietmar Mögenburg	WG	61	2.34i	1)	Madrid	22 Feb
	Jerome Carter	USA	63	2.34	1)	Villanova	08 Jun
	Ján Zvara	Cze	63	2.34	1)	Bratislava	14 Jun
	Doug Nordquist	USA	58	2.34	1)	Moskva	09 Jul
	Valeriy Serena	SU	59	2.34	1)	Kiev	11 Jul
	Patrik Sjöberg	Swe	65	2.34	1)	Catania	13 Sep
1987	Patrik Sjöberg	Swe	65	2.42	1)	Stockholm	30 Jun
	Carlo Thränhardt	WG	57	2.40i	1)	Simmerath	16 Jan
	Igor Paklin	SU	63	2.38i	1)	Indianapolis	07 Mar
	Gennadiy Avdeyenko	SU	63	2.38i	2)	Indianapolis	07 Mar
	Javier Sotomayor	Cub	67	2.37	1)	Athinai	20 Jun
	Jan Zvara	Cze	63	2.36i	1)	Jablonec	14 Feb
	Dietmar Mögenburg	WG	61	2.35	4)	Rome	06 Sep
	Jerome Carter	USA	63	2.34	2)	Eberstadt	07 Jun
	Gerd Nagel	WG	57	2.34	3)	Eberstadt	07 Jun
	Hollis Conway	USA	67	2.34	1)	Formia	11 Jul
1988	Javier Sotomayor	Cub	67	2.43	1)	Salamanca	08 Sep
	Carlo Thränhardt	WG	57	2.42i	1)	Berlin	26 Feb
	Patrik Sjöberg	Swe	65	2.39i	1)	Budapest	05 Mar
	Sergey Malchenko	SU	63	2.38	1)	Banská Bystrica	04 Sep
	Gennadiy Avdeyenko	SU	63	2.38	1)	Seoul	25 Sep
	Dietmar Mögenburg	WG	61	2.37i	2)	Budapest	05 Mar
	Tom McCants	USA	62	2.37	1)	Columbus	08 May
	Jerome Carter	USA	63	2.37	2)	Columbus	08 May
	Sorin Matei	Rum	63	2.37	1)	Bucuresti	11 Jun
	Rudolf Povarnitsyn	SU	62	2.36	1)	Bratislava	09 Jun
	Igor Paklin	SU	63	2.36	1)	Vilnius	28 Aug
	Hollis Conway	USA	67	2.36	2)	Seoul	25 Sep

Year	Name	Nat	Born	Mark	Pos	Venue	Date
1989	Javier Sotomayor	Cub	67	2.44	1)	San Juan	29 Jul
	Patrik Sjöberg	Swe	65	2.40	1)	Bruxelles	05 Aug
	Hollis Conway	USA	67	2.39	1)	Norman	30 Jul
	Gennadiy Avdeyenko	SU	63	2.37	2)	Stockholm	03 Jul
	Carlo Thränhardt	WG	57	2.36i	1)	Berlin	24 Feb
	Gerd Nagel	WG	57	2.36i	1)	Sulingen	17 Mar
	Nick Saunders	Ber	63	2.35i	1)	Hamilton	13 Jan
	Dietmar Mögenburg	WG	61	2.35i	2)	Budapest	04 Mar
	Dalton Grant	GB	66	2.35i	4)	Budapest	04 Mar
	Rudolf Povarnitsyn	SU	62	2.34	2)	Bratislava	14 Jun
1990	Sorin Matei	Rum	63	2.40	1)	Bratislava	20 Jun
	Hollis Conway	USA	67	2.38	1)	Malmö	07 Aug
	Dragutin Topic	Yug	71	2.37	1)	Plovdiv	12 Aug
	Sergey Dymchenko	SU	67	2.37	1)	Kiev	16 Sep
	Nick Saunders	Ber	63	2.36	1)	Auckland	01 Feb
	Ralf Sonnwg	Wg	67	2.36i	1)	Berlin	23 Feb
	Doug Nordquist	USA	58	2.36	2)	Norwalk	15 Jun
	Georgi Dakov	Bul	67	2.36	2)	Bruxelles	10 Aug
	Javier Sotomayor	Cub	67	2.36	1)	Jerez de la Frontera	03 Sep
	Gennadiy Avdeyenko	SU	63	2.35i	1)	Sindelfingen	21 Jan
	Charles Austin	USA	67	2.35	1)	San Marcos	20 May
1991	Hollis Conway	USA	67	2.40i	1)	Sevilla	10 Mar
	Javier Sotomayor	Cub	67	2.40	1)	St. Denis	19 Jul
	Charles Austin	USA	67	2.40	1)	Zurich	07 Aug
	Ralf Sonn	Ger	67	2.39i	1)	Berlin	01 Mar
	Artur Partyka	Pol	69	2.37i	1)	Sulingen	03 Feb
	Dalton Grant	GB	66	2.36	4)	Tokyo	01 Sep
	Brent Harken	USA	61	2.35i	1)	Moskva	15 Feb
	Sorin Matei	Rum	63	2.35	1)	Bucuresti	14 Jun
	Troy Kemp	Bah	66	2.35	1)	Rovereto	13 Jul
	Dragutin Topic	Yug	71	2.34i	1)	Stockholm	19 Feb
	Rolandas Verkys	Lit	67	2.34	1)	Warszawa	16 Jun
	Patrik Sjöberg	Swe	65	2.34	1)	Barcelona	22 Jun
	Arturo Ortiz	Spa	66	2.34	2)	Barcelona	22 Jun
	Marino Drake	Cub	67	2.34	2)	St. Denis	19 Jul
	Exhibition – on ship's deck:						
	Sergey Dymchenko	SU	67	2.34	1)	Sevastopol	25 Sep
1992	Patrik Sjöberg	Swe	65	2.38i	1)	Genova	01 Mar
	Steve Smith	GB	73	2.37	1)	Seoul	20 Sep
	Ralf Sonn	Ger	67	2.36i	1)	Berlin	21 Feb
	Sorin Matei	Rum	63	2.36i	2)	Berlin	21 Feb
	Lambros Papakostas	Gre	69	2.36	1)	Athinai	21 Jun
	Javier Sotomayor	Cub	67	2.36	1)	Eberstadt	04 Jul
	Hollis Conway	USA	67	2.35i	1)	München	23 Feb
	Darrin Plab	USA	70	2.35	2)	New Orleans	28 Jun
	Dragutin Topic	Yug	71	2.35	1)	Beograd	15 Jul
	Troy Kemp	Bah	66	2.34i	2)	Gelsenkirchen	02 Feb
	Tim Forsyth	Aus	73	2.34	1)	Oslo	04 Jul
	Artur Partyka	Pol	69	2.34	3T)	Barcelona	02 Aug
1993	Javier Sotomayor	Cub	67	2.45	1)	Salamanca	27 Jul
	Partrik Sjöberg	Swe	65	2.39i	2)	Toronto	14 Mar
	Hollis Conway	USA	67	2.38	1)	Eberstadt	03 Jul
	Dragutin Topic	Yug	71	2.38	1)	Beograd	01 Aug
	Steve Smith	GB	73	2.37i	3)	Toronto	14 Mar
	Troy Kemp	Bah	66	2.37	1)	Pau	26 Jun
	Artur Partyka	Pol	69	2.37	2)	Stuttgart	22 Aug
	Ralf Sonn	Ger	67	2.36i	1)	Wuppertal	05 Feb
	Hendrik Beyer	Ger	72	2.36i	1)	Berflin	05 Mar
	Charlesm Austin	USA	67	2.35i	1)	Arnstadt	23 Jan
	Tim Forsyth	Aus	73	2.35	1)	Canberra	25 Jan
	Sorin Matei	Rum	63	2.35i	1)	Balingen	06 Feb

Year	Athlete	Nat	Born	Mark	Place	Venue	Date
1994	Javier Sotomayor	Cub	67	2.42	1)	Sevilla	05 Jun
	Steve Smith	GB	73	2.38i	2)	Wuppertal	04 Feb
	Wolf-Hendrik Beyer	Ger	72	2.38i	1)	Weinheim	18 Mar
	Dalton Grant	GB	66	2.37i	1)	Paris	13 Mar
	Steinar Hoen	Nor	71	2.36i	1)	Balingen	12 Feb
	Troy Kemp	Bah	66	2.36i	2)	Weinheim	12 Mar
	Jean-Charles Gicquel	Fra	67	2.35i	2)	Paris	13 Mar
	Ralf Sonn	Ger	67	2.34i	3)	Balingen	12 Feb
	Tim Forsyth	Aus	73	2.33	1)	Sydney	13 Mar
	Artur Partyka	Pol	69	2.33	2T)	Helsinki	09 Aug
	Gilmar Mayo	Col	69	2.33	1)	Pereira	17 Oct
1995	Javier Sotomayor	Cub	67	2.40	1)	Mar del Plata	25 Mar
	Troy Kemp	Bah	66	2.38	1)	Nice	12 Jul
	Sorin Matei	Rum	63	2.38i	1)	Wuppertal	03 Feb
	Artur Partyka	Pol	69	2.37i	1)	Balingen	11 Feb
	Steinar Hoen	Nor	71	2.36i	1)	Berlin	03 Mar
	Lambros Papakostas	Gre	69	2.35i	2)	Barcelona	12 Mar
	Dalton Grant	GB	66	2.35	3)	Eberstadt	09 Jul
	Steve Smith	GB	73	2.35	1)	Birmingham	15 Jul
	Charles Austin	USA	67	2.34i	3)	Balingen	11 Feb
	Håkon Särnblom	Nor	36	2.34i	4)	Balingen	11 Feb
1996	Charles Austin	USA	67	2.39	1)	Atlanta	28 Jul
	Javier Sotomayor	Cub	67	2.38i	1)	Liévin	18 Feb
	Artur Partyka	Pol	69	2.38	1)	Eberstadt	18 Aug
	Steve Smith	GB	73	2.36i	1)	Birmingham	10 Feb
	Dragutin Topic	Yug	71	2.35i	1)	Stockholm	10 Mar
	Partrik Sjöberg	Swe	65	2.35	2)	Eberstadt	18 Aug
	Randy Jenkins	USA	70	2.34i	1)	Montreal	19 Jan
	Dalton Grant	GB	66	2.34i	1)	Birmingham	27 Jan
	Steinar Hoen	Nor	71	2.34i	2)	Birmingham	10 Feb
	Konstantin Matusevich	Isr	71	2.34	1)	Caorle	15 Jun
1997	Javier Sotomayor	Cub	67	2.37	1)	Athinai	06 Aug
	Tim Forsyth	Aus	73	2.36	1)	Melbourne	02 Mar
	Charles Austin	USA	67	2.35i	1)	Paris	09 Mar
	Konstantin Matusevich	Isr	71	2.35	1)	Byrkjelo	13 Jul
	Artur Patyka	Pol	69	2.35	2)	Athinai	06 Aug
	Steve Smith	GB	73	2.34i	1)	Birmingham	23 Feb
	Jin-taek Lee	Kor	72	2.34	1)	Seoul	20 Jun
	Steinar Hoen	Nor	71	2.33i	1	Wuppertal	07 Feb
	Dalton Grant	GB	66	2.33i	2)	Wuppertal	07 Feb
	Lambros Papakostas	Gre	69	2.32i	2)	Paris	09 Mar
	Dragutin Topic	Yug	71	2.32i	3)	Paris	09 Mar
	Charles Lefrançois	Can	72	2.32	2)	Catania	28 Aug
	Town square competition:						
	Steinar Hoen	Nor	71	2.36i	1)	Oslo	01 Jul
1998	Javier Sotomayor	Cub	67	2.37	1)	Maracaibo	20 Aug
	Steve Smith	GB	73	2.36i	1)	Balingen	08 Feb
	Sergey Klyugin	SU	74	2.36	1)	Zurich	12 Aug
	Artur Partyka	Pol	69	2.34	1)	Budapest	21 Aug
	Dalton Grant	GB	66	2.34	2)	Budapest	21 Aug
	Charles Austin	USA	67	2.33i	2)	Balingen	08 Feb
	Stefan Holm	Swe	76	2.33	1)	Eurajoki	18 Jul
	Martin Busse	Ger	76	2.33	2)	Eberstadt	26 Jul
	Dragutin Topic	Yug	71	2.33	1)	Bajina Basta	09 Aug
	Tim Forsyth	Aus	73	2.32i	1)	Wuppertal	06 Feb
	Steinar Hoen	Nor	71	2.32i	2)	Wuppertal	06 Feb
	Vyacheslav Voronin	Rus	74	2.32i	3)	Spala	06 Mar
	Dimitrios Kokotis	Gre	72	2.32	1)	Athinai	19 Jul
	Christian Rhoden	Ger	74	2.32	1)	Luxemburg	19 Jul
1999	Vyacheslav Voronin	Rus	74	2.37	1)	Sevilla	23 Aug
	Javier Sotomayor	Cub	67	2.36i	1)	Maebashi	07 Mar

Year	Athlete	Nat	Born	Mark	Pos	Venue	Date
	Steve Smith	GB	73	2.36	1)	Gateshead	27 Jun
	Martin Busse	Ger	76	2.35	1)	Dortmund	26 Jun
	Mark Boswell	Can	77	2.35	2)	Sevilla	23 Aug
	Wolfgang Kreissig	Ger	70	2.34	1)	Mannheim	11 Sep
	Charles Austin	USA	67	2.33i	3)	Maebashi	07 Mar
	Sergey Klyugin	Rus	74	2.33	1)	Villeneuve d'Ascq	13 Jun
	Henry Patterson	USA	75	2.32	1T)	Nassau	26 May
	Dragutin Topic	Yug	71	2.32	1)	Athinai	16 Jun
	Tomas Janku	Cze	74	2.32	1)	Ostrava	27 Jun
	Abderahmane Hammad	Alg	77	2.32	2)	Rovereto	01 Sep
	Stefan Holm	Swe	76	2.32	2)	Berlin	07 Sep
	Andriy Sokolovskiy	Ukr	78	2.32	1)	Berdichev	16 Sep
2000	Vyacheslav Voronin	Rus	74	2.40	1)	London	05 Aug
	Matt Hemingway	USA	72	2.38i	1)	Atlanta	04 Mar
	Artur Partyka	Pol	69	2.37i	1)	Spala	18 Feb
	Konstantin Matusevich	Isr	71	2.36	1)	Perth	05 Feb
	Nathan Leeper	USA	77	2.35	1)	Sacramento	21 May
	Mark Boswell	Can	77	2.35	2)	Roma	30 Jun
	Sergey Klyugin	Rus	74	2.35	1)	Sydney	24 Sep
	Martin Buss	Ger	76	2.34i	2)	Gent	27 Feb
	Dragutin Topic	Yug	71	2.34i	3)	Gent	27 Feb
	Kwaku Boateng	Can	74	2.34	1)	Zagreb	03 Jul
	Lábros Papakóstas	Gre	69	2.34	1)	Athinai	09 Jul
	Abderahmane Hammad	Alg	77	2.34	1)	Alger	14 Jul
	Stefan Holm	Swe	76	2.34	1)	Helsinki	03 Sep

ALL TIME WORLD LIST AS AT THE END OF 2000

Athlete	Nat	Born	Mark	Pos	Venue	Date
Javier Sotomayor	Cub	67	2.45	1)	Salamanca	27 Jul 93
Patrik Sjöberg	Swe	65	2.42	1)	Stockholm	30 Jun 87
Carlo Thränhardt	WG	57	2.42i	1)	Berlin	28 Feb 88
Igor Paklin	SU	63	2.41	1)	Kobe	04 Sep 85
Rudolf Povarnitsyn	SU	62	2.40	1)	Donetsk	11 Aug 85
Sorin Matei	Rum	63	2.40	1)	Bratislava	20 Jun 90
Hollis Conway	USA	67	2.40i	1)	Sevilla	10 Mar 91
Charles Austin	USA	67	2.40	1)	Zurich	07 Aug 91
Vyacheslav Voronin	Rus	74	2.40	1)	London	05 Aug 00
Jianhua Zhu	Chi	63	2.39	1)	Eberstadt	10 Jun 84
Dietmar Mögenburg	WG	61	2.39i	1)	Köln	24 Feb 85
Ralf Sonn	Ger	67	2.39i	1)	Berlin	01 Mar 91

Year	Athlete	Nat	Born	Mark	Pos	Venue	Date
2001	Vyacheslav Voronin	Rus	74	2.37	1)	Eberstadt	19 Aug
	Martin Buss	Ger	76	2.36	1)	Edmonton	08 Aug
	Andriy Sokolovskiy	Ukr	78	2.35i	1)	Arnstadt	17 Feb
	Charles Clinger	USA	76	2.35	1)	Pocatello	19 May
	Javier Sotomayor	Cub	67	2.35	1)	Somoskö	26 Aug
	Staffan Strand	Swe	76	2.34i	1)	Stockholm	15 Feb
	Stefan Holm	Swe	76	2.34i	2)	Stockholm	15 Feb
	Nathan Leeper	USA	77	2.33i	1)	Manhattan, KS	19 Jan
	Yaroslav Rybakov	Rus	80	2.33i	1)	Moskva	25 Feb
	Gennadiy Moroz	Bye	78	2.33	1)	Brest	21 Jul
	Mark Boswell	Can	77	2.33	2)	Eberstadt	19 Aug
2002	Jacques Freitag	SA	82	2.37	1)	Durban	23 Mar
	Andriy Sokolovskiy	Ukr	78	2.36	1)	Berdichev	07 Sep
	Staffan Strand	Swe	78	2.35i	1)	Stockholm	06 Feb
	Charles Clinger	USA	76	2.35	1)	Eugene	26 May
	Mark Boswell	Can	77	2.35	1)	Roma	12 Jul
	Stefan Holm	Swe	76	2.35	1)	Zurich	16 Aug
	Pavel Fomenko	Rus	76	2.32i	1)	Volgograd	14 Feb
	Nathan Leeper	USA	77	2.32i	1)	New York	02 Mar
	Matt Hemingway	USA	72	2.32	1)	Gresham	18 May
	Andrey Chubsa	Bye	82	2.32	1)	Stockholm	10 Jul

HIGH JUMP 2003 2008

Year	Athlete	Nat	Born	Mark	Pl	Venue	Date
2003	Stefan Holm	Swe	76	2.36i	1)	Arnstadt	08 Feb
	Aleksander Walerianczyk	Pol	82	2.36	1)	Bydgoszcz	20 Jul
	Jacques Freitag	SA	82	2.35	1)	Roma	11 Jul
	Charles Clinger	USA	76	2.34i	1)	Nampa	01 Feb
	Yaroslav Rybakov	Rus	80	2.34i	2)	Arnstadt	08 Feb
	Matt Hemingway	USA	72	2.34	1)	Modesto	10 May
	Germaine Mason	Jam	83	2.34	1)	Santo Domingo	09 Aug
	Andriy Sokolovskiy	Ukr	78	2.33i	1)	Athinai	05 Feb
	Dragutin Topic	S&M	71	2.33i	1)	Athinai	04 Mar
	Jaroslav Bába	Cze	84	2.32i	3)	Arnstadt	08 Feb
	Staffan Strand	Swe	76	2.32i	2)	Satra	02 Mar
	Mark Boswell	Can	77	2.32	3)	St.Denis	25 Aug
2004	Stefan Holm	Swe	76	2.37i	1)	Stockholm	12 Feb
	Andriy Sokolovskiy	Ukr	78	2.35	1)	Langen	13 Jun
	Jaroslav Bába	Cze	84	2.34i	2)	Arnstadt	07 Feb
	Grzegorz Sposób	Pol	76	2.34	1)	Bydgoszcz	05 Jun
	Jacques Freitag	SA	82	2.34	1)	Salamanca	13 Jul
	Matt Hemingway	USA	72	2.34	2)	Athinai	22 Aug
	James Nieto	USA	76	2.34	4)	Athinai	22 Aug
	Svatoslav Ton	Cze	78	2.33	1)	Praha	11 Jun
	Tomás Jankú	Cze	74	2.33	2)	Plzen	26 Jun
	Yaroslav Rybakov	Rus	80	2.32i	2)	Budapest	06 Mar
	Andra Manson	USA	84	2.32	1)	Austin	12 Jun
	Vyacheslav Voronin	Rus	74	2.32	1)	Moskva	07 Aug
2005	Stefan Holm	Swe	76	2.40i	1)	Madrid	06 Mar
	Yaroslav Rybakov	Rus	80	2.38i	1)	Stockholm	15 Feb
	Jacques Freitag	SA	82	2.38	1)	Oudtshoorn	05 Mar
	Andriy Sokolovskiy	Ukr	78	2.38	1)	Roma	08 Jul
	Jaroslav Bába	Cze	84	2.37i	2)	Arnstadt	05 Feb
	Michal Bieniek	Pol	84	2.36	1)	Biala Podlaska	28 May
	Victor Moya	Cub	82	2.35	1)	Monaco	10 Sep
	Aleksey Dmitrik	Rus	84	2.34i	1)	Glasgow	29 Jan
	Svatoslav Ton	Cze	78	2.33i	1)	Brno	22 Feb
	Yuriy Krimarenko	Ukr	83	2.33	1)	Langen	26 Jun
	Vyacheslav Voronin	Rus	74	2.33	1)	Eberstadt	21 Aug
2006	Yaroslav Rybakov	Rus	80	2.37i	1)	Arnstadt	04 Feb
	Ivan Ukhov	Rus	86	2.37i	2)	Arnstadt	04 Feb
	Andrey Silnov	Rus	84	2.37	1)	Monaco	20 Aug
	Andriy Sokolovskiy	Ukr	78	2.36i	1)	Banská Bystrica	14 Feb
	Andrey Tereshin	Rus	82	2.36i	1)	Moskva	17 Feb
	Linus Thörnblad	Swe	85	2.34i	2)	Banská Bystrica	14 Feb
	Stefan Holm	Swe	76	2.34	1)	London	28 Jul
	Tomás Jankú	Cze	74	2.34	2)	Göteborg	09 Aug
	Svatoslav Ton	Cze	78	2.33i	1)	Hustopece	21 Jan
	Tora Harris	USA	78	2.33	1)	Indianapolis	25 Jun
	Naoyuki Daigo	Jap	81	2.33	1)	Kobe	02 Jul
2007	Ivan Ukhov	Rus	86	2.39i	1)	Moskva	28 Jan
	Yarolslav Rybakov	Rus	80	2.38i	1)	Arnstadt	03 Feb
	Stefan Holm	Swe	76	2.38i	1)	Göteborg	25 Feb
	Linus Thörnblad	Swe	85	2.38i	2)	Göteborg	25 Feb
	Andrey Silnov	Rus	84	2.36i	2)	Arnstadt	03 Feb
	Andriy Sokolovskiy	Ukr	78	2.35i	1)	Wuppertal	26 Jan
	Andrey Tereshin	Rus	82	2.35i	3)	Moskva	28 Jan
	Donald Thomas	Bah	84	2.35	1)	Salamanca	04 Jul
	Kyricaos Ioannou	Cyp	84	2.35	3)	Osaka	29 Aug
	Tomás Jankú	Cze	74	2.34i	1)	Brno	06 Feb
	Yuriy Krymarenko	Ukr	83	2.34i	2)	Bydgoszcz	14 Feb
	Eike Onnen	Ger	82	2.34	1)	Garbsen	20 May
2008	Yaroslav Rybakov	Rus	80	2.38i	1)	Moskva	10 Feb
	Andrey Silnov	Rus	84	2.38	1)	London	25 Jul
	Stefan Holm	Swe	76	2.37i	1)	Malmö	24 Feb
	Ivan Ukhov	Rus	86	2.36i	1)	Hustopece	19 Jan

	Andrey Tereshin	Rus	82	2.36i	2)	Moskva	10 Feb
	Dusty Jonas	USA	86	2.36	1)	Boulder	18 May
	Linus Thörnblad	Swe	85	2.35i	2)	Malmö	24 Feb
	Michal Bieniek	Pol	84	2.35	1)	Zamosc	06 Sep
	Kabelo Kgosimang	Bot	86	2.34	1)	Addis Ababa	04 May
	Germaine Manson	USA	84	2.34	2)	Beijing	19 Aug
2009	Ivan Ukhov	Rus	86	2.40i	1)	Pireás	25 Feb
	Linus Thörnblad	Swe	85	2.36i	1)	Banská Bystrica	11 Feb
	Jesse Williams	USA	83	2.36i	2)	Banská Bystrica	11 Feb
	Andra Manson	USA	84	2.35	1)	Austin	04 Apr
	Yaroslav Rybakov	Rus	80	2.35	1)	Cheboksary	25 Jul
	Viktor Shapoval	Ukr	79	2.34	1)	Berdychiv	11 Sep
	Aledksey Dmitrik	Rus	84	2.33	1)	Thessaloniki	10 Jun
	Jaroslav Babá	Cze	84	2.33	1)	London	25 Jul
	Andrey Tereshin	Rus	82	2.33	3)	Cheboksary	25 Jul
	Raul Spank	Ger	88	2.33	1)	Eberstadt	29 Aug
2010	Ivan Ukhov	Rus	86	2.38i	1)	Banska Bystrica	04 Mar
	Jesse Williams	USA	83	2.34i	1)	Albuquerque	27 Feb
	Yaroslav Rybakov	Rus	80	2.33i	2)	Arnstadt	06 Feb
	Dusty Jonas	USA	86	2.33	1)	Lincoln	08 May
	Aleksandr Shustov	Rus	84	2.33	1)	Sochi	28 May
	Andrey Silnov	Rus	84	2.33	1)	Zhukovsky	26 Jun
	Osku Torro	Fin	79	2.32i	1)	Wuppertal	22 Jan
	Andra Manson	USA	84	2.32i	1)	Bydgoszcz	10 Feb
	Aleksey Dmitrik	Rus	84	2.32i	1)	Weinheim	05 Mar
	Donald Thomas	Bah	84	2.32	1)	New Delhi	09 Oct

ALL-TIME WORLD LIST AS AT THE END OF 2010

Javier Sotomayor	Cub	67	2.45	1)	Salamanca	27 Jul 93
Patrik Sjöberg	Swe	66	2.42	1)	Stockholm	30 Jun 87
Carlo Thränhardt	WG	57	2.42i	1)	Berlin	28 Feb 88
Igor Paklin	SU	63	2.41	1)	Kobe	04 Sep 85
Rudolf Povarnitsyn	SU	62	2.40	1)	Donetsk	11 Aug 85
Sorin Matei	Rum	63	2.40	1)	Bratislava	20 Jun 90
Hollis Conway	USA	67	2.40i	1)	Sevilla	10 Mar 91
Charles Austin	USA	67	2.40	1)	Zurich	07 Aug 91
Vyacheslav Voronin	Rus	74	2.40	1)	London	05 Aug 00
Stefan Holm	Swe	76	2.40i	1)	Madrid	06 Mar 05
Ivan Ukhov	Rus	86	2.40i	1)	Pireás	25 Feb 09

POLE VAULT

Note – *Early vaulters, up to and including Richard Dickinson of GB (1891), mostly used the "climbing technique".*

1860	W. S. Gilbert	Aus		3.045	)	Melbourne	06 Feb
	Carruthers	GB		2.79	1)	Addiscombe	28 Apr
	W. Jepson	GB		2.51	1)	Sheffield	07 May
	Professional:						
	Herbert Jamieson	GB		3.125	1)	Jedburgh	27 Jul
1861	Thomas Tyers	GB		2.61	)	Cheltenham	04 May
	Arthur Warrand	GB		2.54	1)	Tonbridge	16 Apr
	Professional:						
	Robert Musgrave	GB	41	3.25	)	Durham	

POLE VAULT 1862 1870

Year	Name	Nat	Born	Mark	Pos	Venue	Date
1862	T. Myles	GB		2.89	1)	Edinburgh	01 Sep
	George Crotch	GB		2.69	1)	Cambridge	28 Mar
	Thomas Hammond	GB		2.69	1)	Camberley Sandhurst	16 Sep
	Professional:						
	David Johnstone	GB		3.10	)	Preston	01 Sep
1863	Andrew Foreman	USA		2.89	)	New York	
	C. W. Earnshaw	GB		2.82	1)	Sheffield	04 May
	F. C. Whitaker	GB		2.69	1)	Wimbledon	30 May
	Professional:						
	Charles Scott	GB		3.10	)	Preston	03 Aug
	Robert Musgrave	GB	41	3.10	)	Preston	04 Aug
	David Johnstone	GB		3.10	)		
1864	T. Lawson	GB		2.84	1)	Stockton / Tees	17 May
	Gracchus Hall	GB		2.83	)	Manchester	27 Aug
	Beaver	GB		2.82	1)	Woolwich	27 Apr
	Professional:						
	Robert Musgrave	GB	41	3.43i	1)	Islington	25 Mar
1865	Avison Scott	GB	48	3.12	1)	Brighton	16 Jun
	Geoge Bayley	GB		2.97	)	Broughton	29 Jul
	Sydney Hyde	GB		2.97	)	Broughton	29 Jul
	Professional:						
	John Allison	GB	43	3.32	1)	Ulverston	04 Aug
1866	John Wheeler	GB		3.05	1)	Beaufort House, London	23 Mar
	Christopher Ewbank	GB	45	2.89	2)	London, BH	23 Mar
	G. A. Bayley	GB		2.89	1)	Llandudno	26 Jun
	Professional:						
	Robert Musgrave	GB	41	3.31	1)	Cockermouth	
1867	Syidney Hyde	GB		3.05	1T)	Manchester	06 Jul
	Robert Horne	GB		3.05	1T)	Manchester	06 Jul
	Edward Bergman	GB	49	2.97	1)	Bristol	
	Professional:						
	Robert Musgrave	GB	41	3.35i	1T)	Islington	19 Apr
	John Allison	GB	43	3.35i	1T)	Islington	19 Apr
1868	Robert Mitchell	GB	47	3.21	1)	Beaufort House, London	19 Jun
	Powell Moore	GB	46	3.06	2)	London, BH	19 Jun
	Alfred Lubbock	GB	46	3.05	1)	Blackheath	06 Jun
	Professional:						
	John Allison	GB	43	3.12	1)		
1869	Robert Mitchell	GB	47	2.99	1)		
	Peter Fraser	USA		2.97	1)	New York	
	Robert Musgrave	GB	41	3.17	1)	Islington	26 Mar
	Edmund Gurney	GB	47	2.94	1)	Norwich	24 May
	Professional:						
	David Anderson	GB	46	3.25	1)		
	Thomas Bell	GB		3.15	1)	Cleator Moor	08 Jun
1870	Robert Mitchell	GB	47	3.12	1)	Lillie Bridge, London, LB	09 Apr
	Charles Leeds	GB	c46	3.12	1)	Nottingham	04 Jun
	Edward Bergman	GB	49	3.05	2)	London, LB	09 Apr
	S. Jackson	GB		3.05	2)	Nottingham	04 Jun
	Professional:						
	David Anderson	GB	46	3.27	1)	Bridge of Allan	06 Aug

1871	Edwin Woodburn	GB	50	3.15	1T)	Douglas	09 Aug
	John Wigfull	GB	51	3.15	1T)	Douglas	09 Aug
	Robert Mitchell	GB	47	3.07	1)	London, LB	03 Apr
	Professional:						
	Thomas Jackson	GB		3.15	1)	New Castle	30 May
1872	Edwin Woodburn	GB	50	3.13	1)	Todmorden	20 Jul
	J. Jackson	GB		3.10	1)	Durham	27 May
	William Kelsey	GB	51	3.05	1)	Newark	27 May
	Professional:						
	W. L. Crichton	GB		3.27	1)	Birnam	29 Aug
1873	Edwin Woodburn	GB	50	3.22	1)	Lancaster	31 May
	William Kelsey	GB	51	3.22	1T)	Sheffield	07 Jul
	John Wigfull	GB	51	3.22	1T)	Sheffield	07 Jul
	Professional:						
	John Richardson	GB		3.20i	1)	Islington	12 Apr
1874	Edwin Woodburn	GB	50	3.22	1)	London, Lillie Bridge	30 Mar
	Charles W. Gaskin	GB	52	3.20	1)	Market Harborough	13 Jul
	Robert Sabin	GB	52	3.20	1T)	Northampton	03 Aug
	Professional:						
	Thomas Newby	GB	43	3.35	1T)	Bolton	11 Jul
	David Anderson	GB	46	3.35	1T)	Bolton	11 Jul
1875	John Wigfull	GB	51	3.22	1)	Sheffield	15 Jul
	Charles W. Gaskin	GB	52	3.20	1)	Olney	26 Jul
	Robert Sabin	GB	52	3.16	1)	Reading	07 Jul
	Professional:						
	David Anderson	GB	46	3.25	)	Morpeth	21 Aug
	F. T. H. Dixon	GB		3.25	)	Morpeth	21 Aug
1876	Edwin Woodburn	GB	50	3.38 °	1)	Ulverston	21 Jul
	Charles Gaskin	GB	52	3.32	1)	Sheffield	03 Jul
	Horace Strachan	GB	55	3.27	1)	Olney	05 Aug
	° = *Probably downhill.*						
	Exhibition:						
	Edwin Woodburn	GB	50	3.40	1)	Ulverston	14 Jul
1877	Harry E. Kyall	GB	55	3.37	1)	Ilkley	11 Aug
	Charles Gaskin	GB	52	3.35	2)	Ilkley	11 Aug
	Thomas Bellamy	GB		3.32	)	Huddersfield	16 Jul
1878	Horace W. Strachan	GB	50	3.31	1T)	Huddersfield	22 Jun
	G. Barker	GB		3.31	1T)	Huddersfield	22 Jun
	W. D. Robinson	GB		3.19	1)	Ipswich	13 Apr
	Professional:						
	William Steel	GB		3.32	1)	Glasgow	08 Sep
1879	Thomas Ray	GB	62	3.42	1)	Ulverston	19 Sep
	George Callow	GB	60	3.27	1)	Husbands Bosworth	06 Aug
	Robert Sabin	GB	52	3.20	)		
1880	Thomas Ray	GB	62	3.35	)	Widnes	19 Jun
	William Van Houten	USA	61	3.32	1)	Mott Haven, NY	25 Sep
	B. F. Richardson	USA		3.22	2)	Mott Haven, NY	25 Sep
	Exhibition:						
	Edward Strachan	GB	58	3.27	1)	Bristol	19 Jun

POLE VAULT 1881 1892

1881	Thomas Ray	GB	62	3.43	1)	Birmingham	16 Jul
	Englesham	GB		3.25	1)	Ayr	07 May
	S. J. Parrington	GB	52	3.25	1)	Milnthorpe	06 Jun
	Professional:						
	P. Simpson	GB		3.30	1)	Grasmere	18 Aug
1882	Thomas Ray	GB	62	3.45	1)	Bradford	12 Aug
	J. G. Pearson	GB		3.22	1T)	London (LB)	08 Apr
	Extra trial:						
	Thomas Ray	GB	62	3.46	-)	Stoke on Trent	01 Jul
	Professional:						
	J. F. Simpson	GB		3.22	1T)	London (LB)	08 Apr
1883	Thomas Ray	GB	62	3.47	1)	Preston	18 Aug
	Hugh Baxter	USA	61	3.36	1)	Mott Haven	02 Jun
1884	Thomas Ray	GB	62	3.40	1)	Newark	02 Jun
	T. H. M. Hobbs	Ire		3.32	1)	Tullamore	17 Jul
1885	Thomas Ray	GB	62	3.48	1)	Grasmere	20 Aug
	Ernest Stones	GB	65	3.27	2)	Ulverston	24 Jul
	E. Newby	GB		3.20	3)	Ulverfston	24 Jul
	Professional:						
	Joseph Thwaites	GB	60	3.32	1)	Warcop	09 Aug
1886	Thomas Ray	GB	62	3.49	1)	Whitehaven	13 Aug
	E. Hinzmann	Ger		3.40	1)	Coblenz	30 May
	Exhibition:						
	Thomas Ray	GB	62	3.53	-)	Grasmere	19 Aug
1887	Thomas Ray	GB	62	3.52	1)	Whitehaven	19 Aug
	Ernest Stones	GB	65	3.50	)	Barrow-on-Furness	07 Sep
	Hugh Baxter	USA	61	3.48	1)	New Haven	15 Oct
1888	Ernest Stones	GB	65	3.53	1)	Southport	02 Jun
	Thomas Ray	GB	62	3.50	1)	Stourbridge	23 Jul
	Not ratified (nails were used to support the bar):						
	Thomas Ray	GB	62	3.55	1)	Barrow	22 Sep
1889	Ernest Stones	GB	65	3.57	1)	Grasmere	23 Aug
	Robert Leavitt	USA		3.53	1)		
	Thomas Ray	GB	62	3.42	2T)	Stourbridge	19 Aug
	Robert Watson	GB	65	3.42	2T)	Stourbridge	19 Aug
	Richard Dickinson	GB	69	3.42	1)	Broughton-in-Furness	08 Sep
1890	Richard Dickinson	GB	69	3.43	1)	Blackburn	09 Aug
	Robert Watson	GB	65	3.42	1)	Ashton-Lyne	06 Sep
	Thomas Ray	GB	62	3.27	2)	Stourbridge	14 Jul
	P. Stokes	Ire		3.27	1)	Limerick	07 Sep
1891	Richard Dickinson	GB	69	3.58	1)	Kidderminster	04 Jul
	Robert Watson	GB	65	3.42	1)	Manchester	27 Jun
	P. Stokes	Ire		3.35	)		
1892	Walter Rodenbaugh	USA	66	3.49	1)	Philadelphia	17 Sep
	Thomas Ray	GB	62	3.46	1)		
	Richard Dickinson	GB	69	3.37	1)	Blackburn	16 Jul
	Robert Watson	GB	65	3.35	1T)	London	02 Jul
	Theodore Luce	USA	72	3.35	1)	NewYork	01 Oct

1893	Richard Dickinson	GB	69	3.50	1)	Bradford	22 Jul
	Theodore Buchholtz	USA	69	3.42	1)	Chicago	16 Sep
	O. G. Cartwright	USA		3.22	2)	New York	27 May
1894	Richard Dickinson	GB	69	3.50i	1)	Windsor	28 Jul
	Theodore Buchholtz	USA	69	3.35	1)	NewYork	15 Sep
	Bernadotte Loomis	USA	73?	3.35	2)	New York	15 Sep
	Robert Watson	GB	65	3.35	1)	Montreal	29 Sep
	W. A. Stewart	USA		3.35	1)		
1895	Theodore Buchholtz	USA	69	3.44	1)	New York	25 May
	Richard Dickinson	GB	69	3.42	1)	Bradford	20 Jul
	William W. Hoyt	USA	75	3.42	2)	New York	25 May
1896	Theodore Buchholtz	USA	69	3.40	1)	Ithaka	09 May
	Franklin Allis	USA	74	3.39	1)	New York	30 May
	W. A. Stewart	USA		3.35	2)	New York	30 May
	C. F. Hamilton	USA		3.35	)	New York	12 Sep
	Professional:						
	Thomas R. Cannon	GB	73	3.58	1)	Ullswater	29 Aug
	Richard Dickinson	GB	69	3.45	1)	Grasmere	20 Aug
1897	Bascom Johnson	USA	78	3.44	1)	New York	29 May
	O. B. Smith	USA		3.42	1)	Bergen Point	31 May
	Charles Van Winckle	USA	72	3.39	1T)	Mott Haven	28 Apr
	William W. Hoyt	USA	75	3.39	2)	New York	29 May
	Professional:						
	Robert Dickinson	GB	69	3.48	)	Sunderland	14 Aug
1898	Raymond Clapp	USA	75	3.62	1)	Chicago	18 Jun
	Jesse Hurlburt	USA	77	3.51	1)	Worcester	21 May
	William Hoyt	USA	75	3.46	1T)	New York	27 May
	Professional:						
	Richard Dickinson	GB	69	3.50	1)	Grasmere	18 Aug
1899	Raymond Clapp	USA	75	3.50	1)	New Haven	22 Apr
	W. E. Selim	USA		3.45	1)	New York	10 Jun
	Bascom Johnson	USA	78	3.43	2T)	New York	27 May
	Robert H. Deming	USA		3.43	2T)	New York	27 May
	E. A. Kenzie	USA		3.43	2T)	New York	27 May
	Professional:						
	Richard Dickinson	GB	69	3.50	)	Morpeth	05 Aug
1900	Bascom Johnson	USA	78	3.55	1)	New York	15 Jun
	Charles Dvorak	USA	78	3.50	1)	Chicago	02 Jun
	A. W. Coleman	USA		3.48	1)	Elmira	30 May
	Dan Horton	USA	79	3.45	2)	Elmira	30 May
	John Holloway	Ire		3.45	1)	Youghal	24 Jun
	Professional:						
	Richard Dickinson	GB	69	3.45	)	Morpeth	04 Aug

ALL TIME WORLD LIST AS AT THE END OF 1900

Raymond Clapp	USA	75	3.62	1)	Chicago	18 Jun 98
Bascom Johnson	USA	78	3.55	1)	New York	15 Jun 00
Jesse Hurlburt	USA	77	3.51	1)	Worcester	21 May 98
Charles Dvorak	USA	78	3.50	1)	Chicago	02 Jun 00
A. W. Coleman	USA		3.48	1)	Elmira	30 May 00
Daniel Horton	USA	79	3.45	2)	Elmira	30 May 00
John Holloway	Ire		3.45	1)	Youghal	24 Jun 00

POLE VAULT 1901 1910

Climbing Climbing Technique:							
Richard Dickinson		GB	69	3.58	1)	Kidderminster	04 Jul 91
Thomas Ray		GB	62	3.57	1)	Barrow	22 Sep 88
Ernest Stones		GB	65	3.57	1)	Grasmere	23 Aug 89
1901	Charles Dvorak	USA	78	3.50	1)	Chicago	01 Jun
	R. W. Albertson	USA		3.45	1)	Louisville	05 Oct
	Albert Anderson	USA		3.44	1)	Buffalo	07 Sep
	Professional:						
	Richard Dickinson	GB	69	3.45	)	Morpeth	03 Aug
1902	Jerome Magee	USA		3.58	1)	Champaign	03 May
	Alexander Gray	USA		3.55	)	Philadelphia	26 Apr
	Danel Horton	USA	79	3.53	1)	New York	31 May
1903	H. Thurman Chapman	USA		3.65	1)	London	12 Apr
	Charles Dvorak	USA	78	3.58	1)	Chicago	30 May
	Norman Dole	USA		3.55	1)	Palo Alto	18 Apr
	Exhibition:						
	H. Thurman Chapman	USA		3.65	-)	Des Moines	23 Apr
1904	Norman Dole	USA		3.69	1)	Berkeley	23 Apr
	Fernand Gonder	Fra	83	3.69	1)	Paris (Pré-Catelan)	26 Jun
	Henry Lawson Moore	USA	81	3.58	)		
	LeRoy Samse	USA	85	3.58	)	St.Louis	31 Aug
	Ward McLanahan	USA	83	3.56	1)	Annapolis	07 May
	Unratified (insufficient number of officials):						
	Fernand Gonder	Fra	83	3.77	1)	Gradignan	31 Jul
1905	Fernand Gonder	Fra	83	3.75	1)	Bordeaux	06 Aug
	Walter Dray	USA	86	3.62	)		
	Edward Glover	USA	85	3.59	1)	Chicago	03 Jun
	Ralph Norris	USA		3.59	2)	Chicago	03 Jun
	Thomas Jackson	USA		3.59	)		
	Unratified (insufficient number of officials):						
	Fernand Gonder	Fra	83	3.83	1)	Gradignan	28 May
	Exhibition:						
	Fernand Gonder	Fra	83	4.00	-)	Bordeaux	Aug
1906	Le Roy Samse	USA	85	3.78	1)	Evanston (Chicago)	09 Jun
	Alfred Gilbert	USA	84	3.73	1)	New York	30 May
	Fernand Gonder	Fra	83	3.72	1)	Agen	05 Aug
1907	Walter Dray	USA	86	3.79	1)	New Haven	18 May
	Fernand Gonder	Fra	83	3.77	)		
	Frederick Lanagan	USA		3.76	)	Berkeley	20 Apr
1908	Walter Dray	USA	86	3.90	1)	Danbury, CT	13 Jun
	Alfred Gilbert	USA	84	3.86	1)	New Haven	12 Jun
	Edward Archibald	Can	84	3.78	1)	Toronto	06 Jun
	Clair Jacobs	USA	72	3.76	1)	Chicago	06 Jun
	Frank Nelson	USA	87	3.72	2T)	Philadelphia	06 Jun
	Unratified:						
	Edward Archibald	Can	84	3.81			
1909	Frank Nelson	USA	87	3.76	1)	New Haven	15 May
	Charles Campbell	USA		3.76	2)	New Haven	15 May
	Clair Jacobs	USA	72	3.73i	1)	Chicago	23 Feb
1910	Leland Scott	USA	88	3.93	1)	Boulder	27 May
	Frank Nelson	USA	87	3.81	1)	Cambridge	14 May
	Samuel Bellah	USA	87	3.79	)		

Year	Athlete	Nat	Born	Mark	Pos	Venue	Date
1911	Harold Babcock	USA	90	3.87	1)	Cambridge, MA	27 May
	Robert Gardner	USA	90	3.86	1)	New Haven	13 May
	Gordon Dukes	USA	88	3.83	1)	Binghampton	17 Jun
	Edward Cook	USA	88	3.81	1T)	Pittsburgh	01 Jul
	Frank Coyle	USA	86	3.81	1T)	Pittsburgh	01 Jul
	Samuel Bellah	USA	87	3.81	1T)	Pittsburgh	01 Jul
	Stanely Wagoner	USA	91	3.80	1)	Pittsburgh	30 Jun
	Frank Murphy	USA	89	3.73	1)	Philadelphia	29 Apr
	William Happenny	Can	85	3.71	1)	Montreal	23 Sep
	Fernand Gonder	Fra	83	3.70	1)	Bruxelles	16 Jul
	Eugene Schobinger	USA		3.68i	1)	Chicago	18 Feb
	Edward Schroth	USA	86	3.68	1)	New Orleans	10 Jun
1912	Marc Wright	USA	90	4.02	1)	Cambridge, MA	08 Jun
	Robert Gardner	USA	90	3.98	1)	Philadelphia	01 Jun
	Harry Babcock	USA	90	3.95	1)	Stockholm	11 Jul
	Stanley Wagoner	USA	91	3.90	1)	New Haven	04 May
	Frank Nelson	USA	87	3.85	2T)	Stockholm	11 Jul
	Sam Bellah	USA	87	3.83	1)	Palo Alto	18 May
	Torrance Fiske	USA	92	3.83	1T)	New Haven	11 May
	Bedrtil Uggla	Swe	90	3.82	1)	Stockholm	25 Aug
	Frank Murphy	USA	89	3.81	1)	Madison	04 May
	William Happenny	Can	85	3.80	4T)	Stockholm	11 Junl
	Exhibition:						
	Sam Bellah	USA	87	3.90	-)	Palo Alto	18 May
1913	Stanley Wagoner	USA	91	3.96	1)	Chicago	05 Jul
	John Gold	USA	90	3.93	1)		
	Torrance Fiske	USA	92	3.86	1)	Cambrige, MA	31 May
	Claes Gille	Swe	88	3.85	1)	Stockholm	14 Sep
	Carl Hårleman	Swe	86	3.83	2)	Stockholm	14 Sep
	Kenneth Curtis	USA		3.82	1)	Philadelphia	26 Apr
	Charles Borgstrom	USA		3.81	1)	Berkeley	04 Apr
	Robert Pasemann	Ger	86	3.79	1)	Berlin	06 Jul
	James Miller	USA		3.76	1)	Palo Alto	28 Mar
	Edward Thomas	USA		3.76	1)	Chicago	24 May
	Marc Wright	USA	90	3.76	2T)	Cambridge, MA	31 May
	Exhibition:						
	Charles Borgstrom	USA		3.90	-)	Los Angeles	22 Mar
1914	Robert Krohn	USA	95	3.87	1)	Palo Alto	18 Apr
	Charles Borgstrom	USA		3.81	1)	Berkeley	28 May
	Marc Wright	USA	90	3.81	1)	Princeton	16 May
	Claes Gille	Swe	88	3.80	1)	Budapest	28 Jun
	Carl Hårleman	Swe	86	3.80	1T)	Stockholm	14 Jul
	Bertil Uggla	Swe	90	3.80	1T)	Stockholm	14 Jul
	Gordon Dukes	USA	88	3.78	1)	Milltown, NJ	07 Sep
	William Fritz	USA	92	3.77	1T)	Ithaca	09 May
	Andis L. Milton	USA		3.77	1T)	Ithaca	09 May
	Knute Rockne	USA	88	3.76i	1)	Evanston	28 Feb
1915	Frank Foss	USA	95	3.91	1T)	Philadelphia	24 Apr
	Wilbur Newstetter	USA		3.91	1T)	Philadelphia	24 Apr
	Sam Bellah	USA	87	3.88	1)	San Francisco	07 Aug
	Percy Graham	USA	96	3.85	1)	Chicago	17 Jul
	Charles Borgstrom	USA		3.85	1)	Los Angeles	22 May
	Florin Floyd	USA		3.81	1)	Urbana	05 Jun
	Edward Knourek	USA	93	3.80	1)	Chicago	03 Jul
	Claes Gille	Swe	88	3.80	1)	Stockholm	13 May
	Jay Camp	USA		3.75	1)	Cambridge, MA	08 May
	Eugene Schobinger	USA		3.73i	1T)	Evanston	20 Mar
	Huston	USA		3.73i	1T)	Evanston	20 Mar
	Andis L. Milton	USA		3.73	1)	Ithaca	15 May
1916	Percy Graham	USA	96	3.92i	1)	Evanston	08 Apr

	Edward Knourek	USA	93	3.92i	2)	Evanston	08 Apr
	Sherman Landers	USA	98	3.88	1)	Newark	09 Sep
	Florin Floyd	USA		3.87i	1)	Kansas City	27 Feb
	Frank Foss	USA	95	3.86	1)	Cambridge, MA	27 May
	Claes Gille	Swe	88	3.86	1)	Kristiania	17 Sep
	Charles Borgstrom	USA		3.83	1)	Los Angeles	15 Apr
	Carl Hårleman	Swe	86	3.83	2)	Stockholm	09 Jul
	Wilbur Newstetter	USA		3.81	1T)	Philadelphia	29 Apr
	Carl Buck	USA	91	3.81	1T)	Cambridge, MA	13 May
	Joseph Nagel	USA	95	3.81	1T)	Cambridge, MA	13 May
	George G. Haydock	USA		3.81	1T)	Cambridge, MA	13 May
1917	Edward Knourek	USA	93	3.88	1)	Saint Louis	01 Sep
	Carl Hårleman	Swe	86	3.88	1)	Kristiania	30 Jun
	B. Wilson	USA		3.81	1)	Los Angeles	14 Apr
	Wilbur Newstetter	USA		3.81	1)	Philadelphia	28 Apr
	Percy Graham	USA	96	3.81	1)	Chicago	09 Jun
	Marc Wright	USA	90	3.81	2)	Saint Louis	01 Sep
	Carl Buck	USA	91	3.81	1)	Saint Louis	03 Sep
	D. J. Fischer	USA		3.73i	1)	Chicago	24 Mar
	Erik Holmstrand	Swe	93	3.70	)	Örebro	01 Jul
	Luther Nichols	USA		3.68	1)	Los Angeles	17 Mar
1918	Georg Högström	Swe	95	3.80	1)	Stockholm	15 Sep
	Edward Knourek	USA	93	3.78	1)	Great Lakes, IL	23 Sep
	Roy Easterday	USA		3.73	1T)	Philadelphia	01 Jun
	John Jordan	USA		3.73	1T)	Philadelphias	01 Jun
	Carl Buck	USA	91	3.73	1)	Great Lakes	21 Sep
	Truman Gardner	USA		3.72	1)	Princeton	11 May
	Georg Morning	Den	93	3.71	2)	Köbenhavn	01 Sep
	Edwin Myers	USA	96	3.69	1)	Cambridge, MA	14 Sep
	Henry Petersen	Den	00	3.69	1)	Köbenhavn	30 Jun
1919	Frank Foss	USA	95	4.05	1)	Chicago	23 Aug
	Ralph Spearow	USA	95	3.98	1)	Portland	03 May
	Edwin Myers	USA	96	3.81	1)	Cambridge, MA	31 May
	Edward Knourek	USA	93	3.81	2)	Chicago	16 Aug
	Percy Graham	USA	96	3.81	2)	Philadelphia	13 Sep
	Henry Petersen	Den	00	3.80	1)	Köbenhavn	15 Jun
	Marc Wright	USA	90	3.77	1)	Cambridge, Ma	23 Aug
	Florin Floyd	USA		3.76	1)	Colombes	01 Jun
	Georg Högström	Swe	95	3.76	)	Karlstad	03 Aug
	John Mattsson	Swe	94	3.75	)	Malmö	
1920	Frank Foss	USA	95	4.09	1)	Antwerpen	20 Aug
	Eldon Jenne	USA	99	3.98	1)	Palo Alto	15 May
	Edwin Myers	USA	96	3.98	2)	Cambridge, MA	17 Jul
	Ralph Spearow	USA	85	3.97	)		
	Edward Knourek	USA	93	3.91	3)	Cambridge, MA	17 Jul
	Truman Gardner	USA		3.88	2)	Chicago	26 Jun
	Dale Merrick	USA		3.85	)		
	Norman Green	USA		3.83	1)	Palo Alto	20 Mar
	Sherman Landers	USA	98	3.81	1)	Philadelphia	24 Apr
	John Mattsson	Swe	94	3.81	1)	Malmö	13 Jun
	Lloyd Wilder	USA		3.81	)		
	Ernfrid Rydberg	Swe	96	3.77	1)	Gävle	26 Sep
	Wooster Webber	USA		3.76	Q)	Philadelphia	28 May

ALL TIME WORLD LIST AS AT THE END OF 1920

Frank Foss	USA	95	4.09	1)	Antwerpen	20 Aug 20
Marc Wright	USA	90	4.02	1)	Cambridge, MA	08 Jun 12
Robert Gardner	USA	90	3.98	1)	Philadelphia	01 Jun 12
Ralph Spearow	USA	95	3.98	1)	Portland	03 May 19
Edwin Myers	USA	96	3.98	2)	Cambridge, MA	17 Jul 20

Year	Athlete	Nat	Born	Mark	Pos	Venue	Date
Eldon Jenne		USA	99	3.98	1)	Palo Alto	15 May 20
Stanley Wagoner		USA	91	3.96	1)	Chicago	05 Jul 13
Harry Babcock		USA	90	3.95	1)	Stockholm	11 Jul 12
Leland Scott		USA	88	3.93	1)	Boulder	27 May 10
Percy Graham		USA	96	3.92i	1)	Evanston	08 Apr 16
Edward Knourek		USA	93	3.92i	2)	Evanston	08 Apr 16
1921	Richard Emmons	USA		3.97	1)	Pasadena, CA	18 Jun
	Truman Gardner	USA		3.90	1)	Princeton	07 May
	Lars Erik Tirén	Swe	01	3.90	1)	Stockholm	21 Aug
	Edward Knourek	USA	93	3.88	1)	Chicago	11 Jun
	Charles Hoff	Nor	02	3.87	1)	Oslo	02 Oct
	Arthur Wilcox	USA		3.86	1)	Los Angeles	19 Mar
	Dale Merrick	USA		3.81	1T)	Philadelphia	30 Apr
	Eldon Jenne	USA	99	3.81	1)	Pullman, WA	07 May
	Percy Graham	USA	96	3.81	2T)	Chicago	11 Jun
	M. Slaughter	USA		3.81	2T)	Chicago	11 Jun
	Richard Gartley	USA		3.81	1)	New Haven, CT	07 Nov
	Henry Petersen	Den	00	3.81	1)	Århus	21 Aug
	Intrasquad meet:						
	Henry Petersen	Den	00	3.88	D)	Köbenhavn	09 Oct
1922	Charles Hoff	Nor	02	4.12	1)	Köbenhavn	03 Sep
	Edward Knourek	USA	93	3.96	1)	Newark, NJ	09 Sep
	Ralph Spearow	USA	95	3.96	2)	Newark, NJ	09 Sep
	Ernfrid Rydberg	Swe	96	3.96	2)	Köbenhavn	03 Sep
	John Landowski	USA		3.89	1T)	Urbana, IL	04 Mar
	Dale Merrick	USA		3.89	1T)	Urbana, IL	04 Mar
	Truman Gardner	USA		3.88	1)	Philadelphia	29 Apr
	Allen Norris	USA	01	3.88	1T)	Berkeley, CA	29 Apr
	William Black	USA		3.88	1T)	Berkeley, CA	29 Apr
	Henry Petersen	Den	00	3.85	1)	Köbenhavn	06 Aug
1923	Charles Hoff	Nor	02	4.21	1)	Köbenhavn	22 Jul
	Dean Brownell	USA		4.01	1)	Ann Arbor, MI	02 Jun
	Edwin Myers	USA	96	3.98	1)	Chicago	01 Sep
	Ralph Spearow	USA	95	3.97	1)	Eugene, OR	18 May
	William Black	USA		3.96	1)	Palo Alto, CA	10 Mar
	Harry Smith	USA	96	3.96	1)	Santa Ana, CA	28 Apr
	James Brooker	USA	02	3.93	2)	Ann Arbor, MI	02 Jun
	Earl McKeown	USA		3.93	1T)	Chicago	16 Jun
	Edward Knourek	USA	93	3.93i	2)	Evanston	30 Mar
	Henry Petersen	Den	00	3.90	1)	Köbenhavn	08 Jul
	Laurits Jörgensen	Den	96	3.90	2)	Köbenhavn	08 Jul
1924	Lee Barnes	USA	06	4.01	1)	Los Angeles	24 May
	Edwin Myers	USA	96	4.00	1)	Ann Arbor, MI	31 May
	Dean Brownell	USA		3.97i	1)	Evanston, IL	15 Mar
	Earl McKeown	USA		3.97	1)	Lawrence, KS	19 Apr
	Charles Bickmore	USA		3.96	2T)	Los Angeles	24 May
	Harry Smith	USA		3.96	2T)	Los Angeles	24 May
	James Brooker	USA	02	3.96	1T)	Cambridge, MA	14 Jun
	Ralph Spearow	USA	95	3.96	1T)	Cambridge, MA	14 Jun
	Glenn Graham	USA	04	3.96	1T)	Cambridge, MA	14 Jun
	Paul Jones	USA		3.94	1)	Richmond, IN	17 May
	Exhibition:						
	Ralph Spearow	USA	95	4.22	-)	Tokyo	05 Nov
1925	Charles Hoff	Nor	02	4.25	1)	Turku	27 Sep
	Earl McKeown	USA		4.03	1)	Lawrence, KS	18 Apr
	Henry Petersen	Den	00	4.03	1)	Köbenhavn	26 Jul
	Jack Williams	USA	07	4.00	1)	Los Angeles	02 May
	Sabin Carr	USA	04	3.98	1)	Princeton	16 May
	Nelson Sherrill	USA		3.98	1)	Philadelphia	09 May
	James Brooker	USA	02	3.96i	1)	Ann Arbor, MI	28 Mar

Year	Athlete	Nat	Born	Mark	Pos	Venue	Date
	Harry Smith	USA		3.96	1)	Los Angeles	28 Feb
	Dean Brownell	USA		3.96	2)	Lawrence, KS	18 Apr
	Vern McDermont	USA	06	3.96	1)	Los Angeles	16 May
	Royal Bouschor	USA		3.96	1)	Columbus, OH	06 Jun
	Edwin Myers	USA	96	3.96	1)	Chicago	20 Jun
	Extra trial:						
	Fred Garner	USA	01	3.98	-)	Claremont, CA	28 Mar
1926	Charles Hoff	Nor	02	4.19	1)	Des Moines, IA	24 Apr
	Lee Barnes	USA	06	4.16	1)	Palo Alto, CA	15 May
	Ralph Smith	USA		4.06	1)	Los Angeles	10 Apr
	Sabin Carr	USA	04	4.04	1)	New Haven, CT	15 May
	Glenn Graham	USA	04	4.04	1)	Los Angeles	15 May
	Paul Harrington	USA		4.04	1)	Chicago	12 Jun
	Roy O'Dell	USA		3.96	2)	Chicago	12 Jun
	Harry Smith	USA		3.96	1)	Los Angeles	19 Jun
	Edwin Myers	USA	96	3.96	2)	Philadelphia	05 Jul
	Frank Wirsig	USA		3.96	1T)	Lawrence, KS	17 Apr
	Frank Potts	USA		3.96	1T)	Lawrence, KS	17 Apr
	J.C.Carter	USA		3.96	1T)	Lawrence, KS	17 Apr
1927	Sabin Carr	USA	04	4.26	1)	Philadelphia	28 May
	Lee Barnes	USA	06	4.20	2)	Philadelphia	28 May
	R.Ward Edmonds	USA		4.12	3)	Philadelphia	28 May
	E. Jack Williams	USA	07	4.11	1T)	Los Angeles	26 Feb
	Frank Wirsig	USA		4.07	1)	Lincoln, NE	21 May
	Xavier Boyles	USA	03	4.05	1)	Iowa City, IA	14 May
	Harold McAtee	USA		4.05	1)	East Lansing, MI	04 Jun
	Charles McGinnis	USA	06	4.04i	1T)	Madison, WI	28 May
	William Droegemuller	USA	06	4.04i	1T)	Madison, WI	28 May
	Clifford Young	USA		4.01	1)	Houston	21 May
	Extra Trial:						
	Earl White	USA	05	4.04	-)	Houston	26 Mar
	Exhibition / Pro:						
	Charles Hoff	Nor	02	4.21i	-)	Brooklyn, NY	26 Mar
1928	Lee Barnes	USA	06	4.30	1)	Fresno, CA	28 Apr
	Sabin Carr	USA	04	4.29i	1)	New York	25 Feb
	R.Ward Edmonds	USA		4.26	2)	Fresno, CA	28 Apr
	William Droegemuller	USA	06	4.19	2)	Cambridge, MA	07 Jul
	Frederic Sturdy	USA	08	4.11	1T)	Travers Island, NY	02 Jun
	E. Jack Williams	USA	07	4.11	1T)	Missoula, MT	02 Jun
	Frank Wirsig	USA		4.11	1)	New York	16 Jun
	Charles McGinnis	USA	06	4.11	1)	Detroit	01 Jul
	Victor Pickard	Can	03	4.11	2)	London	11 Aug
	Lowell Allen	USA		4.04	1)	Chicago	02 Jun
	Paul Harrington	USA		4.04i	1)	Boston	04 Feb
	Ross O'Dell	USA		4.04	1)	Birmingham, AL	12 May
1929	Frederic Sturdy	USA	08	4.26i	1)	New York	18 Feb
	Victor Pickard	Can	03	4.21i	2)	New York	18 Feb
	E. Jack Williams	USA	07	4.21	1)	Palo Alto	06 Apr
	Ward Edmonds	USA		4.19	1T)	Philadelphia	01 Jun
	Tom Warne	USA	09	4.18	1T)	Chicago	08 Jun
	Henry Canby	USA	08	4.15i	1)	Iowa City	09 Mar
	Vern McDermont	USA	06	4.14	1T)	Evanston	25 May
	Shuhei Nishida	Jap	10	4.10	1)	Seoul	17 Oct
	Lucio A.Prado de Castro	Bra	10	4.09	1)	São Paulo	17 Nov
	Bernard Berlinger	USA	08	4.08i	2)	New York	02 Mar
	George Otterness	USA		4.08	1T)	Lawrence	20 Apr
	Harold McAtee	USA		4.08	1)	Denver	03 Jul
	Professional:						
	Charles Hoff	Nor	02	4.28	-)	Trondheim	06 Oct

1930	Tom Warne	USA	09	4.24	1)	Columbus	03 May
	Vern McDermont	USA	06	4.22	1)	Evanston	24 May
	Frederic Sturdy	USA	08	4.19i	1)	New York	18 Mar
	Henry Canby	USA	08	4.15i	1)	Minneapolis	08 Mar
	Shuhei Nishida	Jap	10	4.15	1)	Koshien	01 Jun
	William Hubbard	USA	13	4.11	1)	Berkeley	29 Mar
	Oscar Sutermeister	USA	12	4.11	1)	Cambridge, MA	31 May
	Henry Lindblad	Swe	06	4.10	1)	Stockholm	11 Jul
	Glenn Graham	USA	04	4.06	1)	Los Angeles	15 Feb
	John Wonsowicz	USA	10	4.06	1)	Columbus	02 May
	Lowell Allen	USA		4.06	3)	Pittsburgh	23 Aug
	Marvin Harvey	USA		4.06	4)	Pittsburgh	23 Aug
	Professional:						
	Charles Hoff	Nor	02	4.20	-)	Oslo	23 May
1931	William Graber	USA	11	4.28	1)	Philadelphia	30 May
	Frederic Sturdy	USA	08	4.24i	1)	New York	25 Feb
	Everett Colyer	USA		4.23i	1)	Boston	21 Feb
	Vern McDermont	USA	06	4.22	1T)	Chicago	06 Jun
	Tom Warne	USA	09	4.22	1T)	Chicago	06 Jun
	Lee Barnes	USA	06	4.21	1T)	Berkeley	28 Mar
	George Pool	USA	09	4.21	1T)	Berkeley	28 Mar
	George Jefferson	USA	10	4.19	1T)	Fresno	09 May
	Bernard Berlinger	USA	08	4.17i	1T)	New York	07 Mar
	Clyde Coffman	USA	11	4.15	1)	Lawrence	11 Apr
	Professional:						
	Charles Hoff	Nor	02	4.32	-)	Hönefoss	27 Sep
1932	William Graber	USA	11	4.37	1)	Palo Alto	16 Jul
	William Miller	USA	10	4.31	1)	Los Angeles	03 Aug
	Shuhei Nishida	Jap	10	4.30	2)	Los Angeles	03 Aug
	Keith Brown	USA	13	4.26i	1)	Boston	13 Feb
	Theodore Lee	USA	10	4.23i	1)	Ithaca	12 Mar
	George Jefferson	USA	10	4.22	3T)	Palo Alto	16 Jul
	Don Zimmerman	USA		4.22	3T)	Palo Alto	16 Jul
	Frederic Sturdy	USA	08	4.22	3T)	Palo Alto	16 Jul
	Bernard Deacon	USA	11	4.22	3T)	Palo Alto	16 Jul
	George Pool	USA	09	4.21	1T)	Berkeley	21 May
	Bryce Beecher	USA	10	4.21	1T)	Chicago	11 Jun
	Irving Seely	USA	13	4.21	1T)	Chicago	11 Jun
	Lee Barnes	USA	06	4.21	1)	Los Angeles	18 Jun
	Wirt Thompson	USA	11	4.21	1T)	Berkeley	02 Jul
	Jump-off:						
	Theodore Lee	USA	10	4.26i	-)	Boston	13 Feb
	George Jefferson	USA	10	4.25	-)	Palo Alto	16 Jul
1933	William Graber	USA	11	4.32	1)	Los Angeles	06 May
	Keith Brown	USA	13	4.31i	1)	New York	15 Mar
	William Miller	USA	10	4.26	1)	Palo Alto	04 Mar
	Wirt Thompson	USA	11	4.26i	2)	New York	15 Mar
	Matthew Gordy	USA	09	4.26	1T)	Chicago	30 Jun
	Estel Lennington	USA		4.21i	1)	Chicago	11 Mar
	John Wonsowicz	USA	10	4.21	3)	Chicago	30 Jun
	Bernard Deacon	USA	11	4.21	1)	Berkeley	15 Apr
	Sueo Oe	Jap	14	4.20	1)	Nishinomiya	27 May
	Shuhei Nishida	Jap	10	4.20	1)	Tokyo	11 Jun
1934	Keith Brown	USA	13	4.37i	1)	New York	15 Feb
	Bernard Deacon	USA	11	4.33	1)	Palo Alto	10 Mar
	Wirt Thompson	USA	11	4.29i	1)	Ithaca, N .Y.	24 Feb
	William Graber	USA	11	4.28	1T)	Santa Barbara	28 Apr
	William Sefton	USA	15	4.28	1T)	Santa Barbara	28 Apr
	Jack Rand	USA		4.28	1)	Los Angeles	23 Jun
	Shuhei Nishida	Jap	10	4.25	1)	Nishinomiya	21 Oct
	Ray Lowry	USA		4.22	1)	East Lansing	19 May

Year	Name	Nat	Born	Mark	Place	Venue	Date
	William Miller	USA	10	4.21	1)	Palo Alto	10 Mar
	Sueo Oe	Jap	14	4.20	1)	Tokyo	02 Sep
1935	Keith Brown	USA	13	4.39	1)	Cambridge, MA	01 Jun
	Earle Meadows	USA	13	4.36	1)	Palo Alto	04 May
	William Sefton	USA	15	4.35	1)	Budapest	20 Aug
	Shuhei Nishida	Jap	10	4.30	1)	Budapest	17 Aug
	William Roy	USA		4.29	1)	Alexandria, LA	11 May
	Cornelius Warmerdam	USA	15	4.29	1)	Fresno	20 Apr
	Bernard Deacon	USA	11	4.26	1)	Los Angeles	30 Mar
	William Graber	USA	11	4.26	1T)	Princeton	15 Jun
	Sueo Oe	Jap	14	2.25	1)	Tokyo	16 Jun
	Jack Mauger	USA	12	4.24	1)	Berkeley	20 Apr
	Exhibition / Extra Trial:						
	William Sefton	USA	15	4.35	-)	Fresno	11 May
	Jump-off:						
	William Graber	USA	11	4.34	-)	Princeton	15 Jun
1936	George Varoff	USA	14	4.43	1)	Princeton	04 Jul
	Earle Meadows	USA	13	4.37	1)	Los Angeles	18 Apr
	Albert Haller	USA	16	4.37	1)	Madison	16 May
	William Graber	USA	11	4.35	1)	Helsinki	18 Aug
	David Weichert	USA		4.34	1)	Cambridge, MA	27 Jun
	William Sefton	USA	15	4.34	1T)	Los Angeles	27 Jun
	Sueo Oe	Jap	14	4.34	1)	Tokyo	26 Apr
	Corlnelius Warmerdam	USA	15	4.31	1)	Fresno	16 May
	Shuhei Nishida	Jap	10	4.30	1)	Colombes	23 Aug
	Jack Rand	USA		4.26	)	San Diego	14 Mar
	Loring Day	USA	15	4.26	)	Los Angeles	02 May
	Bernard Deacon	USA	11	4.26	2)	Cambridge, Ma	27 Jun
1937	William Sefton	USA	15	4.54	1)	Los Angeles	29 May
	Earle Meadows	USA	13	4.54	2)	Los Ageles	29 May
	Cornelius Warmerdam	USA	15	4.46	2)	Milwaukee	03 Jul
	George Varoff	USA	14	4.46	4)	Milwaukee	03 Jul
	Jack Mauger	USA	12	4.37	1)	Palo Alto	22 May
	Sueo Oe	Jap	14	4.35	1)	Nishinomiya	26 Sep
	Oscar Sutermeister	USA	12	4.26i	4)	Boston	13 Feb
	Dick Ganslen	USA	17	4.26i	3)	New York	27 Feb
	Albert Haller	USA	16	4.26i	3)	Chicago	06 Mar
	William Harding	USA	15	4.26i	2)	New York	17 Mar
	Kenneth Dills	USA	15	4.26	3)	Palo Alto	22 May
	Nikolay Ozolin	USSR	06	4.26	1)	Moskva	17 Jun
1938	Loring Day	USA	15	4.44	1)	Los Angeles	23 Apr
	Cornelius Warmerdam	USA	15	4.42	1)	Compton	20 May
	Earle Meadows	USA	13	4.42	1)	Princeton	18 Jun
	George Varoff	USA	14	4.38	1)	Milano	11 Sep
	Kenneth Dills	USA	15	4.37	2)	Los Angeles	23 Apr
	Nikolay Ozolin	USSR	06	4.29	1)	Kiev	02 Oct
	Ralph Ross	USA	16	4.26	1)	West Point, NY	23 Apr
	William Harding	USA	15	4.26	3)	Princeton	18 Jun
	Dick Ganslen	USA	17	4.26	4T)	Buffalo	03 Jul
	B. F. Bryan	USA		4.26	1)	Lawrence	23 Apr
1939	Earle Meadows	USA	13	4.44	1)	Compton	02 Jun
	Cornelius Warmerdam	USA	15	4.42i	1)	Boston	11 Feb
	Loring Day	USA	15	4.39	1)	Los Angeles	08 Apr
	Dick Ganslen	USA	17	4.39	1)	Los Angeles	17 Jun
	Gedorge Varoff	USA	14	4.37	1T)	Eugene	22 Apr
	Rod Hansen	USA		4.37	1T)	Eugene	22 Apr
	Robert Cassels	USA		4.33	1)	Ann Arbor	20 May
	Ralph Ross	USA	16	4.31	1)	West Point, NY	22 Apr
	B. F. Bryan	USA		4.31	1)	Lawrence	22 Apr
	Milton Padway	USA	17	4.31	2T)	Los Angeles	17 Jun

Year	Name	Nat	Born	Mark	Pos	Venue	Date
1940	Cornelius Warmerdam	USA	15	4.60	1)	Fresno	29 Jun
	Earle Meadows	USA	13	4.47	1)	Los Angeles	13 Apr
	Kenneth Dills	USA	15	4.47	1)	Compton	07 Jun
	Guinn Smith	USA	20	4.38	2)	Berkeley	18 May
	Dick Ganslen	USA	17	4.37	1)	Travers Island, NY	08 Jun
	Ralph Ross	USA	16	4.32	1)	Philadelphia	27 Apr
	Bernard Deacon	USA	11	4.31	2T)	Berkeley	13 Apr
	Earl Stolberg	USA	18	4.30	1)	Milwaukee	18 May
	B. F. Bryan	USA		4.26	1)	Des Moines	27 Apr
	Carl Clark	USA	18	4.26	1)	Salt Lake City	18 May
	Milton Padway	USA	17	4.26i	2)	New York	03 Feb
	Thomas Lassen	USA	18	4.26i	2)	Boston	10 Feb
	George Hoffman	USA		4.26	2)	Fresno	11 May
	Robert Kenyon	USA		4.26	2T)	Los Angeles	25 May

ALL TIME WORLD LIST AS AT THE END OF 1940

Name	Nat	Born	Mark	Pos	Venue	Date
Cornelius Warmerdam	USA	15	4.60	1)	Fresno	29 Jun 40
Bill Sefton	USA	15	4.54	1)	Los Angeles	29 Jun 37
Earle Meadows	USA	13	4.54	2)	Los Angeles	29 Jun 37
Kenneth Dills	USA	15	4.47	1)	Compton	07 Jun 40
George Varoff	USA	14	4.46	4)	Milwaukee	03 Jul 37
Loring Day	USA	15	4.44	1)	Los Angeles	23 Apr 38
Keith Brown	USA	13	4.39	1)	Cambridge, MA	01 Jun 35
Dick Ganslen	USA	17	4.39	1)	Los Angeles	17 Jun 39
Guinn Smith	USA	20	4.38	2)	Berkeley	18 May 40
William Graber	USA	11	4.37	1)	Palo Alto	16 Jul 32
Albert Haller	USA	16	4.37	1)	Madison	16 May 36
Jack Mauger	USA	12	4.37	1)	Palo Alto	22 May 37
Rod Hansen	USA		4.37	1T)	Eugene	22 Apr 39

Year	Name	Nat	Born	Mark	Pos	Venue	Date
1941	Cornelius Warmerdam	USA	15	4.71	1)	Compton	06 Jun
	Earle Meadows	USA	13	4.44i	1)	New York	08 Mar
	Guinn Smith	USA	20	4.43	1)	Fresno	17 May
	Willard Schaefer	USA	18	4.42	1)	Los Angeles	26 Apr
	Kenneth Dills	USA	15	4.41i	1)	Chicago	22 Mar
	Dick Ganslen	USA	17	4.41i	2)	Chicago	22 Mar
	Harold Hunt	USA	20	4.31	1T)	Palo Alto	21 Jun
	Howard Jensen	USA		4.26i	1)	Boston	25 Jan
	Milton Padway	USA	17	4.26i	3)	New York	08 Mar
	Luther Nichols	USA		4.26	1T)	Berkeley	31 May
1942	Cornelius Warmerdam	USA	15	4.77	1)	Modesto	23 May
	Willard Schaefer	USA	18	4.42	1)	Fresno	16 May
	A. Richmond Morcom	USA	21	4.37i	1)	New York	07 Mar
	Earle Meadows	USA	13	4.37i	2)	Boston	14 Feb
	Jack DeField	USA	17	4.37	2)	New York	20 Jun
	Guinn Smith	USA	20	4.36	1)	Long Beach	21 Mar
	Harold Hunt	USA	20	4.30	1)	Indianapolis	14 Mar
	Bunkichi Sawada	Jap	21	4.30	1)	Dairen	13 Aug
	Luther Nichols	USA		4.26	)		
	Irving Moore	USA	22	4.26	2)	Berkeley	02 May
	Truman Ford	USA		4.26i	2)	New York	07 Mar
1943	Cornelius Warmerdam	USA	15	4.78i	1)	Chicago	20 Mar
	Irving Moore	USA	22	4.42	2)	San Francisco	17 Jul
	A.Richmond Morcom	USA	21	4.37i	1)	Boston	13 Feb
	Jack DeField	USA	17	4.30i	2T)	Chicago	20 Mar
	Harold Hunt	USA	20	4.30i	2T)	Chicago	20 Mar
	Dick Ganslen	USA	17	4.28	)	Des Moines	24 Apr
	William Moore	USA	24	4.26i	2T)	New York	27 Feb
	Keith Groswird	USA		4.21	2)	Evanston	12 Jun
	Nikolay Ozolin	SU	06	4.15	1)	Gorkiy	Sep
	Jan Bém	Cze	17	4.15	1)	Praha	03 Oct

Year	Athlete	Nation	Born	Mark	Place	Venue	Date
1944	Cornelius Warmerdam	USA	15	4.57	1)	New York	18 Jun
	Jack DeField	USA	17	4.29i	2)	Chicago	18 Mar
	Milton Pasway	USA	17	4.26i	1T)	New York	05 Feb
	Nikolay Ozolin	SU	06	4.20	)		
	John Schmidt	USA		4.11i	3)	New York	05 Feb
	Philip Lansing	USA	23	4.11i	1)	New York	19 Feb
	Robert Phelps	USA	23	4.11i	1T)	Chicago	11 Mar
	Keith Groswird	USA		4.11i	)	Cleveland	24 Mar
	Dick Vanderhoof	USA	25	4.11	1)	Los Angeles	13 May
	Del Smith	USA		4.10	1)	Glendale, CA	20 May
	Erling Kaas	Nor	17	4.10	1)	Bollnås	20 Jul
	Birger Hultqvist	Swe	20	4.10	1)	Stockholm	04 Aug
	Exhibition:						
	Earle Meadows	USA	13	4.26	-)		
	Erling Kaas	Nor	17	4.20	-)	Stockhlm	
1945	William Moore	USA	24	4.26	1)	Des Moines, IA	28 Apr
	Robert Phelps	USA	23	4.24i	1T)	Cleveland	23 Mar
	Milton Padway	USA	17	4.21i	1)	New York	17 Feb
	John Schmidt	USA		4.21	)		
	Ray Kring	USA		4.16	1)	Modesto, CA	02 Jun
	Nikolay Ozolin	SU	06	4.15	1)	Moskva	12 Aug
	Rex Felton	USA	23	4.14	)		
	Phil Lansing	USA	23	4.11i	2)	New York	17 Feb
	Irving Moore	USA	22	4.11	1)	Laredo, TX	09 Mar
	Fred Win ter	USA		4.11	1T)	Austin	07 Apr
	John Montgomery	USA	21	4.11	2)	Philadelphia	28 Apr
	Dick Vanderhoof	USA	25	4.11	)		
	A.Richmond Morcom	USA	21	4.11	1T)	New York	30 Jun
1946	Irving Moore	USA	22	4.38	1)	San Antonio	29 Jun
	Guinn Smith	USA	20	4.31	2)	San Antonio	29 Jun
	Fred Winter	USA		4.27	1)	Pasadena, CA	31 May
	Howard Jensen	USA	26	4.26i	1)	Boston	09 Feb
	Bob Hart	USA		4.26	1T)	Compton, CA	07 Jun
	William Moore	USA	24	4.23i	1)	Chicago	16 Mar
	Erling Kaas	Nor	17	4.21	1)	Bergen	07 Sep
	Allan Lindberg	Swe	18	4.20	1)	Praha	20 Sep
	Ray Kring	USA		4.19	2T)	Los Angeles	25 May
	Bob Richards	USA	26	4.16i	1T)	Chicago	30 Mar
	Jan Bém	Cze	17	4.16	1)	Praha	24 Jul
	Lars Andrén	Swe	18	4.16	1)	Luleå	17 Aug
1947	Guinn Smith	USA	20	4.45	1)	Modesto, CA	24 May
	Bob Richards	USA	26	4.35i	1)	Ann Arbor, MI	17 May
	A.Richmond Morcom	USA	21	4.34i	1)	Cleveland	28 Mar
	Earle Meadows	USA	13	4.34	2)	Los Angeles	23 May
	Tom Bennett	USA		4.33i	1)	Iowa City	24 May
	George Rsmussen	USA	28	4.31	1)	Eugene	17 May
	Ray Maggard	USA		4.28	1)	Los Angeles	31 May
	William Moore	USA	24	4.28	1)	Evanston, IL	03 May
	John Montgomery	USA	21	4.27	D)	Alhambra, CA	11 Jul
	Bob Hart	USA		4.26	1T)	Los Angeles	03 May
	Ray Kring	USA		4.26	2T)	Fresno, CA	17 May
	Fred Winter	USA		4.26	2T)	Fresno, CA	17 May
	Exhibition:						
	Cornelius Warmerdam	USA	15	4.37	-)	Palo Alto, CA	19 Apr
1948	A.Richmond Morcom	USA	21	4.47	1)	Evanston, IL	10 Jul
	Guinn Smith	USA	20	4.47	2)	Evanston, IL	10 Jul
	Bob Richards	USA	26	4.42	3)	Evanston, IL	10 Jul
	Earle Meadows	USA	13	4.42i	1)	New York	06 Mar
	John Montgomery	USA	21	4.37	4)	Evanston, IL	10 Jul
	Ragnar Lundberg	Swe	24	4.36	1)	Södertälje	26 Sep
	Don Cooper	USA	26	4.33i	1)	Lincoln, NE	14 Feb

	George Rasmussen	USA	28	4.33	1)	Missoula, MT	22 May
	Erling Kaas	Nor	17	4.31	1)	Oslo	04 Jul
	Harry Cooper	USA	24	4.30	1)	Iowa City	15 May
	Exhibition:						
	Bob Hart	USA		4.39	-)	Compton, CA	04 Jun
1949	Bob Richards	USA	26	4.50	1)	Oslo	29 Jul
	A.Richmond Morcom	USA	21	4.49i	1)	Cleveland	18 Mar
	Harry Cooper	USA	24	4.45i	2T)	Chicago	19 Mar
	John Montgomery	USA	21	4.45	1T)	Inglewood, CA	04 Jun
	George Rasmussen	USA	28	4.42	1)	Klammath Falls, OR	30 Apr
	Tom Bennett	USA		4.35i	4T)	Chicago	19 Mar
	Jack Christopher	USA		4.35i	4T)	Chicago	19 Mar
	Walt Jensen	USA	28	4.35	1)	Modesto, CA	08 Apr
	Bobby Smith	USA	29	4.34	2T)	Compton, CA	03 Jun
	Don Laz	USA	29	4.31	1)	Milwaukee	04 Jun
	Martin Korik	USA		4.31	1)	Gainesville, FL	26 Mar
1950	Bob Richards	USA	26	4.56i	1)	New York	28 Jan
	Don Laz	USA	29	4.42i	2)	New York	28 Jan
	Ragnar Lundberg	Swe	24	4.40	1)	Göteborg	10 Aug
	Bobby Smith	USA	29	4.39	1)	Tempe, AZ	21 Apr
	Bill Carroll	USA	26	4.39	1)	Lawrence, KS	22 Apr
	George Mattos	USA	29	4.39	1)	San Jose, CA	22 Apr
	John Montgomery	USA	21	4.37	1)	Fresno, CA	13 May
	Walt Jensen	USA	28	4.37	3)	Modesto, CA	20 May
	George Rasmussen	USA	28	4.37	1)	Berkeley, CA	27 May
	Don Cooper	USA	26	4.30	1)	Hälsingborg	13 Aug
	Armin Scheurer	Swz	17	4.30	D)	Bruxelles	25 Aug
	Exhibition / Intrasquad meeting:						
	Don Laz	USA	29	4.57i	-)	Champaign, IL	21 Jan
1951	Bob Richards	USA	29	4.69i	1)	Chicago	17 Mar
	Don Laz	USA	29	4.61	1)	Los Angeles	21 Apr
	Don Cooper	USA	26	4.57	1)	Lawrence, KA	21 Apr
	Walt Jensen	USA	28	4.42	1)	Los Angeles	08 Jun
	Pyotr Denisenko	SU	20	4.37	1)	Kiev	05 Sep
	Bobby Smith	USA	29	4.36	1)	San Diego	21 Apr
	Richard Coleman	USA		4.34i	2)	Champaign, IL	03 Mar
	Leroy Poucher	USA		4.34	1)	Birmingham, AL	19 May
	Torfi Bryngeirsson	Ice		4.32	1)	Stockholm	03 Jul
	Richard Shivers	USA		4.31	1)	Los Angeles	28 Apr
1952	Bob Richards	USA	26	4.69i	1)	Milwaukee	01 Feb
	Don Laz	USA	29	4.59i	2)	Milwaukee	01 Feb
	Don Cooper	USA	26	4.49	1)	Fresno	10 May
	George Mattos	USA	29	4.47	1)	Amsterdam	10 Aug
	Ragner Lundberg	Swe	24	4.44	1)	Gävle	01 Aug
	Pyotr Denisenko	SU	20	4.42	1)	Kiev	11 Jun
	Richard Coleman	USA		4.39i	1)	Champaign, IL	01 Mar
	Bobby Smith	USA	29	4.37	3)	Fresno	10 May
	Jack Rowan	USA		4.37	3)	Los Angeles	16 May
	Torfi Bryngeirsson	Ice		4.35	2)	Gävle	01 Aug
1953	Bob Richards	USA	26	4.68i	1)	New York	07 Feb
	Don Laz	USA	29	4.61i	2)	Cleveland	20 Mar
	Fred Barnes	USA	28	4.47	1)	Modesto	16 May
	George Mattos	USA	29	4.47	2)	Compton	05 Jun
	Pyotr Denisenko	SU	20	4.44	1)	Kiev	31 Jun
	Bobby Smith	USA	29	4.37	1)	Fresno	09 May
	Ragnar Lundberg	Swe	24	4,35	2)	Stockholm	02 Jul
	James Harrington	USA		4.34	1)	Notre Dame	07 Mar
	Richard Shivers	USA		4.34	1T)	San Diego	01 May
	Ray Kring	USA		4.31		Stockton, CA	13 Jun
	Len Eilers	USA	32	4.31	1)	Los Angeles	11 Apr

Year	Name	Nat	Born	Mark	Place	Venue	Date
	Dave Kenly	USA		4.31	2)	Lincoln	20 Jun
	Valto Olenius	Fin		4.31	2)	Tampere	06 Jul
	Milan Milakov	Yug	30	4.31	1)	Dortmund	14 Aug
	Vitaliy Chernobay	SU		4.31		Kiev	Oct
1954	Bob Richards	USA	26	4.66	1)	St. Louis	19 Jun
	Don Laz	USA	29	4.62	1)	Columbus	17 Apr
	Jerry Welbourn	USA	32	4.49i	1)	New York	20 Feb
	Bobby Smith	USA	29	4.48	2)	St. Louis	19 Jun
	Pyotr Denisenko	SU	20	4.46	1)	Kiev	13 Sep
	Earl Poucher	USA	34	4.45	1)	Auburn, AL	24 Apr
	Don Bragg	USA	35	4.42i	2)	New York	20 Feb
	Fred Barnes	USA	28	4.42	1)	Fresno	23 Apr
	Ali Albov	SU		4.40	1)	Charkov	Aug
	Eeles Landström	Fin	32	4.40	1)	Bern	28 Aug
	Ragnar Lundberg	Swe	24	4.40	2)	Bern	28 Aug
	Viktor Knyazev	SU		4.40	2)	Kiev	13 Sep
	Vladimir Bulatov	SU	29	4.40	3)	Kiev	13 Sep
1955	Bob Richards	USA	26	4.70i	1)	Philadelphia	21 Jan
	Don Bragg	USA	35	4.59	1)	Los Angeles	18 Jun
	Don Laz	USA	29	4.57i	1T)	Chicago	26 Mar
	Bobby Smith	USA	29	4.54	1)	Los Angeles	05 Feb
	Jerry Welbourn	USA	32	4.52i	2)	Boston	29 Jan
	Earl Poucher	USA	34	4.52i	2)	New York	12 Feb
	Ron Morris	USA	35	4.51	1)	Palo Alto	10 May
	Walt Levack	USA	34	4.51	1)	Palo Alto	10 May
	Eeles Landström	Fin	32	4.50	1)	Helsinki	24 Aug
	Ragnar Lundberg	Swe	24	4.45	1)	Bucuresti	02 Oct
1956	Don Bragg	USA	35	4.70i	1)	New York	03 Mar
	Bob Richards	USA	26	4.70	1T)	Santa Ana, CA	27 Oct
	Bob Gutowski	USA	35	4.70	1T)	Santa Ana, CA	27 Oct
	Jerry Welbourn	USA	32	4.57i	1)	Chicago	24 Mar
	Ron Morris	USA	35	4.57	1T)	Compton	01 Jun
	Georges Mattos	USA	29	4.53	3)	Los Angeles	30 Jun
	Don Laz	USA	29	4.52i	3T)	Philadelphia	20 Jan
	Earl Poucher	USA	34	4.52i	3)	New York	18 Feb
	Eeles Landström	Fin	32	4.51	1)	Hamburg	23 Sep
	Georgios Roubanis	Gre	29	4.50	3)	Melbourne	26 Nov
1957	Bob Gutowski	USA	35	4.82	1)	Austin	15 Jun
	Bob Richards	USA	26	4.72i	1T)	New York	09 Feb
	Don Bragg	USA	35	4.66i	1)	Chicago	
	Ron Morris	USA	35	4.63	1)	Palo Alto	13 Apr
	Joe Rose	USA	33	4.59	1)	Tempe	12 Apr
	Jim Brewer	USA	38	4.57	1)	Phoenix	17 May
	Georgios Roubanis	Gre	29	4.55	1)	Athinai	07 Jul
	Manfred Preussger	EG	32	4.52	1)	Potsdam	19 May
	Vitaliy Chernobay	SU	29	4.52	1)	Odessa	30 Sep
	Eeles Landström	Fin	32	4.50	1)	Helsinki	01 Jul
	Vladimir Bulatov	SU	29	4.50	1)	Moskva	13 Jul
	Exhibition:						
	Georgios Roubanis	Gre	29	4.59	-)	San Diego	23 Mar
1958	Bob Gutowski	USA	35	4.68	1)	Compton	06 Jun
	Ron Morris	USA	35	4.65	1)	Athinai	10 Aug
	Don Bragg	USA	35	4.64i			
	Georgios Roubanis	Gre	29	4.60	1)	München	12 Jul
	Jerry Welbourn	USA	32	4.57i			
	Eeles Landström	Fin	32	4.57	1)	Helsinki	16 Jul
	Mel Schwarz	USA	34	4.56	1)	Columbus	19 Apr
	Jim Brewer	USA	38	4.56	1)	Tempe	30 May
	Vladimir Bulatov	SU	29	4.56	1)	Nalchik	02 May
	Manfred Preussger	EG	32	4.56	1)	Leipzig	26 Jul

Year	Name	Nat	Born	Mark	Pos	Venue	Date
1959	Don Bragg	USA	35	4.81i	1)	Philadelphia	13 Feb
	Aubrey Dooley	USA	37	4.70	1T)	Norman, OK	19 May
	Jim Graham	USA	35	4.70	1T)	Norman, OK	19 May
	Bob Gutowski	USA	35	4.69i	2)	Washington, D.C.	24 Jan
	J. D. Martin	USA	39	4.66	3)	Norman, OK	19 May
	Ron Morris	USA	35	4.65	2)	Boulder	20 Jun
	Mel Schwarz	USA	34	4.65	4)	Boulder	20 Jun
	Vladimir Bulatov	SU	29	4.64	2)	Philadelphia	18 Jul
	Jänis Krasovskis	SU	36	4.58	1)	Yalta	03 Oct
	Joe Rose	USA	33	4.57	1)	Tempe	23 May
	George Mattos	USA	29	4.57	3T)	Modesto	30 May
	Gerhard Jeitner	EG	33	4.57	1)	Leipzig	10 Oct
1960	Don Bragg	USA	35	4.80	1)	Palo Alto	02 Jul
	J. D. Martin	USA	39	4.75i	1)	Kansas City	27 Feb
	Bob Gutowski	USA	35	4.72i	2)	Milwaukee	12 Mar
	Ron Morris	USA	35	4.70	2)	Palo Alto	02 Jul
	Jim Graham	USA	35	4.65	1)	Fayetteville	16 Apr
	Jan Krasovskis	SU	36	4.65	1)	Moskva	17 Jul
	Dave Clark	USA	36	4.65	3)	Palo Alto	02 Jul
	Henry Wadsworth	USA	37	4.65	4)	Palo Alto	02 Jul
	Manfred Preussger	EG	32	4.65	1)	Magdeburg	10 Aug
	Aubrey Dooley	USA	37	4.63	1)	Stillwater	04 May

The following marks could not be listed, since the crossbar was placed in a way to benefit the competitors contrary to the rules:

Name	Nat	Born	Mark	Pos	Venue	Date
J. D. Martin	USA	39	4.82	1)	Norman, OK	12 Apr
Jim Graham	USA	35	4.67	2)	Norman, OK	12 Apr

ALL TIME WORLD LISTS AS AT THE END OF 1960

Name	Nat	Born	Mark	Pos	Venue	Date
Bob Gutowski	USA	35	4.82	1)	Austin	15 Jun 57
Don Bragg	USA	35	4.81i	1)	Philadelphia	13 Feb 59
Cornelius Warmerdam	USA	15	4.78i	1)	Chicago	20 Mar 43
J. D. Martin	USA	39	4.75i	1)	Kansas City	27 Feb 60
Bob Richards	USA	26	4.72i	1T)	New York	09 Feb 57
Ron Morris	USA	35	4.70	2)	Palo Alto	02 Jul 60
Aubrey Dooley	USA	37	4.70	1T)	Norman, OK	19 May 59
Jim Graham	USA	35	4.70	1T)	Norman, OK	19 May 59
Don Laz	USA	29	4.65i	1)	Washington	12 Jan 52
Janis Krasovskis	SU	36	4.65	1)	Moskva	17 Jul 60
Mel Schwarz	USA	34	4.65	4)	Boulder	20 Jun 59
Dave Clark	USA	36	4.65	3)	Palo Alto	02 Jul 60
Henry Wadsworth	USA	37	4.65	4)	Palo Alto	02 Jul 60
Manfred Preussger	EG	32	4.65	1)	Magdeburg	10 Aug 60

Year	Name	Nat	Born	Mark	Pos	Venue	Date
1961	George Davies	USA	40	4.83	1)	Boulder	20 May
	Ron Morris	USA	35	4.77	1)	New York	25 Jun
	Don Bragg	USA	35	4.76i	1)	New York	03 Mar
	John Uelses	USA	37	4.73=	1)	New Orleans	31 Dec
	Henry Wadsworth	USA	37	4.70i	2)	Milwaukee	11 Mar
	Rolando Cruz	PR	39	4.70	1)	Mayagüez	15 Jul
	Manfred Preussger	EG	32	4.70	1)	Magdeburg	14 Oct
	Dick Gear	USA	38	4.67	1T)	Philadelphia	17 Jun
	Jim Brewer	USA	38	4.67	1T)	Philadelphia	17 Jun
	John Cramer	USA	41	4.67	4)	New York	25 Jun

= Made outdoors from a board runway.

Year	Name	Nat	Born	Mark	Pos	Venue	Date
1962	Pentti Nikula	Fin	39	4.94	1)	Kauhava	22 Jun
	Dave Tork	USA	34	4.93	1)	Walnut, CA	28 Apr
	Don Meyers	USA	40	4.91i	1)	Chicago	20 Dec
	Ron Morris	USA	35	4.90	1)	Helsinki	21 Aug
	John Uelses	USA	37	4.89	1)	Santa Barbara	31 Mar
	Dick Plymale	USA	42	4.82	1)	West Point	19 May
	Manfred Preussger	EG	32	4.81	1)	Jena	22 Aug

Year	Name	Nation	Born	Mark	Place	Venue	Date
	John Cramer	USA	41	4.78	2)	Walnut, CA	23 Jun
	John Belitza	USA	40	4.78	4)	Walnut, CA	23 Jun
	Brian Sternberg	USA	43	4.77	1)	Vancouver	25 Aug
1963	John Pennel	USA	40	5.20	1)	Coral Gables	24 Aug
	Pentti Nikula	Fin	39	5.10i	1)	Pajulahti	02 Feb
	Brian Sternberg	USA	43	5.08	1)	Compton	07 Jun
	Ron Morris	USA	35	5.02	1)	Mikkeli	25 Aug
	Yang Chuan-Kwang	For	33	5.00	1)	Bremerhaven	20 Jul
	John Uelses	USA	37	4.95	2)	Warszawa	26 Jul
	Don Meyers	USA	40	4.94	1)	Fort Collins	25 May
	Dave Tork	USA	34	4.93i	1)	Toronto	25 Jan
	Wolfgang Reinhardt	WG	43	4.92	1)	Augsburg	10 Aug
	Warren Brattlof	USA	43	4.91	1)	Houston	08 Jun
1964	Fred Hansen	USA	40	5.28	1)	Los Angeles	25 Jul
	Manfred Preussger	EG	32	5.15	1)	Leipzig	27 Aug
	Wolfgang Reinhardt	WG	43	5.11	1)	Leverkusen	04 Jul
	Don Meyers	USA	40	5.10	1)	Compton	05 Jun
	John Pennel	USA	40	5.09	2)	San Diego	13 Jun
	Dave Tork	USA	34	5.08	2)	New Brunswick	27 Jun
	Wlodzimierz Sokolowski	Pol	41	5.02	1)	Spala	12 Jul
	Wolfgang Nordwig	EG	43	5.01	1)	Berlin	24 Sep
	Mel Hein	USA	41	5.00	3)	San Diego	13 Jun
	Rudolf Tomasek	Cze	37	5.00	1)	Oslo	03 Sep
	Klaus Lehnertz	WG	38	5.00	3)	Tokyo	17 Oct
	Extra trial:						
	John Pennel	USA	40	5.18	-)	Los Angeles	29 Aug
1965	John Pennel	USA	40	5.18	1)	San Diego	26 Jun
	John Cramer	USA	41	5.06	1)	Lohja	22 Aug
	Paul Wilson	USA	47	5.05	1)	Westminster	20 Mar
	Wolfgang Nordwig	EG	43	5.05	1)	Potsdam	11 Aug
	Billy Pemelton	USA		5.03i	1)	Louisville	27 Feb
	Mel Hein	USA	41	5.02i	1)	San Francisco	26 Feb
	Wolfgang Reinhardt	WG	43	5.00i	1)	Kiel	23 Jan
	Rudolf Tomásek	Cze	37	5.00i	1)	Bratislava	05 Mar
	Gennadiy Bliznyetsov	SU	41	5.00	1)	Alma Ata	15 Oct
	Bob Seagren	USA	46	5.00i	2)	São Paulo	22 Oct
	Jeff Chase	USA	40	4.98	1)	Los Angeles	04 Jun
	Exhibition:						
	Jeff Chase	USA	40	5.05	-)	Wichita	23 Jul
1966	John Pennel	USA	40	5.35	1)	Pasadena	12 Jul
	Bob Seagren	USA	46	5.32	1)	Fresno	14 May
	Wolfgand Nordwig	EG	43	5.23	1)	Warszawa	14 Aug
	Sam Kirk	USA	42	5.20	3)	Walnut	09 Apr
	Paul Wilson	USA	47	5.20	1)	Los Angeles	07 May
	Gennadiy Bliznyetsov	SU	41	5.14	1)	Odessa	02 Jul
	Marc Savage	USA	45	5.10	1)	Palo Alto	16 Apr
	Hervé D'Encausse	Fra	43	5.10	1)	Berlin	10 Jul
	Dennis Phillips	USA	46	5.08	1)	Sacramento	11 Jun
	Klaus Lehnertz	WG	38	5.05	1)	Berlin	26 Jun
	Christos Papanicolaou	Gre	41	5.05	2)	Budapest	02 Sep
1967	Paul Wilson	USA	47	5.38	1)	Bakersfield	23 Jun
	Bob Seagren	USA	46	5.36	1)	San Diego	10 Jun
	Christos Papanicolaou	Gre	41	5.30	1)	Mexico City	17 Oct
	Hervé D'Encausse	Fra	43	5.28	1)	Manosque	09 Sep
	Dick Railsback	USA	46	5.20	1)	Eugene	20 May
	Gennadiy Bliznyetsov	SU	41	5.20	D)	Mexico City	19 Oct
	Jim Eshelman	USA	45	5.16	2)	Santa Barbara	25 Mar
	Wolffgang Nordwig	EG	43	5.15	1)	B.Blankenburg	09 Jul
	Igor Fyeld	SU	41	5.15	1)	Moskva	02 Aug
	Risto Ivanoff	Fin	45	5.15	1)	Pori	13 Aug

Year	Athlete	Nat	Born	Mark	Pos	Venue	Date
	Exhibition:						
	Dick Railsback	USA	46	5.28	-)	Los Angeles	15 Apr
	Rick Sloan	USA	46	5.20	-)	Los Angeles	15 Apr
	Irregularity (bar dislodged by rebounding rubber piece):						
	Hervé D'Encausse	Fra	43	5.33	-)	Bellac	11 Jun
1968	Bob Seagren	USA	46	5.41	1)	Soulth Lake Tahoe	12 Sep
	Claus Schiprowski	WG	42	5.40	2)	Mexico City	16 Oct
	Wolfgang Nordwig	Eg	43	5.40	3)	Mexico City	16 Oct
	Hervé D'Encausse	Fra	43	5.37	1)	St. Maur	05 Jun
	Christos Papanicolaou	Gre	41	5.35	4)	Mexico City	16 Oct
	John Pennel	USA	40	5.35	5)	Mexico City	16 Oct
	Jonathan Vaughn	USA	48	5.31	1)	Walnut	10 Aug
	Gennadiy Bliznyetsov	SU	41	5.30	6)	Mexico City	16 Oct
	Altti Alarotu	Fin	45	5.26	1)	Mikkeli	28 Jul
	Kjell Isaksson	Swe	48	5.25	1)	Mexico City	28 Sep
1969	John Pennel	USA	40	5.44	1)	Sacramento	21 Jun
	Bob Seagren	USA	46	5.40	1)	South Lake Tahoe	12 Sep
	Dick Railsback	USA	46	5.40	2)	South Lake Tahoe	12 Sep
	Wolfgang Nordwig	EG	43	5.35	1)	Turku	03 Jul
	Renato Dionisi	Ita	47	5.30	1)	Roma	17 May
	Casey Cardigan	USA	51	5.30	1)	Sacramento	14 Jun
	Erkki Mustkari	Fin	46	5.28	1)	Fresno	12 Apr
	Christos Papanicolaou	Gre	41	5.25	1)	Sofia	31 Aug
	Gennadiy Bliznyetsov	SU	41	5.25	1)	Donyetsk	17 Sep
	Heinfried Engel	WG	47	5.23i	1)	Barcelona	15 Feb
1970	Christos Papanicolaou	Gre	41	5.49	1)	Athinai	24 Oct
	Wolfgang Nordwig	EG	43	5.46	1)	Torino	03 Sep
	François Tracanelli	Fra	51	5.40	1)	Colombes	25 Jul
	Kjell Isaksson	Swe	48	5.37	1)	Victoria	20 Sep
	Jan Johnson	USA	50	5.36i	1)	Des Moines	20 Jun
	Renato Dionisi	Ita	47	5.35	1)	Roma	15 Jul
	John Pennel	USA	40	5.33	1)	Modesto	23 May
	Altti Alarotu	Fin	45	5.31	1)	Turku	01 Jul
	Dick Railsback	USA	46	5.30	1)	Norrköping	17 Aug
	Yuriy Khanafin	SU	46	5.25i	1)	Moskva	13 Feb
	Risto Ivanoff	Fin	45	5.25	2)	Helsinki	30 Jun
	Sam Caruthers	USA	48	5.25	1)	Colombes	08 Jul
1971	Kjell Isaksson	Swe	48	5.43	1)	Siena	19 Sep
	Wolfgeng Nordwig	EG	43	5.40i	1)	Sofia	14 Mar
	Yuriy Isakov	SU	49	5.36	1)	Rostov	23 Jun
	Dick Railsback	USA	46	5.35i	1)	New York	26 Feb
	Renato Dionisi	Ita	47	5.35i	1)	Genova	03 Mar
	Christos Papanicolaou	Gre	41	5.35	1)	Zagreb	05 Sep
	Dave Roberts	USA	51	5.34	1)	Seattle	19 Jun
	Jan Johnson	USA	50	5.33	1)	Cali	04 Aug
	Bob Seagren	USA	46	5.31i	1)	Los Angeles	16 Jan
	Hans-Jürgen Ziegler	WG	51	5.30	1)	Haiger	01 Sep
1972	Bob Seagren	USA	46	5.63	1)	Eugene	02 Jul
	Kjell Isakson	Swe	48	5.59	1)	El Paso	23 May
	Steve Smith	USA	51	5.50	2)	Eugene	02 Jul
	Jan Johnson	USA	50	5.50	3)	Eugene	02 Jul
	Wolfgang Nordwig	EG	43	5.50	1)	München	02 Sep
	Dave Roberts	USA	51	5.49	1)	Seattle	17 Jun
	Renato Dionisi	Ita	47	5.45	1)	Rovereto	25 Jun
	Antti Kalliomäki	Fin	47	5.41	1)	Joensuu	13 Aug
	Hans Lagerqvist	Swe	40	5.40i	2)	Grenoble	12 Mar
	Christos Papanicolaou	Ger	41	5.40	1)	Athinai	14 Jun
	Irregular mark:						
	François Tracanelli	Fra	51	5.43	-)	Vittel	18 Aug

Year	Name	Nat	Born	Mark	Pl	Venue	Date
1973	Steve Smith	USA	51	5.49i	1)	New York	26 Jan
	Antti Kalliomäki	Fin	47	5.47	1)	Hyvinkää	12 Aug
	François Tracanelli	Fra	51	5.42	1)	Moskva	17 Aug
	Yuriy Isakov	SU	49	5.41	1)	Moskva	12 Jul
	Renato Dionisi	Ita	47	5.40i	1)	Genova	28 Feb
	Hans-Jürgen Ziegler	WG	51	5.35i	2)	Rotterdam	10 Mar
	Wladyslaw Kozakiewicz	Pol	53	5.35	1)	Gdynia	12 Jul
	Dave Roberts	USA	51	5.33	1)	Houston	17 Mar
	Mike Cotton	USA	51	5.33	1)	Gainesville	18 Mar
	Bob Richards Jr.	USA	50	5.33	1)	Fresno	12 May
	Pawel Iwinski	Pol	49	5.33	1)	Warszawa	02 Jun
	Don Baird	Aus	51	5.33	1)	Fulda	15 Sep
	Professional:						
	Bob Seagren	USA	46	5.36i	1)	Baltimore	14 Apr
1974	Steve Smith	USA	51	5.53i	1)	Pocatello	03 Feb
	Bob Seagren	USA	46	5.49	2)	El Paso	27 Apr
	Tadeusz Slusarski	Pol	50	5.42	1)	Warszawa	20 Jun
	Renato Dionisi	Ita	47	5.40i	1)	Bra	23 Feb
	Wojciech Buciarski	Pol	50	5.40	1)	Athinai	11 Jul
	Casey Cardigan	USA	51	5.40	1)	Formia	25 Aug
	Vladimir Kishkun	SU	51	5.40	1)	München	12 Sep
	Yuriy Isakov	SU	49	5.40	2)	München	12 Sep
	Vic Dias	USA	47	5.38i	1)	New York	22 Feb
	Buddy Williamson	USA	47	5.38i	1)	Los Angeles	13 Apr
	Dan Ripley	USA	53	5.38	1)	Saskatoon	27 Dec
	Wladyslaw Kozakiewicz	Pol	53	5.38	1)	Gdansk	05 Oct
	Exhibition:						
	Steve Smith	USA	51	5.59	1)	Long Beach	05 May
1975	Dave Roberts	USA	51	5.65	1)	Gainedsville	28 Mar
	Steve Smith	USA	51	5.61i	1)	New York	28 May
	Wladyslaw Kozakiewicz	Pol	53	5.60	1)	Warszawa	20 Jun
	Dan Ripley	USA	53	5.51i	1)	Los Angeles	18 Jan
	Vic Dias	USA	47	5.51	1)	Fresno	10 May
	Earl Bell	USA	55	5.51	1)	Provo	07 Jun
	Wojciech Buciarski	Pol	50	5.50	1)	St.Maur	04 Jun
	Larry Jessee	USA	52	5.48	1)	El Paso	01 Mar
	Bob Seagren	USA	49	5.48	1)	El Paso	10 May
	Russ Rogers	USA	54	5.48	1)	Durham	18 Jul
1976	Dave Roberts	USA	51	5.70	1)	Eugene	22 Jun
	Earl Bell	USA	55	5.67	1)	Wichita	29 May
	Wladyslaw Kozakiewicz	Pol	53	5.62	1)	Bydgoszcz	29 May
	Tadeusz Slusarski	Pol	50	5.62	2)	Bydgoszcz	29 May
	Dan Ripley	USA	53	5.59	1)	San Jose	01 May
	Vladimir Profimyenko	SU	53	5.56	1)	Leningrad	10 Jul
	Larry Jessee	USA	52	5.53	1)	El Paso	02 Jul
	Yuriy Prokhoryenko	SU	51	5.53	1)	München	30 May
	Antti Kalliomäki	Fin	47	5.53	1)	Tampere	16 Aug
	Russ Rogers	USA	54	5.52	1)	Honolulu	27 Mar
	Extra trial:						
	Itsuo Takanezawa	Jap	51	5.52	-)	Walnut	09 Mar
1977	Wladyslaw Kozakiewicz	Pol	53	5.66	1)	Warszawa	17 Jul
	Earl Bell	USA	55	5.60	1)	Stockholm	04 Jul
	Mike Tully	USA	56	5.60	1)	Düsseldorf	03 Sep
	Dan Ripley	USA	53	5.59	1)	Wichita	28 May
	Vladimir Trofimyenko	SU	53	5.59	1)	Sochi	02 Jul
	Tadeusz Slusarski	Pol	50	5.55	1)	Bydgoszcz	05 Jun
	Vladimir Kishkun	SU	51	5.55	1)	Moskva	28 Jul
	Don Baird	Aus	51	5.53	1)	Long Beach	16 Apr
	Mariusz Klinczyk	Pol	56	5.53	1)	Habana	14 Sep
	Larry Jessee	USA	52	5.50	1)	El Paso	02 May

	Yuriy Isakov	SU	49	5.50	1)	Sochi	05 Jun
	François Tracanelli	Fra	51	5.50	2)	Nice	21 Aug
	Bar held on in illegal manner:						
	Antti Kalliomäki	Fin	47	5.50	1)	Handen	05 Jun
	Jean Michel Bellot	Fra	53	5.50	1)	Issy-les-Moulineaux	11 Jun
1978	Mike Tully	USA	56	5.71	1)	Corvallis	19 May
	Wladyslaw Kozakiewciz	Pol	53	5.62	1)	Bratislava	10 Jun
	Larry Jessee	USA	52	5.61	1)	El Paso	29 Apr
	Vladimir Trofimyenko	SU	53	5.61	1)	Vilnius	24 Jun
	Tadeusz Slusarski	Pol	50	5.60	1)	Grudziadz	30 May
	Antti Kalliomäki	Fin	47	5.60	1)	Lohja	08 Aug
	Rauli Pudas	Fin	54	5.56	1)	Nivala	06 Jul
	Jeff Taylor	USA	53	5.55	1)	Westwood	07 May
	Günther Lohre	WG	53	5.51	1)	Frankfurt / M.	05 Sep
	Ralph Haynie	USA	54?	5.50	2)	El Paso	29 Apr
	Yevgeniy Tananika	SU	51	5.50	1)	Kharkov	09 May
	Earl Bell	USA	55	5.50	1)	Walnut	28 May
	Dan Ripley	USA	53	5.50	1)	Athinai	28 Jun
	Bob Pullard	USA	51	5.50	1)	Wien	29 Jul
	Wojciech Buciarski	Pol	50	5.50	1)	Freising	10 Sep
	Extra trial:						
	Dan Ripley	USA	53	5.56	-)	Westwood	10 Jun
	Unsanctioned meet:						
	Philippe Houvion	Fra	57	5.50	1)	Paris	18 Jul
	Exhibition:						
	Thierry Vigneron	Fra	60	5.50	-)	Nice	31 Dec
1979	Patrick Abada	Fra	54	5.65	1)	Paris	04 Jun
	Philippe Houvion	Fra	57	5.65	2)	Paris	04 Jun
	Dan Ripley	USA	53	5.63i	1)	Fort Worth	03 Mar
	Wladyslaw Kozakiewicz	Pol	53	5.61	1)	Bruxelles	04 Sep
	Thierry Vigneron	Fra	60	5.61	1)	Longwy	30 Sep
	Konstantin Volkov	SU	60	5.60	1)	Torino	05 Aug
	Günther Lohre	WG	53	5.60	1)	Berlin	17 Aug
	Larry Jessee	USA	52	5.57	1)	Ruidoso, N.M.	13 Jun
	Yuriy Prokhoryenko	SU	51	5.57i	1)	Leningrad	16 Jan
	Mike Tully	USA	56	5.56	1)	Warszawa	29 Jul
1980	Wladyslaw Kozakiewicz	Pol	53	5.78	1)	Moskva	30 Jul
	Philippe Houvion	Fra	57	5.77	1)	Paris	17 Jul
	Thierry Vigneron	Fra	60	5.75	1)	Colombes	01 Jun
	Jean-Michel Bellot	Fra	53	5.70	2)	Villeneuve d'Ascq	29 Jun
	Konstantin Volkov	SU	60	5.70i	1)	Moskva	06 Jul
	Serge Ferreira	Fra	59	5.70	1)	Nice	17 Aug
	Larry Jessee	USA	52	5.69	1)	El Paso	30 Apr
	Billy Olson	USA	58	5.67	1)	San Angelo	29 Apr
	Antti Kalliomäki	Fin	47	5.66	1)	Raahe	13 Jul
	Mike Tully	USA	56	5.65	2)	Wichita	31 May
	Tadeusz Slusarski	Pol	50	5.65	1)	Warszawa	09 Jun
	Exhibition:						
	Philippe Houvion	Fra	57	5.80	-)	Remiremont	04 Oct

ALL TIME WORLD LIST AS AT THE END OF 1980

Wladyslaw Kozakiewicz	Pol	53	5.78	1)	Moskva	30 Jul 80
Philippe Houvion	Fra	57	5.77	1)	Paris	17 Jul 80
Thierry Vigneron	Fra	60	5.75	1)	Colombes	01 Jun 80
Mike Tully	USA	56	5.71	1)	Corvallis	19 May 78
Dave Roberts	USA	51	5.70	1)	Eugene	22 Jun 76

	Jean-Michel Bellot	Fra	53	5.70	2)	Villeneuve d'Ascq	29 Jun 80
	Konstantin Volkov	SU	60	5.70i	1)	Moskva	06 Jul 80
	Serge Ferreira	Fra	59	5.70	1)	Nice	17 Aug 80
	Larry Jessee	USA	52	5.69	1)	El Paso	30 Apr 80
	Earl Bell	USA	55	5.67	1)	Wichita	29 May 76
	Billy Olson	USA	58	5.67	1)	San Angelo	29 Apr 80
1981	Vladimir Polyakov	SU	60	5.81	1)	Tbilisi	26 Jun
	Thierry Vigneron	Fra	60	5.80	1)	Mâcon	20 Jun
	Konstantin Volkov	SU	60	5.75	1)	Bucuresti	23 Jul
	Philippe Houvion	Fra	57	5.70	1)	Le Tremblay	08 Jun
	Jean-Michel Bellot	Fra	53	5.70	2)	Mâcon	20 Jun
	Sergey Kulibaba	SU	59	5.70	1)	Leningrad	10 Jul
	Aleksandr Krupskiy	SU	60	5.70	1)	Leningrad	25 Jul
	Nikolay Selivanov	SU	58	5.65	1)	Kaunas	30 Jun
	Keith Stock	GB	57	5.65	1)	Stockholm	07 Jul
	Earl Bell	USA	55	5.65	2)	Zurich	19 Aug
	Exhibition:						
	Konstantin Volkov	SU	60	5.84	-)	Irkutsk	02 Aug
1982	Dave Volz	USA	62	5.75	1)	Nice	14 Aug
	Jean-Michel Bellot	Fra	53	5.75	1)	Colombes	25 Sep
	Billy Olson	USA	58	5.74i	1)	Kansas City	27 Feb
	Dan Ripley	USA	53	5.72	1T)	Knoxville	20 Jun
	Larry Jessee	USA	52	5.71	1)	Juarez	31 May
	Thierry Vigneron	Fra	60	5.71	1)	Champs-sur-Marne	26 Sep
	Viktor Spasov	SU	59	5.70i	1)	Milano	07 Mar
	Aleksandr Chernyayev	SU	60	5.70	1)	Sochi	29 May
	Atanas Tarev	Bul	58	5.70	1)	Sofia	03 Jul
	Pierre Quinon	Fra	62	5.70	2)	Nice	14 Aug
	Aleksandr Krupskiy	SU	60	5.70	1)	Podolsk	24 Aug
1983	Thierry Vigneron	Fra	60	5.83	1)	Roma	01 Sep
	Pierre Quinon	Fra	62	5.82	1)	Köln	28 Aug
	Billy Olson	USA	58	5.80i	1)	Toronto	04 Feb
	Jeff Buckingham	USA	60	5.76	1)	Lawrence	16 Jul
	Brad Pursley	USA	60	5.75	1)	Abilene	29 Mar
	Aleksandr Obizhayev	SU	59	5.74i	1)	Moskva	12 Feb
	Pavel Bogatyryov	SU	61	5.74	1)	Irkutsk	06 Jul
	Aleksdandr Krupskiy	SU	60	5.74	1)	Angarsk	12 Jul
	Vladimir Polyakov	SU	60	5.73i	2)	Moskva	12 Feb
	Dan Ripley	USA	53	5.71i	2)	New York	25 Feb
	Felix Böhni	Swz	58	5.71	1)	Bern	11 Jun
	Aleksandr Chernyayev	SU	60	5.71	1)	Chernigov	02 Jul
	Unconfirmed mark:						
	Sergey Bubka	SU	63	5.72	1)	Tallinn	04 Jul
1984	Sergey Bubka	SU	63	5.94	1)	Roma	31 Aug
	Thierry Vigneron	Fra	60	5.91	2)	Roma	31 Aug
	Konstantin Volkov	SU	60	5.85	1)	Kiev	22 Jun
	Mike Tully	USA	56	5.82	1)	Eugene	21 Jul
	Aleksandr Krupskiy	SU	60	5.82	1)	Budapest	20 Aug
	Billy Olson	USA	58	5.80i	2)	Inglewood	10 Feb
	Earl Bell	USA	55	5.80	1)	San Jose	09 Jun
	Pierre Quinon	Fra	62	5.80	1)	Lausanne	10 Jul
	Vladimir Polyakov	SU	60	5.80	1)	Moskva	19 Jul
	Pavel Bogatyryov	SU	61	5.75	2)	Sochi	09 Jun
	Wladyslaw Kozakiewicz	Pol	53	5.75	1)	Edinburgh	17 Jul
1985	Sergey Bubka	SU	63	6.00	1)	Paris	13 Jul
	Pierre Quinon	Fra	62	5.90	2)	Nice	16 Jul
	Billy Olson	USA	58	5.86i	1)	Saskatoon	28 Dec
	Joe Dial	USA	62	5.85	1)	Norman	19 May
	Vasiliy Bubka	SU	60	5.85	1)	Donyetsk	29 Aug
	Aleksandr Parnov	SU	59	5.82	1)	Sumgait	21 Aug

	Mike Tully	USA	56	5.80	1)	Eugene	01 Jun
	Thierry Vigneron	Fra	60	5.80	1)	Nimes	02 Jun
	Pavel Bogatyryov	SU	61	5.80	1)	Schwechat	19 Jun
	Philippe Collet	Fra	63	5.80	1)	Viareggio	07 Aug
	Marian Kolasa	Pol	59	5.80	1)	Kamp-Lintfort	01 Sep

Exhibition (Performance made in irregular conditions – board runway, shopping precinct):

	Larry Jessee	USA	53	5.86	1)	Newcastle, NSW	16 Oct
1986	Sergey Bubka	SU	63	6.01	1)	Moskva	08 Jul
	Billy Olson	USA	58	5.93i	1)	East Rutherford	08 Feb
	Joe Dial	USA	62	5.91i	1)	Columbia, Mo.	01 Feb
	Thierry Vigneron	Fra	60	5.90	1)	Paris	22 Jul
	Radion Gataullin	SU	65	5.85	1)	Kiev	16 Jul
	Philippe Collet	Fra	63	5.85	2)	Paris	22 Jul
	Marian Kolasa	Pol	59	5.81i	1)	Praha	13 Feb
	Earl Bell	USA	55	5.81	1)	Houston	02 Aug
	Dave Volz	USA	62	5.80i	2)	New York	14 Feb
	Mike Tully	USA	56	5.80	1)	Eugene	21 Jun
	Vasiliy Bubka	SU	60	5.80	2)	Kiev	16 Jul
	Atanas Tarev	Bul	58	5.80	2)	Lausanne	02 Sep
1987	Sergey Bubka	SU	63	6.03	1)	Praha	23 Jun
	Joe Dial	USA	62	5.96	1)	Norman	18 Jun
	Ferenc Salbert	Fra	60	5.90i	1)	Grenoble	14 Mar
	Radion Gataullin	SU	65	5.90	1)	Bryansk	17 Jul
	Earl Bell	USA	55	5.86i	1)	Portland	24 Jan
	Thierry Vigneron	Fra	60	5.85i	1)	Liévin	22 Feb
	Mike Tully	USA	56	5.83	1)	Irvine	14 Jun
	Marian Kolasa	Pol	59	5.80i	3)	Liévin	22 Feb
	Phlippe Collet	Fra	63	5.80i	2)	Grenoble	14 Mar
	Billy Olson	USA	58	5.80	1)	Dallas	11 Apr
	Aleksandr Obizhayev	SU	59	5.80	2)	Bryansk	17 Jul
	Kory Tarpenning	USA	62	5.80	2)	Zurich	19 Aug
1988	Sergey Bubka	SU	63	6.06	1)	Nice	10 Jul
	Radion Gataullin	SU	65	5.95	1)	Berlin	26 Aug
	Miroslaw Chmara	Pol	64	5.90	1)	Villeneuve d'Ascq	27 Jun
	Kory Tarpenning	USA	62	5.89	1)	Indianapolis	21 Jul
	Earl Bell	USA	55	5.87	1)	Jonesboro	14 May
	Vasiliy Bubka	SU	60	5.86	1)	Chelyabinsk	16 Jul
	Grigoriy Yegorov	SU	67	5.85	1)	Tallinn	05 Jul
	Mike Tully	USA	56	5.84	1)	Irvine	01 May
	Thierry Vigneron	Fra	60	5.81i	1)	New York	05 Feb
	Philippe Collet	Fra	63	5.80i	2)	Grenoble	12 Mar
1989	Sergey Bubka	SU	63	6.03i	1)	Osaka	11 Feb
	Radion Gataullin	SU	65	6.02i	1)	Gomel	04 Feb
	Philippe Collet	Fra	63	5.92i	2)	Grenoble	11 Mar
	Joe Dial	USA	62	5.90	1)	El Paso	16 Apr
	Miroslaw Chmara	Pol	64	5.85i	1)	Berlin	24 Feb
	Grigoriy Yegorov	SU	67	5.81	2)	Köln	02 Aug
	Tom Bright	USA	60	5.81	1)	Taipei	24 Sep
	Kory Tarpenning	USA	62	5.80	1)	Eugene	13 May
	Vasiliy Bubka	SU	60	5.80	3)	Stockholm	03 Jul
	Maksim Tarasov	SU	70	5.80	1)	Bryansk	14 Jul
1990	Sergey Bubka	SU	63	6.05i	1)	Donyetsk	17 Mar
	Philippe Collet	Fra	63	5.94i	1)	Grenoble	10 Mar
	Radion Gataullin	SU	65	5.92	1)	Seattle	22 Feb
	Grigoriy Yegorov	SU	67	5.90i	1)	Yokohama	11 Mar
	Thierry Vigneron	Fra	60	5.85i	1)	Colombes	24 Feb
	Maksim Tarasov	SU	70	5.85	1)	Bratislava	20 Jun
	Igor Potapovich	SU	67	5.85	2)	Bratislava	20 Jun
	Kory Tarpenning	USA	62	5.83	1)	Sheffield	16 Sep
	Tim Bright	USA	60	5.82	1)	Nice	10 Jul
	Vasiliy Bubka	SU	60	5.81	1)	Lugansk	25 Jul

POLE VAULT 1991 1995

	Name	Nat	Born	Mark	Pl	Venue	Date
	Exhibition:						
	Scott Huffman	USA	64	5.85	-)	Manhattan Beach	17 Jun
1991	Sergey Bubka	SU	63	6.12i	1)	Grenoble	23 Mar
	István Bagyula	Hun	69	5.92	1)	Linz	05 Jul
	Viktor Ryzhenkov	SU	66	5.91i	2)	San Sebastian	15 Mar
	Radion Gataullin	SU	65	5.90	1)	Kiev	11 Jul
	Igor Potapovich	SU	67	5.90	2)	Zurich	07 Aug
	Bill Payne	USA	67	5.86	1)	Houston	19 May
	Maksim Tarasov	SU	70	5.85	2)	Kiev	11 Jul
	Grigoriy Yegorov	SU	67	5.85	3)	Kiev	11 Jul
	Vasiliy Bubka	SU	60	5.82	1)	Bruxelles	13 Sep
	Dean Starkey	USA	67	5.81	1)	Santa Barbara	05 May
	Market square vault competition:						
	Maksim Tarasov	SU	70	5.90	1)	Padova	17 Sep
	Gennadiy Sukharev	SU	65	5.86	1)	Bisceglie	23 Jul
1992	Sergey Bubka	Ukr	63	6.13i	1)	Berlin	21 Feb
	Radion Gataullin	Rus	65	5.95	1)	Köln	16 Aug
	Igor Potapovich	Kaz	67	5.92	2)	Dijon	13 Jun
	Dean Starkey	USA	67	5.91	1)	Modesto	16 May
	Maksim Tarasov	Rus	70	5.90	2)	St. Denis	04 Jun
	Jean Galfione	Fra	71	5.90	3)	St. Denis	04 Jun
	Igor Trandenkov	Rus	66	5.90	2)	Köln	16 Aug
	Kory Tarpenning	USA	62	5.86	2)	Modesto	16 May
	Pyotr Bochkaryov	Rus	67	5.85i	1)	Genova	01 Mar
	Scott Huffman	USA	64	5.85	1)	Austin	09 May
	Grigoriy Yegorov	Kaz	67	5.85	3)	Berlin	21 Aug
1993	Sergey Bubka	Ukr	63	6.15i	1)	Donyetsk	21 Feb
	Radion Gataullin	Rus	65	6.00i	1)	Moskva	02 Feb
	Jean Galfione	Fra	71	5.93	1)	Annecy	25 Jul
	Grigoriy Yegorov	Kaz	67	5.90i	2)	Moskva	02 Feb
	Igor Trandenkov	Rus	66	5.90i	1)	Grenoble	07 Feb
	Maksim Tarasov	Rus	70	5.90i	2)	Madrid	11 Feb
	Denis Petushinskiy	Rus	67	5.90	1)	Moslva	13 Jun
	Scott Huffman	USA	64	5.85	1)	Sheffield	29 Aug
	Jani Lehtonen	Fin	68	5.82	1)	Kuortane	26 Jun
	Valeriy Bukreyev	Est	64	5.81	1)	Riga	29 May
	Exhibition – Market square event:						
	Valeriy Bukreyev	Est	64	5.86	1)	Chiari	05 Sep
1994	Sergey Bubka	Ukr	63	6.14	1)	Sestriere	31 Jul
	Radion Gataullin	Rus	65	6.00	1)	Helsinki	11 Aug
	Scott Huffman	USA	64	5.97	1)	Knoxville	18 Jun
	Jean Galfione	Fra	71	5.94	1)	Dijon	12 Jun
	Dean Starkey	USA	67	5.92	1)	São Paulo	21 May
	Maksim Tarasov	Rus	70	5.90i	1)	Madrid	11 Feb
	Pyotr Bochkaryov	Rus	67	5.90i	1)	Paris	12 Mar
	Igor Trandenkov	Rus	66	5.90	1)	St.Peterburg	25 Jul
	Okkert Brits	SA	73	5.90	1)	London	10 Sep
	Valeri Bukrejev	Est	64	5.86	1)	Somero	03 Jul
	Outdoors on built-up runway:						
	Denis Petushinskiy	Rus	67	5.86	1)	Karlskrona	23 Jul
1995	Okkert Brits	SA	73	6.03	1)	Köln	18 Aug
	Sergey Bubka	Ukr	63	6.00i	1)	Liévin	19 Feb
	Maksim Tarasov	Rus	70	5.91	1)	Salgótarján	11 Sep
	Igor Trandenkov	Rus	66	5.90	1)	Dijon	28 May
	Radion Gataullin	Rus	65	5.90	2)	Tokyo	15 Sep
	Jean Galfione	Fra	71	5.86	3)	Göteborg	11 Aug
	Nick Hysong	USA	71	5.85i	1)	Atlanta	04 Mar
	Viktor Chistyakov	Rus	75	5.85	1)	Helsinki	28 Jun
	Andrej Tiwontschik	Ger	80	5.85	1)	Sheffield	23 Jul

Year	Athlete	Nat	Born	Mark	Pl	Venue	Date
	Pyotr Bochkaryov	Rus	67	5.80i	1)	Grenoble	29 Jan
	Bill Payne	USA	67	5.80i	1)	Reno	10 Feb
	Pat Manson	USA	67	5.80i	2)	Reno	10 Feb
	Tim Bright	USA	60	5.80i	2)	Atlanta	04 Mar
	Igor Potapovich	Kaz	67	5.80i	2)	Barcelona	11 Mar
	Riaan Botha	SA	70	5.80	1)	Cape Town	06 May
	Kory Tarpenning	USA	62	5.80	2)	São Paulo	14 May
	Dean Starkey	USA	67	5.80	4T)	Dijon	28 May
	Scott Huffman	USA	64	5.80	1)	Sacramento	17 Jun
	Exhibition (town square):						
	Igor Potapovich	Kaz	67	5.85	1)	Praha	14 Jun
1996	Sergey Bubka	Ukr	63	6.02	1)	Atlanta	18 May
	Okkert Brits	SA	73	6.01	1)	Stellenbosch	15 Mar
	Igor Trandenkov	Rus	66	6.01	1)	St.Peterburg	04 Jul
	Lawrence Johnson	USA	74	5.98	1)	Knoxville	25 May
	Andrei Tiwontschik	Ger	70	5.95	1)	Köln	16 Aug
	Jean Galfione	Fra	71	5.92	1)	Atlanta	02 Aug
	Tim Lobinger	Ger	72	5.91	1)	Leverkusen	20 Aug
	Radion Gataullin	Rus	65	5.90i	2)	Liévin	18 Feb
	Joe Dial	USA	62	5.90	1)	Stillwater	02 Jun
	Igor Potapovich	Kaz	67	5.90	1)	Nice	10 Jul
	Maksim Tarasov	Rus	70	5.90	2)	Nice	10 Jul
	Scott Huffman	USA	64	5.90	1)	Linz	21 Aug
	Town square (built-up runway):						
	Pyotr Bochkaryov	Rus	67	5.90	1)	Karlskrona	28 Jun
1997	Sergey Bubka	Ukr	63	6.05	1)	Fukuoka	13 Sep
	Maksim Tarasov	Rus	70	6.00	1)	Nice	18 Jul
	Tim Lobinger	Ger	72	6.00	1)	Köln	24 Aug
	Dmitri Markov	Bye	75	5.95	2)	Köln	24 Aug
	Okkert Brits	SA	73	5.92	1)	Hamburg	23 Jul
	Riaan Botha	SA	70	5.91	1)	Pretoria	02 Apr
	Dean Starkey	USA	67	5.91	3)	Athinai	10 Aug
	Igor Potapovich	Kaz	67	5.90i	1)	Paris	08 May
	Lawrence Johnson	USA	74	5.90	1)	Indianapolis	15 Jun
	Jeff Hartwig	USA	67	5.85	1)	Memphis	03 May
	Alain Andji	Fra	74	5.85	1)	Bonneuil-sur-Marne	18 May
	Yevgeniy Smiryagin	Rus	76	5.85	1)	Turku	12 Jun
	Pat Manson	USA	67	5.85	4)	Fukuoka	13 Sep
	Exhibition:						
	Jean Galfione	Fra	71	6.00	-)	Besançon	23 May
1998	Jeff Hartwig	USA	67	6.01	1)	Uniondale, N.Y.	21 Jul
	Dmitri Markov	Bye	75	6.00	1)	Auckland	20 Feb
	Jean Galfione	Fra	71	5.97	1)	Athinai	17 Jun
	Maksim Tarasov	Rus	70	5.95	1)	Moskva	05 Sep
	Danny Ecker	Ger	77	5.93	1)	Ingolstadt	26 Jul
	Igor Potapovich	Kaz	67	5.92i	1T)	Stockholm	19 Feb
	Tim Lobinger	Ger	72	5.92	1)	Nürnberg	11 Jul
	Sergey Bubka	Ukr	63	5.91i	1)	Liévin	22 Feb
	Okkert Brits	SA	73	5.90	1)	Germiston	06 Mar
	Jacob Davis	USA	78	5.90	1)	Austin	04 Apr
1999	Maksim Tarasov	Rus	70	6.05	1)	Athinai	16 Jun
	Jeff Hartwig	USA	67	6.02	1)	Eugene	27 Jun
	Jean Galfione	Fra	71	6.00i	1)	Maebashi	06 Mar
	Tim Lobinger	Ger	72	6.00	1)	Oslo	30 Jun
	Dmitri Markov	Aus	75	5.95	3)	Athinai	16 Jun
	Romain Mesnil	Fra	77	5.93	1)	Göteborg	01 Aug
	Michael Stolle	Ger	74	5.91	1)	Nürnberg	13 Jun
	Danny Ecker	Ger	77	5.90i	1)	Karlsruhe	20 Feb
	Viktor Chistyakov	Aus	75	5.90	1)	Salamanca	15 Jul
	Andrei Tivontchik	Ger	70	5.85i	2)	Karlsruhe	20 Feb

	Nick Hysong	USA	71	5.85i	2)	Atlanta	27 Feb
	Jacob Davis	USA	78	5.85i	1)	Indianapolis	06 Mar
	Lawrence Johnson	USA	74	5.85	1)	Knoxville	08 Apr
	Exhibition (town square event):						
	Viktor Chistyakov	Aus	75	5.95	-)	Chiari	07 Sep
2000	Jeff Hartwig	USA	67	6.03	1)	Jonesboro	14 Jun
	Tim Lobinger	Ger	72	5.95i	1)	Chemnitz	18 Feb
	Michael Stolle	Ger	74	5.95	1)	Monaco	18 Aug
	Lawrence Johnson	USA	74	5.90	1)	Pretoria	24 Mar
	Pavel Gerasimov	Rus	79	5.90	1)	Rüdlingen	12 Aug
	Danny Ecker	Ger	77	5.90	1)	Bruxelles	25 Aug
	Nick Hysong	USA	71	5.90	1)	Sydney	29 Sep
	Maksim Tarasov	Rus	70	5.90	3)	Sydney	29 Sep
	Okkert Brits	SA	73	5.85	1)	Ingolstadt	18 Jun
	Dmitriy Markov	Aus	75	5.85	1)	Lausanne	05 Jul
	Yevgeniy Smiryagin	Rus	76	5.85	1)	Gateshead	16 Jul
	Aleksandr Averbukh	Isr	74	5.85	1)	Tel Aviv	24 Jul

ALL TIME WORLD LIST AS AT THE END OF 2000

Sergey Bubka	Ukr	63	6.15i	1)	Donetsk	21 Feb 93
Maksim Tarasov	Rus	70	6.05	1)	Athinai	16 Jun 99
Okkert Brits	SA	73	6.03	1)	Köln	18 Aug 95
Jeff Hartwig	USA	67	6.03	1)	Jonesboro	14 Jun 00
Radion Gataullin	Rus	65	6.02i	1)	Gomel	04 Feb 89
Igor Trandenkov	Rus	66	6.01	1)	St.Peterburg	04 Jul 96
Tim Lobinger	Ger	72	6.00	1)	Köln	24 Aug 97
Dmitriy Markov	Aus	75	6.00	1)	Auckland	20 Feb 98
Jean Galfione	Fra	71	6.00i	1)	Maebashi	06 Mar 99
Lawrence Johnson	USA	74	5.98	1)	Knoxville	25 May 96

2001	Dmitriy Markov	Aus	75	6.05	1)	Edmonton	09 Aug
	Danny Ecker	Ger	77	6.00i	1)	Dortmund	11 Feb
	Lawrence Johnson	USA	74	5.96i	1)	Atlanta	03 Mar
	Tye Harvey	USA	74	5.93i	2)	Atlanta	03 Mar
	Alex Averbukh	Isr	74	5.91	1)	Gateshead	19 Aug
	Jeff Hartwig	USA	67	5.90	1)	Modesto	12 May
	Romain Mesnil	Fra	77	5.86i	1)	Toulouse	04 Mar
	Pavel Burlachenko	Rus	76	5.86	1)	Pretoria	23 Mar
	Michael Stolle	Ger	74	5.85i	2)	Potsdam	18 Feb
	Richard Spiegelburg	Ger	77	5.85	1)	Stuttgart	30 Jun
	Nick Hysong	USA	71	5.85	3)	Edmonton	09 Aug
2002	Jeff Hartwig	USA	67	6.02i	1)	Sindelfingen	10 Mar
	Tim Lobinger	Ger	72	5.90	2)	Athinai	10 Jun
	Tim Mack	USA	72	5.85i	2)	Donetsk	24 Feb
	Lars Börgeling	Ger	79	5.85	1)	Leverkusen	27 Jul
	Alex Averbukh	Isr	74	5.85	1)	München	10 Aug
	Patrik Kristiansson	Swe	77	5.85	1)	Helsinki	23 Aug
	Derek Miles	USA	72	5.82i	1)	Vermillion	16 Feb
	Dany Ecker	Ger	77	5.82i	1)	Dessau	24 Feb
	Nick Buckfield	GB	73	5.81i	1)	Bad Segeberg	08 Feb
	Tye Harvey	USA	74	5.81i	2)	Flagstaff	17 Feb
	Exhibition (square):						
	Okkert Brits	SA	73	5.81	1)	Hof	22 Jun
2003	Romain Mesnil	Fra	77	5.95	1)	Castres	06 Aug
	Alex Averbukh	Isr	74	5.93	1)	Madrid	19 Jul
	Tim Lobinger	Ger	72	5.91	1)	Monaco	13 Sep
	Giuseppe Gibilisco	Ita	79	5.90	1)	St.Denis	28 Aug
	Oscar Janson	Swe	75	5.87	1)	Somero	29 Jun
	Dmitri Markov	Aus	75	5.86	1)	Berlin	19 Aug

Year	Name	Nat	Born	Mark	Place	Venue	Date
	Okkert Brits	SA	73	5.86	2)	Monaco	13 Sep
	Patrik Kristiansson	Swe	77	5.85	3)	St. Denis	28 Aug
	Adam Ptácek	Cze	80	5.81i	2)	Chemnitz	07 Feb
	Derek Miles	USA	72	5.81	1)	Jonesboro	28 May
	Denis Yurchenko	Ukr	78	5.81	2)	Rieti	07 Sep
2004	Tim Mack	USA	72	6.01	1)	Monaco	18 Sep
	Toby Stevenson	USA	76	6.00	1)	Modesto	08 May
	Jeff Hartwig	USA	67	5.88i	1)	Jonesboro	22 Feb
	Aleksandr Averbukh	Isr	74	5.85	1)	Quortane	27 Jun
	Giuseppe Gibilisco	Ita	79	5.85	3)	Athinai	27 Aug
	Brad Walker	USA	81	5.82	2)	Phoenix	14 May
	Björn Otto	Ger	77	5.82i	1)	Münster	23 Sep
	Nick Hysong	USA	71	5.81	2)	Zaragoza	08 Jun
	Rens Blom	Hol	77	5.81	3)	Zaragoza	08 Jun
	Derek Miles	USA	72	5.81	1)	Jonesboro	13 Jun
2005	Paul Burgess	Aus	79	6.00	1)	Perth	26 Feb
	Brad Walker	USA	81	5.96	1)	Rieti	28 Aug
	Tim Lobinger	Ger	72	5.93	1)	Berlin	04 Sep
	Igor Pavlov	Rus	79	5.90i	1)	Madrid	05 Mar
	Toby Stevenson	USA	76	5.90	2)	Eugene	04 Jun
	Steve Hooker	Aus	82	5.87	1)	Melbourne	12 Mar
	Derek Miles	USA	72	5.85i	1)	Donetsk	12 Feb
	Denis Yurchenko	Ukr	78	5.85i	2)	Madrid	05 Mar
	Tim Mack	USA	72	5.85	1)	Chula Vista	21 May
	Daniel Ryland	USA	79	5.85i	1)	Jonesboro	24 Jul
2006	Brad Walker	USA	81	6.00	1)	Jockgrim	19 Jul
	Steve Hooker	Aus	82	5.96	1)	Berlin	03 Sep
	Paul Burgess	Aus	79	5.92	1)	Mannheim	08 Jul
	Tim Lobinger	Ger	72	5.90	1)	Köln	10 Jun
	Danny Ecker	Ger	77	5.86	1)	Liège	19 Jul
	Jeff Hartwig	USA	67	5.85i	1)	Vermillion, SD	18 Feb
	Björn Otto	Ger	77	5.85	1)	Berlin	02 Sep
	Okkert Brits	SA	73	5.82	2)	Karlsruhe	26 Jul
	Toby Stevenson	USA	76	5.82	2T)	Stuttgart	09 Sep
	Aleksandr Averbukh	Isr	74	5.81i	1)	Gent	28 Feb
	Romani Mesnil	Fra	77	5.81	1)	Bron	04 Jul
	Fabian Schulze	Ger	84	5.81	1)	Ingolstadt	08 Jul
2007	Brad Walker	USA	81	5.95	1)	Brisbane	10 Mar
	Paul Burgess	Aus	79	5.91	1)	Perth	07 Jan
	Steve Hooker	Aus	82	5.91	2)	Perth	07 Jan
	Björn Otto	Ger	77	5.90i	1)	Leipzig	17 Feb
	Danny Ecker	Ger	77	5.87	1)	Monaco	25 Jul
	Tim Mack	USA	72	5.86	1)	Chula Vista	14 Jun
	Romani Mesnil	Fra	77	5.86	2)	Osaka	01 Sep
	Jeff Hartwig	USA	67	5.85i	1)	Jonesboro	19 May
	Fabian Schulze	Ger	84	5.83i	2)	Stuttgart	03 Feb
	Tim Lobinger	Ger	72	5.83	1)	Ingolstadt	16 Jan
2008	Brad Walker	USA	81	6.04	1)	Eugene	08 Jun
	Yevgeniy Lukyanenko	Rus	85	6.01	1)	Bydgoszcz	01 Jul
	Steve Hooker	Aus	82	6.00	1)	Perth	27 Jan
	Denys Yurchenko	Ukr	78	5.83	1)	Kiev	03 Jul
	Maksym Mazuryk	Ukr	83	5.82	1)	Yalta	06 Jun
	Igor Pavlov	Rus	79	5.81i	2)	Stuttgart	02 Feb
	Tim Lobinger	Ger	72	5.81i	1T)	Stockholm	21 Feb
	Sergey Kucheranyu	Rus	85	5.81	1)	Dessau	30 May
	Alexander Straub	Ger	83	5.81	1)	Wattenscheid	01 Aug
	Renaud Lavillenie	Fra	86	5.81i	1)	Aulnay-sous-Bois	05 Dec
	Exhibition (Square):						
	Derek Miles	USA	72	5.85	1)	Berlin	07 Sep
2009	Steve Hooker	Aus	82	6.06i	1)	Boston	07 Feb

	Renaud Lavillenie	Fra	86	6.01	1)	Leiria	21 Jun
	Romain Mesnil	Fra	77	5.85	2)	Berin	22 Aug
	Derek Miles	USA	72	5.82i	1)	Vermillion, SD	24 Jan
	Yevgeniy Lukyanenko	Rus	85	5.82i	2)	Donetsk	15 Feb
	Jeremy Scott	USA	81	5.82i	1)	Jonesboro	14 Jun
	Pavel Gerasimov	Rus	79	5.81i	2)	Stockholm	18 Feb
	Alhaji Jeng	Swe	81	5.81i	3)	Stockholm	18 Feb
	Alexander Straub	Ger	83	5.81	1)	Mannheim	20 Jun
	Danny Ecker	Ger	77	5.80i	1)	Leipzig	21 Feb
	Malte Mohr	Ger	86	5.80	1)	Soest	24 May
	Brad Walker	USA	81	5.80	3)	Monaco	28 Jul
	Maksym Mazuryk	Ukr	83	5.80	4)	Monaco	28 Jul
2010	Steve Hooker	Aus	82	6.01i	1)	Doha	13 May
	Renaud Lavillenie	Fra	86	5.94	1)	Valence	10 Jul
	Malte Mohr	Ger	86	5.85	1)	Bruxelles	27 Aug
	Przemyslaw Czerwinski	Pol	83	5.82i	1)	Donetsk	06 May
	Jedremy Scott	USA	81	5.82i	1)	Jonesboro	18 May
	Derek Miles	USA	72	5.81	1)	Jockgrim	21 Jul
	Raphael Holzdeppe	Ger	89	5.80	1)	Rotterdam-Egern	04 Jul
	Lukasz Michalski	Pol	88	5.80	1)	Bielsko-Biala	10 Jul
	Lukasz Mesnil	Fra	77	5.80	1)	Castres	20 Jul
	Maksym Mazuryk	Ukr	83	5.80	2)	Barcelona	31 Jul
	Exhibition (square):						
	Malte Mohr	Ger	86	5.90	1)	Aachen	01 Sep

ALL TIME WORLD LIST AS AT THE END OF 2010

Sergey Bubka	Ukr	63	6.15i	1)	Donetsk	21 Feb 93
Steve Hooker	Aus	82	6.06i	1)	Boston	07 Feb 09
Maksim Tarasov	Rus	70	6.05	1)	Athinai	16 Jun 99
Dmitriy Markov	Aus	75	6.05	1)	Edmonton	09 Aug 01
Brad Walker	USA	81	6.04	1)	Eugene	08 Jun 08
Okkert Brits	SA	73	6.03	1)	Köln	18 Aug 95
Jeff Hartwig	USA	67	6.03	1)	Jonesboro	14 Jun 00
Radion Gataullin	Rus	65	6.02i	1)	Gomel	04 Feb 89
Igor Trandenkov	Rus	66	6.01	1)	St.Peterburg	04 Jul 96
Tim Mack	USA	72	6.01	1)	Monaco	18 Sep 04
Yevgeniy Lukyanenko	Rus	85	6.01	1)	Bydgoszcz	01 Jul 08
Renaud Lavillenie	Fra	86	6.01	1)	Leiria	21 Jun 09

LONG JUMP

1860	T.J. Treanor	Ire		5.94	1)	Dublin	20 May
	Henry Powell	GB	38	5.69	1)	Oxford	15 Mar
	Professional:						
	William Tait	GB	36	5.95	1)	Biggar	19 Jun
1861	Frederick Stoney	Ire		5.94	)	Dublin	27 May
1862	Rynd	GB		5.79	)	Camberley	16 Sep
	George Osborne	GB		5.79	)	Hurstpierpoint	10 Nov
	Professional:						
	Jones	GB		6.40	1)	Puney	04 Dec

1863	Charles Buller	GB	46	6.37	1)	Harrow	Apr
1864	G. B. Worthington	GB		6.40	)	Manchester	27 Aug
1865	John Sandilands	GB		5.94	)	Uppingham	Apr
	Professional:						
	Samuel Muir	GB		6.25	)		
1866	Thomas Little	GB	45	6.30	1)	Sheffield	07 May
	Robert Mitchell	GB	47	6.25	1)	Llandudno	26 Jun
	Thomas Little	GB	45	6.20	1)	Oxford	10 Mar
	G. A. Bayley	GB		6.09	2)	Llandudno	26 Jun
1867	Robert Mitchell	GB	47	6.22	1)	Liverpool	20 May
	John Duckworth	GB	45	6.22	1)	Haslingden	27 Jul
	F. Foers	GB		6.17	1)	Rotherham	22 Aug
1868	Alick Tosswill	GB	45	6.50	1)	Oxford	14 Mar
	Charles Absolom	GB	46	6.48	1)	Richmond	18 Apr
	Richard Waltham	GB	46	6.42	2)	London, BH	03 Apr
1869	Alick Tosswill	GB	45	6.75	1)	Oxford	27 Feb
	John Duckworth	GB	45	6.44	1)	Burnley	07 Aug
	Edward Bergman	GB	c49	6.44	1)	Oxford	13 Nov
1870	H. S. Ferguson	GB	51	6.46	1)	LondonWoolwich	03 May
	T. Clerk	GB		6.44	2)	LondonWoolwich	03 May
	Percy Rivett-Carnac	GB	52	6.37	1)	Harrow	09 Apr
1871	John MacFarlane	GB		6.40	1)	Edinburgh	27 May
	Edward Hodges	GB	c49	6.39	1)	Oxford	11 Mar
	Charles Shepherd	GB	48	6.30	1)	Camberley	30 May
	Professional:						
	Robert Knox	GB		6.45	)		
1872	E.Jenner Davies	GB	51	6.88	1)	London (LB)	27 Mar
	T. H. Stretch	GB		6.55	1)	Bebington	20 Jul
	A. Court	GB		6.47	2)	Bebington	20 Jul
1873	E. Jenner Davies	GB	51	6.78	1)	Cambridge	19 Nov
	John Goodwin Lane	Ire	53	6.50	1)	Dublin	07 Jul
	A. Mornington	GB		6.50	1)	Market Harborough	14 Jul
1874	John Lane	GB	53	7.05	1)	Dublin	11 Jun
	E. Jenner Davies	GB	51	6.97	1)	London (LB)	27 Mar
	Charles Lockton	GB	56	6.92	1)	London	27 Apr

Note: *In the Dublin meet athletes were allowed "as many attempts as they liked". E. Jenner Davies (GB) did 6.96 on his 4th jump, while Lane's best was after "numerous jumps".*

1875	Charles Lockton	GB	56	6.76	1)	Nuneaton	02 Aug
	J. R. Harper	GB		6.63	1)	Market Weighton	26 Jul
	George Martin Kenny	Ire	55	6.55	1)	Dublin	22 May
1876	Fred Hargreaves	GB	50	6.86	1)	Douglas	30 Aug
	Marshall Brooks	GB	55	6.68	1)	Oxford	18 Mar
	Charles Lockton	GB	56	6.56	1)	Dublin	05 Jun
1877	Gerard Fowler	GB		6.96	)	Birmingham	28 Jul
	John G. Alkin	GB	55	6.96	)	Birmingham	20 Jul
	Charles Lockton	GB	56	6.31	2)	London (SB)	26 May
1878	Charles Lockton	GB	56	6.92	1)	London	27 Apr
	Edmund Baddeley	GB	57	6.91	1)	London (LB)	15 Apr
	Patrick Davin	Ire	57	6.70	1)	Dublin	10 Jun

LONG JUMP 1879 1890

1879	Patrick Davin	Ire	57	6.88	1)	Dublin	02 Jun
	Charles Lockton	GB	56	6.86	)		
	Herbert Massey	GB	57	6.84	1)	Birmingham	26 Jul
1880	E. Jenner J. Davies	Ire	51	6.96	)	Dublin	
	Patrick Davin	Ire	57	6.93	1)	Kilkenny	20 Jul
	Charles Lockton	GB	56	6.75	1)	London (LB)	03 Jul
1881	Patrick Davin	Ire	57	6.98	1)	Birmingham	16 Jul
	John Voorhees	USA		6.90	1)	New York	30 May
	Thomas Malone	Ire	57	6.88	2)	Birmingham	16 Jul
1882	G. W. Rolland	SA		6.85	1)	Queenstown	
	Christopher H. Ware	GB		6.78	1)	Cambridge	20 Mar
	Thomas Malone	Ire	57	6.64	1)	Stoke-on-Trent	01 Jul
1883	Patrick Davin	Ire	57	7.06	1)	Monasterevan	30 Aug
	John W. Parsons	GB	59	7.01	1)	London (LB)	30 Jun
	Ernest Horwood	GB		6.78	1)	Nottingham	16 Jun
	E. Herrod	GB		6.78	1)	Northampton	06 Aug
1884	Malcolm Ford	USA	62	6.78	1)	Mott Haven	07 Jun
	John Purcell	Ire	62	6.74	1)	Kildare	06 Aug
	J. Griffin	Ire		6.65	1)	Lurgan	28 Aug
	Ernest Horwood	GB		6.65	1)	Birminham	21 Jun
	Proffessional:						
	Thomas Malone	Ire	57	7.12	-)	Mansfield, Vic	Jan
1885	John Purcell	Ire	62	6.98	1)	Tralee	17 Jun
	John Voorhees	USA		6.90	1)	Baltimore	05 Aug
	Malcolm Ford	USA	62	6.72	2)	Toronto	26 Sep
	Professional:						
	Thomas Malone	Ire	57	6.88	-)		
1886	Malcolm Ford	USA	62	7.08	1)	Brooklyn, N.Y.	14 Aug
	John Purcell	Ire	62	7.08	1)	Monesterevan	26 Aug
	Paddy Lawless	Ire		7.01	1)	Queenstown	05 Sep
	Alexander Jordan	USA	61	6.94	1)	Mott Haven	02 Oct
	Downhill course:						
	John Purcell	Ire	62	7.30	1)	Ballsbridge	31 Jul
1887	Michael Sweeney	USAIre		6.92	1)	Limerick	09 Jun
	Alexander A. Jordan	USA	61	6.87	1)	New York	01 Oct
	John Purcell	Ire	62	6.84	2)	Limerick	09 Jun
	Francis B. Roberts	GB	64	6.801	1)	Stourbridge	02 Jul
1888	Victor Schifferstein	USA	63	7.07	1)	Oakland	09 Jun
	William Halpin	USA		7.01	1)	Detroit	19 Sep
	Alfred Copland	USA	65	7.00	2)	Detroit	19 Sep
	Alexander Jordan	USA	61	6.95	3)	Detroit	19 Sep
1889	Victor Schifferstein	USA	63	7.02	1)	San Francisco	22 Feb
	P. Shanahan	Ire	66	7.01	)		
	Patrick McGrath	Ire		6.96	1)	Dublin	09 Jun
	Malcolm Ford	USA	62	6.90	1)	Toronto	28 Sep
	Extra trial:						
	Victor Schifferstein	USA	63	7.10	-)	San Francisco	22 Feb
1890	Alfred Copland	USA	65	7.09	1)	Washington, D.C.	11 Oct
	Patrick Davin	Ire	57	7.06	1)	Boston	25 Aug
	James L. Greig	GB		6.90	1)	London, QC	25 Mar
	John Mooney	Ire		6.88	1)	Ballsbridge	26 Jul

Year	Athlete	Nation	Born	Mark	Place	Venue	Date
1891	Charles Reber	USA	70	7.17	1)	Detroit	04 Jul
	Henry L. Williams	USA	69	6.99	1)	New Haven	04 May
	Victor V. Mapes	USA		6.99	1)	New York	31 May
	E. E. Barnes	USA		6.84	1)	New York	16 May
1892	Eugene Goff	USA	72	7.16	1)	New York	08 Oct
	Charles Fry	GB	72	7.13	1)	London	08 Apr
	Dan Bulger	Ire	66	6.96	1)	Dublin	18 Jun
1893	Charles Fry	GB	72	7.17	1)	Oxford	04 Mar
	Eugene Goff	USA	72	7.12	1)	Bergen Point	04 Sep
	Charles Reber	USA	70	7.12	1)	Chicago	16 Sep
	Edward Bloss	USA	70	7.06	)		
1894	John Mooney	Ire		7.21	1)	Mitchelstown	05 Sep
	Charles Fry	GB	72	7.02	1)	Oxford	28 Feb
	Lewis Sheldon	USA	74	6.98	1)	London	16 Jul
	William Oakley	GB	73	6.92	2)	Oxford	28 Feb
1895	Mattehw Roseingrave	Ire		7.13	1)	Gort	15 Aug
	William Rogers	USA	72	7.02	1)	Travers Island, NY	28 Sep
	Lewis Sheldon	USA	74	7.01	1)	New Haven	04 May
1896	Meyer Prinstein	USA	78	7.23	1)	New York	11 Jun
	Matthew Roseingrave	Ire		7.20	1)	Sydney	05 Oct
	Daniel Shanahan	Ire	66	7.16	1)		Jul
	Lewis Sheldon	USA	74	7.10	1)	Travers Island, NY	13 Aug
1897	Walter Newburn	Ire	73	7.16	1)	Maryborough	13 Jul
	Claude Leggatt	GB	76	7.11	1)	Manchester	03 Jul
	Meyer Prinstein	USA	78	7.11	1)	Williamsbridge	07 Aug
	Edward Bloss	USA	70	7.03	1)	Toronto	28 Sep
	William Rogers	USA	72	7.01	1)	Travers Island, NY	05 Jun
	Downhill:						
	Herbert Jones	GB	78	7.17	1)	Framingham	09 Oct
1898	Walter Newburn	Ire	73	7.32	1)	Ballsbridge	16 Jul
	Meyer Prinstein	USA	78	7.23	1)	Traver Island, NY	11 Jun
	Patrick Leahy	Ire	77	7.22	1)	Millstreet	06 Seo
	Jeremiah O'Mahoney	Ire	78	7.21	1)	Kilmallock	29 Jun
	Percy Remington	USA	77	7.17	1)	Philadelphia	21 May
	Unknown irregularity:						
	Walter Newburn	Eir	73	7.47	1)	Clonmel	01 Aug
1899	Alvin Kraenzlein	USA	76	7.43	1)	New York, BO	26 May
	Patrick Leahy	Ire		7.27	1)	Kilcash	06 Aug
	Peter O'Connor	Ire	74	7.19	2)	Kilcash	06 Aug
	Claude Leggatt	GB	76	7.12	1)	London	12 Jul
	Exhibition:						
	Peter O'Connor	Ire	74	7.39	-)	Thurles	17 Sep
1900	Meyer Prinstein	USA	78	7.50	1)	Philadelphia	28 Apr
	Peter O'Connor	Ire	74	7.41	1)	Dublin	13? Aug
	Patrick Leahy	Ire	77	7.21	1)	Yuoghal	27 Apr
	Alvin Kraenzlein	USA	76	7.18	1)	Paris	15 Jul
	Exhibition:						
	Peter O'Connor	Ire	74	7.51#	-)	New Ross	29 Aug
	Patrick Leahy	Ire	77	7.39	-)	Buttevant	14 Oct
	Unknown irregularity:						
	Peter O'Connor	Ire	74	7.43	1)	Ballinasloe	13 Aug

 # = From a board about 4 ins. Wide.

ALL TIME WORLD LIST AS AT THE END OF 1900

Meyer Prinstein		USA	78	7.50	1)	Philadelphia	28 Apr 00
Alvin Kraenzlein		USA	76	7.43	1)	New York	26 May 99
Peter O'Connor		Ire	74	7.41	1)	Dublin	13? Aug 00
Walter Newburn		Ire	74	7.32	1)	Dublin	16 Jul 98
John Mooney		Ire		7.21	1)	Mitchelstown	05 Sep 94
Matthew Roseingrave		Ire		7.20	1)	Sydney	05 Oct 96
Charles Reber		USA	70	7.17	1)	Detroit	04 Jul 91
Charles Fry		GB	72	7.17	1)	Oxford	04 Mar 93
Daniel Shanahan		Ire	66	7.16	1)		Jul 96
1901	Peter O'Connor	Ire	74	7.61	1)	Dublin	05 Aug
	Patrick Leahy	Ire	77	7.11	)		
	Maurice Fitzgerald	Ire		7.11	)	Milltown	
	Alvin Kraenzlein	USA	76	7.08	)		
	Walter Newburn	Ire	73	7.08	1)	Navan, Meath Co	15 Aug
1902	Patrick Leahy	Ire	77	7.29	1)	Listowell	31 Jul
	Cornelius Leahy	Ire	76	7.21	1)	Bruff	29 Jun
	Peter O'Connor	Ire	74	7.20	1)	London SB	05 Jul
	Thomas Kiely	Ire	69	7.00	)		
1903	Meyer Prinstein	USA	78	7.13	)		
	Peter O'Connor	Ire	74	7.08	1)		
	Dan O'Leary	Ire		7.06	1)	Coachford	19 Jul
1904	Meyer Prinstein	USA	78	7.34	1)	St.Louis	01 Sep
	Peter O'Connor	Ire	74	7.33	)		
	Daniel Frank	USA	82	7.30	1)	New York	20 Aug
	Ollie Snedigar	USA		7.29	)		
	Robert Stangland	USA	81	7.17	1)	Philadelphia	27 May
1905	Peter O'Connor	Ire	74	7.31	)	Gorey	24 Jul
	Frank Loveland	USA		7.26	1)	New Haven	14 Oct
	Ollie Snedigar	USA		7.21	)		
	Professional:						
	Bryce Scott	GB		7.36	1)		
1906	Daniel Kelly	USA	83	7.37	1)	Eugene	17 May
	Peter O'Connor	Ire	74	7.36	)		
	Timothy Ahearne	Ire	86	7.29	)		
	Frank Mountpleasant	USA	84	7.24	1)	Carlisle	19 May
	Meyer Prinstein	USA	78	7.20	1)	Athinai	27 Apr
1907	Daniel Kelly	USA	83	7.29	1)	Norfolk	07 Sep
	Timothy Ahearne	Ire	86	7.16	)		
	Edwin Cooke	USA	88	7.07	2)	Norfolk	07 Sep
	Edward French	USA		7.06	1)	Ann Arbor	18 May
	Professional:						
	George Murray	GB		7.24	1)	Dornoch	Aug
1908	Timothy Ahearne	Ire	86	7.57	1)	Kanturk	06 Aug
	Francis Irons	USA	86	7.48	1)	London	22 Jul
	Dan Kelly	USA	83	7.32	)		
	Calvin Bricker	Can	85	7.22	1)	Montreal	06 Jun
1909	Francis Irons	USA	86	7.34	1)	Chicago	07 Aug
	James Thorpe	USA	88	7.16	1)	Carlisle	12 Jun
	Percy Kirwan	Ire		7.11	1)	Mallow	18 Jul
	Frank Mount Pleasant	USA	84	7.09	1)	Philadelphia	24 Apr
	Daniel Ahearn	USA	88	7.09	1)	Montreal	15 Sep

Year	Athlete	Nation	Born	Mark	Place	Venue	Date
1910	Platt Adams	USA	83	7.25	)		
	John Davis	Aus		7.15	)		
	Frans Irons	USA	86	7.13	1)	New Orleans	15 Oct
	Samuel Bellah	USA	87	7.13	)		
	James Wasson	USA		7.10	1)	Philadelphia	30 Apr
1911	Uuno Railo	Fin	87	7.16	1)	Waukegan, IL	04 Jul
	Albert Gutterson	USA	87	7.15	1)	Cambridge, MA	24 Jun
	Percy Kirwan	Ire		7.15	1)	London	01 Jul
	John Davis	Aus		7.12	1)	Adelaide	31 May
	Platt Adams	USA	85	7.12	1)	New York	03 Jun
	Robert Pasemann	Ger	86	7.10	2)	London	01 Jul
	Frederick Allen	USA	90	7.08	1)	Berkeley	15 Apr
	James Wasson	USA		7.08	1)	Philadelphia	29 Apr
	Henri Puncet	Fra	86	7.06	1)	Bordeaux	27 Jul
	Frank Irons	USA	86	7.02	1)	Chicago	04 Jul
	Sidney Abrahams	GB	85	7.01	3)	London	01 Jul
1912	Albert Gutterson	USA	87	7.60	1)	Stockholm	12 Jul
	Eugene Mercer	USA	88	7.27	1)	Philadelphia	31 May
	Calvin Bricker	Can	85	7.21	2)	Sockholm	12 Jul
	Harry Worthington	USA	91	7.20	1)	Cambridge, MA	08 Jun
	Georg Åberg	Swe	93	7.18	3)	Stockholm	12 Jul
	Fred Allen	USA	90	7.15	1)	Berkeley	04 May
	Platt Adams	USA	85	7.12	1)	Celtic Park	20 Oct
	Walters	USA		7.08	1)	Charlottesville	11 May
	James Thorpe	USA	88	7.08	1)	New York (CP)	02 Sep
	Percy Kirwan	Ire		7.07	1)	London (SB)	22 Jun
	Henri Puncet	Fra	86	7.07	1)	Bordeaux	02 Jun
1913	Don Ward Dawson	USA		7.28	1)	Palo Alto	03 Apr
	Philip Stiles	USA		7.20	1)	Chicago	10 May
	Lincoln Prescott	USA		7.17	1)	Cambridge, MA	28 Jun
	H. Bostock	USA		7.16	1)	Pittsburgh	07 Jun
	Henry Ashington	GB	91	7.15	1)	London	14 Mar
	Harry Worthington	USA	91	7.14	1)	Exeter	03 May
	Eugene Mercer	USA	88	7.10	1)	Cambridge, MA	31 Mar
	Platt Adams	USA	85	7.09	1)	New York	27 Sep
	György Kovács	Hun	85	7.07	1)	Budapest	25 May
	Robert Naylor	GB	89	7.07	1)	Aldershot	24 Jul
1914	Otto Egger	Aut	93	7.18	1)	Budapest	12 Jul
	Henry Ashington	GB	91	7.17	1)	London	27 Mar
	Richard Boyd	USA		7.16	1)	Saint Louis	30 May
	H. A. Pogue	USA		7.11	1)	Dayton	04 Jul
	György Kovács	Hun	85	7.10	1)	Budapest	10 May
	Lincoln Prescott	USA		7.09	1)	Exeter	30 May
	Philip Kingsford	GB	91	7.09	1)	London	04 Jul
	William Hunter	GB	92	7.07	1)	Edinburgh	27 Jun
	Willi Düncker	Ger	93	7.06	1)	Münster	14 Jun
	Platt Adams	USA	85	7.06	1)	Baltimore	12 Sep
1915	Solomon Butler	USA	95	7.38	1)	Chicago	17 Jul
	Wesley Oler	USA	92	7.29	1)	New Haven	15 May
	Harry Worthington	USA	92	7.27w	1)	Cambridge, MA	22 May
	Philip Stiles	USA		7.25	1)	Urbana	05 Jun
	Yngve Dahlqvist	Swe	92	7.15	1)	København	15 Jun
	Alma Richards	USA	90	7.12	1)	Ithaca	15 May
	R. D. Gooch	USA		7.11	1)	Charlottesville	15 May
	Platt Adams	USA	85	7.11	1)	New York	19 Jun
	H. Bostock	USA		7.09	2)	Cambridge, MA	26 Jun
	Ollaf Rustad	Nor	94	7.04	1)	Kristiania	19 Sep
	Willi Dünker	Ger	93	7.04	)		
1916	Harry Worthington	USA	92	7.39w	1)	Springfield, MA	20 May
	(Worthington)			7.32	1)	Cambridge, MA	26 May
	Wesley Oler	USA	92	7.19	2)	Cambridge, MA	26 May
	Robert Simpson	USA	92	7.18	1)	Columbia	13 May

Year	Name	Nat	Born	Mark	Pl	Venue	Date
	William Sisson	USA	93	7.17	1)	Palo Alto	15 Apr
	E. F. Jones	USA		7.16	1)	New Brunswick	04 Jul
	Foster Hampton	USA		7.09	1)	Cambridge, MA	13 May
	Frank Maker	USA		7.05	4)	Cambridge, MA	26 May
	Harold Pogue	USA		7.02	1)	Evanston	03 Jun
	Georg Åberg	Swe	93	6.98	1)	Sockholm	08 Jul
	Olaf Rustad	Nor	94	6.96	1)	Krostiania	02 Sep
1917	J. P. Jackson	USA		7.23	1)	Berkeley	14 Apr
	Joseph Irish	USA	94	7.16	1)	Chicago	30 Jun
	Solomon Butler	USA	95	7.15	1)	Philadelphia	28 Apr
	Curt Enhörning	Swe	98	7.15	1)	Stockolm	14 Oct
	Robert Simpson	USA	92	7.10	1)	Chicago	09 Jun
	Rodolfo Hammersley	Chl	89	7.09	)		
	Luther Nichols	USA		7.05	2)	Berkeley	07 Apr
	Ira Dertolet	USA		7.04	2)	Philadelphia	28 Apr
	Olav Frogner	Nor	91	6.96	1)	Kristiania	29 Sep
	E. F. Jones	USA		6.93	1)	New York	25 Aug
1918	Carl Johnson	USA	98	7.29	1)	Chicago	08 Jun
	William Petersson	Swe	95	7.24	1)	Köbenhavn	01 Sep
	David Politzer	USA		7.11	1)	New York	27 Jul
	Olav Frogner	Nor	91	7.08	1)	Stockholm	07 Jul
	William Carter	USA		6.99	1)	Columbia, MO	25 May
	Johan Johansen	Nor	98	6.98	D)	Stavanger	20 Jul
	August Heyneman	Hol	03	6.90	1)	Wormerveer	09 Jun
	A. Lang	USA		6.89	2)	Chicago	08 Jun
	Robert Felter	USA		6.85	1)	Philadelphia	01 Jun
	Daniel Ahearn	USA	88	6.85	1)	Detroit	14 Sep
1919	Solomon Butler	USA	95	7.55w	1)	Paris	29 Jun
	Carl Johnson	USA	98	7.34	1)	Chicago	07 Jul
	William Petersson	Swe	95	7.26	1)	Malmö	13 Jul
	Harry Worthington	USA	92	7.26w	2)	Paris	29 Jun
	(Butler)			7.22	1)	Colombes	19 Jun
	(Worthington)			7.17	2)	Colombes	19 Jun
	Ernst Söllinger	Ger	96	7.15	1)	Wien	06 Jul
	Johan Johansen	Nor	98	7.11	1)	Stavanger	29 Jun
	Gösta Bladin	Swe	94	7.95	1)	Gävle	03 Aug
	Arthur Holz	Ger	96	7.05	1)	Nürnberg	24 Aug
	Jack Merchant	USA	99	7.03	1)	Berkeley	10 May
	Helge Lövevland	Nor	90	7.03	1)	Kristiania	15 Jun
1920	Solomon Butler	USA	95	7.51	1)	Cambridge, MA	17 Jul
	Jack Merchant	USA	99	7.29	1)	Berkeley	08 May
	Henry Foster	USA		7.26	1)	Pullman	22 May
	William Petersson	Swe	95	7.26	1)	Stockholm	11 Jul
	D. D. Malan	SA		7.25	1)	Cape Town	
	Sherman Landers	USA	90	7.21	1)	Philadelphia	29 May
	Carl Johnson	USA	98	7.20	1)	Ann Arbor	04 Jun
	Edwin Gourdin	USA	97	7.19	2)	Philadelphia	29 May
	Karl Hornberger	Ger	00	7.19	1)	Koblenz	27 Jun
	Richard Templeton	USA	97	7.09	3)	Philadelphia	29 May
	Exhibition:						
	Ernst Söllinger	Ger	96	7.17	)		

ALL TIME WORLD LIST AS AT THE END OF 1920

Name	Nat	Born	Mark	Pl	Venue	Date
Patrick O'Coonor	IRE	74	7.61	1)	Dublin	05 Aug 01
ALbert Gutterson	USA	87	7.60	1)	Stockhlm	12 Jul 12
Timothy Ahearne	Ire	86	7.57	1)	Kanturk	06 Aug 08
Solomon Butler	USA	95	7.51	1)	Cambridge, MA	17 Jul 20
Meyer Prinstein	USA	78	7.50	1)	Philadelphia	28 Apr 00
Frank Irons	USA	86	7.48	1)		08

	Alvin Kraenzlein	USA	76	7.43	1)	New York	26 May 99
	Daniel Kelly	USA	83	7.37	1)	Eugene	17 May 06
	Carl Johnson	USA	98	7.34	1)	Chicago	07 Jul 19
1921	Edward Gourdin	USA	97	7.69	1)	Cambridge, MA	23 Jul
	Karl Dickel	Ger	99	7.32	1)	Duisburg	05 Jun
	Paul Courtois	USA		7.26	2)	Philadelphia	30 Apr
	Otto Egger	Aut	93	7.26	1)	Wien	07 Sep
	Carl Schelenz	Ger	90	7.23w	2)	Berlin	24 Jul
	Erling Aastad	Nor	98	7.22	1)	Oslo	04 Sep
	Richard Honner	Aus	97	7.22	1)	Adelaide	31 Dec
	William Petersson (Björneman)	Swe	95	7.15	)	Saint-Cloud	15 May
	Ernst Söllinger	Ger	96	7.14	1)	Hamburg	21 Aug
	Henry Schumacher	Ger	94	7.13	2)	Hamburg	21 Aug
	Extra trial:						
	Karl Hornberger	Ger	00	7.33	-)	Hamburg	21 Aug
	Doubtful conditions:						
	Karl Hornberger	Ger	00	7.50w	1)	Bad Kreuznach	07 Aug
1922	William DeHart Hubbard	USA	03	7.44	1)	Newark, NJ	09 Sep
	Robert LeGendre	USA	97	7.39	1)	Chicago	17 Jun
	Edward Gourdin	USA	97	7.31	2)	Newark NJ	09 Sep
	Karl Hornberger	Ger	00	7.28	1)	Kirn	09 Jul
	Henry Schumacher	Ger	94	7.27	1)	Oslo	17 Sep
	Sverre Hansen	Nor	99	7.24	1)	Oslo	06 Aug
	William Dowding	USA	98	7.22	1)	Chicago	27 May
	Harold Muller	USA	01	7.22	2)	Chicago	17 Jun
	Sol Butler	USA	95	7.20	3)	Newark, NJ	09 Sep
	Albert Rose	USA		7.19	1)	Hanover, NH	06 May
	August Heynemann	Hol		7.19	1)	Recklinghausen	04 Jun
	Measured with linen tape:						
	Paul Couillaud	Fra	93	7.23	1)	Saint-Claude	27 Aug
1923	William DeHart Hubbard	USA	03	7.67	1)	Chicago	16 Jun
	Robert LeGendre	USA	97	7.43w	1)	Cambridge, MA	15 Sep
	William Comins	USA	01	7.41	Q/1)	Philadelphia	25 May
	Charles Hoff	Nor	02	7.32	1)	Oslo	08 Sep
	Albert Rose	USA	01	7.31	2)	Philadelphia	26 May
	Vilho Tuulos	Fin	95	7.31	1)	Göteborg	01 Jul
	Henry Schumacher	Ger	94	7.23	1)	Hannover	10 Jun
	Harold Abrahams	GB	99	7.23	1)	London	07 Jul
	Edward Hamm	USA	06	7.22	1)	Chicago	26 May
	József Haluska	Hun	00	7.22	1)	Budapest	24 Jun
1924	Robert LeGendre	USA	97	7.76	P)	Colombes	07 Jul
	William DeHart Hubbard	USA	03	7.63	1)	Cambride, MA	13 Jun
	Edward Gourdin	USA	97	7.53	1)	London	19 Jul
	William Comins	USA	01	7.51	1)	Cambridge, MA	31 May
	John Paul Jones	USA		7.49	1)	Lawrence, KS	19 Apr
	Sylvio Cator	Hai	00	7.43	1)	Bergerac	16 Aug
	Albert Rose	USA	01	7.41	1)	New Haven, CT	03 May
	William Björneman (Petersson)	Swe	95	7.39	1)	Linköping	03 Aug
	Edward Hamm	USA	06	7.38	1)	Chicago	31 May
	Harold Abrahams	GB	99	7.38	1)	Woolwich	07 Jun
	Exhibition:						
	William DeHart Hubbard	USA	03	7.68	-)	Columbus, OH	19 Apr
1925	William DeHart Hubbard	USA	03	7.89	1)	Chicago	13 Jun
	F. Morgan Taylor	USA	93	7.67w	1)	Norman, OK	30 May
	Sylvio Cator	Hai	00	7.65	1)	Wien	10 Sep
	Erling Aastad	Nor	98	7.45	1)	Oslo	12 Aug

Year	Athlete	Nat	Born	Mark	Place	Venue	Date
	Kenneth Lancaster	USA		7.43	2)	Norman, OK	29 May
	Charles Hoff	Nor	02	7.41	2)	Trondheim	22 Aug
	Edward Hamm	USA	06	7.36	1)	Atlanta	18 Apr
	William Wallace	USA		7.34	2)	Columbus, OH	06 Jun
	Sydney Atkinson	SA	01	7.34	1)	Durban	21 Nov
	Gerald Woods	USA		7.34	1)	Houston	28 Mar
	Paul Jones	USA		7.34	1)	Chicago	31 May
	Exhibition:						
	Sylvio Cator	Hai	00	7.71	-)		25 Aug
1926	William DeHart Hubbard	USA	03	7.72	1)	Cincinnati	05 Jun
	Richard Honner	Aus	97	7.45	1)	London	26 Jun
	Elmer Bondshu	USA	05	7.38	1)	Palo Alto, CA	15 May
	Paul Jones	USA		7.38	2)	Philadelphia	05 Jul
	Rudolf Dobermann	Ger	02	7.36	1)	Leipzig	08 Aug
	George Martin	USA		7.34w	1)	San Francisco	08 May
	Willi Meier	Ger	07	7.32	1)	Lübeck	10 Oct
	Thomas Meeks	USA		7.31	2)	Palo Alto, CA	15 May
	Sydney Atkinson	SA	01	7.31	1)	Durban	04 Dec
	Proctor Flanagan	USA		7.28	3)	Palo Alto, CA	15 May
	Tibor Püspöki	Hun	00	7.28	1)	Colombes	18 Jul
1927	William DeHart Hubbard	USA	03	7.84	1)	Lincoln, NE	02 Jul
	Edward Hamm	USA	06	7.61	1)	Baton Rouge, LA	14 May
	Alfred Bates	USA	05	7.53	1)	Philadelphia	28 May
	Rudolf Dobermann	Ger	02	7.53	1)	Ludwigshafen	26 Jun
	Jesse Hill	USA	07	7.49	1)	Palo Alto, CA	23 Apr
	Olle Hallberg	Swe	03	7.47	1)	Stockholm	21 Aug
	Fred Zombro	USA		7.46	1)	Fresno, CA	30 Apr
	Theodore Mathias	USA		7.46	Q2)	Philadelphia	27 May
	Paul Jones	USA		7.45	2)	Lincoln, NE	02 Jul
	Kimball Dyer	USA	07	7.40	2)	Palo Alto, CA	23 Apr
	Take-off board 1 inch (2.5 cm.) higher than landing pit:						
	William DeHart Hubbard	USA	03	7.98	1)	Cincinnati	17 Sep
	Unconfirmed performance:						
	Sylvio Cator	Hai	00	7.69	)		
1928	Sylvio Cator	Hai	00	7.93	1)	Colombes	09 Sep
	Edward Hamm	USA	06	7.90	1)	Cambridge, MA	07 Jul
	Rudolf Dobermann	Ger	02	7.64	1)	Jena	10 Jun
	Erich Köchermann	Ger	04	7.64	1)	Hamburg	16 Sep
	Edward Gordon	USA	08	7.60	1)	Chicago	09 Jun
	Kimball Dyer	USA	07	7.59	1)	Palo Alto, CA	12 May
	Fred Zombro	USA		7.58	1)	Palo Alto, CA	10 Mar
	Alfred Bates	USA	05	7.58	1)	Cambridge, MA	25 May
	Willi Meier	Ger	07	7.54	1)	Bochum	26 Aug
	Olle Hallberg	Swe	03	7.50	1)	Gävle	23 Sep
	Landing pit lower than take-off board:						
	Helmut Schlöske	Ger	04	7.50	3)	Weimar	09 Jun
1929	Jess Hill	USA	07	7.64	1)	Philadelphia	01 Jun
	Kimball Dyer	USA	07	7.55	1)	San Francisco	04 May
	Chuhei Nambu	Jap	04	7.55w	1)	Mukden	20 Oct
	Edward Gordon	USA	08	7.53	1)	Chicago	08 Jun
	Olof Hallberg	Swe	03	7.51	1)	Stockholm	25 Aug
	George Martin	USA		7.50	1)	Fresno	27 Apr
	Johannes Viljoen	SA	05	7.50	1)	Bloemfontein	31 Aug
	Lamoine Boyle	USA		7.50	2)	Philadelphia	01 Jun
	William Portmess	USA		7.50	1)	Dallas	30 Mar
	Erich Köchermann	Ger	04	7.50	1)	Hamburg	10 Jul
1930	Edward Hamm	USA	06	7.77	1)	Atlanta	10 May
	George Martin	USA		7.69w	1)	San Francisco	03 May

Year	Athlete	Nation	Born	Mark	Place	Venue	Date
	Edward Gordon	USA	08	7.62	1)	Chicago	07 Jun
	Erich Köchermann	Ger	04	7.61	1)	Hamburg	13 Jul
	Chuhei Nambu	Jap	04	7.59	1)	Tokyo	24 May
	Theodore Smith	USA	07	7.51	1)	West Point	May
	Arnold West	USA		7.50	1)	Cambridge, MA	31 May
	Sol Furth	USA	07	7.49	2)	Cambridge, MA	30 May
	T. Kimball Dyer	USA	07	7.46	2)	Palo Alto	08 Mar
	Virgil Dowell	USA		7.46	3)	Cambridge, MA	30 May
	Alfred Bates	USA	05	7.46	1)	Philadelphia	21 Jun
	Mikio Oda	Jap	05	7.46	2)	Tokyo	24 May
1931	Chuhei Nambu	Jap	04	7.98	1)	Tokyo	27 Oct
	Coburn Tomson	USA		7.78w	1)	Lincoln	23 May
	Edward Gordon	USA	08	7.73	1)	Lawrence	18 Apr
	Richard Barber	USA	09	7.71	1)	Philadelphia	30 May
	Lamoine Boyle	USA	13	7.65	2)	Philadelphia	29 May
	Donald Gray	USA		7.62w	2)	Lincoln	23 May
	John Brooks	USA	10	7.53	1)	Lincoln	03 Jul
	Clifford Mell	USA		7.53w	3)	Lincoln	23 May
	Mikio Oda	Jap	05	7.52	2)	Nishinomiya	28 Jun
	Alfred Bates	USA	05	7.49	1)	Lincoln	04 Jul
1932	Lambert Redd	USA	08	7.78	1)	Chicago	11 Jun
	Chuhei Nambu	Jap	04	7.76	1)	Taipei	05 Mar
	Richard Barber	USA	09	7.73	1)	Palo Alto	16 Jul
	Edward Gordon	USA	08	7.70	2)	Palo Alto	16 Jul
	John Brooks	USA	10	7.69	2)	Chicago	11 Jun
	Maurice Walzer	USA		7.60	2)	Fresno	14 May
	Weldon Hale	USA		7.56	1)	Houston	14 May
	Norman Paul	USA	12	7.56	3)	Fresno	14 May
	Sylvio Cator	Hai	00	7.50	1)	Chicago	18 Aug
	Robert Paul	USA	12	7.56	3)	Fresno	14 May
1933	Lutz Long	Ger	13	7.65	1)	Köln	12 Aug
	Jesse Owens	USA	13	7.60	1)	Cleveland	03 Jun
	Chuhei Nambu	Jap	04	7.60	1)	Osaka	04 Jun
	Winfield Whipple	USA	15	7.57	1)	Arkadelphia	22 Apr
	Donald Gray	USA		7.51w	1)	Lincoln	19 May
	Lajos Balogh	Hun	03	7.49	1)	Budapest	19 Aug
	Douglas Taylor	USA		7.48	1)	San Francisco	20 May
	Lewis Hale	USA		7.48	1)	Austin	13 May
	Henrik Koltai	Hun	13	7.48	2)	Budapest	19 Aug
	Masao Harada	Jap	12	7.47	2)	Osaka	04 Jun
1934	Jesse Owens	USA	13	7.81	1)	Milwaukee	30 Jun
	Albert Olson	USA	12	7.72	1)	Los Angeles	22 Jun
	Wilhelm Leichum	Ger	11	7.65w	1)	Stockholm	01 Sep
	H. Moncure Little	USA	12	7.62	1)	Washington, DC	10 Apr
	Robert Clarke	USA	13	7.61	1)	TrAvedrs Island, NY	02 Jun
	Masao Harada	Jap	12	7.59	1)	Nishinomiya	15 Sep
	Henrik Kolltai	Hun	13	7.58	1)	Budapest	05 Aug
	Lutz Long	Ger	13	7.53	1)	Nürnberg	27 Jul
	Otto Berg	Nor	06	7.53	1)	Oslo	26 Aug
	Eric Svensson	Swe	03	7.53	2)	Oslo	26 Aug
	Olle Hallberg	Swe	03	7.53w	1)	Göteborg	23 Sep
1935	Jesse Owens	USA	13	8.13	1)	Ann Arbor	25 May
	Eulace Peacock	USA	14	8.00	1)	Lincoln	04 Jul
	Albert Olson	USA	12	7.84	2)	Berkeley	22 Jun
	John Brooks	USA	10	7.76	3)	Lincoln	04 Jul
	Naoto Tajima	Jap	12	7.74	1)	Nishinomiya	09 Jun
	Wilhelm Leichum	Ger	11	7.73	1)	Berlin	03 Aug
	Robert Paul	Fra	10	7.70	2)	Colombes	04 Aug
	Willis Ward	USA	12	7.65	2)	Ann Arbor	25 May
	Lutz Long	Ger	13	7.64	1)	Jena	30 Jun
	Stanley Johnson	USA		7.59	1)	Lincoln	03 Jul
	Sam Richardson	Can	17	7.59	1)	Winnipeg	09 Aug

LONG JUMP 1936 1940

Year	Name	Nat	Born	Mark	Pl	Venue	Date
1936	Jesse Owens	USA	13	8.06w	1)	Berlin	04 Aug
	(Owens)			8.00	1)	Princeton	04 Jul
	Robert Clark	USA	13	7.91	D)	Milwaukee	26 Jun
	Lutz Long	Ger	13	7.87w	2)	Berlin	04 Aug
	(Long)			7.82	1)	Berlin	11 Jul
	lhelm Leichum	Ger	11	7.76	1)	Jena	07 Jun
	Kermit King	USA	11	7.74	2)	Princeton	04 Jul
	Naoto Tajima	Jap	12	7.74w	3)	Berlin	04 Aug
	Arturo Maffei	Ita	09	7.73w	4)	Berlin	04 Aug
	John Brooks	USA	10	7.70	2)	New York	11 Jul
	Niño Ramirez	Phi	12	7.64	1)	Manila	02 Jun
	Milton Green	USA		7.60	1)	Cambridge, MA	23 May
1937	Lutz Long	Ger	13	7.90	1)	Berlin	01 Aug
	Kermit King	USA	11	7.88	1)	Emporia, KS	04 May
	Mack Robinson	USA	14	7.76	1)	Des Moines	23 Apr
	John Brooks	USA	10	7.73	)		May
	Arnold Nutting	USA	16	7.69	2)	Berkeley	18 Jun
	Arturo Maffei	Ita	09	7.63w?	1)	Colombes	12 Sep
	Robert Clark	USA	13	7.62	1)	Berkeley	20 Mar
	Eulace Peacock	USA	14	7.61	3)	Berkeley	18 Jun
	Charles Walker	USA		7.57	1)	Milwaukee	02 Jul
	Robert Hubbard	USA		7.55	4)	Berkeley	18 Jun
	Exhibition:						
	Tom Lavery	SA	11	7.58	-)	Pretoria	23 Oct
1938	Jackie Robinson	USA	19	7.78	1)	Claremont, CA	07 May
	Arnold Nutting	USA	16	7.67	1)	Evanston	27 Jun
	Guy Manuel	USA	17	7.65	1)	Palo Alto	23 Apr
	Bill Lacefield	USA	17	7.65	1)	Minneapolis	17 Jun
	Kenshi Togami	Jap	13	7.64	1)	Nishinomiya	28 May
	Wilhelm Leichum	Ger	11	7.64	1)	Colombes	03 Sep
	Charles Walker	USA		7.62	1)	Columbus	11 Jun
	Bill Watson	USA	16	7.61	1)	Columbus	20 May
	Arturo Maffei	Ita	09	7.61	2)	Colombes	03 Sep
	Mack Robinson	USA	14	7.58	1)	Eugene	07 May
1939	Bill Watson	USA	16	7.76	1)	Ann Arbor	19 May
	Bill Lacefield	USA	17	7.76w	1)	Lincoln	04 Jul
	Billy Brown	USA	18	7.74	1)	Austin	15 Apr
	Edward Gordon	USA	08	7.65w	3)	Lincoln	04 Jul
	Francis Swaim	USA		7.60	1)	Emporia, KS	07 Jun
	Pat Turner	USA	18	7.59w	4)	Lincoln	04 Jul
	Arturo Maffei	Ita	09	7.58	1)	Milano	16 Jul
	James Mather	USA		7.57	1)		
	Anson Perina	USA	16	7.55	1)	Philadelphia	29 Apr
	Judson Atchison	USA		7.55	1)	Los Angeles	17 Jun
1940	Pat Turner	USA	18	7.78	1)	Evanston	17 Jun
	Genken Kim	Jap	18	7.66	1)	Kashihara	01 Jun
	Billy Brown	USA	18	7.65	1)	Fresno	29 Jun
	Jackie Robinson	USA	19	7.62	1)	Los Angeles	25 May
	Bill Lacefield	USA	17	7.59	3)	Evanston	17 Jun
	Frank Freeman	USA		7.57	1)	Berkeley	18 May
	Norwood Ewell	USA	18	7.52i	1)	New York	02 Mar
	Berton Yates	USA	18	7.51	1)	Lafayette, LA	30 Mar
	Welles Hodgson	USA		7.51	4)	Evanston	17 Jun
	James Mather	USA		7.49	1)	Peru, NB	25 May

ALL TIME WORLD AS AT THE END OF 1940

Name	Nat	Born	Mark	Pl	Venue	Date
Jesse Owens	USA	13	8.13	1)	Ann Arbor	25 May 35
Eulace Peacock	USA	14	8.00	1)	Lincoln	04 Jul 35
Chuhei Nambu	Jap	04	7.98	1)	Tokyo	27 Oct 31

Year	Name	Nat	Born	Mark	Pl	Venue	Date
	Sylvio Cator	Hai	00	7.93	1)	Colombes	09 Sep 28
	Robert Clark	USA	13	7.91	1)	Milwaukee	26 Jun 36
	Edward Hamm	USA	06	7.90	1)	Cambridge, MA	07 Jul 28
	Lutz Long	Ger	13	7.90	1)	Berlin	01 Aug 37
	Willam DeHart Hubbarf	USA	03	7.89	1)	Chicago	13 Jun25
	Kermit King	USA	11	7.88	1)	Emporia, KS	04 May 37
	Albert Olson	USA	12	7.84	2)	Berkeley	22 Jun 35
1941	Billy Brown	USA	18	7.79w?	1)	Austin	05 Apr
	James O'Reilly	USA		7.66	1)	Patterson, NJ	10 Jul
	Ed Vasconcellos	USA		7.62	1)	Berkeley	03 May
	Waldo Clapham	USA		7.61	1)	San Antonio	08 Mar
	Don Anderson	USA	20	7.57	1)	Logan	26 Apr
	José Bento de Assis	Bra	15	7.55	1)	São Paulo	30 Aug
	Jim Jurkovich	USA	21	7.54	1)	Berkeley	26 Apr
	Gerd Wagemanns	Ger	20	7.52	1)	Halle	14 Sep
	Sol Schumitzky	USA	19	7.51	1)	Lincoln	24 May
	Butler Avery	USA		7.51	)		
1942	Norwood Ewell	USA	18	7.68i	1)	New York	07 Mar
	Bill Smith	USA	23	7.62	1)	San Jose	05 May
	Avon Rice	USA		7.59	)		
	James O'Reilly	USA		7.59	)		
	Gerd Wagemanns	Ger	20	7.58	1)	Bedrlin	02 Aug
	Dick Fordham	USA	53	7.53	1)	Los Angeles	15 Apr
	José Bento de Assis	Bra	15	7.51i	1)	New York	28 Feb
	Dallas Dupre	USA	21	7.49	1)	Evanston	16 Jun
	Willie Steele	USA	23	7.46	1)	Fresno	16 May
	Ralph Tate	USA	21	7.45	)		
	Not a bona-fide meet:						
	Willie Steele	USA	23	7.80	1)		04 Jun
1943	Kurt Albert	Ger	20	7.63	1)	Leipzig	14 Nov
	Ralph Tate	USA	21	7.60	1)	Stillwater, OK	29 Apr
	Clarence Lewis	USA		7.57	)		
	Billy Christopher	USA		7.52w	1)	Houston	19 May
	Armand Bour	Fra	16	7.50	1)	Hayange	10 Aug
	Stig Håkansson	Swe	18	7.49w	1)	Örebro	03 Oct
	Pekka Simola	Fin	20	7.40	1)	Lappeenranta	03 Jun
	Lennart Eliaeson	Swe	20	7.40	1)	Helsinki	01 Jul
	Edsel Curry	USA	22	7.39	1)	New York	19 Jun
	Dallas Dupre	USA	21	7.38i	1)	East Lansing	13 Feb
	Jim Jurkovich	USA	21	7.38	1)	Fresno	22 May
1944	Stig Håkansson	Swe	18	7.50	1)	Sigtuna	08 Oct
	Norwood Ewell	USA	18	7.46i	1)	New York	26 Feb
	Claude Young	USA	23	7.42i	1)	Champaign	26 Feb
	Herb Douglas	USA	22	7.42i	2)	New York	26 Feb
	Eulace Peacock	USA	14	7.40i	3)	New York	26 Feb
	Elroy Hirsch	USA		7.37	1)	Ann Arbor	13 May
	Pat Turner	USA	18	7.36	1)	Los Angeles	27 May
	Billy Joe Grimes	USA		7.36	1)	Norman, OK	13 May
	Sergey Kuznyetsov	SU	18	7.36	)		
	Ted Haese	USA		7.31	1)	Austin	01 Apr
	Sloping runway:						
	Jean Balezo	Fra	15	7.44	1)	Vienne	23 Jul
	Unconfirmed performance:						
	James O'Reilly	USA		7.87	1)	College Park, LA	08 Apr
1945	Sylvester Bell	USA		7.57	1)	New York	29 Jun
	Herb Douglas	USA	22	7.53	2)	New York	29 Jun
	Clarence Lewis	USA		7.51	)		
	Sergey Kuznyetsov	SU	18	7.49	1)	Kiev	11 Sep
	Bill Lund	USA		7.44i	2)	Cleveland	23 Mar

Year	Athlete	Nat	Age	Mark	Pos	Venue	Date
	Eulace Peacock	USA	14	7.42	P)	Elizabeth, NJ	04 Jul
	Olle Laessker	Swe	22	7.35	1)	Gävle	30 Sep
	Pekka Simola	Fin	20	7.34	1)	Stockholm	21 Aug
	Fred Bouwman	USA	24	7.30i	1)	New York	03 Mar
	Gustaf Strand	Swe	22	7.30	1)	Karlshamn	30 Sep
	Unconfirmed performance:						
	Harold Brown	Can	17	7.45	-)	Taun	03 Aug
1946	Willie Steele	USA	23	7.66	1)	Los Angeles	25 May
	Alfred Lawrence	USA	25	7.60	1)	Westwood, CA	20 Apr
	John Robertson	USA	21	7.58	1)	Minneapolis	22 Jun
	Herb Douglas	USA	22	7.57	2)	Minneapolis	21 Jun
	Norman Pederson	USA		7.57w	1)	Lincoln	18 May
	Ralph Tate	USA	21	7.56	1)	Austin	06 Apr
	Olle Laessker	Swe	22	7.50	1)	Gävle	18 Jul
	Smith	USA		7.49	1)		
	Sergey Kuznyetsov	SU	18	7.46	1)	Moskva	15/16 Jun
	Lloyd LaBeach	Jam/Pan	23	7.42i	1)	Iowa City	02 Mar
1947	Willie Steele	USA	23	8.07	1)	Salt Lake City, UT	20 Jun
	Lorenzo Wright	USA	26	7.86	2)	Salt Lake City, UT	20 Jun
	George Uyeda	USA		7.63	1)	Honolulu	24 May
	Theodore Bruce	Aus	23	7.58	1)	Perth	25 Jan
	Charles Thompson	Br.Gu		7.55	1)	Georgetown	12 Nov
	Bill Lacefield	USA	17	7.53	1)	Los Angeles	31 May
	Fred Johnson	USA	24	7.50	1)	Philadelphia	30 May
	Paul Miller	USA		7.50	1)	Evanston	30 May
	Herb Douglas	USA	22	7.46i	1)	West Point, NY	25 Jan
	Don Barksdale	USA	23	7.44	2)	Fresno	17 May
	Neville Price	SA	29	7.44	1)	Brakpan	18 Oct
1948	Willie Steele	USA	23	7.97	1)	Evanston	09 Jul
	Lorenzo Wright	USA	26	7.90	1)	Detroit	05 May
	Fred Johnson	USA	24	7.74i	1)	East Lansing, MI	06 Mar
	Herb Douglas	USA	22	7.69	2)	Evanston	10 Jul
	Robert Teel	USA	23	7.65	1)	Dallas	04 Jun
	Jim Holland	USA	24	7.63	1)	Milwaukee	11 Jun
	John Robertson	USA	21	7.62	2)	Dallas	04 Jun
	Eural Davis	USA		7.61	1)	Tuskegee, AL	01 May
	Lloyd Duff	USA	24	7.59	1)	Columbus, OH	08 May
	Denis Hasenjager	SA	24	7.58	1)	Krugersdorp	06 Nov
1949	Gaylord Bryan	USA	27	7.74	1)	Westwood	09 Apr
	George Brown	USA	31	7.68	1)	Los Angeles	01 Apr
	Fred Johnson	USA	24	7.68	1)	Los Angeles	17 Jun
	Neville Price	SA	29	7.63	1)	Kuugersdorp	05 Nov
	Herb Douglas	USA	22	7.61i	1)	New York	19 Feb
	Heinz Kreulich	Ger	20	7.58	1)	Bremen	06 Aug
	Herb Hoskins	USA		7.56	1)	Lawrence, KS	23 Apr
	Henry Aihara	USA	26	7.54	1)	Seattle	29 May
	Gerd Luther	Ger	20	7.53	2)	Bremen	07 Aug
	Denis Hasenjager	SA	24	7.53	2)	Krugersdorp	29 Oct
1950	Jim Holland	USA	24	7.85	1)	College Park, MD	24 Jun
	Jerome Biffle	USA	28	7.81i	1)	Boulder, CO	01 Apr
	Sylvanus Williams	Nig	22	7.69w	1)	Chiswick	17 Jun
	Gaylord Brian	USA	27	7.68	1)	Palo Alto	06 May
	Herb Hoskins	USA		7.68	1)	Manhattan, KS	06 May
	Henry Aihara	USA	26	7.65w	2)	Minneapolis	17 Jun
	Neville Price	SA	29	7.64	1)	Pretoria	11 Mar
	John Simmons	USA		7.59	1)	Fresno	13 May
	Paul Faucher	Fra	20	7.59	1)	Niort	02 Jul
	Andrew Stanfield	USA	27	7.58	1)	Philadelphia	29 Apr
	Bill Albans	USA	25	7.58	2)	Philadelphia	29 Apr
1951	George Brown	USA	31	7.95	1)	Tokyo	18 Jul

	Meredith Gourdine	USA	29	7.86	1)	Philadelphia	25 May
	Andrew Stanfield	USA	27	7.85	2)	Philadelphia	25 May
	Charles Meeks	USA		7.54	1)	Austin	04 May
	William Hairston	USA		7.53	1)		
	Ron Soble	USA		7.51	1)	Ann Arbor	12 May
	Herb Hoskins	USA		7.48	1)		
	Henk Visser	Hol	32	7.48	1)	Ryswyk	09 Sep
	Denis Hasenjager	SA	24	7.45	1)		
	Boris Brnad	Yug		7.45	1)	Beograd	26 Aug
1952	George Brown	USA	31	8.00	1)	Fresno	10 May
	F. Morgan Taylor, Jr.	USA	31	7.77	2)	Berkeley	14 Jun
	Meredith Gourdine	USA	29	7.73	1)	Los Angeles	27 Jun
	Jerome Biffle	USA	28	7.67	2)	Los Angeles	27 Jun
	Ary Façanha de Sá	Bra	28	7.57	1)	São Paulo	08 Jun
	Arthur Scott	USA		7.53	1)	Los Angeles	18 Apr
	Fred Johnson	USA	24	7.53	5)	Los Angeles	27 Jun
	William Albans	USA	25	7.53	2)	Los Angeles	18 Apr
	Sylvanus Williams	Nig	22	7.52	1)	Colombes	24 Aug
	Handadash Madatov	SU		7.50	1)	Baku	29 May
	With assisting wind:						
	Neville Price	SA	27	7.67	1)	Austin	05 Apr
	Henk Visser	Hol	32	7.57	1)	Rotterdam	29 Jun
	Masaji Tajima	Jap		7.52	1)	Tokyo	29 Apr
	Henry Grabowski	Pol		7.51	1)	Leipzig	31 May
1953	George Brown	USA	31	7.89	1)	Dayton	26 Jun
	Ödön Földessy	Hun	29	7.76	1)	Budapest	19 Sep
	John Bennett	USA	30	7.72	1)	Lincoln	20 Jun
	Hector Hogan	Aus	31	7.65	1)	Brisbane	14 Nov
	F. Morgan Taylor, Jr	USA	31	7.63	1)	Philadelphia	25 Apr
	Neville Price	SA	27	7.60	1)	Austin	27 Mar
	Henk Visser	Hol	32	7.52	1)	Ryswyk	07 Jun
	Masaji Tajima	Jap		7.47	1)	Nagoya	03 May
	A. Sheppard	Rho		7.46	1)	Nkana	13 Jul
	Ron Soble	USA		7.43	2)	Dayton	26 Jun
	Ahylton da Conceiçao	Bra		7.43	1)	Curitiba	21 Mar
	Robert Clark	USA		7.43	1)	Albuquerque	06 Jun
	Viktor Leskievich	SU		7.43	1)	Moskva	24 Aug
	With assisting wind:						
	Masaji Tajima	Jap		7.66	1)	Dortmund	13 Aug
	Bobby Ragsdale	USA		7.63	2)	Lawrence	18 Apr
	Eddie Griggs	USA		7.51	1)	Abilene	09 May
	Veryl Switzer	USA		7.50	4)	Lawrence	18 Apr
	Glenn Beerline	USA		7.44	1)	Des Moines	09 May
	Heinz Oberbeck	Ger		7.43	2)	Dortmund	13 Aug
1954	John Bennett	USA	30	7.83	1)	Austin	02 Apr
	Monte Upshaw	USA	36	7.72	1)	Berkeley	29 May
	Ödön Földessy	Hun	29	7.70	1)	Budapest	06 Aug
	Neville Price	SA	27	7.67	2)	Austin	02 Apr
	Rosslyn Range	USA	33	7.63	1)	Fresno	15 May
	George Brown	USA	31	7.63	1)	Compton	04 Jun
	Malachi Andrews	USA	33	7.62	1)	Tucson	27 Mar
	Leonid Grigoryev	SU	26	7.62	1)	Praha	23 Oct
	Jorma Valkama	Fin	28	7.55	1)	Helsinki	11 Sep
	Kenneth Wilmshurst	GB		7.53	1)	Vancouver	05 Aug
	Wilbur Wilson	USA		7.53	1)	Abilene	04 Jun
	With assisting wind:						
	John Bennett	USA	30	7.89	1)	Ann Arbor	12 Jun
	Jon Arnett	USA		7.53	2)	Ann Arbor	12 Jun
	Exhibition:						
	George Brown	USA	31	7.68	-)	Los Angeles	09 Apr

Year	Name	Nat	Born	Mark	Pos	Venue	Date
1955	Rosslyn Range	USA	33	8.03	1)	Mexico City	14 Mar
	John Bennett	USA	30	8.01	2)	Mexico City	14 Mar
	Gregory Bell	USA	30	7.93	1)	Boulder	24 Jun
	Neville Price	SA	27	7.87	1)	Bloemfontein	03 Dec
	Ary Façanha de Sá	Bra	28	7.84	3)	Mexico City	14 Mar
	James Gamble	USA	35	7.69	1)	Prairie View, TX	02 Apr
	Malachi Andrews	USA	33	7.64	1)	Tucson	07 May
	Heinz Oberbeck	Ger		7.62	2)	Bloemfontein	03 Dec
	Donald Stuart	SA		7.57	2)	Pretoria	09 Apr
	Monte Upshaw	USA	36	7.56	1)	Berkeley, CA	16 Apr
	Ödön Földessy	Hun	29	7.56	1)	Budapest	21 Aug
	With assisting wind:						
	Henryk Grabowski	Pol	29	7.73	1)	Budapest	11 Sep
	Malachi Andrews	USA	33	7.72	1)	Albuquerque	02 Apr
	Ödön Földessy	Hun	29	7.61	1)	Budapest	09 Oct
	Erwin Cook	USA		7.59	1)	Lawrence	21 May
	Kermit Ellis	USA		7.56	1)	Austin	01 Apr
1956	Gregory Bell	USA	30	8.09	1)	Ontario, CA	20 Oct
	Henk Visser	Hol	32	7.98	1)	Bucuresti	17 Sep
	Ernest Shelby	USA	37	7.95	1)	Bakersfield	22 Jun
	John Bennett	USA	30	7.83	1T)	Los Angeles	29 Jun
	Jorma Valkama	Fin	28	7.77	1)	Turku	16 Sep
	Rafer Johnson	USA	35	7.76	1)	Los Angeles	05 May
	Olyeg Fyedoseyev	SU	36	7.76	1)	Tashkent	21 Oct
	George Brown	USA	31	7.75	2)	Bakersfield	22 Jun
	Igor Ter-Ovanesyan	SU	38	7.74	2)	Tashkent	21 Oct
	Oscar Bean	USA	38	7.73	1)	Los Angeles	20 Apr
1957	Gregory Bell	USA	30	8.10	1)	Austin	14 Jun
	Henryk Grabowski	Pol	29	7.80	1)	Chorzów	05 Oct
	Ernest Shelby	USA	37	7.78	1)	Compton	31 May
	Igor Ter-Ovanesyan	SU	38	7.77	1)	Kiev	23 Aug
	Carroll Hamilton	USA	36	7.76	1)	Madison, IN	20 Apr
	Jorma Valkama	Fin	28	7.74	1)	Vaasa	06 Sep
	Jim Gamble	USA	35	7.72	2)	Austin	14 Jun
	Frank Herrmann	USA		7.69	1)	Fresno	11 May
	Jim Tate	USA		7.68	1)	San Diego	27 Apr
	Martin Pedigo	USA		7.68	1)	Pullman, WA	11 May
	Ali Brakchi	Fra	34	7.68	2)	Colombes	21 Sep
	With assisting wing:						
	Mike Moroney	Aus	33	7.72	1)	Sydney	16 Feb
1958	Gregory Bell	USA	30	8.00	1)	Kalamazoo	10 May
	Ernest Shelby	USA	37	7.94	1)	Moskva	27 Jul
	Mike Herman	USA	38	7.84	1)	New York	19 Apr
	Henk Visser	Hol	32	7.83	1)	Den Haag	15 Jun
	Ira Davis	USA	36	7.82	1)	Philadelphia	24 May
	Henryk Grabowski	Pol	29	7.81	1)	Bydgoszcz	19 Jul
	Igor Ter-Ovanesyan	SU	38	7.81	1)	Stockholm	20 Aug
	Joel Wiley	USA	35	7.71	1)	Fresno	10 May
	Ronald Krüger	Ger	34	7.70	1)	Kiel	06 Sep
	Willie Davis	USA	40	7.69	1)	Los Angeles	09 May
	Kazimierz Kropidlowski	Pol	31	7.69	2)	Bydgoszcz	19 Jul
	With assisting wind:						
	Ernest Shelby	USA	37	8.01	1)	Austin	28 Mar
	Bill Jackson	USA	39	7.85	1)	Fresno	10 May
	Olyeg Fyedoseyev	SU	36	7.75	1)	Tallinn	19 Jul
	Willy Dawis	USA	40	7.74	1)	Los Angeles	24 May
	Manfred Molzberger	Ger	36	7.72	1)	Hanover	20 Jul
	Attilio Bravi	Ita	36	7.69	1)	Padova	14 Jun
1959	Gregory Bell	USA	30	8.10	1)	Philadelphia	18 Jul
	Igor Ter-Ovanesyan	SU	38	8.01	1)	Moskva	16 May

	Joel Wiley	USA	35	7.99	1)	Modesto	30 May
	Irvin Roberson	USA	35	7.92	1)	Buffalo	23 Aug
	Dmitriy Bondarenko	SU	36	7.82	2)	Moskva	10 Aug
	Kazimierz Kropidlowski	Pol	31	7.82	1)	Gdansk	23 Aug
	Henk Visser	Hol	32	7.79	2)	Modesto	30 May
	Heinz Auga	Ger	33	7.79	1)	Leipzig	11 Jul
	John Buckley	USA	38	7.78	1)	New York	30 May
	Olyeg Fyedoseyev	SU	36	7.77	2)	Moskva	16 May
	With assisting wind:						
	Irvin Roberson	USA	35	7.97	1)	Chicago	29 Aug
	Ernest Shelby	USA	37	7.80	1)	Austin	03 Apr
	Henryk Grabowski	Pol	29	7.80	2)	Warszawa	14 Jun
	Jorma Valkama	Fin	28	7.80	3)	Warszawa	14 Jun
1960	Ralph Boston	USA	39	8.21	1)	Walnut	12 Aug
	Ervin Roberson	USA	35	8.11	2)	Roma	02 Sep
	Igor Ter-Ovanesyan	SU	38	8.04	3)	Roma	02 Sep
	Mike Herman	USA	37	8.00	1)	Eugene	08 Jul
	Manfred Steinbach	Ger	33	8.00	4)	Roma	02 Sep
	Henk Visser	Hol	32	7.97	1)	Santa Barbara	16 Apr
	Anthony Watson	USA	41	7.85	2)	Palo Alto	01 Jul
	Steve Anderson	USA	36	7.85	2)	Eugene	08 Jul
	Manfred Molzberger	Ger	36	7.84	1)	Freiburg	21 Aug
	Kazimierz Kropidlowski	Pol	31	7.81	1)	Rostock	10 Jul
	With assisting wind:						
	Manfred Steinbach	Ger	33	8.14	1)	Berlin	24 Jul

ALL TIME WORLD LIST AS AT THE END OF 1960

Ralph Boston	USA	39	8.21	1)	Walnut	12 Aug 60
Jesse Owens	USA	12	8.13	1)	Ann Arbor	25 May 35
Irvin Roberson	USA	35	8.11	2)	Roma	02 Sep 60
Gregory Bell	USA	30	8.10	1)	Austin	14 Jun 57
Willie Steele	USA	23	8.07	1)	Salt Lake City	21 Jun 47
Igor Ter-Ovanesyan	SU	38	8.04	3)	Roma	02 Sep 60
Rosslyn Range	USA	33	8.03	1)	Mexico City	14 Mar 55
John Bennett	USA	30	8.01	2)	Mexico City	14 Mar 55
George Brown	USA	31	8.00	1)	Fresno	10 May 52
Eulace Peacock	USA	14	8.00	1)	Lincoln	04 Jul 35
Mike Herman	USA	37	8.00	1)	Eugene	08 Jul 60
Manfred Steinbach	Ger	33	8.00	4)	Roma	02 Sep 60
With assisting wind:						
Manfred Steinbach	Ger	33	8.14	1)	Berlin	24 Jul 60
Ernie Shelby	USA	37	8.04	1)	Austin	28 Mar 58

1961	Ralph Boston	USA	39	8.28	1)	Moskva	16 Jul
	Igor Ter-Ovanesyan	SU	38	8.19	1)	Moskva	17 Jun
	Irvin Roberson	USA	35	7.98	2)	Modesto	27 May
	Anthony Watson	USA	41	7.95	2)	New York	24 Jun
	Darrell Horn	USA	39	7.87	1)	Fresno	13 May
	Dmitriy Bondarenko	SU	36	7.84	1)	Kislovodsk	06 May
	Del Blanks	USA	41	7.80	1)	Provo	27 May
	Manfred Steinbach	Ger	33	7.79	1)	Dortmund	03 Sep
	Luther Hayes	USA	40	7.78	2)	Fresno	13 May
	Deryck Taylor	WI	39	7.77	1)	Fayetteville	01 Apr
	Wellesley Clayton	WI	38	7.77	1)	New Orleans	06 May
1962	Igor Ter-Ovanesyan	SU	38	8.31	1)	Erivan	10 Jun
	Ralph Boston	USA	39	8.07	1)	Walnut	22 Jun
	Darrell Horn	USA	39	7.97	1)	Cairo	25 Oct
	Anthony Watson	USA	41	7.93	1)	Eugene	15 Jun
	Paul Warfield	USA	42	7.92	2)	Eugene	16 Jun

Year	Name	Nat	Born	Mark	Place	Venue	Date
	Mel Renfro	USA	41	7.90	3)	Eugene	15 Jun
	Antanas Vaupsas	SU	36	7.90	1)	Erivan	28 Oct
	Dan Moore	USA	40	7.86	4)	Eugene	15 Jun
	Pentti Eskola	Fin	38	7.86	1)	Kurikka	26 Aug
	Leonid Barkovskiy	SU	40	7.86	2)	Erivan	28 Oct
	With assisting wind:						
	Ralph Boston	USA	39	8.15	1)	Palo Alto	21 Jul
	Michael Ahey	Gha	40	8.05	1)	Perth	26 Nov
	Leonid Barkovskiy	SU	40	7.89	1)	Tatabánya	18 Aug
	Made from sloping runway:						
	Michael Ahey	Gha	39	8.17	1)	Kampala	06 Oct
	Charles Mays	USA	41	8.00	1)	Paterson, NJ	08 Jul
1963	Ralph Boston	USA	39	8.20	+)	Modesto	25 May
	Igor Ter-Ovanesyan	SU	38	8.15	1)	Erivan	29 Oct
	Pentti Eskola	Fin	38	8.04	1)	Helsinki	04 Jul
	Darrell Horn	USA	39	8.02	2)	St.Louis	21 Jun
	Bill Miller	USA	41	7.97	+)	Albuquerque	13 Jun
	Ali Brakchi	Alg	34	7.91	1)	Dakar	18 Apr
	Leonid Barkovskiy	SU	40	7.90	4)	Moskva	20 Jul
	Rainer Stenius	Fin	43	7.89	1)	Turku	13 Jun
	Clifton Mayfield	USA	42	7.97i	1)	Granville, OH	16 Mar
	Charlie Mays	USA	41	7.87	3)	St.Louis	21 Jun
	+) *Best legal mark.*						
	With assisting wind:						
	Phil Shinnick	USA	43	8.33	1)	Modesto	25 May
	Ralph Boston	USA	39	8.30	2)	Modesto	25 May
	Pentti Eskola	Fin	38	8.15	1)	Kauhava	21 Jun
	Clifton Mayfield	USA	42	8.10	1)	Albuquerque	13 Jun
	Bill Miller	USA	41	8.04	2)	Albuquerque	13 Jun
	Paul Warfield	USA	42	7.98	3)	Albuquerque	13 Jun
	Józef Schmidt	Pol	35	7.96	1)	Bydgoszcz	16 Jun
	Godfrey Moore	USA	38	7.94	1)	San Antonio	15 Jun
	Charlie Mays	USA	41	7.93	3)	Sioux Falls	31 May
	Charles Moseley	USA	41	7.87	4)	Albuquerque	13 Jun
1964	Ralph Boston	USA	39	8.34	+)	Los Angeles	12 Sep
	Igor Ter-Ovanesyan	SU	38	8.18	1)	Kiev	30 Aug
	Gayle Hopkins	USA	42	8.16	1)	Eugene	19 Jun
	Godfrey Moore	USA	38	8.09	1)	Baltimore	20 Jun
	Lynn Davies	GB	42	8.07	1)	Tokyo	18 Oct
	Leonid Barkovskiy	SU	40	8.03	1)	Los Angeles	25 Jul
	Charles Mays	USA	41	8.01	2)	Modesto	23 May
	Antanas Vaupsas	SU	36	8.01	2)	Kiev	12 Sep
	Phil Shinnick	USA	43	8.01	3)	Los Angeles	12 Sep
	Sid Nickolas	USA	41	7.98	3)	Modesto	23 May
	+) *Best legal mark.*						
	With assisting wind:						
	Ralph Boston	USA	39	8.49	1)	Los Angeles	12 Sep
	Darrell Horn	USA	39	8.22	2)	New York	03 Jul
	Bill Miller	USA	41	8.09	3)	New York	03 Jul
	Charles Mays	USA	41	8.02	4)	New York	03 Jul
1965	Ralph Boston	USA	39	8.35	1)	Modesto	29 May
	Igor Ter-Ovanesyan	SU	38	8.19	1)	Budapest	28 Aug
	Clarence Robinson	USA	42	8.16	1)	Des Moines	23 Apr
	Rainer Stenius	Fin	43	8.04	1)	Jyväskylä	07 Aug
	Leonid Barkovskiy	SU	40	8.00	3)	Kiev	31 Jul
	Dennis Holland	USA	43	7.99	1)	Kalamazoo	29 May
	Wellesley Clayton	Jam	38	7.92	1)	Albuquerque	03 Apr
	Lynn Davies	GB	42	7.89	2)	Budapest	28 Aug
	Hiroomi Yamada	Jap	42	7.88	1)	Tokyo	08 May
	Darrell Horn	USA	39	7.86	4)	Kiev	31 Jul

	With assisting wind:						
	Lynn Davies	GB	42	7.99	1)	Swansea	23 Jun
1966	Igor Ter-Ovanesyan	SU	38	8.23	1)	Leselidze	23 Apr
	Lynn Davies	GB	42	8.18	1)	Bloemfontein	09 Apr
	Ralph Boston	USA	39	8.18	1)	Mexico City	17 Apr
	Rainer Stenius	Fin	43	8.16	1)	Los Angeles	06 May
	Gayle Hopkins	USA	42	8.11	1)	Los Angeles	04 Jun
	Tönu Lepik	SU	46	8.03	1)	Leninakan	02 Oct
	Clarence Robinson	USA	42	8.02	1)	Albuquerque	04 Jun
	Charlie Mays	USA	41	8.00	2)	New York	25 Jun
	Leonid Barkovskiy	SU	40	7.99	1)	Perth	26 Mar
	Freddie Fox	USA	45	7.97	1)	Abilene	01 Apr
	With assisting wind:						
	Ralph Boston	USA	39	8.23	1)	Long Beach	07 Jun
	Tom Chilton	USA	36	8.05	1)	Richmond	21 May
	Andrzej Stalmach	Pol	42	8.00	1)	Warszawa	18 Sep
	Darrell Horn	USA	39	7.97	3)	Modesto	28 May
	Take-off board not up to regulations; suspected wind assistance:						
	Alan Crawley	Aus	41	8.10	1)	Melbourne	18 Oct
1967	Igor Ter-Ovanesyan	SU	38	8.35	1)	Mexico City	19 Oct
	Ralph Boston	USA	39	8.29	1)	Winnipeg	04 Aug
	Lynn Davies	GB	42	8.13	2)	Mexico City	19 Oct
	Bob Beamon	USA	46	8.11	+)	Modesto	27 May
	Alan Crawley	Aus	41	8.07	2)	Los Angeles	09 Jul
	Jacques Pani	Fra	46	8.03	3)	Mexico City	19 Oct
	Tönu Lepik	SU	46	8.02	1)	Leninakan	01 Oct
	Phil Shinnick	USA	43	8.01	4)	Mexico City	19 Oct
	Klaus Beer	EG	42	7.99	1)	Berlin	02 Sep
	Leonid Barkovskiy	SU	40	7.97	1)	Volgograd	06 Sep
	+) *Best legal mark.*						
	With assisting wind:						
	Bob Beamon	USA	46	8.13	2)	Modesto	27 May
	Jerry Proctor	USA	49	8.07	1)	Sacramento	17 Jun
	Jacqaues Pani	Fra	46	8.05	2)	Colombes	24 Jun
1968	Bob Beamon	USA	46	8.90	1)	Mexico City	18 Oct
	Igor Ter-Ovanesyan	SU	38	8.28	1)	Leninakan	17 Aug
	Ralph Boston	USA	39	8.27	Q)	Mexico City	17 Oct
	Lynn Davies	GB	42	8.23	1)	Bern	30 Jun
	Klaus Beer	EG	42	8.19	2)	Mexico City	18 Oct
	Phil Shinnick	USA	43	8.16	2)	Flagstaff	29 Sep
	Andrzej Stalmach	Pol	42	8.11	1)	Chorzów	17 Aug
	Tönu Lepik	SU	46	8.09	5)	Mexico City	18 Oct
	Jacques Pani	Fra	46	8.08	1)	Colombes	28 Jul
	Gayle Hopkins	USA	42	8.07	+)	Sydney	23 Mar
	Max Klauss	EG	47	8.07	1)	Berlin	19 Jun
	+) *Best legal mark.*						
	With assisting wind:						
	Ralph Boston	USA	39	8.37	1)	Flagstaff	29 Sep
	Jacques Pani	Fra	46	8.20	1)	Colombes	22 Jun
	Charlie Mays	USA	41	8.16	3)	South Lake Tahoe	14 Sep
	Gayle Hopkins	USA	42	8.14	1)	Sydney	23 Mar
	Phil May	Aus	44	8.07	1)	Perth	30 nov
1969	Igor Ter-Ovanesyan	SU	38	8.21	1)	Odessa	01 Jul
	Waldemar Stepien	Pol	46	8.21	1)	Chorzów	12 Jul
	Bob Beamon	USA	46	8.20	1)	Miami	28 Jun
	Jacques Pani	Fra	46	8.16	1)	Pulversheim	22 Jun
	Lynn Davies	GB	42	8.14	1)	Berlin	18 Jun
	Stan Whitley	USA	45	8.14	1)	Los Angeles	19 Jul
	Klaus Beer	EG	42	8.07	1)	Berlin	03 Aug

	Henry Hines	USA	49	8.05	1)	Warszawa	29 Aug
	Max Klauss	EG	47	8.05	1)	Berlin	05 Sep
	Aleksey Khlopotnov	SU	46	8.01	+)	Chorzów	12 Jul
	+) *Best legal mark.*						
	With assisting wind:						
	Jerry Proctor	USA	49	8.22	1)	Knoxville	20 Jun
	Jacques Pani	Fra	46	8.22	1)	Colombes	05 Jul
	Gérard Ugolini	Fra	49	8.12	2)	Colombes	05 Jul
	Aleksey Khlopotnov	SU	46	8.11	2)	Chorzów	12 Jul
	Henry Hines	USA	49	8.10	1)	Sacramento	21 Jun
	Marion Anderson	USA		8.06	1)	San Jose	03 May
	Ron Jessie	USA	48	8.04	2)	Des Moines	25 Apr
	Tõnu Lepik	SU	46	8.04	3)	Athinai	18 Sep
	Christian Tourret	Fra	46	8.03	1)	Font Romeu	16 Aug
	Pertti Pousi	Fin	46	8.02	3)	Knoxville	20 Jun
	Leonid Barkovskiy	SU	40	8.02	5)	Athinai	18 Sep
	Take-off board 4 cms. higher than landing pit:						
	Mihai Zaharia	Rum	45	8.01	1)	Košice	07 Sep
1970	Josef Schwarz	WG	41	8.35	1)	Stuttgart	15 Jul
	Jacques Pani	Fra	46	8.16	1)	Lyon	21 Jun
	Klaus Beer	EG	42	8.10	1)	Erfurt	04 Jul
	Christian Tourret	Fra	46	8.09	2)	Colombes	14 Jun
	Henry Jackson	USA	48	8.06	2)	Murfreesboro, TE	15 May
	Phil May	Aus	44	8.04	1)	Perth	05 Dec
	Hiroomi Yamada	Jap	42	8.01	1)	Odawara	07 Jun
	Henry Hines	USA	49	7.99	1)	Modesto	23 May
	Hans Baumgartner	WG	49	7.97	1)	Bonn	30 Aug
	Stanislaw Szudrowicz	Pol		7.96	1)	Poznan	24 May
	Grzegorz Cybulski	Pol	51	7.96	2)	Poznan	24 May
	Bouncy Moore	USA		7.96	1)	Leningrad	24 Jul
	With assisting wind:						
	Jacques Pani	Fra	46	8.20	1)	Font-Romeu	09 Aug
	Phil May	Aus	44	8.15	1)	Perth	25 Nov
	Henry Jackson	USA	48	8.10	1)	Murfreesboro, TE	15 May
	Lynn Davies	GB	42	8.06	1)	Edinburgh	22 Jul
	Larry Reed	USA		8.02	1)	El Paso	11 Apr
	Bill Elliott	USA		8.00	2)	El Paso	11 Apr
	Hans Schicker	WG		8.00	1)	Stuttgart	06 Jun
	John Johnson	USA		7.99	1)	West Los Angeles	11 Apr
	Bouncey Moore	USA		7.99	1)	Bakersfield	26 Jun
	Phil Reaves	USA		7.98	1)	Lawrence	15 May
	Norm Tate	USA	42	7.96	1)	Bakersfield	26 Jun
1971	Jacques Pani	Fra	46	8.15	1)	Madrid	29 Aug
	Henry Hines	USA	49	8.14	1)	Westwood, LA	08 May
	Hans Baumgartner	WG	49	8.12i	1)	Sofia	14 Mar
	Jan Kobuszewski	Pol	47	8.12	1)	Warszawa	20 Jun
	Jameds McAllister	USA	51	8.09	1)	Westwood, LA	03 Apr
	Josef Schwarz	WG	41	8.07	1)	Bonn	24 Jul
	Arnie Robinson	USA	48	8.04	1)	Modesto	29 May
	Henry Jackson	USA	48	8.03	1)	Turku	19 Aug
	Stanislaw Szudrowicz	Pol	47	8.03	1)	Szczecin	02 Oct
	Max Klauss	EG	47	8.00	1)	Leipzig	27 Jun
	With assisting wind:						
	Arnie Robinson	USA	48	8.20	1)	Eugene	25 Jun
	Alan Lerwill	GB	46	8.12	1)	Leicester	31 May
	Danny Brabham	USA	51	8.10	1)	Lubbock, TX	10 Apr
	Bouncy Moore	USA	51	8.09	1)	Seattle	21 May
	Stan Whitley	USA	45	8.08	2)	Walnut	24 Apr
	Randy Willliams	USA	53	8.02	1)	Westwood, LA	05 Jun
	Downhill runway:						
	Ron Coleman	USA	44	8.25	1)	Irvine, CA	16 Jun

	Norm Tate	USA	42	8.23	1)	El Paso	22 May
	Josh Owusu	Gha	48	8.20w	2)	El Paso	22 May
	Henry Jackson	USA	48	8.14	2)	Irvine, CA	16 Jun
	Ralph Boston	USA	39	8.05w	3)	El Paso	22 May
1972	Randy Williams	USA	53	8.34	Q)	München	08 Sep
	Prerston Carrington	USA	49	8.22	Q)	München	08 Sep
	Henry Hines	USA	49	8.19	1)	Athinai	14 Jun
	Hans Baumgartner	WG	49	8.18	2)	München	09 Sep
	Arnie Robinson	USA	48	8.14	1)	Fresno	13 May
	Bill Rea	USA	52	8.11	1)	Pittsburgh	13 May
	Max Klauss	EG	47	8.10	1)	Dresden	28 May
	Christian Tourret	Fra	46	8.08	1)	Vittel	18 Aug
	Phil Shinnick	USA	43	8.07	3)	Modesto	27 May
	Grzegorz Cybulski	Pol	51	8.07	1)	Poznan	03 Jun
	With assisting wind:						
	Henry Hines	USA	49	8.40	1)	Modesto	27 May
	Randy Williams	USA	53	8.34	1)	Sacramento	28 Jul
	Murray Tolbert	Aus	46	8.16	1)	Perth	25 Mar
	Alan Lerwill	GB	46	8.15	1)	Leicester	29 May
	Max Klauss	EG	47	8.12	1)	Erfurt	25 Jun
	Stan Whitley	USA	45	8.11	2)	Modesto	27 May
	Valeriy Podluzhniy	SU	52	8.11	2)	Sacramento	28 Jul
	Bruce Field	Aus	47	8.10	2)	Perth	25 Mar
	Jacques Pani	Fra	46	8.09	1)	Reims	04 Jun
	Ralph Boston	USA	39	8.07	1)	Knoxville	15 Apr
1973	James McAlister	USA	51	8.24	1)	Westwood	05 May
	Randy Williams	USA	53	8.16	-)	Eugene	18 May
	Valeriy Podluzhniy	SU	52	8.15	1)	Moskva	18 Aug
	Hans Baumgartner	WG	49	8.14	1)	München	11 Jul
	Jacques Rousseau	Fra	51	8.11	2)	Colombes	21 Jul
	Stan Whitley	USA	45	8.06	1)	Walnut	28 Apr
	Norm Tate	USA	42	8.06i	2)	New York	23 Feb
	Jerzy Miedzielek	Pol	51	8.03	1)	Warszawa	21 Jun
	Al Lanier	USA	50	8.03	1)	Dakar	04 Aug
	Max Klauss	EG	47	8.03	3)	Edinburgh	08 Sep
	Professional:						
	Henry Hines	USA	49	8.25i	1)	New York	06 Jun
	Bob Beamon	USA	46	8.16i	1)	Salt Lake City	25 May
	With assisting wind:						
	Randy Williams	USA	53	8.46	1)	Eugene	18 May
	Valedriy Podluzhniy	SU	52	8.20	1)	Edinburgh	08 Sep
	Jean-François Bonhème	Fra	49	8.19	1)	Colombes	21 Jul
	Danny Brabham	USA	51	8.16	1)	College Station	24 Mar
	Jaroslav Broz	Cze	50	8.05	1)	Banska Bystrica	01 Sep
	Bill Rea	USA	52	8.04	1)	Des Moines	27 Apr
	Al Lanier	USA	50	8.04	1)	Wichita	01 Jun
1974	Arnie Robinson	USA	48	8.30	1)	Modesto	25 May
	Nenad Stekic	Yug	51	8.24	1)	Rio de Janeiro	27 Oct
	James Moore	USA	51	8.20	2)	Modesto	25 May
	Max Klauss	EG	47	8.18	1)	Berlin	12 Jun
	Jean-François Bonhème	Fra	49	8.17i	1)	Göteborg	09 Mar
	Valeriy Podluzhniy	SU	52	8.17	1)	München	12 Sep
	Grzegorz Cybulski	Pol	51	8.15	1)	Warszawa	26 May
	Tommy Haynes	USA	52	8.14	1)	Murray	17 May
	Jerry Herndon	USA	55	8.11	3)	Modesto	25 May
	Hans Baumgartner	WG	49	8.10i	2)	Göteborg	09 Mar
	With assisting wind:						
	Jerry Proctor	USA	49	8.27	1)	Irvine	24 Mar
	Danny Seay	USA	53	8.15	1)	Lawrence	20 Apr

1975	Nenad Stekic	Yug	51	8.45	1)	Montreal	25 Jul
	Arnie Robinson	USA	48	8.28	1)	Modesto	24 May
	Grzegorz Cybulski	Pol	51	8.27	1)	Warszawa	20 Jun
	Charlton Ehizuelen	Nig	53	8.26i	1)	Bloemfontein	07 Mar
	João Carlos De Oliveira	Bra	54	8.20	1)	Rio de Janeiro	05 Sep
	Danny Seay	USA	53	8.13	+)	Modesto	24 May
	Theo Hamilton	USA	52	8.11i	1)	Detroit	14 Mar
	Luiz Carlos De Souza	Bra		8.08	1)	Rio de Janeiro	06 Jul
	Jacques Rousseau	Fra	51	8.07	1)	Saint-Etienne	29 Jun
	Rolf Bernhard	Swz	49	8.06	1)	Bern	19 Jul
	+) *Best legal mark.*						
	With assisting wind:						
	Arnie Robinson	USA	48	8.35	1)	Fresno	10 May
	Charlton Ehizuelen	Nig	53	8.33	1)	Lawrence	19 Apr
	Danny Seay	USA	53	8.21	2)	Modesto	24 May
	Theo Hamilton	USA	52	8.18	2)	Lawrence	19 Apr
	Valeriy Podluzhniy	SU	52	8.12	1)	Bratislava	07 Jun
	Tommy Haynes	USA	52	8.09	1)	Oakland	06 Jun
	Stan Whitley	USA	45	8.08	2)	Fresno	10 May
	Al Lanier	USA	50	8.07	2)	Oakland	06 Jun
1976	Arnie Robinson	USA	48	8.35	1)	Montreal	29 Jul
	Jacques Rousseau	Fra	51	8.26	+)	Lille	26 Jun
	Aleksey Pereverzyev	SU	49	8.21	1)	Kiev	22 May
	Frank Wartenberg	EG	55	8.18	1)	Berlin	10 Jul
	Valeriy Podluzhniy	SU	52	8.14	2)	Kiev	22 May
	Tommy Haynes	USA	52	8.13	1)	Rio de Janeiro	24 Aug
	Nenad Stekic	Yug	51	8.12	1)	Berlin	20 Aug
	Randy Williams	USA	53	8.11	2)	Montreal	29 Jul
	Theo Hamilton	USA	52	8.10	1)	Atlanta	22 May
	Larry Myricks	USA	56	8.09i	1)	Montgomery	13 Feb
	Grzegorz Cybulski	Pol	51	8.09	1)	Bydgoszcz	22 Jun
	+) *Best legal mark.*						
	With assisting wind:						
	Nenad Stekic	Yug	51	8.39	1)	Torino	02 Jun
	Arnie Robinson	USA	48	8.37	1)	Eugene	25 Jun
	Jacques Rousseau	Fra	51	8.37	1)	Lille	26 Jun
	Larry Myricks	USA	56	8.26	2)	Eugene	25 Jun
	Randy Williams	USA	53	8.18	3)	Eugene	25 Jun
	Philippe Deroche	Fra	54	8.18	2)	Lille	26 Jun
	Roy Mitchell	GB	55	8.16	3)	Lille	26 Jun
	Henry Hines	USA	49	8.11	1)	El Paso	22 May
1977	Nenad Stekic	Yug	51	8.27	1)	Nova Gorica	09 Jul
	Jacques Rousseau	Fra	51	8.25	1)	Fürth	11 Sep
	Arnie Robinson	USA	48	8.24	1)	Westwood	10 Jun
	Larry Doubley	USA	58	8.22	1)	Champaign	03 Jun
	Charlton Ehizuelen	Nig	53	8.18	2)	Champaign	03 Jun
	James Lofton	USA	56	8.15	1)	Mexico City	27 Mar
	David Giralt	Cub	59	8.12	1)	Berlin	15 Jun
	Randy Williams	USA	53	8.10	5)	Westwood	10 Jun
	Erwin Plöger	EG	56	8.10	1)	Dresden	03 Jul
	Philippe Deroche	Fra	54	8.09	1)	Narbonne	03 Jul
	With assisting wind:						
	Jacques Rousseau	Fra	51	8.33	1)	Wolverhampton	02 Jul
	Nenad Stekic	Yug	51	8.32	2)	Wolverhampton	02 Jul
	Rolf Bernhard	Swz	49	8.20	1)	Zofingen	30 May
	Anthony Carter	USA	54	8.14	3)	Westwood	10 Jun
1978	Nenad Stekic	Yug	51	8.32	1)	Rovereto	16 Sep
	James Lofton	USA	56	8.23	2)	Westwood	09 Jun
	João Carlos De Oliveira	Bra	54	8.23	1)	Warszawa	19 Jun
	Arnie Robinson	USA	48	8.21	+)	Westwood	09 Jun
	LaMonte King	USA	59	8.18	2)	Modesto	20 May

Year	Athlete	Nation	Born	Mark	Place	Venue	Date
	Jacques Rousseau	Fra	51	8.18	1)	Praha	02 Sep
	Charlton Ehizuelen	Nig	53	8.11	3)	Modesto	20 May
	Grzegorz Cybulski	Pol	51	8.11	1)	Tarnów	28 May
	Chris Commons	Aus	50	8.08	1)	Sydney	14 Jan
	Tommy Haynes	USA	52	8.07i	1)	Long Beach	07 Jan

+) *Best legal mark.*

With assisting wind:

Athlete	Nation	Born	Mark	Place	Venue	Date
Arnie Robinson	USA	48	8.33	1)	Westwood	09 Jun
Carl Williams	USA	57	8.26	1)	Abilene	19 May
Dannie Jackson	USA	58	8.14	1)	El Paso	05 May
Rick Rock	Can	57	8.13	1)	Carbondale	01 Apr
Daley Thompson	GB	58	8.11	D)	Edmonton	07 Aug
Ken Duncan	USA	53	8.10	1)	San Jose	25 Mar

D) *Made in a decathlon.*

Year	Athlete	Nation	Born	Mark	Place	Venue	Date
1979	Larry Myricks	USA	56	8.52	1)	Montreal	26 Aug
	João Carlos De Oliveira	Bra	54	8.36	1)	Rieti	21 Jul
	Lutz Dombrowski	EG	59	8.31	1)	Torino	04 Aug
	Nenad Stekic	Yug	51	8.27	1)	Rovereto	16 Sep
	Frank Paschek	EG	56	8.25	1)	Moskva	25 Jul
	LaMonte King	USA	59	8.22	1)	San Jose	12 May
	David Giralt	Cub	59	8.22	3)	Montreal	26 Aug
	Valeriy Podluzhniy	SU	52	8.16	1)	Mexico City	09 Sep
	Carl Lewis	USA	61	8.13	3)	San Juan	07 Jul
	Lutz Franke	EG	57	8.13	1)	Dresden	19 Jul

With assisting wind:

Athlete	Nation	Born	Mark	Place	Venue	Date
David Giralt	Cub	59	8.32	1)	Quebec City	11 Aug
LaMonte King	USA	59	8.25	1)	Tempe	26 May

Year	Athlete	Nation	Born	Mark	Place	Venue	Date
1980	Lutz Dombrowski	EG	59	8.54	1)	Moskva	28 Jul
	Larry Myricks	USA	56	8.38i	1)	Johnson City	11 Jan
	Frank Paschek	EG	56	8.36	1)	Berlin	28 May
	Antonio Corgos	Spa	60	8.23	1)	Madrid	24 Aug
	Andrzej Klimaszewski	Pol	60	8.20	1)	Sopot	05 Jul
	Valeriy Podluzhniy	SU	52	8.18	3)	Moskva	28 Jul
	Charlton Ehizuelen	Nig	53	8.14	+)	San Jose	26 Apr
	Jens Knipphals	WG	58	8.14	2)	Berlin	28 May
	Larry Doubley	USA	58	8.13	1)	Los Angeles	01 Mar
	Randy Williams	USA	53	8.13	1)	Tempe	05 Apr
	LaMonte King	USA	59	8.13	1)	Houston	03 May
	László Szalma	Hun	57	8.13	4)	Moskva	28 Jul
	Stanislaw Jaskulka	Pol	58	8.13	5)	Moskva	28 Jul

With assisting wind:

Athlete	Nation	Born	Mark	Place	Venue	Date
Carl Lewis	USA	61	8.35	1)	Austin	06 Jun
Andrzej Klimaszewski	Pol	60	8.33	1)	Warszawa	13 Jun
Larry Doubley	USA	58	8.26	1)	Los Angeles	15 Mar
László Szalma	Hun	57	8.25	1)	Budapest	17 Jul
Charlton Ehizuelen	Nig	53	8.19	1)	San Jose	26 Apr
Nenad Stekic	Yug	51	8.19	1)	Maribor	03 Jun
Rolf Bernhard	Swz	49	8.19	2)	Maribor	03 Jun
David Giralt	Cub	59	8.18	1)	Habana	20 Jan

ALL TIME WORLD LIST AS AT THE END OF 1980

Athlete	Nation	Born	Mark	Place	Venue	Date
Bob Beamon	USA	46	8.90	1)	Mexico City	18 Oct 68
Lutz Dombrowski	EG	59	8.54	1)	Moskva	28 Jul 80
Larry Myricks	USA	56	8.52	1)	Montreal	26 Aug 79
Nenad Stekic	Yug	51	8.45	1)	Montreal	25 Jul 75
João Carlos De Oliveira	Bra	54	8.36	1)	Rieti	21 Jul 79
Frank Paschek	EG	56	8.36	1)	Berlin	28 May 80
Ralph Boston	USA	39	8.35	1)	Modesto	29 May 65
Igor Ter-Ovanesyan	SU	38	8.35	1)	Mexico City	19 Oct 67

Josef Schwarz		WG	41	8.35	1)	Stuttgart	15 Jul 70
Arnie Robinson		USA	48	8.35	1)	Montreal	29 Jul 76
With assisting wind:							
Ralph Boston		USA	39	8.49	1)	Los Angeles	12 Sep 64
Randy Williams		USA	53	8.46	1)	Eugene	18 May 73
Henry Hines		USA	49	8.40	1)	Modesto	27 May 72
Arnie Robinson		USA	48	8.37	1)	Eugene	25 Jun 76
Jacques Rousseau		Fra	51	8.37	1)	Lille	26 Jun 76
Carl Lewis		USA	61	8.35	1)	Austin	06 Jun 80
1981	Carl Lewis	USA	61	8.62	1)	Sacramento	20 Jun
	Larry Myricks	USA	56	8.45	2)	Sacramento	20 Jun
	Hednry Lauterbach	EG	57	8.35	1)	Erfurt	02 Aug
	Winfried Klepsch	WG	56	8.21i	1)	Sindelfingen	07 Feb
	Atanas Chochev	Bul	57	8.19	1)	Sofia	12 Jul
	Shamil Abbyasov	SU	57	8.16	1)	Leningrad	02 Aug
	Rolf Bernhard	Swz	49	8.14	1)	Ebensee	01 Aug
	Jens Knipphals	WG	58	8.13i	2)	Sindelfingen	07 Feb
	László Szalma	Hun	57	8.12	1)	Budapest	31 May
	Joachim Busse	WG	54	8.12	1)	Gelsenkirchen	19 Jul
	Uwe Lange	EG	54	8.12	+)	Erfurt	02 Aug
	With assisting wind:						
	Carl Lewis	USA	61	8.73	Q)	Sacramento	19 Jun
	Mike McCrae	USA	55	8.32	1)	Modesto	16 May
	László Szalma	Hun	57	8.23	1)	Bucuresti	24 Jul
	Yu-Huang Liu	Chi	59	8.22	1)	Beijing	21 Sep
	Andrzej Klmaszewski	Pol	60	8.21	1)	Warszawa	04 Jul
	Uwe Lange	EG	54	8.21	2)	Erfurt	02 Aug
	Rolf Bernhard	Swz	49	8.16	1)	Göteborg	15 Jun
	Gary Honey	Aus	59	8.13	1)	Melbourne	07 Mar
	Greg Artis	USA	59	8.12	Q)	Sacramento	19 Jun
1982	Carl Lewis	USA	61	8.76	1)	Indianapolis	24 Jul
	Larry Myricks	USA	56	8.56	1)	Rhede	01 Sep
	Lutz Dombrowski	EG	59	8.30	+)	Athinai	09 Sep
	Vance Johnson	USA	63	8.21	1)	Provo	04 Jun
	László Szalma	Hun	57	8.20	1)	Debrecen	12 Jun
	Viktor Belskiy	SU	55	8.20	1)	Kiev	21 Aug
	Greg Artis	USA	59	8.19i	1)	Murfreesboro	23 Jan
	Jason Grimes	USA	59	8.19	2)	Walnut	25 Apòr
	Mike Conley	USA	62	8.19	2)	Provo	04 Jun
	Antonio Corgos	Spa	60	8.19	2)	Athinai	09 Sep
	With assisting wind:						
	Jason Grimes	USA	59	8.57	1)	Durham	27 Jun
	Shamil Abbyasov	SU	57	8.41	2)	Indianapolis	03 Jul
	Lutz Dombrowski	EG	59	8.41	1)	Athinai	09 Sep
	Giovanni Evangelisti	Ita	61	8.21	1)	Colombes	29 May
	+) *Best legal mark.*						
1983	Carl Lewis	USA	61	8.79	1)	Indianapolis	19 Jun
	Jason Grimes	USA	59	8.39	2)	Indianapolis	19 Jun
	Sergey Rodin	SU	63	8.33	1)	Leningrad	27 Jul
	Reggie Kelly	USA	62	8.33i	1)	Jackson	03 Dec
	Aleksandr Beskrovniy	SU	60	8.28	1)	Moskva	29 May
	Mike Conley	USA	62	8.28	2)	Houston	03 Jun
	László Szalma	Hun	57	8.24	1)	Budapest	29 Jul
	Larry Myricks	USA	56	8.23	1)	Oxford	09 Apr
	Yusif Alli	Nig	70	8.21	1)	Edmonton	07 Jul
	Mike McRae	USA	55	8.19	1)	San Jose	05 Jun
	With assisting wind:						
	Larry Myricks	USA	56	8.64	1)	Colorado Springs	02 Jul
	Jason Grimes	USA	59	8.41	2)	Colorado Springs	02 Jul
	Mike Conley	USA	62	8.38	3)	Indianapolis	19 Jun
	Ralph Spry	USA	60	8.36	1)	Houston	03 Jun

1984	Carl Lewis	USA	61	8.79i	1)	New York	27 Jan
	Larry Myricks	USA	56	8.59	1)	Rhede	05 Sep
	Lutz Dombrowski	EG	59	8.50	1)	Dresden	27 Jul
	Konstantin Semykin	SU	60	8.38	1)	Moskva	17 Aug
	Jaime Jefferson	Cub	62	8.37	2)	Moskva	17 Aug
	Jason Grimes	USA	59	8.32	2)	Modesto	12 May
	Sergey Layevskiy	SU	59	8.32	1)	Donetsk	08 Sep
	Atanas Atanasov	Bul	56	8.31	1)	Sofia	04 Jul
	Vadim Kobylyanskiy	SU	61	8.28	2)	Donetsk	08 Sep
	Mike McRae	USA	55	8.27	1)	San Jose	09 Jun
	Gary Honey	Aus	59	8.27	1)	Budapest	20 Aug
	László Szalma	Hun	57	8.27	2)	Köln	26 Aug
	With assisting wind:						
	Jason Grimes	USA	59	8.40	1)	Knoxville	19 May
	Gary Honey	Aus	59	8.39	2)	Sacramento	21 Jul
	Sergey Rodin	SU	63	8.37	1)	Moskva	06 Jul
	Mike McRae	USA	55	8.34	1)	Modesto	12 May
	Wind assisted and unknown irregularity:						
	Yuriy Samarin	SU	60	8.28	1)	Kharkov	08 Jul
1985	Carl Lewis	USA	61	8.62	1)	Bruxelles	30 Aug
	Larry Myricks	USA	56	8.44	2)	Bruxelles	30 Aug
	Jason Grimes	USA	59	8.43	+)	Indianapolis	16 Jun
	Mike Conley	USA	62	8.43	1)	Lausanne	10 Jul
	Robert Emmiyan	SU	65	8.30	1)	Moskva	08 Jun
	László Szalma	Hun	57	8.30	1)	Budapest	07 Jul
	Gyula Pálóczi	Hun	62	8.25	1)	Budapest	04 Aug
	James Jefferson	Cub	62	8.24	2)	Lausanne	10 Jul
	Atanas Atanasov	Bul	56	8.24	2)	Budapest	10 Aug
	Khristo Markov	Bul	65	8.23i	1)	Sofia	10 Feb
	+) *Best legal mark.*						
	With assisting wind:						
	Carl Lewis	USA	61	8.77	1)	Westwood	18 May
	Mike Conley	USA	62	8.53	1)	Indianapolis	16 Jun
	Jason Grimes	USA	59	8.50	2)	Indianapolis	16 Jun
	Keith Talley	USA	64	8.44	Q)	Odessa	16 May
	Anthony Bailous	USA	65	8.42	Q)	Odessa	16 May
	Roberrt Emmiyan	SU	65	8.38	1)	Oslo	17 Jul
	Mike Powell	USA	63	8.28	3)	Indianapolis	16 Jun
	Jaime Jefferson	Cub	62	8.28	1)	Ravenna	03 Jul
1986	Robert Emmiyan	SU	65	8.61	1)	Moskva	06 Jul
	Larry Myricks	USA	56	8.50	1)	Rhede	02 Jul
	Jaime Jefferson	Cub	62	8.47	1)	Santiago de Cuba	22 Feb
	Carl Lewis	USA	61	8.37i	1)	East Rutherford	08 Feb
	Mike Conley	USA	62	8.33	+)	Eugene	20 Jun
	Ubaldo Duany	Cub	60	8.32	2)	Santiago de Cuba	22 Feb
	Grigoriy Petrosyan	SU	58	8.29	1)	Yerevan	20 Oct
	Luis Bueno	Cub	69	8.25	1)	Habana	28 Sep
	László Szalma	Hun	57	8.24i	2)	Madrid	22 Feb
	Eric Metcalf	USA	68	8.24	1)	Indianapolis	06 Jun
	Giovanni Evangelisti	Ita	61	8.24	1)	Caorle	27 Jul
	+) *Best legal mark.*						
	With assisting wind:						
	Carl Lewis	USA	61	8.67	1)	Eugene	20 Jun
	Mike Conley	USA	62	8.63	2)	Eugene	20 Jun
	Larry Myricks	USA	56	8.55	1)	Modesto	10 May
	Mike Davis	USA	64	8.31	1)	Houston	18 May
1987	Robert Emmiyan	SU	65	8.86	1)	Tsakhkadzor	22 May
	Carl Lewis	USA	61	8.75	1)	Indianapolis	16 Aug
	Larry Myricks	USA	56	8.66	1)	Tokyo	23 sep
	Jaime Jefferson	Cub	62	8.51	3)	Indianapolis	07 Aug
	Giovanni Evangelisti	Ita	61	8.43	1)	S. Giovanni Valdarno	16 May

	Mike Conley	USA	62	8.32	1)	Berlin	08 Jul
	Sergey Layevskiy	SU	59	8.32	1)	Bryansk	19 Jul
	Mike Powell	USA	63	8.27	1)	Kohriyama	29 Apr
	Marco Delonge	EG	66	8.27	1)	Potsda	06 Jun
	Paul Emordi	Nig	65	8.25	1)	Baton Rouge	05 Jun
	Vladimir Bobylyov	SU	66	8.25	4)	Moskva	07 Jun
	With assisting wind:						
	Carl Lewis	USA	61	8.77	1)	Walnut	26 Apr
	Mike Conley	USA	62	8.55	3)	San Jose	26 Jun
	Andre Ester	USA	65	8.41	1)	Austin	04 Apr
	Yusuf Alli	Nig	60	8.30	1)	El Paso	12 Apr
	Jens Hirschberg	EG	64	8.30	1)	Berlin	25 Aug
	Vladimir Bobylyov	SU	66	8.29	2)	Bryansk	19 Jul
	Gary Honey	Aus	59	8.28	1)	Melbourne	07 Feb
1988	Carl Lewis	USA	61	8.76	1)	Indianapolis	18 Jul
	Larry Myricks	USA	56	8.74	2)	Indianapolis	18 Jul
	Mike Powell	USA	63	8.49	2)	Seoul	26 Sep
	Leonid Voloshin	SU	66	8.46	1)	Tallinn	05 Jul
	Eric Metcalf	USA	68	8.44	1)	Tampa	17 Jun
	Jaime Jefferson	Cub	62	8.37	1)	Mexico City	22 Jul
	Sergey Layevskiy	SU	59	8.35	1)	Dnepropetrovsk	16 Jul
	Vladimir Ochkan	SU	68	8.34	1)	Riga	05 Jun
	Ralph Spry	USA	60	8.32	1)	Albuquerque	09 Jun
	Igor Streltsov	SU	65	8.31	2)	Dnepropetrovsk	16 Jul
	With assisting wind:						
	Giovanni Evangelisti	Ita	61	8.37	1)	S.Giovanni Valdarno	21 May
	Sergey Vasilenko	SU	65	8.33	1)	Leningrad	11 Jun
	Gordon Laine	USA	58	8.31	4)	Indianapolis	18 Jul
1989	Larry Myricks	USA	56	8.70	1)	Houston	17 Jun
	Carl Lewis	USA	61	8.54	1)	New York	22 Jul
	Mike Powell	USA	63	8.49	1)	Bruxelles	25 Aug
	Leroy Burrell	USA	67	8.37	2)	Provo	02 Jun
	Vladimir Ratushkov	SU	65	8.33	1)	Volgograd	11 Jun
	Jaime Jefferson	Cub	62	8.29	1)	Bogota	11 Aug
	Yusuf Alli	Nig	60	8.27	1)	Lagos	08 Aug
	Dietmar Haaf	WG	67	8.25i	2)	Sindelfingen	26 Feb
	Emiel Mellaard	Hol	66	8.23i	1)	den Haag	05 Feb
	Andre Ester	USA	65	8.23	2)	Houston	21 May
	With assisting wind:						
	Mike Powell	USA	63	8.55	1)	San Jose	27 May
	Llewellyn Starks	USA	67	8.48	3)	Houston	17 Jun
	Vernon George	USA	64	8.46	1)	Houston	21 May
	Joe Greene	USA	67	8.41	1)	Provo	02 Jun
	Edrick Floreal	Can	66	8.39	1)	Fayetteville	22 Apr
	Jarmo Kärnä	Fin	58	8.34	1)	Riga	04 Jun
	David Culbert	Aus	67	8.33	1)	Melbourne	11 Nov
	Fraçois Fouche	SA	63	8.32	1)	Johannesburg	15 May
	Andre Ester	USA	65	8.27	4)	Houston	17 Jun
	Marco Delonge	EG	66	8.27	1)	Neubrandenburg	23 Jul
	Gordon Laine	USA	58	8.27	1)	Padova	17 Sep
	Robert Emmiyan	SU	65	8.24	2)	Volgograd	11 Jun
1990	Mike Powell	USA	63	8.66	1)	Villeneuve d'Ascq	29 Jun
	Jaime Jefferson	Cub	62	8.53	1)	Habana	12 May
	Carl Lewis	USA	61	8.51	1)	Barcelona	16 Jul
	Larry Myricks	USA	56	8.45i	1)	Liévin	27 Jan
	Robert Emmiyan	SU	65	8.32	2)	Barcelona	16 Jul
	Sergey Bodgainyi	SU	63	8.25	1)	Kishinyev	18 Aug
	Dietmar Haaf	WG	67	8.25	1)	Split	30 Aug
	Gordon McKee	USA	66	8.24	+)	San Angelo	12 Apr
	Llewellyn Starks	USA	67	8.24	1)	San Juan	09 Jun
	Borut Bilac	Yug	65	8.24	1)	Cagliari	05 Jul

+) *Best legal mark.*

Year	Athlete	Nat	Born	Mark	Pl	Venue	Date
	With assisting wind:						
	Vernon George	USA	64	8.46	1)	Blaine	23 Jun
	Yusuf Alli	Nig	60	8.39	1)	Auckland	01 Feb
	Andre Ester	USA	65	8.37	2)	Blaine	23 Jun
	Gordon McKee	USA	66	8.31	1)	San Angelo	12 Apr
	Joe Greene	USA	67	8.28	1)	Champaign	19 May
1991	Mike Powell	USA	63	8.95	1)	Tokyo	30 Aug
	Carl Lewis	USA	61	8.87	+)	Tokyo	30 Aug
	Larry Myricks	USA	56	8.50	3)	New York	15 Jun
	Llewellyn Starks	USA	67	8.50	2)	Rhede	07 Jul
	Gordon Laine	USA	58	8.28	1)	Sevilla	30 May
	Chen Zunrong	Chi	62	8.26	1)	Beijing	03 Jun
	Konstantinos Koukodimos	Gre	69	8.26	1)	Athinai	08 Jul
	Jaime Jefferson	Cub	62	8.26	1)	Habana	05 Aug
	Keith Talley	USA	64	8.25i	1)	Johnson City	25 Jan
	Gordon McKee	USA	66	8.25	1)	Austin	06 Apr
	+) *Best legal mark.*						
	With assisting wind:						
	Carl Lewis	USA	61	8.91	2)	Tokyo	30 Aug
	Kareem Streete-Thompson	Cay	73	8.40	1)	Houston	05 May
	Giovanni Evangelisti	Ita	61	8.35	2)	Bologna	07 Sep
	Joe Greene	USA	67	8.34	2)	Walnut	20 Apr
	Dietmar Haaf	Ger	67	8.30	1)	Frankfurt	29 Jun
	François Fouchet	SA	63	8.27	1)	Johannesburg	30 Mar
	Robert Emmiyan	SU	65	8.27	3)	Bologna	07 Sep
	Jesús Oliván	Spa	68	8.26	1)	Soria	10 Aug
1992	Carl Lewis	USA	61	8.68	Q)	Barcelona	05 Aug
	Mike Powell	USA	63	8.64	2)	Barcelona	06 Aug
	Ivan Pedroso	Cub	72	8.53	1)	Se villa	17 Jul
	Erick Walder	USA	71	8.47	1)	Austin	05 Jun
	Llewellyn Starks	USA	67	8.40	3)	Modesto	16 May
	Joe Greene	USA	67	8.38	1)	Eugene	06 Jun
	Chen Zunrong	Chi	62	8.36	+)	Shizuoka	05 May
	Dmitriy Bagryanov	Rus	67	8.35	1)	Granada	30 May
	Mike Conley	USA	62	8.34	Q)	New Orleans	22 Jun
	Gordon McKee	USA	66	8.28	1)	El Paso	11 Apr
	+) *Best legal mark.*						
	With assisting wind:						
	Mike Powell	USA	63	8.99	1)	Sestriere	21 Jul
	Ivan Pedroso	Cub	72	8.79	1)	Habana	21 May
	Carl Lewis	USA	61	8.72	1)	New York	24 May
	Joe Greene	USA	67	8.66	2)	Sestriere	21 Jul
	Erick Walder	USA	71	8.58	1)	Starkville	16 May
	Milan Gombala	Cze	68	8.42	3)	Sestriere	21 Jul
	Jaime Jefferson	Cub	62	8.41	2)	Salamanca	13 Jul
	Chen Zunrong	Chi	62	8.39	1)	Shizuoka	05 May
	Kareem Streete-Thompson	Cay	73	8.39	Q)	Austin	03 Jun
	Giovanni Evangelisti	Ita	61	8.29	4)	Sestriere	21 Jul
	Gordon Laine	USA	58	8.28	5)	Sestriere	21 Jul
1993	Mike Powell	USA	63	8.70	1)	Salamanca	27 Jul
	Erick Walzer	USA	71	8.53	1)	New Orleans	03 Jun
	Ivan Pedroso	Cub	72	8.49	1)	Habana	23 May
	Craig Hepburn	Bah	69	8.41	1)	Nassau	17 Jun
	Dion Bentley	USA	71	8.39	2)	Nedw Orleans	03 Jun
	Roland McGhee	USA	71	8.38	1)	Columbus	09 May
	Kareem Streete-Thompson	USA	73	8.36	1)	El Paso	10 Apr
	Nai Hui-Fang	Tai	69	8.34	1)	Shanghai	15 May
	Joe Greene	USA	67	8.33	3)	Eugene	19 Jun
	Huang Geng	Chi	70	8.30	1)	Beijing	09 Sep
	With assisting wind:						
	Anthuan Maybank	USA	69	8.40	1)	Des Moines	24 Apr

Year	Athlete	Nat	Born	Mark	Pl	Venue	Date
	Larry Myricks	USA	56	8.37	1)	Sestriere	28 Jul
	Reggie Jones	USA	71	8.35	2)	Sestriere	28 Jul
	Joe Greene	USA	67	8.35	3)	Sestriere	28 Jul
	Ivailo Mladenov	Bul	73	8.35	1)	Sofia	01 Aug
	Obinna Eregbu	Nig	69	8.32	1)	Durban	27 Jun
	Stacy Brown	USA	72	8.30	1)	Abilene	08 May
1994	Erick Walder	USA	71	8.74	1)	El Paso	02 Apr
	Carl Lewis	USA	61	8.66	+)	Sestriere	31 Jul
	Kareem Streete-Thompson	USA	73	8.63	1)	Linz	04 Jul
	Mike Powell	USA	63	8.58	1)	Bruxelles	19 Aug
	Roland McGhee	USA	71	8.47	1)	Rhede	29 Jul
	Stanislav Tarasenko	Rus	66	8.43i	1)	Moskva	26 Jan
	Konstandinos Koukodimos	Gr	69	8.36	1)	Khania	05 Jun
	Ivailo Mladenov	Bul	73	8.30i	1)	Pireas	28 Feb
	Yevgeniy Tretyak	Rus	71	8.29	1)	Stavropol	28 May
	Dion Bentley	USA	71	8.28	2)	Linz	04 Jul
	+) *Best legal mark.*						
	With assisting wind:						
	Mike Powell	USA	63	8.95	1)	Sestriere	31 Jul
	Carl Lewis	USA	61	8.72	2)	Sestriere	31 Jul
	Kareem Streete-Thompson	USA	73	8.64	2)	Knoxville	18 Jun
	Konstadinos Koukodimos	Gr	69	8.40	1)	Valencia	11 Jun
	Huang Geng	Chi	70	8.34	1)	Hiroshima	11 Oct
	Milko Campus	Ita	69	8.31	4)	Sestriere	31 Jul
	James Beckford	Jam	75	8.29	1)	Tempe	02 Apr
1995	Ivan Pedroso	Cub	72	8.71	1)	Salamanca	18 Jul
	Kareem Streete-Thompson	USA	73	8.56	1)	New York	21 May
	Mike Powell	USA	63	8.52	2)	Paris	03 Jul
	Roland McGhee	USA	71	8.51	2)	São Paulo	14 May
	Joe Greene	USA	67	8.48	3)	São Paulo	14 May
	James Beckford	Jam	75	8.45	2)	Oristano	18 Sep
	Douglas de Souza	Bra	72	8.40	1)	São Paulo	15 Feb
	Huang Geng	Chi	70	8.38	1)	Taiyuan	18 May
	Bogdan Tudor	Rum	70	8.37	2)	Bad Cannstatt	09 Jul
	Andrey Ignatov	Rus	68	8.34	1)	Moskva	16 Jun
	With assisting wind:						
	Ivan Pedroso	Cub	72	8.96	1)	Sestriere	29 Jul
	James Beckford	Jam	75	8.68	1)	Odessa, TX	19 May
	Mike Powell	USA	63	8.55	1)	Sacramento	18 Jun
	Stanislav Tarasenko	Rus	66	8.49	2)	Madrid	20 Jun
	Kiril Sosunov	Rus	75	8.48	1)	Oristano	18 Sep
	Carl Lewis	USA	61	8.45	2)	Sacramento	18 Jun
	Ivailo Mladenov	Bul	73	8.34	3)	Madrid	20 Jun
1996	Erick Walder	USA	71	8.58	1)	Springfield	04 May
	James Beckford	Jam	75	8.52	1)	Innsbruck	29 May
	Carl Lewis	USA	61	8.50	1)	Atlanta	29 Jul
	Kevin Dilworth	USA	74	8.47	1)	Abilene	09 May
	Ivan Pedroso	Cub	72	8.46i	1)	Liévin	18 Feb
	Mike Conley	USA	62	8.46	2)	Springfield	04 May
	Joe Greene	USA	67	8.46	1)	Sestriere	07 Aug
	Mike Powell	USA	63	8.39	1)	Atlanta	19 Jun
	Nelson Ferreira Jr.	Bra	73	8.36	+)	Medellin	10 May
	Kareem Streete-Thompson	USA	73	8.34	1)	Linz	21 Aug
	+) *Best legal mark.*						
	Exhibition:						
	Yuriy Naumkin	Rus	68	8.46	1)	Iglesias	06 Sep
	Irregular (downhill):						
	Sean Robbins	USA	72	8.37i	1)	Bowling Green	10 Feb
	With assisting wind:						
	Nelson Ferreira Jr.	Bra	73	8.41	1)	Medellin	10 May

	Cheikh Tidiane Touré	Sen	70	8.34	3)	Sestriere	07 Aug
1997	Ivan Pedroso	Cub	72	8.63	1)	Padova	08 Jun
	James Beckford	Jam	75	8.62	1)	Orlando	05 Apr
	Erick Walder	USA	71	8.49	1)	Villeneuve d'Ascq	29 Jun
	Joe Greene	USA	67	8.46	1)	Walnut	20 Apr
	Cheikh Tidiane Touré	Sen	70	8.46	1)	Bad Langensalza	15 Jun
	Kirill Sosunov	Rus	75	8.41i	2)	Paris	08 Mar
	Robert Howard	USA	75	8.40	1)	Auburn	17 May
	Gregor Cankar	Slo	75	8.40	1)	Celje	18 May
	Lao Jianfeng	Chi	75	8.40	1)	Zhaoqing	28 May
	Carlos Calado	Por	75	8.36	1)	Lisboa	20 Jun
1998	James Beckford	Jam	75	8.60	1)	Bad Langensalza	06 Jun
	Ivan Pedroso	Cub	72	8.54	1)	Uniondale, NY	20 Jul
	Erick Walder	USA	71	8.48	2)	Villeneuve d'Ascq	11 Jul
	Roland McGhee	USA	71	8.40	3)	Villeneuve d'Ascq	11 Jul
	Kirill Sosunov	Rus	75	8.38	1)	Sankt-Peterburg	27 Jun
	Sean Robbins	USA	72	8.33	4)	Uniondale, NY	20 Jul
	Jai Taurina	Aus	72	8.32	2)	Johannesburg	11 Sep
	Kevin Dilworth	USA	74	8.30	1)	Hania	27 May
	Kader Klouchi	Fra	69	8.30	+)	Dijon	05 Jul
	Carlos Castelbranco	Por	69	8.28	1)	Lisboa	23 May
	+) *Best legal mark.*						
	James Beckford	Jam	75	8.61	1)	Marrubio	12 Sep
	Erick Walder	USA	71	8.54	1)	Salamanca	10 Jul
	Robert Howard	USA	75	8.37	1)	Amherst	04 Jun
	Kader Klouchi	Fra	69	8.33	1)	Dijon	05 Jul
	Tim Bryant	USA	74	8.31	1)	College Station	11 Apr
1999	Ivan Pedroso	Cub	72	8.62i	1)	Maebashi	07 Mar
	Yago Lamela	Spa	77	8.56i	2)	Maebashi	07 Mar
	James Beckford	Jam	75	8.50	2)	Torino	24 Jun
	Gregor Cankar	Slo	75	8.36	3)	Sevilla	28 Aug
	Erick Walder	USA	71	8.35i	2)	Liévin	21 Feb
	Jai Taurina	Aus	72	8.35	4)	Sevilla	28 Aug
	Carlos Calado	Por	75	8.34	1)	Lisboa	19 Jun
	Hatem Mersal	Egy	75	8.31	3)	Oslo	30 Jun
	Roman Shchurenko	Ukr	76	8.30	1)	Belaya Tserkov	25 Jul
	Bogdan Tarus	Rum	75	8.26i	1)	Bucurersti	21 Feb
	Irregular take-off board:						
	Joan Lino Martinez	Cub	78	8.39	1)	La Habana	05 Feb
	With assisting wind:						
	Erick Walder	USA	71	8.50	1)	Oslo	30 Jun
	Shane Hair	Aus	75	8.35	1)	La Laguna	05 Jun
	Emmanuel Bangué	Fra	71	8.32	1)	Pierre-Bénite	11 Jun
	Danial Jahic	Yug	79	8.27	1)	Réthimno	29 May
2000	Ivan Pedroso	Cub	72	8.65	1)	Jena	03 Jun
	Melvin Lister	USA	77	8.49	1)	Baton Rouge	13 May
	Jai Taurima	Aus	72	8.49	2)	Sydney	28 Sep
	Luis Meliz	Cub	79	8.43	2)	Jena	03 Jun
	James Beckford	Jam	75	8.42	1)	Bad Langensalza	01 Jul
	Vitaliy Shkurlatov	Rus	79	8.38i	1)	Samara	30 Jan
	Roman Shchurenko	Ukr	76	8.35	1)	Kiev	25 Jul
	Younès Moudrik	Mar	77	8.34	1)	Alger	13 Jul
	Kirill Sosunov	Rus	75	8.34	1)	Lisboa	05 Aug
	Hussein Al-Sabee	SA	79	8.33	1)	Jakarta	31 Aug
	With assisting wind:						
	Peter Burge	Aus	74	8.48	1)	Gold Coast, RB	10 Sep
	Cheikh Touré	Fra	70	8.43	1)	Nice	06 Aug
	Masaki Morinaga	Jap	72	8.34	1)	Shizuoka	03 May

ALL TIME WORLD LIST AS AT THE END OF 2000

Mike Powell	USA	63	8.95	1)	Tokyo	30 Aug 91
Bob Beamon	USA	46	8.90	1)	Mexico City	18 Oct 68
Carl Lewis	USA	61	8.87	+)	Tokyo	30 Aug 91
Robert Emmiyan	Arm	65	8.86	1)	Tsakhkadzor	22 May 87
Larry Myricks	USA	56	8.74	2)	Indianapolis	18 Jul 88
Erick Walder	USA	71	8.74	1)	El Paso	02 Apr 94
Ivan Pedroso	Cub	72	8.71	1)	Salamanca	18 Jul 95
Kareem Streete-Thompson	Cay/USA	73	8.63	1)	Linz	04 Jul 94
James Beckford	Jam	75	8.62	1)	Orlando	05 Apr 97
Yago Lamela	Spa	77	8.56i	2)	Maebashi	07 Mar 99

With assisting wind:

Mike Powell	USA	63	8.99	1)	Sestriere	21 Jul 92
Ivan Pedroso	Cub	72	8.96	1)	Sestriere	29 Jul 95
Carl Lewis	USA	61	8.91	2)	Tokyo	30 Aug 91
Jameds Beckford	Jam	75	8.68	1)	Odessa, TX	19 May 95
Joe Greene	USA	67	8.66	2)	Sestriere	21 Jul 92
Kareem Streete-Thompson	Cay/USA	73	8.64	2)	Knoxville	18 Jun 94
Mike Conley	USA	62	8.63	2)	Eugene	20 Jun 86
Jason Grimes	USA	59	8.57	1)	Durham	27 Jun 82

2001	Ivan Pedroso	Cub	72	8.43i	1)	Lisboa	11 Mar
	James Beckford	Jam	75	8.41	1)	Torino	09 Jun
	Savanté Stringfellow	USA	78	8.38	1)	Lake Buena Vista	22 Jul
	Hussein Al-Sabee	SA	79	8.31	1)	Doha	18 May
	Danil Burkenya	Rus	78	8.31	1)	Tula	14 Jul
	Kevin Dilworth	USA	74	8.30	3)	Bruxelles	24 Aug
	Grzegorz Marciniszyn	Pol	77	8.28	1)	Malles	14 Jul
	Younès Moudrik	Mor	77	8.23	1)	Melbourne	09 Sep
	Li Dalong	Chi	80	8.22	1)	Baoding	15 Jun
	Vladimir Malyavin	Rus	73	8.22	1)	Moskva	27 Jul
	With assisting wind:						
	Miguel Pate	USA	79	8.48	1)	Fort Worth	21 Apr
	Savanté Stringfellow	USA	78	8.47	1)	Eugene	22 Jun
	Gable Garenamotse	Bot	77	8.26	1)	Ashford	11 Aug
	Kader Klouchi	Fra	69	8.24	1)	St.Etienne	01 Jul
	Yann Doménech	Fra	79	8.24	2)	St.Etienne	01 Jul
	Dwight Phillips	USA	77	8.23	3)	Eugene	22 Jun
2002	Miguel Pateusa	USA	79	8.59i	1)	New York	01 Mar
	Savanté Stringfellow	USA	78	8.52	1)	Stanford	21 Jun
	Dwight Phillips	USA	77	8.38	1)	Linz	19 Aug
	Roman Shchurenko	Ukr	76	8.33i	1)	Brovary	16 Feb
	Ivan Pedroso	Cub	72	8.30	2)	Padova	01 Sep
	Petar Dachev	Bul	79	8.27i	1)	Sofia	10 Feb
	ChrisTomlinson	GB	81	8.27	1)	Tallahassee	13 Apr
	Luis F. Méliz	Cub	79	8.27	1)	La Laguna	14 Sep
	Aleksey Lukasevich	Ukr	77	8.26	1)	Kiev	25 May
	Raúl Fernández	Spa	78	8.26	1)	Monachil	10 Jul
	With assisting wind:						
	Kevin Dilworth	USA	74	8.53	1)	Fort-de-France	27 Apr
	Danil Burkenya	Rus	78	8.35	1)	Lisboa	25 May
	Brian Johnson	USA	80	8.33	1)	New Orleans	16 Mar
	Petar Dachev	Bul	79	8.29	1)	Villeneuve-d'Ascq	16 Jun
2003	Yago Lamela	Spa	77	8.53	1)	Castellón	18 Aug
	Savanté Stringfellow	USA	78	8.46	1)	Oxford, MS	12 Apr
	Miguel Pate	USA	79	8.46	1)	Mexico City	03 May
	Dwight Phillips	USA	77	8.44	1)	Trikala	24 Jun
	Loúis Tsátoumas	Gre	82	8.34	2)	Trikala	24 Jun
	Yahya Berrabah	Mor	81	8.33	1)	Casablanca	12 Aug

Year	Athlete	Nat	Born	Mark	Pos	Venue	Date
	Ivan Pedroso	Cub	72	8.31	1)	Padova	06 Jul
	Nikolay Atanasov	Bul	74	8.31	1)	Pirgos	27 Jul
	Dimitrios Filindras	Gre	73	8.30	1)	Haniá	09 Jun
	Hussein Al-Sabee	SA	79	8.30	2)	Monaco	13 Sep
	Ignisious Gaisah	Gha	83	8.30	1)	Abuja	14 Oct
	With assisting wind:						
	Joan Lino Martinez	Cub	78	8.32	1)	Arona	26 Jul
2004	Dwight Phillips	USA	77	8.60	1)	Linz	02 Aug
	John Moffitt	USA	80	8.47	2)	Athinai	26 Aug
	Savanté Stringfellow	USA	78	8.41i	1)	Fayettteville	13 Feb
	Hussein Al-Sabee	SA	79	8.35	2)	Modesto	08 May
	Victor Castillo	Ven	81	8.34	1)	Cochabamba	30 May
	Joan Lino Martinez	Spa	78	8.32	3)	Athinai	26 Aug
	Ignisious Gaisah	Gha	83	8.32	1)	Monaco	18 Sep
	James Beckford	Jam	75	8.31i	2)	Budapest	06 Mar
	Vitaliy Shkurlatov	Rus	79	8.28i	3)	Budapest	06 Mar
	Yann Doménech	Fra	79	8.28	1)	Vénissieux	07 Jul
	Jonathan Chimier	Mri	82	8.28	Q)	Athinai	24 Aug
	With assisting wind:						
	Hussein Al-Sabee	SA	79	8.41	1)	Carson	22 May
	Loúis Tsátoumas	Gre	82	8.37	1)	Haniá	28 Jun
	Tony Allmond	USA	82	8.35	2)	Austin	10 Jun
	Petr Lampart	Cze	83	8.31	1)	Sestriere	01 Aug
	Ndiss Kaba Badji	Sen	83	8.30	2)	Sestriere	01 Aug
	Gregor Cankar	Slo	75	8.30	3)	Sestriere	01 Aug
	Chris Tomlinson	GB	81	8.28	1)	Bydgoszcz	19 Jun
2005	Dwight Phillips	USA	77	8.60	1)	Helsinki	13 Aug
	Miguel Pate	USA	79	8.45	1)	Sheffield	21 Aug
	Mohamed Salim Al-Khuwalidi	SA	81	8.44	1)	Makkah	13 Apr
	Joan Lino Martinez	Spa	78	8.37i	1)	Madrid	06 Mar
	Khotso Mokoena	SA	85	8.37	1)	Johannesburg	22 Apr
	Ignisious Gaisah	Gha	83	8.34	2)	Helsinki	13 Aug
	Brian Johnson	USA	80	8.33	1)	Bad Langensalza	11 Jun
	Vladimir Zyuskov	Ukr	81	8.31	1)	Kiev	03 Jul
	Irving Saladino	Pan	83	8.29	1)	Sevilla	04 Jun
	James Beckford	Jam	75	8.28	3)	Monaco	10 Sep
	With assisting wind:						
	Irving Saladino	Pan	83	8.51	1)	São Paulo	02 Apr
	James Beckford	Jam	75	8.36	1)	Glasgow	27 Aug
	Arnaud Casquette	Mri	78	8.28	1)	Sestriere	24 Jul
2006	Irving Saladino	Pan	83	8.56	1)	Rio de Janeiro	14 May
	Mohamed Salim Al-Khuwalidi	SA	81	8.48	1)	Sotteville	02 Jul
	Ignisious Gaisah	Gha	83	8.43	2)	Roma	14 Jul
	Andrew Howe	Ita	85	8.41	3)	Roma	14 Jul
	Khotso Mokoena	SA	85	8.39	1)	Lapinlahti	16 Jul
	Ahmad Fayez Marzouk	SA	79	8.39	1)	Lemgo	13 Aug
	Walter Davis	USA	79	8.36	1)	Fort-de-France	29 Apr
	Ibrahim Camejo	Cub	82	8.34	1)	Habana	24 Feb
	Brian Johnson	USA	80	8.33	2)	Fort-de-France	29 Apr
	Dwight Phillips	USA	77	8.32	4)	Roma	14 Jul
	With assisting wind:						
	Irving Saladino	Pan	83	8.65	1)	Athinai	03 Jul
	Ignisious Gaisah	Gha	83	8.51	1)	Bambous	09 Aug
	Khotso Mokoena	SA	85	8.45	2)	Bambous	09 Aug
	Issam Nima	Alg	79	8.37	3)	Bambous	09 Aug
	Ibrahin Camejo	Cub	82	8.35	1)	Habana	03 Feb
	Rogério Bispo	Bra	85	8.32	1)	Tunja	29 Sep
2007	Louis Tsátoumas	Gre	82	8.66	1)	Kalamáta	02 Jun
	Irving Saladino	Pan	83	8.57	1)	Osaka	30 Aug

Year	Name	Nat	Born	Mark	Pos	Venue	Date
	Andrew Howe	Ita	85	8.47	2)	Osaka	30 Aug
	James Beckford	Jam	75	8.37	1)	Warszawa	17 Jun
	Khotso Mokoena	SA	85	8.34	1)	Pretoria	09 Mar
	Dwight Phillips	USA	77	8.31	1)	Réthimno	18 Jul
	Brian Johnson	USA	80	8.31	2)	Réthimno	18 Jul
	Ruslan Gataullin	Rus	79	8.29	1)	Sochi	27 May
	Chris Tomlinson	GB	81	8.29	2)	Bad Langensalza	07 Jul
	Issam Nima	Alg	79	8.26	3)	Zaragoza	28 Jul
	With assisting wind:						
	Tommi Evilä	Fin	80	8.41	1)	Göteborg	08 Sep
	Dwight Phillips	USA	77	8.37	1)	Zaragoza	28 Jul
	Tareq Bougtaib	Mor	81	8.35	1)	Khémisset	14 Jul
	Gable Garenamotse	Bot	77	8.34	1)	Bad Langensalza	07 Jul
	Jadel Gregório	Bra	80	8.26	2)	Dakar	28 Apr
	Thiago Dias	Bra	84	8.26w?	1)	São Paulo	22 Jul
	Trevell Quinley	USA	83	8.26	2)	Zaragoza	28 Jul
2008	Irving Saladino	Pan	83	8.73	1)	Hengelo	24 May
	Ibrahin Camejo	Cub	82	8.46	1)	Bilbao	21 Jun
	Loúis Tsátoumas	Gre	82	8.44	1)	Athinai	13 Jul
	Mohamed Al-Khuwalidi	SA	81	8.37	1)	Riyadh	16 Apr
	Trevell Quinley	USA	83	8.36	1)	Eugene	29 Jun
	Hussein Al-Sabee	SA	79	8.35	1)	Zurich	29 Aug
	Wilfredo Martinez	Cub	85	8.31	1)	Cali	06 Jul
	Brian Johnson	USA	80	8.30	1)	Baie Mahault	01 May
	Ngonidzashe Makusha	Zim	87	8.30	1)	Des Moines	12 Jun
	Khotso Mokoena	SA	85	8.25	2)	Stellenbosch	14 Mar
	Dwight Phillips	USA	77	8.25	2)	Ponce	17 May
	With assisting wind:						
	Brian Johnson	USA	80	8.48	1)	Fort-de-France	08 May
	Dwight Phillips	USA	77	8.47	2)	Fort-de-France	08 May
	Miguel Pate	USA	79	8.39	3)	Fort-de-France	08 May
	Khotso Mokoena	SA	85	8.35	2)	Hengelo	24 May
	Keenan Watson	SA	88	8.26	1)	Stellenbosch	14 Mar
2009	Dwight Phillips	USA	77	8.74	1)	Eugene	07 Jun
	Sebastian Bayer	Ger	86	8.71i	1)	Torino	08 Mar
	Irving Saladino	Pam	83	8.63	2)	Eugene	07 Jun
	Khotso Mokoena	SA	85	8.50	2)	Madrid	04 Jul
	Mitchell Watt	Aus	88	8.43	1)	Réthimno	20 Jul
	Salim Sdiri	Fra	78	8.42	1)	Pierre-Bénite	12 Jun
	Yahya Berrabah	Mor	81	8.40	1)	Beirut	02 Oct
	Fabrice Lapierre	Aus	83	8.35	+)	Madrid	04 Jul
	Ndiss Kaba Badji	Sen	83	8.32	2)	Beirut	02 Oct
	Ibrahin Camejo	Cub	82	8.30	1)	Malles	28 Jun
	Greg Rutherford	GB	86	8.30	Q)	Berlin	20 Aug
	+) *Best legal mark.*						
	With assisting wind:						
	Fabrice Lapierre	Aus	83	8.57	1)	Madrid	04 Jul
	Kim Duk-hyun	Kor	85	8.41	1)	Beograd	12 Jul
2010	Christian Reif	Ger	84	8.47	1)	Barcelona	01 Aug
	Dwight Phillips	USA	77	8.46	1)	Monaco	22 Jul
	Fabrice Lapierre	Aus	83	8.40	1)	Nuoro	14 Jul
	Alain Bailey	Jam	87	8.35	1)	Knoxville	15 May
	Chris Noffke	Aus	88	8.33	2)	Perth	18 Apr
	Irving Saladino	Pan	83	8.30	1)	Bad Langensalza	05 Jun
	Su Xiongfeng	Chi	87	8.27i	1)	Nanjing	11 Mar
	Ndiss Kaba Badji	Sen	83	8.27	1)	Dakar	24 Apr
	Eusebio Cáceres	Spa	91	8.27	Q)	Barcelona	30 Jul
	Pavel Shalin	Rus	87	8.25	1)	Moskva	06 Jun
	With assisting wind:						
	Fabrice Lapierre	Aus	83	8.78	1)	Perth	18 Apr

Irving Saladino	Pan	83	8.46	1)	Eugene	03 Jul
Li Jinzhe	Chi	89	8.29	3)	Eugene	03 Jul
Salim Sdiri	Fra	78	8.28	1)	Valence	10 Jul
Pavel Shalin	Rus	87	8.26	1)	Bergen	19 Jun

ALL TIME WORLD LIST AS AT THE END OF 2010

Mike Powell	USA	63	8.95	1)	Tokyo	30 Aug 91
Bob Beamon	USA	46	8.90	1)	Mexico City	18 Oct 68
Carl Lewis	USA	61	8.87	+)	Tokyo	30 Aug 91
Robert Emmiyan	Arm	65	8.86	1)	Tsakhkadzor	22 May 87
Larry Myricks	USA	56	8.74	2)	Indianapolis	18 Jul 88
Erick Walder	USA	71	8.74	1)	El Paso	02 Apr 94
Dwight Phillips	USA	77	8.74	1)	Eugene	07 Jun 09
Irving Saladino	Pan	83	8.73	1)	Hengelo	24 May 08
Ivan Pedroso	Cub	72	8.71	1)	Salamanca	18 Jul 95
Sebastian Bayer	Ger	86	8.71i	1)	Torino	08 Mar 09

+) *Best legal mark.*

With assisting wing:

Mike Powell	USA	63	8.99	1)	Sestriere	21 Jul 92
Ivan Pedroso	Cub	72	8.96	1)	Sestriere	29 Jul 95
Carl Lewis	USA	61	8.91	2)	Tokyo	30 Aug 91

TRIPLE JUMP

Note - *Throughout the 19th century and prior to the first world record officially ratified by the IAAF (Daniel Ahearn's 15.52, made in 1911) the prevailing form, especially in Great Britain and Ireland - pioneer countries of the event - consisted in two hops and a jump (denoted with a *). I have tried, as far as possible, to list only marks made with the hop, step and jump style.*

ALL TIME WORLD BEST AS AT THE END OF 1860

John Overland	Can		12.24	1)	Toronto	Nov 39
Hamner Webb	GB	37	12.19	1)	Cheltenham	30 Apr 56

Professional: (first known "hop, step and leap" mark):

Andrew Beatty	GB		12.95	1)	Mount Benger	17 Mar 26

ALL TIME WORLD BEST AS AT THE END OF 1880

John Hargreaves	GB	50	13.56	1)	Manchester	30 Jul 77
P. Johnson	USA		13.26	1)	Boston	29 Jun 78

Professional:

Samuel Muir	GB		14.15	1)	Bridge of Alan	03 Aug 67

ALL TIME WORLD BEST AS AT THE END OF 1900

James Connolly	USA	65	14.94	1)	New York	19 Sep 96

1911	Daniel Ahearn	USA	88	15.52*	-)	New York	30 May
	Timothy Ahearne	Ire	86	14.67*	-)	New York	30 May
	Dennis Lane	Aus		14.40	1)	Sydney	25 Nov

Year	Athlete	Nat	Born	Mark	Pl	Venue	Date
	Daniel O'Leary	Ire		14.22*	)	Banteer	16 Jul
	Edward Southee	Aus		14.22	2)	Sydney	25 Nov
	M. J. Teahan	Ire		14.20*	)	Kilgarvan	22 Aug
	Gustaf Nordén	Swe	84	14.17w	1)	Stockholm	10 Sep
	Erling Vinne	Nor	92	14.12	-)	Kristiania	11 Jun
1912	Karl Baaske	Ger	91	14.87	1)	Osterode	25 Aug
	Gustaf Lindblom	Swe	91	14.76	1)	Stockholm	15 Jul
	Georg Åberg	Swe	93	14.51	2)	Stockholm	15 Jul
	Charles Brickley	USA	91	14.45	1)	Cambridge, MA	08 Jun
	Percy Kirwan	Ire		14.35*	1)	Dublin	27 May
	Gustaf Nordén	Swe	84	14.33	2)	Stockholm	17 Jun
	M. J. Cullinan	USA		14.32	)		
	Erling Vinne	Nor	92	14.30	1)	Kristiania	23 Jun
	Nils Fixdal	Nor	89	14.27	1)	Haugesund	04 Aug
	Erik Almlöf	Swe	91	14.18	3)	Stockholm	17 Jun
1913	Daniel Ahearn	USA	88	15.24*	1)	Chicago	05 Jul
	Timothy Ahearne	Ire	86	14.80*	2)	Chicago	05 Jul
	Vilho Tuulos	Fin	95	14.71	1)	Turku	04 Aug
	Erling Vinne	Nor	92	14.49	2)	Turku	04 Aug
	Frank Roche	Ire		14.48*	)	Kinsale	27 Jul
	P. P. O'Sullivan	Ire		14.39*	)	Kinsale	27 Jul
	Nils Fixdal	Nor	89	14.34	1)	Haugesund	13 Jul
	Timothy Carroll	Ire	87	14.32*	)	Kinsale	15 Aug
	Platt Adams	USA	85	14.32	1)	New York	20 Sep
	Ivar Sahlin	Swe	95	14.30	1)	Sundsvall	08 Jun
1914	Daniel Ahearn	USA	88	14.79	1)	Baltimore	12 Sep
	Vilho Tuulos	Fin	95	14.62	1)	Malmö	09 Jul
	Platt Adams	USA	85	14.59	1)	New York	03 Oct
	Timothy Ahearne	Ire	86	14.57	2)	Baltimore	12 Sep
	Ivar Sahlin	Swe	95	14.52	1)	Stockholm	14 Jun
	Juho Halme	Fin	88	14.51	1)	Kotka	07 Jun
	Emil Liljeberg	Fin	95	14.38	2)	Malmö	09 Jul
	Karl Baaske	Ger	91	14.36	1)	Berlin	12 Jul
	Erik Almlöf	Swe	91	14.25	4)	Malmö	09 Jul
	Cristoph Kretzschmar	Ger		14.19	1)	Dresden	12 Jul
1915	Daniel Ahearn	USA	88	15.52w	1)	San Francisco	07 Aug
	(D. Ahearn)			15.18	1)	Chicago	17 Jul
	Ivar Sahlin	Swe	95	14.77	1)	Sundsvall	08 Aug
	Sherman Landers	USA	98	14.36w	1)	San Francisco	06 Aug
	Platt Adams	USA	85	14.22	1)	New York	19 Jun
	Lauritz Schibbye	Nor	92	14.21	1)	Fredrikstad	29 Aug
	Ephraim Levin	Swe	96	14.19	1)	Stockholm	24 May
	M. J. Fahey	USA		14.14	2)	New York	19 Jun
	Folke Jansson	Swe	97	14.12	)	Jönköping	06 Jun
	Valter Olsson	Swe		14.07	)	Jönköping	06 Jun
	John Andersson	Swe	96	14.06	)	Jönköping	06 Jun
1916	Curt Enhörning	Swe	98	14.75	1)	Stockholm	15 Oct
	Ephraim Levin	Swe	96	14.71	1)	Malmö	27 Aug
	Vilho Tuulos	Fin	95	14.67	1)	Vaasa	16 Jul
	Georg Danielsen	Nor	94	14.49	1)	Kristiania	03 Sep
	Sven Runström	Swe	96	14.48	)	Gävle	30 Jul
	Thorvig Svahn	Swe	93	14.41	2)	Malmö	27 Aug
	Daniel Ahearn	USA	88	14.32	1)	Chicago	26 Aug
	William Britton	Ire		14.25	1)	Killorglin	
	Eric Abrahamsson	Swe	98	14.20	)	Stockholm	15 Oct
	Harry Svensson	Swe	94	14.07	)	Stockholm	28 May
	Ivar Sahlin	Swe	95	14.07	)	Stockholm	09 Jul
1917	Daniel Ahearn	USA	88	14.79	1)	Chicago	30 Jun
	Folke Jansson	Swe	97	14.75	1)	Malmö	17 Jun
	William Overbee	USA		14.74	1)	Philadelphia	28 Apr
	Erling Vinne	Nor	92	14.65	1)	Kristiania	23 Sep

Year	Name	Nat	Born	Mark	Pos	Venue	Date
	Sherman Landers	USA	98	14.50	2)	Philadelphia	28 Apr
	Erling Thorsnaes	Nor	96	14.29	2)	Bergen	16 Sep
	Georg Danielsen	Nor	95	14.28	1)	Kristiania	02 Sep
	Kurt Enhörning	Swe	98	14.25	)	Stockholm	08 Sep
	Ephraim Levin	Swe	96	14.19	)	Stockholm	18 Aug
	Hugo Lilliér	Swe	94	14.15	)	Stockholm	04 Aug
1918	Folke Janson	Swe	97	14.92	1)	Kristiania	29 Jun
	Erling Vinne	Nor	92	14.54	2)	Kristiania	19 Jun
	Sven Runström	Swe	96	14.25	3)	København	01 Sep
	Johan Johansen	Nor	98	14.18	1)	Bergen	30 Jun
	Daniel Ahearn	USA	88	14.11	1)	Great Lakes	21 Sep
	Ephraim Levin	Swe	96	14.05	)	Stockholm	18 Aug
	Aarne Gulbrandsen	Nor		13.99	-)	Kristiania	18 Aug
	Erik Almlöf	Swe	91	13.98	)	Stockholm	18 Aug
	Hugo Lindberg	Swe	96	13.92	)	Stockholm	03 Aug
	Gustaf Bäckman	Swe	93	13.92	)		
1919	Vilho Tuulos	Fin	95	15.30	1)	Tampere	20 Jul
	Folke Janson	Swe	97	14.71	1)	Karlstad	17 Aug
	Erling Vinne	Nor	92	14.58	1)	Kristiania	07 Jun
	Sven Runström	Swe	96	14.55	1)	Kristiania	07 Sep
	Sherman Landers	USA	98	14.54	1)	Philadelphia	13 Sep
	Anthony Winter	Aus	94	14.50	1)	Sydney	13 Dec
	T. O'Donovan	Ire		14.26*	1)	Brandon	13 Jul
	Gustaf Bäckman	Swe	93	14.25	)	Stockholm	10 Aug
	Kaare Bache	Nor	98	14.23	2)	Kristiania	21 Sep
	Hugo Lindberg	Swe	96	14.14	)	Uppsala	18 May
1920	Folke Jansson	Swe	97	15.09	1)	Colombes	28 Aug
	Vilho Tuulos	Fin	95	14.97	2)	Colombes	28 Aug
	Sherman Landers	USA	98	14.83	1)	Cambridge, MA	17 Jul
	Erling Juul	Nor	97	14.83	1)	Kristiania	25 Jul
	Anthony Winter	Aus	94	14.69	1)	Sydney	04 Dec
	Kaare Bache	Nor	98	14.63	2)	Kristiania	25 Jul
	Sven Runström	Swe	96	14.60	2)	Stockholm	12 Sep
	Daniel Ahearn	USA	88	14.55	2)	Cambridge, MA	17 Jul
	Eric Almlöf	Swe	91	14.44	3)	Colombes	28 Aug
	Erling Vinne	Nor	92	14.26	1)	Kristiania	19 Jun

ALL TIME WORLD LIST AS AT THE END OF 1920

Name	Nat	Born	Mark	Pos	Venue	Date
Daniel Ahearn	USA	88	15.52		New York	30 May 11
Vilho Tuulos	Fin	95	15.30	1)	Tampere	20 Jul 19
Folke Jansson	Swe	97	15.09	1)	Colombes	28 Aug 20
James Connolly	USA	65	14.94	1)	New York	19 Sep 96
Timothy Ahearne	GB	86	14.92	1)	London	25 Jul 08
Karl Baaske	Ger	91	14.87	1)	Osterode	25 Aug 12
Sherman Landers	USA	98	14.83	1)	Cambridge, MA	17 Jul 20
Erling Juul	Nor	97	14.83	1)	Kristiania	25 Jul 20
Edward Bloss	USA	70	14.78	1)	Chicago	16 Sep 93
Ivar Sahlin	Swe	85	14.77	1)	Sundsvall	08 Aug 15

Year	Name	Nat	Born	Mark	Pos	Venue	Date
1921	Anthony Winter	Aus	94	15.15	1)	Sydney	10 Dec
	Vilho Tuulos	Fin	95	15.02	1)	Turku	29 May
	Folke Janson	Swe	97	14.60	1)	Oslo	04 Sep
	Elemér Somfay	Hun	98	14.51	1)	Budapest	21 Aug
	Arthur Holz	Ger	96	14.47	1)	Hamburg	12 Jun
	Erling Vinne	Nor	92	14.45	1)	Oslo	19 Jun
	Robert Kelley	USA	97	14.39	1)	Berkeley	14 May
	Sven Runström	Swe	96	14.39	1)	Stockholm	10 Jul
	Lauritz Bryhn	Nor	95	14.28	1)	Fredrikstad	20 Aug
	Harold Osborn	USA	99	14.27	1)	Philadelphia	29 Apr
	Kaufman Geist	USA	95	14.27	1)	Jersey City, NJ	19 Jun
	Leo Gabriel	Aus		14.27	2)	Sydney	10 Dec

	Name	Nat	Born	Mark	Pos	Venue	Date
	Unknown irregularity:						
	Gerald Plummer	NZ		14.32	1)	Auckland	17 Mar
1922	Arthur Holz	Ger	96	14.99	1)	Berlin	01 Jul
	Vilho Tuulos	Fin	95	14.98	1)	Kuopio	29 Jul
	Anthony Winter	Aus	94	14.73	1)	Sydney	18 Mar
	William DeHart Hubbard	USA	03	14.67	1)	Newark, NJ	09 Sep
	K. Oakes	Aus		14.60	1)	Sydney	04 Mar
	Karl Baaske	Ger	91	14.55*	2)	Berlin	01 Jul
	Hubert Gädda (Haukia)	Fin	96	14.51	2)	Kuopio	29 Jul
	Elemér Somfay	Hun	98	14.51	1)	Dolrog	06 Aug
	Erik Almlöf	Swe	91	14.48	1)	Gävle	13 Aug
	Folke Janson	Swe	97	14.46	1)	Köbenhavn	03 Sep
	Extra trial:						
	Karl Baaske	Ger	91	14.70*	-)	Berlin	01 Jul
	***)** *German style of jumping.*						
1923	Vilho Tuulos	Fin	95	15.48	1)	Borås	06 Jul
	Luis A. Brunetto	Arg	01	15.15	1)	Rosario	27 Oct
	William DeHart Hubbard	USA	03	14.90	1)	Philadelphia	27 Apr
	Folke Janson	Swe	97	14.72	1)	Borås	23 Sep
	Väinö Rainio	Fin	96	14.71	1)	Helsinki	26 Aug
	Anthony Winter	Aus	94	14.58	1)	Sydney	08 Dec
	Arthur Holz	Ger	96	14.55	1)	Oslo	17 Jun
	Ferenc Molnár	Hun	04	14.46	1)	Debrecen	13 Oct
	Kaufman Geist	USA	95	14.39	1)	New York	08 Sep
	Louis Lundgren	Dan	01	14.35	1)	Randers	19 Aug
1924	Anthony Winter	Aus	94	15.52	1)	Colombes	12 Jul
	Luis A. Brunetto	Arg	01	15.42	2)	Colombes	12 Jul
	Vilho Tuulos	Fin	95	15.37	3)	Colombes	12 Jul
	Väinö Rainio	Fin	96	15.01	4)	Colombes	12 Jul
	Folke Janson	Swe	97	14.97	5)	Colombes	12 Jul
	Erik Manskow	Nor	00	14.63	1)	Oslo	17 Aug
	Kaufman Geist	USA	95	14.46	1)	New York	07 Jun
	Ivar Sahlin	Swe	95	14.44	1)	Stockholm	09 Jun
	Mikio Oda	Jap	05	14.35	6)	Colombes	12 Jul
	Aleksander Klumberg (Kolmpere)	Est	99	14.33	2)	Helsinki	21 Sep
	Extra trial:						
	Rudolf Mühleis	Ger	95	14.42*	-)	Hannover	31 Aug
	***)** *German style of jumping.*						
1925	Vilho Tuulos	Fin	95	15.06	1)	Helsinki	31 May
	Luis A. Brunetto	Arg	01	15.00	1)	Rosario	11 Oct
	Anthony Winter	Aus	94	14.87	1)	Sydney	14 Mar
	Mikio Oda	Jap	05	14.80	1)	Tokyo	22 Nov
	Homer Martin	USA	01	14.71	1)	Chicago	20 Jun
	Gustaf Nilsson	Swed	03	14.63	1)	Strängnäs	04 Oct
	Merwin Graham	USA	03	14.54	1)	Des Moines	25 Apr
	Elemér Somfay	Hun	98	14.53	1)	Prešov	05 Jul
	John Connor	Eir	93	14.45	1)	Dublin	27 Jun
	Louis Minsky	USA		14.45w	1)	San Francisco	03 Jul
1926	Luis A. Brunetto	Arg	01	15.10	1)	Montevideo	18 Apr
	Levi Casey	USA	02	15.04	1)	Philadelphia	05 Jul
	Vilho Tuulos	Fin	95	14.69	1)	Turku	29 Aug
	Mikio Oda	Jap	05	14.65	1)	Tokyo	18 Apr
	Eric Svensson	Swe	03	14.63	1)	Huskvarna	29 Aug
	Erkki Järvinen	Fin	04	14.59	1)	Tampere	15 Aug
	Väinö Rainio	Fin	96	14.57	1)	Helsinki	22 Aug
	Gunnar Hagen	Nor	04	14.57	1)	Oslo	22 Aug
	Anthony Winter	Aus	94	14.56	1)	Sydney	13 Jan
	Willem Peters	Hol	03	14.50	1)	Groningen	24 Jul
1927	Willem Peters	Hol	03	15.48	1)	London	04 Jul
	Mikio Oda	Jap	05	15.35	1)	Shanghai	29 Aug

	Vilho Tuulos	Fin	95	15.08	1)	Turku	21 Aug
	Väinö Rainio	Fin	96	14.80	1)	Helsinki	14 Aug
	Eric Svensson	Swe	03	14.76	1)	Falkenberg	19 Jun
	Levi Casey	USA	02	14.75	1)	Lincoln	02 Jul
	Luis A. Brunetto	Arg	01	14.64	1)	Santiago de Chile	15 Apr
	Kenkichi Oshima	Jap	08	14.63	2)	Tokyo	07 Aug
	Erkki Järvinen	Fin	04	14.61	2)	Turku	21 Aug
	Anthony Winter	Aus	94	14.58	1)	Camden	01 Oct
1928	Vilho Tuulos	Fin	95	15.58w	1)	Helsinki	08 Jul
	Mikio Oda	Jap	05	15.41	1)	Osaka	19 May
	Erkki Järvinen	Fin	04	15.40w	2)	Helsinki	08 Jul
	Levi Casey	USA	02	15.17	2)	Amsterdam	02 Aug
	(Tuulos			15.11	3)	Amsterdam	02 Aug
	Willem Peters	Hol	03	15.10	1)	Enschede	02 Sep
	Anthony Winter	Aus	94	15.02	1)	Dublin	25 Aug
	Chuhei Nambu	Jap	04	15.01	4)	Amsterdam	02 Aug
	Sidney Bowman	USA	07	14.96	1)	Dallas	02 Jun
	Cecil Smith	USA		14.83	)		
	Toimi Tulikoura	Fin	05	14.83w	3)	Helsinki	08 Jul
1929	Mikio Oda	Jap	05	15.45	1)	Koshien	26 May
	Chuhei Nambu	Jap	04	15.24	1)	Dairen	17 Aug
	Robert Kelley	USA	97	14.97	1)	San Francisco	04 May
	Willem Peters	Hol	03	14.87	1)	Amsterdam	24 Aug
	Luis A. Brunetto	Arg	01	14.77	1)	Lima	07 May
	Kenkichi Oshima	Jap	08	14.74	1)	Osaka	19 Oct
	Vilho Tuulos	Fin	95	14.73	1)	Helsinki	07 Sep
	Sol Furth	USA	07	14.66	2)	Denver	04 Jul
	Toimi Tulikoura	Fin	05	14.66	1)	Viipuri	18 Aug
	Yo Ejiri	Jap		14.60	1)	Osaka	28 Apr
1930	Willem Peters	Hol	03	15.30	1)	Zwolle	15 Jun
	Levi Casey	USA	02	15.18	1)	Chicago	17 Aug
	Mikio Oda	Jap	05	14.90	1)	Helsinki	17 Jul
	Onni Rajasaari	Fin	10	14.88	1)	Helsinki	24 Jun
	Kenkichi Oshima	Jap	08	14.88	2)	Helsinki	17 Jul
	Eamonn Fitzgerald	Eir		14.86	1)	Killorglin	07 Sep
	Heikki Mäkinen	Fin	08	14.85	1)	Tampere	17 Aug
	Anders Hanson	Swe	09	14.80	1)	Malmö	15 Jun
	Gordon Smallacombe	Can		14.75	1)	Hamilton	16 Aug
	Sol Furth	USA	07	14.70	1)	Travers Island, NY	20 Sep
	Exhibition / Extra trial:						
	Eamonn Fitzgerald	Eir		15.54	-)	Dublin	29 Jun
1931	Mikio Oda	Jap	05	15.58	1)	Tokyo	27 Oct
	Kenkichi Oshima	Jap	08	15.44	2)	Tokyo	27 Oct
	Willem Peters	Hol	03	15.22	1)	Arnhem	09 Aug
	Eric Svensson	Swe	03	15.13	1)	Stockholm	29 Aug
	Chuhei Nambu	Jap	04	15.07	1)	Koshien	28 Jun
	Yoshitoshi Shibata	Jap		14.93	1)	Tokyo	02 Nov
	Erkki Järvinen	Fin	04	14.90	1)	Lahti	09 Aug
	Heikki Mäkinen	Fin	08	14.75	1)	Helsinki	16 Aug
	Péter Bácsalmási	Hun	08	14.74	1)	Budapest	25 May
	Shigetsuna Fukunaga	Jap		14.71	2)	Koshien	30 May
1932	Chuhei Nambu	Jap	04	15.72	1)	Los Angeles	04 Aug
	Mikio Oda	Jap	05	15.55	1)	Taipei	05 Mar
	Eric Svensson	Swe	03	15.32	2)	Los Angeles	04 Aug
	Kenkichi Oshima	Jap	08	15.21	1)	Nishinomiya	01 May
	Rolland Romero	USA	14	15.20	1)		
	Onni Rajasaari	Fin	10	15.16	1)	Helsinki	19 Jun
	Sidney Bowman	USA	07	15.12	1)	New Orleans	04 Jun
	Villem Peters	Hol	03	15.10	1)	Haarlem	05 Jun
	John Metcalfe	Aus	12	15.08	1)	Sydney	26 Dec
	Eamonn Fitzgerald	Eir		15.01	4)	Los Angeles	04 Aug

TRIPLE JUMP 1933 1938

1933	John Metcalfe	Aus	12	15.30	1)	Sydney	31 May
	Eric Svensson	Swe	03	15.18	1)	Stockholm	26 Aug
	Willem Peters	Hol	03	15.14	1)	Apeldoorn	13 Aug
	Kenkichi Oshima	Jap	08	15.13	1)	Osaka	04 Jun
	Onni Rajasaari	Fin	10	15.09	1)	Turku	06 Aug
	Masao Harada	Jap	12	15.09	1)	Tokyo	02 Nov
	Naoto Tajima	Jap	12	15.05	1)	Osaka	08 Oct
	Yukio Miyagawa	Jap		14.85	2)	Nishinomiya	27 May
	Shuhei Nishida	Jap	10	14.80	3)	Nishinomiya	27 May
	Hjalmar Holmberg	Swe	11	14.79	1)	Katrineholm	13 Aug
	Tokio Fukuda	Jap		14.79	2)	Osaka	08 Oct
	Exhibition / Extra trial:						
	John Metcalfe	Aus	12	15.36	-)	Sydney	27 May
	Ernest Baker	Aus		15.33	-)	Sydney	22 Oct
	Folco Guglielmi	Ita	10	14.82	-)	Pisa	29 Jun
1934	Kenkichi Oshima	Jap	08	15.82w	1)	Nishinomiya	16 Sep
	Masao Harada	Jap	12	15.75w	2)	Nishinomiya	16 Sep
	John Metcalfe	Aus	63	15.63	1)	London	04 Aug
	(Oshima)			15.63	1)	Seoul	01 Oct
	Kaneyuki Togami	Jap	13	15.37	1)	Hiyoshi	11 Nov
	(Harada)			15.32	2)	Nishinomiya	21 Oct
	Sidney Bowman	USA	07	15.19	)		
	Kenneth Teague	Aus		15.15w	1)	Melbourne	24 Feb
	Harold Brainsby	NZ		15.15	1)	Auckland	24 Mar
	Willem Peters	Hol	03	15.15w	1)	Malmö	23 Sep
	Yoshitoshi Kaneko	Jap		15.11	2)	Dairen	24 Sep
	Eugen Haugland	Nor	12	15.09	1)	Haugesund	30 Sep
1935	John Metcalfe	Aus	12	15.78	1)	Sydney	14 Dec
	Basil Dickinson	Aus	15	15.64	2)	Sydney	14 Dec
	Kenkichi Oshima	Jap	08	15.54	1)	Nishinomiya	09 Jun
	Rolland Romero	USA	14	15.36	1)	Lincoln	04 Jul
	Kaneyuki Togami	Jap	13	15.34	1)	Nishinomiya	06 Oct
	Yukio Miyagawa	Jap		15.30	2)	Nishinomiya	09 Jun
	Onni Rajasaari	Fin	10	15.28	1)	Helsinki	24 Aug
	Dudley Wilkins	USA	14	15.16	1)	Baton Rouge	04 May
	Naoto Tajima	Jap	12	15.16	2)	Nishinomiya	06 Oct
	Masao Harada	Jap	12	15.15	1)	Nishinomiya	26 May
1936	Naotro Tajima	Jap	12	16.00	1)	Berlin	06 Aug
	Kaneyuki Togami	Jap	13	15.67	1)	Nishinomiya	31 May
	Masao Harada	Jap	12	15.67	1)	Tallinn	10 Jul
	Yasuji Furuta	Jap	14	15.52	1)	Kasugahara	10 May
	John Metcalfe	Aus	12	15.50	3)	Berlin	06 Aug
	Rolland Romero	USA	14	15.46	1)	Houston	05 Jun
	Heinz Wöllner	Ger	13	15.27	4)	Berlin	06 Aug
	Kenkichi Oshima	Jap	08	15.24	2)	Koshien	03 May
	Edward Luckhaus	Pol	10	15.21	1)	Bialystok	14 Jun
	Eugen Haugland	Nolr	12	15.21	1)	Haugesund	15 Aug
1937	Kaneyuki Togami	Jap	13	15.86	1)	Nishinomiya	23 May
	Kaarlo Ilovaara	Fin	13	15.62w	1)	Pori	19 Sep
	Onni Rajasaari	Fin	10	15.29	1)	Viipuri	08 Aug
	Kimio Yada	Jap	13	15.27	2)	Nishinomiya	26 Sep
	Genken Kim	Jap	18	15.23	1)	Seoul	17 Oct
	(Ilovaara)			15.22	1)	Hanko	22 Jul
	John Mecalfe	Aus	12	15.16	1)	Brisbane	04 Dec
	Kazuyoshi Okada	Jap		15.14	1)	Dairen	03 Oct
	Billy Brown	USA	18	15.12	1)	Milwaukee	03 Jul
	Kalevi Luoma	Fin	17	15.12	2)	Viipuri	08 Aug
	Basil Dickinson	Aus	15	15.02	1)	Sydney	20 Nov
1938	Genken Kim	Jap	18	15.63	1)	Fengtian	21 Aug
	John Metcalfe	Aus	12	15.49	1)	Sydney	12 Feb
	Lloyd Miller	Aus	15	15.41	2)	Sydney	12 Feb

	Oscar Bringas	Per	20?	15.40	1)	Bogota	10 Aug
	Onni Rajasaari	Fin	10	15.32	1)	Colombes	04 Sep
	Basil Dickinson	Aus	15	15.28	3)	Sydney	12 Feb
	Karl Kotratschek	Aut	14	15.28	1)	Berlin	19 Jul
	Kaare Ström	Nor	15	15.28	1)	Oslo	08 Aug
	Yoshiie Miyazaki	Jap		15.23	1)	Nishinomiya	07 Aug
	Eugen Haugland	Nor	12	15.23	1)	Haugesund	13 Aug
1939	Kaare Ström	Nor	15	15.82w	1)	Göteborg	17 Sep
	Masao Harada	Jap	12	15.73	1)	Nishinomiya	30 Jul
	Lloyd Miller	Aus	15	15.70	1)	Sydney	11 Feb
	Onni Rajasaari	Fin	10	15.52	1)	Lahti	16 Jul
	(Ström)			15.49	1)	Oslo	20 Aug
	Genken Kim	Jap	18	15.43	1)	Stuttgart	30 Jul
	Wakaki Maeda	Jap	20	15.28	1)	Nishinomiya	24 Sep
	Oscar Bringas	Per	20?	15.21	1)	Lima	26 May
	Kaarlo Ilovaara	Fin	13	15.21	2)	Helsinki	28 Aug
	Néstor Tenorio	Arg	16	15.19	1)	La Plata	23 Apr
	Civico Granado	Phi		15.15	)	Manila	26 Feb
1940	Genkin Kim	Jap	18	15.68	1)	Kashihara	02 Jun
	Masahiko Omuro	Jap	18	15.56	1)	Nishinomiya	17 Oct
	Lloyd Miller	Aus	15	15.54	1)	Sydney	10 Feb
	Masao Harada	Jap	12	15.52	2)	Kashihara	02 Jun
	Billy Brown	USA	18	15.30	1)	Fresno	29 Jun
	Onni Rajasaari	Fin	10	15.22	1)	Helsinki	08 Sep
	L. T. Boosey	Ind		15.18	1)	Colombo	25 Oct
	Bertil Johnsson	Swe	15	15.11w	1)	Göteborg	29 Sep
	Åke Hallgren	Swe	18	15.10	2)	Helsinki	08 Sep
	Seiji Saito	Jap		15.03	2)	Tokyo	09 Jun

ALL TIME WORLD LIST AS AT THE END OF 1940

Naoto Tajima	Jap	12	16.00	1)	Berlin	06 Aug 36
Kaneyuki Togami	Jap	13	15.86	1)	Nishinomiya	23 May 37
Kenkichi Oshima	Jap	08	15.82w	1)	Nishinomiya	16 Sep 34
John Metcalfe	Aus	12	15.78	1)	Sydney	14 Dec 35
Masao Harada	Jap	12	15.75w	2)	Nishinomiya	16 Sep 34
Chuhei Nambu	Jap	04	15.72	1)	Los Angeles	04 Aug 32
Lloyd Miller	Aus	15	15.70	1)	Sydney	11 Feb 39
Genken Kim	Jap	18	15.68	1)	Kashihara	02 Jun 40
Basil Dickinson	Aus	15	15.64	2)	Sydney	14 Dec 35
(Oshima)			15.63	1)	Seoul	01 Oct 34
Mikio Oda	Jap	05	15.58	1)	Tokyo	27 Oct 31

1941	Genken (Kim) Kanayama	Jap	18	15.82	1)	Tokyo	25 Oct
	Masahiko Omuro	Jap	18	15.63	1)	Sakai	17 Oct
	Billy Brown	USA	18	15.53	1)	Philadelphia	29 Jun
	Tetsuzo Satomi	Jap		15.28	2)	Tokyo	05 Oct
	Carlos Eugenio Pinto	Bra		15.10	1)	Buenos Aires	01 May
	B. Bañez	Phi		15.02	1)	Manila	23 Feb
	Jouko Norén	Fin	14	15.01	1)	Hyvinkää	15 Jun
	Olev Salum	Est/SU	18	14.91	1)	Narva	22 Jun
	Néstor Tenorio	Arg	16	14.90	2)	Buenos Aires	01 May
	Wakaki Maeda	Jap	20	14.87	1)	Kobe	26 Apr
1942	Genken (Kim) Kanayama	Jap	18	15.64	1)	Sakai	12 Jul
	Chu Takahashi	Jap		15.22	2)	Sakai	12 Jul
	Masahiko Omuro	Jap	18	15.10	2)	Sakai	19 Jul
	Bertil Johnsson	Swe	15	15.00	1)	Göteborg	04 Aug
	Eric Hellstrand	Swe	23	14.97	1)	Borås	26 Jul
	Billy Brown	USA	18	14.92	1)	New York	20 Jun
	Wakaki Maeda	Jap	20	14.88	)		
	Sune Axelsson	Swe	16	14.88	2)	Göteborg	04 Aug
	Jouko Norén	Fin	14	14.80	1)	Helsinki	30 Aug
	Yoshiie Miyazaki	Jap		14.67	2)	Tokyo	31 May

Year	Athlete	Nat	Born	Mark	Pos	Venue	Date
1943	Genken (Kim) Kanayama	Jap	18	15.86	1)	Tokyo	20 Jun
	Bertil Johnsson	Swe	15	15.04	1)	Stockholm	15 Aug
	Åke Hallgren	Swe	18	14.98	1)	Linköping	17 Aug
	George Avery	Aus	26	14.79	1)	Sydney	13 Nov
	Hannes Sonck	Fin	19	14.77	1)	Helsinki	15 Aug
	Sune Axelsson	Swe	16	14.76	1)	Malmö	05 Sep
	Geraldo de Oliveira	Bra	19	14.71	1)	São Paulo	31 Oct
	Jouko Norén	Fin	14	14.71	1)		
	Eric Hellstrand	Swe	23	14.66	1)	Ulricehamn	04 Jul
	Esko Jalava	Fin	20	14.63	1)		Jul
1944	Boris Zambrimborts	SU	19	15.23	1)	Moskva	17 Aug
	Eric Hellstrand	Swe	23	15.05	1)	Alingsås	03 Sep
	Bertil Johnsson	Swe	15	14.90	2)	Alingsås	03 Sep
	Åke Hallgren	Swe	18	14.82	1)	Örebro	15 Sep
	Lennart Moberg	Swe	18	14.71	2)	Stockholm	20 Aug
	Preben Larsen	Dan	22	14.60	1)	Odense	11 Aug
	John Joe Lavin	Eir		14.60	1)	Riverstown	13 Aug
	Toivo Pöyry	Fin	11	14.48	Q)	Helsinki	24 Sep
	Don Barksdale	USA	23	14.40	1)	New York	18 Jun
	Ragnar Åberg	Swe	21	14.38	1)	Umeå	30 Jul
	Unconfirmed performance:						
	Billy Brown	USA	18	15.43	-)	Bainbridge, MD	May
1945	Valdemar Rautio	Fin	21	15.48w	1)	Turku	14 Jun
	Bertil Jonhsson	Swe	15	15.38w	1)	København	25 Aug
	(Johnsson)			15.27	1)	Göteborg	07 Oct
	Lennart Moberg	Swe	18	15.11	1)	Helsinki	21 Jun
	Preben Larsen	Den	22	15.10w	2)	København	25 Aug
	Boris Zambrimborts	SU	19	15.05	1)	Kiev	Sep
	Hannes Sonck	Fin	19	15.04	2)	Helsinki	21 Jun
	Åke Hallgren	Swe	18	14.95	1)	Stockholm	12 Aug
	(Larsen)			14.90	1)	Stockholm	12 Jul
	Arne Åhman	Swe	25	14.79	1)	Örebro	14 Jul
	Güner Frik	Tur	25	14.78	1)	Istanbul	23 Sep
	Esko Jalava	Fin	20	14.77	1)	Turku	12 Aug
1946	Valdemar Rautio	Fin	21	15.17	1)	Oslo	22 Aug
	Bertil Johnsson	Swe	15	15.15	2)	Oslo	22 Aug
	Arne Åhman	Swe	25	15.10	1)	Stockhlolm	11 Aug
	Lennart Moberg	Swe	18	15.04w	1)	Skövde	15 Sep
	Garaldo de Oliveira	Bra	19	15.00	1)	Santiago de Chile	30 Apr
	(Moberg)			14.94	2)	Stockholm	11 Aug
	Hélio Coutinho da Silva	Bra	23	14.84	2)	Santiago de Chile	30 Apr
	Hannes Sonck	Fin	19	14.81	2)	Helsinki	12 Aug
	Eric Hellstrand	Swe	23	14.72	1)	Uppsala	29 Sep
	Åke Hallgren	Swe	18	14.71	2)	Lidköping	26 Jun
	Eugen Haugland	Nor	12	14.70	4)	Oslo	22 Aug
1947	Arne Åhman	Swe	25	15.26	1)	Stockholm	17 Aug
	Lennart Moberg	Swe	18	15.17	1)	Lidköping	28 Sep
	Geraldo de Oliveira	Bra	19	15.16	1)	Rio de Janeiro	29 Apr
	Valdemar Rautio	Fin	21	15.14	2)	Stockholm	07 Sep
	Bertil Johnsson	Swe	15	15.07	1)	Göteborg	14 Sep
	Carlos Vera	Chl	28	15.03	2)	Rio de Janeiro	29 Apr
	Åke Hallgren	Swe	18	15.02	3)	Stockholm	07 Sep
	George Avery	Aus	25	14.93	1)	Sydney	Apr
	Lloyd Miller	Aus	15	14.87	1)	Sydney	27 Dec
	Keizo Hasegawa	Jap	23	14.77	1)	Kanazawa	01 Nov
	Unconfirmed performance:						
	Charles Thompson	BGU		14.93	)		
1948	Keizo Hasegawa	Jap	23	15.62	1)	Yamagata	15 Aug
	Geraldo de Oliveira	Bra	19	15.41	1)	São Paulo	19 Jun
	Arne Åhman	Swe	25	15.40	1)	London	03 Aug

Year	Athlete	Nat	Age	Mark	Place	Venue	Date
	George Avery	Aus	25	15.36	2)	London	03 Aug
	Henry Rebello	Ind		15.29	1)	Lucknow	21 Feb
	Lennart Moberg	Swe	18	15.27	1)	Södertälje	19 Jun
	Ruhi Sarialp	Tur	24	15.07	1)	Ankara	22 May
	Les McKeand	Aus	24	15.06	1)	Sydney	28 Feb
	Preben Larsen	Den	22	15.03	1)	Göteborg	20 Jun
	Adhemar Ferreira da Silva	Bra	27	15.00	2)	São Paulo	19 Jun
1949	Adhemar Ferreira da Silva	Bra	27	15.51	1)	São Paulo	04 Dec
	Leonid Shcherbakov	SU	27	15.43	1)	Tbilisi	16 Oct
	Arne Åhman	Swe	25	15.33	1)	Oslo	27 Jul
	Brian Oliver	Aus	29	15.29	1)	Perth	26 Nov
	Hélio Coutinho da Silva	Bra	23	15.26	1)	Lima	20 Apr
	Wakaki Maeda	Jap	20	15.22	1)	Tokyo	17 Apr
	Geraldo de Oliveira	Bra	19	15.20	2)	Såo Paulo	15 Mar
	Lennart Moberg	Swe	18	15.15	1)	Sollefteå	14 Aug
	Valdemar Rautio	Fin	21	15.09	1)	Pori	17 Jul
	Yoshio Iimuro	Jap	25	15.07	1)	Musashino	25 Sep
1950	Adhemar Ferriera da Silva	Bra	27	16.00	1)	São Paulo	13 Dec
	Leonid Shcherbakov	SU	27	15.70	1)	Moskva	20 Jul
	Boris Zambrimborts	SU	19	15.66	1)	Kiev	24 Aug
	Brian Oliver	Aus	29	15.60	1)	Auckland	09 Feb
	Les McKeand	Aus	24	15.35	1)	Adelaide	02 Jan
	Yoshio Iimuro	Jap	25	15.22	1)	Matsumoto	30 Jul
	Geraldo de Oliveira	Bra	19	15.18	2)	São Paulo	12 Nov
	Mankichiro Kawano	Jap		15.15	1)	Oita	04 Jun
	Lennart Moberg	Swe	18	15.11	1)	Stockholm	17 Sep
	Keizo Hasegawa	Jap	23	15.00	2)	Matsumoto	30 Jul
1951	Adhemar Ferreira da Silva	Bra	27	16.01	1)	Rio de Janeiro	30 Sep
	Helio Coutinho da Silva	Bra	23	15.99	1)	Rio de Janeiro	18 Nov
	Keizo Hasegawa	Jap	23	15.48	1)	Fukuoka	22 Apr
	Yoshio Iimuro	Jap	25	15.45	1)	Nagoya	02 Aug
	Reino Hiltunen	Fin		15.24	1)	Vaasa	17 Jun
	Leonid Shcherbakov	URSS	27	15.23	1)	Minsk	30 Aug
	Pentti Uusihauta	Fin		15.13	1)	Laihia	15 Jul
	Akira Nishimura	Jap		15.09	3)	Tokyo	16 Jul
	Jun Nakayama	Jap		15.08	)	Tokyo	29 Apr
	Kichigoro Fujihashi	Jap		15.07	)	Tokyo	03 Jun
1952	Adhemar Ferreira da Silva	Bra	27	16.22	1)	Helsinki	23 Jul
	Leonid Shcherbakov	SU	27	15.98	2)	Helsinki	23 Jul
	Rui Ramos	Por		15.54	1)	Lisboa	22 Jun
	Arnoldo Devonish	Ven	33	15.52	3)	Helsinki	23 Jul
	Yoshio Iimuro	Jap	25	15.50	1)	Morioka	12 Oct
	Walter Ashbaugh	USA	29	15.39	4)	Helsinki	23 Jul
	George Shaw	USA	31	15.38	1)	Los Angeles	28 Jun
	Noriaki Sagawa	Jap		15.36	2)	Gifu	05 Oct
	Boris Zambrimborts	SU		15.24	)	Kiev	May
	Shoji Kogake	Jap		15.16	3)	Gifu	05 Oct
	Exhibition:						
	Brian Oliver	Aus		15.17	-)	Perth	06 Dec
	With assisting wind:						
	Walter Ashbaugh	USA	29	15.46	1)	Long Beach, CA	21 Jun
	Keizo Hasegawa	Jap	22	15.43	2)	Tokyo	29 Apr
	Salvatore Mazzocca	USA		15.42	2)	Long Beach, CA	21 Jun
	James Gerhardt	USA		15.23	3)	Long Beach, CA	21 Jun
	Roger Norman	Swe		15.21	1)	Stockholm	24 Aug
1953	Leonid Shcherbakov	SU	27	16.23	1)	Moskva	19 Jul
	Adhemar Ferreira da Silva	Bra	27	15.92	1)	Dortmund	13 Aug
	Noriaki Sagawa	Jap		15.35	1)	Takamatsu	24 Oct
	Elles West	SA		15.34	1)	Salisbury	06 Apr
	Brian Oliver	Aus	29	15.29	1)	Perth	26 Jan

Year	Athlete	Nat	Born	Mark	Pl	Venue	Date
	Yoshio Iimuro	Jap	25	15.21	2)	Tokyo	03 Nov
	Kevin Salt	Aus		15.19	2)	Perth	10 Jan
	Chuji Yamamoto	Jap		15.19	2)	Suzuka	24 May
	Roger Norman	Swe		15.15	1)	Budapest	12 Sep
	Sten Eriksson	Swe		15.14	1)	Härnösand	04 Sep
1954	Adhemar Ferreira da Silva	Bra	27	16.22	1)	São Paulo	21 Apr
	Leonid Shcherbakov	SU	27	16.08	1)	Kiev	16 Sep
	Valentin Dementyev	SU	32	15.63	2)	Kiev	16 Sep
	Konstantin Samokhvalov	SU	28	15.50	1)	Odessa	Oct
	Jorgely dos Santos Figueira	Bra		15.48	2)	São Paulo	21 Feb
	Martin Rehák	Cze	33	15.48	1)	Praha	01 Oct
	Teruji Kogake	Jap	32	15.43	1)	Osaka	17 Oct
	Konstantin Tsigankov	SU		15.39	3)	Kiev	16 Sep
	Tapio Lehto	Fin		15.36	1)	Budapest	02 Oct
	Arnis Bute	SU		15.34	4)	Kiev	16 Sep
1955	Adhemar Ferreira da Silva	Bra	27	16.56	1)	Mexico City	16 Mar
	Leonid Shcherbakov	SU	27	16.35	1)	Warszawa	03 Aug
	Arnoldo Devonish	Ven	33	16.13	2)	Mexico City	16 Mar
	Yevgeniy Chen	SU	34	15.85	1)	Moskva	26 Jun
	Martin Rehák	Cze	33	15.80	2)	Bucuresti	03 Oct
	Valentin Dementyev	SU	32	15.78	2)	Tbilisi	17 Nov
	Oleg Fyedoseyev	SU	36	15.69	3)	Tbilisi	17 Nov
	Victor Hernández	Cub	29	15.60	3)	Mexico City	16 Mar
	Teruji Kogake	Jap	32	15.52	1)	Odawara	09 Oct
	Vlastimil Kalecky	Cze		15.50	1)	Bratislava	24 Sep
1956	Teruji Kogake	Jap	32	16.48	1)	Sendai	07 Oct
	Leonid Shcherbakov	SU	27	16.46	1)	Moskva	04 Jul
	Adhemar Ferreira da Silva	Bra	27	16.35	1)	Melbourne	27 Nov
	Vilhjálmur Einarsson	Ice	34	16.26	2)	Melbourne	27 Nov
	Vitold Kreyer	SU	32	16.02	3)	Melbourne	27 Nov
	Yevgeniy Chen	SU	34	15.95	1)	Tashkent	22 Oct
	Oleg Ryakhovskiy	SU	33	15.93	2)	Tashkent	22 Oct
	Viktor Kobelyev	SU	36	15.92	3)	Tashkent	22 Oct
	Hiroshi Shibata	Jap	35	15.88	2)	Sendai	07 Oct
	William Sharpe	USA	32	15.88	4)	Melbourne	27 Nov
1957	Oleg Ryakhovskiy	SU	33	16.29	1)	Moskva	02 Sep
	Konstantin Tsigankov	SU	31	16.04	1)	Moskva	06 Jul
	Vitold Kreyer	SU	32	16.00	1)	Kharkov	17 Sep
	Dmitriy Yefremov	SU	37	16.00	1)	Odessa	03 Oct
	Leonid Shcherbakov	SU	27	15.98	2)	Moskva	02 Sep
	Arsentiy Tyerkel	SU	33	15.95	1)	Moskva	02 Jun
	Vilhjálmur Einarsson	Ice	34	15.95	1)	Athinai	06 Oct
	Yevgeniy Chen	SU	34	15.94	1)	Moskva	12 May
	Adhemar Ferreira da Silva	Bra	27	15.92	1)	Moskva	04 Aug
	Motomitsu Kogake °	Jap	32	15.90	1)	Tokyo	24 nov
	° = Formerly Teruji Kogake.						
1958	Oleg Ryakhovskiy	SU	33	16.59	1)	Moskva	28 Jul
	Józef Schmidt	Pol	35	16.43	1)	Stockholm	23 Aug
	Vitold Kreyer	SU	32	16.43	1)	Tbilisi	02 Nov
	Adhemar Ferreira da Silva	Bra	27	16.25	1)	Rio de Janeiro	09 Nov
	Konstantin Tsigankov	SU	31	16.19	1)	Moskva	07 Aug
	Leonid Shcherbakov	SU	27	16.12	1)	Kiev	02 Aug
	Yegeniy Chen	SU	34	16.00	1)	Sofia	25 May
	Vilhjálmur Einarsson	Ice	34	16.00	3)	Stockholm	23 Aug
	Kari Rahkamo	Fin	33	15.96	1)	Varkaus	31 Aug
	Yevgeniy Mikhailov	SU	37	15.92	1)	Karkov	27 Sep
1959	Oleg Fyedoseyev	SU	36	16.70	1)	Nalchik	03 May
	Vladimir Goryayev	SU	39	16.51	1)	Krasnodar	12 Sep
	Vitold Kreyer	SU	32	16.46	2)	Lrasnodar	12 Sep
	Ryszard Malcherczyk	Pol	34	16.44	1)	Warszawa	14 Jun
	Oleg Ryakhovskiy	SU	33	16.38	2)	Moskva	13 Aug

	Józef Schnidt	Pol	35	16.29	1)	Sosnowiec	16 May
	Lev Karpushenko	SU	38	16.20	4)	Moskva	13 Aug
	Konstantin Tsigankov	SU	31	16.17	1)	Moskva	05 Jul
	Enzo Cavalli	Ita	37	16.10	2)	Warszawa	14 Jun
	Manfred Hinze	Ger	33	16.04	1)	Leipzig	13 Aug
	With assisting wind:						
	Ryszard Malcherczyk	Pol	34	16.48	1)	Lódz	07 Jun
1960	Józef Schmidt	Pol	35	17.03	1)	Olsztyn	05 Aug
	Vilhjálmur Einarsson	Ice	34	16.70	1)	Reykjavik	07 Aug
	Vladimir Goryayev	SU	39	16.63	2)	Roma	06 Sep
	Vitold Kreyer	SU	32	16.49	2)	Kiev	19 Oct
	Ryszard Malcherczyk	Pol	34	16.44	1)	Beograd	23 Oct
	Ira Davis	USA	36	16.41	4)	Roma	06 Sep
	Kari Rahkamo	Fin	33	16.40	1)	Colombes	25 Sep
	Yevgeniy Mikhailov	SU	37	16.39	3)	Tula	26 Jun
	Tien Chao-Chung	Chi	37	16.35	1)	Beijing	14 Sep
	Aleksandr Vyereshchagin	SU	32	16.18	1)	Sverdlovsk	05 Aug
	With assisting wind:						
	John Baguley	Aus	40	16.37	1)	Perth	07 Mar

ALL TIME WORLD LIST AS AT THE END OF 1960

Józef Schmidt	Pol	35	17.03	1)	Olsztyn	05 Aug 60
Oleg Fyedoseyev	SU	36	16.70	1)	Nalchik	03 May 59
Vilhjálmur Einarsson	Ice	34	16.70	1)	Reykjavik	07 Aug 60
Vladimir Goryayev	SU	39	16.63	2)	Roma	06 Sep 60
Oleg Ryakhovskiy	SU	33	16.59	1)	Moskva	28 Jul 58
Adhemar Ferreira da Silva	Bra	27	16.56	1)	Mexico City	16 Mar 55
Vitold Kreyer	SU	32	16.49	2)	Kiev	19 Oct 60
Motomitsu Kogake	Jap	32	16.48	1)	Sendai	07 Oct 56
Leonid Shcherbakov	SU	27	16.46	1)	Moskva	04 Jul 56
Ryszard Malcherczyk	Pol	34	16.44	1)	Warszawa	14 Jun 59
With assisting wind:						
Ryszard Malcherczyk	Pol	34	16.48	1)	Lodz	07 Jun 59

1961	Vitold Kreyer	SU	32	16.71	1)	Moskva	25 Jul
	Ryszard Malcherczyk	Pol	34	16.53	1)	Szczecin	16 Jul
	Vladimir Goryayev	SU	39	16.52	2)	Tbilisi	06 Oct
	Józef Schnidt	Pol	35	16.40	1)	Siena	22 Oct
	Oleg Ryakhovskiy	SU	33	16.33	2)	Kiev	28 May
	Adil Dementyev	SU	36	16.26	3)	Tbilisi	06 Oct
	Yuriy Okunkov	SU	38	16.20	1)	Frunze	28 May
	Vilhjálmur Einarsson	Ice	34	16.17	1)	Reykjavik	12 Aug
	Aleksandr Zolotaryev	SU	40	16.15	1)	Voronezh	25 Jul
	Aleksandr Vyereshchagin	SU	31	16.13	1)	Krasnodar	25 Apr
	Yevgeniy Mikhailov	SU	37	16.13	1)	Rostov	06 May
	Oleg Fyedoseyev	SU	36	16.13	Q)	Tbilisi	06 Oct
	With assisting wind:						
	Ryszard Malcherczyk	Pol	34	16.71	1)	Palermo	08 Oct
	Enzo Cavalli	Ita	37	16.17	2)	Palermo	08 Oct
	Tomio Ota	Jap	36	16.14	1)	Tobata City	21 May
1962	Vladimir Goryayev	SU	39	16.65	1)	Kiev	17 Jun
	Józef Schmidt	Pol	35	16.55	1)	Beograd	13 Sep
	Aleksandr Zolotaryev	SU	40	16.51	1)	Makhach Kala	21 Sep
	Ryszard Malcherczyk	Pol	34	16.50	1)	Warszawa	09 Jun
	Oleg Fyedoseyev	SU	36	16.48	1)	Moskva	01 Jul
	Vitold Kreyer	SU	32	16.38	2)	Moskva	11 Aug
	John Baguley	Aus	40	16.36	+)	Perth	24 Feb
	Ian Tomlinson	Aus	36	16.27	+)	Perth	24 Feb

	Pierre William	Sen	28	16.27	1)	Paris	10 Jun
	Tomio Ota	Jap	36	16.25	1)	Wetzlar	07 Jul
	Oleg Zotov	SU	37	16.25	1)	Adler	19 Sep
	+) *Best legal mark.*						
	With assisting wind:						
	Józef Schmidt	Pol	35	16.57	1)	Warszawa	18 Aug
	John Baguley	Aus	40	16.46	1)	Perth	24 Feb
	Ian Tomlinson	Aus	36	16.29	2)	Perth	24 Feb
1963	Józef Schmidt	Pol	35	16.99	1)	Bydgoszcz	25 Aug
	Aleksandr Zolotaryev	SU	40	16.60	1)	Moskva	18 May
	Vitold Kreyer	SU	32	16.45	1)	Moskva	02 Jul
	Anatoliy Alyabyev	SU	38	16.39	1)	Kiev	12 Jul
	Hans-Joachim Ruckborn	Ger	40	16.35	1)	Bydgoszcz	21 Sep
	Oleg Fyedoseyev	SU	36	16.34	2)	Moskva	02 Jul
	Vladimir Goryayev	SU	39	16.34	1)	Moskva	13 Aug
	Ryszard Malcherczyk	Pol	34	16.30	2)	Bydgoszcz	21 Sep
	Aleksandr Lazarenko	SU	37	16.29	1)	Yalta	23 Apr
	Ian Tomlinson	Aus	36	16.23	2)	Adelaide	25 Mar
	With assisting wind:						
	Mahoney Samuels	Jam	40	16.59	1)	Fresno	11 May
	Jan Jaskolski	Pol	39	16.33	2)	Warszawa	27 Jul
	Graham Boase	Aus	42	16.31	1)	Adelaide	25 Mar
1964	Józef Schmidt	Pol	35	16.85	1)	Tokyo	16 Oct
	Chao-chung Tien	Chi	37	16.58	1)	Beijing	03 Jun
	Oleg Fyedoseyev	SU	36	16.58	2)	Tokyo	16 Oct
	Viktor Kravchenko	SU	41	16.57	3)	Tokyo	16 Oct
	Takayuki Okazaki	Jap	40	16.48	1)	Kita-Kyushu	19 Apr
	Adil Dementyev	SU	35	16.47	1)	Krasnodar	15 Oct
	Fred Alsop	GB	38	16.46	4)	Tokyo	16 Oct
	Ira Davis	USA	36	16.43	1)	Los Angeles	26 Jul
	Günther Krivec	Ger	42	16.29	1)	Berlin	23 Aug
	Serban Ciochina	Rum	39	16.28	1)	Bucuresti	19 Aug
	Extra trial:						
	Art Walker	USA	41	16.49	-)	Palo Alto	29 Aug
	With assisting wind:						
	Ian Tomlinson	Aus	36	16.29	1)	Melbourne	04 Jan
1965	Józef Schmidt	Pol	35	16.74	1)	London	30 Jul
	Henrik Kalocsai	Hun	40	16.54	1)	Warszawa	20 Jun
	Hans-Jürgen Rückborn	EG	40	16.51	1)	Stuttgart	12 Sep
	Aleksandr Zolotaryev	SU	40	16.50	1)	Kiev	01 Aug
	Chao-chung Tien	Chi	37	16.41	1)	Beijing	15 Sep
	Fred Alsop	GB	38	16.39	4)	Stuttgart	12 Sep
	Dragan Ivanov	Hun	42	16.35	2)	Budapest	29 Aug
	Michael Sauer	WG	41	16.35	3)	Budapest	29 Aug
	Art Walker	USA	41	16.34	2)	Kiev	01 Aug
	Aleksandr Lazarenko	SU	38	16.32	1)	Alma-Ata	17 Oct
	With assisting wind:						
	Fred Alsop	GB	38	16.65	1)	London	13 Aug
	Art Walker	USA	41	16.56	1)	Modesto	29 May
1966	Jan Jaskolki	Pol	39	16.76	1)	Bydgoszcz	05 Jun
	Art Walker	USA	41	16.74	1)	Los Angeles	23 Jul
	Georgi Stoikovski	Bul	41	16.67	1)	Budapest	04 Sep
	Hans-Jürgen Rückborn	EG	40	16.66	2)	Budapest	04 Sep
	Józef Schmidt	Pol	35	16.64	1)	Poznan	07 Aug
	Henrik Kalocsai	Hun	40	16.59	3)	Budapest	04 Sep
	Vladimir Kurkyevich	SU	43	16.56	1)	Leninakan	03 Oct
	Michael Sauer	WG	41	16.46	Q)	Budapest	03 Sep
	Serban Ciochina	Rum	39	16.46	2)	Mexico City	20 Oct
	Adil Dementyev	SU	35	16.44	1)	Baku	20 Jun

Year	Athlete	Nation	Born	Mark	Place	Venue	Date
1967	Aleksandr Zolotaryev	SU	40	16.92	1)	Chorzów	01 Jul
	Józef Schmidt	Pol	35	16.84	1)	Chorzów	19 Aug
	Henrik Kalocsai	Hun	40	16.73	1)	Budapest	18 Jun
	Jan Jaskólski	Pol	39	16.72	1)	Sofia	04 Jun
	Vladimir Korkyevich	SU	43	16.69	1)	Leninakan	02 Oct
	Viktor Saneyev	SU	45	16.67	1)	Kiev	17 Sep
	Michael Sauer	WG	41	16.65	1)	Stuttgart	06 Aug
	Serban Ciochina	Rum	39	16.59	2)	Sofia	04 Jun
	Hans-Jürgen Rückborn	EG	40	16.57	3)	Sofia	04 Jun
	Nikolay Dudkin	SU	47	16.56	1)	Moskva	03 Aug
	With assisting wind:						
	Hans-Jürgen Rückborn	EG	40	16.62	3)	Budapest	18 Jun
	Dragan Ivanov	Hun	42	16.60	4)	Budapest	18 Jun
	Art Walker	USA	41	16.56	1)	Walnut	29 Apr
	Phil May	Aus	45	16.56	1)	Honolulu	03 Jul
1968	Viktor Saneyev	SU	45	17.39	1)	Mexico City	17 Oct
	Nelson Prudencio	Bra	44	17.27	2)	Mexico City	17 Oct
	Giuseppe Gentile	Ita	43	17.22	3)	Mexico City	17 Oct
	Phil May	Aus	45	17.02	6)	Mexico City	17 Oct
	Pertti Pousi	Fin	46	17.00	1)	Kuortane	23 Jun
	Józef Schmidt	Pol	35	16.89	7)	Mexico City	17 Oct
	Klaus Neumann	EG	42	16.82	1)	Jena	22 Jun
	Art Walker	USA	41	16.81	1)	Los Angeles	30 Jun
	Nikolay Dudkin	SU	47	16.77	2)	Leningrad	21 Jul
	Mansour Dia	Sen	40	16.71	+)	Mexico City	17 Oct
	+) *Best legal mark.*						
	With asssting wind:						
	Art Walker	USA	41	17.12	4)	Mexico City	17 Oct
	Nikolay Dudkin	SU	47	17.09	5)	Mexico City	17 Oct
	Mansour Dia	Sen	40	16.73	8)	Mexico City	17 Oct
1969	Viktor Saneyev	SU	45	17.15	1)	Sukhumi	18 Oct
	Phil May	Aus	45	16.82	1)	Perth	01 Feb
	Nikolay Dudkin	SU	47	16.68	+)	Chorzów	13 Jul
	Zoltán Cziffra	Hun	42	16.68	1)	Budapest	29 Aug
	Henrik Kalocsai	Hun	40	16.65	2)	Budapest	29 Aug
	Jörg Drehmel	EG	45	16.64	1)	Sofia	01 Jun
	Klaus Neumann	EG	42	16.59	1)	Berlin	05 Sep
	Masato Muraki	Jap	45	16.58	1)	Musashino	03 Aug
	Georgi Stoikovski	Bul	41	16.57	1)	Sofia	31 Aug
	Mike McGrath	Aus	47	16.53	1)	Melbourne	15 Feb
	+) *Best legal mark.*						
	With assisting wind:						
	Viktor Saneyev	SU	45	17.34	1)	Athinai	17 Sep
	Phil May	Aus	45	16.86	1)	Melbourne	30 Mar
	Zoltán Cziffra	Hun	42	16.85	2)	Athinai	17 Sep
	Jörg Drehmel	EG	45	16.78	1)	Berlin	02 Aug
	Klaus Neumann	EG	42	16.78	Q)	Athinai	16 Sep
	Carol Corbu	Rum	46	16.76	Q)	Athinai	16 Sep
	Mike McGrath	Aus	47	16.69	2)	Melbourne	30 Mar
	Nikolay Dudkin	SU	47	16.69	3)	Chorzów	13 Jul
1970	Viktor Saneyev	SU	45	17.34	1)	Sukhumi	17 Oct
	Jörg Drehmel	EG	45	17.13	1)	Stockholm	30 Aug
	Nikolay Dudkin	SU	47	17.01	1)	Moskva	26 Jul
	Phil May	Aus	45	16.89	1)	Perth	28 Nov
	Carol Corbu	Rum	46	16.76	1)	Athinai	14 Jun
	Giuseppe Gentile	Ita	43	16.72	1)	Sarajevo	02 Aug
	Norm Tate	USA	42	16.70	1)	Stuttgart	16 Jul
	Józef Schmidt	Pol	35	16.65	3)	Stockholm	30 Aug
	Vladimir Kurkyevich	SU	43	16.60	1)	Leningrad	23 Jul
	Andrzej Lasocki	Pol	45	16.55	1)	Warszawa	20 Jun
	Michael Sauer	WG	41	16.55	2)	Stuttgart	16 Jul

TRIPLE JUMP 1971 1974

	With assissting wind:						
	Dave Smith	USA	47	16.56	1)	San Jose	02 May
	Zoltán Cziffra	Hun	42	16.56	1)	Budapest	24 May
1971	Pedro Pérez	Cub	52	17.40	1)	Cali	05 Aug
	Viktor Saneyev	SU	45	17.29	1)	Madrid	11 Sep
	Carol Corbu	Rum	46	17.12	1)	Torino	13 Jun
	Jörg Drehmel	EG	45	16.93	2)	Torino	13 Jun
	Nelson Prudencio	Bra	44	16.82	2)	Cali	05 Aug
	Mohinder Singh Gill	Ind	47	16.79	1)	Fresno	08 May
	Heinz-Günther Schenk	EG	42	16.79	1)	Berlin	23 Jul
	Michael Sauer	WG	41	16.64	1)	Stuttgart	11 Jul
	John Craft	USA	47	16.53	1)	Eugene	26 Jun
	Dave Smith	USA	47	16.60	2)	Eugene	26 Jun
	With assisting wind:						
	Jörg Drehmel	EG	45	17.16	1)	Helsinki	15 Aug
	Phil May	Aus	45	17.10	1)	Perth	09 Jan
	Gennadiy Byessonov	SU	44	16.86	2)	Berkeley	02 Jul
	Dave Smith	USA	47	16.82	3)	Berkeley	02 Jul
1972	Viktor Saneyev	SU	45	17.44	1)	Sukhumi	17 Oct
	Jörg Drehmel	EG	45	17.31	2)	München	04 Sep
	Carol Corbu	Rum	46	17.10	1)	Milano	17 Jun
	Dave Smith	USA	47	17.07	2)	Eugene	01 Jul
	Nelson Prudencio	Bra	44	17.05	3)	München	04 Sep
	Michal Joachimowski	Pol	50	16.95	1)	Warszawa	10 Jun
	Hein-Günter Schenk	EG	42	16.94	2)	Potsdam	15 Jun
	John Craft	USA	47	16.89i	1)	Richmond	17 Mar
	Mikhail Bariban	SU	49	16.86i	2)	Richmond	17 Mar
	Gennadiy Byessonov	SU	44	16.82	2)	Milano	17 Jun
	With assisting wind:						
	John Craft	USA	47	17.12	1)	Eugene	01 Jul
	Mansour Dia	Sen	40	16.83	6)	München	04 Sep
1973	Mikhail Bariban	SU	49	17.20	1)	Moskva	19 Aug
	Viktor Saneyev	SU	45	17.12	1)	Sukhumi	17 Oct
	Michal Joachimowski	Pol	50	17.06	1)	Warszawa	02 Jun
	Gustavo Platt	Cub	54	17.00	1)	Habana	05 May
	John Craft	USA	47	16.98	1)	Bakersfield	16 Jun
	Carol Corbu	Rum	46	16.91i	1)	Bucuresti	10 Feb
	Andrzej Sontag	Pol	52	16.84	2)	Warszawa	10 Aug
	Heinz-Günter Schenk	EG	42	16.79	1)	Dresden	21 Jun
	Jörg Drehmel	EG	45	16.76	3)	Moskva	19 Aug
	Nikolay Sinichkin	SU	48	16.76	2)	Baku	01 Oct
	With assisting wind:						
	Jörg Drehmel	EG	45	16.89	2)	Edinburgh	09 Sep
1974	Viktor Saneyev	SU	45	17.23	1)	Roma	08 Sep
	Jörg Drehmel	EG	45	17.06	1)	Potsdam	13 Jun
	Michal Joachimowski	Pol	50	17.03i	1)	Göteborg	09 Mar
	Michail Bariban	SU	49	16.88i	2)	Göteborg	09 Mar
	Pedro Pérez	Cub	52	16.83	+)	Santo Domingo	09 Mar
	Nikolay Sinichkin	SU	48	16.83	1)	Moskva	22 Jun
	Charlton Ehizuelen	Nig	53	16.82	1)	Des Moines	27 Apr
	Milan Spasojevic	Yug	50	16.77	2)	Bratislava	30 May
	Clarence Taylor	USA	52	16.76	1)	Westwood	17 Mar
	Mikhail Syegal	SU	52	16.74	2)	Moskva	26 Jul
	Stanislav Penyayev	SU	48	16.74	1)	Baku	29 Sep
	+) *Best legal mark.*						
	With assisting wind:						
	Pedro Pérez	Cub	52	17.01	1)	Santo Domingo	09 Mar
	Michal Joachimowski	Pol	50	16.89	1)	Warszawa	24 Aug
	Milan Tiff	USA	49	16.82	1)	Walnut	27 Apr
	John Craft	USA	47	16.79	1)	Lawrence	19 Apr

Year	Athlete	Nation	Born	Mark	Place	Venue	Date
1975	João Carlos de Oliveira	Bra	54	17.89	1)	Mexico City	15 Oct
	Viktor Saneyev	SU	45	17.33	1)	Moskva	30 Jul
	Tommy Haynes	USA	52	17.20	2)	Mexico City	15 Oct
	Jörg Drahmel	EG	45	16.98	1)	Dresden	22 Jun
	Caleb Abdul Rahman #	USA	49	16.98	3)	Mexico City	15 Oct
	Andrzej Sontag	Pol	52	16.96	1)	Bydgoszcz	03 Aug
	Nelson Prudencio	Bra	44	16.93	1)	Rio de Janeiro	06 Sep
	Michal Joachimowski	Pol	50	16.90i	2)	Katowice	08 Mar
	Pentti Kuukasjärvi	Fin	46	16.87	1)	Helsinki	31 Aug
	Arnold Grimes	USA	53	16.86i	1)	Detroit	14 Mar
	#) *Rahman – former name Milan Tiff.*						
	With assisting wind:						
	Michal Joachimowski	Pol	50	17.04	1)	Bydgoszcz	21 Jun
	Eugeniusz Biskupski	Pol	47	16.92	2)	Bydgoszcz	21 Jun
1976	João Carlos de Oliveira	Bra	54	17.38	1)	Rio de Janeiro	26 Aug
	Viktor Saneyev	SU	45	17.29	1)	Montreal	30 Jul
	James Butts	USA	50	17.18	2)	Montreal	30 Jul
	Tommy Haynes	USA	52	16.90i	1)	New York	27 Feb
	Jiri Vycichlc	Cze	46	16.87	1)	Praha	16 May
	Michal Joachimowski	Pol	50	16.86	11)	Bydgoszcz	27 Jun
	Andrzej Sontag	Pol	52	16.81	2)	Bydgoszcz	27 Jun
	Pedro Pérez	Cub	52	16.81	4)	Montreal	30 Jul
	Bernard Lamitié	Fra	46	16.80	1)	Lille	27 Jun
	Armando Herrera	Cub	55	16.77	1)	Habana	18 Apr
	With assisting wind:						
	James Butts	USA	50	17.29	1)	Eugene	26 Jun
	Tommy Haynes	USA	52	17.02	2)	Eugene	26 Jun
	Rayfield Dupree	USA	53	17.01	3)	Eugene	26 Jun
	Phil Robins	Bah	54	16.90	1)	Lawrence	16 Apr
	Willie Banks	USA	55	16.88	4)	Eugene	26 Jun
	Ron Livers	USA	55	16.87	5)	Eugene	26 Jun
	John Craft	USA	47	16.77	6)	Eugene	26 Jun
1977	Ron Livers	USA	55	17.19	1)	Sochi	01 Jul
	Anatoliy Piskulin	SU	52	17.04	2)	Sochi	01 Jul
	Viktor Saneyev	SU	45	16.90	3)	Sochi	01 Jul
	Juan Velazquez	Cub	52	16.90	4)	Sofia	22 Aug
	Willie Banks	USA	56	16.88	4)	Westwood	11 Jun
	Tommy Haynes	USA	52	16.84i	1)	Toronto	04 Mar
	Aleksandr Yakovlyev	SU	57	16.83	5)	Sofia	22 Aug
	James Butts	USA	50	16.82	4)	Sochi	01 Jul
	Milan Tiff	USA	49	16.81	1)	Walnut	24 Apr
	João Carlos de Oliveira	Bra	54	16.81	1)	Guadalajara	11 Aug
	With assisting wind:						
	Milan Tiff	USA	49	17.38	1)	Westwood	11 Jun
	Anatoliy Piskulin	SU	52	17.30	1)	Sofia	22 Aug
	James Butts	USA	50	17.00	2)	Westwood	11 Jun
	Willie Banks	USA	56	16.94	3)	Sofia	22 Aug
	Tommy Haynes	USA	52	16.90	1)	Norwalk	30 May
	João Carlos de Oliveira	Bra	54	16.85	1)	Nice	21 Aug
1978	João Carlos de Oliveira	Bra	54	17.44	1)	Bratislava	10 Jun
	James Butts	USA	50	17.24	1)	Helsinki	29 Jun
	Ron Livers	USA	55	17.15	1)	Eugene	03 Jun
	Anatoliy Piskulin	SU	52	17.07	1)	Vilnius	24 Jun
	Willie Banks	USA	56	17.05	2)	Westwood	07 May
	Viktor Saneyev	SU	45	17.03	1)	Tbilisi	10 Sep
	Gennadiy Valyukevich	SU	58	17.02	1)	Vilnius	20 Jul
	Aleksandr Lisichonok	SU	58	17.00	1)	Kishinyov	18 Aug
	Ian Campbell	Aus	57	16.97i	1)	Detroit	10 Mar
	Gennadiy Kovtunov	SU	56	16.94	3)	Kishinyov	18 Aug
	Miloš Srejovic	Yug	56	16.94	1)	Praha	03 Sep

	With assisting wind:						
	Keith Connor	GB	57	17.21	1)	Edmonton	12 Aug
1979	Gennadiy Valyukevich	SU	58	17.29i	1)	Minsk	12 Feb
	João Carlos de Oliveira	Bra	54	17.27	1)	San Juan	09 Jul
	Willie Banks	USA	56	17.23	1)	Mexico City	11 Sep
	Jaak Uudmäe	SU	54	17.20	2)	Mexico City	11 Sep
	Tommy Haynes	USA	52	17.12	1)	Alger	06 Jul
	Nate Cooper	USA	57	17.10	1)	Champaign	02 Jun
	Ron Livers	USA	55	17.06	1)	Tokyo	23 Sep
	Zou Zhenxian	Chi	55	17.02	1)	Tokyo	02 Jun
	Anatoliy Piskulin	SU	52	17.00i	3)	Minsk	12 Feb
	Viktor Saneyev	SU	45	17.00	1)	Tbilisi	30 May
	With assisting wind:						
	Ron Livers	USA	55	17.56	1)	Walnut	17 Jun
	Willie Banks	USA	56	17.43	2)	Walnut	17 Jun
	Milan Tiff	USA	49	17.11	1)	Walnut	21 Apr
1980	Jaak Uudmäe	SU	54	17.35	1)	Moskva	25 Jul
	Viktor Saneyev	SU	45	17.24	2)	Moskva	25 Jul
	João Carlos de Oliveira	Bra	54	17.22	3)	Moskva	25 Jul
	Keith Condor	GB	57	17.16	1)	Melbourne	17 Jan
	Willie Banks	USA	56	17.13	1)	Westwood	11 May
	Ron Livers	USA	55	17.11	1)	Hiroshima	29 Apr
	Ian Campbell	Aus	57	17.09	2)	Melbourne	17 Jan
	Mike Marlow	USA	56	17.09	2)	San Jose	12 Apr
	Yevgeniy Anikin	SU	58	17.07	1)	Moskva	05 Jul
	Vince Parrette	USA	57	17.03i	1)	Lincoln	29 Feb
	With assisting wind:						
	Willie Banks	USA	56	17.36	1)	Walnut	15 Jun
	Ken Lorraway	Aus	56	17.35	1)	Perth	13 Jan
	Ron Livers	USA	55	17.34	1)	San Jose	12 Apr
	Ian Campbell	Aus	57	17.19	2)	Perth	13 Jan
	Zhen-Xian Zou	Chi	55	17.04	3)	San Jose	12 Apr

ALL TIME WORLD LIST AS AT THE END OF 1980

João Carlos de Oliveira	Bra	54	17.89	1)	Mexico City	15 Oct 75
Viktor Saneyev	SU	45	17.44	1)	Sukhumi	17 Oct 72
Pedro Pérez	Cub	52	17.40	1)	Cali	05 Aug 71
Jaak Uudmäe	SU	54	17.35	1)	Moskva	25 Jul 80
Jörg Drehmel	EG	45	17.31	2)	München	04 Sep 72
Gennadiy Valyukevich	SU	58	17.29i	1)	Minsk	12 Feb 79
Nelson Prudencio	Bra	44	17.27	2)	Mexico City	17 Oct 68
James Butts	USA	50	17.24	1)	Helsinki	29 Jun 78
Willie Banks	USA	56	17.23	1)	Mexico City	11 Sep 79
Giuseppe Gentile	Ita	43	17.22	3)	Mexico City	17 Oct 68
With assisting wind:						
Ron Livers	USA	55	17.56	1)	Walnut	17 Jun 79
Willie Banks	USA	56	17.43	2)	Walnut	17 Jun 79
Milan Tiff	USA	49	17.38	1)	Westwood	11 Jun 77
Ken Lorraway	Aus	56	17.35	1)	Perth	13 Jan 80
Anatoliy Piskulin	SU	52	17.30	1)	Sofia	22 Aug 77
James Butts	USA	50	17.29	1)	Eugene	26 Jun 76

1981	Willie Banks	USA	56	17.56	1)	Sacramento	21 Jun
	João Carlos de Oliveira	Bra	54	17.37	1)	Roma	05 Sep
	Zhen-Xian Zou	Chi	55	17.34	2)	Roma	05 Sep
	Keith Connor	GB	57	17.31i	1)	Detroit	13 Mar
	Shamil Abbyasov	SU	57	17.30i	1)	Grenoble	21 Feb
	Aleksandr Beskrovniy	SU	60	17.21	1)	Moskva	06 Jul
	Gennadiy Valyukevich	SU	58	17.18	1)	Leningrad	10 Jul

	Mike Marlow	USA	56	17.17	2)	Sacramento	21 Jun
	Vasiliy Isayev	SU	59	17.16	1)	Tallinn	15 Jun
	Béla Bakosi	Hun	57	17.13	1)	Berlin	21 Aug
	With assisting wind:						
	Vasiliy Grishchenkov	SU	58	17.24	2)	Bratislava	06 Jun
	Béla Bakosi	Hun	57	17.21	1)	Praha	24 Jun
	Mike Marlow	USA	56	17.20	1)	Auckland	25 Jan
1982	Keith Connor	GB	57	17.57	1)	Provo	05 Jun
	Ken Lorraway	Aus	56	17.46	1)	London	07 Aug
	Gennadiy Valyukevich	SU	58	17.42	1)	Kiev	22 Aug
	Willie Banks	USA	56	17.41i	1)	San Diego	19 Feb
	Aleksandr Beskrovniy	SU	60	17.37	2)	Kiev	22 Aug
	Vasiliy Grishchenkov	SU	58	17.26	3)	Kiev	22 Aug
	Béla Bakosi	Hun	57	17.20	1)	Budapest	21 Aug
	Robert Cannon	USA	58	17.18	1)	Indianapolis	25 Jul
	Jaak Uudmäe	SU	54	17.17	1)	Tbilisi	30 Sep
	Nikolay Musiyenko	SU	59	17.16i	1)	Moskva	20 Feb
	Vyacheslav Bordukov	SU	59	17.16	1)	Kishinyov	25 Sep
	With assisting wind:						
	Keith Connor	GB	57	17.81	1)	Brisbane	09 Oct
	Ken Lorraway	Aus	56	17.54	2)	Brisbane	09 Oct
	Béla Bakosi	Hun	57	17.29	1)	Hiroshima	05 May
	Henry Ellard	USA	61	17.23	1)	Fresno	01 May
1983	Vasiliy Grishchenkov	SU	58	17.55	1)	Moskva	19 Jun
	Aleksandr Beskrovniy	SU	60	17.53	2)	Moskva	19 Jun
	Zdzislaw Hoffmann	Pol	59	17.42	1)	Helsinki	08 Aug
	Lázaro Betancourt	Cub	63	17.40	1)	Formia	30 Jul
	Ken Lorraway	Aus	56	17.35	1)	Adelaide	25 Jun
	Peter Bouschen	WG	60	17.33	1)	Bremen	25 Jun
	Vyacheslav Bordukov	SU	59	17.30	1)	Kiev	27 Aug
	Shamil Abbyasov	SU	57	17.27	1)	Tashkent	13 May
	Grigoriy Yemets	SU	57	17.27	3)	Moskva	19 Jun
	Oleg Protsenko	SU	63	17.27	1)	Kishinev	17 Aug
	With assisting wind:						
	Lázaro Betancourt	Cub	63	17.50	1)	Habana	22 May
	Keith Connor	GB	57	17.48	1)	San Jose	28 May
	Mike Conley	USA	62	17.37	1)	Bruxelles	26 Aug
	Willie Banks	USA	56	17.32	2)	Bruxelles	26 Aug
1984	Oleg Protsenko	SU	63	17.52	1)	Kiev	21 Jun
	Aleksandr Yakovlev	SU	57	17.50	1)	Sochi	10 Jun
	Mike Conley	USA	62	17.50	1)	Los Angeles	17 Jun
	Gednnadiy Valyukevich	SU	58	17.47	1)	Moskva	19 Jul
	Lázaro Betancourt	Cub	63	17.45	1)	Köln	26 Aug
	Khristo Markov	Bul	65	17.42	1)	Sofia	19 May
	Willie Banks	USA	56	17.39	1)	Koblenz	29 Aug
	Vyacheslav Bordukov	SU	59	17.37	2)	Sofia	19 May
	Jan Cado	Cze	63	17.34	1)	Bratislava	26 May
	Zdzislaw Hoffmann	Pol	59	17.34	1)	St.Denis	02 Jun
	With assisting wind:						
	Zdzislaw Hoffmann	Pol	59	17.55	1)	Warszawa	09 Jun
1985	Willie Banks	USA	56	17.97	1)	Indianapolis	16 Jun
	Charles Simpkins	USA	63	17.86	1)	Kobe	02 Sep
	Khristo Markov	Bul	65	17.77	1)	Budapest	11 Aug
	Mike Conley	USA	62	17.71	2)	Indianapolis	16 Jun
	Oleg Protsenko	SU	63	17.69	1)	Leningrad	04 Aug
	Vladimir Plekhanov	SU	58	17.60	2)	Leningrad	04 Aug
	Lázaro Betancourt	Cub	63	17.57	1)	Habana	23 Mar
	Zdzislaw Hoffmann	Pol	59	17.53	1)	Madrid	04 Jun
	Volker Mai	EG	66	17.50	1)	Erfurt	23 Jun
	Gennadiy Valyukevich	SU	58	17.48	1)	Bydgoszcz	20 Aug

	With assisting wind:						
	Mike Conley	USA	62	17.72	1)	Austin	01 Jun
1986	Khristo Markov	Bul	65	17.80	1)	Budapest	11 Aug
	Nikolay Musiyenko	SU	59	17.78	1)	Leningrad	07 Jun
	Lázaro Betancourt	Cub	63	17.78	1)	Habana	15 Jun
	Mike Conley	USA	62	17.69	1)	Moskva	09 Jul
	Oleg Protsenko	SU	63	17.59	1)	Kiev	17 Jul
	Willie Banks	USA	56	17.58	1)	El Paso	20 Apr
	Maris Bruziks	SU	62	17.54i	1)	Madrid	23 Feb
	Gennadiy Valyukevich	SU	58	17.53	1)	Erfurt	01 Jun
	Charles Simpkins	USA	63	17.50i	1)	Los Angeles	17 Jan
	Vladimir Inozemtsev	SU	64	17.43i	1)	Kiev	26 Jan
	With assisting wind:						
	Charles Simpkins	USA	63	17.91	1)	Eugene	21 Jun
	Mike Conley	USA	62	17.84	2)	Eugene	21 Jun
	Willie Banks	USA	56	17.82	1)	San Jose	31 May
	Gennadiy Valyukevich	SU	58	17.75	1)	Uzhgorod	27 Apr
1987	Khristo Markov	Bul	65	17.92	1)	Roma	31 Aug
	Mike Conley	USA	62	17.87	1)	San Jose	27 Jun
	Aleksandr Kovalenko	SU	63	17.77	1)	Bryansk	18 Jul
	Oleg Protsenko	SU	63	17.67i	1)	Osaka	15 Jan
	Aleksandr Yakovlev	SU	57	17.65	1)	Moskva	06 Jun
	Al Joyner	USA	60	17.53	Q)	San Jose	26 Jun
	Willie Banks	USA	56	17.49	+)	San Jose	27 Jun
	Jorge Reyna	Cub	63	17.48	1)	Santiago de Cuba	27 Feb
	Aleksandr Leonov	SU	62	17.45	1)	Sochi	24 May
	Oleg Sakirkin	SU	66	17.43	3)	Roma	31 Aug
	+) *Best legal mark.*						
	With assisting wind:						
	Willie Banks	USA	56	17.60	2)	San Jose	27 Jun
	Charlie Simpkins	USA	63	17.59	3)	San Jose	27 Jun
1988	Khristo Markov	Bul	65	17.77	1)	Sofia	03 Sep
	Igor Lapshin	SU	63	17.69	1)	Staiki	31 Jul
	Oleg Protsenko	SU	63	17.68	1)	Helsinki	30 Jun
	Mike Conley	USA	62	17.59	1)	Berlin	26 Aug
	Maris Bruziks	USSDR	62	17.56	1)	Riga	03 Sep
	Milan Mikulás	Cze	63	17.53	1)	Praha	17 Jul
	Oleg Sakirkin	SU	66	17.50	1)	Barcelona	13 Jul
	Aleksandr Kovalenko	SU	63	17.47	1)	Tallinn	07 Jul
	Gennadiy Valyukevich	SU	58	17.44	1)	Jena	04 Jun
	Peter Bouschen	WG	60	17.43	1)	Düsseldorf	02 Jun
	With assisting wind:						
	Willie Banks	USA	56	18.20	1)	Indianapolis	16 Jul
	Charles Simpkins	USA	63	17.93	2)	Indianapolis	16 Jul
	Robert Cannon	USA	58	17.63	3)	Indianapolis	16 Jul
	Mike Conley	USA	62	17.62	4)	Indianapolis	16 Jul
	Al Joyner	USA	60	17.58	5)	Indianapolis	16 Jul
	Kenny Harrison	USA	65	17.56	6)	Indianapolis	16 Jul
	Ray Kimble	USA	53	17.53	7)	Indianapolis	16 Jul
1989	Mike Conley	USA	62	17.65i	1)	Budapest	05 Mar
	Vladimir Inozemtsev	SU	64	17.62	1)	Gorkiy	23 Jul
	Oleg Sakirkin	SU	66	17.58	2)	Gorkiy	23 Jul
	Charles Simpkins	USA	63	17.53	1)	Columbus	13 May
	Kenny Harrison	USA	65	17.47	1)	São Paulo	21 May
	Jorge Reyna	Cub	63	17.44	1)	Bogota	13 Aug
	Igor Lapshin	SU	63	17.40	1)	Duisburg	29 Aug
	Vasiliy Sokov	SU	68	17.37	1)	Irkutsk	06 Aug
	Nikolay Musiyenko	SU	59	17.34	1)	Volgograd	10 Jun
	Edrick Floreal	Can	66	17.29	1)	Provo	03 Jun

	With azssisting wind:						
	Kenny Harrison	USA	65	17.74	1)	Hiroshima	03 May
	Vasiliy Sokov	SU	68	17.73	1)	Riga	03 Jun
	Maris Bruzhiks	SU	62	17.42	2)	Riga	03 Jun
	Dainis Berzhinsa	SU	66	17.31	3)	Riga	03 Jun
1990	Kenny Harrison	USA	65	17.93	1)	Stockholm	02 Jul
	Vladimir Inozemtsev	SU	64	17.90	1)	Bratislava	20 Jun
	Oleg Protsenko	SU	63	17.75	1)	Moskva	10 Jun
	Leonid Voloshin	SU	66	17.74	1)	Split	31 Aug
	Mike Conley	USA	62	17.56	1)	Zurich	15 Aug
	Vasiliy Sokov	SU	68	17.47	2)	Moskva	10 Jun
	Kristo Markov	Bul	65	17.43	2)	Split	31 Aug
	Oleg Sakirkin	SU	66	17.36i	1)	Chelyabinsk	04 Feb
	Igor Lapshin	SU	63	17.35i	2)	Chelyabink	04 Feb
	Vasif Asadov	SU	65	17.33	1)	Bryansk	18 Jun
	With assisting wind:						
	Chen Yanping	Chi	66	17.51	1)	Beijing	03 Oct
1991	Kerry Harrison	USA	65	17.78	1)	Tokyo	26 Aug
	Leonid Voloshin	SU	66	17.75	2)	Tokyo	26 Aug
	Ralf Jaros	Ger	65	17.66	1)	Frankfurth	30 jun
	Mike Conley	USA	62	17.62	3)	Tokyo	26 Aug
	Vladimir Inozemtsev	SU	64	17.53i	1)	Stockholm	19 Feb
	Oleg Denishchik	SU	69	17.53	2)	Kiev	12 Jul
	Vasiliy Sokov	SU	68	17.52	3)	Kiev	12 Jul
	Serge Hélan	Fra	64	17.45	1)	Dijon	27 Jul
	Jonathan Edwards	GB	66	17.43	1)	Carlisle	22 Jun
	Oleg Sakirkin	SU	66	17.43	1)	Alma-Ata	08 sep
	With assisting wind:						
	Georges Sainte-Rose	Fra	69	17.48	1)	Montgeron	23 Jun
1992	Mike Conley	USA	62	17.72	1)	Zurich	19 Aug
	Charles Simpkins	USA	63	17.60	2)	Barcelona	03 Aug
	Leonid Voloshin	Rus	66	17.53i	1)	Madrid	14 Feb
	Denis Kapustin	Rus	70	17.48	1)	Bryansk	05 Jun
	Frank Rutherford	Bah	64	17.41	2)	São Paulo	17 May
	Pierre Camara	Fra	65	17.34	Q)	Barcelona	01 Aug
	Jonathan Edwards	GB	66	17.34	1)	Habana	25 Sep
	Aleksandr Kovalenko	Bye	63	17.32	1)	Moskva	23 Jun
	Milan Mikulás	Cze	63	17.31	1)	Nitra	05 Jul
	Vasiliy Sokov	Rus	68	17.30i	1)	Mopskva	02 Feb
	With assisting wind:						
	Mike Conley	USA	62	18.17	1)	Barcelona	03 Aug
	Charles Simpkins	USA	63	17.86	1)	New Orleans	21 Jun
	Leonid Voloshin	Rus	66	17.64	1)	Sevilla	06 Jun
	Kenny Harrison	USA	65	17.58	1)	Hiroshima	29 Apr
	Joseph Taiwo	Nig	59	17.47	1)	São Paulo	17 May
	Brian Wellman	Ber	67	17.30	1)	Austin	06 Jun
1993	Mike Conley	USA	62	17.86	1)	Stuttgart	16 Aug
	Yoelvis Queseda	Cub	73	17.68	1)	Habana	23 May
	Leonid Voloshin	Rus	66	17.65	2)	Stuttgart	16 Aug
	Pierre Camara	Fra	65	17.59i	1)	Toronto	13 Mar
	Vasiliy Sokov	Rus	68	17.59	1)	Moskva	19 Jun
	Denis Kapustin	Rus	70	17.54	2)	Bad Cannstatt	04 Jul
	Jonathan Edwards	GB	66	17.44	3)	Stuttgart	16 Aug
	Maris Bruzhiks	Lat	62	17.36i	2)	Toronto	13 Mar
	Ralf Jaros	Ger	65	17.34	4)	Stuttgart	16 Aug
	Anisio Souza Silva	Bra	69	17.32	1)	Chaux-de-Fonds	08 Oct
	With assisting wind:						
	Jonathan Edwards	GB	66	17.70	1)	Edinburgh	02 Jul

TRIPLE JUMP 1994 1998

1994	Leonid Voloshin	Rus	66	17.77i	1)	Grenoble	06 Feb
	Mike Conley	USA	62	17.68	1)	Paris	03 Sep
	Denis Kapustin	Rus	70	17.62	11)	Helsinki	13 Aug
	Yoelbi Queseda	Cub	73	17.62	1)	London	10 Sep
	Serge Hélan	Fra	64	17.55	2)	Helsinki	13 Aug
	Vasiliy Sokov	Rus	68	17.43	1)	Bratislava	01 Jun
	Kenny Harrison	USA	65	17.43	1)	St. Peterburg	29 Jul
	Brian Wellman	Ber	67	17.41	1)	El Paso	16 Apr
	Jonathan Edwards	GB	66	17.39	1)	Sheffield	12 Jun
	Gennadiy Markov	Rus	66	17.38	1)	Stavropol	29 May
	With assisting wind:						
	Denis Kapustin	Rus	70	17.86	1)	Sevilla	05 Jun
	Vladimir Melikhov	Rus	69	17.49	2)	Sevilla	05 Jun
	Oleg Sakirkin	Kaz	66	17.49	1)	Dijon	12 Jun
1995	Jonathan Edwards	GB	66	18.29	1)	Göteborg	07 Aug
	James Beckford	Jam	75	17.92	1)	Odessa, TX	20 May
	Brian Wellman	Ber	67	17.72i	1)	Barcelona	12 Mar
	Yoelvis Quesada	Cub	73	17.67	1)	Mar del Plata	24 Mar
	Jerome Romain	Dom	71	17.48	Q)	Göteborg	05 Aug
	Yoel Garcia	Cub	73	17.47	1)	Bad Cannstatt	09 Jul
	Denis Kapustin	Rus	70	17.42	1)	Moskva	05 Jun
	Maris Bruziks	Lat	62	17.40	1)	Valniera	19 Aug
	Andrey Kurennoy	Rus	72	17.30	1)	Fukuoka	30 Aug
	Zeng Lizhi	Chi	73	17.30	1)	Changchun	07 Sep
	With assisting wind:						
	Jonathan Edwards	GB	66	18.43	1)	Villeneuve d'Ascq	25 Jun
	Yoelvis Quesada	Cub	73	17.97	1)	Madrid	20 Jun
	Brian Wellman	Ber	67	17.75	2)	Madrid	20 Jun
	Jerome Romain	Dom	71	17.59	3)	Göteborg	07 Aug
	Mohamed Karim Sassi	Tun	68	17.32	1)	Tunis	02 Jul
1996	Kenny Harrison	USA	65	18.09	1)	Atlanta	27 Jul
	Jonathan Edwards	GB	66	17.88	2)	Atlanta	27 Jul
	Yoelvis Quesada	Cub	73	17.75	1)	Granada	29 May
	Aliecer Urrutia	Cub	74	17.70	1)	Sevilla	06 Jun
	Mike Conley	USA	62	17.57	2)	Atlanta	15 Jun
	Brian Wellman	Ber	67	17.51	+)	Sestriere	07 Aug
	Yoel Garcia	Cub	73	17.36	2)	Granada	29 May
	Malis Bruziks	Lat	62	17.31	1)	Riga	02 Jun
	Sergey Kochkin	Rus	70	17.30	1)	Rostov	16 Jun
	Viktor Sazankov	Bye	68	17.20	1)	Minsk	31 May
	+) *Best legal mark.*						
	With assisting wind:						
	Brian Wellman	Ber	67	17.56	1)	El Paso	13 Apr
	Vladimir Kravchenko	Ukr	69	17.29	2)	Madrid	02 Jun
	Andrew Murphy	Aus	69	17.28	1)	Sydney	11 Feb
	Francis Agyepong	GB	65	17.22	1)	Florö	25 May
1997	Yoelbi Quesada	Cub	73	17.85	1)	Athinai	08 Aug
	Aliecer Urrutia	Cub	74	17.83i	1)	Sindelfingen	01 Mar
	Jonathan Edwards	GB	66	17.74	1)	München	22 Jun
	Yoel Garcia	Cub	73	17.62i	2)	Sindelfingen	01 Mar
	Charles-Michael Friedek	Ger	71	17.59	1)	Hamburg	23 Jul
	Denis Capustin	Rus	70	17.59	4)	Athinai	08 Aug
	Kenny Harrison	USA	65	17.51	1)	Oslo	04 Jul
	Andrey Kurennoy	Rus	72	17.44	1)	Tula	09 Jul
	Vasiliy Sokov	Rus	68	17.36	2)	Tula	09 Jul
	Vyacheslav Taranov	Rus	75	17.33	1)	Vladimir	22 Jun
	With assisting wind:						
	Jerome Romain	Dom	71	17.53	1)	San Juan	28 Jun
1998	Jonathan Edwards	GB	66	18.01	1)	Oslo	09 Jul

	Denis Kapustin	Rus	70	17.65	2)	Oslo	09 Jul
	Aleksandr Glavatskiy	Bye	70	17.53	2)	Zurich	12 Aug
	LaMark Carter	USA	70	17.44	1)	New Orleans	20 Jun
	Yoelvi Quesada	Cub	73	17.43i	1)	Sindelfingen	08 Mar
	Charles Friedek	Ger	71	17.42	1)	Johannesburg	12 Sep
	Armen Martirosyan	Arm	69	17.41	1)	Gyumri	05 Jun
	Ndabazinhle Mdhlongwa	Zim	73	17.34	1)	Lafayette, LA	28 Mar
	Andrey Kurennoy	Rus	72	17.27	1)	Tivoli	31 May
	Zsolt Czinglar	Hun	71	17.24	2)	Tivoli	31 May
	With assisting wind:						
	Rostislav Dimitrov	Bul	74	17.26	3)	Budapest	23 Aug
1999	Charles Friedek	Ger	71	17.59	1)	Sevilla	25 Aug
	Jonathan Edwards	GB	66	17.52	1)	Lahti	28 Jul
	Rostislav Dimitrov	Bul	74	17.49	2)	Sevilla	25 Aug
	Denis Kapustin	Rus	70	17.40	1)	Paris	20 Jun
	Yoelbi Quesada	Cub	73	17.40	1)	Palma de Mallorca	10 Jul
	Andrew Murphy	Aus	69	17.32	4)	Sevilla	25 Aug
	Jerome Romain	Fra	71	17.31	1)	Castres	08 Aug
	Jiri Kuntos	Cze	73	17.29	1)	Ostrava	26 Jun
	Paolo Camossi	Ita	74	17.29	5)	Sevilla	25 Aug
	Ketill Hanstveit	Nor	73	17.27	1)	Byrkjelo	08 Aug
	With assisting wind:						
	Jonathan Edwards	GB	66	17.71	1)	Salamanca	15 Jul
	Denis Kapustin	Rus	70	17.65	1)	Thessaloniki	23 Jun
	Vasiliy Sokov	Rus	68	17.40	2)	Thessaloniki	23 Jun
2000	Jonathan Edwards	GB	66	17.71	1)	Sydney	25 Sep
	Fabrizio Donato	Ita	76	17.60	1)	Milano	07 Jun
	Yoel Garcia	Cub	73	17.47	2)	Sydney	25 Sep
	Denis Kapustin	Rus	70	17.46	3)	Sydney	25 Sep
	Paolo Camossi	Ita	74	17.45	2)	Milano	07 Jun
	Charles Friedek	Ger	71	17.41	1)	Wesel	12 Jun
	Yoelbi Quesada	Cub	73	17.37	4)	Sydney	25 Sep
	Rostislav Dimitrov	Bul	74	17.30	1)	Stockholm	01 Aug
	Larry Achike	GB	75	17.30	Q)	Sydney	23 Sep
	Michael Calvo	Cub	77	17.26	1)	Habana	17 Jun
	With assisting wind:						
	Larry Achike	GB	75	17.31	1)	Gateshead	15 Jul

ALL TIME WORLD LIST AS AT THE END OF 2000

Jonathan Edwards	GB	66	18.29	1)	Göteborg	07 Aug 95
Kenny Harrison	USA	65	18.09	1)	Atlanta	27 Jul 96
Willie Banks	USA	56	17.97	1)	Indianapolis	16 Jun 85
Khristo Markov	Bul	65	17.92	1)	Roma	31 Aug 87
James Beckford	Jam	75	17.92	1)	Odessa, TX	20 May 95
Vladimir Inozemtsev	Ukr	64	17.90	1)	Bratislava	20 Jun 90
João Carlos de Oliveira	Bra	54	17.89	1)	Mexico City	15 Oct 75
Mike Conley	USA	62	17.87	1)	San Jose	27 Jun 87
Charles Simpkins	USA	63	17.86	1)	Kobe	02 Sep 85
Yoelbi Quesada	Cub	73	17.85	1)	Athinai	08 Aug 97
With assisting wind:						
Jonathan Edwards	GB	66	18.43	1)	Villeneuve d'Ascq	25 Jun 95
Willie Banks	USA	56	18.20	1)	Indianapolis	16 Jul 88
Mike Conley	USA	62	18.17	1)	Barcelona	23 Aug 92
Yoelbi Quesada	Cub	73	17.97	1)	Madrid	20 Jun 95
Charles Simpkins	USA	63	17.93	2)	Indianapolis	16 Jul 88
Denis Kapustin	Rus	70	17.86	1)	Sevilla	05 Jun 94

2001	Jonathan Edwards	GB	66	17.92	1)	Edmonton	06 Aug

Year	Athlete	Nat	Born	Mark	Pos	Venue	Date
	Christian Olsson	Swe	80	17.49	1)	Réthimno	01 Jul
	Igor Spasovkhodskiy	Rus	79	17.44	3)	Edmonton	06 Aug
	Yoel Garcia	Cub	73	17.40	4)	Edmonton	06 Aug
	Paolo Camossi	Ita	74	17.34	1)	Bressanone	17 Jun
	Phillips Idowu	GB	78	17.33	1)	Haniá	04 Jun
	Michael Calvo	Cub	77	17.30	1)	Habana	27 May
	Brian Wellman	Ber	67	17.24	1)	C. de Guatemala	21 Jul
	Walter Davis	USA	79	17.22	Q)	Edmonton	04 Aug
	Kenta Bell	USA	77	17.22	1)	Beijing	31 Aug
	With assisting wind:						
	Phillips Idowu	GB	78	17.38	2)	Glasgow	01 Jul
	Andrew Murphy	Aus	69	17.28	1)	Perth	04 Mar
2002	Jonathan Edwards	GB	66	17.86	1)	Manchester	28 Jul
	Christian Olsson	Swe	80	17.80i	1)	Göteborg	05 Mar
	Phillips Idowu	GB	78	17.68	2)	Manchester	28 Jul
	Kenta Bell	USA	77	17.63	1)	Walnut	21 Apr
	Walter Davis	USA	79	17.59	1)	Stanford	23 Jun
	Leevan Sands	Bah	81	17.50	1)	Odessa	18 May
	Konstadinos Zalaggitis	Gre	80	17.43	1)	Haniá	30 Jun
	Yoelbi Quesada	Cub	73	17.42	1)	Rivas	11 Jun
	Igor Spasovkhodskiy	Rus	79	17.39	+)	Lisboa	26 May
	Jadel Gregório	Bra	80	17.35i	1)	Samara	03 Feb
	+) *Best legal mark.*						
	With assisting wind:						
	Igor Spasovkhodskiy	Rus	79	17.42	1)	Lisboa	26 May
	LeJuan Simon	USA	81	17.39	2)	Odessa	18 May
	Marian Oprea	Rum	82	17.39	2)	Milano	05 Jun
2003	Christian Olsson	Swe	80	17.77	1)	Haniá	09 Jun
	Marian Oprea	Rum	82	17.63	1)	Bucuresti	07 Jun
	Jonathan Edwards	GB	66	17.61	2)	Gateshead	13 Jul
	Kenta Bell	USA	77	17.59	1)	Stanford	22 Jun
	Dmitriy Valyukevich	Bye	81	17.57	1)	Bydgoszcz	19 Jul
	Walter Davis	USA	79	17.55	2)	Stanford	22 Jun
	Tim Rusan	USA	77	17.45i	1)	Boston	01 Mar
	Leevan Sands	Bah	81	17.40	1)	London	08 Aug
	Arnie David Giralt Jr.	Cub	84	17.31	Q)	St.Denis	23 Aug
	Yoandri Betanzos	Cub	82	17.28	2)	St.Denis	25 Aug
	With assisting wind:						
	Christian Olsson	Swe	80	17.92	1)	Gateshead	13 Jul
	Jadel Gregório	Bra	80	17.37	3)	Gateshead	13 Jul
2004	Christian Olsson	Swe	80	17.83i	1)	Budapest	07 Mar
	Melvin Lister	USA	77	17.78	1)	Sacramento	17 Jul
	Jadel Gregório	Bra	80	17.72	1)	São Paulo	06 Jun
	Danil Burkenya	Rus	78	17.68	1)	Tula	31 Jul
	Walter Davis	USA	79	17.63	2)	Sacramento	17 Jul
	Kenta Bell	USA	77	17.58	3)	Sacramento	17 Jul
	Marian Oprea	Rum	82	17.55	2)	Athinai	22 Aug
	Yoandri Betanzos	Cub	82	17.53	Q)	Athinai	20 Aug
	Phillips Idowu	GB	78	17.47	1)	London	30 Jul
	Leevan Sands	Bah	81	17.41	2)	London	30 Jul
	With assisting wind:						
	Kenta Bell	USA	77	17.76	1)	El Paso	10 Apr
2005	Marian Oprea	Rum	82	17.81	1)	Lausanne	05 Jul
	Jadel Gregório	Bra	80	17.73	1)	São Paulo	19 Jun
	Nathan Douglas	GB	82	17.64	1)	Manchester	10 Jul
	Walter Davis	USA	79	17.62i	1)	Baton Rouge	18 Feb
	Alexander Martinez	Cub	77	17.51	1)	Bern	23 Jul
	Yoandri Betanzos	Cub	82	17.46	1)	Monaco	09 Sep
	Karl Taillepierre	Fra	76	17.45	1)	Angers	16 Jul

	Igor Spasovkhodskiy	Rus	79	17.40	1)	Moskva	18 Jun
	Charles-Michael Friedek	Ger	71	17.39	1)	Bad Schwalbach	10 Jun
	Phillips Idowu	GB	78	17.30i	1)	Sheffield	13 Feb
	Leevan Sands	Bah	81	17.30	+)	Helsinki	11 Aug
	+) *Best legal mark.*						
	With assisting wind:						
	Rodrigo Mendes	Bra	68	17.54	Q)	Sacramento	10 Jun
	Leevan Sands	Bah	81	17.39	4)	Helsinki	11 Aug
	Momchil Karailiev	Bul	82	17.36	2)	Lausanne	05 Jul
2006	Marian Oprea	Rum	82	17.74i	1)	Bucuresti	18 Feb
	Walter Davis	USA	79	17.73i	1)	Moskva	12 Mar
	Christian Olsson	Swe	80	17.67	1)	Göteborg	12 Aug
	Yoandri Betanzos	Cub	82	17.63	1)	Habana	04 Feb
	Jadel Gregório	Bra	80	17.56i	2)	Moskva	12 Mar
	Dimitrios Tsiámis	Gre	82	17.55	1)	Thessaloniki	18 Jun
	Phillips Idowu	GB	78	17.50	1)	Manchester	16 Jul
	Nathan Douglas	GB	82	17.42	1)	Génève	11 Jun
	Danil Burkenya	Rus	78	17.42	1)	Tula	15 Jun
	Alexis Copello	Cub	85	17.38	1)	Habana	05 May
	Julien Kapek	Fra	79	17.38	1)	Tomblaine	21 Jul
	With assisting wind:						
	Yoandri Betanzos	Cub	82	17.67	1)	Bilbao	01 Jul
	Kenta Bell	USA	77	17.58	1)	Zaragoza	03 Jun
	Yoelbi Quesada	Cub	73	17.38	1)	Habana	04 Feb
2007	Jadel Gregório	Bra	80	17.90	1)	Belém	20 May
	Nelson Évora	Por	84	17.74	1)	Osaka	27 Aug
	Aarik Wilson	USA	82	17.58	1)	London	03 Aug
	Phillips Idowu	GB	78	17.56i	1)	Birmingham	03 Mar
	Christian Olsson	Swe	80	17.56	1)	St.Denis	06 Jul
	Osniel Tosca	Cub	84	17.52	1)	Caracas	10 May
	Danil Burkenya	Rus	78	17.48	1)	Warszawa	17 Jun
	Nathan Douglas	GB	82	17.47i	2)	Birmingham	03 Mar
	Randy Lewis	Grn	80	17.43	3)	London	03 Aug
	Arnie David Giralt Jr.	Cub	84	17.39i	1)	Samara	03 Feb
	With assisting wind:						
	Leevan Sands	Bah	81	17.55	2)	London	03 Aug
	Aleksandr Petrenko	Rus	83	17.41	1)	Haniá	09 Jun
2008	Phillips Idowu	GB	78	17.75i	1)	Valencia	09 Mar
	Nelson Évora	Por	84	17.67	1)	Beijing	21 Aug
	Leevan Sands	Bah	81	17.59	3)	Beijing	21 Aug
	Arnie David Giralt Jr.	Cub	84	17.52	4)	Beijing	21 Aug
	Alexis Copello	Cub	85	17.50	1)	Habana	19 Jul
	Randy Lewis	Grn	80	17.49	1)	São Paulo	22 May
	Danil Burkenya	Rus	78	17.48	1)	Kazan	20 Jul
	Dmitriy Valyukevich #	Svk	81	17.46	1)	Zhukovskiy	15 Jun
	Aarik Wilson	USA	82	17.43	1)	Eugene	06 Jun
	Héctor Dayro Fuentes	Cub	88	17.43	2)	Habana	19 Jul
	Aleksandr Petrenko	Rus	83	17.43	2)	Kazan	20 Jul
	#) *formerly of Byelarus.*						
2009	Phillips Idowu	GB	78	17.73	1)	Berlin	18 Aug
	Nelson Évora	Por	84	17.66	1)	Belém	24 May
	Yoandri Betanzos	Cub	82	17.65	2)	Habana	25 Apr
	Alexis Copello	Cub	85	17.65	1)	Habana	30 May
	Arnie David Giralt Jr.	Cub	84	17.62	3)	Habana	25 Apr
	Fabrizio Donato	Ita	76	17.59i	1)	Torino	07 Mar
	Li Yanxi	Chi	84	17.59	1)	Jinan	26 Oct
	Teddy Tamgho	Fra	89	17.58i	1)	Paris	13 Feb
	Momchil Karailiev	Bul	82	17.41	1)	Sofia	27 Jun
	Zhu Shujing	Chi	85	17.41	2)	Jinan	26 Oct

With assisting wind:

Nelson Évora	Por	84	17.82	1)	Seixal	26 Jul
Alexis Copello	Cub	85	17.69	1)	Habana	25 Apr
Samyr Laine	Hai	84	17.45	1)	Bogotá	24 Jul
Brandon Roulhac	USA	83	17.44	1)	Eugene	25 Jun

2010

Teddy Tamgho	Fra	89	17.98	1)	New York	12 Jun
Phillips Idowu	GB	78	17.81	1)	Barcelona	29 Jul
Yoandri Betanzos	Cub	82	17.69i	2)	Doha	14 Mar
Alexis Copello	Cub	85	17.55	1)	Zhukovskiy	26 Jun
Marian Oprea	Rum	82	17.51	2)	Barcelona	29 Jul
Arnie David Giralt Jr.	Cub	84	17.49	1)	Paris	16 Jul
Christian Olsson	Swe	80	17.41	1)	London	13 Aug
Fabrizio Donato	Ita	76	17.39i	1)	Ancona	28 Feb
Randy Lewis	Gra	80	17.29	2)	Gateshead	10 Jul
Viktor Kuznyetsov	Ukr	86	17.29	4)	Barcelona	29 Jul

With assisting wind:

Christian Olsson	Swe	80	17.62	2)	New York	12 Jun

ALL TIME WORLD LIST AS AT THE END OF 2010

Jonathan Edwards	GB	66	18.29	1)	Göteborg	07 Aug 95
Kenny Harrison	USA	65	18.09	1)	Atlanta	27 Jul 96
Teddy Tamgho	Fra	89	17.98	1)	New York	12 Jun 10
Villie Banks	USA	56	17.97	1)	Indianapolis	16 Jun 85
Khristo Markov	Bul	65	17.92	1)	Roma	31 Aug 87
James Beckford	Jam	75	17.92	1)	Odessa, TX	20 May 95
Vladimir Inozemtsev	Ukr	64	17.90	1)	Bratislava	20 Jun 90
Jadel Gregório	Bra	80	17.90	1)	Belém	20 May 07
João Carlos de Oliveira	Bra	54	17.89	1)	Mexico City	15 Oct 75
Mike Conley	USA	62	17.87	1)	San Jose	27 Jun 87

With assisting wind:

Jonathan Edwards	GB	66	18.43	1)	Villeneuve d'Ascq	25 Jun 95
Willie Banks	USA	56	18.20	1)	Indianapolis	16 Jul 88
Mike Conley	USA	62	18.17	1)	Barcelona	03 Aug 92
Yoelbi Quesada	Cub	73	17.97	1)	Madrid	20 Jun 95
Charles Simpkins	USA	63	17.93	2)	Indianapolis	16 Jul 88
Christian Olsson	Swe	80	17.92	1)	Gateshead	13 Jul 03

STATISTICS WOMEN

HIGH JUMP

	Best mark as at the end of 1900:						
	Bessie De Graff	USA	77	1.23	1)	Poughkeepsie	12 May 00
	Best mark as at the end of 1920:						
	Elise Constant	Fra	05	1.42	1)	Caen	13 Nov 20
1921	Waltraude Schmidt	Ger	00	1.50	1)	Dresden	17 Jul
	Elise Constant	Fra	05	1.47	2)	Caen	26 Mar
	Else Radenberg	Ger		1.45	1T)	Langenberg	12 Jun
	Else Retthagen	Ger		1.45	1T)	Lagenberg	12 Jun
	Elfriede Lübbers	Ger		1.45	1)	Nürnberg	16 Jul
	Angelika Finn	Ger		1.44	1)	Lübeck	28 Aug
	Cécile Maugars	Fra		1.41	1)	Paris	03 Jul
	Vera Blankfeld	USSR		1.41	1)	Yekaterinburg	07 Aug
	Unconfirmed mark:						
	Hilda Hatt	GB	03	1.447	1)	London	12 Mar
1922	Sophie Eliott-Lynn	GB	96	1.473	1)	Torquay	02 Aug
	Nancy Vorhees	USA	06	1.463	1)	Simsbury, CT	20 May
	Hilda Hatt	GB	03	1.45	1T)	Paris	20 Aug
	Ivy Lowman	GB	98	1.43	1T)	Bruxelles	27 Aug
	Over a rope:						
	Mercedes LeCorgne	USA		1.46	1)	New Orleans	Jun
1923	Gertrud Döring	Ger		1.51	1)	Berlin	10 Jun
	Hiilda Hatt	GB	03	1.498	1)	London	14 Jul
	Catherine Lee	USA		1.495	1)	Chicago	03 Sep
	Elizabeth Stine	USA	05	1.485	1)	Leonia, NJ	26 May
	Ivy Lowma	GB	98	1.485	2)	London	14 Jul
	Zélie Heurarrd	Fra		1.48	1)	St. Denis	05 Aug
	Bunny Beth Scott	USA		1.473	1)	St. Louis	09 Jun
	Sophie Eliott-Lynn	GB	96	1.473	3)	London	14 Jul
	Eunice Thumley	USA		1.473	2)	Chicago	03 Sep
	Wulke	Ger		1.47	1)	Essen	17 Jun
	Exhibition:						
	Elisa Van Truyen	Bel	06	1.55	-)	Amsterdam	01 Jul
	Unconfirmed mark:						
	Viola Baldwin	USA		1.473	)	Petaluma, CA	
1924	Elisa Van Truyen	Bel	06	1.511	1)	London	04 Aug
	Grete Sommer	Ger	06	1.50	1)	Hannover	01 Jun
	Katherine Lee	USA		1.498i	1)	Chicago	19 Mar
	Marguerite Patouillet	Fra	99	1.498	2)	London	04 Aug

Year	Name	Nat	Born	Mark	Pos	Venue	Date
	Ivy Lowman	GB	98	1.485	3)	London	04 Aug
	Frieda Heister	Ger	06	1.48	1)	Hannover	19 Jul
	Katherine Maguire	USA	06	1.473	1)	St. Louis	
	Sylvia Stone	GB		1.460	1)	London	
	Doubtful conditions:						
	Phyllis Green	GB	08	1.574	1)	London	Jul
1925	Phyllis Green	GB	08	1.524	1)	London	11 Jul
	Marguerite Patouillet	Fra	99	1.50	1)	Ezy	26 Jul
	Gerda Müller	Ger	08	1.50	1)	Giessen	02 Aug
	Anna Urban	Ger	05	1.50	2)	Giessen	02 Aug
	Amy Jordan	GB	08	1.498	1)	Hull	17 Jun
	Dora Gardner	GB	12	1.498	1)	Epsom	17 Jul
	Hilda Hatt	GB	03	1.485	2)	London	11 Jul
	Marie Teichmann	USA		1.473	1)	Chicago	05 Jul
	Elizabeth Stine	USA	05	1.473	1)	Pasadena, CA	11 Jul
	Violet Krubaeck	USA		1.473	1)	Chicago	05 Sep
	Eleanor Egg	USA	09	1.473	-)hcp	New York	19 Sep
	Not measured with steel tape:						
	Innes Bramley	Can		1.498i	1)	Toronto	28 Mar
	Unconfirmed mark:						
	Elaine Paterson	USA		1.524	)	Mamaroneck, NJ	May
1926	Ethel Catherwood	Can	10	1.585	1)mix	Regina	06 Sep
	Phyllis Green	GB	08	1.552	1)	London	02 Aug
	Viola Edwards	USA	12	1.536	1)	Chicago	21 Jul
	Barbara Holliday	GB	08	1.524	1)	Romford	18 Sep
	Catherine Maguire	USA	06	1.505	1)	Philadelphia	10 Jul
	Grete Sommer	Ger	06	1.50	1)	Hannover	20 Jun
	Elizabeth Stine	USA	05	1.498	2)	Philadelphia	10 Jul
	Hilda Hatt	GB	03	1.498	3)	Romford	18 Sep
	Mildred Wiley	USA	01	1.498	1)	Melrose, MA	18 sep
	Eva von Bredow	Ger	04	1.49	1)	Braunschweig	22 Aug
	Mix = *competition with men.*						
	Jump-off:						
	Hélène Bones	Fra	03	1.50	-)	Göteborg	27 Aug
1927	Marjorie Clark	SA	09	1.587	1)	Pietermaritzburg	03 Oct
	Phyllis Green	GB	08	1.581	1)	Reading	09 Jul
	Ethel Catherwood	Can	10	1.574	1)	Toronto	03 Sep
	Catherine Maguire	USA	06	1.536	1)	Eureka, CA	03 Sep
	Helma Notte	Ger	11	1.53	1)	Berlin	14 Aug
	Elisabeth Bonetsmüller	Ger	07	1.52	°)	München	19 Jun
	Jean McKay	Can	10	1.52	1)	Toronto	20 Aug
	Marie Amthor	Ger	06	1.51	1)	Nürnberg	15 May
	Hanny Elser	Ger	05	1.50	1)	Stuttgart	02 Jul
	Lucienne Laudré	Fra	07	1.50	1)	Bruxelles	15 Aug
	Nina Yanushkovskaya	USSR		1.50	1)	Moskva	29 Aug
	Leni Junker	Ger	05	1.50	1)	Duisburg	11 Sep
	°) *Special record attempt.*						
1928	Ethel Catherwood	Can	10	1.60	1)	Halifax	02 Jul
	Caroline Gisolf	Hol	13	1.58	1)	Bruxelles	03 Jun
	Marjorie Clark	SA	09	1.562	1)	Capetown	07 Apr
	Mildred Wiley	USA	01	1.56	3)	Amsterdam	05 Aug
	Mariya Shamanova	USSR	08	1.55	1)	Moskva	15 Jul
	Helma Notte	Ger	11	1.54	1)	Leipzig	17 Jun
	Leonine Stevens	Bel	07	1.51	1)	Schaerbeek	12 Aug
	Jean Shiley	USA	11	1.536	1)	Philadelphia	16 May
	Hilda Hatt	GB	03	1.524	1)	London	23 Jun
	Eva Dawes	Can	12	1.524	2)	Halifax	02 Jul
	Exhibition:						
	Marjorie Clark	SA	09	1.600	-)	London	23 Jun

Year	Name	Nat	Born	Mark	Pos	Venue	Date
Unconfirmed mark:							
	Dora Gardner	GB	12	1.600	1)	Epsom	Jul
1929	Caroline Gisolf	Hol	13	1.608	1)	Maaastricht	18 Aug
	Jean Shiley	USA	11	1.603i	1)	Boston	30 Mar
	Ethel Catherwood	Can	10	1.562	1)	Saskatoon	15 Jul
	Eva Dawes	Can	12	1.555	1)	Toronto	27 Jul
	Marjorie Clark	SA	09	1.549	1)	Maritzburg	14 Oct
	Marjorie O'Kell	GB	08	1.536	1)	London	31 Aug
	Mildred Wiley	USA	01	1.530i	2)	Boston	30 Mar
	Connie Coulson	Can	09	1.530	1)	Montreal	01 Jul
	Rose Winter	Aus	08	1.528	1)hcp	Sydney	07 Oct
	Mollie Ellis	GB	16	1.524	1)	Ruthin	17 Jun
	Mary Milne (Dumbrill)	GB	14	1.524	1)	London	24 Jun
1930	Jean Shiley	USA	11	1.612i	1)	Boston	19 Apr
	Helma Notte	Ger	11	1.59	1)	Düsseldorf	25 Jul
	Ethel Catherwood	Can	10	1.587	1)	Winnipeg	19 Aug
	Caroline Gisolf	Hol	10	1.574	1)	London	16 Aug
	Ingeborg Braumüller	Ger	09	1.57	1)	Praha	07 Sep
	Mildred Didrikson	USA	14	1.549	1)	Dallas	21 Jun
	Eva Dawes	Can	12	1.549	1)	Cornwall	04 Aug
	Mary Milne (Dumbrill)	GB	14	1.549	2)	London	16 Aug
	Elsie Harris	GB	15	1.549	1)	London	20 Sep
	Hedwig Geiling	Ger	10	1.54	2)	Leipzig	17 Aug
1931	Jean Shiley	USA	11	1.600i	1)	Newark	14 Mar
	Helma Notte	Ger	11	1.58	1)	Krefeld	14 Jun
	Marjorie O'Kell	GB	08	1.574	1)	Leamington	03 Aug
	Connie Coulson	Can	09	1.568	1)	Cornwall	04 Aug
	Genevieve Valvoda	USA	15	1.552i	1)	Chicago	27 Mar
	Caroline Gisolf	Hol	10	1.55	1)	Amsterdam	09 Aug
	Doris Anderson	USA	12	1.549	1T)	Milwaukee	20 Jun
	Annette Rogers-Kelly	USA	13	1.549	1T)	Milwaukee	20 Jun
	Susannah Bowyer	GB	12	1.549	1)	London	Jun
	Mary Seary	GB	09	1.549	2)	Leamington	03 Aug
	Eva Dawes	Can	12	1.549	2)	Cornwall	04 Aug
1932	Jean Shiley	USA	11	1.65	1)	Los Angeles	07 Aug
	Mildred Didrikson	USA	11	1.65	2)	Los Angeles	07 Aug
	Caroline Gisolf	Hol	10	1.623	1)	Amsterdam	12 Jun
	Eva Dawes	Can	12	1.60	3)	Los Angeles	07 Aug
	Genevieve Valvoda	USA	15	1.594	1)	Chicago	21 Jul
	Helma Notte	Ger	11	1.59	2)	Amsterdam	12 Jun
	Catherine Maguire	USA	06	1.587	1)	St.Louis	18 Jun
	Ilse Niederhoff	Ger	13	1.58	1)	Bielefeld	17 Jun
	Marjorie Clark	SA	09	1.575	5)	Los Angeles	07 Aug
	Annette Rogers	USA	13	1.575	6)	Los Angeles	07 Aug
Jump-off:							
	Jean Shiley	USA	11	1.675	-)	Los Angeles	07 Aug
1933	Dora Greenwood	GB	12	1.651	1)	Southend	08 Jun
	Alice Arden	USA	14	1.606	1)	Chicago	30 Jun
	Ilse Niederhoff	Ger	13	1.60	1)	Krefeld	21 May
	Genevieve Valvoda	USA	15	1.581	2)	Chicago	30 Jun
	Helma Notte	Ger	11	1.58	2)	Krefeld	21 May
	Elizabeth Greener	GB	14	1.574	2T)	Brentwood	05 Jun
	Hilda Thorogood	GB	12	1.574	2T)	Brentwood	05 Jun
	Eva Dawes	Can	12	1.574	1)	Toronto	15 Jul
	Mary Milne-Dumbrill	GB	14	1.574	1)	London	07 Aug
	Marjorie O'Kell	GB	08	1.562	1)	Luton	29 Jul
	Marjorie Clark	SA	09	1.562	1)	Pietermaritzburg	Sep
1934	Marjorie Clark	SA	09	1.606	1)	Ladysmith	17 Dec
	Doris Carter	Aus	12	1.600	1)	Melbourne	17 Mar
	Margaret Bell	Can	17	1.597	1)	Vancouver	23 May

	Eva Dawes	Can	12	1.584	1)	London, Ont.	07 Jul
	Selma Grieme	Ger	10	1.58	1)	Nürnberg	28 Jul
	Erna Steinberg-Boeck	Ger	11	1.58	1)	Frankfurt/O.	23 Sep
	Mary Milne-Dumbrill	GB	14	1.575	1)	Schaerbeek	15 Aug
	Isabella Miller	Can	17	1.574	2)	London, Ont.	07 Jul
	Ilse Niederhoff	Ger	13	1.56	1)	Lennep	24 Jun
	Elfriede Kaun	Ger	14	1.56	2)	Nürnberg	28 Jul
	Later identified as man:						
	Dora Ratjen	Ger	18	1.56	1)	Hannover	07/08 Jul
1935	Alice Arden	USA	14	1.612	1)		
	Doris Carter	Aus	12	1.609	1)	Melbourne	06 Apr
	Mary Milne-Dumbrill	GB	14	1.606	1)	Mitcham	27 Jul
	Elfriede Kaun	Ger	14	1.60	1)	Wuppertal	21 Jul
	Dorothy Odam	GB	20	1.600	1)	London	05 Aug
	Mary Guess	USA	16	1.600	1)		
	Nellie Carrington	GB	16	1.574	1T)	Morecambe	10 Jun
	Dorothy Cosnett	GB	18	1.574	1T)	Morecambe	10 Jun
	Margaret Bell	Can	17	1.574	1)	Vancouver	01 Jul
	Sophie Scheibe	Ger	14	1.56	1)	Erfurt	07 Jul
	Ilse Niederhoff	Ger	13	1.56	2)	Wuppertal	21 Jul
	Ibolya Csák	Hun	15	1.56	1)	Budapest	28 Jul
	Later identified as man:						
	Dora Ratjen	Ger	18	1.57	1)	Bremen	23 Jun
1936	Dorothy Odam	GB	20	1.651	1)	Brentwood	01 Jun
	Doris Carter	Aus	12	1.615	1)	Melbourne	01 Feb
	Ibolya Csák	Hun	15	1.61	1)	Budapest	14 Jun
	Francina Blankers-Koen	Hol	18	1.605	1)	Amsterdam	12 Jul
	Mary Milne-Dumbrill	GB	14	1.600	2)	Brentwood	01 Jun
	Margarete Bergmann	Ger	14	1.60	1)	Stutetgart	27 Nov
	Margaret Bell	Can	17	1.600	1)	Vancouver	01 Jul
	Elfriede Kaun	Ger	14	1.60	3)	Berlin	09 Aug
	Annette Rogers	USA	13	1.587	1)	Providence, RI	04 Jul
	Theodora "Tidye" Pickett	USA	14	1.581i	1)	New Westminster	25 Feb
	Marguerite Nicolas	Fra	16	1.58	4)	Berlin	09 Aug
	Jump-off:						
	Ibolya Csák	Hun	15	1.62	-)	Berlin	09 Aug
	Later identified as a man:						
	Dora Ratjen	Ger	18	1.60	1)	Berlin	11 Jul
1937	Dorothy Odam	GB	20	1.635	1)	London	07 Aug
	Ibolya Csák	Hun	15	1.63	1)	Pancevo	20 Jun
	Elfriede Kaun	Ger	14	1.60	3)	Krefeld	04 Jul
	Dora Gardner	GB	12	1.600	2)	London	07 Aug
	Feodora Solms	Ger	20	1.60	1)	Berlin	29 Aug
	Hertha König	Ger	18	1.59	1)	Karlsruhe	12 Sep
	Maggie de Klerk	SA		1.581	1)	Port Elizabeteh	13 Nov
	Francina Blankers-Koen	Hol	18	1.58	P)	Rotterdam	12 Sep
	Margarete Bergmann	Ger/USA	14	1.574	1)	New York	26 Jun
	Margaret Bell	Can	17	1.574	1)	Vancouver	03 Aug
	Doris Carter	Aus	12	1.574	1)	Melbourne	27 Nov
	Later identified as man:						
	Dora Ratjen	Ger	18	1.65	1)	Krefeld	04 Jul
1938	Ibolya Csák	Hun	15	1.64	1)	Wien	18 Sep
	Nelly Van Balen Blanken	Hol	13	1.64	2)	Wien	18 Sep
	Feodora Solms	Ger	20	1.64	3)	Wien	18 Sep
	Dorothy Odam	GB	20	1.625	1)	London	23 Jul
	Gunda Friedrich	Ger	20	1.60	1)	Würzburg	12 Jun
	Francina Blankers-Koen	Hol	18	1.60	1)	Rotterdam	10 Jul
	Ilsebill Pfenning	Swz	16	1.60	1)	Varese	04 Sep

	Name	Nat	Born	Mark	Pos	Venue	Date
	Margaret Bell	Can	17	1.587	1)	New Westminster	02 Jul
	Dorothy Cosnett	GB	18	1.58	4)	Wien	18 Sep
	Dora Gardner	GB	12	1.58	5)	Wien	18 Sep
	Later identified as man:						
	Dora Ratjen	Ger	18	1.70	-)	Wien	18 Sep
1939	Dorothy Odam	GB	20	1.660	1)	Brentwood	29 May
	Alice Coachman	USA	23	1.635	1)	Tuskegee	May
	Feodora Solms	Ger	20	1.63	1)	Dresden	04 Jun
	Elfriede Kaun	Ger	14	1.63	3)	Berlin	29 Jul
	Esther Van Heerden	SA	24	1.612	1)	Krugersdorp	08 Apr
	Rie Yamanouchi	Jap	22	1.61	1)	Nagoya	01 Oct
	Dora Gardner	GB	12	1.60	1T)	London	17 Jul
	Francina Blankers-Koen	Hol	18	1.60	2)	Aachen	06 Aug
	Margaret Quarry	SA		1.600	1)	Johannesburg	25 Nov
	Christine Momberg	SA		1.587	1)	Bloemfontein	10 Mar
	Elizabeth Duke	GB	21	1.587	1)	London	23 Jun
	Exhibition:						
	Dorothy Cosnett	GB	18	1.600	-)	Birmingham	Aug
1940	Esther Van Heerden	SA	24	1.651	1)	Stellenbosch	30 Mar
	Ilsebill Pfenning	Swz	16	1.63	1)	Torino	09 May
	Francina Blankers-Koen	Hol	18	1.63	1)	Wiermgerwoord	21 Jul
	Rie Yamanouchi	Jap	22	1.60	1)	Tokyo	09 Jun
	Nelly Van Balen Blanken	Hol	13	1.60	1)	Utrecht	23 Jun
	Feodora Solms	Ger	20	1.60	1)	Parma	28 Jul
	Gunda Friedrich	Ger	20	1.60	1)	Berlin	11 Aug
	Galina Ganeker	USSR	17	1.57	1)	Kiev	23 Jun
	Luise Lockemann	Ger	17	1.57	1)	Jena	23 Jun
	Elfriede Kaun	Ger	14	1.57	2)	Parma	28 Jul

ALL TIME WORLD LIST AS AT THE END OF 1940

Name	Nat	Born	Mark	Pos	Venue	Date
Dorothy Odam	GB	20	1.660	1)	Brentwood	29 May 39
Esther Van Heerden	SA	24	1.651	1)	Stellenbosch	30 Mar 40
Jean Shiley	USA	11	1.65	1)	Los Angeles	07 Aug 32
Mildred Didrikson	USA	11	1.65	2)	Los Angeles	07 Aug 32
Ibolya Csák	Hun	15	1.64	1)	Wien	18 Sep 38
Nelly Van Balen Blanken	Hol	13	1.64	2)	Wien	18 Sep 38
Feodora Solms	Ger	20	1.64	3)	Wien	18 Sep 38
Elfriede Kaun	Ger	14	1.63	3)	Berlin	29 Jul 39
Ilsebill Pfenning	Swz	16	1.63	1)	Torino	09 May 40
Francina Blankers-Koen	Hol	18	1.63	1)	Wiermgerwoord	21 Jul 40
Later identified as man:						
Dora Ratjen	Ger	18	1.70	-)	Wien	18 Sep 38

	Name	Nat	Born	Mark	Pos	Venue	Date
1941	Esther Van Heerden	SA	24	1.660	1)	Stellenbosch	29 Mar
	Ilsebill Pfenning	Swz	16	1.66	1)	Lugano	27 Jul
	Feodora Solms	Ger	20	1.62	1)	Berlin	07 Sep
	Alice Coachman	USA	23	1.593	1)	Ocean City	05 Jul
	Luise Lockemann	Ger	17	1.57	1)	Jena	24 Aug
	Gwsen Beech	Can	25	1.562	1)	Vancouver	12 Jul
	Christel Schulz	Ger	21	1.56	1)	Darmstadt	27 Jul
	Lelia Spuhr	Arg		1.55	1)	Buenos Aires	03 May
	Yelena Voyt	SU		1.55	1)	Moskva	25 May
	Alida de Vries	Hol	14	1.55	1)	Amsterdam	25 May
	Nelly Van Balen-Blanken	Hol	13	1.55	1)	Rotterdam	02 Jul
	Gertrud Pagalies	Ger	20	1.55	1)	Duisburg	27 Jul
1942	Alice Coachman	USA	23	1.651	1)	Tuskegee	08 May
	Francina Blankers-Koen	Hol	18	1.63	1)	Amsterdam	31 May
	Rie Yamanouchi	Jap	22	1.62	1)	Sakai	12 Jul

Year	Athlete	Nation	Born	Mark	Place	Venue	Date
	Nelly Van Balen Blanken	Hol	13	1.60	2)	Amsterdam	31 May
	Feodora Solms	Ger	20	1.60	1)	Berlin	30 Aug
	Ingrid Leonhard	Ger	25	1.59	1)	Breslau	26 Aug
	Elfriede Schall	Ger	23	1.58	1)	Berlin	26 Jul
	Christel Schulz	Ger	21	1.58	3T)	Berlin	26 Jul
	Editha Evers	Ger	20	1.58	3T)	Berlin	26 Jul
	Noemi Simonetto	Arg	26	1.56	1)	Buenos Aires	26 Sep
1943	Francina Blankers-Koen	Hol	18	1.71	1)	Amsterdam	30 May
	Rie Yamanouchi	Jap	22	1.62	1)	Kokuru	20 Nov
	Nelly Van Balen Blanken	Hol	13	1.60	1)	Amsterdam	04 Jul
	Ingrid Leonhard	Ger	25	1.60	1)	Iserlohn	Jul
	Gunda Friedrich	Ger	20	1.60	1)	Berlin	25 Jul
	Luise Lockemann	Ger	17	1.58	1)	Weissenfels	26 Jun
	Maria Staudt	Ger	20	1.58	1)	Andernach	22 Aug
	Anne Feldges	Ger	24	1.58	1)	Köln	26 Sep
	Galina Ganeker	SU	17	1.58	1)	Yerevan	06 Oct
	Erika Eckelt	Ger	24	1.56	1)	München	18 Jul
	Springboard:						
	Helga Pinnau	Ger	25	1.60i	1)	Hamburg	28 Feb
	Ruth Hagemann-Sievert	Ger	13	1.58i	2)	Hamburg	13 Mar
1944	Francina Blankers-Koen	Hol	18	1.65	1)	Enschede	28 May
	Nelly Van Balen Blanken	Hol	13	1.60	1)	Amsterdam	29 Jul
	Noemi Simonetto	Arg	26	1.57	1)	Buenos Aires	02 Dec
	Alice Coachman	USA	23	1.565	1)	Harrisburg	08 Jul
	Vlasta Pisová	Cze/BM	23	1.55	P)	Chocen	06 Aug
	Galina Ganeker	SU	17	1.55	1)	Moskva	14 Aug
	Anne Feldges	Ger	24	1.55	1)	Andernach	27 Aug
	Ilse Barends-Heck	Chl	21	1.545	1)		12 Nov
	Helga Pinnau	Ger	25	1.54	1)	Hamburg	20 May
	Gertrud Pagalies	Ger	20	1.54	1)	Krefeld	28 May
	Viola McGhan	Can	28	1.540	1)	Edmonton	05 Aug
1945	Galina Ganeker	SU	17	1.59	1)	Tbilisi	14 Oct
	Ilse Barends-Heck	Chl	21	1.58	1)	Montevideo	21 Apr
	Dorothy Tyler-Odam	GB	20	1.562	1)	London	04 Aug
	Vlasta Pisová	Cze	23	1.56	P)	Brno	23 Sep
	Aleksandra Caudina	SU	23	1.55	1)	Moskva	15 Aug
	Noemi Simonetto	Arg	26	1.55	1)	Buenos Aires	08 Sep
	Phylis Decker	Can	29	1.524	1)	New Westminster	28 May
	Alice Coachman	USA	23	1.524	1)	Harrisburg, PA	30 Jun
	Pat Fleming	Can	28	1.524	1)	Vancouver	03 Jul
	Dora Gardner	GB	12	1.524	1)	London	18 Aug
1946	Ilse Barends-Heck	Chl	21	1.63	1)	Santiago de Chile	04 May
	Aleksandra Chudina	SU	23	1.63	P)	Dnyepropetrovsk	12 Sep
	Rie Yamanouchi	Jap	22	1.63	1)	Kitakyushu	20 Nov
	Erika Eckelt	Gern	24	1.61	1)	Fürstenfeldbruck	01 Sep
	Micheline Ostermeyer	Fra	22	1.61	1)	Colombes	29 Sep
	Noemi Simonetto	Arg	26	1.61	1)	Buenos Aires	02 Nov
	Anne-Marie Colchen	Fra	25	1.60	1)	Oslo	22 Aug
	Francina Blankers-Koen	Hol	18	1.60	1)	Colombes	06 Oct
	Alice Coachman	USA	23	1.581	1)	Tuskegeee, AL	10 May
	Anne Iversen	Dan	23	1.57	3)	Oslo	22 Aug
	Triny Bourkel	Lux	27	1.57	6)	Oslo	22 Aug
	Dora Gardner	GB	12	1.57	1)	Sandvika	26 Aug
1947	Aleksandra Chudina	SU	23	1.65	P)	Kharkov	02 Sep
	Margaret Ring	GB	21	1.625	1)	Uxbridge	15 Aug
	Anne Iversen	Den	23	1.61	1)	Oslo	12 Jun
	Francina Blankers-Koen	Hol	18	1.61	1)	Sittard	07 Aug
	Micheline Ostermeyer	Fra	22	1.61	2)	Strasbourg	10 Aug
	Ilse Barends-Heck	Chl	23	1.60	1)	Rio de Janeiro	03 May
	Galina Ganeker	SU	17	1.60	1)	Moskva	04 Aug
	Erika Eckelt	Ger	24	1.60	1)	Köln	10 Aug

Year	Name	Nat	Age	Mark	Pos	Venue	Date
	Rie Yamanouchi	Jap	22	1.60	1)	Kanazawa	01 Nov
	Ilse Steinegger	Aut	25	1.58	1)	Innsbruck	20 Jul
1948	Alice Coachman	USA	23	1.68	1)	London	07 Aug
	Dorothy Odam-Tyler	GB	20	1.68	2)	London	07 Aug
	Galina Ganeker	SU	17	1.64	P)	Kharkov	11 Sep
	Aleksandra Chudina	SU	23	1.63	1)	Leningrad	28/29 May
	Dora Gardner	GB	12	1.625	1)	Worthing	15 May
	Micheline Ostermeyer	Fra	22	1.61	3)	London	07 Aug
	Carmen Phipps	Jam		1.609	1)	Kingston	24 May
	Doreen Dredge	Can	31	1.600	1)	Winnipeg	25 Jun
	Bertha Crowther	GB	21	1.600	2)	Chiswick	26 Jun
	Francina Blankers-Koen	Hol	18	1.60	1)	Roma	27 Jun
	Anne Iversen	Den	23	1.60	1)	Amsterdam	14 Aug
	Extra trial:						
	Vinton Beckett	Jam		1.625	-)	Kingston	Jun
1949	Dorothy Odam-Tyler	GB	20	1.657	1)	London	20 Aug
	Anne-Marie Colchen	Fra	25	1.638	2)	London	20 Aug
	Aleksandra Chudina	SU	23	1.63	1)	Moskva	29 May
	Galina Ganeker	SU	17	1.62	)		
	Margarete von Buchholtz	Ger	24	1.61	1)	Bremen	07 Aug
	Joan Cowan	GB	31	1.600	1)	Chiswick	11 Jun
	Sheila Alexander	GB	28	1.600	2)	London	09 Jul
	Bertha Crowther	GB	21	1.600	3)	London	09 Jul
	Lena Stumpf	Ger	24	1.60	P)	Bremen	24 Jul
	Hilde Gerschler	Ger	14	1.60	2)	Bremen	07 Aug
	Rie Yamanouchi	Jap	22	1.60	1)	Musashino	25 Sep
1950	Sheila Alexander	GB	28	1.692	1)	Aylesford	05 Aug
	Aleksandra Chudina	SU	23	1.68	1)	Kiev	18 Sep
	Dorothy Odam-Tyler	GB	20	1.651	2)	Aylesford	05 Aug
	Galina Ganeker	SU	17	1.63	3)	Bruxelles	26 Aug
	Anne Knudsen-Iversen	Den	23	1.62	1)	Helsingör	03 Sep
	Vinton Beckett	Jam		1.615	1)	Guatemala City	27 Feb
	Feodora Schenk	Aut	20	1.61	1)	Graz	11 Jun
	Bertha Crowther	GB	21	1.600	2)	Auckland	07 Feb
	Francina Blankers-Koen	Hol	18	1.60	1)	Brescia	29 Jun
	Lidiya Tsitko	SU	28	1.60	P)	Kiev	30 Jul
	Jean Cowan	GB	31	1.600	3)	London	10 Sep
	Olga Gyarmati	Hun	24	1.60	1)	Budapest	15 Oct
1951	Sheila Alexander-Lerwill	GB	28	1.717	1)	London	07 Jul
	Aleksandra Chudina	SU	23	1.66	P)	Minsk	30 Aug
	Esther Van Heerden-Brand	SA	24	1.635	1)	Pretoria	26 Mar
	Feodora Solms-Schenk	Aut	20	1.63	1)	Wien	31 Jul
	Dorothy Odam-Tyler	GB	20	1.625	1)	Chiswick	05 May
	Maria Pisaryeva	SU	34	1.62	1)	Bucuresti	30 Sep
	Galina Ganeker	SU	17	1.61	2)	Minsk	27 Aug
	Francina Blankers-Koen	Hol	18	1.605	1)	Amsterdam	15 Sep
	Lidia Chaurskaya	SU	28	1.60	)	Rostov / Don	28 May
	Olga Modrachova	Cze	30	1.60	1)	Brno	16 Jun
	Arleen Weeks	Can		1.600	1)	Toronto	07 Jul
	Ursula Hynes	GB	33	1.600	1)	Birmingham	09 Aug
	Lidiya Tsitko	SU	28	1.60	)		
1952	Esther Van Heerden-Brand	SA	24	1.67	1)	Helsinki	27 Jul
	Aleksandra Chudina	SU	23	1.66	1)	Kiev	Jun
	Sheila Alexander-Lerwill	GB	28	1.651	1)	Chiswick	10 May
	Dorothy Odam-Tyler	GB	20	1.651	1)	London	14 Jun
	Lyudmila Mochilina	SU	35	1.63	1)	Minsk	27 Jul
	Galina Ganeker	SU	17	1.63	)		
	Thelma Hopkins	GB	36	1.63	2)	Napoli	05 Oct
	Natalya Kossova	SU	35	1.62	1)	Kiev	26 May
	Ursula Schmückle	WG	33	1.61	1)	Ulm	01 Jun
	Feodora Solms-Schenk	Aut	20	1.61	1)	Graz	08 Jun

Year	Athlete	Nat	Born	Mark	Pos	Venue	Date
	Hilde Gerschler	WG	14	1.61	1)	Karlsruhe	15 Jun
1953	Aleksandra Chudina	SU	23	1.69	1)	Moskva	24 Aug
	Sheila Alexander-Lerwill	GB	28	1.689	1)	London	23 Sep
	Lyudmila Mochilina	SU	35	1.67	1)	Kharkov	23 Sep
	Thelma Hopkins	GB	36	1.651	2)	London	04 Jul
	Dorothy Odam-Tyler	GB	20	1.651	1)	London	19 Sep
	Olga Modrachova	Cze	30	1.65	1)	Praha	17 Jun
	Natalya Kossova	SU	35	1.64	)		
	Deyse Jurdelina De Castro	Bra	33	1.64	1)	São Paulo	17 Oct
	Gunhild Larking	Swe	36	1.61	1)	Stockholm	19 Sep
1954	Aleksandra Chudina	SU	23	1.73	1)	Kiev	22 May
	Thelma Hopkins	GB	36	1.676	1)	Vancouver	03 Aug
	Olga Modrachovā	Cze	30	1.67	P)	Stara Boleslav	03 Jun
	Nina Kossova	SU	35	1.66	2)	Praha	23 Oct
	Sheila Alexander-Lerwill	GB	28	1.651	1)	Southampton	26 Jun
	Hermina Geyser	SA	38	1.651	1)	Paarl	27 Dec
	Iolanda Balas	Rum	36	1.65	1)	Bucuresti	07 Jul
	Gunhild Larking	Swe	36	1.64	1)	Stockholm	25 Sep
	Lyudmila Mochilina	SU	35	1.63	2)	Kiev	15 Sep
	Dorothy Odam-Tyler	GB	20	1.63	2)	Ostrava	07 Oct
	Exhibition:						
	Iolanda Balas	Rum	36	1.66	-)	Bucuresti	27 Sep
1955	Thelma Hopkins	GB	36	1.71	1)	Praha	14 Sep
	Iolanda Balas	Rum	36	1.70	1)	Oslo	25 Jul
	Mildred McDaniel	USA	33	1.69	1)	Ponca City, OK	19 Jun
	Olga Modrachová	Cze	30	1.69	2)	Praha	14 Sep
	Maria Pisaryeva-Grigalka	SU	34	1.67	)		
	Aleksandra Chudina	SU	23	1.66	1)	Moskva	Jul
	Dorothy Odam-Tyler	GB	20	1.66	3)	Praha	14 Sep
	Herfmina Geyser	SA	38	1.657	1)	Pretoria	10 Dec
	Nina Kossova	SU	35	1.65	)	Moskva	Aug
	Sofia Garms	SU		1.64	)		
1956	Mildred McDaniel	USA	33	1.76	1)	Melbourne	01 Dec
	Iolanda Balas	Rum	36	1.75	1)	Bucuresti	14 Jul
	Thelma Hopkins	GB	36	1.739	1)	Belfast	05 May
	Micheline Mason	Aus	39	1.727	1)	Melbourne	17 Nov
	Valentina Ballod	SU	37	1.70	1)	Bucuresti	17 Sep
	Maria Pisaryeva-Grigalka	SU	34	1.70	2)	Taashkent	30 Oct
	Jessie Mary Donaghy	NZ	39	1.676	1)	Wellington	17 Nov
	Olga Modrachová	Cze	30	1.67	1)	Napoli	24 Jun
	Aleksandra Chudina	SU	23	1.67	)	Moskva	Jul
	Gunhild Larking	Swe	36	1.67	4T)	Melbourne	01 Dec
	Extra trial:						
	Maria Pisaryeva-Grigalka	SU	34	1.74	-)	Tashkent	29 Oct
	Non-competitive trial:						
	Mildred McDaniel	USA	33	1.767	-)	Los Angeles	26 Oct
1957	Cheng Feng-jung	Chi	33	1.77	1)	Beijing	17 Nov
	Iolanda Balas	Rum	36	1.76	1)	Bucuresti	13 Oct
	Taisia Chenchik	SU	36	1.75	1)	Bucuresti	17 Sep
	Ludmila Nabatova	SU	38	1.70i	1)	Orenburg	19 Jan
	Maria Pisaryeva-Grigalka	SU	34	1.70	1)	Kharkov	15 Sep
	Ludmila Mochilina	SU	35	1.70	P)	Kharkov	17 Sep
	Jessie Mary Donaghy	NZ	39	1.683	1)	Dunedin	02 Mar
	Thelma Hopkins	Gb	36	1.68	2)	Warszawa	08 Jun
	Valentina Ballod	SU	37	1.68	2)	Moskva	02 Sep
	Hermina Geyser	SA	38	1.676	1)	Pietersburg	09 Feb
	Made from a raised take-off:						
	Dorothy Odam-Tyler	Gb	20	1.676	1)	London	15 Jun

Year	Athlete	Nat	Born	Mark	Pl	Venue	Date
1958	Iolanda Balas	Rum	36	1.83	1)	Bucuresti	18 Oct
	Taisia Chenchik	SU	36	1.765	1)	Chelyabinsk	14 Jun
	Cheng Feng-jung	Chi	33	1.75	1)		
	Micheline Mason	Aus	39	1.727	1)	Sydney	15 Sep
	Mary Donaghy	NZ	39	1.707	2)	Cardiff	22 Jul
	Maria Pisaryeva-Grigalka	SU	34	1.70	1)	Budapest	24 May
	Luiza Slobozhanina	SU	35	1.70	P)	Minsk	13 Aug
	Hermina Geyser	SA	38	1.689	1)	Pretoria	22 Mar
	Helen Frith	Aus	39	1.689	1)	Portland	07 Dec
	Inge Killian	WG	35	1.68	1)	Delmenhorst	28 Jun
	Tatyana Talisheva	SU	37	1.68	P)	Moskva	08 Aug
	Ludmila Nabatova	SU	38	1.68	2)	Krasnodar	08 Sep
	Margarita Nekunde	SU	37	1.68	2)	Tbilisi	02 Nov

Officially declared as illegal (built-up-shoe) marks:

Athlete	Nat	Born	Mark	Pl	Venue	Date
Ludmila Nabatova	SU	38	1.70i	1)	Orenburg	19 Jan
Inge Killian	WG	35	1.69	1)	Mainz	24 May

Year	Athlete	Nat	Born	Mark	Pl	Venue	Date
1959	Iolanda Balas	Rum	36	1.84	1)	Bucurersti	21 Sep
	Taisia Chenchik	SU	36	1.78	1)	Moskva	22 Aug
	Cheng Feng-Yung	Chi	37	1.75	P)	Beijing	27 Sep
	Valentina Ballod	SU	37	1.73	2)	Torino	06 Sep
	Micheline Mason	Aus	39	1.727	1)	Sydney	10 Jan
	Helen Frith	Aus	39	1.727	1)	Sydney	31 Oct
	Galina Dolya	SU	33	1.71	2)	Moskva	16 May
	Galina Akimova	SU	36	1.71	2)	Moskva	20 Aug
	Inga-Britt Gybom-Lorentzon	Swe	36	1.68	1)	Norrköping	31 Aug
	Yumei Yang	Chi	41	1.68	2)	Beijing	20 Sep
	Florence Pedtry-Amiel	Fra	42	1.68	1)	Paris	04 Oct
1960	Iolanda Balas	Rum	36	1.86	1)	Bucuresti	09 Jul
	Galina Dolya	SU	33	1.77	1)	Tula	21 May
	Cheng Feng-Yung	Chi	37	1.75	1)	Praha	19 Jun
	Taisia Chenchik	SU	36	1.75	1)	Moskva	13 Aug
	Robyn Woodhouse	Aus	43	1.74	1)	Wollongong	29 Oct
	Valentina Ballod	SU	37	1.73	2)	Moskva	17 Jul
	Micheline Mason	Aus	39	1.727	1)	Brisbane	26 Mar
	Helen Frith	Aus	39	1.727	2)	Brisbane	26 Mar
	Lidia Shmakova-Lyakhova	SU	33	1.72	P)	Tula	21 May
	Yang Yu-mei	Chi	41	1.72	1)	Canton	20 Nov

ALL TIME WORLD LIST AS AT THE END OF 1960

Athlete	Nat	Born	Mark	Pl	Venue	Date
Iolanda Balas	Rum	36	1.86	1)	Bucuresti	10 Jul 60
Taisia Chenchik	SU	36	1.78	1)	Moskva	22 Aug 59
Cheng Feng-Yung	Chi	37	1.77	1)	Beijing	17 Nov 57
Galina Dolya	SU	33	1.77	1)	Tula	21 May 60
Mildred McDaniel	USA	33	1.76	1)	Melbourne	01 Dec 56
Robyn Woodhouse	Aus	43	1.74	1)	Wollongong	29 Oct 60
Thelma Hopkins	GB	36	1.739	1)	Belfast	05 May 56
Aleksandra Chudina	SU	23	1.73	1)	Kiev	21 May 54
Valentina Ballod	SU	37	1.73	2)	Torino	06 Sep 59
Micheline Mason	Aus	39	1.727	1)	Melbourne	17 Nov 56
Helen Frith	Aus	39	1.727	1)	Sydney	31 Oct 59

Year	Athlete	Nat	Born	Mark	Pl	Venue	Date
1961	Iolanda Balas	Rum	36	1.91	1)	Sofia	16 Jul
	Micheline Mason	Aus	39	1.753	1)	Nowra	19 Mar
	Valentina Ballod	SU	37	1.74	1)	Tbilisi	04 Oct
	Taisia Chenchik	SU	36	1.74	P)	Tbilisi	08 Oct
	Galina Dolya	SU	33	1.73	2)	Moskva	01 Jul
	Robyn Woodhouse	Aus	43	1.727	1)	Sydney	28 Jan
	Mary Donaghy	NZ	40	1.71	1)	Hamilton	12 Mar
	Ingrid Becker	WG	42	1.71	P)	Hamm	17 Jun
	Thelma Hopkins	GB	36	1.71	1)	Paris	23 Sep
	Galina Ploashenko-Yevsyukova	SU	39	1.71	2)	Tbilisi	04 Oct

Year	Name	Nat	Born	Mark	Pos	Venue	Date
1962	Iolanda Balas	Rum	36	1.87	1)	Praha	22 Jun
	Robyn Woodhouse	Aus	43	1.778	1)	Perth	26 Nov
	Olga Pulic-Gere	Yug	42	1.76	2)	Beograd	14 Sep
	Galina Dolya	SU	33	1.76	1)	Baku	21 Sep
	Taisia Chenchik	SU	36	1.76	1)	Tashkent	15 Oct
	Helen Frith	Aus	39	1.753	1)	Auckland	17 Feb
	Micheline Mason-Brown	Aus	39	1.753	1)	Melbourne	14 Oct
	Frances Mary Slaap	Gb	41	1.753i	1)	Stanmore	03 Nov
	Galina Kostyenko	SU	38	1.74	1)	Moskva	13 May
	Linda Knowles	GB	46	1.73	3)	Beograd	14 Sep
	Carolyn Wright	Aus	46	1.727	1)	Adelaide	29 Jan
1963	Iolanda Balas	Rum	36	1.88	1)	Oradea	22 Jun
	Cheng Feng-Yung	Chi	37	1.78	1)	Nanking	26 Jun
	Micheline Mason-Brown	Aus	39	1.75	1)	Sydney	16 Mar
	Robyn Woodhouse	Aus	43	1.75i	1)	Tokyo	31 Mar
	Wu Fu-Shan	Chi	43	1.75	1)	Beijing	19 May
	Klara Pushkaryeva	SU	41	1.75	1)	Moskva	14 Sep
	Taisia Chenchik	SU	36	1.74	1)	Odessa	22 Sep
	Ilia Hans	WG	37	1.73i	1)	Stuttgart	23 Mar
	Linda Knowles	GB	46	1.73i	2)	Stuttgart	23 Mar
	Jaroslava Bieda	Pol	37	1.73	1)	Spala	14 Jul
	Eleanor Montgomery	USA	46	1.73	1)	Warszawa	26 Jul
	Extra trial:						
	Lesley Wilson	NZ	43	1.727	-)	Christchurch	23 Nov
1964	Iolanda Balas	Rum	36	1.90	1)	Bucuresti	19 Aug
	Michele Brown	Aus	39	1.835	1)	Sydney	01 Nov
	Wu Fu-Shan	Chi	43	1.79	1)	Taiyuan	09 Jun
	Taisia Chenchik	SU	36	1.78	3)	Tokyo	15 Oct
	Cheng Feng-Yung	Chi	37	1.77	1)	Lushun-Dairen	22 Aug
	Karin Rüger	EG	44	1.76	1)	Potsdam	15 Aug
	Wu Yun-Hsin	Chi		1.76	P)	Beijing	25 Sep
	Frances Slaap	GB	41	1.76	1)	Portsmouth	26 Sep
	Diane Gerace	Can	43	1.75	1)	Vancouver	09 May
	Gerda Kupferschmied	EG	42	1.75	1)	Jena	11 Jul
	Jaroslava Bieda	Pol	37	1.75	1)	Warszawa	16 Jul
	Extra trial:						
	Cheng Feng-Yung	Chi	37	1.80	-)	Beijing	25 Sep
1965	Iolanda Balas	Rum	36	1.86	1)	Bucuresti	02 Sep
	Hsuan Hsiao-Mei	Chi	43	1.81	1)	Beijing	01 Sep
	Wu Fu-Shan	Chi	43	1.80	1)	Beijing	16 May
	Cheng Feng-Yung	Chi	37	1.77	2)	Beijing	14 Sep
	Taisia Chenchik	SU	36	1.76	1)	Moskva	15 May
	Galina Kostyenko	SU	38	1.76	1)	Moskva	06 Sep
	Karin Rüger	EG	44	1.76	1)	Leipzig	22 Sep
	Robyn Woodhouse	Aus	43	1.75	1)	Sydney	06 Feb
	Chang Ching-Ying	Chi	40	1.75	2)	Tsinan	18 May
	Eleanor Montgomery	USA	46	1.74i	2)	Cleveland	19 Mar
	Tatyana Kuznyetsova	SU	44	1.73	1)	Leningrad	07 Mar
	Olga Pulic	Yug	42	1.73	1)	Beograd	23 Jul
	Linda Knowles	GB	46	1.73	1)	Berlin	05 Sep
	Jaroslava Bieda	Pol	37	1.73	1)	Krakow	02 Oct
1966	Iolanda Balas	Rum	36	1.84	1)	Cluj	07 Aug
	Maria Faithova	Cze	46	1.77	1)	Trinec	07 Aug
	Antonina Okorokova	SU	41	1.76	1)	Nizhniy Tagil	26 Aug
	Michele Brown	Aus	39	1.75	1)	Sydney	12 Mar
	Klara Pushkaryeva	SU	41	1.75	1)	Moskva	03 Jun
	Valentina Kozyr	SU	50	1.75	1)	Chernovtsi	14 Jun
	Taisia Chenchik	SU	36	1.75	1)	Odessa	03 Jul
	Robyn Woodhouse	Aus	43	1.75	2)	Los Angeles	23 Jul
	Eleanor Montgomery	USA	46	1.745i	1)	Los Angeles	12 Feb
	Lyudmila Komlyeva	SU	43	1.74	1)	Leselidze	15 May

Year	Athlete	Nat	Born	Mark	Pos	Venue	Date
1967	Antonina Okorokova	SU	41	1.82	1)	Chorzow	02 Jul
	Eleanor Montgomery	USA	46	1.78	1)	Winnipeg	05 Aug
	Taisia Chenchik	SU	36	1.76i	1)	Praha	12 Mar
	Klara Pushkaryeva	SU	41	1.76	1)	Sedvastopol	06 Apr
	Rita Schmidt	EG	50	1.76	1)	Dresden	16 Jul
	Maria Faithova	Cze	46	1.76	1)	Povazská Bystrica	27 Aug
	Karin Schulze	EG	44	1.75	1)	Leipzig	30 Sep
	Valentina Kozyr	SU	50	1.74i	1)	Moskva	30 Jan
	Dagmar Melzer	EG	45	1.74i	1)	Berlin	19 Feb
	Galina Kostyenko	SU	38	1.74	2)	Leningrad	20 May
	Ilona Gusenbauer	Aut	47	1.74	1)	Praha	30 Jun
	Alena Proskova	Cze	48	1.74	1)	Plzen	26 Sep
	Extra trial:						
	Lyudmila Komlyeva	SU	43	1.75	-)	Kharfkov	28 May
1968	Rita Schmidt	EG	50	1.87	1)	Sofia	01 Jun
	Antonina Okorokova	SU	41	1.84	1)	Mexico City	04 Oct
	Karin Schulze	EG	44	1.83	2)	Sofia	01 Jun
	Miloslava Rezkova	Cze	50	1.82	1)	Jablonec	28 Jul
	Valentina Kozyr	SU	50	1.82	2)	Mexico City	04 Oct
	Jaroslava Valentova	Cze	45	1.82	3)	Mexico City	04 Oct
	Vyera Gruzhkina	SU	48	1.80	1)	Leningrad	21 Jul
	Ilona Gusenbauer	Aut	47	1.80	1)	Innsbruck	07 Sep
	Yordanka Blagoyeva	Bul	47	1.79	1)	Sofia	11 May
	Nina Brintseva	SU	50	1.78	1)	Baku	15 Mar
	Maria Faithova	Cze	46	1.78	1)	Bratislava	07 May
1969	Rita Schmidt	EG	50	1.86	1)	Leipzig	27 Jul
	Ilona Gusenbauer	Aut	47	1.84	1)	Sofia	01 Jun
	Miloslava Rezkova	Cze	50	1.84	1)	Povazská Bystrica	20 Jul
	Yordanka Blagoyeva	Bul	47	1.83	1)	Athinai	15 Jun
	Maria Mracnova	Cze	46	1.83	2)	Athinai	15 Jun
	Antonina Lazaryeva	SU	41	1.83	1)	Berlin	18 Jun
	Karin Schulze	EG	44	1.82	1)	Warszawa	29 Aug
	Valentina Kozyr	SU	50	1.81i	2)	Moskva	14 Mar
	Nina Bryntseva	SU	50	1.80	1)	Baku	15 May
	Ghislaine Barnay	Fra	45	1.80	1)	Paris	11 Jun
	Eleanor Montgomery	USA	46	1.80	1)	Dayton	06 Jul
1970	Ilona Gusenbauer	Aut	47	1.88i	1)	Wien	15 Mar
	Antonina Lazaryeva	SU	41	1.87	1)	Kiev	02 Jul
	Snezana Hrepevnik	Yug	48	1.86	1)	Torino	05 Sep
	Miloslava Hubnerová	Cze	50	1.85	1)	Ostrava	28 May
	Rita Schmidt	EG	50	1.85	1)	London	11 Jul
	Cornelia Popescu	Rum	50	1.85	1)	Bucuresti	16 Aug
	Yordanka Blagoyeva	Bul	47	1.84i	3)	Berlin	01 Mar
	Magdolna Komka	Hun	49	1.84	1)	Salgotarjan	18 Apr
	Debbie Brill	Can	53	1.835	1)	Modesto	23 May
	Karen Mack	WG	47	1.82	1)	Berlin	08 Aug
1971	Ilona Gusenbauer	Aut	47	1.92	1)	Wien	04 Sep
	Antonina Lazaryeva	SU	41	1.88	1)	Orel	20 Aug
	Cornelia Popescu	Rum	50	1.87	1)	Bucuresti	25 Jul
	Valentina Chulkova	SU	49	1.87	1)	Moskva	01 Aug
	Rita Schmidt	EG	50	1.86i	1)	Berlin	20 Feb
	Snezana Hrepevnik	Yug	48	1.855i	1)	Vancouver	20 Feb
	Debbie Brill	Ca	53	1.855i	2)	Vancouver	20 Feb
	Miloslava Hübnerová	Cze	50	1.85	1)	Bratislava	31 Jul
	Debbie Brill	Can	53	1.85	1)	Cali	02 Aug
	Barbara Inkpen	GB	49	1.85	2)	Helsinki	12 Aug
	Alena Proskova	Cze	48	1.84	1)	Trinec	06 Jul
1972	Yordanka Blagoyeva	Bul	47	1.94	1)	Zagreb	24 Sep
	Ilona Gusembauer	Aut	47	1.93	1)	Wien	07 Oct
	Ulrikke Meyfarth	WG	56	1.92	1)	München	04 Sep
	Rita Schmidt	EG	50	1.90i	1)	Grenoble	12 Mar

	Rita Gildemeister	EG	47	1.87i	1)	Berlin	23 Jan
	Miroslava Hübnerová	Cze	50	1.87	1)	Praha	19 Aug
	Debbie Brill	Can	53	1.86	1)	London	05 Aug
	Barbara Inkpen	GB	49	1.86	1)	London	15 Sep
	Galina Filatova	SU	49	1.855i	1T)	Richmond	17 Mar
	Antonina Lazaryeva	SU	41	1.855i	1T)	Richmond	17 Mar
	Beatrix Rechner	Swi	51	1.85	1)	Bucuresti	27 Feb
	Mandolna Komka	Hun	49	1.85	1)	Budapest	10 Jun
	Grith Eistrup	Den	53	1.85	1)	Köbenhavn	12 Aug
	Rosemarie Witschas	EG	52	1.85	1)	Berlin	13 Aug
	Sara Simeoni	Ita	53	1.85	6)	München	04 Sep
1973	Yordanka Blagoyeva	Bul	47	1.92i	1)	Rotterdam	11 Mar
	Rosemarie Witschas	EG	52	1.91i	1)	Berlin	28 Jan
	Ilona Gusenbauer	Aut	47	1.91	1)	Wien	04 Jul
	Rita Kirst	EG	50	1.90	1)	Sofia	26 May
	Virginia Ioan	Rum	49	1.90	1)	Athinai	26 Aug
	Milada Karbanová	Cze	48	1.88	1)	Praha	12 Aug
	Cornelia Popescu	Rum	50	1.88	1)	Sofia	06 Oct
	Rita Gildemeister	EG	47	1.87	1)	Leipzig	16 Sep
	Barbara Lawton	GB	49	1.87	1)	London	22 Sep
	Erika Rudolf	Hun	54	1.86i	1)	Moskva	04 Mar
	Marie-Christine Wartel	Fra	51	1.86	1)	Sittard	05 Aug
	Sara Simeoni	Ita	53	1.86	1)	Milano	02 Sep
1974	Rosemarie Witschas	EG	52	1.95	1)	Roma	08 Sep
	Rita Kirst	EG	50	1.92i	1)	Sofia	17 Feb
	Virginia Ioan	Rum	49	1.92	1)	Bucuresti	09 Jun
	Milada Karbanová	Cze	48	1.91	2)	Roma	08 Sep
	Sara Simeoni	Ita	53	1.90	1)	Avezzano	22 Sep
	Cornelia Popa	Rum	50	1.89i	1)	Trinec	28 Feb
	Erika Rudolf	Hun	54	1.87i	1)	Budapest	07 Feb
	Maria Mracnová	Cze		1.87	1)	Praha	29 Jun
	Miloslava Hübnerová	Cze		1.87	1)	Praha	20 Jul
	Debbie Brill	Can		1.87	1)	Richmond	10 Aug
1975	Rosemarie Ackermann	EG	52	1.94i	1)	Berlin	09 Feb
	Ulrike Meyfarth	WG	56	1.92	2)	Nice	17 Aug
	J. Huntley	USA		1.90	1)	Christchurch	26 Jan
	Debbie Brill	Can	53	1.89	1)	Oslo	03 Jul
	Sara Simeoni	Ita	53	1.89	1)	Alger	26 Aug
	Nadyezhda Oskolok	SU	55	1.89	1)	Nikolayev	06 Sep
	M. van Doorn	Hol		1.88	1)	Utrecht	17 Aug
	Alla Fedorchuk	SU	57	1.88	1)	Athinai	22 Aug
	Galina Filotova	SU	49	1.88	1)	Roma	20 Sep
	Tamara Galka	SU	44	1.87	1)	Sochi	29 May
	Rita Kirst	EG	50	1.87	2)	Oslo	25 Jun
	E. Rudolf	Hun		1.87	1)	Sofia	13 Jul
	L. Walker	Can		1.87	2)	Montreal	25 Jul
	V. Joan	Rum		1.87	1)	Bucuresti	10 Aug
	D. Jones	Can		1.87	P)	Sudbury	23 Aug
1976	Rosemarie Ackermann	EG	52	1.96	1)	Dresden	08 May
	Cornelia Popa	Rum	50	1.93	1)	Athinai	30 Jun
	Maria Mracnová	Cze		1.92	1)	Trinec	28 Aug
	Brigitte Holzapfel	WG	58	1.91	1)	Düsseldorf	08 Jun
	Sara Simeoni	Ita	53	1.91	2)	Montreal	28 Jul
	J. Blagoyeva	Bul		1.91	3)	Montreal	28 Jul
	Rita Kirst	EG	50	1.90i	2)	Berlin	25 Jan
	Debbie Brill	Can	53	1.90	1)	Walnut	24 Apr
	V. Bradácová	Cze		1.90	1)	Praha	09 May
	Galina Filatova	SU	49	1.90	1)	Kiev	22 May
	Tatyana Shlyakhto	SU	55	1.90	1)	Kiev	24 Jun
	Ulrike Meyfarth	EG	56	1.90	1)	Köln	26 Jun
1977	Rosedmarie Ackermann	EG	52	2.00	1)	Berlin	26 Aug
	Jutta Kirst	EG	54	1.94	1)	Linz	27 Aug

	Sara Simeoni	Ita	53	1.93	1)	Formia	15 May
	Brigitte Holzapfel	WG	58	1.93	1)	Stuttgart	16 Jul
	Anne-Marie Pira	Bel	55	1.92	1)	Torino	05 Jun
	Milada Karbanová	Cze	48	1.92	2)	Trinec	06 Aug
	Cornelia Popa	Rum	50	1.91i	1)	Praha	02 Mar
	Debbie Brill	Can	53	1.91	1)	Walnut	23 Apr
	Erika Rudolf	Hun	54	1.90i	1)	Budapest	24 Feb
	Kristine Nitzsche	EG	59	1.90	1)	Erfurt	10 Jul
	Andrea Reichstein	EG	59	1.90	1)	Halle	27 Aug
1978	Sara Simeoni	Ita	53	2.01	1)	Brescia	04 Aug
	Rosemarie Ackermann	EG	52	1.99	2)	Praha	31 Aug
	Brigitte Holzapfel	WG	58	1.95	1)	Köln	12 Aug
	Ulrike Meyfarth	WG	56	1.95	2)	Köln	12 Aug
	Joni Huntley	USA	56	1.93i	1)	College Park	13 Jan
	Katrina Gibbs	Aus		1.93	1)	Edmonton	11 Aug
	Jutta Kirst	EG	54	1.93	4)	Praha	31 Aug
	Kristine Nitzsche	EG	59	1.93	P)	Praha	02 Sep
	Debbie Brill	Can	53	1.925i	1)	Richfield	11 Feb
	Cornelia Popa	Rum	50	1.91	1)	Thessaloniki	13 Aug
1979	Rosemarie Ackermann	EG	52	1.99	1)	Torino	05 Aug
	Andrea Mátay	Hun	55	1.98i	1)	Budapest	17 Feb
	Sara Simeoni	Ita	53	1.98	1)	Split	25 Sep
	Debbie Brill	Can	53	1.96	1)	Montreal	26 Aug
	Pristine Nitzsche	EG	59	1.95	P)	Schielleiten	14 Jul
	Yelena Goloborodko	SU	55	1.95	1)	Donyetsk	14 Sep
	Nina Serbina	SU	51	1.94	1)	Donyetsk	04 Aug
	Ulrike Meyfarth	WG	56	1.93i	1)	Berlin	09 Feb
	Urszula Kielan	Pol	60	1.93i	1)	Trinec	16 Feb
	Kerstin Dedner	EG	61	1.93	1)	Erfurt	24 Jun
	Louise Ritter	USA	58	1.93	1)	San Juan	13 Jul
	Elzbieta Krawczuk	Pol	60	1.93	1)	Poznan	12 Aug
	Extra trial:						
	Marina Syerkova	SU	61	1.93i	-)	Minsk	12 Feb
1980	Sara Simeoni	Ita	53	1.98	1)	Torino	01 Jun
	Debbie Brill	Can	53	1.97	1)	Bern	19 Jul
	Tamara Bykova	SU	58	1.97	1)	Donyetsk	07 Sep
	Nina Serbina	SU	52	1.96	1)	Chernigov	03 Jun
	Rosedmarie Ackermann	EG	52	1.95i	1)	Senftenberg	27 Jan
	Urszula Kielan	Pol	60	1.95	1)	Grudziadz	28 May
	Louise Ritter	USA	58	1.95	1)	Wichita	30 May
	Valentina Poluyko	SU	55	1.95	1)	Tallinn	18 Jun
	Jutta Kirst	EG	54	1.95	1)	Linz	09 Aug
	Joni Huntley	USA	56	1.94i	1)	New York	08 Feb
	Elzbieta Krawczuk	Pol	60	1.94	1)	Madrid	17 May
	Louise Miller	GB	60	1.94	2)	Napoli	25 May
	Ulrike Meyfarth	WG	56	1.94	1T)	Warszawa	10 Jun
	Andrea Reichstein	EG	59	1.94	2)	Cottbus	16 Jul

ALL TIME WORLD LIST AS AT THE END OF 1980

Sara Simeoni	Ita	53	2.01	1)	Brescia	04 Aug 78
Rosemarie Ackermann	EG	52	2.00	1)	Berlin	26 Aug 77
Andrea Matay	Hun	55	1.98i	1)	Budapest	17 Feb 79
Debbie Brill	Can	53	1.97	1)	Bern	19 Jul 80
Tamara Bykova	SU	58	1.97	1)	Donyetsk	07 Sep 80
Nina Serbino	SU	52	1.96	1)	Chernigov	03 Jun 80
Brigitte Holzapfel	WG	58	1.95	1)	Köln	12 Aug 78
Ulrike Meyfarth	WG	56	1.95	2)	Köln	12 Aug 78
Kristine Nitzsche	EG	59	1.95	P)	Schielleiten	14 Jul 79
Yelena Goloborodko	SU	55	1.95	1)	Donyetsk	14 Sep 79
Urszula Kielan	Pol	60	1.95	1)	Grudziadz	28 May 80

Louise Ritter		USA	58	1.95	1)	Wichita	30 May 80
Valentina Poluyko		SU	55	1.95	1)	Tallinn	18 Jun 80
Jutta Kirst		EG	54	1.95	1)	Linz	09 Aug 80
1981	Sara Simeoni	Ita	53	1.97i	1)	Grenoble	22 Feb
	Pam Spencer	USA	57	1.97	1)	Bruxelles	28 Aug
	Charmaine Gale	SA	64	1.96	1)	Bloemfontein	04 Apr
	Kerstin Dedner	EG	61	1.96	1)	Tbilisi	27 Jun
	Ulrike Meyfarth	WG	56	1.96	1)	Rhede	07 Aug
	Tamara Bykova	SU	58	1.96	2)	Roma	04 Sep
	Joni Huntley	USA	56	1.95i	1)	New York	06 Feb
	Andrea Reichstein	EG	59	1.95	1)	Leipzig	06 Jun
	Lyudmila Zhecheva	Bul	60	1.95	1)	Sarajevo	20 Sep
	Elzbieta Krawczuk	Pol	60	1.94i	2)	Grenoble	22 Feb
	Urszula Kielan	Pol	60	1.94i	3)	Grenoble	22 Feb
	Valentina Poluyko	SU	55	1.94	2)	Tbilisi	27 Jun
	Louise Ritter	USA	58	1.94	1)	Leningrad	11 Jul
1982	Ulrike Meyfarth	WG	56	2.02	1)	Athinai	08 Sep
	Coleen Sommer	USA	60	2.00i	1)	Ottawa	14 Feb
	Debbie Brill	Can	53	1.99i	1)	Edmonton	23 Jan
	Andrea Bienias	EG	59	1.99i	2)	Milano	07 Mar
	Katalin Sterk	Hun	61	1.99i	3)	Milano	07 Mar
	Tamara Bykova	SU	58	1.98	1)	Leningrad	26 Jun
	Sara Simeoni	Ita	53	1.98	1)	Formia	28 Aug
	Zhanna Nekrasova	SU	57	1.97i	1)	Moskva	13 Feb
	Jutta Kirst	EG	54	1.97	1)	Karl-Marx-Stadt	10 Jul
	Yelena Popkova	SU	55	1.97	2)	Kiev	21 Aug
1983	Tamara Bykova	SU	58	2.04	1)	Pisa	25 Aug
	Ulrike Meyfarth	WG	56	2.03	1)	London	21 Aug
	Louise Ritter	USA	58	2.01	1)	Roma	01 Sep
	Kerstin Brandt	EG	61	1.99	3)	London	21 Aug
	Larisa Kosytsina	SU	63	1.98	2)	Sofia	21 May
	Silvia Costa	Cub	64	1.98	2)	Edmonton	11 Jul
	Valentina Poluyko	SU	55	1.98	1)	Leningrad	26 Jul
	Niculina Vasile	Rum	58	1.97	1)	Bucuresti	15 May
	Susanne Helm	EG	61	1.97	1)	Berlin	08 Jun
	Andrea Bienias	EG	59	1.97	1)	Leipzig	27 Jul
	Olga Juha	Rum	62	1.97	4)	London	21 Aug
1984	Lyudmila Andonova	Bul	60	2.07	1)	Berlin	20 Jul
	Tamara Bykova	SU	58	2.05	1)	Kiev	22 Jun
	Ulrike Meyfarth	WG	56	2.02	1)	Los Angeles	10 Aug
	Sara Simeoni	Ita	53	2.00	2)	Los Angeles	10 Aug
	Stefka Kostadinova	Bul	65	2.00	1)	Sofia	25 Aug
	Silvia Costa	Cub	64	1.99	1)	Verona	01 Jun
	Lyudmila Butuzova	SU	57	1.98	2)	Sochi	10 Jun
	Debbie Brill	Can	53	1.98	2)	Rieti	02 Sep
	Marina Doronina	SU	61	1.97i	1)	Vilnius	14 Jan
	Canuta Bulkowska	Pol	59	1.97	1)	Wörrstadt	09 Jun
	Olga Belkova	SU	56	1.97	2)	Kiev	22 Jun
	Joni Huntley	USA	56	1.97	3)	Los Angeles	10 Aug
1985	Stefka Kostadinova	Bul	65	2.06	1)	Moskva	18 Aug
	Tamara Bykova	SU	58	2.02	2)	Moskva	18 Aug
	Silvia Costa	Cub	64	2.01	1)	Kobe	03 Sep
	Charmaine Gale	SA	64	2.00	1)	Pretoria	25 Mar
	Louise Ritter	USA	58	2.00	2)	Paris	13 Jul
	Niculina Vasile	Rum	58	1.98	1)	Bucuresti	02 Jun
	Larisa Kosytsina	SU	63	1.97	3)	Leningrad	01 Aug
	Susanne Helm	EG	61	1.97	3)	Canberra	04 Oct
	Chris Stanton	Aus	59	1.96	H)	Adelaide	26 Jan
	Gabriele Günz	EG	61	1.96i	1)	Senftenberg	17 Feb
	Wenqing Yang	Chi	60	1.96	1)	Beijing	26 May
	Lyudmila Andonova	Bul	60	1.96	2)	Heidenheim	15 Jujn
	Debbie Brill	Can	53	1.96i	1)	Montreal	28 Jun

	Maryse Ewanje-Epée	Fra	64	1.96	1)	Colombes	21 Jul
	Galina Brigadnaya	SU	58	1.96	1)	Alma-Ata	13 Sep
1986	Stefka Kostadinova	Bul	65	2.08	1)	Sofia	31 May
	Olga Turchak	SU	67	2.01	2)	Moskva	07 Jul
	Desiree du Plessis	SA	65	2.01	1)	Johannesburg	16 Sep
	Charmaine Gale	SA	64	1.99	1)	Johannesburg	18 Apr
	Silvia Costa	Cub	64	1.99	1)	Tokyo	11 May
	Gabriele Günz	EG	61	1.98i	1)	Berlin	26 Jan
	Andrea Bienias	EG	59	1.98i	2)	Berlin	26 Jan
	Larisa Kositsyna	SU	63	1.98i	1)	Moskva	07 Feb
	Katalin Sterk	Hun	61	1.98	1)	Budapest	17 Aug
	Debbie Brill	Can	53	1.97i	1)	New York	28 Feb
	Svetlana Isaeva	Bul	67	1.97	2)	Sofia	25 May
1987	Stefka Kostadinova	Bul	65	2.09	1)	Roma	30 Aug
	Tamara Bykova	SU	58	2.04	2)	Roma	30 Aug
	Susanne Beyer	EG	62	2.02i	2)	Indianapolis	08 Mar
	Louise Ritter	USA	58	2.01	1)	Zurich	19 Aug
	Emilia Dragieva	Bul	65	2.00i	3)	Indianapolis	08 Mar
	Desirée du Plessis	SA	65	2.00	1)	Stellenbosch	11 Apr
	Lyudmila Avdeyenko	SU	63	2.00	1)	Bryansk	17 Jul
	Svetlana Isaeva	Bul	67	2.00	2)	Drama	08 Aug
	Lisa Bernhagen	USA	66	1.97i	1)	Flagstaff	21 Feb
	Gabriele Günz	EG	61	1.97	1)	Halle	26 Jun
1988	Stefka Kostadinova	Bul	65	2.07	1)	Sofia	03 Sep
	Louise Ritter	USA	58	2.03	1)	Austin	08 Jul
	Silvia Costa	Cub	64	2.02	1)	Nice	10 Jul
	Gabriele Günz	EG	61	2.01i	2)	Stuttgart	31 Jan
	Lyudmila Avdeyenko	SU	63	2.00i	1)	Volgograd	11 Feb
	Larisa Kositsyna	SU	63	2.00i	2)	Volgograd	11 Feb
	Olga Turchak	SU	67	2.00	1)	Portsmouth	19 Jun
	Alina Astafei	Rum	69	2.00	1)	Sudbury	29 Jul
	Tamara Bykova	SU	58	1.99	3)	Seoul	30 Sep
	Coleen Sommer	USA	60	1.98	1)	Austin	07 May
	Heike Redetzky	WG	64	1.98	1)	Düsseldorf	20 Jun
	Yelena Yelesina	SU	70	1.98	1)	Nyiregyháza	13 Aug
1989	Stefka Kostadinova	Bul	65	2.04i	1)	Athinai	08 Mar
	Silvia Costa	Cub	64	2.04	1)	Barcelona	09 Sep
	Heike Balck	EG	70	2.01	1)	Karl-Marx-Stadt	18 Jun
	Tamara Bykova	SU	58	2.00i	2)	Budapest	05 Mar
	Jan Wohlschlag	USA	58	2.00	1)	Oslo	01 Jul
	Alina Astafei	Rum	69	2.00	1)	Gateshead	06 Aug
	Heike Henkel	WG	64	2.00	2)	Köln	20 Aug
	Louise Ritter	USA	58	1.98i	1)	Jonaesboro	13 Jan
	Vanessa Ward	Aus	63	1.98	1)	Perth	12 Feb
	Biljana Petrovic	Yug	61	1.98	1)	Split	17 Jun
	Andrea Arens	WG	67	1.98	1)	Hamburg	12 Aug
1990	Yelena Yelesina	SU	70	2.02	1)	Seattle	23 Jul
	Heike Henkel	WG	64	2.01i	1)	Berlin	23 Feb
	Yolanda Henry	USA	64	2.00	1)	Sevilla	30 May
	Biljana Petrovic	Yug	61	2.00	1)	St.Denis	22 Jun
	Tamara Bykova	SU	58	1.98i	1)	Chelyabinsk	04 Feb
	Yelena Panikarovskikh	SU	59	1.98i	1)	Moskva	25 Feb
	Alina Astafei	Rum	69	1.98i	2)	München	25 Feb
	Jan Wohlschlag	USA	58	1.97	3)	Sevilla	30 May
	Heike Balck	EG	70	1.97	2)	Berlin	04 Jul
	Valentina Gotovskaya	SU	65	1.97	1)	Vilnius	04 Aug
1991	Heike Henkel	Ger	64	2.05	1)	Tokyo	31 Aug
	Stefka Kostadinova	Bul	65	2.03	1)	Padova	15 Sep
	Inga Babakova	SU	67	2.02	2)	Berlin	10 Sep
	Yelena Rodina	SU	67	1.99	1)	Moskva	09 Jun
	Svetlana Leseva	Bul	67	1.98	1)	Zagreb	12 Jun

Year	Name	Nat	Born	Mark	Pos	Venue	Date
	Yelena Yelesina	SU	70	1.98	2)	Tokyo	31 Aug
	Tamara Bykova	SU	58	1.97i	2)	Sevilla	09 Mar
	Silvia Costa	Cub	64	1.96i	2)	Stuttgart	10 Feb
	Yolanda Henry	USA	64	1.96i	1)	New York	22 Feb
	Hanne Haugland	Nor	70	1.96i	2)	Arnstadt	02 Feb
	Heike Balck	Ger	70	1.96i	1)	Berlin	01 Mar
	Sue Rembao	USA	62	1.96	1)	San Jose	25 May
	Beata Holub	Pol	67	1.96	4)	Tokyo	31 Aug
1992	Heike Henkel	Ger	64	2.07i	1)	Karlsruhe	08 Feb
	Stefka Kostadinova	Bul	65	2.05i	1)	Sofia	01 Feb
	Inga Babakova	Ukr	67	2.00	2)	Nice	15 Jul
	Alina Astafei	Rum	69	2.00	2)	Barcelona	08 Aug
	Ioamnet Quintero	Cub	72	1.98	3)	Wörrstadt	30 May
	Tanya Hughes	USA	72	1.97	1)	Eugene	22 May
	Tatyana Shevchik	Bye	69	1.96i	2)	Berlin	21 Feb
	Angie Bradburn	USA	68	1.96i	1)	New York	28 Feb
	Galina Isachenko	Bye	65	1.96	2)	Gomel	16 Jul
	Alison Inverarity	Aus	70	1.96	1)	Gateshead	17 Jul
	Yelena Gribanova	Rus	72	1.96	1)	Khimki	09 Aug
1993	Stefka Kostadinova	Bul	65	2.05	1)	Fukuoka	18 Sep
	Heike Henkel	Ger	64	2.02i	2)	Toronto	13 Mar
	Ioamnet Quintero	Cub	72	2.01i	1)	Berlin	05 Mar
	Alina Astafei	Rum	69	2.00i	2)	München	12 Feb
	Inga Babakova	Ukr	67	2.00i	3)	Toronto	13 Mar
	Tatyana Shevchik	Bye	69	2.00	1)	Gomel	14 May
	Yelena Topchina	Rus	66	1.99	1)	Rieti	05 Sep
	Yelena Rodina-Gulyayeva	Rus	67	1.98	1)	Moskva	24 Jul
	Silvia Costa	Cub	64	1.98	3)	Zurich	04 Aug
	Melena Gribanova	Rus	72	1.97i	3)	München	12 Feb
	Britta Bilac	Slo	68	1.97i	3)	Sindelfingen	14 Feb
	Alison Inverarity	Aus	70	1.97i	5)	Toronto	13 Mar
	Sigrid Kirchmann	Aut	66	1.97	3)	Stuttgart	21 Aug
	Olga Bolshova	Mol	68	1.97	3)	Rieti	05 Sep
1994	Alina Astafei	Rum	69	2.02i	1)	Berlin	04 Mar
	Yelena Gulyayeva	Rus	67	2.00i	1)	Moskva	27 Jan
	Britta Bilac	Slo	68	2.00i	1)	Frankfurt/M.	09 Feb
	Stefka Kostadinova	Bul	65	2.00i	1)	Stockholm	08 Mar
	Silvia Costa	Cub	64	2.00	1)	Habana	24 Jun
	Inga Babakova	Ukr	67	2.00	1)	Moskva	31 Jul
	Antonella Bevilacqua	Ita	71	1.98i	1)	Pireas	28 Feb
	Hanne Haugland	Nor	67	1.98i	2)	Pireas	28 Feb
	Angie Bradbum	USA	68	1.98i	1)	Atlanta	05 Mar
	Yevgenia Zhdanova	Rus	66	1.98	2)	Moskva	05 Jun
	Alison Inverarity	Aus	70	1.98	1)	Ingolstadt	17 Jul
1995	Inga Babakova	Ukr	67	2.05	1)	Tokyo	15 Sep
	Alina Astafei	Rum	69	2.04i	1)	Berlin	03 Mar
	Tatyana Motkova	Rus	68	2.03	2)	Bratislava	30 May
	Stefka Kostadinova	Bul	65	2.01	1)	Göteborg	13 Aug
	Hanne Haugland	Nor	67	2.00i	1)	Spala	17 Feb
	Yelena Gulyayeva	Rus	67	1.99i	2)	Berlin	03 Mar
	Britta Bilac	Slo	68	1.99i	2)	Barcelona	11 Mar
	Heike Henkel	Ger	64	1.99i	3)	Barcelona	11 Mar
	Amy Acuff	USA	75	1.98	1)	Tucson	19 May
	Tatyana Khramova	Bye	70	1.98	1)	Gomel	26 May
	Tisha Waller	USA	70	1.98	1)	San Jose	27 May
1996	Stefka Kostadinova	Bul	65	2.05	1)	Atlanta	03 Aug
	Niki Bakoyanni	Gre	68	2.03	2)	Atlanta	03 Aug
	Inga Babakova	Ukr	67	2.03	2)	Bruxelles	23 Aug
	Alina Astafei	Ger	69	2.02i	1T)	Arnstadt	09 Feb
	Tatyana Motkova	Rus	68	2.00i	3)	Arnstadt	09 Feb
	Yelena Gulyayeva	Rus	67	2.00	1)	Grenada	29 May
	Tisha Waller	USA	70	1.99i	1)	Atlanta	02 Mar

	Svetlana Zalevskaya	Kaz	73	1.98i	1)	Samara	02 Mar
	Antonella Bevilacqua	Ita	71	1.98	1)	Milano	04 May
	Hanne Haugland	Nor	67	1.98	1)	Kristiansand	18 Aug
	Drugs disqualication:						
	Antonella Bevilacqua	Ita	71	1.99	-)	Atlanta	03 Aug
1997	Stefka Kostadinova	Bul	65	2.02i	1)	Paris	08 Mar
	Inga Babakova	Ukr	67	2.02	1)	Fukuoka	13 Sep
	Hanne Haugland	Nor	67	2.01	1)	Zurich	13 Aug
	Monica Iagar	Rum	73	2.00	1)	Bruxelles	22 Aug
	Amy Acuff	USA	75	2.00	2)	Bruxellaes	22 Aug
	Yulia Lyakhova	Rus	77	1.99	2)	Fukuoka	13 Sep
	Tatyana Motkova	Rus	68	1.98	1)	Sevilla	29 May
	Antonella Bevilacqua	Ita	71	1.98	1)	Valencia	31 May
	Viktoria Fyodorova	Rus	73	1.98	1)	Tartu	20 Jun
	Alina Astafei	Ger	69	1.97	2)	Köln	24 Aug
1998	Venelina Veneva	Bul	74	2.03	1)	Kalamata	23 May
	Monica Iagar-Dinescu	Rum	73	2.02	1)	Budapest	06 Jun
	Tisha Waller	USA	70	2.01i	1)	Atlanta	28 Feb
	Yelena Gulyayeva	Rus	67	2.01	2)	Kalamata	23 May
	Khristina Kalcheva	Bul	77	1.99	1)	Sofia	13 May
	Melena Yelesina	Rus	70	1.98i	1)	Moskva	13 Feb
	Zuzana Kovácikovä	Cze	73	1.98	1)	St.Peterburg	28 Jun
	Erin Aldrich	USA	77	1.97i	1)	Indianapolis	14 Feb
	Viktoriya Seryogina	Rus	73	1.97	1)	Berdichev	11 Sep
	Alina Astafei	Ger	69	1.96i	1)	Sindelfingen	14 Feb
	Yulia Lyakhova	Rus	77	1.96i	3)	Moskva	13 Feb
	Yekaterina Aleksandrova	Rus	77	1.96i	4)	Moskva	13 Feb
	Hestrie Storbeck-Cloete	SA	78	1.96	1)	Rhede	19 Jun
1999	Hestrie Cloete	SA	78	2.04	1)	Monaco	04 Aug
	Monica Dinescu	Rum	73	2.03i	1)	Bucuresti	23 Jan
	Yelena Yelesina	Rus	70	2.01	1)	St.Denis	03 Jul
	Inga Babakova	Ukr	67	2.01	1)	Zurich	11 Aug
	Yulia Lyakhova	Rus	77	2,00i	1)	Wuppertal	05 Feb
	Tisha Waller	USA	70	2.00	1)	Walnut	18 Apr
	Khristina Kalcheva	Bul	77	1.99i	1)	Maebashi	05 Mar
	Yedlena Gulyayeva	Rus	67	1.99	1)	Paris	20 Jun
	Zuzana Kovácikovä-Hlavonova	Cze	73	1.99	3)	Zurich	11 Aug
	Svetlana Lapina	Rus	78	1.99	3)	Sevilla	29 Aug
2000	Monica Iagar-Dinescu	Rum	73	2.02	1)	Villeneuve d'Ascq	17 Jun
	Velenina Veneva	Bul	74	2.01	1)	Kalamáta	04 Jun
	Kajsa Bergqvist	Swe	76	2.01	1)	Uppsala	19 Aug
	Yelena Yelesina	Rus	70	2.01	1)	Sydney	30 Sep
	Hestrie Cloete	SA	78	2.01	2)	Sydney	30 Sep
	Zuzana Hlavonova	Cze	73	2.00	1)	Praha	05 Jun
	Inga Babakova	Ukr	67	2.00	2)	Villeneuve d'Ascq	17 Jun
	Oana Pantelimon	Rum	72	1.99	3T)	Sydney	30 Sep
	Khristina Kalcheva	Bul	77	1.98	2)	Kalamáta	04 Jun
	Irina Mikhalchenko	Ukr	72	1.98	1)	Kiev	05 Aug
	Viketoriya Palamar	Ukr	77	1.98	2)	Kiev	05 Aug

ALL TIME WORLD LIST AS AT THE END OF 2000

Stefka Kostadinova	Bul	65	2.09	1)	Roma	30 Aug 87
Lyudmila Andonova	Bul	60	2.07	1)	Berlin	20 Jul 84
Heike Henkel	Ger	64	2.07i	1)	Karlsruhe	08 Feb 92
Tamara Bykova	Rus	58	2.05	1)	Kiev	22 Jun 84
Inga Babakova	Ukr	67	2.05	1)	Tokyo	15 Sep 95
Silvia Costa	Cub	64	2.04	1)	Barcelona	09 Sep 89
Alina Astafei	Ger	69	2.04i	1)	Berlin	03 Mar 95
Hestrie Cloete	SA	78	2.04	1)	Monaco	04 Aug 99

Year	Athlete	Nat	Born	Mark	Pos	Venue	Date
	Ulrike Meyfarth	WG	56	2.03	1)	London	21 Aug 83
	Louise Ritter	USA	58	2.03	1)	Austin	08 Jul 88
	Tatyana Motkova	Rus	68	2.03	2)	Bratislava	30 May 95
	Niki Bakoyiánni	Gre	68	2.03	2)	Atlanta	03 Aug 96
	Venelina Veneva	Bul	74	2.03	1)	Kalamáta	23 May 98
	Monica Iagar-Dinescu	Rum	73	2.03i	1)	Bucuresti	23 Jan 99
2001	Venelina Veneva	Bul	74	2.04	1)	Kalamáta	02 Jun
	Inga Babakova	Ukr	67	2.03	1)	Lausanne	04 Jul
	Hestrie Cloete	SA	78	2.01	1)	Zurich	17 Aug
	Kajsa Bergqvist	Swe	76	2.00i	1)	Lisboa	09 Mar
	Dóra Györffy	Hun	78	2.00	1)	Nyiregyháza	26 Jul
	Vita Palamar	Ukr	77	1.99	2)	Zurich	17 Aug
	Amy Acuff	USA	75	1.98	1)	Eugene	27 May
	Antonietta Di Martino	Ita	78	1.98	1)	Catania	07 Jul
	Monica Iagar	Rum	73	1.97i	1)	Liévin	25 Feb
	Viktoriya Seryogina	Rus	73	1.96i	1)	Wien	12 Feb
	Yuliya Lyakhova	Rus	77	1.96i	1)	Moskva	18 Feb
	Olga Kaliturina	Rus	76	1.96	1)	Tula	09 Jun
	Yekaterina Aleksandrova	Rus	77	1.96	1)	Moskva	23 Jun
	Miki Imai	Jap	75	1.96	2)	Yokohama	15 Sep
	Drugs disqualification:						
	SolangebWitteveen	Arg	76	1.97	1)	Manaus	19 May
2002	Kajsa Bergqvist	Swe	76	2.05	1)	Poznan	18 Aug
	Marina Kuptsova	Rus	81	2.03i	1)	Wien	02 Mar
	Venelina Veneva	Bul	74	2.02i	1)	Lódz	02 Feb
	Hestrie Cloete	SA	78	2.02	1)	Madrid	21 Sep
	Irina Mikhalchenko	Ukr	72	2.00	1)	Kiev	25 May
	Viktoriya Seryogina	Rus	73	2.00	1)	Bryansk	11 Jun
	Anna Chicherova	Rus	82	2.00i	1)	Bryansk	26 Dec
	Yuliya Lyakhova	Rus	77	1.98	1)	Moskva	29 Jun
	Yelena Gulyayeva	Rus	67	1.97i	1)	Moskva	17 Jan
	Dóra Györffy	Hun	78	1.97i	1)	Stuttgart	03 Feb
	Olga Kaliturina	Rus	76	1.97i	2)	Stockholm	06 Feb
	Yelena Sivushenko-Slesarenko	Rus	82	1.97	2)	Athens, F.	29 May
	Juana Arrendel	Dom	78	1.97	1)	San Salvador	02 Dec
2003	Kajsa Bergqvist	Swe	76	2.06	1)	Eberstadt	26 Jul
	Hestrie Cloete	SA	78	2.06	1)	St.Denis	31 Aug
	Anna Chicherova	Rus	82	2.04i	1)	Yekaterinburg	07 Jan
	Marina Kuptsova	Rus	81	2.02i	1)	Arnstadt	08 Feb
	Yelena Yelesina	Rus	70	2.02i	1)	Moskva	26 Feb
	Inga Babakova	Ukr	67	2.01	1)	Oslo	27 Jun
	Vita Palamar	Ukr	77	2.01	2T)	Zurich	15 Aug
	Blanka Vlasic	Cro	83	2.01	2T)	Zurich	15 Aug
	Ami Acuff	USA	75	2.01	4)	Zurich	15 Aug
	Venelina Veneva	Bul	74	2.01	1)	Rieti	07 Sep
2004	Yelena Slesarenko	Rus	82	2.06	1)	Athinai	28 Aug
	Anna Chicherova	Rus	82	2.04i	1)	Arnstadt	07 Feb
	Hestrie Cloete	SA	78	2.04	1)	Zurich	06 Aug
	Blanka Vlasic	Cro	83	2.03	1)	Ljubljana	10 Aug
	Kajsa Bergqvist	Swe	76	2.02i	2)	Arnstadt	07 Feb
	Viktoria Styopina	Ukr	76	2.02	3)	Athinai	28 Aug
	Venelina Veneva	Bul	74	2.01	1)	Plovdiv	06 Jun
	Irina Mikhalchenko	Ukr	72	2.01	1)	Eberstadt	18 Jul
	Daniela Rath	Ger	77	2.00i	1)	Wuppertal	23 Jan
	Vita Palamar	Ukr	77	2.00i	3)	Arnstadt	07 Feb
	Ruth Beitia	Spa	79	2.00i	1)	Valencia	21 Feb
	Viktoriya Seryogina	Rus	73	2.00	1)	Moskva	07 Aug
	Amy Acuff	USA	75	2.00	1)	München	08 Aug
2005	Kajsa Bergqvist	Swe	76	2.03	1)	Sheffield	21 Aug
	Anna Chicherova	Rus	82	2.01i	1)	Madrid	06 Mar
	Yelena Slesarenko	Rus	82	2.00	1)	Tula	12 Jul

Year	Athlete	Nat	Born	Mark	Place	Venue	Date
	Chaunte Howard	USA	84	2.00	1)	Liège	20 Jul
	Ruth Beitia	Spa	79	1.99i	2)	Madrid	06 Mar
	Venelina Veneva	Bul	74	1.98	1)	Istanbul	04 Jun
	Tatyana Kivimyagi	Rus	84	1.98	19	Firenze	19 Jun
	Yekaterina Aleksan.-Savchenko	Rus	77	1.97	1)	Tula	14 Jun
	Irina Mikhalchenko	Ukr	72	1.97	1)	Kiev	02 Jul
	Emma Green	Swe	84	1.97	1)	Helsingborg	20 Aug
2006	Kajsa Bergqvist	Swe	76	2.08i	1)	Arnstadt	04 Feb
	Blanka Vlasic	Cro	83	2.05i	1)	Banská Bystrica	14 Feb
	Venelina Veneva	Bul	74	2.04	1)	Zurich	18 Aug
	Tia Hellebaut	Bel	78	2.03	1)	Göteborg	11 Aug
	Yelena Slesarenko	Rus	82	2.02i	1)	Moskva	12 Mar
	Chaunte Howard	USA	84	2.01	1)	Indianapolis	24 Jun
	Vita Styopina	Ukr	76	1.99i	3)	Arnstadt	04 Feb
	Barbora Laláková	Cze	81	1.99i	2)	Banská Bystrica	14 Feb
	Ruth Bestia	Spa	79	1.98	3)	Moskva	12 Mar
	Yekaterina Savchenko	Rus	77	1.98i	4)	Moskva	12 Mar
2007	Blanda Vlasic	Cro	83	2.07	1)	Stockholm	07 Aug
	Tia Hellebaut	Bel	78	2.05i	1)	Birmingham	03 Mar
	Antonietta Di Martino	Ita	78	2.03	1)	Milano	24 Jun
	Anna Chicherova	Rus	82	2.03	2T)	Osaka	02 Sep
	Kajsa Bergqvist	Swe	76	2.02	1)	Torino	08 Jun
	Yelena Slesarenko	Rus	82	2.02	1)	Oslo	15 Jun
	Ruth Beitia	Spa	79	2.02	1)	San Sebastián	04 Aug
	Yekaterina Savchenko	Rus	77	2.00	1)	Dudelange	01 Jul
	Vita Palamar	Ukr	77	2.00	2)	Shanghai	28 Sep
	Viktoriya Klyugina-Slivka	Rus	80	1.97i	1)	Moskva	25 Jan
	Mélanie Skotnik	Fra	82	1.97i	1)	Aubière	18 Feb
	Nicole Forrester	Can	76	1.97	2)	Thessaloniki	30 Jul
	Drugs disqualification:						
	Venelina Veneva	Bul	74	2.02i	1)	Banská Bystrica	13 Feb
2008	Blanka Vlasic	Cro	83	2.06	1)	Istanbul	22 Jun
	Tia Hellebaut	Bel	78	2.05	1)	Beijing	23 Aug
	Anna Chicherova	Rus	82	2.04	2)	Zagreb	09 Sep
	Ariane Friedrich	Ger	84	2.03	1)	Annecy	22 Jun
	Yelena Slesarenko	Rus	82	2.03	2)	Kazan	20 Jul
	Vita Palamar	Ukr	77	2.01i	3)	Valencia	09 Mar
	Ruth Beitia	Spa	79	2.01	2)	Madrid	05 Jul
	Yekaterina Savchenko	Rus	77	2.00i	1)	Bucuresti	17 Feb
	Chaunté Howard	USA	84	2.00	1)	Rieti	07 Sep
	Tatyana Kivimyagi	Rus	84	1.98i	1)	Moskva	20 Jan
	Emma Green	Swe	84	1.98i	1)	Malmö	23 Feb
	Iva Straková	Cze	80	1.98i	1)	Cejkovice	14 Mar
	Viktoriya Klyugina	Rus	80	1.98	2)	Buhi	11 Jul
	Svetlana Shkolina	Rus	86	1.98	3)	Kazan	20 Jul
2009	Blanda Vlasic	Cro	83	2.08	1)	Zagreb	31 Aug
	Ariane Friedrich	Ger	84	2.06	1)	Berlin	14 Jun
	Anna Chicherova	Rus	82	2.02	2)	Berlin	20 Aug
	Irina Gordeyeva	Rus	86	2.02	1)	Eberstadt	30 Aug
	Ruth Beitia	Spa	79	2.01	1)	Zaragoza	18 Jul
	Viktoriya Klyugina	Rus	80	2.00i	2)	Arnstadt	07 Feb
	Antonietta Di Martino	Ita	78	2.00	3)	Leiria	21 Jun
	Marina Aitova	Kaz	82	1.99	1)	Athinai	13 Jul
	Svetlana Shkolina	Rus	86	1.98i	3)	Rijeka	26 Jan
	Destinee Hooker	USA	87	1.98i	1)	College Station	13 Mar
	Chaunté Howard	USA	84	1.98	1)	Athens	09 May
2010	Blanka Vlasic	Cro	83	2.06i	1)	Arnstadt	06 Feb
	Chaunté Howard-Lowe	USA	84	2.05	1)	Des Moines	26 Jun
	Ariane Friedrich	Ger	84	2.02i	1)	Karlsruhe	28 Feb
	Anetonietta Di Martino	Ita	78	2.01	1)	Grosseto	30 Jun
	Emma Green	Swe	84	2.01	2)	Barcelona	01 Aug

Svetlana Shkolina	Rus	86	2.00i	2)	Arnstadt	06 Feb
Meike Kröger	Ger	86	2.00i	2)	Karlsruhe	28 Feb
Ruth Beitia	Spa	79	2.00	1)	Santander	20 Feb
Lavern Spencer	StL	84	1.98	1)	Athens, Ga	08 May
Irina Gordeyeva	Rus	86	1.97	1)	Torino	12 Jun
Tia Hellebaut	Bel	78	1.97	5)	Barcelona	01 Aug

ALL TIME WORLD LIST AS AT THE END OF 2010

Stefka Kostadinova	Bul	65	2.09	1)	Roma	30 Aug 87
Kajsa Bergqvist	Swe	76	2.08i	1)	Arnstadt	04 Feb 06
Blanka Vlasic	Cro	83	2.08	1)	Zagreb	31 Aug 09
Lyudmila Andonova	Bul	60	2.07	1)	Berlin	20 Jul 84
Heike Henkel	Ger	64	2.07i	1)	Karlsruhe	08 Feb 92
Hestrie Cloete	SA	78	2.06	1)	St.Denis	31 Aug 03
Yelena Slesarenko	Rus	82	2.06	1)	Athinai	28 Aug 04
Ariane Friedrich	Ger	84	2.06	1)	Berlin	14 Jun 09
Tamara Bykova	Rus	58	2.05	1)	Kiev	22 Jun 84
Inga Babakova	Ukr	67	2.05	1)	Tokyo	15 Sep 95
Tia Hellebaut	Bel	78	2.05i	1)	Birmingham	03 Mar 07
Chaunté Howard-Lowe	USA	84	2.05	1)	Des Moines	26 Jun 10

POLE VAULT

ALL TIME WORLD BEST AS AT THE END OF 1990

	Zhang Chunzhen	Chi	70	3.81	1)	Guangzhou	24 Mar 90
1991	Zhang Chunzhen	Chi	70	4.05	1)	Guangzhou	10 Aug
	Nicole Rieger	Ger	72	3.90	1)	Berlin	21 Jul
	Jingwen Shao Jingwen	Chi	71	3.90	2)	Guangzhou	10 Aug
	Sun Caiyun	Chi	73	3.83	)	Guangzhou	24 Mar
1992	Sun Caiyun	Chi	73	4.05	1)	Nanjing	21 May
	Cai Weiyan	Chi	73	4.00	1)	Wuhan	19 Oct
	Nicole Rieger	Ger	72	3.92	1)	Landau	22 Jul
	Carmen Haage	Ger	71	3.90	1)	Spaichigen	15 Aug
	Tanja Cors	Ger	71	3.83i	1)	Berlin	02 Feb
	Daniela Köpernick	Ger	73	3.80	1)	München	21 Jun
	Shao Jingwen	Chi	71	3.80	)	Beijing	15 Aug
	Zhu Rong	Chi	72	3.80	)	Beijing	15 Aug
	Chen Xiaoli	Chi	73	3.70	3)	Nanjing	21 May
	Fang Fang	Chi	72	3.70	4)	Nanjing	21 May
	Zhang Lihong	Chi		3.70	5)	Nanjing	21 May
	Christine Adams	Ger	74	3.70	3)	München	21 Jun

NB. *The first mark ratified as a world record by the IAAF was Sun Caiyun's 4.05.*

1993	Sun Caiyun	Chi	73	4.11	1)	Guangzhou	21 Mar
	Shao Jingwen	Chi	71	3.95i	2)	Landau	31 Jan
	Tanja Cors	Ger	71	3.93	1)	Bad Gendersheim	23 May
	Svetlana Abramova	Rus	70	3.90	1)	Schwechat	30 May
	Cai Weiyan	Chi	73	3.85	2)	Jinan	05 Jun
	Carmen Haage	Ger	71	3.85	1)	Duisburg	11 Jul
	Nicole Rieger	Ger	72	3.80	1)	Dillingen	04 Jun
	Wu Weili	Chi	70	3.80	3)	Jinan	05 Jun
	Galina Yenvarenko	Rus	70	3.80	2)	Moskva	18 Jun
	Christine Adams	Ger	74	3.80	1)	Gladbeck	18 Jul

1994	Sun Caiyun	Chi	73	4.12	1)	Guangzhou	22 Oct
	Nicole Rieger	Ger	72	4.08i	1)	Karlsruhe	01 Mar
	Marina Andreyeva	Rus	73	4.01	1)	Voronezh	18 Jun
	Cai Weiyan	Chi	73	4.01	1)	Hefei	03 Aug
	Andrea Müller	Ger	74	4.00i	1)	Sindelfingen	06 Mar
	Gabriela Mihalcea	Rum	64	3.96i	1)	Bucuresti	06 Feb
	Caroline Ammel	Fra	73	3.91	1)	La Roche-sur-Yon	14 Jul
	Svetlana Abramova	Rus	70	3.90i	1)	Donyetsk	20 Feb
	Carmen Haage	Ger	71	3.90	2)	Worms	05 Jun
	Christine Adams	Ger	74	3.90	2)	Erfurt	03 Jul
	Daniela Köpernick	Ger	73	3.90	2)	Ahlen	06 Aug
	Tanja Cors	Ger	71	3.90	1)	Lehrte	04 Sep
1995	Emma George	Aus	74	4.28	1)	Perth	17 Dec
	Sun Caiyun	Chi	73	4.23	1)	Shenzhen	04 Nov
	Daniela Bártová	Cze	74	4.21	1)	Linz	21 Aug
	Andrea Müller	Ger	74	4.18	1)	Zittau	05 Aug
	Cai Weiyan	Chi	73	4.12	2)	Nanjing	23 Oct
	Zhong Guiqing	Chi	77	4.08	1)	Taiyuan	18 May
	Marina Andreyeva	Rus	73	4.06i	1)	Volgograd	25 Feb
	Christine Adams	Ger	74	4.02	2)	Duisburg	18 Jun
	Gabriela Mihalcea	Rum	64	4.01i	1)	Bucuresti	04 Mar
	Melissa Price	USA	77	4.01	1)	Walnut	24 Jun
	Nicole Rieger	Ger	72	4.01	1)	Jockgrim	19 Jul
	Town square meetings:						
	Andrea Müller	Ger	74	4.40	1)	Zweibrücken	08 Oct
	Daniela Bártová	Cze	74	4.22	1)	Salógtarján	11 Sep
1996	Emma George	Aus	74	4.45	1)	Sapporo	14 Jul
	Cai Weiyan	Chi	73	4.33	1)	Shenzhen	05 Oct
	Sun Caiyun	Chi	73	4.28i	1)	Tianjin	27 Feb
	Daniela Bártová	Cze	74	4.27	1)	Oristano	18 Sep
	Marina Andreyeva	Rus	73	4.20i	1)	Moskva	23 Feb
	Stacy Dragila	USA	71	4.20	1)	Atlanta	19 Jun
	Vala Flosadottir	Ice	78	4.17	1)	Bordeaux	28 Sep
	Nicole Rieger	Ger	72	4.16	1)	Ludwigshafen	18 Jul
	Christinen Adams	Ger	74	4.15i	1)	Bielefeld	17 Feb
	Nastja Ryshich	Ger	77	4.15	2)	Köln	21 Jun
	Zhong Quiqing	Chi	77	4.15	2)	Zhunde	11 Oct
1997	Emma George	Aus	74	4.55	1)	Melbourne	20 Feb
	Stacy Dragila	USA	71	4.45	1)	Modesto	10 May
	Anzhela Balakhonova	Ukr	72	4.36	1)	Weissach-im-Tal	27 Jul
	Cai Weiyan	Chi	73	4.35i	3)	Paris	09 Mar
	Daniela Bártová	Cze	74	4.33	1)	Trinec	05 Jul
	Eszter Szemerédi	Hun	76	4.32i	1)	Budapest	31 Jan
	Andrea Müller	Ger	74	4.30	1)	Worms	31 May
	Caroline Ammel	Fra	73	4.21	1)	Bondoufle	04 Oct
	Vala Flosadottir	Ice	78	4.20i	2)	Reykjavik	25 Jan
	Sun Caiyun	Chi	73	4.20i	2)	Eaubonne	28 Feb
	Town square meetings:						
	Anzhela Balakhonova	Ukr	72	4.45	1)	Iglesias	07 Sep
	Daniela Bartová	Cze	74	4.40	1)	Praha	18 Jun
	Janet Zach	Ger	75	4.31	1)	Recklinghausen	30 May
	Janine Whitlock	GB	73	4.23	2)	Salgótarján	17 Sep
	Sabine Schulte	Ger	76	4.21	2)	Recklinghausen	30 May
1998	Emma George	Aus	74	4.59	1)	Brisbane	21 Mar
	Daniela Bartová	Cze	74	4.51	1)	Bratislava	09 Jun
	Stacy Dragila	USA	71	4.48i	1)	Sindelfingen	08 Mar
	Anzhela Balakhonova	Ukr	72	4.45i	1)	Valencia	01 Mar
	Vala Flosadottir	Ice	78	4.44i	1)	Eskilstuna	14 Feb
	Yelena Belyakova	Rus	76	4.38	1)	Uniondale, NY	19 Jul
	Melissa Price	USA	77	4.36	1)	Houston	23 May
	Tatyana Grigorieva	Rus/Aus	75	4.35	2)	Brisbane	21 Mar

	Nicole Humbert-Rieger	Ger	72	4.35	3)	Cottbus	27 May
	Zsuzsa Szabó	Hun	73	4.34i	1)	Budapest	20 Feb
	Exhibition:						
	Nastja Ryshich	Ger	77	4.42	-)	Jockgrim	22 Jun
	Nicole Humbert	Ger	72	4.40	-)	Iglesias	13 Sep
1999	Emma George	Aus	74	4.60	1)	Sydney	20 Feb
	Stacy Dragila	USA	71	4.60	1)	Sevilla	21 Aug
	Nicole Humbert	Ger	72	4.56i	1)	Stockholm	25 Feb
	Anzhela Balakhonova	Ukr	72	4.55	1)	St.Denis	03 Jul
	Zsuzsanna Szabó	Hun	73	4.51i	1)	Budapest	04 Feb
	Melaine Mueller	USA	72	4.50i	1)	Roxbury	07 Feb
	Nastja Ryshich	Ger	77	4.50i	1)	Maebashi	05 Mar
	Tatyana Grigorieva	Aus	75	4.50	1)	Salamanca	15 Jul
	Kellie Suttle	USA	73	4.46i	1)	Jonesboro	17 Jul
	Yelena Belyakova	Rus	76	4.46	2)	Ingolstadt	11 Jul
	Exhibition:						
	Tatyana Grigorieva	Aus	75	4.55	-)	Iglesias	04 Sep
2000	Stacy Dragila	USA	71	4.63	1)	Sacramento	23 Jul
	Anzhela Balakhonova	Ukr	72	4.56	1)	Linz	08 Aug
	Tatyana Grigorieva	Aus	75	4.55	2)	Sydney	25 Sep
	Kellie Suttle	USA	73	4.53	2)	Palo Alto	01 Jul
	Emma George	Aus	74	4.50	1)	Perth	05 Feb
	Svetlana Feofanova	Rus	80	4.50	1)	Helsinki	15 Jun
	Daniela Bártová	Cze	74	4.50	2)	Athinai	28 Jun
	Melena Belyakova	Rus	76	4.50	3)	Athinai	28 Jun
	Nicole Humbert	Ger	72	4.50	1)	Salamanca	20 Jul
	Vala Flosadóttir	Ice	78	4.50	3)	Sydney	25 Sep
	Made on a platform runway, unacceptable for world records:						
	Stacy Dragila	USA	71	4.70	1)	Santa Barbara	11 Jun
	Melanine Mueller	USA	72	4.50	2)	Santa Barbara	11 Jun

ALL TIME WORLD LIST AS AT THE END OF 2000

Stacy Dragila	USA	71	4.63	1)	Sacramento	23 Jul 00
Emma George	Aus	74	4.60	1)	Sydney	20 Feb 99
Nicole Rieger-Humbert	Ger	72	4.56i	1)	Stockholm	25 Feb 99
Anzhela Balakhonova	Ukr	72	4.56	1)	Linz	08 Aug 00
Tatyana Grigorieva	Aus	75	4.55	2)	Sydney	25 Sep 00
Kellie Suttle	USA	73	4.53	2)	Palo Alto	01 Jul 00
Daniela Bártová	Cze	74	4.51	1)	Bratislava	09 Jun 98
Zsuzsanna Szabó	Hun	73	4.51i	1)	Budapest	04 Feb 99
Melissa Mueller	USA	72	4.50i	1)	Roxbury	07 Feb 99
Nastia Ryshich	Ger	77	4.50i	1)	Maebashi	05 Mar 99
Svetlana Feofanova	Rus	80	4.50	1)	Helsinki	15 Jun 00
Yelena Belyakova	Rus	76	4.50	3)	Athinai	28 Jun 00
Vala Flosadóttir	Ice	78	4.50	3)	Sydney	25 Sep 00
Made on a platform runway, unacceptable for world records:						
Stacy Dragila	USA	71	4.70	-)	Santa Barbara	11 Jun 00

2001	Stacy Dragila	USA	71	4.81	1)	Palo Alto	09 Jun
	Svetlana Feofanova	Rus	80	4.75	2)	Edmonton	06 Aug
	Mary Sauer	USA	75	4.61	1)	Irvine	16 Jun
	Monka Pyrek	Pol	80	4.61	1)	Bydgoszcz	01 Jul
	Kellie Suttle	USA	73	4.60	1)	Modesto	12 May
	Pavla Hamácková	Cze	78	4.56i	1)	Lisboa	09 Mar
	Tatyana Grigorieva	Aus	75	4.56	1)	Yokohama	15 Sep
	Yelena Belyakova	Rus	76	4.55i	2)	Pireás	21 Feb
	Annika Becker	Ger	81	4.55	1)	Stuttgart	01 Jul
	Anzhela Balakhonova	Ukr	72	4.52	2)	Athinai	11 Jun
	Gao Shuying	Chi	79	4.52	1)	Beijing	29 Aug

Year	Name	Nat	Born	Mark	Pos	Venue	Date
	Street competition, raised runway, slightly uphill:						
	Melissa Mueller	USA	72	4.62	1)	Clovis	04 Aug
2002	Svetlana Feofanova	Rus	80	4.78	1)	Stockholm	16 Jul
	Annika Becker	Ger	81	4.77	1)	Wattenscheid	07 Jul
	Stacy Dragila	USA	71	4.72	1)	Eugene	26 May
	Christine Adams	Ger	74	4.66i	1)	Sindelfingen	10 Mar
	Yvonne Buschbaum	Ger	80	4.65i	2)	Wien	03 Mar
	Mary Sauer	USA	75	4.65	2)	Madrid	03 Jul
	Monika Pyrek	Pol	80	4.62	2)	London	23 Aug
	Mel Mueller	USA	72	4.60i	1)	Flagstaff	09 Feb
	Yelena Isinbayeva	Rus	82	4.60	1)	Dreux	14 Jun
	Tatyana Polnova	Rus	79	4.60	1)	Lappeenranta	18 Aug
	Exhibition, town square:						
	Yelena Isinbayeva	Rus	82	4.65	1)	Praha	19 Jun
2003	Yelena Isinbayeva	Rus	82	4.82	1)	Gateshead	13 Jul
	Svetlana Feofanova	Rus	80	4.80i	1)	Birmingham	16 Mar
	Stacy Dragila	USA	71	4.78i	1)	Boston	02 Mar
	Tatyana Polnova	Rus	79	4.70i	1)	Moskva	11 Feb
	Yvonne Buschbaum	Ger	80	4.70	1)	Ulm	29 Jun
	Annika Becker	Ger	81	4.70	2)	St.Denis	25 Aug
	Pavla Hamácková	Cze	78	4.60	1)	Velenje	21 Jun
	Monika Pyrek	Pol	80	4.60	3)	Trikala	24 Jun
	Melissa Mueller	USA	72	4.60	1)	Atascadero	09 Jul
	Yelena Belyakova	Rus	76	4.60	1)	Tula	10 Aug
2004	Yelena Isinbayeva	Rus	82	4.92	1)	Bruxelles	03 Sep
	Svetlana Feofanova	Rus	80	4.88	1)	Iráklio	04 Jul
	Stacy Dragila	USA	71	4.83	1)	Ostrava	08 Jun
	Tatyana Polnova	Rus	79	4.78	2)	Monaco	19 Sep
	Monika Pyrek	Pol	80	4.72	2T)	Bruxelles	03 Sep
	Anna Rogowska	Pol	81	4.71	1)	Thessaloniki	19 Jul
	Annika Becker	Ger	81	4.68i	2)	Dortmund	04 Feb
	Kellie Suttle	USA	73	4.67	1)	Jonesboro	16 Jun
	Carolin Hingst	Ger	80	4.66	1)	Karlsruhe	21 Jul
	Jillian Schwartz	USA	79	4.60i	4)	Budapest	06 Mar
	Andrea DuToit	USA	78	4.60	1)	Albuquerque	01 May
	Thórey Edda Elisdóttir	Ice	77	4.60	2)	Madrid	17 Jul
2005	Yelena Isinbayeva	Rus	82	5.01	1)	Helsinki	12 Aug
	Anna Rogowska	Pol	81	4.83	2)	Bruxelles	26 Aug
	Monika Pyrek	Pol	80	4.70i	3)	Donyetsk	12 Feb
	Svetlana Feofanova	Rus	80	4.70i	2)	Birmingham	18 Feb
	Carolin Hingst	Ger	80	4.65i	4)	Madrid	06 Mar
	Tatyana Polnova	Rus	79	4.60i	4T)	Donyetsk	12 Feb
	Tracy O'Hara	USA	80	4.60	1)	Stanford	30 May
	Mary Sauer	USA	75	4.60	1)	Atascadero	29 Jun
	Stacy Dragila	USA	71	4.60	2)	Lausanne	05 Jul
	Vanessa Boslak	Fra	82	4.60	1)	Angers	15 Jul
2006	Yelena Isinbayeva	Rus	82	4.91i	1)	Donyetsk	12 Feb
	Anna Rogowska	Pol	81	4.80i	1)	Liévin	05 Mar
	Monika Pyrek	Pol	80	4.76i	2)	Donyetsk	12 Feb
	Svetlana Feofanova	Rus	80	4.70i	3)	Moskva	11 Mar
	Vanessa Boslak	Fra	82	4.70	2)	Málaga	28 Jun
	Jennifer Stuczynski	USA	82	4.68i	1)	Ypsilanti	14 Jan
	Fabiana Murer	Bra	81	4.66	1)	Monaco	20 Aug
	Tatyana Polnova	Rus	79	4.65	3)	Göteborg	12 Aug
	Nastia Ryshich	Ger	77	4.63	1)	Nürnberg	29 Jul
	Kym Howe	Aus	80	4.62	1)	Melbourne	25 Mar
	Yvonne Buschbaum	Ger	80	4.62	1)	Wipperfürth	02 Jul
2007	Yelena Isinbayeva	Rus	82	4.93i	1)	Donyetsk	10 Feb
	Jennifer Stuczynski	USA	82	4.88	1)	New York	02 Jun
	Monika Pyrek	Pol	80	4.82	2)	Stuttgart	22 Sep

	Svetlana Feofanova	Rus	80	4.82	3)	Stuttgart	22 Sep
	Katerina Badurová	Cze	82	4.75	2)	Osaka	28 Aug
	Kym Howe	Aus	80	4.72i	2)	Donyetsk	10 Feb
	Anna Rogowska	Pol	81	4.72i	3)	Donyetsk	10 Feb
	Tatyana Polnova	Rus	79	4.72	1)	Rivas-Vaciamadrid	29 Jun
	Yuliya Golubchikova	Rus	83	4.71i	2)	Birmingham	04 Mar
	Carolin Hingst	Ger	80	4.70i	1)	Ludwigshafen	14 Jan
	Vanessa Boslak	Fra	82	4.70	5)	Osaka	28 Aug
2008	Yelena Isinbayeva	Rus	82	5.05	1)	Beijing	18 Aug
	Jennifer Stuczynski	USA	82	4.92	1)	Eugene	06 Jul
	Fabiana Murer	Bra	81	4.80	1)	São Paulo	29 Jun
	Yuliya Goluchikova	Rus	83	4.75i	1)	Athinai	13 Feb
	Monika Pyrek	Pol	80	4.75	1)	Sopot	29 Jun
	Svetlana Feofanova	Rus	80	4.75	1)	Madrid	05 Jul
	Chelsea Johnson	USA	83	4.73	1)	Los Gatos	26 Jun
	Jillian Schwartz	USA	79	4.72i	1)	Jonesboro	15 Jun
	Stacy Dragila	USA	71	4.70	1)	Chula Vista	22 Jun
	Tatyana Polnova	Rus	79	4.70	1)	Salamanca	02 Jul
	Silke Spiegelburg	Ger	86	4.70	3)	Roma	11 Jul
	Square competition:						
	Tatyana Polnova	Rus	79	4.71	-)	Sopot	06 Jun
	Exhibition:						
	Anastasiya Shvedova	Rus	79	4.72	1)	Aosta	05 Jul
2009	Yelena Isinbayeva	Rus	82	5.06	1)	Zurich	28 Aug
	Jennifer Stuczynski	USA	82	4.83i	1)	Boston	01 Mar
	Fabiana Murer	Bra	81	4.82	1)	Rio de Janeiro	07 Jun
	Anna Rogowska	Pol	81	4.80	1)	Bydgoszcz	01 Aug
	Monika Pyrek	Pol	80	4.78	2)	Berlin	14 Jun
	Yuliya Golubchikova	Rus	83	4.75i	1)	Torino	07 Mar
	Silke Spiegelburg	Ger	86	4.75i	2)	Torino	07 Mar
	Svetlana Feofanova	Rus	80	4.70	3)	Roma	10 Jul
	Anna Batte	Ger	85	4.68	5)	Berlin	14 Jun
	Aleksandra Kiryashova	Rus	85	4.65	1)	Tula	01 Aug
	Chelsea Johnson	USA	83	4.65	2)	Berlin	17 Aug
2010	Jenn Suhr	USA	82	4.89	1)	Des Moines	27 Jun
	Yelena Isinbayeva	Rus	82	4.85i	1)	Moskva	07 Feb
	Fabiana Murer	Bra	81	4.85	1)	San Fernando	04 Jun
	Anna Rogowska	Pol	81	4.81i	1)	Bydgoszcz	10 Feb
	Svetlana Feofanova	Rus	80	4.80i	2)	Doha	14 Mar
	Carolin Hingst	Ger	80	4.72	1)	Biberach	09 Jul
	Silke Spiegelburg	Ger	86	4.71	2)	Wattenscheid	26 Jun
	Yuliya Golubchikova	Rus	83	4.70i	2)	Moskva	07 Feb
	Tatyana Polnova	Rus	79	4.70i	2)	Moskva	26 Feb
	Lacy Janson	USA	83	4.66i	1)	Fayetteville	12 Feb
	Jirina Ptácnikova	Cze	86	4.66	1)	Trinec	17 Jul

ALL TIME WORLD LIST AS AT THE END OF 2010

Yelena Isinbayeva	Rus	82	5.06	1)	Zurich	28 Aug 09
Jennifer Stuczynski	USA	82	4.92	1)	Eugene	06 Jul 08
Jenn Suhr	USA	82	4.89	1)	Des Moines	27 Jun 10
Svetlana Feofanova	Rus	80	4.88	1)	Iráklio	04 Jul 04
Fabiana Murer	Bra	81	4.85	1)	San Fernando	04 Jun 10
Stacy Dragila	USA	71	4.83	1)	Ostrava	08 Jun 04
Anna Rogowska	Pol	81	4.83	2)	Bruxelles	26 Aug 05
Monika Pyrek	Pol	80	4.82	2)	Stuttgart	22 Sep 07
Tatyana Polnova	Rus	79	4.78	2)	Monaco	19 Sep 04
Annida Becker	Ger	81	4.77	1)	Wattenscheid	07 Jul 02

LONG JUMP

Best mark as at the end of 1920:

	Maria Kiessling	Ger	94	5.41	1)	München	17 Jul 20
1921	Maria Kiessling	Ger	94	5.54	1)	München	29 May
	Helene Seeliger	Ger		5.46	2)	Hamburg	21 Aug
	Anna Pieper	Ger	01	5.15	1)	Bielefeld	05 Jun
	Marie Keller	Aut	93	5.12	1)	Berlin	24 Jul
	Lotte Wolk	Ger		5.12	1)	Duisburg	18 Sep
	Luise Cron	Ger		5.10	1)	Hanau	15 May
	Zenta Bauer	Ger		5.06	1)	München	17 Jul
	Margarete Furchheim	Ger	00	5.00	2)	Berlin	03 Jul
	Hedwig Drees	Ger		4.95	2)	Bielefeld	05 Jun
	Alice Swigardi	Ger		4.90	1)	Erfurt	22 May
	Sloping runway:						
	Eckert	Ger		5.54	1)	Taubenberg	
1922	Margarete Furchheim	Ger	00	5.28	1)	Duisburg	20 Aug
	Anna Pieper	Ger	01	5.26	1)	Bochum	10 Sep
	Marie Mejzliková II	Cze	03	5.16	1)	Praha	06 Aug
	Melene Seeliger	Ger		5.09	1)	Hannover	30 Jul
	Loef	Ger		5.09	2)	Duisburg	20 Aug
	Mary Lines	GB	93	5.06	1)	Paris	20 Aug
	Maria Nill	Ger		5.05	1)	Stuttgart	14 Aug
	Rademacher	Ger		5.02	1)	Berlin	30 Jul
	Camilia Sabie	USA	03	5.02	2)	Paris	20 Aug
	Gertrud Döring	Ger		5.00	1)	Berlin	11 Jun
	Anni Stender	Ger		5.00	1)	Heide	16 Jul

Note – *Mejzliková's 5.16 was the first mark officially ratified as a world record by the FSFI.*

1923	Anna Pieper	Ger	01	5.31	1)	Hamm	15 Jul
	Marie Mejzliková II	Cze	03	5.30	1)	Praha	23 Sep
	Alma Höppner	Ger	00	5.21i	1)	Krefeld	28 Jan
	Margarete Furchheim	Ger	00	5.11	1)	Berlin	03 Jun
	Loef	Ger		5.10	1)	Köln	15 Jul
	Ingrid Albertsen	Ger		5.07	1)	Hannover	29 Jul
	Vera Jacobson	Swe	06	5.06	1)	Stockholm	09 Sep
	Mary Lines	GB	93	5.04	1)	Antwerpen	13 Aug
	Helen Filkey	USA	08	5.03	1)	Chicago	03 Sep
	Elisa Van Truyen	Bel	06	5.01	1)	Bruxelles	29 Jul
1924	Gerda Müller	Ger	08	5.43	+)	Hannover	31 Aug
	Margarete Furchheim	Ger	00	5.26	1)	Brandenburg	06 Jul
	Frieda Heister	Ger	06	5.21	1)	Hannover	20 Jul
	Mary Lines	GB	93	5.16	1)	London	28 Jun
	Anna Pieper	Ger	01	5.15	1)	Krefeld	12 Jul
	Gladys Elliott	GB	11	5.11	2)	London	28 Jun
	Mavis Howard	USSR		5.10	1)	Cape Town	16 Dec
	Marie Mejzliková II	Cze	03	5.09	1)	Paris	14 Sep
	Ingrid Albertsen	Ger		5.08	2)	Hannover	31 Aug
	Emmy Haux	Ger	04	5.07	1)	Frankfurrt/M.	29 Jun
	Georgette Gagneux	Fra	07	5.07	1)	Le Bourget	06 Jul

+) *Made in a special record attempt. Not ratified by the FSFI.*

1925	Margarete Furchheim	Ger	00	5.50	1)	Leipzig	29 Aug
	Gerda Müller	Ger	08	5.49	+)	Leipzig	29 Aug
	Block	Ger		5.31	1)	Osnabrück	09 Aug
	Helen Filkey	USA	08	5.28	1)	Chicago	23 Aug
	Leni Junker	Ger	05	5.25	3)	Leipzig	29 Aug
	Phyllis Green	GB	08	5.23	1)	London	06 Jun
	Maud Schilling	Hol		5.19	1)	Eindhoven	23 Aug
	Elizabeth Stine	USA	05	5.18	1)	Paterson, NJ	20 Jun
	Zinaida Liepina	Lat	07	5.18	1)	Liepaja	09 Aug
	Margaret Hull	GB	02	5.15	1)	London	01 Aug

+) *Made in a special record attempt.*

1926	Kinue Hitomi	Jap	07	5.75	1)	Tokyo	05 Jun
	Muriel Gunn	GB	06	5.57	1)	London	21 Sep
	Leni Junker	Ger	05	5.41	1)	Hannover	29 Aug
	Eva von Bredow	Ger	04	5.34	1)	Berlin	26 Sep
	Gerda Müller	Ger	08	5.33	1)	Düsseldorf	14 Aug
	Dolly Wagner	Aut	06	5.33	1)	Wien	25 Sep
	Gertrud Gladitsch	Ger	03	5.31	1)	Worms	29 Aug
	Zdenka Smolová	Cze	08	5.28	3)	Göteborg	28 Aug
	Block	Ger		5.27	1)	Hannover	20 Jun
	Mariya Shamanova	USSR	08	5.26	1)	Moskva	27 Jun
	Extra trial:						
	Gisela Pöting	Ger		5.40	-)	Braunschweig	22 Aug
1927	Gertrud Gladitsch	Ger	03	5.60	1)	Schwenningen	26 Jun
	Muriel Gunn-Cornell	Gb	06	5.57	1)	London	01 Aug
	Käthe Alpen	Ger	10	5.54	2)	Hannover	04 Sep
	Phyllis Green	GB	08	5.52	1)	London	01 Jul
	Elsa Gehring	Ger	06	5.49	1)	Anklam	21 Jul
	Gerda Müller	Ger	08	5.47	1)	Berlin	13 Aug
	Eva von Bredow	Ger	04	5.45	1)	Breslau	07 Aug
	Helene Junker	Ger	05	5.45	2)	Berlin	13 Aug
	Elta Cartwright	USA	07	5.43	1)	Arcata, CA	23 Apr
	Elisabeth Bonetsmüller	Ger	07	5.41	1)	Rottaci-Egern	31 Jul
	Extra trial:						
	Helene Junker-Thymm	Ger	05	5.51	-)	Hannover	19 Jun
	Irregular:						
	Gertrud Gladitsch	Ger	03	5.62	-)	Hannover	04 Sep
	Unconfirmed:						
	Phyllis Green	GB	08	5.60	-)	London	Jun
1928	Kinue Hitomi	Jap	07	5.98	1)	Osaka	20 May
	Muriel Cornell-Gunn	GB	06	5.68	1)	London	14 Jul
	Fanny Rosenfeld	Can	03	5.56	1)	Halifax	02 Jul
	Nellie Todd	USA	10	5.53	1)	Cicero, IL.	15 Sep
	Mariya Shamanova	USSR	08	5.51	1)	Leningrad	30 Jul
	Elizabeth Grobes	USA		5.43	1)	Kearny, NJ	15 Sep
	Luise Gröneveld	Ger	12	5.40	1)	Bremen	30 Jun
	Georgette Gagneux	Fra	07	5.37	1)	Paris	15 Jul
	Evavon Bredow	Gerf	04	5.36	2)	Berlin	18 Aug
	Anne Zondervaan	Hol		5.36	)		

Note – *Hitomi's 5.98 was the first world record ratified by the IAAF.*

1929	Kinue Hitomi	Jap	07	6.07w	1)	Mukden	20 Oct
	(Hitomi			5.91	1)	Tokyo	03 Nov
	Muriel Gunn-Cornell	GB	06	5.78	1)	London	13 Jul
	Selma Grieme	Ger	10	5.69	1)	Düsseldorf	18 Aug
	Felicitas Schlarp	Ger		5.65	1)	Frankfurt/M.	21 Jul
	Rie Briejer	Hol	10	5.56	1)	Leiden	01 Sep
	Marie Amthor	Ger	06	5.55	1)	Nürnberg	16 Jun
	Hedwig Bauschulte	Ger	08	5.51	1)	Meppen	14 Jul
	Stanislawa Walasiewicz *	Pol	11	5.50	1)	Królewska Huta	28 Jul
	Gertrud Gladitsch	Ger	03	5.49	1)	Freiburg	16 Jun
	Ingeborg Braumüller	Ger	09	5.45	1)	Berlin	23 Jun
	Marga Wittkowski	Ger	05	5.45	1)	Hamburg	23 Juu

Note – *Hitomi's 6.07 was made with an assisting wind of 5.8 m/s. The IAAF had no "wind rule" at the time, yet the mark was not ratified as a world record.*

** Her actual name at birth was Stefania, but she was known as Stanislawa throughout her career. At the time of her death (1980), an autopsy revealed a situation "not compatible with participation in women's sports".*

1930	Stanislawa Walasiewicz	Pol	11	6.02w	1)	Cleveland	10 Jul
	Kinue Hitomi	Jap	07	5.90w	1)	Praha	08 Sep
	Muriel Gunn-Cornell	GB	06	5.85	1)	Birmngham	26 Jul

	Selma Grieme-Heldenmaier	Ger	10	5.74w	1)	Lennep	03 Aug
	(Walasiewicz)			5.72	1)	Dallas	04 Jul
	(Grieme)			5.72	2)	Birmingham	26 Jul
	Mildred Didrikson-Zaharias	USA	11	5.69	2)	Dallas	04 Jul
	Tanja Heuvelmann	Ger		5.69	1)	Leipzig	17 Aug
	Maj Jacobsson-Patriksson	Swe	09	5.65w	4)	Praha	08 Sep
	(Hitomi)			5.61	1)	Paris	21 Sep
	Lina Weigele	Ger		5.63	1)	Stuttgart	14 Aug
	Mary Seary-Hartley	GB	09	5.52	1)	London	07 Jun
	Felicitas Schlarp	Ger	07	5.52w	5)	Praha	08 Sep
1931	Selma Grieme-Heidenmaier	Gerr	10	5.91	1)	Hannover	23 Aug
	Muriel Gunn-Cornell	GB	06	5.77	2)	Hannover	23 Aug
	Stanislawa Walasiewicz	Pol	11	5.72	1)	Cleveland	23 Ma
	Jean Knight	GB	11	5.68	1)	St. Albans	18 Jul
	Mary Seary-Hartley	GB	09	5.68	2)	St.Albans	18 Jul
	Mildred Didrikson-Zahariaas	USA	11	5.67	1)	Dallas	04 Jul
	Lina Weigele	Ger		5.61	1)	Cannstatt	28 Jun
	Felicitas Schlarp-Schubeck	Ger	07	5.61	1)	Magdeburg	02 Aug
	Helene Junker-Thymm	Ger	05	5.53	1)	Erfurt	12 Jul
	HerthA Wolff	Ger		5.52	1)	Hamburg	14 Jun
	Ilse Luttermann	Ger	11	5.52	1)	Hamburg	05 Jul
1932	Selma Grieme-Heldenmaier	Ger	10	5.74	1)	Bremen	11 Sep
	Stanislawa Walasiewicz	Pol	11	5.71	1)	Chicago	18 Aug
	Phyllis Bartholomew	GB	14	5.69	1)	London	09 Jul
	Erika Mascher	Ger		5.62	1)	Erfurt	07 Aug
	Rie Briejer	Hol	10	5.55	1)	Amsterdam	18 Sep
	Gerda Laue-Lähnemann	Ger	08	5.53	1)	Berlin	18 Jun
	Hertha Wolff	Ger		5.50i	1)	Heidelberg	07 Feb
	Katharina Krauss	Ger	06	5.50	1)	Görlitz	21 Aug
	Lina Weigele	Ger		5.49	)	Nürnberg	10 Jul
	Maria Dollinger	Ger	10	5.48	1)	Nürnberg	21 Jun
1933	Stanislawa Walasiewicz	Pol	11	5.84	1)	Lwów	24 Sep
	Selma Grieme	Ger	10	5.79	1)	Weimar	20 Aug
	Erika Mascher	Ger		5.78	1)	Coburg	09 Jul
	Ingeborg Braumüller	Ger	09	5.73	1)	Berlin	23 Jul
	Veronika Kohlbach	Aut	06	5.65	1)	Wien	13 Jul
	Traude Göppner	Ger	11	5.65	1)	Danzig	27 Aug
	Sumiko Watanabe	Jap	16	5.64	1)	Tokyo	02 Nov
	Erna Steinberg-Boeck	Ger	11	5.53	2)	Berlin	23 Jul
	Katharina Krauss	Ger	06	5.52	P)	Zurich	27 Aug
	A. Preysinger	Ger		5.50	1)	München	25 Jun
1934	Selma Grieme	Ger	10	5.85	1)	Wuppertal	15 Aug
	Käthe Krauss	Ger	06	5.82	1)	Dresden	17 Jun
	Traude Göppner	Ger	11	5.80	1)	London	11 Aug
	Galina Turova	USSR	12	5.80	1)	Moskva	01 Aug
	Hedwig Bauschulte	Ger	08	5.79	2)	London	11 Aug
	Stanislawa Walasiewicz	Pol	11	5.77	1)	Warszawa	23 Jun
	Liesel Vey	Ger	15	5.67	1)	München	24 Sep
	Sumiko Watanabe	Jap	16	5.66	1)	Koshien	29 Apr
	Gisela Mauermayer	Ger	13	5.63	3)	Berlin	01 Jul
	Mariya Shamanova	USSR	08	5.61	1)	Moskva	01 Jul
	Later identified as a man:						
	Zdenka Koubková	Cze	13	5.83	1)	Praha	13 Oct
1935	Traude Göppner	Ger	11	5.89	1)	Dresden	25 Aug
	Stanislawa Walasiewicz	Pol	11	5.84	1)	Lwów	24 Sep
	Hedwig Bauschulte	Ger	08	5.70	2T)	Dresden	25 Aug
	Vyera Istomina	SU		5.60	1)	Moskva	11 Sep
	Rie Briejer	Hol	10	5.56	1)	Amsterdam	15 Sep
	Ronny Kohlbach	Aut	06	5.51	1)	Wien	17 Aug
	Ethel Raby	GB	14	5.50	1)	London	10 Aug
	Nellie Carrington	GB	16	5.49w	2)	London	10 Aug

Year	Name	Nat	Born	Mark	Pos	Venue	Date
	Fusako Takino	Jap		5.48	1)	Kyoto	12 Oct
	Erna Eltermane	Lat		5.47	1)	Riga	02 Sep
	Later identified as a man:						
	Zdenka Koubková	Cze	13	5.56	1)	Praha	26 May
	Stepánka Pekarová	Cze	13	5.49	P)	Ceske Budejovice	26 Sep
1936	Käthe Krauss	Ger	06	5.78	1)	Wuppertal	19 Jun
	Traude Göppner	Ger	11	5.76	2)	Wuppertal	19 Jun
	Stanislawa Walasiewicz	Pol	11	5.71	1)	Wuppertal	19 Aug
	Rie Briejer	Hol	10	5.62w	1)	Amsterdam	12 Jul
	Madeleine Renaud	Fra	13	5.51	1)	Colombes	13 Jul
	Galina Turova	SU	12	5.51	1)	Leningrad	28 Jul
	Wanda Nowak	Aut	13	5.51	1)	Wien	13 Sep
	Mabel Smith	USA	17	5.48	1)	Providence	05 Jul
	Thelma Peake	Aus	14	5.48	1)	Sydney	18 Jan
	Erna Eltermane	Lat		5.47	1)	Riga	07 Sep
1937	Stanislawa Walasiewicz	Pol	11	6.09	1)	Worcester, MA	28 Jun
	Käthe Krauss	Ger	06	5.85	P)	Frankfurt/M.	10 Jul
	Ethel Raby	GB	14	5.79	1)	London	07 Aug
	Thelma Peake	Aus	14	5.76	1)	Brisbane	01 Oct
	Elfriede Kaun	Ger	14	5.65i	1)	Kiel	21 Mar
	Traude Göppner	Ger	11	5.65	1)		Jun
	Claudia Testoni	Ita	15	5.65	1)	Paris	08 Aug
	Margarete Trenkner-Kuhlmann	Ger	15	5.61	1)	Hamburg	26 Jun
	Veronika Kohlbach	Aut	06	5.61	1)	Wien	28 Aug
	Sophie Hagg	Ger	10	5.60	2)	München	29 Aug
	With assisting wind:						
	Käthe Krauss	Ger	06	5.96	1)	Berlin	25 Jul
	Hilde Franke	Ger	18	5.71	2)	Berlin	25 Jul
	Traude Göppner	Ger	11	5.69	3)	Berlin	25 Jul

Note: *The IAAF introduced a "wind rule" (maximum allowable, 2.0 m/s) late in 1936.*

Year	Name	Nat	Born	Mark	Pos	Venue	Date
	Sloping runway:						
	Ilse Holze	Ger	19	5.70w	1)	Wetter	01 Aug
1938	Erika Junghanns	Ger	19	6.07	1)	Weissenfels	02 Oct
	Stanislawa Walasiewicz	Pol	11	6.05	1)	Cleveland	12 Jun
	Irmgard Praetz	Ger	20	5.88	1)	Wien	17 Sep
	Gisela Voss	Ger	17	5.84	1)	Cottbus	19 Jun
	Gisela Mauermayer	Ger	13	5.84	1)	Mannheim	07 Aug
	Decima Norman	Aus	15	5.80	1)	Sydney	07 Feb
	Ruth Hagermann	Ger	13	5.74	1)	Braunschweig	19 Jun
	Vedder Schenck	GB	20	5.74	1)	London	03 Sep
	Walburga Wilkening	Ger	20	5.73	1)	Wuppertal	19 Jun
	Hilde Franke	Ger	18	5.71	2)	Cottbus	19 Jun
1939	Christel Schulz	Ger	21	6.12	1)	Berlin	30 Jul
	Francina Blankers-Koen	Hol	18	5.97	2)	Berlin	30 Jul
	Stanislawa Walasiewicz	Pol	11	5.89	1)	Waterbury	03 Sep
	Gisela Voss	Ger	17	5.88	1)	Berlin	11 Jun
	Edeltraut Boeck-Landsberg	Ger	18	5.88	1)	Dresden	13 Aug
	Rie Yamauchi	Jap	22	5.86	1)	Nagoya	01 Oct
	Erika Junghanns	Ger	19	5.77	1)	Erfurt	18 Jun
	Elfriede Kaun	Ger	14	5.76	1)	Kiel	20 Aug
	Irmgard Praetz	Ger	20	5.73	1)	Tangerhütte	06 Aug
	Irmgard Herholdt	Ger	19	5.67	1)	Wittten	04 Jun
	With assisting wind:						
	Stanislawa Walasiewicz	Pol	11	6.12	1)	Cleveland	18 Jun
	E. Mengel	Ger	21	5.72	1)	Frankfurt/M.	01 Jul
	Dorothy Vedder-Schenk	GB	20	5.69	2)	London	03 Jun
1940	Erika Junghanns	Ger	19	5.92	1)	Naumburg	25 Aug
	Christel Schulz	Ger	21	5.87	1)	Parma	28 Jul

Francina Blankers-Koen	Hol	18	5.87	1)	Ryswyk	18 Aug
Gisela Voss-Jahn	Ger	17	5.81	1)	Berlin	13 Jul
Edeltraut Boeck-Landsberg	Ger	18	5.78	2)	Parma	28 Jul
Rie Yamauchi	Jap	22	5.75	1)	Ome	23 Aug
Decima Norman	Aus	09	5.71	1)	Perth	09 Mar
Toyoko Yoshino	Jap	20	5.67	1)	Tokyo	02 Nov
Erika Nerlich	Ger	18	5.64	1)	Hindenburg	23 Jun
Valentina Vasilyeva	SU	21	5.64	1)	Leningrad	Aug

ALL TIME WORLD LIST AS AT THE END OF 1940

Christel Schulz		Ger	21	6.12	1)	Berlin	30 Jul 39
Stanislawa Walasiewicz		Pol	11	6.09	1)	Worcester, MA	28 Jun 37
Erika Junghanns		Ger	19	6.07	1)	Weissenfels	02 Oct 38
Kinue Hitomi		Jap	07	5.98	1)	Osaka	20 May 28
Francina Blankers-Koen		Hol	18	5.97	2)	Berlin	30 Jul 39
Selma Grieme-Heldenmaier		Ger	10	5.91	1)	Hannover	23 Aug 31
Traude Göppner		Ger	11	5.89	1)	Dresden	25 Aug 35
Irmgard Praetz		Ger	20	5.88	1)	Wien	17 Sep 38
Gisela Voss		Ger	17	5.88	1)	Berlin	11 Jun 39
Edeltraut Boeck-Landsberg		Ger	18	5.88	1)	Dresden	13 Aug 39
With assisting wind:							
Stanislawa Walasiewicz		Pol	11	6.12	1)	Cleveland	18 Jun 39
Kinue Hitomi		Jap	07	6.07	1)	Mukden	20 Oct 29
Käthe Krauss		Ger	06	5.96	1)	Berlin	25 Jul 37
1941	Christel Schulz	Ger	21	5.90	1)	Berlin	20 Jul
	Irmgard Kirchhoff	Ger	21	5.85	1)	Kassel	15 Jun
	Gisela Voss-Jahn	Ger	17	5.84	1)	Berlin	07 Sep
	Irmgard Herholdt	Ger	19	5.75	1)	Hagen	27 Sep
	Elfriede Brunemann	Ger	20	5.71	1)	Braunschweig	14 Jun
	Erika Junghanns	Ger	19	5.65	1)	Halle	14 Sep
	Stanislawa Walasiewicz	Pol	11	5.65	1)	Ocean City	05 Jul
	Felicitas Schmidt	Ger	20	5.62	3)	Berlin	19 Jul
	Inge Schmidt-Nielsen	Den	15	5.61	1)	Köbenhavn	28 Sep
	Lucy Newell	USA	22	5.56	1)		
	Edeltraud Boeck	Ger	18	5.56	3)	Berlin	29 Jun
	Hilde Ranke	Ger	24	5.56	1)	Nürnberg	29 Jun
	Helma Renker	Ger	21	5.56	)	Fürth	17 Aug
1942	Christel Schulz	Ger	21	6.04	1)	Göttingen	18 Jul
	Francina Blankers-Koen	Hol	18	6.00	1)	Eindhoven	26 Jul
	Hertha Prade	Ger	22	5.83	1)	Usti-nad-Labem	12 Jul
	Irmgard Herholdt	Ger	19	5.74i	1)	Dortmund	14 Mar
	Eva Thiel	Ger	23	5.71	1)	Leipzig	13 Jun
	Luise Lockemann	Ger	17	5.68	1)	Halle	05 Jul
	Elfriede Brunemann	Ger	20	5.68	2)	Berlin	25 Jul
	Gisela Voss-Jahn	Ger	17	5.67	1)	Berlin	07 Jun
	Rie Yamauchi	Jap	22	5.66	1)	Sakai	12 Jul
	Erika Janghanns	Ger	19	5.63	1)	Königsberg	28 Jun
1943	Francina Blankers-Koen	Hol	18	6.25	1)	Leiden	19 Sep
	Christel Schulz	Ger	21	5.83	1)	Göttingen	18 Jul
	Stanislawa Walasiewicz	Pol	11	5.81	1)	Cleveland	15 Aug
	Lieselotte Siemsen	Ger	22	5.79	1)	Hamburg	27 Jun
	Elfriede Brunnemann	Ger	20	5.76	1)	Hannover	15 Aug
	Hertha Prade	Ger	22	5.74	-)	Liberec	18 Jul
	Gerda Koudijs	Hol	23	5.73	1)	Roosendaal	01 Aug
	Anni-Luzie Schirmer	Ger	24	5.71	1)	Wien	30 Jun
	Annemarie Kreter-Clausner	Ger	21	5.69	1)	Radom	11 Jul
	Edeltraut Boeck	Ger	18	5.69	2)	Berlin	24 Jul
1944	Elfriede Brunnemann	Ger	20	5.85	1)	Hannover	25 Jun
	Francina Blankers-Koen	Hol	18	5.82	1)	Amsterdam	20 Aug

Year	Name	Nat	Born	Mark	Pl	Venue	Date
	Joy Quist	Aus	27	5.78	1)	Sydney	14 Feb
	Annemarie Kreter-Clausner	Ger	21	5.70	1)	Kraków	23 Jul
	Edeltraut Boeck	Ger	18	5.69	1)	Berlin	15 Jul
	Lena Stumpf	Ger	24	5.68	1)	Praha	25 Jun
	Felicitas Schmidt	Ger	20	5.63	2)	Berlin	15 Jul
	Gerda Koudijs	Hol	23	5.62	1)	Leiden	04 Jun
	Christel Schulz	Ger	21	5.62	1)	Bochum	27 Aug
	Renate Griesshammer	Ger	24	5.60	1)	Würzburg	16 Jul
1945	Noemi Simonetto	Arg	26	5.76	1)	San Fernando	16 Sep
	Galina Turova	SU	12	5.61	1)	Kiev	11 Sep
	Yelena Gokieli	SU	18	5.58	1)	Moskva	15 Aug
	Stanislawa Walasiewicz	Pol	11	5.56	1)	Harrisburg	30 Jun
	Lidiya Gaile-Leimane	SU	22	5.51	3)	Kiev	11 Sep
	Lieselotte Siemsen	Ger	20	5.50	1)	Hamburg	16 Sep
	Yevgeniya Sechenova	SU	19	5.45	-)		
	Rowena Harrison	USA	23	5.42	2)	Harrisburg	30 Jun
	Zoya Dukhovich	SU		5.42	-)		
	Elfriede Brunemann	Ger	20	5.41	1)	Hannover	30 Sep
1946	Rie Yamauchi	Jap	22	5.86	1)	Kitakyushu	20 Nov
	Elfriede Brunemann	Ger	20	5.79	P)	Braunschweig	29 Sep
	Francina Blankers-Koen	Hol	18	5.74	1)	Amsterdam	23 Jun
	Lidiya Gaile Leimane	SU	22	5.72	1)	Moskva	23 Jul
	Valentina Vasiilyeva	SU	21	5.69	1)	Moskva	05 Aug
	Gerda Koudijs	Hol	23	5.67	1)	Oslo	23 Aug
	Noemi Simonetto	Arg	26	5.64	1)	Buenos Aires	16 Nov
	Yelena Gokieli	SU	18	5.56	2)	Moskva	23 Jul
	Maria Trösch	Aut	21	5.55	1)	Wien	20 Jul
	Galina Turova	SU	12	5.54	3)	Moskva	23 Jul
1947	Rie Yamauchi	Jap	22	6.07	1)	Sakai	31 Aug
	Gerda Koudijs	Hol	23	5.76	1)	Rotterdam	21 Sep
	Francina Blankers-Koen	Hol	18	5.75	1)	Amsterdam	24 Aug
	Elfriede Brunemann	Ger	20	5.70	1)	Braunschweig	20 Jul
	Aleksandra Chudina	SU	23	5.67	P)	Kharkov	02 Sep
	Yelena Gokieli	SU	18	5.62	2)	Kharkov	31 Aug
	Ursula Ehrhardt	Ger	28	5.61	1)	Schweinfurt	31 Aug
	Lidija Gaile-Leimane	SU	22	5.59	3)	Kharkov	31 Aug
	Loma Lee	GB	31	5.55	1)	Hull	19 Jul
	Ilona Fekete	Hun	26	5.55	1)	Budapest	17 Aug
	With assisting wind:						
	Kaisa Parviainen	Fin	14	5.69	1)	Pori	07 Sep
	Unconfirmed:						
	Elfriede Brunemann	Ger	20	5.75	)		
1948	Olga Gyarmati	Hun	24	5.99	1)	Budapest	29 May
	Francina Blankers-Koen	Hol	18	5.89	1)	Zwolle	04 Jul
	Rie Yamauchi	Jap	22	5.88	1)	Tokyo	28 Aug
	Irmgard Kirchhoff	Ger	21	5.84	1)	Kassel	25 Sep
	Gerda Koudijs-Van der Kade	Hol	23	5.73	1)	Roma	27 Jun
	Nelly Karelse	Hol	26	5.71	1)	Rotterdam	18 Jul
	Joan Shepherd	GB	24	5.70	1)	Chiswick	26 Jun
	Yvonne Chabot-Curtet	Fra	20	5.67	1)	Colombes	15 Aug
	Aleksandra Chudina	SU	23	5.66	P)	Kharkov	10 Sep
	Noemi Simonetto	Arg	28	5.65	Q)	London	04 Aug
	Spomenka Koledin	Yug	29	5.65	1)	Beograd	19 Sep
	With assisting wind:						
	Lena Stumpf	Ger	24	5.72	P)	Hamburg	18 Sep
1949	Elfriede Brunemann-Von Nitzsch	Ger	20	6.21	1)	Hannover	04 Sep
	Lena Stumpf	Ger	24	5.96	2)	Bremen	06 Aug
	Olga Gyarmati	Hun	24	5.95	1)	Budapest	21 Aug
	Irmgard Kirchhoff	Ger	21	5.92	3)	Bremen	06 Aug

Year	Name	Nat	Born	Mark	Pos	Venue	Date
	Nadezhda Khnykina	SU	33	5.82	1)	Tbilisi	17 Oct
	Aleksandra Caudina	SU	23	5.78	1)	Moskva	08 Sep
	Judy Canty	Aus	32	5.77	1)	Sydney	10 Dec
	Yvette Corlett-Williams	NZ	29	5.77	1)	Napier	31 Dec
	Valentina Bogdanova	SU	30	5.76	2)	Tbilisi	17 Oct
	Yvonne Chabot-Curtet	Fra	20	5.71	1)	Colombes	10 Jul
	Ruth Klüver	Ger	27	5.71	4)	Bremen	06 Aug
	Rie Yamauchi	Jap	22	5.71	1)	Tokyo	02 Nov
	With assisting wind:						
	Olga Gyarmati	Hun	24	5.95	1)	Budapest	20 Aug
	Valentina Vasilyeva	SU	21	5.80	2)	Budapest	20 Aug
1950	Aleksandra Chudina	SU	23	5.95	1)	Berlin	27 May
	Leni Hofknecht	WG	29	5.91	1)	München	01 Jul
	Yvette Corlett-Williams	NZ	29	5.90	1)	Auckland	11 Feb
	Olga Gyarmati	Hun	24	5.90	1)	Warszawa	15 Jul
	Valentina Bogdanova	SU	30	5.87	1)	Moskva	20 May
	Kiyoko Sugimura	Jap	29	5.86	1)	Chiba	15 Jul
	Lena Stumpf	WG	24	5.86	1)	Stuttgart	05 Aug
	Judy Canty	Aus	31	5.82	1)	Sydney	21 Jan
	Nadezhda Khnykina	SU	33	5.77	1)	Tbilisi	May
	Yvonne Chabot-Curtet	Fra	20	5.76	1)	Albi	21 Jun
	Exhibition:						
	Judy Canty	Aus	31	5.89	-)	Sydney	22 Feb
	With assisting wind:						
	Judy Canty	Aus	31	6.00	1)	Sydney	18 Feb
	Lena Stumpf	WG	24	5.92	1)	Wilhelmshaven	17 Sep
	Yvonne Chabot-Curtet	Fra	20	5.79	1)	Albi	18 Jun
	Exhibition (and assisting wind):						
	Yvette Corlett-Williams	NZ	29	6.24	-)	Balclutha	09 Dec
1951	Yvette Corlett-Williams	NZ	29	6.13	1)	Melbourne	21 Jan
	Aleksandra Chudina	SU	23	6.11	1)	Minsk	29 Aug
	Kiyoko Sugimura	Jap	29	6.05	1)	Niigata	06 Aug
	Lena Stumpf	WG	24	6.01	1)	Leer	30 Sep
	Olga Gyarmati	Hun	24	5.99	1)	Budapest	19 Oct
	Francina Blankers-Koen	Hol	18	5.90	1)	Amsterdam	22 Jul
	Nadezhda Khnykina	SU	33	5.90	)	Moskva	28 Jul
	Judy Canty	Aus	31	5.86	1)	Sydney	13 Jan
	Lore Fauth	WG	26	5.80	1)	Düsseldorf	29 Jul
	Irmgard Kirchhoff-Schmelzer	WG	21	5.78	1)	Kassel	02 Sep
	Elfriede Brunemann-Von Nietzsch	WG	20	5.78	1)	Braunschweig	08 Sep
1952	Yvette Corlett-Williams	NZ	29	6.24	1)	Helsinki	23 Jul
	Aleksandra Chudina	SU	23	6.14	2)	Helsinki	23 Jul
	Francina Blankers-Koen	Hol	18	6.05	1)	Amsterdam	17 Aug
	Kathleen Russell	Jam	27	6.02	1)	Kingston	30 May
	Valentina Bogdanova-Lituyeva	SU	30	5.98	1)	Leningrad	24 Aug
	Olga Gyarmati	Hun	24	5.96	2)	Kiev	11 Jun
	Ludmila Tsurevich	SU		5.96	3)	Kiev	11 Jun
	Irmgard Kirchhoff-Schmelzer	WG	21	5.94	1)	Kassel	10 Aug
	Verna Johnston	Aus	30	5.93	1)	Belfast	25 Jun
	Anneliese Seonbuchner	WG	29	5.93	)	München	05 Oct
	With assisting wind:						
	Yvette Corlett-Williams	NZ	29	6.29	1)	Hamilton	22 Feb
	Anneliese Seonbuchner	WG	29	5.93	1)	München	04 Oct
1953	Aleksandra Chudina	SU	23	6.24	1)	Budapest	23 Sep
	Olga Gyarmati	Hun	24	6.23	1)	Budapest	20 Sep
	Nadezhda Khnykina-Dvalishvili	SU	33	6.14	2)	Budapest	23 Sep
	Jean Desforges	GB	29	6.10	1)	Nürnberg	30 Aug
	Yvette Corlett-Williams	NZ	29	5.94	)		18 Apr

	Lena Stumpf	WG	24	5.91	1)	Leer	23 Aug
	Tamara Finogenova	SU		5.90	)		
	Anneliese Seonbuchner	WG	29	5.89	1)	Augsburg	26 Jul
	Galina Segen-Sliva	SU	30	5.87	3)	Moskva	23 Aug
	Erika Fisch	WG	34	5.86	2)	Augsburg	26 Jul
	With assisting wind:						
	Fenna Van Heerden	SA		6.04	1)	Tsumeb	25 Apr
	Wilhelmina Lust	Hol	32	5.91	1)	Den Haag	18 Jul
1954	Yvette Corlett-Williams	NZ	29	6.28	1)	Gisborne	20 Feb
	Nadezhda Khnykina-Dvalishvili	SU	33	6.25	1)	Tbilisi	19 May
	Elzbieta Dunska	Pol	33	6.12	1)	Budapest	05 Aug
	Jean Desforges-Pickering	GB	29	6.04	1)	Bern	26 Aug
	Maria Kusion	Pol	36	6.00	2)	Budapest	05 Aug
	Aleksandra Chudina	SU	23	5.99	1)	Kiev	12 Sep
	Galina Segen-Sliva	SU	30	5.97	)		
	Galina Vinogradova-Popova	SU	32	5.97	2)	Kiev	12 Sep
	Erika Fisch	WG	34	5.95i	1)	Frankfurt/M.	20 Mar
	Valentina Bogdanova-Lituyeva	SU	30	5.93	3)	Kiev	12 Sep
1955	Galina Vinogradova-Popova	SU	32	6.31	1)	Tbilisi	18 Nov
	Galina Besborodova	SU	29	6.09	2)	Tbilisi	18 Nov
	Valentina Bogdanova-Liyuyeva	SU	30	6.07	3)	Tbilisi	18 Nov
	Thelma Hopkins	GB	36	6.06	1)	Praha	15 Sep
	Elzbieta Dunska-Krzesinska	Pol	33	6.05	1)	Poznan	05 May
	Aleksandra Caudina	SU	23	6.05	)		
	Nina Tyurkina	SU	31	6.04	1)	Moskva	03 Sep
	Nina Martynenko-Vinogradova	SU	33	6.03	)		
	Maria Sturm	WG	35	5.98	1)	Rosenheim	03 Jul
	Erika Fisch	WG	34	5.98	1)	Bad Pyrmont	16 Oct
1956	Elzbieta Dunska-Krzesinska	Pol	33	6.35	1)	Budapest	20 Aug
	Erika Fisch	WG	34	6.19	1)	Berlin	19 Aug
	Marga Weidner	WG	32	6.15	2)	Berlin	19 Aug
	Nadezhda Khnykina-Dvalishvili	SU	33	6.15	1)	Tashkent	13 Oct
	Sheila Turner-Hoskin	GB	36	6.14	1)	Tooting	05 May
	Galina Segen-Sliva	SU	30	6.14	1)	Kiev	24 Jun
	Ludmila Radchenko-Chen	SU	32	6.14	1)	Kiev	28 Jul
	Nancy Borwick	Aus	35	6.13	1)	Melbourne	17 Nov
	Galina Vinogradova-Popova	SU	32	6.12	1)	Bucuresti	20 Sep
	Thelma Hopkins	GB	36	6.11	1)	Budapest	29 Sep
	With assisting wind:						
	Sheila Turner-Hoskin	GB	36	6.26	1)	Maidstone	07 Jul
	Nancy Borwick	Aus		6.13	1)	Melbourne	17 Apr
	Thelma Hopkins	GB	36	6.12	)	Belfast	05 May
1957	Nina Kazmina	SU	35	6.28	1)	Moskva	17 Aug
	Elzbieta Dunska-Krzesinska	Pol	33	6.27	1)	Chorzów	06 Oct
	Beverly Weigel	NZ	40	6.23	1)	Auckland	09 Feb
	Galina Dolshenkova-Bystrova	SU	34	6.17	P)	Odessa	16 Oct
	Anneliese Seonbuchner	WG	29	6.15	1)	Lindau	08 Sep
	Vilve Maremäe	SU	38	6.11	1)	Leningrad	11 Jul
	Vera Kalashnikova-Krepkina	SU	33	6.03	1)	Paris	05 Sep
	Galina Vinogradova-Popova	SU	32	6.03	1)		
	Christa Seliger-Stubnick	EG	33	6.03	1)	Brno	12 Oct
	Tatyana Demidova	SU	36	6.03	1)	Baku	12 Oct
	With assisting wind:						
	Zlata Rozkosna	Cze	28	6.09	1)	Praha	25 Aug
1958	Beverly Weigel	NZ	40	6.28	1)	Papakura	29 Jun
	Ludmila Radchenko-Chen	SU	32	6.28	1)	Kiev	07 Sep
	Erika Fisch	WG	34	6.21	1)	Köln	29 Aug
	Margaret Matthews	USA	35	6.18	1)	Budapest	06 Aug

	Willye White	USA	39	6.16	1)	Warszawa	02 Aug
	Nina Kazmina-Protshenko	SU	35	6.16	1)	Moskva	28 Aug
	Liesel Jakobi	WG	39	6.14	1)	Stockholm	22 Aug
	Marthe Lambert-Djian	Fra	36	6.13	Q)	Stockholm	21 Aug
	Valentina Shaprunova	SU	37	6.13	1)	Leningrad	31 Aug
	Nelly Yeliseyeva	SU	37	6.11	1)	Moskva	10 May
1959	Valentina Shaprunova	SU	37	6.27	1)	Moskva	17 May
	Gudrun Scheller	WG	40	6.22	1)	Berlin	21 Jun
	Wemmy Scholtmeyer-Spierenberg	Hol	36	6.20	1)	Maastricht	21 Jun
	Zenta Gastl-Kopp	WG	33	6.20	1)	Stuttgart	25 Jul
	Tatiana Demidova-Frolova	SU	36	6.20	2)	Moskva	02 Aug
	Mary Bignal	GB	40	6.19	1)	London	01 Aug
	Waltraud Paluszkiewicz	EG	32	6.19	1)	Bydgoszcz	20 Sep
	Maria Kusion-Bibro	Pol	36	6.18	1)	Kraków	23 May
	Vera Kalashnikova-Krepkina	SU	33	6.17	1)	Philadelphia	19 Jul
	Joke Bijleveld	Hol	40	6.15	1)	Amsterdam	14 Jun
	With assisting wind:						
	Valentina Shaprunova	SU	37	6.38	1)	Warszawa	14 Jun
	Mary Bignal	GB	40	6.30	1)	Chiswick	06 Jun
	Galina Vinogradova-Popova	SU	32	6.19	2)	Warszawa	14 Jun
	Joke Bijleveld	Hol	40	6.16	1)	Den Haag	28 May
	Maria Ilwicka-Chojnacka	Pol	31	6.16	3)	Warszawa	14 Jun
	Renate Junker	WG	38	6.16	1)	Pretoria	28 Nov
1960	Hildrun Claus	EG	39	6.40	1)	Erfurt	07 Aug
	Vera Kalashnikova-Krepkina	SU	33	6.37	1)	Roma	31 Aug
	Mary Bignal	GB	40	6.33	Q)	Roma	31 Aug
	Elzbieta Dunska-Krzesinska	Pol	33	6.32	1)	Moskva	03 Jul
	Valentina Shaprunova	SU	37	6.31	1)	Nalchik	01 May
	Joke Bijleveld	Hol	40	6.28	1)	Frechen	12 Jun
	Ludmila Iyevlyeva	SU	41	6.25	1)	Kharkov	26 Jul
	Maria Kusion-Bibro	Pol	36	6.25	1)	Lódz	31 Aug
	Ludmila Radchenko-Chen	SU	32	6.25	1)	Krasnodar	27 Sep
	Renate Junker	WG	38	6.23	2)	Erfurt	07 Aug
	With assisting wind:						
	Mary Bignal	GB	40	6.39	1)	Warszawa	17 Sep
	Elzbieta Dunska-Krzesinska	Pol	33	6.33	2)	Warszawa	17 Sep
	Sylvia Mitchell	Aus	37	6.24	1)	Sydney	27 Feb
	Hildrun Claus	EG	39	6.24	1)	Budapest	02 Oct

ALL TIME WORLD LIST AS AT THE END OF 1960

Hildrun Claus	EG	39	6.40	1)	Erfurt	07 Aug 60
Vera Kalashnikova-Krepkina	SU	33	6.37	1)	Roma	31 Aug 60
Elzbieta Dunska-Krzesinska	Pol	33	6.35	1)	Budapest	20 Aug 56
Mary Bignal	GB	40	6.33	2)	Roma	31 Aug 60
Galina Vinogradova-Popova	SU	32	6.31	1)	Tbilisi	18 Nov 55
Valentina Shaprunova	SU	37	6.31	1)	Nalchik	01 May 60
Yvette Corlett-Williams	NZ	29	6.28	1)	Gisborne	20 Feb 54
Beverly Weigel	NZ	40	6.28	1)	Papakura	29 Jun 58
Nina Kazmina	SU	35	6.28	1)	Moskva	17 Aug 57
Ludmila Radchenko-Chen	SU	32	6.28	1)	Kiev	07 Sep 58
Joke Bijleveld	Hol	40	6.28	1)	Frechen	12 Jun 60
With assisting wind:						
Mary Bignal	GB	40	6.39	1)	Warszawa	17 Sep 60
Valentina Shaprunova	SU	37	6.38	1)	Warszawa	14 Jun 59
Yvette Corlett-Williams	NZ	29	6.29	1)	Hamilton	22 Feb 52

1961	Tamara Shchelkanova	SU	37	6.48	1)	Moskva	16 Jul
	Willye White	USA	39	6.44	1)	London	21 Jul
	Hildrun Claus	EG	39	6.42	3)	Berlin	23 Jun

	Maria Kusion-Bibro	Pol	36	6.38	1)	Lódz	13 Aug
	Valentina Shaprunova	SU	37	6.36	2)	Tbilisi	03 Oct
	Joke Bijleveld	Hol	40	6.31	1)	Weimar	22 May
	Irina Press	SU	39	6.24	P)	Tbilisi	09 Oct
	Aida Sukhoryabova-Chuyko	SU	36	6.22	1)	Moskva	01 Aug
	Pamela Kilborn	Aus	39	6.21	1)	Melbourne	26 Dec
	Nadezhda Markova	SU	40	6.19	1)	Nalchik	10 May
	Helda Hoffmann	WG	37	6.19	1)	Saarbrücken	10 Jul
	With assisting wind:						
	Tatyana Shchelkanova	SU	37	6.56	1)	Tbilisi	03 Oct
	Valentina Shaprunova	SU	37	6.46	2)	Berlin	23 Jun
	Nina Kazmina-Protschenko	SU	35	6.27	3)	Tbilisi	03 Oct
	Doubtful mark:						
	Helga Hoffmann	WG	37	6.21i	1)	Stuttgart	11 Mar
1962	Tatyana Shchelkanova	SU	37	6.62	1)	Bruxelles	01 Oct
	Helga Hoffmann	WG	37	6.35	1)	Hamburg	27 Jul
	Hildrun Laufer-Claus	EG	39	6.34	1)	Praha	11 Aug
	Joke Bijleveld	Hol	40	6.30	1)	Den Haag	29 Apr
	Elzbieta Dunska-Krzesinska	Pol	33	6.30	1)	Lódz	02 Sep
	Mary Bignal-Rand	GB	40	6.29	Q)	Beograd	14 Sep
	Ingrid Becker	WG	42	6.26	2)	Hamburg	27 Jul
	Teresa Wieczorek-Ciepla	Pol	38	6.22	1)	Poznan	23 Sep
	Renate Junker-Potgieter	WG	38	6.21	2)	Berlin	09 Jun
	Vera Kalashnikova-Krepkina	SU	33	6.21	1)	Kiev	17 Jun
	Bärbel Geissler	EG	42	6.21	3)	Praha	11 Aug
	With assisting wind:						
	Hildrun Laufer-Claus	EG	39	6.41	1)	Praha	03 Jun
	Pamela Kilborn	Aus	39	6.26	1)	Perth	01 Dec
	Helen Frith	Aus	39	6.24	2)	Perth	01 Dec
	Doubtful mark:						
	Edith McGuire	USA	44	6.24	)		
1963	Tatyana Shchelkanova	SU	37	6.60	1)	Kurayoshi	19 Oct
	Vlasta Prikrylova	Cze	43	6.47	1)	Hradec Králove	14 Jul
	Mary Bignal-Rand	GB	40	6.44	1)	London	05 Aug
	Cornelia Bakker	Hol	45	6.34	1)	Den Haag	21 Jul
	Willye White	USA	39	6.34	1)	Braunschweig	30 Jul
	Helga Hoffmann	WG	37	6.32	1)	Augsburg	09 Aug
	Bärbel Geissler	EG	42	6.31	1)	Leipzig	05 Aug
	Claude Bouix	Fra	46	6.26	2)	Den Haag	21 Jul
	Tatyana Kotsar	SU	39	6.26	Q)	Moskva	11 Aug
	Berit Töien	Nor	44	6.23	2)	Tokyo	14 Oct
	With assisting wind:						
	Willye White	USA	39	6.42	1)	Warszawa	27 Jul
1964	Mary Rand	GB	40	6.76	1)	Tokyo	14 Oct
	Tatyana Shchelkanova	SU	37	6.70	1)	Moskva	04 Jul
	Irena Kirszenstein	Pol	46	6.60	2)	Tokyo	14 Oct
	Willye White	USA	39	6.55	-)	Los Angeles	26 Jul
	Aida Chuyko	SU	36	6.49	1)	Kiev	12 Sep
	Hildrun Laufer-Claus	EG	39	6.48	1)	Liberec	18 Jul
	Berit Berthelsen	Nor	44	6.46	2)	London	04 Jul
	Viorica Viscopoleanu	Rum	39	6.46	1)	Bucuresti	12 Sep
	Helga Hoffmann	WG	37	6.45	1)	Lódz	13 Sep
	Ingrid Becker	WG	42	6.40	1)	Kassel	28 May
	With assisting wind:						
	Martha Watson	USA	46	6.47	2)	New York	08 Aug
1965	Tatyana Shchelkanova	SU	37	6.71	1)	Kiev	01 Aug
	Irena Kirszenstein	Pol	46	6.54	1)	Warszawa	20 Jun
	Viorica Viscopoleanu	Rum	39	6.52	1)	Constanza	22 Aug

Year	Name	Nat	Born	Mark	Pos	Venue	Date
	Hsiao Chieh-Ping	Chi	43	6.44	1)	Beijing	30 Jul
	Willye White	USA	39	6.44	1)	München	13 Aug
	Tatyana Talisheva	SU	37	6.41	2)	Kiev	01 Aug
	Mary Rand	GB	40	6.40	1)	London	03 Jul
	Berit Berthelsen	Nor	44	6.40	1)	Oslo	10 Aug
	Helen Frith	Aus	39	6.33	1)	Sydney	13 Feb
	Ingrid Becker	WG	42	6.30	P)	Celje	27 Jun
	Deana Yorgova	Bul	42	6.30	2)	Neon Faliron	11 Sep
	With assisting wind:						
	Ursula Wittmann	WG	44	6.36	1)	Duisburg	06 Aug
	Helga Hoffmann	WG	37	6.30	3)	Kassel	19 Sep
1966	Tatyana Shchelkanova	SU	37	6.73i	1)	Dortmund	27 Mar
	Viorica Viscopoleanu	Rum	39	6.59	1)	Bucuresti	16 Jul
	Irena Kirszenstein	Pol	46	6.55	2)	Minsk	26 Jul
	Mary Rand	GB	40	6.53i	2)	Dortmund	27 Mar
	Heide Rosendahl	WG	47	6.49i	3)	Dortmund	27 Mar
	Deana Yorgova-Prodanova	Bul	42	6.47	1)	Sofia	26 Jun
	Berit Berthelsen	Nor	44	6.39	1)	Oslo	01 Jun
	Maria Vittoria Trio	Ita	39	6.39	1)	Macerata	31 Jul
	Helga Hoffmann	WG	37	6.38	3)	Budapest	03 Sep
	Burghild Wieczorek	EG	43	6.34	1)	Neubrandenburg	05 Jun
	Corrie Bakker	Hol	45	6.34	4)	Budapest	03 Sep
	With assisting wind:						
	Tatyana Shchelkanova	SU	37	6.96	P)	Dnyepropetrovsk	14 Aug
	Ingrid Becker	WG	42	6.51	1)	Osnabrück	22 May
	Tatyana Talisheva	SU	37	6.39	3)	London	17 Jun
1967	Ingrid Becker	WG	42	6.63	1)	Kiev	15 Sep
	Irena Kirszenstein	Pol	46	6.62	1)	Sofia	04 Jun
	Viorica Viscopoleanu	Rum	39	6.56	1)	Mexico City	17 Oct
	Tatyana Talisheva	SU	37	6.56	2)	Mexico City	17 Oct
	Maria Vittoria Trio	Ita	47	6.52	1)	Torino	24 Sep
	Berit Berthelsen	Nor	44	6.51i	1)	Praha	12 Mar
	Mary Rand	GB	40	6.45	1)	Los Angeles	09 Jul
	Eva Kucmanova	Cze	46	6.45	1)	Trinec	02 Sep
	Barbel Lohnert	EG	42	6.43	1)	Frankfurt/O.	02 Jul
	Sheila Parkin	GB	45	6.42	1)	Liverpool	01 Jul
	With assisting wind:						
	Ingrid Becker	WG	42	6.65	1)	Stuttgart	06 Aug
	Corrie Bakker	Hol	45	6.49	1)	Den Haag	15 Oct
1968	Viorica Viscopoleanu	Rum	39	6.82	1)	Mexico City	14 Oct
	Sheila Sherwood	GB	45	6.68	2)	Mexico City	14 Oct
	Irena Kirszenstein-Szewinska	Pol	46	6.67	1)	Warszawa	27 Aug
	Tatyana Talisheva	SU	37	6.66	3)	Mexico City	14 Oct
	Heide Rosendahl	WG	47	6.62	1)	Berlin	18 Aug
	Burghild Wieczorek	EG	43	6.57	1)	Sokolov	21 Jul
	Berit Berthelsen	Nor	44	6.56	1)	Oslo	10 Sep
	Barbel Lohnert	EG	42	6.53	P)	Erfurt	09 Aug
	Ingrid Becker	WG	42	6.52	P)	Hannover	01 Sep
	Manon Bornholdt	WG	50	6.51	2)	Berlin	18 Aug
	With assisting wind:						
	Berit Berthelsen	Nor	44	6.68	1)	Warszawa	29 Jun
	Maria Vittoria Trio	Ita	47	6.58	1)	Roma	18 May
1969	Heide Riosendahl	WG	47	6.64	1)	Leverkusen	08 Jun
	Sieglinde Ammann	Swz	46	6.64	1)	Wien	27 Sep
	Irena Kirszenstein-Szewinska	Pol	46	6.56	1)	Warszawa	20 Jun
	Meta Antenne	Swz	49	6.49	P)	Liestel	06 Jul
	Miroslawa Sarna	Pol	42	6.49	1)	Athinai	19 Sep
	Eva Kucmanova	Cze	46	6.48	2)	Warszawa	20 Jun
	Liese Prokop	Aut	41	6.48	2)	Wien	27 Sep
	Sheila Sherwood	GB	45	6.47	1)	Brno	06 Jul

Year	Athlete	Nation	Born	Mark	Place	Venue	Date
	Viorica Viscopoleanu	Rum	39	6.45	2)	Athinai	19 Sep
	Berit Berthelsen	Nor	44	6.44	3)	Athinai	19 Sep
	With assisting wind:						
	Liese Prokop	Aut	41	6.62	P)	Wien	05 Oct
1970	Heide Rosendahl	WG	47	6.84	1)	Torino	03 Sep
	Sheila Sherwood	GB	45	6.73	1)	Edinburgh	23 Jul
	Ingrid Becker-Mickler	WG	42	6.73	2)	Mainz	19 Sep
	Viorica Viscopoleanu	Rum	39	6.67	1)	Pitesti	03 Oct
	Margrit Herbst	EG	47	6.65	1)	Erfurt	27 Sep
	Ann Wilson	GB	49	6.55	P)	Edinburgh	22 Jul
	Meta Antenen	Swz	49	6.55	1)	Winterthur	12 Sep
	Miroslawa Sarna	Pol	42	6.54i	3)	Wien	14 Mar
	Burghild Wieczorek	EG	43	6.53i	4)	Wien	14 Mar
	Odette Ducas	Fra	40	6.47	1)	Paris	17 Jul
	With assisting wind:						
	Marcia Garbey	Cub	49	6.60	1)	Panama City	01 Mar
	Ann Wilson	GB	49	6.57	2)	Budapest	22 Aug
	Moira Walls	GB	52	6.48	1)	Den Haag	17 May
1971	Margrit Herbst	EG	47	6.81	P)	Leipzig	26 Jul
	Ingrid Becker-Mickler	WG	42	6.76	1)	Helsinki	14 Aug
	Meta Antenen	Swz	49	6.73	2)	Helsinki	14 Aug
	Heide Rosendahl	WG	47	6.72	1)	München	04 Sep
	Sheila Sherwood	GB	45	6.69	1)	Praha	30 Jun
	Irena Kirszenstein-Szewinska	Pol	46	6.62	5)	Helsinki	14 Aug
	Christa Herzog	WG	49	6.60	3)	Stuttgart	10 Jul
	Viorica Viscopoleanu	Rum	39	6.53i	3)	Sofia	13 Mar
	Heidi Schuller	WG	50	6.52i	2)	Kiel	27 Feb
	Helena Ringa	SU	47	6.51	1)	Yerevan	09 Oct
	With assisting wind:						
	Meta Antenen	Swz	49	6.81	1)	Basel	25 Jul
	Irena Kirszenstein-Szewinska	Pol	46	6.67	1)	Edinburgh	12 Jun
1972	Heide Rosendahl	WG	47	6.78	1)	München	31 Aug
	Deana Yorgova	Bul	42	6.77	2)	München	31 Aug
	Margrit Olfert	EG	47	6.72	1)	Dresden	12 Aug
	Angelika Liebsch	EG	50	6.69	Q)	München	31 Aug
	Eva Suranová	Cze	46	6.67	3)	München	31 Aug
	Lynnette Tillett	Aus	53	6.60	1)	München	23 Aug
	Brigitte Roesen	WG	44	6.58i	1)	Grenoble	12 Mar
	Kristina Albertus	EG	45	6.58	1)	Dresden	28 May
	Heidi Räbiger	EG	49	6.57	1)	Berlin	13 Aug
	Martha Watson	USA	46	6.55	1)	Modesto	27 May
	With assisting wind:						
	Heide Rosendahl	WG	47	6.83	P)	München	03 Sep
	Lynnette Tillett	Aus	53	6.62	1)	Perth	25 Mar
	Kristina Albertus	EG	45	6.59	1)	Jena	20 May
	Irena Kirszenstein-Szewinska	Pol	46	6.57	1)	Edinburgh	16 Jun
1973	Angela Schmalfeld	EG	51	6.76	1)	Dresden	21 Jul
	Margrit Olfert	EG	47	6.63	1)	Moskva	20 Aug
	Margarite Treinite	SU	49	6.62	1)	Vilnius	02 Sep
	Tuula Rautanen	Fin	42	6.60	1)	Warszawa	04 Aug
	Deana Yorgova	Bul	42	6.58i	1)	Sofia	03 Mar
	Martha Watson	USA	46	6.58	1)	Minsk	24 Jul
	Radojka Franzoti	Yug	52	6.55	1)	Fürth	10 Jun
	Kristina Albertus	EG	45	6.54	[illegible])	Dresden	21 Jul
	Djurdica Focic	Yug	48	6.54	1)	Zagreb	21 Jul
	Erica Nixon	Aus	53	6.53	P)	Sydney	28 Oct
	With assisting wind:						
	Ilona Bruzsenyák	Hun	50	6.83	P)	Innsbruck	11 Aug
	Kristina Albertus	EG	45	6.61	2)	Dresden	21 Jul

Year	Name	Nat	Born	Mark	Pl	Venue	Date
1974	Angela Schmalfeld	EG	51	6.77	1)	Berlin	24 Aug
	Marianne Voelzke	EG	56	6.77	2)	Berlin	24 Aug
	Meta Antenen	Swz	49	6.69i	1)	Göterborg	10 Mar
	Eva Suranová	Cze	46	6.67	1)	München	11 Sep
	Lidia Alfeyeva	SU	46	6.66	1)	Moskva	24 Jul
	Ilona Bruzsenyak	Hun	50	6.65	1)	Roma	03 Sep
	Maroula Lambrou	Gre	53	6.62	1)	Sofia	02 Aug
	Martha Watson	USA	46	6.59	1)	Stockholm	18 Jul
	Ildiko Szabó	Hun		6.59	2)	Budapest	21 Jul
	Pirkko Helenius	Fin		6.59	3)	Roma	03 Sep
	With assisting wind:						
	Eva Suranová	Cze	46	6.74	1)	Edinburgh	27 Jul
	Jarmila Nygrynova	Cze	53	6.66	1)	Praha	19 Jun
	Martha Watson	USA	46	6.65	1)	Modesto	24 May
	Tuula Rautanen	Fin		6.62	1)	Tampere	18 Jun
	Brenda Eisler	Can		6.60	2)	Modesto	24 May
1975	Lidia Alfeyeva	SU	46	6.76	1)	Nice	17 Aug
	Ildiko Szabo	Hun		6.66	1)	Budapest	25 Jul
	Isabella Keller-Lusti	Swz	53	6.65	-)	Winterthur	07 Jun
	A. Alexander	Cub		6.63	1)	Mexico City	14 Oct
	M. Garbey	Cub		6.62	1)	Habana	05 Sep
	Angela Voigt	EG	51	6.61	1)	Erfurt	23 Aug
	Kathyy McMillan	USA	57	6.58	1)	Praha	08 Jul
	Martha Watson	USA	46	6.57	2)	Mexico City	14 Oct
	Ch. Striezel	WG		6.56	2)	Nice	17 Aug
	M. Dlugosielska	Pol		6.54	1)	Bydgoszcz	29 Jun
	With assisting wind:						
	Isabella Keller-Lusti	Swz	53	6.82	1)	Winterthur	07 Jun
	Ilona Bruszenyák	Hun	50	6.61	1)	Budapest	04 Jun
1976	Siegrun Siegl	EG	54	6.99	1)	Dresden	19 May
	Angela Voigt	EG	51	6.92	1)	Dresden	09 May
	Lidia Alfeyeva	SU	46	6.79	1)	Paris	10 Jul
	Kathy McMillan	USA	57	6.78	1)	Los Angeles	12 Jun
	Lilyana Panajotova	Bul	56	6.71	1)	Sofia	09 May
	Heidemarie Wycisk	EG	49	6.71	2)	Berlin	10 Jul
	Jarmila Nygrynova	Cze	53	6.70	1)	Praha	22 Aug
	Ildiko Erdelyi	Hun	55	6.66	1)	Budapest	22 Aug
	Brigitte Künzel-Wujak	EG	55	6.64	1)	Berlin	02 Jun
	D. Spinu	Rum		6.60	1)	Pescara	06 Jun
	L. Barsuk	SU		6.60	2)	Kiev	22 Jun
	With assisting wind:						
	Heidemarie Wycisk	EG	49	6.86	2)	Dresden	09 May
	Marianne Voelzke	EG	56	6.75	3)	Dresden	09 May
	Elena Vintila	Rum	46	6.74	1)	Athinai	01 Jul
	Maroula Lambrou	Gre	53	6.71	1)	Athinai	05 Sep
	D. Catineanu	Rum		6.63	2)	Athinai	01 Jul
	S. Walker	USA		6.61	2)	Eugene	19 Jun
1977	Vilma Bardauskiene	SU	53	6.82	1)	Krasnodar	22 Sep
	Brigitte Künzel-Wujak	EG	55	6.76	-)	Dresden	03 Jul
	Heidemarie Wycisk	EG	49	6.76	2)	Dresden	03 Jul
	Ildikó Erdelyi	Hun	55	6.76	1)	Nyiregiháza	09 Oct
	Jodi Anderson	USA	57	6.68	1)	Sochi	02 Jul
	Alina Gheorghiu	Rum	51	6.68	1)	Bucuresti	17 Jul
	Jarmila Nygrynová	Cze	53	6.68	1)	Trinec	06 Aug
	Tatyana Skachko	SU	54	6.67i	1)	Donetsk	18 Jan
	M. Krauze ??	SU		6.62	1)	Donetsk	11 Sep
	Irina Timofeyeva	SU	53	6.62	1)	Dnyepropetrovsk	11 Sep
	With assisting wind:						
	Brigitte Künzel-Wujak	EG	55	6.87	1)	Dresden	03 Jul
	Susan Reeve	GB	51	6.84	1)	Edinburgh	25 Jun

	Alina Gheorghiu	Rum	51	6.72	1)	Budapest	14 Jun
	Maryna van Niekerk	SA	54	6.67	1)	Pretoria	01 Dec
1978	Vilma Bardauskiene	SU	53	7.09	Q)	Praha	29 Aug
	Jodi Anderson	USA	57	6.90	1)	Westwood	10 Jun
	Sigrun Siegl	EG	54	6.79	2)	Dresden	12 Aug
	Angela Voigt	EG	51	6.79	2)	Praha	30 Aug
	Jarmila Nygrynová	Cze	53	6.74	1)	Praha	12 Aug
	Brigitte Wujak	EG	55	6.73	3)	Dresden	12 Aug
	Kathy McMillan	USA	57	6.72	2)	Westwood	10 Jun
	Gina Panait	Rum	58	6.71	19	Bucuresti	03 Jun
	Lynette Jacenko	Aus	53	6.70	1)	Brisbane	18 Mar
	Anita Stukane	SU	54	6.69	1)	Kishinyov	23 Aug
	With assisting wind:						
	Angela Voigt	EG	51	6.87	1)	Dresden	12 Aug
1979	Brigitte Künzel-Wujak	EG	55	6.90	1)	Potsdam	29 Jul
	Anita Stukane	SU	54	6.80	1)	Mexico City	12 Sep
	Yekaterina Smirnova	SU	56	6.78	P)	Quebec City	12 Aug
	Angela Voigt	EG	51	6.77	2)	Potsdam	29 Jul
	Ramona Neubert	EG	58	6.73	1)	Dresden	13 Jun
	Siegrun Siegel	EG	54	6.70i	1)	Wien	24 Feb
	Irina Palyenko	SU	55	6.70	1)	Baku	23 Sep
	Susan Reeve	GB	51	6.69	1)	Fürth	10 Jun
	Susan Hearnshaw	GB	61	6.68	1)	London	22 Sep
	Jodi Anderson	USA	57	6.67	2)	Mexico City	12 Sep
	With assisting wind:						
	Jodi Anderson	USA	57	6.89	1)	Colorado Springs	30 Jul
	Sabine Everts	WG	61	6.69	P)	Wilhelmshaven	14 Jul
	Maroula Lambrou	Gre	53	6.67	1)	Athinai	10 Aug
1980	Tatyana Kolpakova	SU	59	7.06	1)	Moskva	31 Jul
	Brigitte Künzel-Wujak	EG	55	7.04	2)	Moskva	31 Jul
	Tatyana Skachko	SU	54	7.01	3)	Moskva	31 Jul
	Jodi Anderson	USA	57	7.00	1)	Eugene	28 Jun
	Anna Wlodarczyk	Pol	51	6.95	4)	Moskva	31 Jul
	Siegrun Siegel	EG	54	6.87	5)	Moskva	31 Jul
	Sigrid Heimann	EG	58	6.85	1)	Potsdam	10 May
	Lidiya Alfeyeva	SU	46	6.84	2)	Moskva	12 Jun
	Yarmila Nygrynová	Cze	53	6.83	6)	Moskva	31 Jul
	Natalya Alyoshina	SU	56	6.81	P)	Moskva	20 Jun
	Margarita Butkiene	SU	49	6.81	1)	Vilnius	17 Aug
	With assisting wind:						
	Kathy McMillan	USA	57	6.91	1)	Houston	03 May
	Ramona Neubert	EG	58	6.83	P)	Halle	04 May

ALL TIME WORLD LIST AS AT THE END OF 1980

Vilma Bardauskiene	SU	53	7.09	Q)	Praha	29 Aug 78
Tatyana Kolpakova	SU	59	7.06	1)	Moskva	31 Jul 80
Brigitte Künzel-Wujak	EG	55	7.04	2)	Moskva	31 Jul 80
Tatyana Skachko	SU	54	7.01	3)	Moskva	31 Jul 80
Jodi Anderson	USA	57	7.00	1)	Eugene	28 Jun 80
Siegrun Siegl	EG	54	6.99	1)	Dresden	19 May 76
Anna Wlodarczyk	Pol	51	6.95	4)	Moskva	31 Jul 80
Angela Voigt	EG	51	6.92	1)	Dresden	09 May 76
Sigrid Heimann	EG	58	6.85	1)	Potsdam	10 May 80
Heide Rosendahl	WG	47	6.84	1)	Torino	03 Se0p 70
Lidiya Alfeyeva	SU	46	6.84	2)	Moskva	12 Jun 80
With assisting wind:						
Tatyana Shchelkanova	SU	37	6.96	P)	Dnyepropetrowsk	14 Aug 66

Year	Name	Nation	Born	Mark	Place	Venue	Date
	Kathy McMillan	USA	57	6.91	1)	Houston	03 May 80
	Heidemarie Wycisk	EG	49	6.86	2)	Dresden	09 May 76
	Susan Reeve	GB	51	6.84	1)	Edinburgh	25 Jun 77
1981	Jodi Anderson	USA	57	6.96	1)	Colorado Springs	23 Jul
	Anisoara Cusmir	Rum	62	6.91	1)	Bucuresti	23 May
	Heike Daute	EG	64	6.91	1)	Jena	09 Aug
	Ramona Neubert	EG	58	6.90	-)	Dresden	14 Jun
	Sigrid Ulbricht	EG	58	6.90	2)	Jena	09 Aug
	Anna Wlodarczyk	Pol	51	6.88	1)	Warszawa	23 Jul
	Margarita Butkiene	SU	49	6.83	1)	Kishinyov	29 Jun
	Tatyana Kolpakova	SU	59	6.83	1)	Bucuresti	25 Jul
	Tatyana Skachko	SU	54	6.80	1)	Tbilisi	26 Jun
	Irina Timofeyeva	SU	53	6.78	1)	Kharkov	27 Aug
	With assisting wind:						
	Heike Daute	EG	64	7.02	1)	Utrecht	20 Aug
	Ramona Neubert	EG	58	7.00	1)	Dresden	14 Jun
	Anke Weigt	WG	57	6.81	1)	Rhede	17 May
	Christina Sussiek	WG	60	6.81	1)	Gelsenkirchen	18 Jul
1982	Vali Ionescu	Rum	60	7.20	1)	Bucuresti	01 Aug
	Anisoara Cusmir	Rum	62	7.15	2)	Bucuresti	01 Aug
	Heike Daute	EG	64	6.98	1)	Potsdam	18 Aug
	Tatyana Skachko	SU	54	6.92	1)	Voroshilovgrad	23 Aug
	Jodi Anderson	USA	57	6.91	-)	Indianapolis	25 Jul
	Sabine Möbius	EG	57	6.90	H)	Magdeburg	23 May
	Jarmila Strejcková	Cze	53	6.89	1)	Praha	18 Sep
	Ramona Neubert	EG	58	6.88	1)	Potsdam	10 Jun
	Brigitte Wujak	EG	55	6.86	2)	Potsdam	18 Aug
	Svetlana Zorina	SU	60	6.86	1)	Kiev	21 Aug
	With assisting wind:						
	Jodi Anderson	USA	57	6.93	1)	Indianapolis	25 Jul
	Shonel Ferguson	Bah	57	6.91	1)	Brisbane	08 Oct
	Robyne Strong	Aus	61	6.88	2)	Brisbane	08 Oct
1983	Anisoara Cusmir	Rum	62	7.43	1)	Bucuresti	04 Jun
	Heike Daute	EG	64	7.14	1)	Bratislava	04 Jun
	Svetlana Zorina	SU	60	7.04	1)	Moskva	20 Jun
	Tatyana Proskuryakova	SU	56	7.04	1)	Kiev	25 Aug
	Margarita Butkiené	SU	49	7.00	1)	Vilnius	25 May
	Carol Lewis	USA	63	6.97	1)	Luxemburg	20 Jul
	Vali Ionescu	Rum	60	6.92i	2)	Bucuresti	19 Feb
	Eva Murková	Cze	62	6.9\2	1)	Banska Bystrica	11 Jun
	Tatyana Turulina	SU	58	6.90	1)	Krasnodar	26 May
	Bev Kinch	GB	64	6.90	-)	Helsinki	14 Aug
	With assisting wind:						
	Heike Daute	EG	64	7.27	1)	Helsinki	14 Aug
	Carol Lewis	USA	63	7.04	3)	Helsinki	14 Aug
	Bev Kinch	GB	64	6.99	5)	Helsinki	14 Aug
1984	Heike Daute	EG	64	7.40	1)	Dresden	26 Jul
	Galina Chistyakova	SU	62	7.29	1)	Moskva	06 Aug
	Anisoara Cusmir-Stanciu	Rum	62	7.27	1)	Sofia	17 Jun
	Helga Radtke	EG	62	7.21	2)	Dresden	26 Jul
	Sabine Paetz	EG	57	7.12	2)	Dresden	19 May
	Vali Ionescu	Rum	60	7.11	1)	Madrid	21 Jun
	Yelena Kokonova	SU	63	7.09	1)	Donyetsk	09 Sep
	Tatyana Proskuryakova	SU	56	7.02	1)	Moskva	09 Jul
	Niole Medvedyeva	SU	60	7.02	4)	Praha	17 Aug
	Eva Murkova	Cze	62	7.01	1)	Bratislava	26 May
	Yelena Ivanova	SU	61	7.01	2)	Moskva	09 Jul
	With assisting wind:						
	Eva Murkova	Cze	62	7.17	1)	Nitra	26 Aug
	Carol Lewis	USA	63	7.03	1)	San Jose	26 May

Year	Athlete	Nation	Born	Mark	Place	Venue	Date
1985	Heike Drechsler	EG	64	7.44	1)	Berlin	22 Sep
	Yelena Kokonova	SU	63	7.31	1)	Alma-Ata	12 Sep
	Galina Chistyakova	SU	62	7.28	1)	Moskva	18 Aug
	Jackie Joyner	USA	62	7.24	2)	Zurich	21 Aug
	Helga Radtke	EG	62	7.19	4)	Zurich	21 Aug
	Irina Valyukevich	SU	59	7.07	2)	Leningrad	01 Aug
	Yelena Yatsuk	SU	61	7.04	1)	Moskva	08 Jun
	Carol Lewis	USA	63	7.04	5)	Zurich	21 Aug
	Marina Kibakina	SU	60	7.01	1)	Krasnoyarsk	10 Aug
	Yelena Belevskaya	SU	63	7.00	3)	Leningrad	01 Aug
1986	Heike Drechsler	EG	64	7.45	1)	Tallinn	21 Jun
	Galina Chistyakova	SU	62	7.34	2)	Tallinn	21 Jun
	Yelena Belevskaya	SU	63	7.31	1)	Kiev	15 Jul
	Irena Ozhenko	SU	62	7.20	1)	Budapest	12 Sep
	Larisa Berezhnaya	SU	61	7.19	1)	Krasnodar	22 Jun
	Helga Radtke	EG	62	7.17	1)	Rieti	07 Sep
	Jackie Joyner	USA	62	7.12	2)	Bruxelles	05 Sep
	Vali Ionescu	Rum	60	7.10	1)	Pitesti	28 Jun
	Irina Valyukevich	SU	59	7.07	3)	Moskva	07 Jul
	Svetlana Zorina	SU	60	7.01	1)	Volgograd	06 Sep
	With assisting wind:						
	Jackie Joyner	USA	62	7.15	2)	Rieti	07 Sep
	Irina Valyukevic	SU	59	7.10	4)	Tallinn	21 Jun
1987	Jackie Joyner-Kersee	USA	62	7.45	1)	Indianapolis	13 Aug
	Heike Drechsler	EG	64	7.40	1)	Potsdam	21 Aug
	Yelena Byelevskaya	SU	63	7.39	1)	Bryansk	18 Jul
	Galina Chistyakova	SU	62	7.27	1)	Moskva	22 Aug
	Irina Valyukevich	SU	59	7.17	2)	Bryansk	18 Jul
	Helga Radtke	EG	62	7.16	2)	Berlin	08 Jul
	Svetlana Zorina	SU	60	7.07	1)	Krasnodar	15 Aug
	Yelena Ivanova	SU	61	7.05	2)	Moskva	07 Jun
	Vali Ionescu	Rum	60	7.04	1)	Pitesti	09 Aug
	Niole Medvedyeva	SU	60	7.01i	1)	Vilnius	25 Jan
	With assisting wind:						
	Helga Radtke	EG	62	7.19	1)	Berlin	25 Aug
1988	Galina Chistyakova	SU	62	7.52	1)	Leningrad	11 Jun
	Heike Drechsler	EG	64	7.48	1)	Neubrandenburg	09 Jul
	Jackie Joyner-Kersee	USA	62	7.40	1)	Seoul	29 Sep
	Yelena Byelevskaya	SU	63	7.36	2)	Leningrad	11 Jun
	Yeledna Kokonova	SU	63	7.29	1)	Alma-Ata	18 Jun
	Inessa Kravets	SU	66	7.27	1)	Kiev	22 May
	Yolanda Chen	SU	61	7.16	1)	Moskva	30 Jul
	Niole Medvedyeva	SU	60	7.14	1)	Riga	04 Jun
	Valy Ionescu	Rum	60	7.08	1)	Bucuresti	19 Jun
	Larisa Bereznaya	SU	61	7.07	4)	Leningrad	11 Jun
	With assisting wind:						
	Jackie Joyner-Kersee	USA	62	7.45	1)	Indianapolis	23 Jul
	Irina Valyukevich	SU	59	7.07	5)	Leningrad	11 Jun
1989	Galina Chistyakova	SU	62	7.30i	1)	Lipetsk	28 Jan
	Larisa Berezhnaya	SU	61	7.20i	1)	Gomel	04 Feb
	Helga Radtke	EG	62	7.15	1)	Rostock	22 Jun
	Marieta Ilcu	Rum	62	7.08	1)	Potesti	25 Jun
	Yolanda Chen	SU	61	7.05i	2)	Gomel	04 Feb
	Niole Medvedyeva	SU	60	6.98	1)	Vilnius	06 Aug
	Vali Ionescu	Rum	60	6.93	1)	Bucuresti	17 Sep
	Yelena Kokonova	SU	63	6.89i	1)	Karaganda	28 Jan
	Liu Shuzhen	Chi	66	6.89	1)	Qingdao	03 Jun
	Inessa Kravets	SU	66	6.88i	3)	Gomel	04 Feb
	With assisting wind:						
	Galina Chistyakova	SU	62	7.36	1)	Volgograd	11 Jun

Year	Athlete	Nat	Born	Mark	Pos	Venue	Date
	Fiona May	GB	69	6.98	1)	Jarrow	04 Jun
1990	Galina Chistyakova	SU	62	7.35	1)	Bratislava	20 Jun
	Heike Drechsler	EG	64	7.30	1)	Split	28 Aug
	Jackie Joyner-Kersee	USA	62	7.12	2)	Rieti	09 Sep
	Inessa Kravets	SU	66	7.10	1)	São Paulo	20 May
	Larisa Berezhnaya	SU	61	7.10	2)	São Paulo	20 May
	Yelena Khlopotnova	SU	63	7.06i	1)	Chelyabinsk	03 Feb
	Marita Ilcu	Rum	62	7.06	3)	Bratislava	20 Jun
	Yolanda Chen	SU	61	7.03i	2)	Chelyabinsk	03 Feb
	Helga Radtkle	EG	62	6.97	1)	Leipzig	16 May
	Liu Shuzhen	Chi	66	6.92	1)	Beijing	24 Jun
	With assisting wind:						
	Larisa Berezhnaya	SU	61	7.13	1)	Chiba	10 Jun
	Yolanda Chen	SU	61	7.11	1)	Lahti	09 Aug
1991	Heike Drechsler	Ger	64	7.37	1)	Sestriere	31 Jul
	Jackie Joyner-Kersee	USA	62	7.32	1)	Tokyo	25 Aug
	Larisa Berezhnaya	SU	61	7.24	1)	Granada	25 May
	Yelena Sinchukova	SU	61	7.20	1)	Budapest	20 Jun
	Susen Tiedtke	Ger	69	7.00	2)	Seoul	18 Aug
	Inessa Kravets	SU	66	6.95	2)	Granata	25 May
	Ludmila Ninova	Aut	60	6.95	4)	Sevilla	30 May
	Yelana Khlopotnova	SU	63	6.94	1)	Kiev	19 Jun
	Helga Radtke	Ger	62	6.94	)	Hamburg	14 Jul
	Marieta Ilcu	Rum	62	6.89i	1)	Bacau	17 Feb
	With assisting wind:						
	Heike Drechsler	Ger	64	7.39	1)	Padova	15 Sep
	Yelena Byelevskaya	SU	63	7.21	1)	Lisboa	28 Jul
	Fiona May	GB	69	6.91	1)	Derby	07 Jul
1992	Heike Drechsler	Ger	64	7.48	1)	Lausanne	08 Jul
	Inessa Kravets	Ukr	66	7.37	1)	Kiev	13 Jun
	Jackie Joyner-Kersee	USA	62	7.17	1)	New York	24 May
	Mirela Dulgheru	Rum	66	7.14	1)	Sofia	05 Jul
	Larisa Berezhnaya	Ukr	61	7.08i	2)	Moskva	01 Feb
	Chioma Ajunwa	Nig	70	7.06	1)	Lagos	12 Jun
	Yelena Sinchukova	Rus	61	7.04	2)	Duisburg	07 Jun
	Marita Ilcu	Rum	62	6.98	1)	Potesti	12 Jun
	Yelena Khlopotnova	Ukr	63	6.95	1)	Kiev	30 May
	Ludmila Ninova	Aut	60	6.92	1)	St.Denis	04 Jun
	Doubtful measurement:						
	Antonella Capriotti	Ita	62	7.09	1)	Roma	02 Jul
	With assisting wind:						
	Heike Drechsler	Ger	64	7.63	1)	Sestriere	21 Jul
	Larisa Berezhnaya	Ukr	61	7.15	3)	Villeneuve d'Ascq	06 Jul
	Susen Tiedtke	Ger	69	7.02	2)	Sestriere	21 Jul
	Ludmila Ninova	Aut	60	7.00	1)	São Paulo	17 May
	Ringa Ropo	Fin	66	6.93	3)	Sestriere	21 Jul
1993	Heike Drechsler	Ger	64	7.21	1)	Zurich	04 Aug
	Jackie Joyner-Kersee	USA	62	7.08	1)	Berlin	27 Aug
	Ludmila Ninova	Aut	60	7.06	2)	Sevilla	05 Jun
	Irina Mushayilova	Rus	67	7.02	2)	Lausanne	07 Jul
	Yao Weili	Chi	68	7.01	1)	Jinan	03 Jun
	Mirela Dulghero	Rum	66	6.99i	1)	Bacau	23 Jan
	Larisa Berezhnaya	Ukr	61	6.99	5)	Sevilla	05 Jun
	Ma Miaolan	Chi	70	6.97	1)	Beijing	10 Sep
	Marieta Ilcu	Rum	62	6.94i	1)	Liévin	13 Feb
	Yolanda Chen	Rus	61	6.90i	2)	Moskva	27 Feb
	With assisting wind:						
	Susan Tiedtke	Ger	69	7.19	1)	Sestriere	28 Jul
	Jakie Joyner-Kersee	USA	62	7.09	1)	San Jose	29 May

Year	Athlete	Nat	Born	Mark	Pos	Venue	Date
	Ma Miaolan	Chi	70	7.06	1)	Beijing	10 Sep
	Inessa Kravets	Ukr	66	7.02	3)	Sevilla	05 Jun
	Yelena Khlopotnova	Ukr	63	7.01	4)	Sevilla	05 Jun
	Yelena Sinchukova	Rus	61	6.94	6)	Sevilla	05 Jun
1994	Jackie Joyner-Kersee	USA	62	7.49	1)	New York	22 May
	Heike Drechsler	Ger	64	7.29	2)	Oslo	22 Jul
	Irina Mushayilova	Rus	67	7.20	1)	St.Peterburg	14 Jul
	Ludmila Ninova	Aut	60	7.09	1)	Sevilla	05 Jun
	Inessa Kravets	Ukr	66	7.09	1)	Zurich	17 Aug
	Yelena Khlopotnova	Ukr	63	7.03	1)	Kharkov	30 May
	Renata Nielsen	Den	66	6.96	-)	Sevilla	05 Jun
	Fiona May	Ita	69	6.95	-)	Sestriere	31 Jul
	Yao Weili	Chi	68	6.91	1)	Hiroshima	15 Oct
	Larisa Berezhnaya	Ukr	61	6.89i	2)	Sindelfingen	06 Mar
	Agata Karczmarek	Pol	63	6.89	1)	Valencia	12 Jun
	With assisting wind:						
	Heike Drechsler	Ger	64	7.39	2)	Sestriere	31 Jul
	Renata Nielsen	Den	66	7.09	2)	Sevilla	05 Jun
	Fiona May	Ita	69	7.00	3)	Sestriere	31 Jul
	Valentina Uccheddu	Ita	66	6.96	4)	Sestriere	31 Jul
	Iva Prandzheva	Bul	72	6.95	1)	Sofia	15 May
	Viktoria Vershinina	Ukr	71	6.90	2)	Duisburg	12 Jun
1995	Heike Drechsler	Ger	64	7.09i	1)	Liévin	19 Feb
	Inessa Kravets	Ukr	66	6.97	1)	Moskva	05 Jun
	Fiona May	Ita	69	6.96	-)	Villeneuve d'Ascq	25 Jun
	Lyudmila Galkina	Rus	72	6.95i	1)	Barcelona	12 Mar
	Nadine Caster	Fra	64	6.94	3)	Villeneuve d'Ascq	25 Jun
	Niki Xanthou	Gre	73	6.94	1)	Patra	23 Jul
	Svetlana Moskalets	Rus	69	6.93	1)	Götzis	28 May
	Yelena Khlopotnova	Ukr	63	6.92	1)	Kiev	26 May
	Irina Mushayilova	Rus	67	6.90i	2)	Barcelona	12 Mar
	Susen Tiedtke-Greene	Ger	69	6.90i	3)	Barcelona	12 Mar
	Sharon Couch	USA	67	6.90	1)	Houston	19 May
	Olga Rublyova	Rus	74	6.90	-)	Villeneuve d'Ascq	25 Jun
	Exhibition:						
	Viktoria Vershinina	Ukr	71	6.98	1)	Iglesias	10 Sep
	Valentina Uccheddu	Ita	66	6.90	2)	Iglesias	10 Sep
	With assisting wind:						
	Fiona May	Ita	69	7.23	1)	Sestriere	29 Jul
	Marieke Veltman	USA	71	7.14	2)	Sestriere	29 Jul
	Niki Xanthou	Gre	73	7.12	3)	Sestriere	29 Jul
	Nicole Boegman	Aus	67	7.12	4)	Sestriere	29 Jul
	Valentina Uccheddu	Ita	66	7.07	5)	Sestriere	29 Jul
	Olga Rublyova	Rus	74	7.01	1)	Moskva	16 Jun
	Diane Guthrie-Gresham	Jam	71	6.92	H)	Knoxville	03 Jun
1996	Jackie Joyner-Kersee	USA	62	7.20	1)	Atlanta	18 May
	Chioma Ajunwa	Nig	71	7.12	1)	Atlanta	02 Aug
	Inessa Kravets	Ukr	66	7.05	1)	Bellinzona	12 Jul
	Fiona May	Ita	69	7.02	2)	Atlanta	02 Aug
	Niki Xanthou	Gre	73	7.01	1)	Hania	08 Jun
	Shana Williams	USA	72	7.01	Q)	Atlanta	21 Jun
	Yelena Shekhovtsova	Ukr	72	6.97	5)	Atlanta	02 Aug
	Heike Drechsler	Ger	64	6.96i	1)	Stuttgart	04 Feb
	Magdalna Khristova	Bul	77	6.94	2)	Kalamata	22 Jun
	Viktoriya Vershinina	Ukr	71	6.93	1)	Kiev	10 May
	Exhibition:						
	Viktoriya Vershinina	Ukr	71	6.94	-)	Iglesias	06 Sep
	With assisting wind:						
	Fiona May	Ita	69	7.12	1)	Bologna	25 May

Year	Athlete	Nat	Born	Mark	Pos	Venue	Date
	Inessa Kravets	Ukr	66	7.07	1)	Padova	07 Jul
	Ludmila Ninova	Aut	60	7.01	2)	Atlanta	18 May
1997	Lyudmila Galkina	Rus	72	7.05	1)	Athinai	09 Aug
	Niki Xanthou	Gre	73	7.03	1)	Bellinzona	18 Aug
	Xiong Qiying	Chi	67	7.03	Q)	Shanghai	21 Oct
	Chioma Ajunwa	Nig	70	7.01	Q)	Athinai	07 Aug
	Fiona May	Ita	69	6.97	1)	Torino	24 Jun
	Heike Drechsler	Ger	64	6.95i	1)	Stuttgart	02 Feb
	Agata Karczmarek	Pol	63	6.95	1)	Bydgoszcz	21 Jun
	Marion Jones	USA	75	6.93	1)	Indianapolis	15 Jun
	Yelena Shekhovtsova	Ukr	72	6.88	1)	Kiev	12 Jul
	Susen Tiedtke-Greene	Ger	69	6.86	1)	Frankfurt	28 Jun
	Guan Yingnan	Chi	77	6.86	2)	Shanghai	22 Oct
	With assisting wind:						
	Sharon Couch	USA	67	7.07	1)	El Paso	12 Apr
	Heike Drechsler	Ger	64	7.02	1)	Jena	25 May
	Fiona May	Ita	69	6.98	1)	Padova	08 Jun
	Jackie Joyner-Kersee	USA	62	6.91	2)	Indianapolis	15 Jun
	Viktoriya Vershinina	Ukr	71	6.88	1)	Hania	31 May
	Questionable circumstances:						
	Valerie Williams	USA	79	6.89w	1)	Rockville	16 May
1998	Marion Jones	USA	75	7.31	1)	Eugene	31 May
	Heike Drechsler	Ger	64	7.16	1)	Budapest	22 Aug
	Fiona May	Ita	69	7.11	2)	Budapest	22 Aug
	Lyudmila Galkina	Rus	72	6.99	1)	Helsinki	13 Jun
	Shana Williams	USA	72	6.97	1)	Philadelphia	25 Apr
	Tatyana Ter-Mesrobyan	Rus	68	6.94	2)	Hania	27 May
	Niurka Montalvo	Cub	68	6.93	1)	Rieti	30 Aug
	Dawn Burrell	USA	73	6.92i	1)	Atlanta	28 Feb
	Magdalena Khristova	Bul	77	6.91i	1)	Stockholm	19 Feb
	Susen Tiedtke	Ger	69	6.91	3)	Athinai	17 Jun
	Guan Yingnan	Chi	77	6.91	1)	Linz	05 Jul
	With assisting wind:						
	Lyudmila Galkina	Rus	72	7.06	3)	Budapest	22 Aug
	Tatyana Kotova	Rus	76	6.97	1)	Hania	27 May
1999	Mauren Maggi	Bra	76	7.26	1)	Bogotá	26 Jun
	Niurka Montalvo	Spa	68	7.06	1)	Sevilla	23 Aug
	Fiona May	Ita	69	7.04	Q)	Sevilla	21 Aug
	Marion Jones	USA	75	7.01	1)	Raleigh	12 Jun
	Eunice Barber	Fra	74	7.01	1)	Paris	21 Jul
	Tatyana Kotova	Rus	76	6.99	1)	Leverkusen	05 Sep
	Niki Xanthou	Gre	73	6.98	1)	Kalamáta	22 May
	Dawn Burrell	USA	73	6.96	1)	Eugene	25 Jun
	Lyudmila Galkina	Rus	72	6.95	1)	Moskva	05 Jun
	Paraskevi Tsiamita	Gre	72	6.93	1)	Patra	01 Aug
	With assisting wind:						
	Lyudmila Galkina	Rus	72	7.08	1)	Thessaloniki	23 Jun
	Tatyana Kotova	Rus	76	7.01	2)	Thessaloniki	23 Jun
	Niki Xanthou	Gre	73	7.01	3)	Thessaloniki	23 Jun
	Iva Prandzheva	Bul	72	6.97	1)	Ankara	23 May
	Erica Johansson	Swe	74	6.95	1)	Göteborg	04 Sep
2000	Fiona May	Ita	69	7.09	1)	Rio de Janeiro	14 May
	Tatyana Kotova	Rus	76	7.04	1)	St.Denis	23 Jun
	Marion Jones	USA	75	7.02	1)	Sacramento	16 Jul
	Inessa Kravets	Ukr	66	7.00	1)	Kiev	15 Jul
	Lissette Cuza	Cub	75	6.99	1)	Jena	03 Jun
	Erica Johansson	Swe	74	6.99	-)	Lausanne	05 Jul
	Heike Drechsler	Ger	64	6.99	1)	Sydney	29 Sep
	Dawn Burrell	USA	73	6.98	1)	Stockholm	01 Aug

Guan Yingnan	Chi	77	6.95	1)	Tianjin	03 May
Maurren Maggi	Bra	76	6.93	2)	Rio de Janeiro	14 May

With assisting wind:

Erica Johansson	Swe	74	7.07	1)	Vygieskraal	15 Jan
Heike Drechsler	Ger	64	7.07	1)	Doha	05 Oct
Dawn Burrell	USA	73	6.99	2)	Doha	05 Oct
Niurka Montalvo	Spa	68	6.95	1)	La Laguna	15 Jul

Pending - Positive drugs test:

Inessa Kravets	Ukr	66	7.10w	1)	Barcelona	25 Jul

ALL TIME WORLD LIST AS AT THE END OF 2000

Galina Chistyakova	Rus	62	7.52	1)	Leningrad	11 Jun 88
Jackie Joyner-Kersee	USA	62	7.49	1)	New York	22 May 94
Heike Drechsler	Ger	64	7.48	1)	Neubrandenburg	09 Jul 88
Anisoara Cusmir-Stanciu	Rum	62	7.43	1)	Bucuresti	04 Jun 83
Yelena Byelevskaya	Bye	63	7.39	1)	Bryansk	18 Jul 87
Inessa Kravets	Ukr	66	7.37	1)	Kiev	13 Jun 92
Yelena Kokonova	Ukr	63	7.31	1)	Alma-Ata	12 Sep 85
Marion Jones	USA	75	7.31	1)	Eugene	31 May 98
Maurren Maggi	Bra	76	7.26	1)	Bogotá	26 Jun 99
Larisa Berezhnaya	Ukr	61	7.24	1)	Granada	25 May 91

With assisting wind:

Heike Drechsler	Ger	64	7.63	1)	Sestriere	21 Jul 92

2001	Tatyana Kotova	Rus	76	7.12	1)	Torino	09 Jun
	Dawn Burrell	USA	73	7.03i	1)	Lisboa	10 Mar
	Lyudmila Galkina	Rus	72	7.00i	1)	Moskva	16 Feb
	Fiona May	Ita	69	6.97	-)	Edmonton	07 Aug
	Eunice Barber	Fra	74	6.97	1)	Zurich	17 Aug
	Maurren Maggi	Bra	76	6.94	1)	Brisbane	07 Sep
	Niurka Montalvo	Spa	68	6.91	3)	Thessaloniki	22 Aug
	Valentina Gotovska	Lat	65	6.88	2)	Torino	09 Jun
	Bronwyn Thompson	Aus	78	6.88	2)	Brisbane	07 Sep
	Erica Johansson	Swe	74	6.87	1)	Fort-de-France	28 Apr
	With assisting wind:						
	Fiona May	Ita	69	7.02	1)	Edmonton	07 Aug
	Maurren Maggi	Bra	76	6.98	1)	São Caetano do Sul	21 Apr
	Elva Goulbourne	Jam	80	6.90	1)	Odessa, TX	11 May
2002	Tatyana Kotova	Rus	76	7.42	1)	Annecy	23 Jun
	Tatyana Ter-Mesrobyan	Rus	68	7.06	1)	St.Peterburg	22 May
	Maurren Maggi	Bra	76	7.02	1)	Paris	14 Sep
	Bronwyn Thompson	Aus	78	7.00	1)	Melbourne	07 Mar
	Elva Goulbourne	Jam	80	6.91i	1)	Fayetteville	23 Feb
	Concepción Montaner	Spa	81	6.89	1)	Castellón	01 Jun
	Niki Xanthou	Gre	73	6.85	1)	Patra	14 Jul
	Heike Drechsler	Ger	64	6.85	1)	Leverkusen	27 Jul
	Niurka Montalvo	Spa	68	6.83	1)	Madrid	03 Jul
	Oksana Rogova	Rus	78	6.79	1)	Bryansk	12 Jun
	With assisting wind:						
	Maurren Maggi	Bra	76	7.17	1)	São Paulo	13 Apr
	Niurka Montalvo	Spa	68	7.00	1)	Valencia	15 Jun
2003	Maurren Maggi	Bra	76	7.06	1)	Milano	03 Jun
	Eunice Barber	Fra	74	7.05	1)	Monaco	14 Sep
	Tatyana Kotova	Rus	76	6.94	1)	Réthimno	06 Jul
	Olga Rublyova	Rus	74	6.89	1)	Tula	09 Aug
	Carolina Klüft	Swe	83	6.86	1)	Bydgoszcz	19 Jul
	Elva Goulbourne	Jam	80	6.83	1)	Knoxville	17 May

Year	Name	Nat	Born	Mark	Pl	Venue	Date
	Irina Simagina	Rus	82	6.83	1)	Cheboksary	28 Jun
	Tatyana Lebedeva	Rus	76	6.82	1)	Moskva	20 Sep
	Stiliani Pilátou	Gre	80	6.80i	1)	Athinai	04 Mar
	Inessa Kravets	Ukr	66	6.79i	1)	Sumy	23 Feb
	With assisting wind:						
	Grace Upshaw	USA	75	6.99	1)	Glasgow	29 Jun
	Elva Goulbourne	Jam	80	6.96	1)	St.George's	05 Jul
2004	Tatyana Lebedeva	Rus	76	7.33	1)	Tula	31 Jul
	Irina Simagina	Rus	82	7.27	2)	Tula	31 Jul
	Elva Goulbourne	Jam	80	7.16	1)	Mexico City	22 May
	Marion Jones	USA	75	7.11	1)	Sacramento	15 Jul
	Tatyana Kotova	Rus	76	7.05	3)	Athinai	27 Aug
	Carolina Klüft	Swe	83	6.97	H)	Tallinn	04 Jul
	Bronwyn Thompson	Aus	78	6.96	4)	Athinai	27 Aug
	Olga Rublyova	Rus	74	6.88	2)	Réthimno	23 Jun
	Grace Upshaw	USA	75	6.84	-)	Eugene	19 Jun
	Anju Bobby George	Ind	77	6.83	6)	Athinai	27 Aug
	With assisting wind:						
	Marion Jones	USA	75	7.13	1)	Carson	22 May
	Grace Upshaw	USA	75	6.88	2)	Eugene	19 Jun
2005	Irina Simagina	Rus	82	7.04	1)	Sochi	26 May
	Tatyana Kotova	Rus	76	6.96	1)	Tula	13 Jul
	Concepción Montaner	Spa	81	6.92	2)	Madrid	16 Jul
	Tianna Madison	USA	85	6.89	1)	Helsinki	10 Aug
	Carolina Klüft	Swe	83	6.87	H)	Helsinki	07 Aug
	Oksana Udmurtova	Rus	82	6.86	1)	Kazan	25 Jun
	Viktoriya Molchanova	Ukr	82	6.81i	1)	Kharkov	19 Jan
	Ineta Radevica	Lat	81	6.80	1)	Tallinn	19 Jun
	Eunice Barber	Fra	74	6.80	1)	Paris	03 Sep
	Lyudmila Kolchanova	Rus	79	6.79	1)	Izmir	16 Aug
	With assisting wind:						
	Tatyana Kotova	Rus	76	7.20	1)	Madrid	16 Jul
	Tianna Madison	USA	85	6.92	1)	Nashville	14 May
	Carolina Klüft	Swe	83	6.92	1)	Göteborg	28 Aug
	Marshevet Hooker	USA	84	6.89	1)	Manhattan,KS	14 May
	Yargelis Savigne	Cub	84	6.88	1)	Nassau	11 Jul
	Grace Upshaw	USA	75	6.87	3)	Madrid	16 Jul
	Niurka Montalvo	Spa	68	6.87	4)	Madrid	16 Jul
	Maho Hanaoka	Jap	76	6.82	1)	Osaka	07 May
	Eva Goulbourne	Jam	80	6.81	6)	Madrid	16 Jul
	Rose Richmond	USA	81	6.79	7)	Madrid	16 Jul
2006	Tatyana Kotova	Rus	76	7.12	1)	Novosibirsk	26 Aug
	Lyudmila Kolchanova	Rus	79	7.11	1)	Tula	15 Jul
	Oksana Udmurtova	Rus	82	7.02	2)	Doha	12 May
	Bronwyn Thompson	Aus	78	6.97	1)	Melbourne	24 Mar
	Tatyana Lebedeva	Rus	76	6.97	2)	Doha	12 May
	Natalya Lebusova	Rus	78	6.93	2)	Tula	15 Jul
	Kumiko Ikeda	Jap	81	6.86	1)	Osaka	06 May
	Rose Richmond	USA	81	6.84	-)	Indianapolis	24 Jun
	Maurren Maggi	Bra	76	6.84	1)	Bogotá	15 Jul
	Akiba McKinney	USA	79	6.83	1)	Walnut	15 Apr
	Hrisopiyi Devetzi	Gre	76	6.83	1)	Trikala	10 Jun
	With assisting wind:						
	Tatyana Lebedeva	Rus	76	7.09	1)	Zaragoza	03 Jun
	Rose Richmond	USA	81	6.93	1)	Indianapolis	24 Jun
	Viktoriya Rybalko	Ukr	82	6.87	1)	Kiev	21 Jul
	Maurren Maggi	Bra	76	6.86	1)	Tunja	30 Sep
	Naide Gomes	Por	79	6.84	2)	Göteborg	01 Aug
2007	Lyudmila Kolchanova	Rus	79	7.21	1)	Sochi	27 May
	Tatyana Lebedeva	Rus	76	7.15	1)	Madrid	21 Jul

	Irina Simagina	Rus	82	7.11	2)	Sochi	27 May
	Naide Gomes	Por	79	7.01	2)	Madrid	21 Jul
	Maurren Maggi	Bra	76	6.95	Q)	Osaka	27 Aug
	Karen Mey	SA	84	6.93	1)	Bad Langensalza	07 Jul
	Oksana Udmurtova	Rus	82	6.92	2)	Moskva	29 Jun
	Tatyana Kotova	Rus	76	6.90	3)	Moskva	29 Jun
	Bianca Kappler	Ger	77	6.90	2)	Bag Langensalza	07 Jul
	Natalya Lebusova	Rus	78	6.89	3)	Sochi	27 May
	With assisting wind:						
	Tatyana Kotova	Rus	76	7.10	1)	Albufeira	27 May
	Rhonda Watkins	Tri	87	6.96	1)	Sacramento	07 Jun
2008	Naide Gomes	Por	79	7.12	1)	Monaco	29 Jul
	Lyudmila Kolchanova	Rus	79	7.04	1)	Annecy	22 Jun
	Maurren Maggi	Bra	76	7.04	1)	Beijing	22 Aug
	Tatyana Lebedeva	Rus	76	7.03	2)	Beijing	22 Aug
	Irina Simagina	Rus	82	6.96i	1)	Stockholm	21 Feb
	Brittney Reese	USA	86	6.95	1)	Eugene	03 Jul
	Karen Mey-Melis	Tur/SA	84	6.93	2)	Bad Langensalza	07 Jun
	Funmi Jimoh	USA	84	6.91	1)	Houston	29 May
	Blessing Okagbare	Nig	86	6.91	3)	Beijing	22 Aug
	Concepción Montaner	Spa	81	6.89	1)	Ávila	20 Jul
	With assisting wind:						
	Bianca Kappler	Ger	77	6.97	1)	Bad Langensalza	07 Jun
2009	Brittney Reese	USA	86	7.10	1)	Berlin	23 Aug
	Naide Gomes	Por	79	6.99	1)	London	25 Jul
	Tatyana Lebedeva	Rus	76	6.97	2)	Berlin	23 Aug
	Funmi Jimoh	USA	84	6.96	2)	Doha	08 May
	Yelena Sokolova	Rus	86	6.92	1)	Cheboksary	24 Jul
	Olga Kucherenko	Rus	85	6.91	4)	Moskva	01 Jul
	Irina Meleshina	Rus	82	6.91	1)	Rieti	06 Sep
	Maurren Maggi	Bra	76	6.90	3)	Doha	08 May
	Hyleas Fountain	USA	81	6.89	1)	Luzern	15 Jul
	Ksenija Baita	Est	86	6.87i	1)	Torino	07 Mar
	Karin Mey-Melis	Tur	84	6.87	1)	Leverkusen	31 Jul
	With assisting wind:						
	Hyleas Fountain	USA	81	6.95	H)	Eugene	28 Jun
	Blessing Okagbare	Nig	86	6.90	1)	Tulsa	15 May
2010	Olga Kucherenko	Rus	85	7.13	1)	Sochi	27 May
	Darya Klishina	Rus	91	7.03	1)	Zhukovskiy	26 Jun
	Lyudmila Kolchanova	Rus	79	7.01	1)	Saransk	13 Jul
	Brittney Reese	USA	86	6.94	1)	Lausanne	08 Jul
	Ineta Radevica	Lat	81	6.92	1)	Barcelona	28 Jul
	Naide Gomes	Por	79	6.92	2)	Barcelona	28 Jul
	Yargelis Saligne	Cub	84	6.91	1)	Reims	30 Jun
	Chaunté Lowe	USA	84	6.90	2)	Des Moines	26 Jun
	Tatyana Kotova	Rus	76	6.90	2)	Saransk	13 Jul
	Hyleas Fountain	USA	81	6.89	2)	Nottwil	08 Aug
	With assisting wind:						
	Brittney Reese	USA	86	7.08	1)	Des Moines	26 Jun
	Yelena Sokolova	Rus	86	6.90	3)	Zhukovskiy	26 Jun

ALL TIME WORLD LIST AS AT THE END OF 2010

Galina Chistyakova	Rus	62	7.52	1)	Leningrad	11 Jun 88
Jackie Joyner-Kersee	USA	62	7.49	1)	New York	22 May 94
Heike Drechsler	Ger	64	7.48	1)	Neubrandenburg	09 Jul 88
Anisoara Cusmir-Stanciu	Rum	62	7.43	1)	Bucuresti	04 Jun 83
Tatyana Kotova	Rus	76	7.42	1)	Annecy	23 Jun 02

Yelena Byelevskaya	Bye	63	7.39	1)	Bryansk	18 Jul 87
Inessa Kravets	Ukr	66	7.37	1)	Kiev	13 Jun 92
Tatyana Lebedeva	Rus	76	7.33	1)	Tula	31 Jul 04
Yelena Kokonova	Ukr	83	7.31	1)	Alma-Ata	12 Sep 85
Marion Jones	USA	75	7.31	1)	Eugene	31 May 98
With assisting wind:						
Heike Drechsler	Gerr	64	7.63	1)	Sestriere	21 Jul 92

TRIPLE JUMP

Best mark as at the end of 1900:							
Mary Ayer		USA		6.72i	1)	Bryn Mawr	21 Apr 99
Best mark as at the end of 1920:							
Ellen Hayes		USA		10.21	1)	Sweetbriar	07 Apr 13
Best mark as at the end of 1980:							
Rie Yamaguchi		Jap	22	11.66	)		21 Oct 39
1987	Li Huirong	Chi	65	14.04	1)	Hamamatsu	11 Oct
	Galina Chistyakova	SU	62	13.98i	1)	Moskva	25 Jan
	Vali Ionescu	Rum	60	13.93i	1)	Inglewood	21 Feb
1988	Li Huirong	Chi	65	14.16	1)	Shijazhuang	23 Apr
	Wendy Brown	USA	66	13.82	1)	Tampa	17 Jun
	Sheila Hudson	USA	67	13.79	1)	Modesto	07 May
	Yvette Bates	USA	65	13.64i	1)	Oklahoma City	12 Mar
	Renita Robinson	USA	67	13.56i	1)	Lincoln	13 Feb
	With assisting wind:						
	Sheila Hudson	USA	67	13.92	1)	Eugene	04 Jun
1989	Galina Chistyakova	SU	62	14.52	1)	Stockholm	03 Jul
	Inna Lisovskaya	SU	69	14.40i	1)	Moskva	26 Feb
	Li Huirong	Chi	65	14.34	1)	Shanghai	16 Sep
	Sheila Hudson	USA	67	13.90	1)	San Jose	15 Apr
	Inara Tsurko	SU	66	13.88	1)	Bryansk	10 Sep
	Natalya Kayukova	SU	68	13.78	2)	Bryansk	10 Sep
	Tatyana Fyodorova	SU	67	13.74	1)	Sochi	14 May
	Irina Privalova	SU	68	13.72i	2)	Moskva	26 Feb
	Rina Babakova	SU	65	13.69i	1)	Donyetsk	04 Mar
	Yelena Chicherova	SU	58	13.68i	1)	Lipetsk	22 Jan
	Yelena Semiraz	SU	65	13.68	1)	Temopol	27 May
	With assisting wind:						
	Sheila Hudson	USA	67	14.01	2)	Hiroshima	03 May
1990	Li Huirong	Chi	65	14.54	1)	Sapporo	25 Aug
	Galina Chistyakova	SU	62	14.15i	1)	Moskva	14 Jan
	Inna Lasovskaya	SU	69	14.09i	1)	Moskva	25 Feb
	Inessa Kravets	SU	66	14.08i	2)	Moskva	25 Feb
	Sofia Bozhanova	Bul	67	14.06	1)	Sofia	03 Jun
	Sheila Hudson	USA	67	14.04	1)	Durham	02 Jun
	Li Jing	Chi	69	13.97	2)	Beijing	26 Jun
	Irina Babakova	SU	65	13.92	1)	Moskva	03 Jun
	Tatyana Fyodorova	SU	67	13.83i	3)	Moskva	25 Feb
	Olga Kontsevaya	SU	72	13.80	1)	Sochi	13 May
	With assisting wind:						
	Sheila Hudson	USA	67	14.07	1)	Norwalk	15 Jun

Note: From 1 Jan. 1990 the women's triple jump became an event officially recognized by the IAAF.
The first mark ratified as a world record was Li Huirong's 14.54, made at the Chuhei Nambu Memorial in Sapporo.

Year	Name	Nat	Born	Mark	Pos	Venue	Date
1991	Inessa Kravets	SU	66	14.95	1)	Moskva	10 Jun
	Li Huirong	Chi	65	14.42	1)	Beijing	04 Jun
	Yelena Semiraz	SU	65	14.35	2)	Kiev	13 Jul
	Natalya Kayukova	SU	66	14.09	1)	Vladivostok	18 Aug
	Sofia Bozhanova	Bul	67	14.08	1)	Plovdiv	02 Jun
	Inna Lasovskaya	SU	69	14.05	3)	Kiev	13 Jul
	Galina Chistyakova	SU	62	14.04	2)	Malmö	05 Aug
	Tatyana Matyashova	SU	73	13.85	1)	Sochi	25 May
	Svetlana Davydova	SU	71	13.84	1)	Samara	02 Jun
	Zhanna Gureyeva	SU	70	13.84	1)	Staiki	26 Jun
	With assisting wind:						
	Concepción Paredes	Spa	70	13.90	1)	Soria	10 Aug
1992	Galina Chistyakova	Rus	62	14.62	1)	Villeneuve-d'Ascq	13 Sep
	Li Huirong	Chi	65	14.55	1)	Sapporo	19 Jul
	Inessa Kravets	Ukr	66	14.41	1)	Oslo	04 Jul
	Helga Radtke	Ger	62	14.30	1)	Rostock	20 May
	Sheila Hudson	USA	67	14.23	1)	New Orleans	20 Jun
	Natalya Kayukova	Rus	66	14.21i	1)	Moskva	28 Feb
	Zhang Yan	Chi	72	14.14	1)	Wuhan	18 Oct
	Inna Lasovskaya	Rus	69	14.13i	1)	Moskva	18 Jan
	Yelena Sinchukova	Rus	61	14.09	2)	Villeneuve d'Ascq	13 Sep
	Eloisa Echevarria	Cub	61	14.07	1)	Habana	14 May
	With assisting wind:						
	Helga Radtke	Ger	62	14.44	1)	Rostock	01 May
1993	Ana Biryukova	Rus	67	15.09	1)	Stuttgart	21 Aug
	Yolanda Chen	Rus	61	14.97	1)	Moskva	18 Jun
	Irina Mushailova	Rus	67	14.79	1)	Stockholm	05 Jul
	Irina Lasovskaya	Rus	69	14.70	2)	Bratislava	01 Jun
	Niurka Montalvo	Cub	68	14.51	1)	Habana	22 May
	Inessa Kravets	Ukr	66	14.49	3)	Stockholm	05 Jul
	Galina Chistyakova	Rus	62	14.40	2)	London	23 Jul
	Ren Ruiping	Chi	76	14.29	1)	Beijing	13 Sep
	Zhang Yan	Chi	72	14.28	2)	Beijing	13 Sep
	Iva Prandzheva	Bul	72	14.23	3)	Stuttgart	21 Aug
	With assisting wind:						
	Iva Prandzheva	Bul	72	14.32	1)	Sofia	03 Jul
	Previously disqualified for drugs use:						
	Inessa Kravets	Ukr	66	14.70	1)	Nice	21 Jul
1994	Sofia Bozhanova	Bul	67	14.98	1)	Stara Zagora	16 Jul
	Inna Lasovskaya	Rus	69	14.94	1)	Bratislava	01 Jun
	Inessa Kravets	Ukr	66	14.91	2)	Bratislava	01 Jun
	Anna Biryukova	Rus	67	14.89	1)	Helsinki	08 Aug
	Niurka Montalvo	Cub	68	14.60	1)	Habana	24 Jun
	Yolanda Chen	Rus	61	14.58	2)	Stockholm	12 Jul
	Rodica Petrescu	Rum	71	14.47	1)	Bucuresti	18 Jun
	Natalya Kayukova	Rus	66	14.47	1)	Sochi	10 Sep
	Sárka Kaspárková	Cze	71	14.46i	4)	Paris	13 Mar
	Helga Radtke	Ger	62	14.46	1)	Erfurt	03 Jul
1995	Inessa Kravets	Ukr	66	15.50	1)	Göteborg	10 Aug
	Iva Prandzheva	Bul	72	15.18	2)	Göteborg	10 Aug
	Anna Biryukova	Rus	67	15.08	3)	Göteborg	10 Aug
	Yolanda Chen	Rus	61	15.03i	1)	Barcelona	11 Mar
	Inna Lasovskaya	Rus	69	14.90	1)	Göteborg	10 Aug
	Rodica Petrescu	Rum	71	14.80	1)	Bucuresti	19 Jul
	Galina Chistyakova	Rus	62	14.76	1)	Luzern	27 Jun
	Ashia Hansen	GB	71	14.66	1)	Gateshead	21 Aug
	Mariya Sokova	Rus	70	14.54i	1)	Volgograd	24 Feb
	Irina Mushayilova	Rus	67	14.46i	2)	Volgograd	24 Feb

	With assisting wind:						
	Inna Lasovskaya	Rus	69	15.05	1)	Sevilla	03 Jun
	Galina Chistyakova	Rus	62	14.84	1)	Innsbruck	28 Jun
	Ren Ruiping	Chi	76	14.83	1)	Taiyuan	21 May
	Rodica Pertrescu	Rum	71	14.82	5)	Göteborg	10 Aug
	Sheila Hudson	USA	67	14.66	1)	Sacramento	17 Jun
1996	Inessa Kravets	Ukr	66	15.33	1)	Atlanta	31 Jul
	Inna Lasovskaya	Rus	69	15.08	1)	Madrid	12 Jun
	Sárka Kaspárková	Cze	71	14.98	3)	Atlanta	31 Jul
	Iva Prandzheva	Bul	72	14.82i	1)	Liévin	18 Feb
	Ashia Hansen	GB	71	14.78	2)	Sheffield	25 Aug
	Teresa Marinova	Bul	77	14.62	1)	Sydney	25 Aug
	Yelena Govorova	Ukr	73	14.60	Q)	Atlanta	29 Jul
	Anna Biryukova	Rus	67	14.56	1)	Mito	06 May
	Ren Ruiping	Chi	76	14.56	Q)	Atlanta	29 Jul
	Jelena Blazevica	Lat	70	14.55	1)	Riga	08 Jun
	With assisting wind:						
	Yelena Govorova	Ukr	73	14.75	1)	Kiev	07 Jun
	Sheila Hudson	USA	67	14.56	1)	El Paso	13 Apr
	Drugs disqualification:						
	Iva Prandzheva	Bul	72	14.72	4)	Atlanta	31 Jul
1997	Sárka Kaspárková	Cze	71	15.20	1)	Athinai	04 Aug
	Rodica Petrescu-Mateescu	Rum	71	15.16	2)	Athinai	04 Aug
	Ashia Hansen	GB	71	15.15	1)	Fukuoka	13 Sep
	Inna Lasovskaya	Rus	69	15.09	1)	Valencia	31 May
	Gundega Sproge	Lat	72	14.76	3)	Sheffield	29 Jun
	Yelena Govorova	Ukr	73	14.67	3)	Athinai	04 Aug
	Ren Ruiping	Chi	76	14.66	1)	Hiroshima	29 Apr
	Anna Biryukova	Rus	67	14.64	1)	Tula	10 Jul
	Olga Vasdeki	Gre	73	14.62	4)	Athinai	04 Aug
	Yelena Donkina	Rus	73	14.58	2)	Tula	10 Jul
	With assisting wind:						
	Jelena Blazevica	Lat	70	14.75	1)	Kaunas	23 Aug
1998	Ashia Hansen	GB	71	15.16i	1)	Valencia	28 Feb
	Iva Prandzheva	Bul	72	15.12	1)	Tokyo	19 Sep
	Rodica Mateescu	Rum	71	15.01	1)	Villeneuve d'Ascq	11 Jul
	Sárka Kaspárková	Cze	71	14.98	1)	Rovereto	26 Aug
	Tereza Marinova	Bul	77	14.67	2)	Athinai	17 Jun
	Fiona May	Ita	69	14.65	1)	St.Peterburg	27 Jun
	Olga Vasdeki	Gre	73	14.64	1)	Johannesburg	11 Sep
	Yelena Lebedenko	Rus	71	14.57i	1)	Moskva	13 Feb
	Yamilé Aldama	Cub	72	14.55	1)	La Habana	02 Aug
	Adelina Gavrila	Rum	78	14.53	2)	Bucuresti	02 Aug
	With assisting wind:						
	Tatyana Lebedeva	Rus	76	14.58	1)	Formia	12 Jul
1999	Paraskevi Tsiamita	Gre	72	15.07	Q)	Sevilla	22 Aug
	Ashia Hansen	GB	71	15.02i	1)	Maebashi	07 Mar
	Iva Prandzheva	Bul	72	14.94i	2)	Maebashi	07 Mar
	Tatyana Lebedeva	Rus	76	14.89	1)	Moskva	05 Jun
	Sárka Kaspárková	Cze	71	14.87i	3)	Maebashi	07 Mar
	Yamilé Aldama	Cub	72	14.77	1)	Winnipeg	28 Jul
	Tereza Marinova	Bul	77	14.76i	1)	Pireás	24 Feb
	Yelena Lebedenko	Rus	71	14.74i	1)	Moskva	15 Jan
	Adelina Gavrila	Rum	78	14.71	1)	Bucuresti	12 Jun
	Cristina Nicolau	Rum	77	14.70	1)	Göteborg	01 Aug
	Françoise Mbango	Cam	76	14.70	1)	Johannesburg	18 Sep
	With assisting wind:						
	Yelena Govorova	Ukr	73	14.99	1)	Palma de Mallorca	11 Jul

2000	Tatyana Lebedeva	Rus	76	15.32	1)	Yokohama	09 Sep
	Tereza Marinova	Bul	77	15.20	1)	Sydney	24 Sep
	Iva Prandzheva	Bul	72	15.04	1)	Sofia	17 Jun
	Yelena Govorova	Ukr	73	14.96	4)	Sydney	24 Sep
	Cristina Nicolau	Rum	77	14.94i	1)	Bucuresti	05 Feb
	Anja Valant	Slo	77	14.69	3)	Kalamáta	04 Jun
	Yelena Lebedenko	Rus	71	14.66i	1)	Samara	30 Jan
	Natalya Safronova	Bye	74	14.65	1)	Stayki	03 Jun
	Inessa Kravets	Ukr	66	14.57	1)	Ljubljana	10 Jun
	Anastasiya Ilyima	Rus	82	14.52	Q)	Santiago de Chile	20 Oct

ALL TIME WORLD LIST AS AT THE END OF 2000

Inessa Kravets	Ukr	66	15.50	1)	Göteborg	10 Aug 95
Tatyana Lebedeva	Rus	76	15.32	1)	Yokohama	09 Sep 00
Sarká Kaspárková	Cze	71	15.20	1)	Athinai	04 Aug 97
Tereza Marinova	Bul	77	15.20	1)	Sydney	24 Sep 00
Iva Prandzheva	Bul	72	15.18	2)	Göteborg	10 Aug 95
Rodica Mateescu	Rum	71	15.16	2)	Athinai	04 Aug 97
Ashia Hansen	GB	71	15.16i	1)	Valencia	28 Feb 98
Anna Biryukova	Rus	67	15.09	1)	Stuttgart	21 Aug 93
Inna Lasovskaya	Rus	69	15.09	1)	Valencia	31 May 97
Paraskevi Tsiamita	Gre	72	15.07	Q)	Sevilla	22 Aug 99

2001	Tatyana Lebedeva	Rus	76	15.25	1)	Edmonton	10 Aug
	Tereza Marinova	Bul	77	14.91i	1)	Lisboa	11 Mar
	Yelena Lebedenko	Rus	71	14.83i	1)	Samara	01 Feb
	Huang Qiuyan	Chi	80	14.72	1)	Guangzhou	22 Nov
	Françoise Mbango	Cam	76	14.65	1)	St.Etienne	30 Jun
	Cristina Nicolau	Rum	77	14.62	1)	Ottawa	22 Jul
	Nadezhda Bazhenova	Rus	78	14.60	1)	Moskva	23 Jun
	Yelena Oleynikova	Rus	76	14.59	2)	Tula	15 Jul
	Magdelin Martinez	Ita	76	14.59	Q)	Edmonton	08 Aug
	Irina Vasilyeva	Rus	79	14.57	2)	Moskva	23 Jun
	Natalya Safronova	Bye	74	14.57	2)	Beijing	01 Sep
	With assisting wind:						
	Trecia Smith	Jam	75	14.88	1)	Lawrence	21 Apr
2002	Françoise Mbango	Cam	76	14.95	1)	Radés	06 Aug
	Ashia Hansen	GB	71	14.86	1)	Manchester	31 Jul
	Yelena Oleynikova	Rus	76	14.83	1)	Praha	17 Jun
	Tereza Marinova	Bul	77	14.81i	1)	Wien	02 Mar
	Magdelin Martinez	Ita	76	14.73	1)	Rieti	08 Sep
	Oksana Rogova	Rus	78	14.70i	1)	Volgograd	06 Feb
	Anna Pyatykh	Rus	81	14.67	1)	Annecy	22 Jun
	Nadezhda Bazhenova	Rus	78	14.65i	1)	Pireás	20 Feb
	Huang Qiuyan	Chi	80	14.60	1)	Shizuoka	03 May
	Yelena Lebedenko	Rus	71	14.56i	2)	Moskva	07 Jan
	With assisting wind:						
	Ashia Hansen	GB	71	15.00	1)	München	10 Aug
	Heli Koivula	Fin	75	14.83	2)	München	10 Aug
2003	Yamilé Aldama	Sud	72	15.29	1)	Roma	11 Jul
	Tatyana Lebedeva	Rus	76	15.18	1)	St.Denis	26 Aug
	Françoise Mbango	Cam	76	15.05	2)	St.Denis	26 Aug
	Ashia Hansen	GB	71	15.01i	1)	Birmingham	15 Mar
	Kène Ndoye	Sen	78	14.91	1)	Villeneuve d'Ascq	15 Jun
	Magdelin Martinez	Ita	76	14.90	3)	St.Denis	26 Aug
	Hrisopiyi Devetzi	Gre	76	14.84i	1)	Athinai	04 Mar
	Yelena Govorova	Ukr	73	14.81	2)	Villeneuve d'Ascq	15 Jun
	Anna Pyatykh	Rus	81	14.79	1)	Firenze	21 Jun
	Adelina Gavrila	Rum	78	14.76i	1)	Bucuresti	22 Feb

Year	Athlete	Nat	Born	Mark	Pos	Venue	Date
2004	Tatyana Lebedeva	Rus	76	15.36i	1)	Budapest	06 Mar
	Hrisopiyi Devetzi	Gre	76	15.32	Q)	Athinai	21 Aug
	Françoise Mango-Etone	Cam	76	15.30	1)	Athinai	23 Aug
	Yamilé Aldama	Sud	72	15.28	1)	Linz	02 Aug
	Trecia Smith	Jam	75	15.16	2)	Linz	02 Aug
	Magdelin Martinez	Ita	76	15.03	1)	Roma	26 Jun
	Kène Ndoye	Sen	78	15.00	2)	Iráklio	04 Jul
	Baya Rahouli	Alg	79	14.89	Q)	Athinai	21 Aug
	Anna Pyatykh	Rus	81	14.85	1)	Bydgoszcz	19 Jun
	Yelena Govorova	Ukr	73	14.78	3)	Bydgoszcz	19 Jun
	With assisting wind:						
	Magdelin Martinez	Ita	76	15.24	1)	Sestriere	01 Aug
2005	Tatyana Lebedeva	Rus	76	15.11	1)	St.Denis	01 Jul
	Trecia Smith	Jam	75	15.11	1)	Helsinki	07 Aug
	Baya Rahouli	Alg	79	14.98	1)	Almeria	01 Jul
	Hrisopiyi Devetzi	Gre	76	14.89	1)	Monaco	10 Sep
	Anna Pyatykh	Rus	81	14.88	2)	Lausanne	05 Jul
	Yargelis Savigne	Cub	84	14.82	2)	Helsinki	07 Aug
	Yamilé Aldama	Sud	72	14.82	2)	Berlin	04 Sep
	Viktoriya Gurova	Rus	82	14.74i	1)	Madrid	06 Mar
	Simona La Mantia	Ita	83	14.69	1)	Palermo	22 May
	Magdelin Martinez	Ita	76	14.69	1)	Padova	03 Jul
2006	Tatyana Lebedeva	Rus	76	15.23	1)	Athinai	03 Jul
	Trecia Smith	Jam	75	15.05	1)	Helsinki	26 Jul
	Hrisopiyi Devetzi	Gre	76	15.05	2)	Göteborg	08 Sep
	Anna Pyatykh	Rus	81	15.02	3)	Göteborg	08 Sep
	Yargelis Savigne	Cub	84	14.91	3)	Athinai	03 Jul
	Yamilé Aldama	Sud	72	14.86i	3)	Moskva	11 Mar
	Yelena Oleynikova	Rus	76	14.63	2)	Tula	12 Jun
	Viktoriya Gurova	Rus	82	14.60	1)	Sochi	28 May
	Xie Limei	Chi	86	14.54	1)	Shijuazhuang	06 Aug
	Anastasiya Zhuravlyeva	Uzb	81	14.54	5)	Athinai	16 Sep
	With assisting wind:						
	Anna Pyatykh	Rus	81	15.17	2)	Athinai	03 Jul
2007	Yargelis Savigne	Cub	84	15.28	1)	Osaka	31 Aug
	Tatyana Lebedeva	Rus	76	15.14	1)	Athinai	02 Jul
	Hrisopiyi Devetzi	Gre	76	15.09	Q)	Osaka	29 Aug
	Marija Sestak	Slo	79	14.92	1)	Ljubljana	03 Jun
	Xie Limei	Chi	86	14.90	1)	Urumqi	20 Sep
	Anna Pyatykh	Rus	81	14.88	4)	Osaka	31 Aug
	Olga Saladuha	Ukr	83	14.79	1)	Bangkok	13 Aug
	Magdelin Martinez	Ita	76	14.71	6)	Osaka	31 Aug
	Teresa N'zola Meso	Fra	83	14.69	1)	München	23 Jun
	Olga Rypakova	Kaz	84	14.69	1)	Amman	28 Jul
	With assisting wind:						
	Keila Costa	Bra	83	15.10	1)	Uberlândia	06 May
2008	Françoise Mbango	Cam	76	15.39	1)	Beijing	17 Aug
	Tatyana Lebedeva	Rus	76	15.32	2)	Beijing	17 Aug
	Hrisopiyi Devetzi	Gre	76	15.23	3)	Beijing	17 Aug
	Yargelis Savigne	Cub	84	15.20	1)	Rethimno	14 Jul
	Olga Rypakova	Kaz	84	15.11	4)	Beijing	17 Aug
	Marija Sestak	Slo	79	15.08i	1)	Athinai	13 Feb
	Oksana Udmurtova	Rus	82	14.94i	1)	Tartu	20 Feb
	Anna Pyatykh	Rus	81	14.91	2)	Rieti	07 Sep
	Viktoriya Gurova	Rus	82	14.85	3)	Kazan	19 Jul
	Olga Saladuha	Ukr	83	14.84	1)	Kiev	03 Jul
2009	Nadezhda Alekhina	Rus	78	15.14	1)	Cheboksary	26 Jul
	Yargelis Savigne	Cub	84	15.00	1)	Athinai	13 Jul
	Tatyana Lebedeva	Rus	76	14.72	1)	Shanghai	20 Sep

	Anastasiya Taranova-Potapova	Rus	85	14.68	1)	Torino	04 Mar
	Anna Pyatykh	Rus	81	14.67	2)	Cheboksary	26 Jul
	Yekaterina Kayukova	Rus	86	14.64	3)	Cheboksary	26 Jul
	Mabel Gay	Cub	83	14.64	1)	Tallinn	25 Aug
	Oksana Udmurtova	Rus	82	14.62i	2)	Volgograd	24 Jan
	Athanasia Pérra	Gre	83	14.62	1)	Pescara	02 Jul
	Xie Limei	Chi	86	14.62	Q)	Berlin	15 Aug
	With assisting wind:						
	Tatyana Lebedeva	Rus	76	15.01	1)	Madrid	04 Jul
	Anna Pyatykh	Rus	81	14.84	2)	Madrid	04 Jul
	Olga Rypakova	Kaz	84	14.69	3)	Madrid	04 Jul
	Yamilé Aldama	Sud	72	14.68	4)	Madrid	04 Jul
	Hrisopiyi Devetzi	Gre	76	14.67	1)	Yalta	05 Jun
2010	Olga Rypakova	Kaz	84	15.25	1)	Split	04 Sep
	Yargelis Savigne	Cub	84	15.09	1)	Monaco	22 Jul
	Olha Saladuha	Ukr	83	14.81	1)	Barcelona	31 Jul
	Nadezhda Alekhina	Rus	78	14.77	Q)	Saransk	15 Jul
	Anna Pyatykh	Rus	81	14.68	1)	Rabat	06 Jun
	Athanasia Pérra	Gre	83	14.61	1)	Kalamáta	29 May
	Simona La Matia	Ita	83	14.56	2)	Barcelona	31 Jul
	Natalya Kutyakova	Rus	86	14.55	1)	Istanbul	12 Jun
	Svetlana Bolshakova	Bye	84	14.55	3)	Barcelona	31 Jul
	Adelina Gavrilá	Rum		14.48	Q)	Barcelona	29 Jul
	With assisting wind:						
	Nadezhda Alekhina	Rus	78	15.00	1)	Saransk	15 Jul
	Alsu Murtazina	Rus	87	14.63	2)	Saransk	15 Jul
	Dana Veld'áková	Svk	81	14.59	Q)	Barcelona	29 Jul
	Dailenis Alcántara	Cub	91	14.55	1)	Habana	21 Mar
	Ksenia Dzetsuk	Bye	86	14.54	1)	Grodno	27 Jun
	Snezana Rodic	Slo	82	14.52	2)	Budapest	19 Jun

ALL TIME WORLD LIST AS AT THE END OF 2010

Inessa Kravets	Ukr	66	15.50	1)	Göteborg	10 Aug 95
Françoise Mbango	Cam	76	15.39	1)	Beijing	17 Aug 08
Tatyana Lebedeva	Rus	76	15.36i	1)	Budapest	06 Mar 04
Hrisopiyi Devetzi	Ger	76	15.32	Q)	Athinai	21 Aug 04
Yamilé Aldama	Cub/Sud	72	15.29	1)	Roma	11 Jul 03
Yargelis Savigne	Cub	84	15.28	1)	Osaka	31 Ago 07
Olga Rypakova	Kaz	84	15.25	1)	Split	04 Sep 10
Sarká Kaspárková	Cze	71	15.20	1)	Athinai	04 Ago 97
Tereza Marinova	Bul	77	15.20	1)	Sydney	24 Sep 00
Iva Pradzheva	Bul	72	15.18	2)	Göteborg	10 Aug 95
With assisting wind:						
Magdelin Martinez	Ita	76	15.24	1)	Sestriere	01 Aug 04

INDEX MEN

(names mentioned in the written text)

C

D

E

F

G

H

I

J

K

L

M

N

S

X

Y

Z

INDEX WOMEN

(names mentioned in the written text)

Surnames given in the following index are those under which the athletes were generally known at the peak of their career. In the case of married women their maiden name is given alongside.

D

E

F

G

H

T

U

V

W

X

Y

Z

BIBLIOGRAPHY

Berendonk, B. "Doping, von der Forschung zum Betrug", Rowohlt Sport, 1992.

Brant, J. and Wasko, J. "World Women's Athletics – 100 Best Performers Year Lists, 1926-1962. Zamosc, 2010.

Doherty, K. "Track & Field Omnibook". Tafnews Press, Los Altos, CA. 1980.

Hamacher, H. "Leichtathletik in 19. Jahrhundert (Band 1: 1891-1900; Band II: 1881-1890).

Hymans, R. "Progression of World Best Performances and Official IAAF World Records (IAAF, Monaco, 2003).

Kök, N., Magnusson, R., Potts D.H., Quercetani, R.L. "Track & Field Performances Through the Years", Volumes 1, 2, 3 and 4, ATFS, Firenze/Köbenhavn (1986, '89, '92 and '97).

Matthews, P. "Athletics 2011", the International Track and Field Annual (ATFS), Sports Books Ltd. (2011).

Mengoni, L., Magnusson, R., Sykora, M., Terry, D. "World and National Leaders in Track & Field Athletics", 1860-1972 ATFS

Shearman, M. "Athletics and Football", Longmans, Green and Co., London, 1888

Watman, M. "Encyclopaedia of Track and Field Athletics", St.Martin's Press, New York, and Robert Hale Ltd., London, 1981.

Printed in July 2011